UNEARTHING THE PAST

UNEARTHING THE PAST:

ARCHAEOLOGY AND AESTHETICS

IN THE MAKING OF

RENAISSANCE CULTURE

LEONARD BARKAN

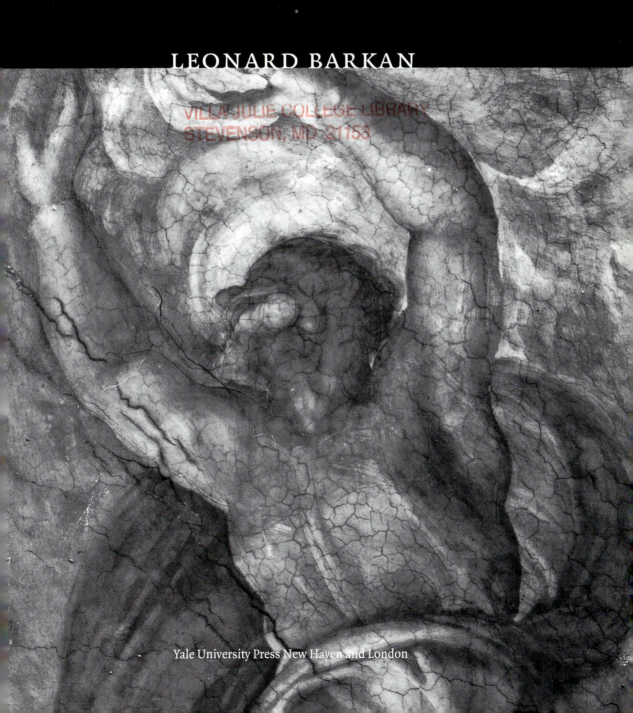

Yale University Press New Haven and London

Published with assistance from the Elizabethan
Club, Yale University, and from the Kingsley
Trust Association Publication Fund established
by the Scroll and Key Society of Yale College.

Sections of this book, in earlier form, appeared in
Raritan 11 (1991) and *Representations* 44 (1993).
Permission to reprint these materials is gratefully
acknowledged.

Title page: Michelangelo, *Separation of Light from Darkness*
(detail), fresco, 1511–12, Sistine Chapel, Rome

Designed by Gregg Chase. Set in Quadraat type.
Printed in the United States of America
by Vail-Ballou Press, Binghamton, New York.

Library of Congress Cataloging-in-Publication Data

Barkan, Leonard
    Unearthing the past : archaeology and
    aesthetics in the making of Renaissance
    culture / Leonard Barkan
        p. cm.
    Includes bibliographic references
    and index.
    ISBN 0–300–07677–0 (alk. paper)
    1. Sculpture, Classical.
    2. Sculpture, Classical—Reproduction.
    3. Art, Renaissance—Classical influences.
    4. Classical antiquities in art.
    I. Title.
    NB85.B37 1999
    709'.02'4—dc21   99—24893
                                   CIP

A catalogue record for this book is available from
the British Library.

The paper in this book meets the guidelines for
permanence and durability of the Committee
on Production Guidelines for Book Longevity of
the Council on Library Resources.

10 9 8 7 6 5 4 3 2 1

Agli amici di Roma
Dal 1987 al 1992
E per sempre

ACKNOWLEDGMENTS

It's scary to do the math, but numbers don't lie: I have spent about a quarter of my life researching and writing this book. Or let's say a quarter of the *years* of my life, since, however satisfying the accomplishment may be, I hope the book does not represent the whole of my existence during that time. Yet that statement, too, should perhaps be qualified. A long and absorbing labor like the present one can never be separated from the whole of one's existence. As I try to remember the persons, places, and institutions whose influence brought this work into being, I discover that I am recalling thirteen years of friendship, support, and love, all of which are as inseparable from each other as they are from the book. So, in spite of the usual neatly organized rubrics of gratitude that I have composed below, I really wish to thank everyone for *all* their generosities. But perhaps that is best done in life rather than on an acknowledgments page.

This book would not be possible without the *Census of Antique Works Known to Renaissance Artists*, courtesy of Phyllis Bober and the Warburg Institute (of which I have more to say in the Introduction); nor could I have written it without a fellowship from the Howard Foundation, which first cast me loose upon Rome. Generous leave times from my various academic homes—Northwestern University, the University of Michigan, and New York University—have also been indispensable, though no more so than the years spent on the job in all these places (as well as at Washington University in St. Louis, where I was a Fannie Hurst Visiting Professor), since I benefited at least as much from great conversations with students and colleagues as from the chance to escape them. While on the subject of students, I am delighted to celebrate a sequence of brilliant individuals who have served as my research assistants: William West, Ann Flower, and Philip Lorenz. I cannot list all the libraries without which there would have been no research, but I want to single out that of N.Y.U.'s Institute of Fine Arts and especially its reference librarian, Clare Hills-Nova. I wish as well to recognize the long-term support and encouragement of Yale University Press, notably from two editors, as different as they are great: Ellen Graham and Jonathan Brent. In the more recent term, the production of this book owes a great debt to the care and enthusiasm of Karen Gangel. And, in a category both material and spiritual, it is a special pleasure to acknowledge the grant from the Yale Elizabethan Club, place of happiest New Haven memories and now of inestimable assistance.

Perhaps the definitive case of my personal and professional gratitude, however, is bound up with the multidisciplinary nature of the book. Whether owing to the breadth of my curiosity or to the brevity of my attention span, I have never been able to stay inside my training as a scholar of English Literature. What is remarkable in this story, though, is not my determination to delve in other fields but the extraordinary generosity—that is, both the sharing of expertise and the invitations to colleague-ship—that I have received from those who are the great recognized experts in those disciplines upon which I have poached.

I have, first of all, been blessed with collaborative support from a worldwide network of art historians: Northwestern colleagues Larry Silver and Whitney Davis; Michigan colleagues Celeste Brusati and Pat Simons; N.Y.U. colleagues Marvin Trachtenberg, Linda Nochlin, Colin Eisler, and A. Richard Turner. In wider geographies I have picked up such companions as James Ackerman, Nicole Dacos, Rona Goffen, Michael Koortbojian, Marilyn Lavin, Irving Lavin, Joseph Rykwert, and Philip Sohm. Classicists, perhaps even more than art historians, might have reason to run when they see me coming; miraculously, they have been full of welcome and wisdom. Again I have been favored with colleagues: at Michigan, John D'Arms and H.D. Cameron; at N.Y.U., Michele Lowrie, Matthew Santirocco, and Seth Benardete. Farther afield, a stint as Walker-Ames Professor at the University of Washington gave me a chance to play classicist for real and to see some very fine ones in action, especially Stephen Hinds. Elsewhere in my travels, I have had the great pleasure of support from Alessandro Barchiesi, Alessandro Schiesaro, and Froma Zeitlin.

Nor, even though English Literature may have been left behind, have my colleagues in that field ever abandoned me. To cite a very small portion of those who have managed to bear with me: Marjorie Levinson, Joseph Loewenstein, David Lee Miller, Martin Mueller, Peter Platt, Michael Schoenfeldt, Tobin Siebers, Richard Strier, and Michael Warner, who, as I recall, gave me the book's title before a word of it had been written. What life or liveliness has emerged in these writings about old stones I owe in part to the challenging interventions of Chris King, writer, editor, friend.

Then there are those persons who defy all categories. They are my friends, my mentors (or mentees, but what's the difference?), examples of what a scholar can be, readers and encouragers of my work, makers of my life, all of the above. May they forgive the indignity of group listing: Albert Ascoli, Harry Berger, Philip Blumberg, Jonathan Freedman, Anthony Grafton, John Hollander, Richard Howard, Jon Koslow, Thomas Laqueur, Dan Lewis, Alexander Nagel, Stephen Orgel, Michael Putnam, Mary Beth Rose, Richard Sennett, David Silverman, Benjamin Taylor, William Wallace, Robert Weisbuch.

Finally, I elaborate on the book's dedication as I record the greatest, if most diffuse, debt of all. When I arrived in Rome in 1987, I knew not a single person, nor did I have any institutional affiliation. In the subsequent years I came to feel, like certain very fortunate ancients, that I could declare myself a Roman citizen. Such miraculous naturalization was owing to an extraordinary group of newly made friends, most of them not academics (their professions range from housekeeper to historian, from pediatrician to barkeep) but, rather, lovers of their city, of good wine, good food, good talk, and, by felicitous extension, of this foreigner who would be Roman. I name some of these glorious people and offer this book as a small return for their kindnesses of mind and soul: Vincenzo Anelli, Michele Bernardini, Sergio Bonetti, Stefano Bonilli, Andrea Carlino, Sergio Ceccarelli, Daniele Cernilli, Ian d'Agata, Massimo d'Alessandro, Giovanni Gregoletto, Silvia Imparato, Giovanni Levi, Paola di Mauro, Mara Memo, Giovanna Pantellini, Sandro Sangiorgi, Rosalba Spagnoletti, Edward Steinberg, Clara Viscogliosi, Paolo Zaccaria.

INTRODUCTION

The conditions under which an object of discourse may appear, the historical conditions which make it possible to "say something about it" and for many people to say different things about it, the conditions under which such a thing inscribes itself into a network of relations with other objects, so that it can establish with them relations of resemblance, nearness, distance, difference, transformation—these conditions, as is clear, are numerous and imposing. All of which means that one cannot simply talk about any old thing in any old time period; it is not easy to say something new; it is not enough just to open one's eyes, to pay attention, or to become aware so that new objects light up and emerge from the surface of the ground in their first clarity.

—MICHEL FOUCAULT

Whether there are new things to be said and thought at any given moment, and what the conditions might be for saying them: these are among Foucault's fundamental questions about history and knowledge. No novelty is so radical, he tells us, that it can be perceived independently of the time-bound conditions of discourse. That would be like something that emerged from the ground into the light of day with no more cause or context than its own self-generated will; such things never happen.

This is a book about a group of objects that actually *did* emerge from the ground into the light of day. The objects, as it happens, are not new, but they are radical, which is to say that they appear literally and figuratively at the root level of the civilization that unearths them and provide a fundamental alternative that must be encountered. But if this book tortures Foucault's metaphor by translating it into a material reality, it nonetheless shares his project of narrating history by chronicling the possibilities of discourse as they define the old and the new. The finding of ancient sculpture in the ground during early modern times, followed by the decoding, the restoring, the imitating, the reimagining, the weaving together of a grand narrative of history from these material remains and their textual traces—what happens if we entertain the possibility that this was precisely the impossibly new thing that produces, or at the very least signals, historical change?

Habent libelli sua fata. If the Latin grammarian was right to assert that even a little thing like a book has a destiny, it is bound to be even more certain that a book has a history. When the book is *about* history and about the ways a set of cultural objects can be made into a history, then the book's own past may offer the surest key to what it is. Further, when the book uses metaphors of forward and backward time travel almost compulsively, then a retrospective glimpse into its own origins would seem only appropriate. After the author has spent a dozen years on finding art in the ground, perhaps it is normal that the subject seems to him inevitable and universal, that it appears to provide a kind of key to all knowledge concerning history, art, and culture. The ensuing pages are unlikely to persuade even the most enthusiastic reader of anything quite so absolute. Still, it is precisely this conviction of the author—itself a kind of miniature *mentalité*—which demands to be historically unpacked, so that its own strands can be disentangled, its layers unsedimented, and its internal relations mapped. With this in mind, I present, by way of this Introduction, a series of origins.

As I write these words, it is precisely fifty years since Phyllis Bober, working under Fritz Saxl and in the worldwide orbit of the Warburg Institute, began collecting the materials for what soon came to be known as the *Census of Antique Works Known to Renaissance Artists*.[1] (It is extraordinary, a case perhaps unequalled in the annals of scholarship, that the same remarkable individual remains today the erudite, imaginative, and indefatigable spirit behind this enterprise.) The plan was to make as complete a record as possible, principally photographic and to a lesser extent textual, of the pieces of ancient sculpture known in the fifteenth and sixteenth centuries, and equally to document the drawings and imitations of these works which proved their familiarity in this period. What is perhaps most notable is that Professor Bober was by training a classical archaeologist and not (to begin with, at least) a Renaissance scholar at all. Thus the twentieth-century act of recuperation was a kind of archaeology—a careful mapping of material artifacts on a grid of time and space—which was itself being applied to a rather different sort of Renaissance archaeology, a recovery of the past that was as unsystematic as it was passionate.

In my own experience of the Warburg enterprise, which included not only the *Census* but also analogous projects of documentation on subjects like astrology, Platonism, and classical iconography, the catalyst for these mutually reflective recordings of the past was, as my opening quotation suggests, a third archaeology. At some point in the late 1970s I was by day a researcher in the collections of the Warburg Library and by night a reader of *The Order of Things* and *The Archaeology of Knowledge*. Which is to say that I was encountering in my research a nested history of attempts to archive the past, from Phyllis Bober and her colleagues back to the sixteenth-century antiquarians and the collections of Renaissance sketchbooks after antiquity, back to the discoverers of everything from mass-produced sarcophagi to the *Laocoön*, back to the humanists from Petrarch to Alberti, who constructed an ideology of the past, back to the Romans themselves, who had in the first place created or plundered or collected the art objects as an act of retrieving a more glorious Greek past. Meanwhile I was learning a different set of meanings for *archive*, seeing it not as the sum total of events and things that had been recorded but as the system that governed what could be recorded. The real archive, in other words, might not be the *Census* or the sketchbooks or the antiquarian records or even the recovered works of art but rather the sequence of mentalities that had made this list possible, both then and now. And archaeology might not be the science of collecting and preserving these material things but "the never completed, never wholly achieved uncovering of the archive."[2] I found myself, in short, stranded between an archive being assiduously completed and an archive that was by definition uncompletable but constantly acting as a commentary on itself. Yet I felt far less conflicted when I realized that archaeology, which was in a sense my topic, could now be understood as the very principle or method with which I approached my topic and which I hoped it would in turn illuminate.

The result is a documentary history that aspires to rigor but that is properly skeptical about the discursive practices that are called history; it also seeks to tell one story among many—that is, of one moment that might be called "archaeology"—while investigating what the larger archaeological paradigms of *story* and *history* might be. Foucault, of course, repeatedly discounts the conventional meaning of the term he uses in his title—just as I will say pointedly in the first chapter that the Renaissance rediscovery of art in the ground is *not* archaeology in the normal modern sense—but that does not prevent his work from being steeped in the metaphorics of depth, of layers, and of excavation. What he cannot have anticipated is the uncanny appropriateness of his metaphors to the particular case recounted in this book, that is, of the unearthing of the past via a set of artistic representations that were once lost, dormant, and unreadable but were now being awakened, interpreted, and transformed into culture.

> These four terms: reading—trace—decipherment—memory . . . define the system that usually makes it possible to snatch past discourse from its inertia and, for a moment, to rediscover something of its lost vitality.

> Now, the function of enunciative analysis is not to awaken texts from their present sleep, and, by reciting the marks still legible on their surface, to rediscover the flash of their birth; on the contrary, its function is to follow them through their sleep, or rather to take up the related themes of sleep, oblivion, and lost origin, and to discover what mode of existence may characterize statements, independently of their enunciation, in the density of time in which they are preserved, in which they are reactivated, and used, in which they are also—but this was not their original destiny—forgotten, and possibly even destroyed.[3]

I would only add—as with many Foucauldian formulations—that in practice it is not so easy to separate those procedures that he disparages from those that he champions. Whether ancient sculpture is being awakened from its sleep or followed through its sleep, whether one is rediscovering the flash of its birth or rediscovering something of its lost vitality: these are not either/or possibilities but instead the continuing set of methodological questions we must ask, questions concerning both what the Renaissance did to its past and what we are doing to the Renaissance.

Another origin for this work emerges from a quite different world of theory and method. Those poststructuralist theories of reading which see texts not as collocations of themes but as sequences of tropes proved unexpectedly illuminating as I began to consider matters less global than the entire conceptual or historical field of archaeology. This book is even less deconstructionist than it is Foucauldian, but my sense of how to decipher the reception of individual works of art has been much influenced by a movement in literary criticism that has sought to denaturalize imaginative language. When Paul de Man and J. Hillis Miller read text, they do not assume that voice is an attribute that merely belongs in some automatic or uncomplicated way to any fictive or real person; rather, they follow the process by which the text has created personhood out of voice.[4] While this work seems very remote from rediscovered ancient sculpture, it is noteworthy that deconstructive reading reveals a kind of obsession with the boundary lines between animate and inanimate objects, specifically with the ways in which something like a block of marble—say, Pygmalion's statue or a gravestone—might be figured as speaking.

In fact, the very basis of recuperating ancient sculpture that represented the human form was to endow the object with a voice. In an effort both to make these enigmatic works live and to fix a particular identity upon them, Renaissance viewers responded not only by describing the works in their own voices but also by giving the objects voices of their own. For students of rhetoric, this is the trope of prosopopoeia, which has been defined as "the fiction of an apostrophe to an absent, deceased, or voiceless entity, which posits the possibility of the latter's reply and confers upon it the power of speech. Voice assumes mouth, eye, and finally face, a chain that is manifest in the etymology of the trope's name, *prosopon poien*, to confer a mask or a face (*prosopon*)."[5]

De Man traces this definition back from Wordsworth's *Essays upon Epitaphs*, which he sees as problematizing the questions of how the poet lives from beyond the grave or how a poet's name "is made as intelligible and memorable as a face." The material of the trope, in Wordsworth and in the important precursor of Milton's early poem "On Shakespeare," is the stone of the tomb upon which an epitaph is written. Milton, composing his sonnet for the Second Folio of Shakespeare's plays, had discounted the value of the marble monument ("weak witness of thy name"), whereas Wordsworth—to follow de Man's argument—rhetorically reanimates the stone even while he argues against the efficacy of such tropes. De Man focuses Wordsworth's real anxiety upon an issue addressed in lines that the poet leaves out of his Milton quotation: "Then thou, our fancy of itself bereaving, / Dost make us marble with too much conceiving."[6] If the inanimate are permitted to speak, then, symmetrically, the living must be turned to stone. Milton's source for *that* image, which de Man leaves out,

is Shakespeare's own fiction in *The Winter's Tale*, the reanimation of the statue /
Hermione, of which her formerly hard-hearted husband says, "Does not the stone
rebuke me / For being more stone than it?"[7] Of course, the onlookers at those final
moments of the romance are astonished—*astonied*, as Shakespeare would say—just as
observers of newly discovered ancient marble often were.[8] At the same time, by this
process of deconstructive declension, the act of writing, which is in effect making a
self out of a voice, has been defined through a movement back to personification,
apostrophe, and prosopopoeia, at the end of which is the poetic fiction of a statue that
comes to life. Italian Renaissance culture at the beginning of the sixteenth century was
just discovering a world of stony figures not invented by poets and not even by sculptors within their own Christian tradition. These figures already had mouth, eye, and
face (or some remnants thereof), while the voices that emanated from them, even if
fictional and created by writers rather than by stonemasons, may well have seemed not
merely responses made possible by a living person's apostrophe but initiations of a
historical—and transhistorical—dialogue.

Archaeology and prosopopoeia are to be found throughout this book; a quite
different set of informing origins is to be sought in what is *not* found here. At a very
early stage, the working title of this project was "Gilded Monuments, Powerful
Rhymes." The allusion is to the opening of Shakespeare's Sonnet 55: "Not marble,
nor the gilded monuments / Of princes, shall outlive this powerful rhyme." It was a
neat conceit on the visual arts in the Renaissance as viewed through the eyes of a poet,
that is, inscribed in competition and defined by decay. The book that might have
resulted was designed on a kind of Solomonic balance between the verbal—consisting
of Dantean and Petrarchan archaeology, ekphrasis from late antiquity to the
Renaissance, and the poetically imagined monumentalism of such works as the
Hypnerotomachia or *The Faerie Queene*—and the visual, consisting of the rediscovery of
actual ancient art objects. It is not so much the case that half of this chapter outline
simply dropped out, though that should be in itself comforting to a reader who faces
the sheer bulk of the present volume. Rather it became clear that these were subjects
that could not be coordinated; in other words, they needed to be presented in the full
dynamic of their cultural interactions. The baby could not be split in two: I had to
write a book about one of these systems, in which I would record the informing and
competitive presence of the other.

Why it became a book about monuments and not a book about rhymes is perhaps more interesting to the author than to the reader. Certainly it has something to
do with archaeology itself, as I have discussed it above, and the sense that I wished to
move from a textual to a material revival of antiquity. But the deeper answer to the
question is, once again, not in coordination but in subordination. Leonardo pointed
out (quite resentfully) that poets always had the chance to speak for themselves but
that painters were forced to be the objects of other people's speech.[9] Although that is
too simple—Leonardo is himself speaking, and so do many other visual artists, from

Ghiberti to Michelangelo to Vasari and onward—I suppose I was redressing a kind of disequilibrium. On the other hand, it was the poets themselves who gave me the clues to understand how the system of subordination might work.

Ariosto, for instance:

> Timagora, Parrasio, Polignoto,
> Protogene, Timante, Apollodoro,
> Apelle, più di tutti questi noto,
> e Zeusi, e gli altri ch'a quei tempi foro;
> di quai la fama . . .
> sempre starà, fin che si legge e scriva
> mercé degli scrittori, al mondo viva.[10]

> Timagoras, Parrhasius, Polygnotus, Protogenes, Timanthes, Apollodorus, Apelles, more famous than all the rest, and Zeuxis, along with the others of that age, whose reputation, . . . thanks to authors, shall remain always alive in the world, so long as man reads and writes.

In faithfully reproducing the topos, indeed the cliché, of the poet's eternizing power, Ariosto makes one of his characteristically ironic jokes. When Ovid inaugurates the topos by concluding the *Metamorphoses* with the boast of his own immortality, he engages in a kind of sublime tautology (or sublime self-referentiality): my writing will immortalize my writing. By shifting the object to a canonical list of great visual artists of Hellenic antiquity whose actual works are unrecoverable, Ariosto turns tautology into incongruity and bathos. How can visual masterpieces be immortal *thanks to authors*—that is, in words rather than in pictures? Does not this process of immortalization ridicule both artist and writer and thus render the immortality of both a bit suspect? These states of doubt are intensified in the immediately following stanzas when the greatness of living artists (Leonardo, Mantegna, Giovanni Bellini, Michelangelo, etc.: "questi che noi *veggian* [as opposed to *leggem*] pittori") is made contingent upon the fugitive achievements of the ancient masters whose work "si legge e crede"—that is, we can only read about and take on faith. Further doubt is raised when the poet gets to his real point, the failure of the visual arts to depict the future. In the case of Apelles et al., the future is their own nonexistence, a fate that presumably also awaits Leonardo et al., except once again for the quixotic job of recovery *mercé degli scrittori*.

But Ariosto's list of artists is very selective indeed: they are all painters. Meanwhile the poet himself flourishes in a patronage world of Gonzaga and Este that is pursuing with every resource the work of ancient sculptors, attempting to buy them, to make casts of them, to copy them in miniature. All the ironic relations that Ariosto establishes here, between words and images, between genius and oblivion, between time and immortality, depend upon the exclusion of a vast middle term of objects that by their very nature question the categories. When he homologizes two cross-cultural encounters—one between ancients and moderns, the other between the art of the image and the art of the word—and when he undertakes to stage a drama of attempted communication that struggles in the face of the untranslatability of signs and the irrecoverability of past masterpieces, he does so by suppressing a set of artworks that *are* recoverable and *may* speak for themselves.

If Ariosto writes from the midpoint of the rediscovery of ancient sculpture, then a somewhat later poet yet more removed from the scene looks back on the phenomenon as though it were a closed book:

> Ne vous pouvant donner ces ouvrages antiques
> Pour vostre Sainct-Germain ou pour Fontainebleau,
> Je les vous donne (Sire) en ce petit tableau
> Peint, le mieux que j'ay peu, de couleurs poëtiques,
>   Qui, mis sous vostre nom devant les yeux publiques,
> Si vous le daignez voir en son jour le plus beau,
> Se pourra bien vanter d'avoir hors du tombeau
> Tiré des vieux Romains les poudreuses reliques.[11]

> Not being able to give you those antique works for your palace of Saint Germain or for Fontainebleau, I give you them, Sire, in this little tablet, painted, as best I can, in poetical colors. The which, if you deign to see it in its sharpest light, may well boast of having extracted from the tomb the crumbling relics of the ancient Romans.

Ariosto pretends that there is no surviving ancient sculpture. Du Bellay, here beginning his sonnet sequence on the antiquities of Rome, can make no such simple gesture of exclusion, since the failed attempt to import works like those in the Vatican Belvedere was a determining cultural circumstance during the reign of Francis I, and, by the time of Henry II when these poems are written, their unattainability must be viewed as definitive. Excluded they nevertheless are, and if any poet could have a complex attitude toward this heritage, it would be du Bellay, theorist of influence and of translation—indeed, of the impossibility of translation and the worthiness of the vernacular—in his *Deffence et illustration de la langue françoyse*.[12] These lines open the *Antiquitez* with an admission of failure and an act of substitution. The "tableau peint" and the "couleurs poëtiques" ostensibly signal the limits of literary language, but they also define a task of compensation. As the poem engages in a vast cultural act of *enargeia*, it will make absent things present and will overcome its own belatedness in relation to the unobtainable material remains of antiquity; it will present these things both as ruined and as (to use the Renaissance term) repristinated—that is, like new.

For du Bellay, it is not only that antique works are unprocurable and that translation is itself a kind of plundering or profanation of classical relics. Rome is the very name of what cannot be enunciated.

Nouveau venu, qui cherches Rome en Rome
Et rien de Rome en Rome n'apperçois:
Ces vieux palais, ces vieux arcz que tu vois,
Et ces vieux murs, c'est ce que Rome on nomme.
. . . .
Rome de Rome est le seul monument,
Et Rome Rome a vaincu seulement. [3]

Thou stranger, which for *Rome* in *Rome* thou seekest,
And nought of *Rome* in *Rome* perceiv'st at all,
These same olde walls, olde arches, which thou seest
Olde Palaces, is that which *Rome* men call.
. . . .
Rome now of *Rome* is th'onely funerall,
And onely *Rome* of *Rome* hath victorie.

Rome seule pouvoit à Rome ressembler,
Rome seule pouvoit Rome faire trembler. [6]

Rome onely might to *Rome* compared bee,
And onely *Rome* could make great *Rome* to tremble.

Rome fut tout le monde, et tout le monde est Rome.
Et si par mesmes noms mesmes choses on nomme,
Comme du nom de Rome on se pourroit passer
La nommant par le nom de la terre et de l'onde,
Ainsi le monde on peult sur Rome compasser,
Puisque le plan de Rome est la carte du monde. [26]

Rome was th' whole world, and al the world was *Rome*,
And if things nam'd their names doo equalize,
When land and sea ye name, then name ye *Rome*,
And naming *Rome* ye land and sea comprize:
For th'auncient Plot of *Rome* displayed plaine,
The map of all the wide world doth containe.

Rome is unfindable, the nonpareil. It is the map of the world, but it cannot be mapped and therefore renders the world unmappable. It is the only possible vanquisher of itself, but it is also the tomb of itself: the living Rome was entombed in or under the seven hills; what survives of Rome is literally tombs, while to render Rome in poetry may be to extract it from the tomb or simply to provide another kind of tomb. Rome is the very definition of name—that is, of language—a claim that is abetted by all the rhymes available among *Rome*, *nomme*, and *nom*; but if it is the quintessential name, it can only be the name of itself, and therefore it defines but also defies signification.

Easy for him to say. Du Bellay writes these lines during a stay of several years in Rome, when he goes native to the extent of producing considerable quantities of Latin verse that even his contemporaries recognized as a contradiction to the manifesto in favor of the native muse in the *Deffence*. In response, he wrote an introductory verse, *Ad lectorem*, in which he compares the writing of verse in French to legitimate marriage and the writing of verse in Latin to a delicious episode of adultery; the metaphorics are doubtless connected with the poet's decision to write nostalgic elegy in sonnet form, historically associated with eros. In fact writing in itself, writing about Rome, and writing about a supposedly nonexistent Rome *is* eros in a tradition that goes back to a letter of Petrarch that verbally reconstructs a tabula rasa version of the city.[13] The less there is of material Rome, whether historical, urbanological, or aesthetic, the greater the space for the poet. The mantra of *Rome, Rome*, as well as the scorched-earth policy that the poet exercises on the physical remains of the city, clears the space for literary inspiration.

All this poetic compensation—and to Shakespeare, Ariosto, and du Bellay one might add, among others, Dante, Petrarch, Spenser (whose very first work was a set of translations from du Bellay's *Antiquitez*)—cleared some space for me, I felt. Rome is not impossible, even if it is ineffable: whatever du Bellay might say, it was being very effectively mapped from the fourteenth century onward. Many monuments of its architecture and its urban topography were in fine condition and formed the basis of whole libraries of humanistic study. And, most relevantly, its artistic monuments in marble and bronze existed in magnificent profusion and attracted massive attention. Still, if for these writers they were the very central trope of the unattainable, the invisible, and that which language must complete or supplement, then what related senses of loss might inhabit those places where the objects were, in whatever condition, actually present? This particular origin of the present volume, then, is as a kind of response to the poets: by calling their bluff, I hoped to say something about the culture in which both writers and artists were constructing their past and about the ways language and visuality are interdependent.

The remaining tales of origin for this book have less to do with theory or history and more to do with personal experience and taste. It is difficult to find nice housing in the *centro storico* of Rome that an academic can afford. By some sort of uncanny predestination, in the first years when I was plotting and researching this book, I secured a little attic apartment near the Campo de' Fiori in the Piazza dei Satiri, named, it is said (probably erroneously), for two statues of satyrs that had been discovered in its environs. Small wonder that it should be an archaeological site, since this corner of the city, bounded by the Via dei Chiavari, the Via dei Giubbonari, the Piazza del Biscione, and the Piazza Paradiso, is entirely constructed on the foundations of Pompey's Theater, one of ancient Rome's most glorious and most enduring monuments. Textual records from Pliny, Suetonius, and Tertullian, among others, reveal many details of its magnificence; from Pompey's own time down to the sixth-century pope Symmachus, it was one of the city's great showpieces. And it was loaded with statues: fourteen subdued nations sculpted by Coponius, a bronze representation of Sejanus, icons in four or five shrines to the gods, and, of course, the statue of Pompey himself, under which on the fateful Ides of March Julius Caesar was murdered.[14] Many stories beneath me, in other words, reposed the ancient world *sub specie statuarum*.

And not only beneath me. The façade of the Palazzo Pio-Righetti, which I could glimpse through a front window, and the whole sequence of buildings that followed into the Via di Grotta Pinta, all basically seventeenth-century constructions, maintained the perfect semicircle that had characterized Pompey's Theater in 55 B.C. My own rather undistinguished building, probably of medieval origins, was in part supported by the top of a classical column whose capital was about waist high on me but whose base doubtless extended deep into the ground where ancient Rome lay buried. Noisy ditchdigging work in the Via dei Chiavari that frequently disrupted telephone service churned up a steady stream of marble fragments—or so it was rumored in the shops—too small and ordinary to merit the attention of the archaeologists. I was, in short, living among the strata of history, and I could be expected to be in awe of the very spot on which I paid rent.

The truth is, I wasn't entirely in awe. Certainly the sense that the very ground of Rome was layered with multiple real and symbolic significances, which I will elevate to a historical principle in the first chapter of this book, came to me as a lived experience (and not a particularly original one). Yet what struck me more, at least after a few weeks, was the delicious banality of conducting daily life at such an active and monumental nexus point of history. That I was hanging out my wash or grilling sausages or rushing to a dental appointment on a spot successively adorned by the complete personnel of *I, Claudius* put me in touch with a Rome that lived its sedimented past as the most mundane condition of existence. I don't think I could have written this book, at least in the way I did, without the sense that the adventures I would chronicle here—of discovery, history writing, mythmaking, artistic inspiration—reposed on a foundation of the ordinary. And I have tried to maintain a sense of the distance between the story I am telling and the ground out of which it springs.

But there is a more radical set of implicit claims for the ordinary in this book. I recall a pair of scholarly and convivial conversations—they took place on the same day, as it happens—early in the life of the project. I explained that I was writing about ancient sculpture and Renaissance response. Nicole Dacos, herself the author of magisterial work on the Domus Aurea and the classical sources of Raphael's work in the Vatican Logge, urged me to move quickly through the antique part of the subject since its artistic value was so patently inferior to what would follow. Robert Durling, who has masterfully woven Dante and Petrarch into the fabric of earlier culture, pulled even fewer punches about the rediscovered sculpture: "Why do you want to write a whole book about third-rate stuff?" Now, personally I would not want to argue for or against this proposition (though I have been known to refer to some of these materials as Late

Imperial Schlock). But it raised questions that proved to be a central part of the book's dynamic. If the *Apollo Belvedere*, so universal an icon in Renaissance art and so celebrated in the encomia of Winckelmann and his contemporaries, strikes me as just a little bit stagy and vapid, if I allow myself to notice that the larger-than-life central figure of the *Laocoön* is a man about five feet high and that the whole group is slightly histrionic, if the Bacchic sarcophagus so extolled by Donatello that the awe-struck Brunelleschi trudged fifty miles from Florence to Cortona in his clogs just to see it [15] turns out to have been (like most of them) a factory-made knockoff produced for the rising lower middle class of Imperial Rome, what does it all mean?

What it meant to me was that I was writing a book about a gap. Not just the space between ancient and modern or between objects and the discourse about them but what we might call the energy gap—the sparking distance—that exists between an artistic source and its destination. It is in the nature of imitation, influence, and inspiration that they may seek to efface their origins, or even that they may unconsciously seek readily effaceable origins. That is certainly what Petrarch, Ariosto, and du Bellay were doing when they constructed their poetics on an emptied out field of classical art and architecture. Renaissance artists certainly did not make the antiques go away. And even if that were possible, this book does nothing to cooperate in the project, since it defies all my friends' good advice and approaches the subject more from the point of view of the ancient sources than from that of the modern works they inspired. Yet I remain with a certain consciousness that the modern culture which appropriates the classical past in part seeks to make something out of nothing. That "nothing" may in the end be less about artistic quality than about historic distance and all the inevitable erasures that come with fragmentation, loss of context, and illegibility.

Each of the chapters that follow attempts to map the gap. First, discovery itself: the opening chapter pursues the narratives of finding antique valuables in the ground, attempts to historicize and theorize this fundamental cultural activity of the early moderns, places the discovery of art objects in the context of other finds, and asks what makes representational art a special category. Chapter 2 steps back from the fifteenth and sixteenth centuries to follow the written traces of ancient art as they themselves resurfaced, particularly in the *Natural History* of Pliny and the traditions in which it was read. Then in the third chapter the book goes on to ask what may be the most fundamental set of questions about the rediscovered objects: what constitutes a fragment, what kinds of things are known and not known about these imperfect objects, and what are the systems for decoding and assimilating them? Chapter 4, by way of complement, concentrates on the reintegrating of fragments; it focuses on three significant discoveries that illustrate a range of discursive systems for weaving the past into the present. The final chapter takes the example of one Renaissance artist, who is in some ways typical and some ways unique; by telling the story of his career it attempts to present the situation of art in culture at the middle of the sixteenth century when those figures exist upon a ground that is defined by the ancient objects that have been found within it.

Finally, in case it hasn't emerged from that summary, in my focus on these spaces of inspiration, there is a darker purpose that, sooner or later, must be confessed. The archaeological recovery of ancient art, enabling it to arrive out of the earth with almost autochthonic independence—just what Foucault said couldn't happen—offers us a glimpse at a set of creative acts with quite particular valences. When Renaissance artists look at works in the tradition of their own Christian civilization, whether religious or secular, they see a complex picture of the origins of their own society. Such art radiates meaning by reflecting the society's past. Excavated works seem by comparison almost nonrepresentational. Their alienness and the fragmentary nature of their exhumation create a new arena for art as independent from clear denotation, artistic conventions, conceptual significance, and sociological function. What does that leave? We may quote from an eyewitness to the discovery of the *Laocoön*: "The moment we saw it we started to draw, all the time talking about antique works, discussing the ones in Florence as well."[16] The discovery of the great fragments of ancient art puts Renaissance artists in mind of—art. The cultural production that results becomes a sign that art can be made not only out of dogma, out of natural observation, or out of historical events but also out of what we might in the fullest sense call *aesthetics*—which is to say a philosophy, a history, and a phenomenology proper to art itself.

To focus on a set of events like these, and to view them in this way, is to make some quite conscious intellectual choices. It is a feature of our fin-de-siècle moment in the history of scholarship that a project many years in the making should traverse a wide arc of method. The citation of diverse names like Warburg, Foucault, and de Man, along with the worrying of the term *history*, stands as a sign that this book embraces not only the archaeology of monuments but also the archaeology of critical approaches. Looking back on it myself, I see a palimpsest of theories and practices that have formed, fragmented, crumbled to dust in some cases, and left their recombinable traces throughout the field of scholarship in these years. One of these approaches—not really in ruins at all—deserves special mention. Critics of recent decades, particularly in regard to the Renaissance, have brought about a revolution in method, proposing new ways of reading the presence of history inside aesthetic objects. Many of these scholars have worked under the assumption—explicit, implicit, fully thematized, or taken for granted—that history is essentially the workings of power in society. I want to separate what seems to me a brilliant methodology from what can be an underinvestigated set of assumptions. It is not only politics, society, and economics that generate the impulses of art; it is also art itself. I hesitate to speak up for a New Aestheticism—slogans, after all, are better born than made—but perhaps the history that follows in these many pages can speak in that language for itself.

In the pages that follow, the citation of texts in foreign languages follows a case-by-case determination by the author rather than a simple uniformity. Poetry and other forms of imaginative literature are cited in both original and translation within the text, and the same practice is followed for any significant writings in which artists themselves discuss their lives and practices. Pliny, whose prose is itself the subject of Chapter 2, is cited in both languages in the body of the text. Vasari's Italian is included either alongside the English in the text or else in notes, depending on the importance of the vocabulary in making the argument. Other classical and Renaissance writings are sometimes cited in both languages in the text, but more often only in English, with the originals given in the notes when the wording is of direct scholarly relevance. Brief passages in foreign languages whose meaning is evident from the context are occasionally left without translation, as are some quotations from modern scholarship that appear only in the notes.

1.1. *Laocoön*, marble, Roman copy, first century A.D., after Hellenistic original, Vatican Museums, Rome

CHAPTER 1

DISCOVERIES

Love . . . needs no incentives, being self-sufficient, its own stimulus and reward; if it enjoys added benefits, it is due not to friendship but to fortune. Thus, the man who finds a gem inside a fish is not a better, but a more fortunate, fisherman. . . . The farmer who while tilling the soil happened to discover under the Janiculum seven Greek and seven Latin books and the tomb of King Numa Pompilius was really doing something else; often there came to me in Rome a vinedigger, holding in his hands an ancient jewel or a golden Latin coin, sometimes scratched by the hard edge of a hoe, urging me either to buy it or to identify the heroic faces inscribed on them; and often while putting in supports for a more sound foundation a builder has discovered a golden urn or a treasure hidden in the ground. Which of these with their unusual treasure became famous for his artistry or talent? For these are the gifts of fortune, not the laudable merits of men. Much more worthy of the name of artist is the man who is stopped short, while performing his rightful labor, by a serpent sliding from a cave than the man working blindly who is happily bedazzled by the unexpected brilliance of hidden gold.

—PETRARCH, *Familiar Letters*

The *Apollo Belvedere* reentered the world around 1490 unannounced—at least in any document that comes down to us. A trove of statues in the Pergamene style, depicting various wounded and dead warriors, was unearthed in September 1514: this we know from a Filippo Strozzi letter, though we have little other evidence that the event excited much attention. The *Tiber* may have been discovered twice, first in the 1440s, when Poggio Bracciolini reported such huge crowds that the owner of the property reinterred the statue, and again in 1512, when according to a detailed account by Grossino the piece was identified and brought triumphantly to Pope Julius; in other words, both times documented, and both times the subject of much popular notice.[1] A few bronzes and scores of friezes, sarcophagi, and sculpted triumphal arches were never discovered at all because they were never under ground. For many centuries they had decorated—or, depending on one's point of view, littered—the Roman cityscape, but throughout these earlier times, interest in them seems to have been sporadic. The *Torso Belvedere*, for us one of the definitive examples of the inspired and inspiring ancient masterpiece, was probably above ground for nearly a century before it received much attention.[2]

GREEKS BEARING GIFTS

The discovery on 14 January 1506 of the Laocoön (fig. 1.1), another of these definitive works, is the most famous case of all, the very model of a high-publicity artistic event such as we are familiar with in our own time.[3] Almost instantly the news traveled to Pope Julius II, who dispatched experts to make the identification. In March the pope bought the statue; by the first of July it was installed in a specially built niche in the Cortile Belvedere at the Vatican Palace near where it is exhibited today. It appears, in fact, that this installation for antiquities was already under construction even as the Laocoön was being found—which would clearly define the Laocoön as an idea whose time had come.[4] Indeed, the opportune moment may have arrived quite precisely. Only eighteen years earlier, we hear in a letter to Lorenzo de' Medici of the nocturnal discovery of a small statue "with three beautiful little fauns on a marble base, all three belted around by a huge serpent"; but the author hazards no guess as to the subject of the work.[5] As for the Esquiline find of 1506, there are many other indicators of fame: a flood of correspondence within the first month and a series of poetic responses throughout the sixteenth century; scores of drawings, copies, and re-creations in the work of virtually every Renaissance artist; instant political valorization as far in the future as the time of Napoleon, who procured the Laocoön for the Louvre, where it flourished for about as long as the emperor who brought it there.[6]

The Laocoön is not unique. Doubtless it has been used too often as a paradigm, and in the service of too many divergent aesthetics. Indeed, the artistic and historical life of ancient sculpture in modern times has probably depended overmuch on elevating individual works to paradigmatic status, and not only the Laocoön. The Apollo Belvedere, adored by Winckelmann and associated with the famous "stille Einfalt und edle Grösse," has been the very emblem of Neoclassicism.[7] The Torso Belvedere, sublime in its fragmentariness, has stood as the (literal) embodiment of an art based on inward struggle. For Hawthorne, it is the Marble Faun that symbolizes all the wayward eros of ancient and modern Rome.[8] George Eliot has the Vatican Sleeping Ariadne define the heroine of Middlemarch as she is first perceived by her future husband.[9] Rilke—slightly more generic in his tastes—hears the voice of an archaic torso of Apollo declaring "Du mußt dein Leben ändern."[10]

Not that the present volume promises universality or even novel examples. It is nevertheless worth establishing from the outset that hundreds, perhaps thousands of ancient sculptural objects were found, placed in commerce, gazed at, written about, and copied in the course of the Renaissance. To emphasize those of special and enduring fame offers the same promises and pitfalls as does any other focus on a traditional canon: it records the cases that are most fully documented and that have touched the greatest number of individuals most deeply, but it tends to take their status for granted and fails to give a full picture of the culture where the canon itself is in the process of formation.

Now the rediscovery of ancient sculpture is not only the place where a canon is being formed; it is also a place where canonicity itself is receiving some of its crucial modern definitions. For that reason it seems appropriate, at least briefly, to allow the *Laocoön* exemplary status, since it is not only the most famous of all antiquities in the sixteenth century but also comes, through Gotthold Ephraim Lessing and others, to be the very symbol of art as a subject. Before Lessing, indeed before January of 1506, Laocoön was a pivotal but not very fully delineated character in the *Aeneid*, the Trojan priest who vehemently advises against accepting the wooden horse into the city and who is punished by the visitation of serpents that convinces the onlookers to disregard his advice.[11] He does get to say the poem's most famous line—"timeo Danaos et dona ferentis"—which, along with the statue itself, earns him a potentially high recognition factor on two counts. But the Virgilian character can hardly be said to haunt the Renaissance imagination. When Filippino Lippi, who died in 1504, depicts Laocoön in a fresco at the Medici Villa Poggio a Caiano—an almost unique instance of this subject prior to 1506—it is more as a classicizing reference to sacred customs than to the subject of the Trojan War.[12] Laocoön's life really does change on that winter day on the Esquiline Hill, for which we have an eyewitness account, a letter written sixty years later by Francesco da Sangallo, son of the famous architect Giuliano. Both father and son were present at the scene of discovery:

> The first time I was in Rome when I was very young, the pope was told about the discovery of some very beautiful statues in a vineyard near S. Maria Maggiore. The pope ordered one of his officers to run and tell Giuliano da Sangallo to go and see them. He set off immediately. Since Michelangelo Buonarroti was always to be found at our house, my father having summoned him and having assigned him the commission of the pope's tomb, my father wanted him to come along, too. I joined up with my father and off we went. I climbed down to where the statues were when immediately my father said, "That is the Laocoön, which Pliny mentions." Then they dug the hole wider so that they could pull the statue out. As soon as it was visible everyone started to draw, all the while discoursing on ancient things, chatting as well about the ones in Florence.[13]

It is a great narrative of discovery. The Florentine Sangallo family is appropriating Roman antiquities, while the presence of Michelangelo has all the makings of a great artist-myth, a Cinquecento visual-arts equivalent to the moment in the *Commedia* when Dante first sees Virgil, whose voice "seems faint from long silence." The young Michelangelo, fresh from the Florentine triumph of the *David*, arrives for his first adult stay in Rome only to be present at the discovery and identification of the greatest sculptural masterpiece of antiquity and to establish thereby a personal link with his ancient colleagues.

So far as the *Laocoön* itself is concerned, what should strike us at once is the means of identification. Pliny the Elder wrote a *Natural History* in thirty-seven volumes, toward the end of which he included a history and description of the visual arts from early Greece to his own time, with particular attention to the objects visible in then-contemporary Rome.[14] Pliny's volume was fairly widely read, especially by painters and sculptors, though it was hardly as well known as Virgil's *Aeneid.* Yet what these Renaissance Romans see first in that hole on the Esquiline is not Virgil's Trojan martyr who said "Beware of Greeks bearing gifts" but a famous work of art as canonized by Pliny. Renaissance viewers of the *Laocoön* will not forget the *Aeneid,* of course. On the contrary, they will place Virgil's text in a highly charged comparative relation to the statue. Lodovico Dolce, for instance, attempts to destabilize the chronological priorities between Raphael and his literary sources by declaring that Virgil based his Laocoön on the statue; "it is a matter of mutual exchange," he declares, "that painters often seize their inventions from poets, and poets from painters."[15] Actually, he uses the word *cavare*—to dig.

But the key term is *exchange*: the material object that emerges from the ground becomes the nexus point for the discourse of ancient narrative or history, as contained in the *Aeneid,* and the discourse of art as contained in the *Natural History.* As a consequence the visible work of art develops its own privilege and priority, not merely as the contingent material representation of a remoter but truer historical reality but rather as a reality of its own. In the face of these new interrelations, Sangallo and the other onlookers respond in two ways: they draw and they talk. They create more works of art, and they conduct an impromptu seminar on the history of art. The words are a sign that art has a history that deserves to stand alongside the history of power or of nature, while the establishment of a past history of art directs the course of art's future history. The images are a sign that art can be made not only out of dogma, out of natural observation, or out of historical events, but also out of art itself. The words and images together produce *aesthetics*—which is to say a philosophy and a phenomenology proper to art itself. The unearthed object becomes the place of exchange not only between words and pictures but also between antiquity and modern times and between one artist and another.

A piece of marble is being rediscovered, but at the same time a fabric of texts about art is being restitched. Writings from later antiquity—Ovidian poetry, Roman novels, Greek romances, lyrics, and rhetorical exercises—turn out to be filled with passages, typically what are called *ekphrases,* in which narrative is framed not as reality but as the contents of an artist's picture.[16] These passages stand in ambiguous relation to the actual objects emerging from the ground. Ekphrases are categorically different from the works of art they supposedly describe; indeed, the poetic description of an imaginary sculpted Laocoön would doubtless not resemble the statue in Rome any more than Virgil's narrative does. Yet this fabric of texts tantalizes readers with the possibility that, together with the rediscovered works themselves, it will reconstruct a complete visual antiquity. In addition, the ekphrastic literature brings with it a set of ways to look at the visual arts and a set of relations between aesthetic representation and language.

As it happens, the Pliny text that springs to Sangallo's mind and enables him to identify the statue is notably un-ekphrastic:

> Nec deinde multo plurium fama est, quorundam claritati in operibus eximiis obstante numero artificum, quoniam nec unus occupat gloriam nec plures pariter nuncupari possunt, sicut in Laocoonte, qui est in Titi imperatoris domo, opus omnibus et picturae et statuariae artis praeferendum. Ex uno lapide eum ac liberos draconumque mirabiles nexus de consilii sententia fecere summi artifices Hagesander et Polydorus et Athenodorus Rhodii.[17]   [36.37]

> The reputation of some works of art has been obscured by the number of artists engaged with them on a single task, because no individual monopolizes the credit nor again can several of them be named on equal terms. This is the case with the Laocoon in the palace of Titus, a work superior to any painting and any bronze. Laocoon, his children, and the wonderful clasping coils of the snakes were carved from a single block in accordance with an agreed plan by those eminent craftsmen Hagesander, Polydorus, and Athenodorus, all of Rhodes.

There is a kind of entropy in the conjunction of these words with the found object. The *Natural History* becomes a treasure map when the object is discovered just where Pliny says it will be, and this piece of fortune (which does not frequently repeat itself) confers special authority on the text's account of aesthetic history. Pliny presents the *Laocoön* as a unity in multiplicity, an object made from a single piece of marble but by three different sculptors who somehow managed to work together, to the glory of their creation but the detriment of their personal fame. Both of these claims reverberate loudly. The object itself is the most complexly articulated of ancient statues; hence the notion that it is constructed out of a single piece of stone amounts to an assertion of almost magical status. Further, the idea of collaboration on a work so stylistically unified reflects powerfully on the individualist and fame-obsessed world in which the object was rediscovered.

Still more important is Pliny's statement that the *Laocoön* is the greatest of all works of art; it is a marble statue that is "superior to any painting and any bronze." He puts it in those terms because he has divided art objects rigorously into these generic categories that correspond to the materials out of which they are made.[18] For a Renaissance reader this way of assigning the first prize cannot help but summon up a consciousness of medium or genre and especially of the rivalry among the media, often referred to as the *paragone*, which means both "comparison" and "competition." It is just in these years that Leonardo is filling notebook pages with discussions of the superiority of painting over sculpture or of the visual arts over music, while in the near future the whole career of Michelangelo will be read (perhaps even by the artist himself) as an agon among artistic media.[19] The paragone, in other words, is a hot topic, and the *Laocoön* emerges from the ground as the embodiment of triumph in the comparison of the arts.

But it is the making of new words—the talking that Sangallo reports at the discovery site—that really testifies to the unearthing of aesthetic consciousness. The *Laocoön* statue figures in countless verbal artifacts of the early sixteenth century, letters describing the discovery, poems extolling the work itself, representations of the statue in Renaissance histories of art.[20] The question of Pliny's single piece of marble, for instance, turns out to have been the center of considerable discussion, as is evident from a letter by Cesare Trivulzio written about six months after the discovery, in which he asserts that Giancristoforo Romano and Michelangelo, "the leading sculptors of Rome," have denied absolutely that the work could be a single stone. "They say that Pliny was deceived, or wished to deceive others, in order to render the work more impressive. . . . The authority of Pliny is great, but our artists can also be right; nor should one undervalue that ancient saying: how fortunate the arts would be if they were judged solely by artists."[21] Once again Michelangelo is invoked, here as part of a complicated construction of authority. The text of Pliny can be disproved by the ocular experience of unearthing the objects themselves, though only when evaluated, as Trivulzio says, "da persone peritissime"—by supreme experts. The conjunction of text and object (curiously, on the very subject of conjunction) raises questions about textual authority itself by exposing the rhetoricity of the text. The solution to these uncertainties is to find truth in the object rather than in the text and to place the discourse of art in the hands of artists themselves.

Poetic responses to the newly unearthed statue often betray a desire to place art in the hands of artists. Like those present at the discovery, these writers say less about the Trojan War than about the history and emotional power of art. On a number of occasions, the form, medium, and condition of the material object come to be part of the narrative rather than merely its external representation. The humanist and papal courtier Jacopo Sadoleto, after celebrating the artwork itself and the miracle of its rediscovery in a newly reborn Rome, begins his account of the narrative with a rhetoricized list of emotional topics; the climactic phrase, after father, children, snakes, and wounds, is "veros, saxo moriente, dolores."[22] "Dying in stone" is syntactically ambiguous: as it is enveloped by the "true sufferings," it suggests at once that marble is in opposition to the reality of the anguish and also that stone is the fitting medium for the individual's death. Evangelista Maddaleni Capodiferro (another figure of the papal court, of whom we shall hear more) makes the point more directly by suggesting that it is part of Laocoön's punishment at the hands of Athena that he continue to live his life in Parian marble—in effect, a further metaphorical turn on the much praised longevity of the art object, thus rendered as a pleasure to the modern viewer but as a pain to the (fictive) person under view.[23] An anonymous contemporary epigram goes furthest to make the art object into the story:

Laocoon natique cadunt Trionidis ira:
Ille qui ad Troiam vulnere laesit equum.
Nec satis hoc: Rhodi artifices mirabile visu
marmore restituunt. Hos dea condit humo.
Ecce iterum redeunt. Quanta est iam numinis ira,
dextera, qua laesa est machina, trunca perit.[24]

Laocoön and his sons fall owing to the wrath of the goddess: he who brought
Troy down with the harm done by the horse. Nor is that all. The Rhodian
artists, amazing to see, have brought them back in marble. The goddess laid
them in the earth, and here they are again returned to us. How great is even
now the wrath of the divinity: the mangled right hand, in which the statue was
harmed, has been destroyed.

The making of the original statue, its loss in the ground, and the lack of Laocoön's
right arm when it is unearthed all become continuing episodes in the original tale of
the goddess's wrath. Even the thousand years of neglect that have mutilated the statue
become part of its narrative.

Implicit in all these responses—perhaps in all ekphrasis—is a sort of
paragone a tre. Poet-observers are in competition both with the narrative material (itself
generally deriving from other poets) and with the mediating art object. But they may
also make alliances with either of their competitors against the other—that is, they
may declare words to be the superior and necessary medium, or they may identify their
task as the verbal celebration of the visual artist's triumph over the original material.
In the same letter quoted above, Cesare Trivulzio finishes his attempt at capturing the
statue for his son who has not seen it by relying on Sadoleto, "who has described
Laocoön and his sons no less elegantly with his pen than the very makers of the work
realized him with their chisel. In the end, those who read Sadoleto's verses won't have
all that much need to see the statue itself, so well does he place every detail before your
eyes."[25] Curiously similar is Lessing's statement in the appendix to Laocoön that he is
publishing the Sadoleto poem in its entirety because "it can well serve in place of an
engraving."[26] Such a casual reference to the exchangeability of a poem and a picture
sorts ill with all Lessing's intricate differentiations between visual and poetic art. Or is
an engraving itself a kind of inferior ekphrasis? Lessing, it should be remembered,
had never seen the thing itself.

What places the unearthed object at the center of these aesthetic debates is its
specially elliptical quality. That the statue emerges from the ground, that it is to some
extent deprived of physical and historical context, that it is imperfect—all these circumstances contribute to a sense that the image is in itself incomplete. The experience
must be finished; and words play their role not only by describing or praising the
object as work of art but also by assigning emotions and words to the characters as
people. In fact, there is a two-thousand-year-long debate as to what sounds Laocoön
ought to be emitting.[27] Virgil has him making horrible cries to heaven like the bel-

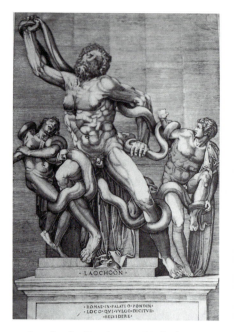 

1.2. *Laocoön*, after Bartolommeo Marliani, *Topographiae urbis Romae*, Rome, 1544

1.3. *Laocoön*, with unfinished arm attached, as put in place by Filippo Magi, Vatican Museums, Rome

lowing of a sacrificial animal, whereas Sadoleto hears him faintly moaning.[28] Winckelmann marveled at the stoicism of a figure who could suffer so greatly yet (apparently) not bellow, as Virgil's Laocoön does.[29] Lessing, on the other hand, took the *Laocoön* to be the very keystone of the difference between art and poetry because the figure in his control and silence epitomizes an ideal visual beauty that is not involved with the realistic particulars of verbal description or the realistic outpourings of verbal agony.[30] The *Laocoön*'s medium, once again, determines the message.

The visual and material aspect of the statue demands completion as much as the verbal. The power of the work in three dimensions exercised a kind of imperative on painters and draughtsmen that they re-create it in two dimensions; while its fragmentary condition exercised a similar imperative on sculptors that they complete it—either in replicas or upon the thing itself. Its power and its history as a great Roman icon further inspired architects and designers to "stage" it—that is, to give it an appropriate setting, whether it be the eventual canonical location in the Belvedere courtyard of Pope Julius or placement in a mythic version of the rediscovery site.[31] These responses initiate what we might call a participatory art. Such an encounter erases the distinction between connoisseurship and creativity and creates an independent history of art by which a Renaissance painter is related to the sculptors of the *Laocoön* not only because of a school, a style, or a common patronage network but also because the artists exist in a collective realm of inspiration.

Artists could participate in the *Laocoön* much more directly, however, than by simply sketching it. We know both from early documents and from observation of the statue in its present state that the only significant pieces missing in 1506 were the right arms of Laocoön and the younger son; as ancient sculpture goes, in other words, the *Laocoön* was almost pristine.[32] Still, it was a fragment, in a state somewhere between that of its two perennial companions, the *Apollo* and the *Torso*. And fragmentariness is perhaps the most crucial fact of all about rediscovered sculpture. If Laocoön's emotional expression seems to require a completion, his body requires it even more. It is the physical incompleteness of so much ancient sculpture that enables both artists and viewers to enter into the works, to decide what the works depict, to define or alter the narrative, to view the works as beautiful shapes rather than only as narratives, and, finally, to take part literally in the creation by restoring the objects in a particular way.

These processes of reimagining and restoring demonstrate just how difficult it was for the Renaissance—and is for us—to arrive at the concept of an authentic original, let alone at its embodiment in stone. Most of the statues the Renaissance could unearth, and certainly the *Laocoön*, were themselves Roman copies after Greek originals.[33] This is a fact that Renaissance viewers did, and did not, confront. The particular gap, say, between the objects in the Belvedere collection and the legendary oeuvres of Phidias or Praxiteles, will carry a powerful charge for a culture just beginning to make painful distinctions between anachronism and historicism.[34] (All the more potent in the case of the *Laocoön*, which, almost uniquely, comes with a correct attribution—though to artists of little fame.) Meanwhile, the Renaissance busies itself by altering the form in which posterity will define the "true" *Laocoön*. Different projects for restoring Laocoön's right arm succeed one another thick and fast in the middle of the sixteenth century; these range from the diagonal, which dramatically replicates the left leg, to the nearly vertical, which seems especially heroic, to the slightly flexed, which is perhaps the most tortured. The *Laocoön* of the seventeenth, eighteenth, and nineteenth centuries—in effect, the canonical *Laocoön* for the modern imagination—is of the diagonal type (fig. 1.2; see also fig. 5.4). And as though to usher in our own revisionist century, in 1905 a German archaeologist discovered in a Roman stonemason's shop what is almost certainly an authentic piece from the real *Laocoön's* elbow, which turns out to be more flexed than any of the reconstructions; curiously, it resembles most closely some of the earliest ideas of reconstruction.[35]

What is of particular interest here is not so much the choice of a certain arm position as the way the Renaissance understands the project of completing or solving the riddle of the statue. Around 1510, the great architect and keeper of the Vatican treasures Donato Bramante seems to have conducted a contest among a group of fledgling artists hanging around Rome, asking each to make a wax version of the *Laocoön* suitable for casting. Raphael, acting as judge, awarded first prize to Jacopo Sansovino, who ultimately became one of the leading architects of Venice. This episode, as reported by Vasari, demonstrates that within four years of its discovery the *Laocoön* has already become the basis for an academy of design—just as these famous ancient statues and their copies will continue to be for another four hundred years. The winning entry is cast in bronze and becomes a valuable work of art with its own history; but for the moment, at least, the pope's *Laocoön* remains as it is, and the replica is understood to be a work by Sansovino.[36]

Ten years on, things have changed. It is Vasari, once again, who will eventually tell the story:

> There had recently returned from France Cardinal Bernardo Divizio of Bibbiena, who, perceiving that King Francis possessed not a single work in marble, whether ancient or modern, although he much delighted in such things, had promised his Majesty that he would prevail on the Pope to send him some beautiful work. After this Cardinal there came to the Pope two Ambassadors from King Francis, and they, having seen the statues of the Belvedere, lavished all the praise at their command on the Laocoon. Cardinals de' Medici and Bibbiena, who were with them, asked them whether the King would be glad to have a work of that kind; and they answered that it would be too great a gift. Then the Cardinal said to them: "There shall be sent to his Majesty either this one or one so like it that there shall be no difference." And, having resolved to have another made in imitation of it, he remembered Baccio [Bandinelli], whom he sent for and asked whether he had the courage to make a Laocoon equal to the original. Baccio answered that he was confident that he could make one not merely equal to it, but even surpassing it in perfection.[37]

The *Laocoön* (among other art objects) has become an important pawn in international politics. The elaborate verbal negotiations hide—and reveal—just how much the French want the statue and how little the pope is willing to give it up. At this moment is born the idea of a replica that is worth just as much as the original. Bandinelli, of whom we shall hear much in the present volume, is the ferocious competitor who thinks he can outdo everybody, notably his contemporary Michelangelo; at the same time, he derives his only great successes from copying ancient works. True to his reputation, he boasts that he will produce a *Laocoön* that is better than the *Laocoön*. The political valorizing of the *Laocoön* quite naturally adds to its aesthetic value the status of currency (in every sense of the word). The *Laocoön* becomes exchangeable for diplomatic goods and services and also interchangeable with other *Laocoöns*. Fittingly, Bandinelli not only creates this improved *Laocoön* but also constructs a new right arm for the actual Belvedere statue—presumably, to bring it in line with his own complete version of the work. (In the end Francis I gets neither of these *Laocoöns*. The pope likes Bandinelli's *Laocoön* and ships it back to his native Florence; the French king has to make do with a bunch of plaster casts provided by Primaticcio and Cellini—which may tell us a good deal about the future history of French art.)[38]

Ten years later the right arm of the *Laocoön* needs to be invented once again—

either the Bandinelli arm was never attached or it was damaged—and in 1532 there is no doubt but that the newly commissioned limb will be joined directly to the ancient work. The process of replicating has, in other words, imposed itself even more strongly upon the original. According to one tradition, Michelangelo was asked to provide this new arm, but he declined and passed the commission on to a younger associate, Montorsoli—altogether a more tractable figure than Bandinelli. It is certain that Montorsoli did execute an arm that was attached, corresponding to the familiar diagonal position.[39] It is appropriate to surmise that Michelangelo did not wish to touch so directly upon the marble of the ancient work itself, just as it has been said that he was opposed to restoring the *Torso Belvedere* for similar reasons.[40] But the arm needs to be made yet once more around 1540, and many believe that this newest limb (fig. 1.3), with its powerful upright flex that seems like a cross between Bandinelli and the modern version, was actually executed by Michelangelo.[41] Perhaps he changed his mind during those ten years and decided to put aside his reverence and impose himself on the *Laocoön*. Whoever planned this work certainly did impose on the statue: in order for the new arm to fit, the statue's original shoulder was severely sliced back. In these various approaches we may see both a diachronic history—that is, a movement toward ever-increasing imposition of the modern artist on the ancient work—and at the same time a set of synchronic alternatives that define Renaissance theory and the practice of imitation, emulation, and (a term we hear less of in the literary discourse of this topic) mutilation.

The full life of the *Laocoön* in the visual culture of the Renaissance goes far beyond restorations, copies, or sketches of the statue itself; from the time of its discovery it inserts itself into the visual imagination and becomes the basis for new image making. This kind of story—often using this very example—has been recounted many times. A succession of historical insights from the work of Aby Warburg to that of Fritz Saxl and Ernst Gombrich, among others, has taught us to see in antique images and motifs qualities of inherent attractiveness through which creative artists of the fifteenth and sixteenth centuries measured themselves and discovered their own originality.[42] For our present purposes, let us say that it is necessary to look ever more closely at the historical machine that takes in the *Laocoön* at one end and extrudes the Sistine Ceiling at the other. It isn't a machine at all, of course, but—just to keep the metaphor alive—one might say that it is a mechanism of very complex circuitry. None of the stages can be taken for granted. Not all the ancient sources are masterpieces, nor are all individuals who operate under their influence inspired. And the processes of transmission are anything but smooth: in the encounter between the moderns and the ancients there may be more friction than flow, more fealty than freedom. Just where the friction rubs, and upon whom the fealty depends—these are the larger concerns of this book.

Titian, to cite one canonical example, quotes and develops the body of Laocoön throughout his career.[43] A quarter century, along with many compositional

1.4. Titian, *Crowning with Thorns*, oil on wood, 1540s, Louvre, Paris

1.5. Titian, *Crowning with Thorns*, oil on canvas, 1560s, Alte Pinakothek, Munich

differences, separates the two versions of the *Crowning with Thorns* (figs. 1.4, 1.5); but in both cases the Christ is a Laocoön with slightly recombined limbs, and the most original element in the disposition of the body is the right arm, precisely where the original statue was silent. The particular combination of turned waist and spread legs appears frequently in Titian's oeuvre: in the *Sacrifice of Isaac* (fig. 1.6) from Santa Maria della Salute in Venice or the Madrid *Gloria* (fig. 1.7), and somewhat less directly in many other instances, including the Madrid *Fall of Man*, the Washington *Saint John on Patmos*, and any of the various Adonises taking leave from Venus. This persistence of the *Laocoön* body is teasingly ambiguous. Are we to see the figure as an attempt to appropriate the *classic* image, in both senses of the word: that is, of a greatness that transcends time while simultaneously being stylishly identified with the time of antiquity? Are we to see it as meant to evoke typologically either the iconography or the emotional significance of the *Laocoön* statue itself, perhaps filtered through Virgil, Servius, or Landino? Are we to see that this constellation of limbs satisfies some special psychic needs of artist, patron, or contemporary viewers?

I don't know. What I do see in some other instances is the explicit entry of the *Laocoön* into the discursive practice of Titian's art. Well before any of the previously mentioned sculptural quotations, the painter includes in his *Bacchus and Ariadne* (fig. 1.8) a kind of profile version of Laocoön entwined with (somewhat rearranged) snakes. The sophistications of modern iconographic reading enable us to see in this figure an importation, thanks to the Belvedere collections, of an authentic Dionysiac

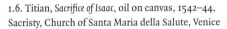

1.6. Titian, *Sacrifice of Isaac*, oil on canvas, 1542–44, Sacristy, Church of Santa Maria della Salute, Venice

1.7. Titian, *The Glory of the Holy Trinity* (detail), oil on canvas, 1551–54, Prado, Madrid

representation appropriately decorating the mythological narrative. But Annibale Roncaglia, whose documentation of this group of paintings in 1598 was reliable enough for Cesare d'Este and for some modern attempts to reconstruct the full program, entitles this work not *Bacchus and Ariadne* but "un quadro di mano di Tiziano dove era dipinto il Lacoonte."[44] What's a young genius to do? He attempts to be inspired, to be influenced by, to assimilate, to transcend past masterpieces, but ends up, at least in some viewers' eyes, assimilated and transcended by them. The clearest way that Titian attempts to seize control of the process and of his source is by parody. It is in his simian *Laocoön* (fig. 1.9), known to us only from a woodcut copy,[45] that he fully explores the historicity of his own aesthetics: by rendering the *Laocoön* as a trio of monkeys in a landscape, he represents ancient sculpture, modern painterliness, and—most important—the process of imitation-emulation-assimilation—read, *aping*—that occupies the space between.

But one cannot recount the story of these aesthetic relations as merely one-on-one. To render Laocoön and his sons as apes, in all their muscular corporeality, is to parody not only the process of transmission but also its principal mediator. Michelangelo, as we have seen, was present at the discovery. Later, he will be cited as an expert on the statue; he will refuse to restore it and then (perhaps) accept the task. It has been argued that Michelangelo did not simply imitate the *Laocoön* but somehow held it within him; and it may be that while in Florence and almost a prisoner of his Medici projects at San Lorenzo, he re-created from memory the head of the *Laocoön* as

a sketch on the wall.[46] As with Titian, Michelangelo offers a career-long history of *Laocoön* quotations and appropriations.[47] Shortly after 1506, works like the *Saint Matthew* and certain of the Sistine *ignudi* (fig. 1.10) derive their energies from reproducing the muscular turned torso and the protruding knee; much later, with the Florentine *Pietà* (see fig. 5.48) and in drawings for Vittoria Colonna of the Crucified Christ (fig. 1.11) the same muscular body has been rendered wholly limp.

Rather than see the matter as a set of individual choices, we should understand Michelangelo as establishing a kind of ownership of the image. Although everyone might be privileged to look at the *Laocoön* on the Esquiline, the image does not stay in the public domain any more than the object does. Michelangelo's situation at the papal court as well as his own personal vision will in a short time make it impossible for his contemporaries (and us) to look at the *Laocoön* except as always having been a work by Michelangelo. We may get a glimpse at the process by considering first a very early appropriation of the statue, Antonio Lombardo's frieze of *Vulcan's Forge* (fig.

1.10. Michelangelo,
Ignudi surrounding the
*Separation of Light from
Darkness*, fresco, 1511–12,
Sistine Chapel, Rome

1.12), which includes a graceful, relaxed Laocoön figure with the familiar position of
torso and limbs but without any dynamic sense of what renders the body so powerful—and, as it happens, without the snakes. In another work in relief of some years
later, the *Flagellation of Christ*, by Moderno (fig. 1.13), not only is the body authentically
re-created; but the sculptor also understands the driving force of tension that causes
all the muscles to flex.[48] In fact, the work is influenced by Michelangelo's composition
for Sebastiano del Piombo's *Flagellation* in San Pietro in Montorio, itself a rather softened version of the Belvedere statue, but Moderno has re-Laocoön-ized the figure,
replacing the snakes with ropes that almost literally hold the tension inside the body.
It is Michelangelo, with the whole of his highly visible career, who makes sense out of
the muscular torsion and the struggle against external bonds. The great sculptural
forms that he creates out of this inspiration are not imitations but responses to a set of
qualities in the *Laocoön* that he has himself defined. In turn, his status canonizes the
vision while rendering it almost inimitable.

1.11. Michelangelo, *Crucified Christ*,
black chalk, ca. 1540,
British Museum, London

1.12. Antonio Lombardo, *Vulcan's
Forge*, marble relief, ca. 1508,
Hermitage, St. Petersburg

Though not quite inimitable; just copyrighted. Through the *Laocoön*, along
with the *Torso Belvedere* and a few other ancient works, Michelangelo will have rights to
the contemporary life of the rediscovered antiquities. Titian may once again stand as
the fitting competitor. His *Laocoön* figures, including the Isaac and the King David of
the *Gloria*, are references to Michelangelo as much as to the ancient statue; and, as we
have seen, the ape-*Laocoön* is as much a parody of Titian's contemporary as of the
ancient original. What is significant in this set of transmissions is not so much the
fact of personal difference as the opportunities it offers to pursue in visual language
the discourses of artistic theory and practice. The artistic culture of the earlier sixteenth century is obsessively self-defining and self-referential; one battleground of
this war is the Belvedere courtyard and all the other collections and reproductions that
it spawns. Let one document speak for the whole scene of aesthetic and social struggle. Titian's *Averoldi Altarpiece* (fig. 1.14) from the 1520s includes a variety of *Laocoön*
images.[49] The resurrected Christ is a direct quotation but, like the Lombardo frieze, it
removes nearly all the internal electricity of the body; indeed to turn Laocoön into a
floating Christ is to make this removal of tension the very subject of the image, to the-
matize it. The Saint Sebastian, on the other hand, is a post-Michelangelo *Laocoön*
figure, a profile version of the Belvedere figure rendered as a very direct quotation
from Michelangelo's *Rebellious Slave* (fig. 1.15). Titian is engaging in the paragone on
two counts: painting and sculpture; himself and Michelangelo. The broken column
under Saint Sebastian signals the heavy, massive, and fragmentary quality of sculpture
(ancient or modern) and contrasts it with the lightness of the painter's art, which

1.13. Galeazzo Mondella,
called Moderno, *Flagellation
of Christ*, silver and gold relief,
ca. 1530, Kunsthistorisches
Museum, Vienna

finds its expression in the rising Christ. What the sculptor's medium is good for, according to Titian, is a place of graffitti. And as his personal graffitto, Titian chooses to inscribe it with his own name. To declare of ancient sculpture (as Titian is doing) "dust thou art, to dust thou shalt return" is only to confirm that Renaissance art discovered itself—in words—as a subject when the masterpieces of antiquity emerged from that dust.

VERTICAL HISTORY

The *Laocoön*, as I have repeatedly suggested, is not unique. From at least the 1480s onward modern Romans were encountering in extraordinary profusion those products of their ancient predecessors that had best withstood the destructions and constructions of the intervening centuries; for the most part, these durable goods (or at least those worth writing about) were works of art. A mid-sixteenth-century guide book to sculpture visible in Roman collections lists dozens of objects as having had specific discovery sites, as well as hundreds of others that can only have appeared by the same means.[50] It seems, then, reasonable to say that the unearthing of ancient sculpture was virtually a commonplace event.

 Yet what defined the nature of that object was, in some important ways, the fact that it was *discovered*, and this is a chapter about the conditions that made discovery possible and gave it meanings. The unearthing of an ancient statue is conditioned in part by circumstances that have their own histories behind them. Why was a certain

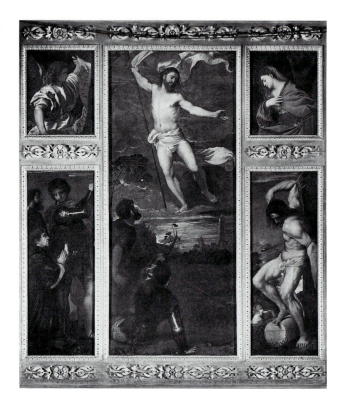

1.14. Titian, *Averoldi Altarpiece*, oil on wood, 1520–22, Church of Santi Nazzaro e Celso, Brescia

person digging in a certain place? Was there a lot of digging going on—so much that the probability of finding things underground was suddenly high? Were there reasons for the location in which the digging took place, such that the turf containing a high proportion of thousand-year-old statues was now reassuming some of the importance that led to the statues being there in the first place? These questions need not be thought of as too minute or too statistical for respectable humanist study, and indeed we shall consider some of them below. But, important as they are, they take it for granted that these particular diggings are worth our attention. What gives the discovery of ancient statues a collective identity as a subject is not a sequence of events that caused it but rather a set of predispositions, a *mundus significans* that made and makes it worthy of attention.[51]

Of course the phenomenology or sociology of digging impinges retrospectively upon the mundus significans in which the digging is defined. Still, one must enter this circle somewhere, and it is our predisposition here to say that the point of entry should be a prior history of ways in which the past was defined. As a first step in considering the history of the idea of the past as a mundus significans for the discovery of ancient statues, let us ask a naive, rather anachronistic question. Given the hundreds of accidental discoveries of ancient art in the Renaissance, and given the historical importance assigned to these objects as well as their monetary value, why is it that the discoveries remained *accidental?* How could it be that such an enormous industry of intellect, aesthetics, politics, and economy in a city notorious for poor intrinsic

1.15. Michelangelo, *Rebellious Slave,*
marble, ca. 1514, Louvre, Paris

resources should *not* give rise to the professional enterprise of archaeology such as
waited another two centuries to be born? I ask the question not as part of a historical
comparison but as a way of isolating the Renaissance from our own presuppositions.
The ultimate *uses* of the discovered objects in the sixteenth century—scholarship, artistic inspiration, economic and political valorization—have much in common with the
uses of classical archaeology two hundred years later, or indeed with some equivalent
activity of our own time (moon rocks?). The difference is that in the sixteenth century
these utilities could not so readily be induced. Indeed we must assume that the assignment of value to the objects—their utility—depended in part on the chance circumstances of their procurement. And if that is the case, then the often repeated circumstance of Renaissance Romans coming upon statues accidentally in a vineyard will
point to a very different mentality from the mythic surroundings of the career of
Heinrich Schliemann or, for that matter, of Neil Armstrong.

    An earnest comparison of these cases would presumably make a great deal of
the differences among social relations and levels of technological development. It
seems to me, however, that the real difference is in the operations of symbolism, that
is, both with the nature of the central symbol and with the hermeneutics according to
which the symbol is understood. The discoveries of ancient statues had to remain
accidental, because the objects would lose something of their authenticity if they were
procured as the result of aggressive and individualistic industry. This authenticity is
derived from the soil in which they are found. Although there are discoveries all over

Italy, and although there is interest in these discoveries in far-off northern capitals, the ground is above all that of the eternal city itself: the symbol is Rome, and the hermeneutics are, roughly speaking, chthonic.[52]

In what ways, then, is Rome a symbol? The answer is, in almost all ways; that is, Rome is almost purely a symbol. With the exception of a very brief period, the history of Rome is a history of the idea of a city that used to be. Through a simple mechanism, the more depressed the reality of Rome, the more potent the symbolization. This is, of course, a universal phenomenon in regard to any widely perceived historical construction; Rome merely happens to be among the most extravagant examples. Students of the geopolitical scene in the early modern period can point to many obvious instances both of the loss of Rome's greatness and of the persistence of nostalgia for that greatness. We might take as an example the relation between the exile of the papacy to Avignon in the fourteenth century and the contemporary flourishing of intellectual and literary activity with a passionately pan-Italian and symbolically Roman slant. The combination is surely not fortuitous, and the two circumstances are the more closely related for the fact that Dante and Petrarch are double exiles: first, they are not Romans and second, they spend much of their lives banished even from that other city which, for all its sedulous mythmaking about itself, is an upstart in the Rome-centered history of the world. One cannot explain away the birth and growth of geniuses, but one can hazard to say that the existence of a great argument can act as an inspiration; in the case of the fourteenth-century Florentines, one of the great arguments is patently the unattainability of Rome, which alternates as tenor and vehicle with the unattainability of Italy. It may be too much to claim that the grand projects of these two men, in the one case a reinvention of the universe in the vulgar tongue, in the other a reinvention of antiquity in the Latin tongue, are compensations for the loss of the reality of Rome; but it is certainly not too much to say that their explicit concerns with Rome maintain this form of potent symbolization.

Dante and Petrarch point to many facets of Rome's infinite regress from reality into symbol: the economic and political decay of medieval Rome, the special nature of the papacy as both more and less powerful than secular hegemonies, the combined sense of brashness and inferiority that comes with the shift of Italian cultural determination to the north—not to mention the net loss occasioned by the growth of international powers outside of (and preying upon) Italy. In the subsequent century and a half Rome is strengthened as a reality: the papacy returns, and some able and aggressive figures occupy the Holy See. But it could be argued that the competition, both in Italy and abroad, both political and cultural, strengthens itself even more. As a consequence, the Rome of Nicholas V, who imports Fra Angelico, or of Sixtus IV, who imports Botticelli, or of Julius II, who imports Raphael and Michelangelo, uses its cultural force not so much to build a new reality as to realize an old myth.

It is even more instructive to move backward from Dante and Petrarch than forward, for the habit of seeing Rome as perpetually a symbol whose reality is in the past has itself a perpetually regressing past. The furthest of these regressions concerns the ancient Roman attitude toward its own prehistory. From early times—and persisting throughout antiquity—Roman culture understands itself as derivative from the Greek and relates to that consciousness with a mixture of self-effacement and arrogance. The *locus classicus*, which epitomizes an already deeply ingrained mentality and codifies it for the future, is the parting shot of Anchises to his son, Aeneas, who has come to the underworld to hear prophesies:

> "Excudent alii spirantia mollius aera,
>   (credo equidem), vivos ducent de marmore voltus;
>   orabunt causas melius, caelique meatus
>   describent radio et surgentia sidera dicent:
>   tu regere imperio populos, Romane, memento
>   (haec tibi erunt artes) pacique imponere morem,
>   parcere subiectis et debellare superbos."[53]

> "Others, I assuredly believe, will fashion bronze images with a tenderer breath of life and will shape living faces out of marble; others will plead more eloquently in court or, gauging with instruments the movements of heaven, will predict the rising of the stars. But remember, Roman, that you must rule diverse peoples in an empire—these will be your arts—to impose the rule of peace, to spare the conquered, and to subdue the proud."

So far as the visual arts are concerned (and perhaps those of rhetoric and astronomy as well), there can be no doubt who these "others" are: the fictional date of this declaration, in the eighth century B.C., precedes and prophesies the glorious age of Greek culture as much as it does that of Roman power. Viewed in terms of the real date of this utterance—during the reign of Augustus—the prophesy is self-justifying and compensatory. "Haec tibi erunt artes" is the same sort of half-pun in Latin that it would be in English: *ars* is essentially the practice of visual representation, while lawyers and astronomers practice their *artes*—skills—only at one remove, with governors of territories perhaps at a second remove. That the *Aeneid* seeks to situate these last *artes* in the highest place should not make us overlook the poem's insecurities about what it considers to be the essential *ars*, of which Roman skills are but a reflection.

Roman taste in the visual arts conforms to the awareness that Anchises codifies. We shall speak elsewhere of the competition within the Renaissance imagination among the respective aesthetics of Periclean Athens, Hellenistic Greece, and imperial Rome.[54] For the present it suffices to observe that high culture, particularly of the visual arts, was defined in this central moment of the central literary expression of the Roman people as quintessentially foreign. As Virgil retrospectively invents a Rome that does not exist yet, he declares already that its cultural production will always be a reflection of an absent essence. And the practice, both in Virgil's time and later, follows this definition. For the most part the representational arts—in other words, the kind of object that the Renaissance will unearth—are brought over from the Greek world. Artists were imported; alternatively, objects were purchased, plundered, or copied. There is, of course, powerful native art in Rome—sarcophagi will interest us later; architecture is beyond the scope of this book—but ancient Romans themselves had reason to look upon their own visual arts as being removed in time and place from a source and a reality.

Anchises' prospective vision of an absent reality should be balanced with a retrospective vision from the later imperial period. The growth and proliferation of Roman political power well after Virgil's time has its own ways of attenuating the reality of Rome.[55] A city that stands at the head of a vast empire is both strengthened and weakened by the proliferation of territories: strengthened as the symbolic *caput mundi*, weakened as a center of real power. By the third century this state of affairs receives de facto recognition with the establishment of alternative loci of administration from the Caucasus to Yorkshire. These appear to have been real working centers of government. They tended to denude Rome of imperial functionaries and to produce a class of circuit-riding government workers. Meanwhile the Senate continued, but largely as a ceremonial institution, embodying ancient wealth and symbolizing pagan glories. Rome thus signified much as a center, but in practice it contained neither emperor nor imperial court. The establishment of Christianity and, later, of Constantinople strengthened this trend. Not only the particulars of imperial rule but even the official seat of the emperor was now outside of Rome; yet at the same time the state religion, particularly with the special prominence given to the veneration of Saint Paul and Saint Peter, derived its symbolic power from its presence in Rome.

Just as real power recedes from Rome, so the graven images of that power become increasingly pure symbols. By the end of the third century, the Palatine and the Capitoline, the Forum and the Colosseum, were almost entirely showpieces; indeed, they functioned for an imperial tourist trade not unlike that of our own time.[56] This type of social utility increasingly dictated what sort of building, rebuilding, or restoring was practiced in these areas of the city; in addition it defined high artistic ambition as more concerned with image making than with use. It is around this time that these monumental works start to show signs of decay. From the age of Constantine onward, Roman letters are full of an awareness that buildings and works of art are crumbling: time itself is one of the culprits but no more so than Christianity, which placed imperial power in an ambiguous relation to the pagan cultural heritage and inspired the spoliation of ancient buildings in the cause of erecting new churches; in addition, there was much individual theft of valuable works of art and more particularly of valuable materials out of which works of art had been made.[57]

That visible ruins should have more symbolic force and less reality than functioning structures is fairly obvious; what is less obvious is that ruins are manufactured (that is, grand constructions are allowed to decay) by societies that treat themselves more as symbols than as realities. The experience of an imperial tourist who sees a purely ceremonial but perfectly preserved Forum is similar to that of a later tourist who sees a ruin of past grandeur. Two reflections upon the condition of Rome from late antiquity will demonstrate how closely these points of view embrace each other. The first is Ammianus Marcellinus describing the visit of the eastern emperor Constantius II to Rome in 357:

> So then he entered Rome, the home of empire and of every virtue, and when he had come to the Rostra, the most renowned forum of ancient dominion, he stood amazed; and on every side on which his eyes rested he was dazzled by the array of marvellous sights. [There follows a description of several wonders of Rome, a list of names of other wonders, and a climactic account of the Forum of Trajan.] When Ormisda [Prince of Persia, traveling with Constantius] was asked directly what he thought of Rome, he said that he took comfort in the fact alone, that he had learned that even these men were mortal. So then, when the emperor had viewed many objects with awe and amazement, he complained of Fame as either incapable or spiteful, because while always exaggerating everything, in describing what there is in Rome she becomes shabby.[58]

The second, about a hundred and fifty years later, is one of Cassiodorus's many letters written for Theodoric on the subject of the ruination of the city, in this case part of what we would call the infrastructure:

> We have directed John to repair the Cloacae of the City, those splendid works which strike astonishment into the hearts of all beholders. There you see rivers as it were shut in by concave mountains, flowing down through mighty rafters. There you see men steering their ships with the utmost possible care, lest they should suffer shipwreck. Hence may the greatness of Rome be inferred. What other city may compare with her in her heights when even her depths are so incomparable?[59]

In both cases Rome is a remote and fundamentally unlifelike object of symbolic value, an exemplum. Emperor Constantius and his entourage see a Rome that, so far as we can tell, is in perfect condition. But its very grandeur and symbolic force make the beholders think of ruin: the mortality of the individuals who built these monuments and the feebleness and fickleness of Fama. Cassiodorus, on the other hand, sees the time line in retrospection: faced with a ruined sewer, he imagines it as a mini-Roman Empire and uses it to infer the same monumentality from which the earlier visitors had inferred decay.

These accounts of a Rome that is absent or symbolic even in antiquity are important to us because such symbol making continues as individuals contemplate the physical remains of the city, whether they live in 400, 1400, or 1600. Or even earlier: the first encounter of Virgil's band of Trojans with the space that will become Rome is structured in a series of layers that are both temporal and spatial. Aeneas is led by a vision of the future to a place where Evander and his Arcadians are engaging in the ritual retelling and celebration of an event in their ancient past.[60] According to this history, Hercules vanquished the monster Cacus, who was associated with primordial evils rooted in a deep underground cave. Hercules laid bare and exorcised these earthbound monstrosities; in the almost uncountable ages between that event and this moment in the *Aeneid* (itself of ancient days when Virgil is writing), the underground cave has become a craggy mountain. The surroundings of the mountain become the scene for a primordial history of the human race as well as an implied "future" history, complete with familiar place names, of the Roman people. The mountain itself, though savage when Aeneas sees it, is already implanted with the Jovian divinity that will become visible as the glorious adornments of the Capitol, which stands at the topmost level of Augustan Rome. The history of Rome, in other words, is morally, chronologically, and spatially vertical; and the metaphor is grounded in the literal terrain of Virgil's city.

Fourteen hundred years later, when the seven hills are nearly as desolate as they were in the fictional time of Evander, the history of Rome is barely visible to the naked eye. In a letter to his friend Giovanni Colonna, Petrarch uses the emptiness of the city (which he somewhat exaggerates) as a tabula rasa on which to impose a massive verbal text detailing the events that took place in each piece of this geography.[61] The inhabitants of Rome know nothing of this, he says, presumably because it is the act of the historical and metaphorical imagination, and not the few crumbling objects themselves, that creates a vision of Rome. Like many of Petrarch's writings, the letter enacts a double distancing: historical Rome was absent when he and his friend walked through the ruins, while at the moment of writing the letter, the speaker is absent even from those ruins. When in Rome Petrarch was able to conjure up the text of the city's history from the ruins, and even now he can remember that text. But his friend has asked for something more—a discourse on the origins of the arts that sprang so readily to Petrarch's lips while contemplating Rome; that text, Petrarch teasingly announces, is unrecoverable at this second remove. The technique is drawn from the *Aeneid*. Petrarch is looking through Virgil's time telescope the other way, re-creating a physical Rome as Evander pre-created it. But while Virgil wants his readers to recognize their familiar space, Petrarch takes advantage of centuries of ruin and further obliterates the landmarks so that they become little more than an excuse for demonstrating his discursive ability to envisage the golden age.[62]

The terms of Petrarch's metaphorics will remain powerful well into the Renaissance. According to this model, the absent monumental Rome is a set of images, but like all images from antiquity, these have perished almost to the point of being immaterial. They can be reimagined by the application of ancient verbal texts—which have survived in vastly better material condition—and this process in turn generates modern verbal texts. Words, following this logic, are relatively easy to come by and to produce afresh; images, on the other hand, are the (largely) unattainable object of desire, fugitive and perishable but possessed of some more essential truth. In Petrarch's time the objects of desire that are attainable are for the most part textual: manuscripts are found, forgeries detected, the science of philology envisaged. The succeeding century witnesses first of all great constructs of antiquarian words that almost smother the images, whether mental or physical. But the same period also sees the birth of the possibility of attaining authentic ancient images—that is, of matching verbal iconography with classical forms of representation, as the brilliant formulation of Erwin Panofsky and Fritz Saxl long ago suggested.[63] Yet creating pictures of pagan myths in the fifteenth century that conform roughly to the vast repertoire of ancient icons known to scholars at the Warburg Institute is one thing and encountering that repertoire in the flesh is quite another. In one of those circular patterns in which cultural history tends to shape itself, the attaining of classical images—that is, the ability to make them—is inspired by some early discoveries of the real thing, while that ability in turn makes possible more discoveries and new visions of what has been discovered.

But in what sort of vehicle does one proceed along this metaphorical circle? As Petrarch has rewritten Virgil, the distance between glorious Rome in its heyday and the empty landscape of other times is symbolic. To travel across it, Virgil conjures, Petrarch imagines, the antiquarian Poggio Bracciolini researches, the Dugento sculptor Nicola da Pisano extrapolates.[64] The Renaissance inherits the supposition that ancient flourishing Rome and desolate modern Rome do not exist in the same dimension. If they are not in the same dimension, then one cannot literally travel between them, however much one can contemplate their parallel relationship. Yet to find ancient statues in the ground of modern Rome—not just once or twice but so frequently as to become a commonplace event—is to come face-to-face with the fact that there is a dimension that both Romes share. Just as Proust's narrator dates his mature awareness to the realization that the Méséglise Way and the Guermantes' Way exist in the same space,[65] so we might date the Renaissance *sub specie statuarum*. Yet this is not a twentieth-century perception; and what characterizes the discovery of statues is the tenacity with which the Renaissance adhered to the old symbolism in the face of the new data. Consider what unwieldy hypotheses had to be created to ignore the (to us) obvious fact that ancient Rome was some twenty to fifty feet below modern Rome. Placing the Domus Aurea underground or in a grotto (hence, its paintings *grotteschi*) is approximately the equivalent of the superstructure of epicycles that was needed in its final days to correlate Ptolemaic cosmology with observation. Archaeology does not develop in 1480 for the same reason: you cannot travel through symbolic space with a shovel.

The discovery of ancient statues in the ground places the ultimate test on a millennium and a half of belief in the purely symbolic nature of Roman space. Suddenly the space of Rome is both real and symbolic; the past is both an idea and a buried physical reality. The metaphors do not die but become enriched. So long as the geological has not subdued the metaphorical, the field is rich with imaginative possibilities. There is a moment (in our subject let us call it fifty years, more or less) when the images that have been the unattainable objects of desire *may perhaps* be attainable. (We shall see in later chapters how they *may perhaps* be decipherable or *may perhaps* be re-creatable.) It is in this period that an extended metaphorics of symbolic space will be created to explain the new and more complicated relation between ancient and modern Roman space. As we have seen, the Renaissance resists the archaeological—or evolutionary—belief that ancient Rome simply got buried under fifteen hundred years of debris. Even so, for the antique city to exist below the modern is an emblem of its ruin, physical, moral, or spiritual. Yet the space underneath is also an emblem of the origins of the present-day world perpetually existing at its core, just as Virgil had narrated the subterranean origins of the Capitol and as Ovid had done for the whole Mediterranean world with his metamorphic science of etiology.[66] A third, and more modern, canonical text, Dante's *Inferno*, created a universe of the past living underground; and while that universe is damned, it is pointedly alive with the glories of pagan antiquity. That may be the most relevant vision of all, offering the modern matrix of time and space, of linear history rendered as vertical geography.[67]

FINDINGS AND LOSSES

The story I want to tell about finding statues in the Roman turf around the year 1500 impinges on quite a few other stories that are concerned with different times, different places, and different materials for discovery. Some of these I have already touched on: Petrarch, who lived a century and a half earlier, whose geographical roots were in Florence and Avignon, and whose interests were far more literary than visual, can stand as an example of these larger fields of study. But it will be useful to sketch in these relations more fully.

It is perhaps easiest to separate out the other objects of discovery, not the least because they have been so magisterially chronicled by Roberto Weiss in *The Renaissance Discovery of Classical Antiquity*.[68] As it turns out, any of these sets of materials has a history that manages both to parallel and to intersect at every turn with the history of rediscovering sculpture. Perhaps the object of greatest priority is the classical inscription.[69] Like statues, these are visible everywhere in Italy throughout the Middle Ages; also like statues, however, they are newly unearthed, more greatly valorized, and submitted to changing forms of rigorous study from the fourteenth century onward. Petrarch's friend Giovanni Dondi copies Roman inscriptions during his trip to the city in 1375.[70] By the fifteenth century we hear of many exploratory journeys (usually quite far from Rome) organized for the sole purpose of collecting epigraphic remains. Mantegna spends some days in September of 1464 with the antiquarian Felice Feliciano and others transcribing monumental writings around the Lago di Garda. Feliciano describes the events in his journal as a ritual classicizing pilgrimage, complete with a flower-bedecked boat and quasi-pagan religious ceremonies.[71] Feliciano's elder contemporary Ciriaco d'Ancona was first inspired, he tells us, by the triumphal arch of Trajan in his native city; from there he went off to a lifetime of travels—including to Greece, where almost no one ventured during this period—in search primarily of inscriptions but also of ruins, architectural monuments, and art objects.[72] Andrea Alciati began his career at the opening of the sixteenth century by writing a history of his native Milan, for which his principal research activity was the assiduous collecting of epigraphy throughout the region; it is not surprising that this work might lead to his later and more famous interest in emblems.[73]

Inscriptions have a significantly pivotal role among ancient material remains: that is, they are at once a form of text and a form of image. On the text side, as the example of Alciati's history and dozens of other historical-propagandistic projects attest, inscriptions stand as a set of reliable antique data much like more extensive forms of literary remains. But if manuscript material comes to the Renaissance as a succession of earlier transcriptions, epigraphic materials carved in stone are more like the thing itself. As text construed in a philological sense, they represent a lexicon of authentic ancient language that might stand, even in the pre-Renaissance period, as an enduring witness of the falling off between classical Latin and its degraded modern forms. Yet the fact is that inscriptions, whether ancient or modern, come in a specialized language quite unlike other written modes. Viewed through Renaissance eyes, epigraphy becomes doubly enigmatic: mysterious in the way of all remnants from an alien culture and at the same time composed in a style that may have been intentionally elliptical to begin with.[74] Because these enigmas are coded as primarily linguistic, they become a particularly rich field for analysis among scholars trained in all the philological and rhetorical modes of the medieval trivium. So inscriptions are directly understood as a hermeneutic site: matter for interpretive decoding and about which it is difficult to arrive at a definitive answer. They are also a site for humanist correspondence, discussion, and debate, as in the fight between Poliziano and Battista Mantovano about "Virgil" versus "Vergil" or between Ciriaco d'Ancona and Poggio Bracciolini concerning the form *Iunonibus*. But it is not always a question of grammatical pedantry: many volumes of correspondence reveal that epigraphy was understood as an important set of antique questions that demanded modern answers.[75]

At the same time, inscriptions form parts of images and are also images themselves. In fact, all this protoarchaeology—not only epigraphy but also many other objects of discovery—stands at the threshold of words and images. Decidedly logocentric humanists like Giovanni Mansionario or Ciriaco d'Ancona find it necessary and useful to produce drawings in the midst of the verbal texts they compose in order to record their discoveries; nor should it be surprising that artists like Pisanello and Mantegna take part in collecting and recording constructions of words.[76] Viewed as purely linguistic objects, inscriptions might be reproduced in whatever scribal hand happened to be comfortable. But often they appear on monuments that need to be recorded as visual objects; and even when they are disconnected from a physical setting, their very enigmatic quality makes it necessary that they be transcribed in a visual approximation of their original lapidary lettering. By the end of the fifteenth century a number of humanists are producing pattern books for the making of authentic capital letters *all'antica*.[77] Throughout the period the whole rediscovery of antiquity will remain in important ways rooted in the revival and reinvention of epigraphy. The "picture" of the pagan world that the Renaissance cultivates, say, in the works of Mantegna or in the *Hypnerotomachia Poliphili*, is decorated with inscriptions. Where objects are recovered without them (as is generally the case), Renaissance viewers will attempt to supply the explanatory epigraphy by imagining it, falsifying it, or cobbling it together from unrelated sources. The actual recovered words in stone thus provide a model for newly classicizing verbal responses from the moderns.

Coins provide an analogous, though distinctive, object of discovery. Like inscriptions and statues (along with many other forms of ancient remains), they were widely known throughout the Middle Ages, but they came to be valued in new ways in the Renaissance. What links them especially with sculpture is the fact that they are above all found objects, generally dug for in the ground, as is clear already from the Petrarch letter used as this chapter's epigraph: "Often there came to me in Rome a vinedigger, holding in his hands an ancient jewel or a golden Latin coin, sometimes scratched by the hard edge of a hoe." The paradigmatic narrative for epigraphy is the travel across the land to some far-off place where marble slabs are to be found in profusion; the numismatic stories, on the other hand, tend to be concerned with accidental excavation on the home front—precisely what we have already seen as central in the finding of statues. Petrarch's rhetoric in this passage depends on separating the ignorant finder of the object from its learned recipient. That distinction points to the special quality of coins: they are of obvious material value, even to a vinedigger, but they also contain arcane historical information. This information consists typically in portraits of emperors with, as it happens, inscriptions, rendering them once again a mixture of pictures and words in need of decoding.

The deployment of these numismatic materials can be glimpsed in another of Petrarch's letters, when he speaks of his meeting with Charles IV in Mantua: "I gave him as a gift some gold and silver coins bearing the portraits of our ancient rulers and inscriptions in tiny and ancient lettering, coins that I treasured, and among them was the head of Caesar Augustus, who almost appeared to be breathing. 'Here, O Caesar,' I said, 'are the men whom you have succeeded, here are those whom you must try to imitate and admire, whose ways and character you should emulate: I would have given these coins to no other save yourself.'"[78] Although the event took place in 1354, Petrarch's account contains in miniature all the elements of prestige that coins will enjoy in the Renaissance: they are aesthetically pleasing; they require expert philological and historical knowledge to be properly deciphered; they are understood as the objects par excellence of exemplarity, to be contemplated by rulers so that they understand the proper uses of power as sanctioned by the ancients. The diffusion of interest in coins follows along these lines of force. They are universally sought after because of their obvious material value. They hold great fascination for artists, including Pisanello, Filarete, and Ghiberti,[79] not only as generic classical remains but also because they represent specimens of portraiture so perfect that their subjects—in the tried-and-true formulation—seem to be alive. They are decoded, transcribed, drawn, and published because, like inscriptions, they contain authentic historical information, but, even more important, they provide likenesses of Roman emperors that can become the bases for the visual aspect of a whole exemplary literature concerned with illustrious men. And, even more than sculpture, they become the identifying object for princely collecting, including such individuals as Lorenzo de' Medici and Pietro Barbo, who would become Pope Paul II.[80]

Objects of discovery other than inscriptions, coins, or statues are far less detachable—in both the material and the intellectual sense. Rome of the fifteenth and sixteenth centuries (along with many other sites in Italy) is, after all, a gigantic archaeological playground crowded with antique remains, including architectural monuments, ruins, and the more abstract vestiges of classical city planning. The broadest context for the rediscovery of sculpture is therefore not so much other analogous transportables or collectibles as the very ground in which all these things are located. These grander remains of ancient Rome had always been to some extent visible. We have already considered the remarks about them made in late antiquity by Ammianus Marcellinus and Cassiodorus. A ninth-century monk from Einsiedeln who provided a much used itinerary to the city is no less aware that Rome is filled with massive ancient structures.[81] But he has far less interest in reading them: in the earlier medieval accounts antique buildings are mentioned almost exclusively as points of reference for a tourist who is understood to be making a pilgrimage among the city's principal churches.

By the twelfth and thirteenth centuries, accounts of the *Mirabilia* of Rome take far more notice of ancient landmarks—indeed, one work by the English monk known as Magister Gregorius is almost wholly devoted to classical remains[82]—but in other respects the formula has not greatly changed. In the manner of medieval historiography, these descriptive works ground the objects in a relatively undifferentiated mass of textual materials, including folk legend, Christianized versions of classical history, and snatches of (usually irrelevant) literary ekphrasis, generally taken from Ovid or Virgil. Even into the fifteenth century, with the anonymous *Tractatus de rebus antiquis*, works in this genre tend to describe a Rome whose pagan and Christian monuments coexist but without a logical set of geographical or chronological relations.[83] Thus we hear of Octavius largely in regard to his encounter with the Sibyl who predicted the Virgin birth; Ovid's ekphrasis of the Palace of the Sun in book 2 of the *Metamorphoses* is treated as a description of the Septizonium; and the Viminal Hill is described as the place "where the Church of Sant' Agata is and where Virgil, being taken by the Romans, escaped invisibly and went to Naples."[84]

One way to understand the change that comes about in the 1420s and 1430s with Poggio Bracciolini is to see it as a species of a newly historicized philology.[85] At any time after these monuments had become more symbolic than real—to use the terms I offered above—contemplating them means searching for a verbal text that explains them. The authors of the *Mirabilia* accounts, deficient in the quantity of ancient writings at their disposal, tend to treat imaginative descriptions out of the *Fasti* or the *Aeneid* as though they were topographical accounts of the living city—that is, when they are not using wholly anachronistic legendary materials. Poggio, who was in and out of Rome from the beginning of the fifteenth century as he followed the fortunes of the schismatic papacy, made a specialty of searching for manuscripts of classical works that would contribute to an accurate version of Rome's historical topography. His volumes of correspondence document tireless efforts to procure manuscripts at Monte Cassino that include the work of Ammianus Marcellinus, whose accounts of Roman history and geography we have already cited, and of Frontinus, the chronicler of the city's water system.[86] These are in turn cited as evidence in his own description of the ancient city. In the succeeding century, authors like Plutarch, Varro, Pliny, and Vitruvius will be similarly scanned for information that could bring to life the mute signs of classical Rome—and, reciprocally, be brought to life by them.

But this description should not suggest our own model of professional archaeologists trained in material culture and making instrumental use of texts; it would be more accurate to say that for these founders of a humanistic approach to classical remains, archaeology is a subset of the study of texts. Flavio Biondo, Poggio's great successor, whose *Roma instaurata* was to remain for at least a century the major work on Rome's urban topography in relation to ancient texts, began his career with a study of the spoken language of ancient Romans. Giovanni Tortelli provided his description of ancient Rome as a chapter within a larger text on spelling.[87] Indeed, for many of the more au courant writers of the later fifteenth century, archaeology is a linguistic activity, a kind of materialistic etymology. The word *Rome* itself must have its origins and its correct orthography properly specified; and from there it follows that the names for the buildings and geographical structure of the city will become the key to their nature.[88] In that sense, it is also worth distinguishing among *kinds* of texts: more than one archaeological dispute in this period is resolved by contrasting the relevance of ancient books with that of the inscriptions actually found on the remains themselves.[89] The up-to-date study of epigraphy thus becomes a form of empiricism that displaces an older tradition according to which inscriptions are ephemeral and books have primary authority.

Not all approaches to the materials from antiquity are so resolutely textual. From the earliest signs of humanist interest in the buildings and structure of the ancient city, individuals devote considerable attention to systems of measuring and mapping that seem to be generated out of the objects themselves. The earliest post-classical account of the city we have—the ninth-century Einsiedeln travel guide—is in the form of a verbal map, with separate itineraries radiating out from a (not clearly identified) central point. And, to turn to the beginnings of the Renaissance, much of the description by Giovanni Dondi of his jubilee trip in 1375 is devoted to measurements of the buildings, along with a brief discussion of the mechanics of measurement and comparisons with other people's results—suggesting that there existed already a lively conversation in this field.⁹⁰ The central figure in the enterprises of both maps and measurements is Alberti, who spent some time in the 1430s at the Roman Curia.⁹¹ Spurred on by some learned colleagues there, he designed a system of measurement that would integrate the placement and shape of individual monuments with the larger structure of the city walls so as to provide the basis for an overall map of Rome. While Alberti's plan owes much to an up-to-date awareness of such disciplines as mathematics, navigation, and astronomy, it remains a highly abstract account of the city, probably less revealing about its physical features than were many of the medieval itineraries. In fact, though it acted as a sort of prolegomenon to a map of Rome, we are aware of no such map being made from it. And even when more concrete panoramas of the city begin to be created in the later fifteenth century, it is worth noting that like Alberti's plan they are ahistorical—that is, they map the complete city as it exists in the present moment without reference to the different ages of the buildings or different shapes of the urban space through time.

Alberti's other contribution to the humanist study of ancient remains, the enormously influential *De re aedificatoria*, is possessed of a quite different historical consciousness.⁹² One of the book's running strategies of argument is the careful marshaling of ancient verbal data, from Vitruvius and others, which the author nevertheless privileges less than his own empirical investigation of ancient buildings themselves (e.g., "Examples of ancient temples and theaters have survived that may teach us as much as any professor" [6.1, ed. cit., 154]; "I have learned more on my own than I have from the author of any book" [3.16, ed. cit., 89]). In fact, this claim is rather rhetorical: passages of detailed mathematical description in the *De re aedificatoria* tend to be derived more from earlier written accounts than from Alberti's own travels among the ruins with a measuring rod. Yet Alberti's authority as a master of both theory and practice will continue to validate the empirical aspect of measuring and mapping the classical city. In his compendium on Roman topography, *De urbe Roma*, composed at the end of the century, Bernardo Rucellai will make up-to-date use of all the disciplines—history, philology, epigraphy, mechanical systems of measurement—but will reserve a special place for Alberti, both as the theorist who wrote the book on architecture and as Rucellai's personal, hands-on guide to the city twenty years earlier.⁹³ Like many other approaches to the material remains of antiquity, topography and architectural measurement will remain in that charged space between authoritative written texts and individual modern experience.

Both philology and topography are learned enterprises in regard to antiquity's material remains, but their force and persistence in Renaissance culture cannot be fully explained without recognizing what one might describe as a more popular sentiment—that is, various forms of fascination with ruins. We have already touched on the Petrarchan version of this experience. The sentiment gains rather than loses strength as the study of ancient materials becomes more scholarly and technical. Poggio Bracciolini's work, which inaugurates the archaeological revolution, is, after all, entitled *De varietate fortunae*. In good medieval fashion, Poggio treats the ruins as exempla of mutability and proceeds to his efforts at philological reconstruction as a response to the visible signs of decay. The elegiac note may be more characteristic of Poggio than of any of his successors—among his later works is a *De miseria humanae conditionis*—but virtually all writers in this field gain rhetorical force from apostrophes to a Rome in decline; and the physical evidence for this falling off is often linked with laments at the loss of knowledge concerning antique culture.[94]

A more aggressive interest in the question of ruin is also to be heard among those responding to Roman antiquities. In its most traditional form, the *ubi sunt* topos is free of particular agency: the world is in an undifferentiated process of decay, and the observer indulges in a (frequently pleasurable) lamentation. But throughout the Middle Ages and the Renaissance, the decay of ancient Roman remains is not at all free of personal agency, and those watching the process from at least the twelfth century are fully capable of seeing the forms of destruction being actively practiced. The reasons for this activity vary through time. Roughly speaking, in the earlier period, ancient buildings and monuments were despoiled largely for the value of their building materials; later, acquisition of the newly valorized classical objects as collectibles became an additional motive.[95]

Like many chronological formulations, however, this is a bit simple. It may be that in the eyes of medieval builders nonfigural architectural remnants appear to be nothing more than high-quality raw materials to be used for propping up some new structure made of shaky bricks and wood. But other kinds of remains—sarcophagi, columns, statue fragments—do not seem to have ever been completely emptied of the significance originally attached to them. Charlemagne is no less aware than Julius II that the possession of ancient marble pieces confers some sort of imperial worthiness.[96] And if ninth-century marbles express their value chiefly in a purely material sense—that is, only because marble is a rare commodity—one cannot say the same for the practice that begins from at least the eleventh century of collecting and exhibiting many figural works in the walls of churches, where, incidentally, they have no structural function. Yet another form of reuse and revalidation is to be seen in the approach toward three-dimensional objects, like ancient sarcophagi used for modern burials or urns used as dispensers of holy water.[97] And finally there are numerous legends of what we might call negative validation, like those concerning the fourth-century Pope Silvester (similar stories are told of Gregory the Great), who is supposed to have destroyed the Colosseum so as to prevent sun worship while keeping the colossal bronze head of the sun god on exhibit as an apotropaic warning lest anyone reinstate the practice of pagan religious abominations.[98] The ironic possibilities of both condemning and profiting from ancient artworks seem already to be apparent in the twelfth century, when John of Salisbury tells how the Bishop of Winchester had considerable quantities of antique sculpture shipped back to England on the slender and mendacious excuse that he was thereby preventing the return of pagan worship in Rome.[99]

This mixture of reactions suggests that from early times the same impulses that bestowed value on the material remains of antiquity also led to their physical undoing. It is not a war between lovers of antiquity, who carefully preserve remains, and Christian zealots, who destroy them; rather, the very history of the values that come to be attached to ancient material culture carries within itself the potential for furthering the process of ruin. Although there are early signs of an awareness of this problem (in 1162 the Roman senate decrees capital punishment for anyone who damages Trajan's Column), the issue comes to be part of general humanist conversation only in the fifteenth century.[100] Which is no coincidence: throughout this period, it is the imperial ascendancy of the papacy, despite all its classicizing trappings, that tends to ride roughshod over the very field of ancient remains it is using to validate itself. This history has been eloquently documented several times. Eugène Müntz has lamented with great fervor the destruction of the Colosseum, the Septizonium, the Forum of Nerva, and the Triumphal Arch of Marcus Aurelius under even the most enlightened of pontiffs.[101] To that list one might add earlier removals of marble from the Colosseum in the time of Eugenius IV, plus the demolition of the Hercules temple in the Forum Boarium under Paul II, of the Meta Romuli under Alexander VI, and further destructive building projects under the most celebrated classicizing popes of all, Julius II and Leo X. In short, to quote another sensitive modern observer: "The Renaissance passion for building on classical lines was the main cause for the destruction of what still remained of ancient Rome."[102]

In fact, the cultural paradox of valuing ancient remains by destroying them is itself perceptible to some observers at the time. The Renaissance version of these jeremiads is initiated by Pier Paolo Vergerio (1370–1444), whose career as a classical and civic humanist spans the period from Petrarch, whose *Africa* he edits, to the intellectually liberal milieu of the anti-pope John XXIII and beyond.[103] When Vergerio first visits Rome in 1398, he composes an epistolary account that is almost a completion of Petrarch's letter to Giovanni Colonna (*Familiar Letters*, 6.2; indeed the two texts are woven together in several of the manuscripts), offering in more pedestrian terms the historical travelogue that Petrarch had not fully delivered. Vergerio begins with the generic *ubi sunt*—so many great cities have fallen into decay; Rome's greatness is to be measured by the extent of its ruins—but he soon turns to a more specifically humanist lament. "Nusquam minus Romam cognosci quam Rome" (Nowhere is Rome less known than in Rome itself), he declares, quoting the *Familiar Letters* directly in an argument that joins the diffused sadness of general physical decay to a degradation for which modern individuals can be held more directly responsible. The Roman people make up stories about the ruins and speak a corrupted version of the language in which the historical landmarks are named.

The physical depradations by the Romans occupy Vergerio even more: "Both in books and in buildings, the [modern] Romans struggle in their will toward the ruin and destruction of these arts. That is, of painted manuscript pages which, in order that pilgrims have something useful to wipe their sweat with, those of the city tear apart large numbers of books of uncommon value. Also, those who work the stoves, lest they have to go too far to bring stones, destroy buildings, such that they transform marble and virgin stone into lime. For this reason, a large number of extraordinary buildings have already been demolished, and continue to be demolished every day" (4.97). The Petrarch-inspired move is a geographical distancing of the speaker from modern Romans which produces a concomitant historical identification with the ancients. Vergerio will influence a long line of humanists who see modern culture as Petrarch saw it: that is, as debased and ordinary. For humanists through the rest of the century, the ignorance, avarice, and bigotry of modern Romans becomes a crucial foil to their own more ambitious and paganizing philological impulses. This is a bold claim, because the industry of debased modern Rome is the church and because the authors of these laments are almost always in the employ of the Curia, but, especially in the earlier period, they do not seem to shy away from the contradictions. Vergerio's most evocative detail—picked up by others writing on the same theme—concerning the manuscript pages that are ripped out in order to provide souvenir veils of Veronica for pilgrims,[104] places a popular form of Christian religion in harsh contrast to humanist bibliophilic efforts; it also suggests the triviality of modern art in comparison both to ancient art and to the real imprinting of Christ's face on Veronica's veil.

Twenty years later, Cencio da Rustici exposes these issues even more directly in an eloquent attack on these same "modern" impulses in a letter to his mentor, Francesco da Fiano, known for his almost religious devotion to ancient writings and material objects:

> Every day you see citizens (if indeed a man should be called a citizen who is so degraded by abominable deeds) demolishing the Amphitheater or the Hippodrome or the Colosseum or statues or walls made with marvelous skill and marvelous stone and showing that old and almost divine power and dignity. Truly I would prefer and would pay more for a small marble figure by Phidias or Praxiteles than for a living and breathing image of the man who turns the statues of those glorious men into dust or gravel. But if anyone asks these men why they are led to destroy marble statues, they answer that they abominate the images of false gods [falsorum deorum idola]. Oh voice of savages, who flee from one error to another! For it is not contrary to our religion if we contemplate a statue of Venus or of Hercules made with the greatest of skill and admire the almost divine art of the ancient sculptors. But mistakes of this kind are to be blamed not only on those we have just mentioned but on the former governors of the city and on the popes, who have continually consented to this destructive behavior which lowers the dignity of mankind.[105]

Once again, the diatribe depends on separating the despised race of modern Romans from ownership of the Latin language and therefore true citizenship all'antica. But

Cencio takes the implication of Vergerio's comment on the Veronica veils and confronts the theological issue more directly. He ignores the prevailing materialist explanation for the plundering of ruins and chooses instead to see the matter as doctrinal, referring back to the whole tradition centering on Pope Sylvester, according to which it was Christian zeal that directed the destruction of the pagan idols. (He goes on to argue ecumenically that priests have been responsible for the destruction of Christian monuments and texts as well.) In what is clearly a Plinian formulation, Cencio declares that he would rather have a small work from one of the great Greek sculptors—it will be at least a century before the impossibility of fulfilling that wish is manifest—than any representation of those who destroy artworks. What we should hear in this attack is, I think, less a record of widespread Counter-Reformation-style piety *avant la lettre* than the argumentative mode of early fifteenth-century humanism that sought to further its classicizing aims by a sort of elitist attack on unlettered forms of Christian piety.

Not that Cencio altogether succeeds in Christianizing the contemplation of statues depicting Venus or Hercules simply by ascribing to Phidias and Praxiteles *ingenia pene divina*. The claim is clearly a rhetorical one, and as one moves more into the mainstream of the humanism that regards the city's ruins from the perspective of the papal court, one hears less invective against zealous Christianity and more abstractions about human greed. As I have already suggested, Poggio Bracciolini, who begins writing his *De varietate fortunae* in the 1430s, takes a very neutral approach to the causes of ruin, concentrating on fate, age, and mutability. His more archaeologically sophisticated successor, Flavio Biondo, writing his *Roma instaurata* at mid-century, recognizes (as had Vergerio and Cencio) that the decay of ancient remains is both a sign and an effect of widespread ignorance as to the meaning and value of the monuments. As his title suggests, Biondo's project responds to this state of affairs by in effect designing a philological reconstruction of the ancient city that has been—and continues to be—lost. The very notion of reconstruction weaves the humanist project back into the papal agenda of imperializing its own place in the caput mundi. Thus in *Roma instaurata*, Biondo forcefully juxtaposes the Rome of the Caesars with the Rome of the Christian martyrs, which tends not to be part of the earlier humanist account of the ancient city at all, while in his later work, *Roma triumphans*, he goes even further by arguing for the absolute typological unity between the present-day Vatican and some of the holiest places of Roman antiquity.[106] He is, in other words, searching for a syncretic historical account of the two Romes that can stand as the basis for a modern city that is both Christian and imperial.

By the time one enters the half-century that stretches from the accession of Sixtus IV to the death of Leo X, the humanist project of the city's philological reconstruction comes to be inextricable from the political—and artistic—project of the city's physical reconstruction. In many respects, these can be understood as harmonious goals, just as Biondo had imagined. A succession of humanists from Bernardo

Rucellai to Castiglione could document the ancient urban space with sufficient accuracy that modern building projects might renew these glories, while the latest written topographies of the city, like that of Francesco Albertini in 1510, could include recent monumental construction as part of the full panoply of Rome's wonders, thereby recreating the mixture of pagan and Christian marvels that characterized the medieval itineraries, though now with a firmer sense of history.[107] On the other hand, we have already seen how these goals could also be in conflict, because building the new city inevitably meant destroying the old.

This, then, is the contested space occupied by the material remains of Roman antiquity during the four decades surrounding 1500. In the time of Sixtus IV, when the building projects begin in earnest, we hear some complaints from the humanists concerning the losses. Pomponio Leto, Lucio Fauno, and Andrea Fulvio note the destruction of the Hercules temple in the Forum Boarium and the triumphal arch near the Palazzo Sciarra-Colonna with telling indications of the pope's own involvement.[108] Even more significant, because it comes from a Roman nobleman who will have a long career of both currying papal favor and epigrammatizing ancient and modern art, is the response of Evangelista Maddaleni Capodiferro, expressing himself with great acerbity in regard to the building of the Ponte Sisto, which included marble removed from the Colosseum:

> ut parvi starent fondamina pontis,
> Ampla tuae quatiant amphitheatra manus?

> In order that the foundations of a little bridge be erected,
> must your hands bring down great amphitheaters?[109]

It is noteworthy that we possess no such invectives against the contemporaneous building of the Vatican Library, whose architects were given permission to dig up marble wherever they pleased,[110] nor against any of the other ambitious constructions that earned Sixtus the title *gran fabbricatore*. The Ponte Sisto, built merely to solve traffic problems anticipated in the jubilee year of 1475, had none of the cachet of these grander efforts, whether secular or sacred, and could therefore be dismissed as trivial in comparison to a Colosseum that is rendered as both a magnificent ancient monument and a sanctified space.[111]

In the end, perhaps the most remarkable thing about Capodiferro's response is its rarity. Throughout the period, lament over the destruction of ancient monuments continues to be directed, as it was in the fourteenth century, either against mutability in general or against a boorish Roman populace associated with the barbarians who had visited their own forms of destruction upon the city. As the projects emanating from the papacy become more monumental and more "classicizing," the humanists come to be more thoroughly implicated in the ventures. By the pontificates of Julius II and Leo X, as we shall see, Capodiferro himself is recording the imperial glory conferred upon the popes by newly found art objects, which were themselves often discovered owing to the demolition of structures in which they were originally housed.

But it would be wrong to see the project of responding to ancient material remains as merely an unholy patronage alliance. In August 1514, Leo X appointed Raphael to be *maestro della fabbrica*, or chief architect, of Saint Peter's, and a year later he was named *commissario delle antichità*, in effect protector of ancient marble.[112] Raphael would not seem an obvious candidate for either job. The 1514 letter of appointment declares that he is being named as *architect* because of his excellence as a *painter*;[113] nor, despite his judging of the *Laocoön* contest, has he by this time gained any great fame as a student of antiquities. In addition, the combination of jobs is noteworthy. We have no trouble recognizing in the papal commission the humanist language respecting ancient remains: "Since we have been informed that masons unheedingly cut and use ancient pieces of marble and stone that bear inscriptions or other remains which often contain things memorable, and which deserve to be preserved for the progress of classical studies and the elegance of the Latin tongue, but that get lost in this fashion, we order all stone quarries of Rome not to break or saw stones bearing inscriptions without your order and permission." But the reason for all this authority tells a somewhat different story: "It is of the utmost importance for the work on the Roman temple of the Prince of the Apostles that the stones and marble, of which a great quantity are needed, be easily obtained in the neighborhood rather than imported from afar. . . . We create you, because we have entrusted you with the direction of the work, inspector in chief for all the marble and all the stone which will be excavated from now on within Rome or within ten miles around it, so that you can purchase them if they are useful for the work on the temple."[114]

Raphael's power, in other words, has more to do with eminent domain in acquiring marble for the construction of Saint Peter's than with humanist preservation. Indeed, we know of only one prosecution, when Raphael attempted to intervene not because ancient marble was being wantonly destroyed but because a collection was to be diverted from the pope's grasp for use in the Conservators' Palace, where ancient art objects had been exhibited since the time of Sixtus IV.[115] Whatever the results in this case, Raphael's efforts in general, like those of a succession of well-meaning decrees going back to 1162 and to papal bulls from Pius II (1462) and Sixtus IV (1474), do not seem to have done anything to halt the despoiling of ancient remains.[116]

In fact, the election of Raphael to this status has less to do with the practicalities of saving the ruins or of building Saint Peter's than with the wish to promulgate a vision of artistic production and humanist study consolidated in the service of ambitious papal propaganda and under the leadership of the leading painter of the age. The key word is *consolidate*: the hindsight of Vasari's *Life*, which praises Raphael above all as a principle of harmony among conflicting colleagues, enables us to notice that in both his jobs Raphael became the center of a vast collaborative network.[117] The immediate reasons for his appointments had to do with his connections to his predecessors in their respective jobs, Bramante and Fra Giocondo, and he went on to enlarge these groupings. As papal architect, besides his stewardship of the heritage of Bramante, Raphael employed Giovanni da Udine, Giulio Romano, and a host of others listed by Vasari;[118] as protector of antiquities, he continued the work of Fra Giocondo, in addition to which he came to be closely associated with Giacomo Mazzocchi for epigraphy, Fabio Calvo for his translation of Vitruvius, Andrea Fulvio for his topographical studies, and—most significantly—Castiglione as humanist and courtier.

The same syncretizing conceptual ambition leads to a great expansion of the commissionership. Whether the impetus came from Raphael himself, from the humanist circle around him, or from the aggrandizing ambition of Leo, the simple mandate to watch over the reuse of ancient marble turns into nothing less than the production of a complete visual record of the ancient and modern palimpsest that was Rome. Writing of these activities around 1519, Celio Calcagnini, who was associated with Fabio Calvo and the translation of Vitruvius, declares them to be the culmination of Raphael's career. Raphael is the "prince of all painters, both in theory and practice." He can expound Vitruvius, both defending and attacking him—though attacking so gently that there is no rancor. He can act as the overseer of the Vatican's architecture, "but now, in truth, he is accomplishing an admirable work which will be astonishing to future ages. . . . He is revealing in a plan the very face of the ancient city with its grandeur and proportion in large part recreated. For he has excavated the highest pinnacles and the deepest foundations with everything called back into being according to the descriptions and explanations of the ancient writers—so much so that Pope Leo and his nobles stand in admiration, almost as though everyone were beholding a divine godhead sent from heaven to the eternal city to bring back its former glory."[119] The coordinates of Raphael's venture consist, first, of humanist verbal discourse, in his learned and civil interpretation of Vitruvius; second, of very real architectural production, in the new Saint Peter's; and, finally, of a much more abstract and unrealized kind of production, the divinely sanctioned repristination of ancient Rome.

The terms in which this project is generally understood come from a famous letter to Pope Leo, which is the subject of much textual uncertainty but is now generally understood to be Raphael's thoughts as polished by Castiglione.[120] There, Raphael declares that he will produce drawings of everything one can determine about the look of ancient Rome, "facendo quelli membri, che sono in tutto ruinati nè si veggono punto, corrispondenti a quelli che restano in piedi e che si veggono" ("those that are completely ruined and no longer visible may be understood by the study of those that still stand and can be seen" [84]). As his very language suggests, the acts of recording, decoding, and reconstructing the ancient city—with all the problematics that operate in the multiple time lines embodied in the successive constructions of different ages—are inextricably interwoven. Raphael proves himself, to begin with, quite conscious of ancient verbal authority, as Calcagnini suggested, though his means of invoking it are often somewhat indirect. Vitruvius is in fact generally cited as a way of *avoiding* a discussion—that is, as rendering unnecessary a more specific description of architectural features. One thinks in this connection of the haunting expression in Raphael's earlier letter to Castiglione: "Vorrei trovar le belle forme degli edifici antichi, né so se il volo sarà d'Icaro. Me ne porge una gran luce Vitruvio, ma non tanto che basti" ("I should like to revive the handsome forms of the buildings of the ancients. Nor do I know whether my flight will be a flight of Icarus. Vitruvius affords me much light, but not sufficient").[121] That distance between the promise of illumination and the need for something beyond ancient sources remains characteristic of Raphael's thinking.

The fullest account of sources in the letter to the pope does not mention Vitruvius at all:

> E ben ch'io habbia cavato da molti auctori Latini quello ch'io intendo di dimostrare, tra gli altri nondimeno ho principalmente seguitato P. Victore, el qual per esser stato degli ultimi, può dar più particolar notizia delle ultime cose, [non pretermettendo anchor le antiche, et vedesi che concorda nel scriver le regioni con alcuni marmi antichi nelle quali medesimamente son descripte].   [84]

> I have studied in many Latin authors these things that I mean to set forth, but among all those I have chiefly followed P. Victore, since he was one of the latest of them all, and can give more particular information on the works of that time, while not neglecting the older ones, [not omitting again the ancients, as it can be seen that they agree in their writings with certain antique pieces of marble which are themselves described].

The passage is textually problematic: the last half-sentence appears in only one of the versions, while the name of the author whom Raphael principally followed is blank in the other version. Nor does the name Publius Victor point to anything very definitive when it is cited.[122] It was invented by Pomponio Leto to identify the anonymous author of the late antique *Notitia regionum urbis*, which set out most fully the ancient division of Rome that would develop into the modern *rioni*, or districts. That Raphael cites Publius Victor as "one of the latest of them all," in apologetic contrast to the more authoritative classical writers, already demonstrates his difficulties in dating the verbal source materials that were themselves transmitted through modern commentaries. This uncertainty goes hand in hand with competing sources of authority—that is, between the textual claims of the ancients, like Vitruvius, with their experience of Rome in its fullness, and the experiential claims of the moderns, who have seen it as it is now. The authority of present experience predominates in the letter, proving itself largely by a very detailed account of the artist's procedures in mapping and measuring. Although Raphael does not invent new methods, he gives one of the fullest practical accounts yet proposed of the procedures both for determining the size and shape of individual buildings and for representing the complete result on paper. Following his mentor, Fra Giocondo, he adapts the magnetic compass to the surveying of land; then, like Leonardo before him, he plots the results in compass directions defined by the winds; finally, in a Vitruvian tradition, he divides the modes of representation into the flat plane, the section, and the elevation.[123]

These modes of intervention in regard to Rome's antiquities—Raphael comments that "havendo posto non piccola cura in cercarle minutamente et in misurarle con diligentia, e leggendo di continuo di buoni auctori et conferendo l'opere con le loro scripture" ("I have taken no small effort to look them over with care and to measure them with diligence. I have read the best authors of that age and compared what they had written with the works which they described")—are grounded in what may be the boldest and most eloquent of jeremiads in response to Rome's decay. He passes through the typical sources of ruin, including *tempus edax rerum* and the Goths and Vandals, to reach a cause yet closer to home:

> Quanti pontefici, padre santo, quali havevano il medesimo officio, che ha V. Santità ma non già 'l medesimo valore et grandezza di animo, quanti, dico, pontefici hanno permesso le ruine et disfacimenti delli templi antichi, delle statue, delli archi et altri edificii, gloria delli loro fondatori? Quanti hanno comportato, che solamente per pigliare terra pozzolana si siano scavati i fondamenti, onde in poco tempo poi li edificii sono venuti a terra? Quanta calcina si è fatta di statue et d'altri ornamenti antichi? che ardirei dire, che tutta questa nuova Roma, che hor si vede, quanto grande ch'ella vi sia, quanto bella, quanto ornata di palazzi, di chiese et di altri edificii sia fabricata di calcina fatta di marmi antichi.   [82–83]

> How many pontiffs, Holy Father, who held the same office as yourself, though without the same knowledge, the same valour or greatness of soul—how many, I say, of these Pontiffs have permitted the ruin and defacement of the ancient temples, of statues and arches and other edifices that were the glory of their builders? How many allowed the very foundations to be undermined that pozzolana may be dug from them, so that, in but a little time, the buildings fell to the ground? How much lime has been burned from the statues and ornaments of ancient time? I am bold to ask how much of all this new Rome that we see today, however great, however beautiful, however adorned with palaces and churches and other buildings has been built with lime made from ancient marbles?

In making this simple, direct, and indeed revolutionary declaration that the glories of the new Rome are built on the ruination of old Rome, Raphael is not inhibited by the fact that such acts are precisely part of his job description. He is participating in a humanist redefinition of papal ambitions with regard to antiquity and the arts.

What renders this assertion so powerful is not only that it is made to Leo but also that it is made by Raphael—that is, by an artist rather than an archaeologist and by an individual who is more associated with building the new Rome than with contemplating the old. In fact, the special authority of everything in the letter is bound up with Raphael's privileges as a great artist. His is a *practical* understanding of Vitruvius or "P. Victor"; his mapping and measuring are based, as he frequently asserts, on an understanding of artistic draughtsmanship, including the differences between the painter's and the architect's systems of perspective; and he is representing himself in a certain sense as altruistic, as willing to humble his own independent ambitions in the service of recording and preserving the work of the ancients. The letter reveals the vision of the artist in other, more direct ways. When Raphael looks at the ruins, he sees not just a mass of timeless materials worthy of preservation but rather a whole progressive and regressive history of styles, ranging from the golden age of the empire to successive diminutions under the barbarians and the medievals. It is the history told roughly by Ghiberti and precisely by Vasari—all three, notably, invoking their privilege as visual artists.[124]

At the same time, it is probably more significant how little there is in the letter of Raphael the artist, as we know him, and how little the letter conforms to some preconceived model for sixteenth-century art as a rebirth of antiquity. Painting, sculpture, and literature, Raphael tells the pope, declined much faster than did architecture. The reliefs on the Arch of Constantine are "sciocchissime"—utterly insipid—as are the statuary and painting (presumably mosaic) from the Baths of Diocletian. Only those things from the columns of Trajan and Antoninus Pius are "excellentissime e di perfetta maniera." Perhaps, having drawn all these implicit parallels between the larger aspect of the ruins and the sculpture that is the real subject of this book, we had better in the end notice the differences. The marbles over which Raphael is given protective custody are those containing inscriptions that will benefit the improvement of Latin linguistic culture, with no mention made of representational objects. When Raphael looks at the grander urban fragments that constitute ancient Rome, he stands in subservience and awe; when he looks at the sculpture on the Arch of Constantine, he turns up his nose in disdain. There are, to be sure, some uncomplicated reasons for the difference. Raphael is more a figural artist than an architect; his contemporaries have attained higher standards in their own exercises of representational art than in their buildings or city-planning ventures; and—most important of all—the ancient Romans produced greater architecture than sculpture in the first place. Yet there are other categorical differences, at least in degree if not in kind. The inscriptions, the coins, and above all the larger topography of the city participate in a discourse of reinscription—that is, they tell the broader historical narrative that will fit the pieces back together and thus enable observers to create a new version through humanistic study, practical technologies, and artistic inspiration. But the fragmentary works of figural art, though contemporaries are equally desirous of recording and completing their story, turn out to be far more resistant. The ancient texts that render them in words are even more enigmatic; compasses do not measure them so well; the modes of reconstructing them in two or three dimensions are fraught with greater artistic license; and their status as ruined or mutilated takes on different, more anthropomorphic resonances.

In a larger respect, one can look back on the whole Raphael-based project as less a reality than an idea. Although manuscripts of the letter mention illustratory images,[125] none has been preserved. More significantly, Raphael's premature death cuts short all efforts of mapping and reconstruction; and indeed the great cultural outpouring of sorrow after 1520 attaches itself with special poignancy to the artist's lost classicizing project, almost as an alibi for the inability to create a new Rome as grand as the old and as faithful to it—an alibi that will be strengthened by the disasters of the Sack in 1527.[126] But perhaps no part of the venture is more elusive than its relation to Raphael the painter. There is, as the *Laocoön* story already began to suggest, no shortage among Raphael's contemporaries of artists whose inspiration can be traced to their encounter with both the monumental *and* the representational remains of the ancients. But there remains a considerable gap between the humanist discourse of antiquities and the making of aesthetics. To whatever degree statues respond less to the imperializing concern of humanists and popes than do urban monuments, they may turn out to have a broader, more insidious, and more powerful diffusion in the imaginative culture of the Renaissance.

ROME'S OTHER POPULATION

Notwithstanding analogies to New World exploration or to developments in astronomy, the great breakthroughs in the discovery of ancient sculpture cannot be so easily pinpointed on the calendar. The unearthing of the *Laocoön* in 1506 is more a defining than an inaugural moment. What renders that event salient is the fact that people have for some time been in the habit of discovering objects when they plant vines, that there are humanists ready to be dispatched to the scene, that the particular ground (in this instance the Esquiline) has already proven to be significant excavational territory, and that the pope is already in the process of constructing a gallery to display antique sculpture. Yet it is important to remember that these people had also lived in the presence of artistic remains that had not suddenly appeared out of the ground but had contributed significantly to the visual scene more or less as long as anyone could remember. Sculpture formed an integral part of the monumental Rome that remained uninterruptedly visible throughout the Middle Ages. No piles of debris, however high, could obscure Trajan's Column or any number of triumphal arches; richly carved burial containers of various kinds were so numerous that they never ceased to form part of the cityscape (often to be reused); and a small number of freestanding statues were so massive as to have avoided removal, plundering, or decay. Before the twelfth century these objects seem to enter into discourse even less than the architectural and topographical remains of the ancient city. Objects made of valuable materials occasionally figure as spoils of war in the very early period, while the ninth-century Einsiedeln itinerary makes reference to a river god and an equestrian statue that are probably the *Marforio* (see fig. 3.5) and the Capitoline *Marcus Aurelius* (fig. 1.16), though the *Tigris* and the *Nile* (fig. 1.17) were already known at that time; nevertheless, as with the itinerary's other classical references, these objects appear as signposts rather than as

1.16. *Equestrian Portrait of Marcus Aurelius*, bronze, second century A.D., Museo Capitolino, Rome

1.17. River Gods, *Tigris/Tiber* (left) and *Nile*, colossal Roman statues, second century A.D., Capitol, Rome

matters of intrinsic interest to the tourist. And there are retrospective accounts—but, so far as I can tell, no contemporary ones—of how certain early popes (e.g., Silvester I, Gregory I) treated pagan statues as dangerous idols.[127]

If one strings together all the extant responses to ancient art objects dating from the twelfth to the fourteenth centuries, one can make a case for a remarkably proto-Renaissance set of perceptions and relations. Individual documents testify, for instance, to the economic value of sculptural works in circulation: we have already spoken about the export of statues to England in the time of John of Salisbury, while in the fourteenth century a precise and well-informed shopping list for antiquities will be

composed by the moneylender Oliviero Forzetta of Treviso.[128] During the same period in Rome certain of the statues take on political associations. It is a notable irony that the ascendancy of Cola di Rienzo is justified in part by his status as a publicist of antiquities, as his anonymous biographer declares,[129] while his eventual death sentence is read out in front of the Capitoline *Lion Attacking a Horse* (fig. 1.18), understood as a classical symbol of justice.[130]

A different kind of appreciation is evidenced in the remarkable *Narracio de mirabilibus urbis Romae* of the English monk Magister Gregorius (otherwise unidentified), who visited Rome somewhere around the year 1200.[131] Although the work is a tissue of medieval legends and greatly wanting in the eventual refinements of classical learning, the text reveals aesthetic and intellectual sensibilities of a decidedly humanist kind. Despite its formal similarities to descriptions of the city intended for pious pilgrims, the *Narracio* is almost exclusively devoted to Rome's classical wonders, and within that already surprising field of concentration it places exceptional emphasis on the sculpture as against the architecture, which suggests that the author is more interested in the city's art than its grandeur. There are lengthy accounts of the *Marcus Aurelius*, the colossal bronze head (see fig. 3.3), the *Spinario* (see fig. 3.26), and the reliefs on various triumphal arches. The works are emphatically not framed by Christian typology but contextualized within what the author knows of their own classical culture. Even the bronze head, cited here and everywhere else as an idol anathematized by Pope Gregory, is declared to be admirable for the skill of the artist. Concerning a marble Venus (perhaps the *Capitoline Venus*), Magister Gregorius waxes especially eloquent: "The image is made from Parian marble with such wonderful and intricate skill, that she seems more like a living creature than a statue; indeed she seems to blush in her nakedness, a reddish tinge colouring her face, and it appears to those who take a close look that blood flows in her snowy complexion. Because of this wonderful image, and perhaps some magic spell that I am unaware of, I was drawn back three times to look at it despite the fact that it was two *stadia* from my inn."[132] Two hundred years later the magic would be more explicitly metaphorical, but the terms of praise—that is, the temptation to leave doctrinal considerations behind in an erotically tinged set of aesthetic responses—would not be so different.

Where Gregorius reveals his limitations (at least from the Renaissance perspective) is in the masses of legendary material that he adduces to explain the statues. Several fantastic narratives are advanced to explain the *Marcus Aurelius*, while other statues, like a *Bellerophon*, are allegorized and the *Spinario* is named as Priapus because of its (inaccurately observed) oversized genitals.[133] But even as we are amused by these misappropriations of the material or simple failures to record what is actually there, we must notice certain predispositions that will be significant in a humanist view of these works. Objects are capable of more than one exegesis without the necessity of a unique orthodox reading. That the bronze equestrian statue may represent either Theodoric or Constantine or a soldier who battled the Miseni or a Roman citizen who dared to visit the underworld not only sanctions multiple readings—that is, after all, the habit of medieval textual hermeneutics from Augustine onward—but also puts viewers in a position to read objects with their own eyes and independently of a preexisting narrative: "The rider raises his right hand, as if to address the people or to give orders; his left hand holds a rein, which turns the horse's head to the right, as if he were about to ride away in another direction."[134] And even certain of Gregorius's errors of learning—as when he sees the Septizonium as Ovid's Palace of the Sun or describes the (quite possibly nonexistent) carvings on some triumphal arch precisely as the Antony and Cleopatra story that appears on the shield of Virgil's Aeneas—are still efforts to correlate the material remains of antiquity with its verbal record, as Renaissance humanists will continue to do, only more successfully.[135]

These rather jagged efforts to correlate text and material object serve as an appropriate context for a figure who has played a considerable historiographical role in telling the story of early humanism, that is, Petrarch's learned medical friend Giovanni Dondi. We have already encountered him as a visitor to Rome who measured buildings and copied inscriptions. He also found himself at the center of an epistolary network in which he acted as spokesperson for the glories of the ancients as opposed to the moderns. In an extensive and often cited letter on this theme, Dondi celebrates antiquity by echoing a Petrarchan-style distaste for the present, which is really *contemptus mundi* in disguise:

> But who and what sort of men those Ancients were, by what customs they lived, what virtues they had, what sorts of actions gained reward, and what sorts of things were given to those who deserved well, all belong to a bygone age and cannot, like present things, be seen by our eyes or touched with our hands; they can, however, be recognized by great testimonies and reliable evidence, so that no one who looks carefully can doubt them. The best evidence consists of the writings which outstanding minds have left to the memory of posterity; their authority and majesty is so great that no one can fail to trust them. If you should ask my own opinion, their credit is so great, believe me, that I seem somehow to have seen those things that I have read.[136]

For Dondi, material antiquity is completely lost to the senses and can be recaptured only in writings, but these writings are so grand and authoritative that they almost manage to produce visual experience.

Such a response might be described as pure logocentrism, ignoring the physical traces of the ancients in favor of verbal materials upon which an imaginary antiquity can be projected—rather like Petrarch's technique in the letter to Giovanni Colonna. In fact, in a compelling argument by Richard and Trude Krautheimer, Dondi's letter has served to define a wholly text-based approach to antiquity that has blinded all humanist thinkers, whether from the Renaissance or in our own time, to a purely visual approach, understood as the special province of artists.[137] I would argue, however, that rather than postulate a special painters' and sculptors' consciousness that is independent of the word, we would do better to understand Renaissance—even early Renaissance—classicism as the search for a common ground between the writings that permit moderns to imagine antiquity and the material remains that might, in however limited a way, satisfy the senses. It is the very desire for ocular experience and the hope that text can achieve real presence ("quodam modo illa putem vidisse que legi") that focuses humanist attention on surviving art objects.

In this regard Dondi cites ancient sculpture and invokes a decidedly nonliterary consciousness:

Moreover, proof of [the greatness of the ancients] is given by those objects which remain in Rome to this day as testimony to the honors that used to be conferred upon outstanding actions. For although time has consumed many of them—even many of the more magnificent—and only ruins of others appear, which present certain traces of what formerly stood, still, those things that remain, fewer and less magnificent, testify abundantly that those who decreed them must have been of great virtue. . . . I mean the statues which, either cast in bronze or chiseled in marble, have lasted to the present, and the many fragments of those that have been shattered lying about everywhere, the marble triumphal arches of impressive workmanship and the sculptured columns showing the histories of great deeds, and so many other things of this kind publicly built in honor of men who were distinguished, whether because they had established peace or because they had liberated the fatherland from imminent peril or had extended empire over subjected peoples, as I recall having read in some of them, not without a certain notable pleasure.   [342]

Dondi's response is nonvisual in the sense that he looks to ancient sculpture to provide signs of the glories that attached themselves to those who commissioned the works or whose greatness was recorded in them. But it is risky, even by implication and even in the fourteenth century, to write this set of responses out of the history of art—that is, to declare as visual only those responses that are unconcerned with representation and devoted exclusively to aesthetics or the celebration of the artist.

Not that Dondi is insensitive to this form of response, either:

Of the artistic products of ancient genius, few survive. But those that do remain anywhere are eagerly sought and seen and highly prized by those who feel strongly about such things. . . . I knew a certain well-known worker in marble who was famous for his ability in that art among those whom Italy had at the time, especially in the creation of figures. I have heard this man tell many times about the statues and sculptures that he had seen at Rome, with such admiration and veneration that he seemed in recalling it to be transported beyond himself from the wonder of the thing. For he used to say that sometimes, passing with his friends by a place where some images of this sort could be seen, he had held back, looking in astonishment at their artistry, and, forgetting his company, had stood still so long that his companions had passed on five hundred steps and more. And when he would tell of the great excellence of these figures, and praise their authors beyond measure, he used to add in the end (in his own words): "If only these images did not lack life, they would be better than living ones," as if to say that nature had been not only imitated by the genius of such artists but even surpassed.   [344–45]

That Dondi may be distancing himself from this point of view by fobbing it off on an unnamed artist or by characterizing lovers of classical sculpture as those "who like

1.18. *Lion Attacking a Horse*, third-century B.C. group, as restored in sixteenth century, Palazzo dei Conservatori, Rome

that kind of thing" matters rather little. What is significant is that in making the complete argument for the greatness of antiquity he joins together the literary argument of exemplarity—that is, the reading of ancient remains as signifiers of unrecapturable history—with the aesthetic pleasure of contemplating objects independently of what they mean or represent. In fact, both his personae have in common the experience of pleasure in looking and in interpreting what their eyes have read. And for Dondi, at least, the principal nexus of the two approaches is not so much inscriptions, buildings, or urban topography as representational sculpture.

But despite the rhetorical gestures that Dondi uses to imply a large number of like-minded humanists and artists, these enthusiastic and well-informed views of ancient sculpture are probably not typical of their time. It is noteworthy that both Magister Gregorius and Dondi—not to mention Petrarch—are tourists rather than residents in Rome (Forzetta is also a traveler, though to Venice) and that their responses are dictated in part by the special forms of decontextualizing and recontextualizing that come with writing a letter home. If we wish to plant ourselves more firmly in the Eternal City, then we must consider the in situ sculptural topography of Rome prior to the fifteenth century. *In situ*, of course, is a relative term, since even among the small number of statues above ground throughout this period, few are likely to have been in their original ancient places of installation. A sculptural map of visible antiquities would highlight above all the Quirinal Hill, site of several massive statues, probably forming part of the Baths of Constantine and the Temple of Salus.[138] The *Dioscuri* (see

1.19. View of the Lateran from Codex made for Giovanni Marcanova ("Quaedam Antiquitatum Fragmenta"), ca. 1465, fol. 29v, Biblioteca Estense, Modena

fig. 3.4), of all Roman statues, perhaps, the ones that have been moved the least from antiquity to the present, were known for centuries and gave to the Quirinal its medieval name of Monte Cavallo. The *River Gods* (see fig. 1.17), which have been displayed on either side of the Capitoline senatorial palace since the sixteenth century, were visible in the Middle Ages near the *Dioscuri* and are already recorded in the *Mirabilia* as the idols of Saturn and Bacchus to be found in their temple. But if we follow a more scientific and less legendary version of their history, they are to be named more probably the *Tigris* and the *Nile*, and it becomes less clear whether they were originally installed on the Quirinal, even if they are recorded there as early as the twelfth century.[139]

The Capitol is a more problematic originary location.[140] We have already considered its value as a perpetually retrospective symbol of Rome's primordial glories, and we know that by the middle of the sixteenth century it will take on official status as material repository for these glories—specifically of a sculptural kind. Whether it played any such role in the real life of antiquity is more difficult to determine. The widely known account in Livy of the Capitol's founding and naming depends on a circumstance that is prophetic in more ways than one: it seems that having begun excavations on the hill for a temple to Jupiter, Tarquin discovered a perfectly preserved human head of gigantic size. In the tradition that follows from Livy this signifies that the place will be *caput imperii* and hence *Capitol*.[141] In longer retrospect, of course, it prefigures all the Renaissance modes of discovery as we are applying them to statues, fragments, and bodies; it is noteworthy, as we shall soon see, that the gigantic bronze head known throughout the Middle Ages was made part of the Capitoline collection in the late fifteenth century. But we are getting ahead of ourselves. Partly because of its elemental significance, the real Capitol of later antiquity—the period, that is, from which artistic remains might have survived—is likely to have been rather empty of the kind of materials that abounded on the Quirinal. What did survive, at least beginning in the later Middle Ages, was an awareness that the Tarpeian Rock (probably on the southwest corner of the hill) was the place of execution for capital criminals. Not surprisingly, therefore, the only ancient sculpture locatable on the Capitol before the Renaissance is the *Lion Attacking a Horse* (see fig. 1.18), which, as we have seen, was both site and symbol for the administering of justice as early as the fourteenth century.[142] But as with the *River Gods* of the Quirinal, we cannot determine whether it was found or brought there.[143]

In short, while the status of original location has the potential to bestow enormous significance on a piece of sculptural antiquity even during the Middle Ages, in practice it is a condition that is more manipulable than real and more legendary than documentable. In fact, the statues that excite the most interest during the earlier period are generally those that already in the unrecorded mists of (postclassical) time have been brought within the structures of Christian Rome. There is the lone instance of the *Pine Cone*—the earliest documented sculpture of all—that was housed in the forecourt of the old Saint Peter's from the late fifth century.[144] More significant, how-

1.20. *Capitoline Wolf*, mid-Italic bronze, fifth century B.C., Palazzo dei Conservatori, Rome

ever, is the collection of antiquities housed at the Lateran (fig. 1.19). By the year 1200 (and beginning perhaps as much as four centuries earlier) there was displayed in front of the papal palace a group of bronze sculptures that included the equestrian figure we now call *Marcus Aurelius* (see fig. 1.16); the *She-Wolf* (fig. 1.20), named by reference to its later provenance as the *Lupa Capitolina*; the colossal head and hand we now generally associate with Constantine; and the *Spinario*, or *Thornpuller* (see fig. 3.26). I list them in (conjectural) order of their placement at the Lateran—really the order in which we first hear of them in that setting, ranging from the tenth to the twelfth centuries—but we are unable to document any single moment during the Middle Ages when there was a concerted effort to bring them all together.[145] However the assemblage came about, the choice of the Lateran suggests a particular threshhold relationship between Christian Rome and pagan Rome. Unlike Saint Peter's, which has no pre-Christian significance, the Lateran was understood to be an imperial site and figured significantly as a property transferred from emperor to pope in the Donation of Constantine. So, while the *Pine Cone* of Saint Peter's counts as merely a magnificent decorative object, most of the Lateran antiquities are ripe for ideological interpretation—by both medieval onlookers and modern scholars.

This collection, with several of the objects placed on columns, has in a sense been all too easy to read as a set of efforts to Christianize ancient relics in the medieval decontextualizing manner and to render them as propaganda for papal power. Both Tilmann Buddensieg and W. S. Heckscher write sensitively about the way this installation seems to give material form to the centuries-old claims that the pagan gods were to be identified with biblical idols and demons.[146] Yet neither the collection itself nor the hermeneutic systems likely to be applied to it ought to be seen as monolithic. The bronze head atop a pillar embodies idolatry perfectly, to be sure. The *Spinario*, however, becomes the beautiful Absalom for a Jewish traveler in the twelfth century and, as we have seen, a "ridiculous" figure of Priapus for Magister Gregorius: neither of these reactions involves simple contempt for pagan worship or art.[147] The equestrian figure, as we have also seen, comes to be named as Constantine, which brings him within the Christian pantheon, but he is also capable of being given several other names and narratives, most of which redound to the glory of a Rome that is transhistorical. The *She-Wolf*'s placement on a column does not so much render her an anathematized idol as a symbol of Roman justice and power, with, once again, no very strong distinctions made between the pagan and Christian expression of such forces.[148] In short, one can place classical art objects in Christian settings, but one cannot control all the ways in which they will be seen. Indeed as Heckscher points out, the Lateran display is itself classicizing—that is, it resembles "a Roman forum, rostrum, or harbour installation," rendering it "both a survival and a revival of antiquity."[149]

Antique sculptural objects are thus arrayed in a variety of ways during these earlier centuries in Rome—some of them in significant locations where the ancients had placed them, some of them moved about at random in the forgotten past, some of them organized in Christian contexts but in an *all'antica* design, not to mention the greater number of surviving monumental constructions that could never have been moved. The aggregate becomes not so much a landscape in which Christian power and doctrine impose themselves on pagan art as a set of conditions in which—narrow theological questions aside—a historical awareness of pagan versus Christian ages is not easily readable. These matters become easier to decipher with Renaissance hindsight. The Lateran collection in particular has generally (and justly) been defined from the moment of its dissolution: that is, the gift by Sixtus IV of the whole collection to the Roman people in 1471, when it began to be placed in the Conservators' Palace and to form the basis for an extensive collection of antiquities still housed there. This momentous shift has been seen to embody many of the defining features of the Renaissance humanist approach to ancient artistic culture. The inscription accompanying the transfer declares that the collection is at once *given* to the Roman people and *returned* to them ("aeneas insignes statuas . . . restituendas condonandasque"): from this turn of phrase itself we can see the pope both glorifying his own temporal ambitions and flattering the *populus Romanus* as imperial subjects already. In effect, he is presenting himself simultaneously as the restorer of a glorious ancient Rome and as its modern protector. It has also been suggested that the pope wishes to be understood as reversing medieval traditions of indifference to these objects, or, in the case of some of his famous predecessors, of determinedly destroying them.[150]

Whatever the political value of instituting the Capitoline collection, the move must also be seen as part of a new humanistic climate. In the twenty-five years preceding the transfer of the Lateran bronzes, important developments take place in the historicizing of these objects, familiar for so many centuries but shrouded in legend. The two portrait figures begin to be given names of specific (and plausible) Roman emperors; the *Spinario* starts showing up as a genre figure rather than as an allegorical personification; and Poggio Bracciolini's new archaeological awareness takes note for the first time of the difference between genuinely in situ antiquities and those that earlier Christians had moved around. Taking account of all these developments, Buddensieg argues persuasively that in retrospect the Lateran arrangement could be seen as accidental and driven by theological rather than scholarly necessity. The establishment of the Capitoline collection, on the other hand, formed part of a genuinely topographical awareness of Roman history that would render the sculptural objects no longer homeless and give them an authentically urban function.

All of which is the truth, though perhaps not the whole truth. The Conservators' Palace is not an ancient or archaeologically correct setting any more than is the Lateran—indeed, less. And the collection of sculpture that comes to be displayed there, for all that it is ideologically bound up with transhistorical notions of Rome, is, in the process, as sequestered as ever it was in the Middle Ages. To which we might add the other, even greater collection, the pope's Belvedere courtyard, which begins to be assembled about thirty years later: once again, as with the Lateran, the items are removed from their sites of discovery and enshrined in a Christian setting. I am not arguing that these are neomedieval operations. What we are in fact seeing is a variety of purposes or consequences with regard to ancient art objects, all of which can be associated with the Renaissance, though they may be in tension with one another. To begin with, the assertions of papal power and the newly historicist reading of urban topography may stand in an uneasy relationship. This is really another version of the conflict we observed earlier between exploiting the grandeur of ancient ruins and demolishing them so as to build a new Rome in the ancient style. From at least 1471 onward, virtually any ancient statue that *could* be moved *was* moved, whether it was visible throughout the Middle Ages or newly dug up. Generally, these are privatizing moves, which, if one may speak of them as a group, have a primary purpose of glorifying the (new) possessor. It may be that humanists envisaging an authentic map of ancient Rome are benefited by this commerce and these new collocations; on the other hand, the reality they are trying to map is being obliterated in the process. What makes this less of a crisis than my schematic terms imply is that sculpture per se tends to exist apart from humanist historicism; and this—to return after many pages to the uniqueness of this volume's subject—may be the most important fact of all. Granted that Poggio (more than any of the other protoarchaeologists) has an interest in statues and that certain discovered works like the *Laocoön* and the *Hercules* of the Forum Boarium are associated with their imperial locations. But on the whole the historicist enterprise is fueled by all those other material elements we catalogued in the revival of antiquity: buildings, inscriptions, coins, and surviving topography. In regard to sculpture, the developments from 1471 consist not only of the conflicting aims of papal possession and humanist historiography but of a third notion intimately bound up with museum-style forms of display: the reception of aesthetic pleasure.[151]

The transfer of the statues to the Capitoline removed them from their columns;[152] it collapsed the distance between art object and viewer; and it led to a great increase in the number of works being exhibited together. All these changes could be seen in even more decisive form in the yet more aesthetically organized display of the Belvedere and, eventually, numerous private sculpture gardens, where relatively complete works were mixed together with fragments and occasionally with modern works. These developments arise from and contribute to the possibility that for statues, at any rate, the mediating experience between antiquity and modern times is the visual pleasure of the onlooker. Further, when the onlooker happens to be a modern artist, that experience becomes an arena of professional study through all the modalities of imitation and mimesis. In neither case should these relations be casually equated with other ways in which the Renaissance seized upon the classical past. That popes or members of powerful secular families appropriated ancient objects to legitimize and glorify their own present condition, or that humanists sought in the material remains around them an ever more historically contingent account of antiquity—these are what we might call public actions, directed toward the management of and by a whole culture. The beholder's pleasure and the artist's inspiration, while ultimately inseparable from those things that the broader culture makes possible and legitimizes, are different in kind—even subversive in the way that they privatize aesthetic experience and collapse the official diachronic line of historiography.

There is another reason why statues might form the site for a less culturally determined mode of relating to antiquity. Granted, Renaissance viewers could (and did) cultivate private and aesthetic responses to ruins, buildings, even to inscriptions and topography. But sculptural works are representations of human beings—many of the most famous ones in fact three-dimensional. Underlying all the possible relations in front of art objects, whether characterized by medieval notions of idolatry or by Renaissance notions of ancient glory, historical recuperation, and aesthetic pleasure, is a sense that, in the act of looking at ancient statues, modern individuals are encountering their own mirror images from the classical past, not in bronze or marble but in the flesh.

The moment when a statue is unearthed thus becomes a kind of face-to-face encounter. In the story of finding the *Laocoön*, the meeting between the Trojan priest and his Renaissance discoverers is relatively distanced and impersonal: as we saw, the moderns treat him as a document in Pliny. Other occasions are different. Ghiberti, for instance, narrates the laborious removal of a statue of Hermaphroditus (see fig. 3.44) from deep within a Roman sewer. The work, he tells us, revealed both male and female natures: "era sanza testa, nessuna altra cosa aueua manco. In questa era moltissime dolceze, nessuna cosa il uiso scorgeua, se non col tatto la mano la trouaua" (It was headless, but nothing else was lacking. In this statue there were a great many lovelinesses: the eye could not perceive anything if the hand did not find it with the touch).[153] Three quarters of a century later, Federico Gonzaga's representative excitedly narrates the unearthing of the *Tiber* (see fig. 3.64) near Santa Maria sopra Minerva, "una statua marmorea dil più grande huomo che si possa ritrovare, e anche magior assai . . . , la qual ho visto con li ochi mei et tocho tuta com le mane" (a marble statue of the largest man who could possibly be found, and perhaps even larger . . . , which I saw with my own eyes and touched all over with my hands).[154] We shall consider a wider range of responses below in Chapter 3, but it is worth pointing out here that statues could stand as vividly corporeal objects to which an observer might develop a decidedly sensuous relation, as though to a living thing.

To understand what it means to find statues in the ground, we must relate them to other *objets trouvés*. For instance:

> At that time [1065] the body of Pallas, the son of Evander, of whom Virgil speaks, was found entire at Rome, to the great astonishment of all, for having escaped corruption so many ages. Such, however, is the nature of bodies embalmed, that, when the flesh decays, the skin preserves the nerves, and the nerves the bones. The gash which Turnus had made in the middle of his breast measured four feet and a half. His epitaph was found to this effect,

> > Pallas, Evander's son, lies buried here
> > In order due, transfix'd by Turnus' spear.

> Which epitaph I should not think made at the time, though Carmentis the mother of Evander is reported to have discovered the Roman letters, but that it was composed by Ennius, or some other ancient poet. There was a burning lamp at his head, constructed by magical art; so that no violent blast, no dripping of water could extinguish it. While many were lost in admiration of this, one person, as there are always some people expert in mischief, made an aperture beneath the flame with an iron style, which introducing the air, the light vanished. The body, when set up against the wall, surpassed it in height, but some days afterward, being drenched with the drip of the eves [sic], it acknowledged the corruption common to mortals; the skin and the nerves dissolving.[155]

I quote at some length from a source not contemporary to the period we are considering—it is William of Malmesbury's twelfth-century chronicle of English kings—to show that these tropes of discovery have an appeal independent of Renaissance humanism. Modern Romans find—and through the fifteenth century will continue to find—more than classical objects in the ground; they also find classical persons. As in all sorts of past-life regression, these persons are not merely hoi polloi of ancient times but the most celebrated of heroic figures. That fame is signaled by text: specifically, a combination of already known documents—in this case the *Aeneid*—

together with newly found authenticating inscriptions. In the instance of Pallas (and not many other "discoveries" will be quite so perfect), historical uniqueness and hence truth is clinched by something more absolute than text: the sign on the body, his four-foot wound, as a result of which the newly found object and Virgil can authenticate each other reciprocally. Of course the marker that certifies all this truth is also the sign of death; the ancient hero, in other words, can prove who he is only by being a corpse. Yet there is something transhistorically alive about this discovery; the body is uncorrupted, and, more important, it is found in the company of another object that is not dead—namely, the ever burning lamp. Nor should we be surprised that all these materials succeed in maintaining their perfect aura of antiquity so very briefly. As we have already observed in other connections, the fragility of antiquity's material remains is an integral part of its value while it helps to set the learned humanist observers apart from the unappreciative laity who participate in its destruction.

In 1283 the skeleton of Antenor was found near Padua, and in 1500 a still burning ancient lamp was found among the tombs in the town of Este.[156] But the episode that best exemplifies this form of discovery mania, and also draws the parallels to sculpture most fully, took place on the Appian Way in 1485. Leaving aside matters of obvious and immediate political significance, it may be the most fully documented event to take place in Rome during the fifteenth century, with at least twelve full-scale narratives in extant contemporary writings.[157] Among the great nineteenth-century historians, including Burckhardt, Gregorovius, and Lanciani, it stood as one of the salient moments in defining the relation between antiquity and Renaissance; nor has it been forgotten more recently, though it does not always occupy center stage.[158] I offer the account by a cleric writing a letter to a fellow Veronese citizen, Giacomo Maffei:

> Three marble tombs have been discovered during these last days. . . . One of them contained a young girl, intact in all her members, covered from head to foot with a coating of aromatic paste, one inch thick. On the removal of this coating, which we believe to be composed of myrrh, frankincense, aloe, and other priceless drugs, a face appeared, so lovely, so pleasing, so attractive, that, although the girl had certainly been dead fifteen hundred years, she appeared to have been laid to rest that very day. The thick masses of hair, collected on the top of the head in the old style, seemed to have been combed then and there. The eyelids could be opened and shut; the ears and the nose were so well preserved that, after being bent to one side or the other, they instantly resumed their original shape. By pressing the flesh of the cheeks the color would disappear as in a living body. The tongue could be seen through the pink lips; the articulations of the hands and feet still retained their elasticity. The whole of Rome, men and women, to the number of twenty thousand, visited the marvel of Santa Maria Nova that day. I hasten to inform you of this event, because I want you to understand how the ancients took care to prepare not only their

souls but also their bodies for immortality. I am sure that if you had had the privilege of beholding that lovely young face, the pleasure would have equalled your astonishment.[159]

The recipient of the above letter was a member of a distinguished humanist family recently transferred to Rome. Indeed much of the paper trail surrounding the event is composed by individuals in the avant garde of classical and antiquarian enthusiasm (often in the circle of Pomponio Leto), among them the archaeological commentator Volaterrano (another member of the Maffei family), the antipapal polemicist Stefano Infessura, and the connoisseur of ancient monuments and inscriptions Bartolommeo Fonzio (fig. 1.21).[160] They all tell pretty much the same story, though one anonymous diarist stands out by declaring "non si sa certo, se fusse maschio o femmina" (one doesn't know for sure if it is male or female).[161] Several of them add crucial later developments, including the discovery along with the body of several identifying inscriptions (not accepted by modern epigraphers), the various attempts to name the individual, the transport of the body to the Conservators' Palace, and finally its rapid decay and reinterment owing either to its corruption or to the pious intervention of Pope Innocent VIII.

Whatever *really* happened in April 1485, it was a good and an important story that needed to be constantly retold, embellished, and interpreted. Although I assume the event was more substantial and capable of being authenticated than the finding of Pallas's body four centuries earlier, the outlines are remarkably similar: the body that is dead yet still lifelike, the web of texts, and even the identification with one of antiquity's most important canonical authors, since it comes to be widely accepted that the girl was Tulliola, Cicero's daughter, on the grounds that she had to be important to be so carefully buried, that the Cicero family owned lands nearby, and that other tombs and inscriptions relevant to them were found in the vicinity.[162] I wish to look at this event through the eyes of another chronicler (almost never cited when this story is told, presumably because he is thought to be unreliable) who will set the matter more fully in the context of our present concerns. Paolo Pompilio was a Roman humanist closely associated with the Spanish ascendancy surrounding the papal court in this period.[163] He lectured on grammar, both Greek and Latin, and seems to have been connected with some particularly radical notions of paganizing Christian culture, including a translation into more classical language of the Nicene Creed. Within the memoirs from the latter years of his life, he presents the month of April 1485 in Rome as exceptionally rich in *ostentis*—shows, wonders, signs. Pompilio declares that certain people have thought them to be of trifling significance, whereas many others, presumably himself included, think they are of some moment.

Pompilio structures his account as a rising series of four miraculous events, each of which occupies more space and is more dramatic than the last. The discovery of the perfectly preserved corpse in the Appian Way represents the climax. First, however, there is a half-witted hermit (other contemporaries suggest it was a Franciscan) who

Ceterum hoc corpus cum .XVIII.
cal. maij anno à natiuitate Christi
millesimo quadringentesimo octogesimo quinto
Innocentij uero Pape octaui anno
eius pontificatus primo repertum
fit apud casale fratrum sanctæ
mariæ nouæ in uia appia ad sextu
ab urbe lapidem : biduo post dela-
tum est in capitolium maximo populi concursu iussu conseruatorum
urbis .

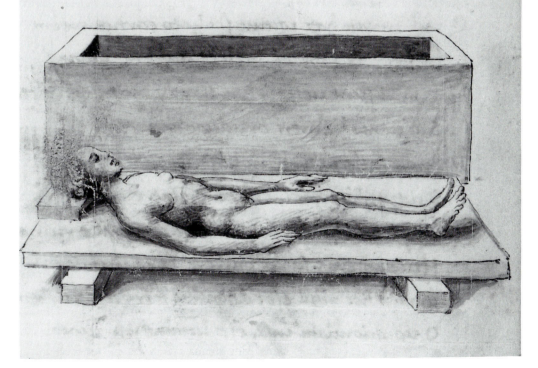

1.21. Bartolommeo Fonzio, Body of a Roman Girl, ca. 1490, MS Lat. Misc. d.85, fol. 161v, Bodleian Library, Oxford

came riding through Rome on a bull. Pompilio marvels at the animal's having been reduced to such servitude and suggests that the Franciscan was trying to bring the beast down to his own idiotic level; he adds that the bull had been fitted with a packsaddle, which rendered the performance more comfortable but less holy. Next there appeared a nine-year-old Benedictine preacher who exhibited so much learning, acuteness, and rhetorical flair, doing everything from memory and with the appropriate gestures, that he could not possibly have been coached; what adds to Pompilio's amazement at this event is that the authorities permitted the boy to continue preaching in Rome for many days. The third wonder begins with a backward look at events several months earlier, when the papal tiara had been stolen and not recovered. The wonder itself is juxtaposed to that circumstance: it seems that a marble statue of a figure carrying a club and with imperial emblems sculpted on its breastplate was drawn from the ground directly at the front door of the Vatican palace.[164] It is still visible there at the time Pompilio writes and is daily strewn with flowers and herbs by the papal guard.

That these events, including the discovery of a Hercules statue, form the windup to the events of the Appian Way places them all in a powerful epistemic context. Pompilio's story consists in a set of encounters with antiquity that is also a kind of history of such encounters. The idiot Franciscan mounted on a bull has certain qualities of traditional or medieval religious *mirabilia* about it. What then distinguishes the boy preacher is that he is so clearly not an idiot but rather a master of classical rhetoric (Pompilio cites his "clever anacephaleosis," a technical term he gets from Quintilian),[165] even though this mastery may be an act of ventriloquism. The real pivot comes with miracle three: not only is a statue excavated directly in front of the papal palace, but it is understood to be some sort of response to or recompense for the earlier theft of the pontifical tiara. The fact that the pope's guards should be daily anointing it with herbs—here, if nowhere else, Pompilio strains one's credulity—makes sense only if we construe the event as bridging the ages of pagan and Christian. The last and most important miraculous event consists in an appearance not of mere classical discourse, nor of an ancient marble simulacrum, but of an unmediated—though brief—encounter with a Roman citizen. From idiot to dummy spouting Ciceronian rhetoric to archaeological excavation to the authentic flesh-and-blood classical undead.

Whether the objects are bodies or representations of bodies, what Renaissance Romans can discover in the ground is a function of what ancient Romans left there to *be* discovered. Through the centuries of the Roman republic and the early empire, the universal practice with the dead was cremation, leaving urns but no bodies to be found. Beginning in the first couple of centuries A.D.—in practice, the earliest time from which any materials could be found in the Renaissance—inhumation becomes more the rule, with bodies being placed in sarcophagi, and those, in turn, often inside larger tombs of various kinds.[166] (Elaborate embalming, clearly relevant to the corpse on the Appian Way, is not a widespread practice and gets associated with Egypt.) All these stone funerary remains, and especially the ubiquitous sarcophagi, become by far the most numerous objects of any substantial kind that stand for Renaissance Italians as the relics of antiquity. Medieval Italians saw ancient sarcophagi immured in their churches; from the time of Dante and Giotto onward they were visible everywhere, having been described in words and quoted in pictures passim.[167] So, despite the value assigned to special discoveries like the Laocoöns and Herculeses, the bulk of classical art to be seen in the Renaissance is death-related, and the moderns who seek out this art are understood as necromancers.

The encounter with the past—in any of Pompilio's miracles, but increasingly as one progresses from the first to the last—is the encounter with the dead. But the encounter itself becomes a way of raising the dead. The labile geology that characterizes the rediscovery of ancient Rome applies to bodies and statues alike. Whether ancient civilization was lived underground or not, it exists there at the present time. Tombs are above ground, but the bodies inside them are below. The discovery of a perfectly preserved body in a tomb along the Appian Way is meant to herald the beginning of a much more radical resurrection than that of statues and sarcophagi, namely, the real life of antiquity—for which, in any event, the sculptural objects are metonymic. The map of these events is important because it provides keys to the kind of hermeneutic that will direct acts of translation or interpretation between moderns and ancients. These chthonic poetics of which I speak—that is, all the uncertain locations and statuses characterized by burial, necromancy, and the undead—exist in relation to a cultural predisposition according to which the past might be considered as though it were present. I say "might be" because I think that what Renaissance culture wanted was a past that was just living enough so that it might be made to speak to the present, through certain interpreters, or else to listen when certain voices in the present spoke to it. (That is why the figure of prosopopoeia is so central to these matters; it will be considered in Chapter 4.)

The process of raising the dead is, perhaps first of all, a process of reading or identifying the remains. As it happens, Pompilio presents all his prodigious events as in one way or another requiring interpretation. The idiot presumably babbles, but his very appearance demands explanation. The boy preacher might be a sort of carnival trick unless one recognizes the cleverness of his anacephaleosis. As for the statue, Pompilio himself gives this event its astonishing twist when he introduces it by saying that it *respondet* to the theft of the papal tiara—that is, it answers, compensates, or offers something in return. In one sense, this is a very radical proposition: however much Renaissance Romans valued ancient art, few would declare that it possessed numinous significance equal to an emblem of what Christ had given to Peter or that the two could possibly be interchangeable. Yet in another sense it is a very traditional proposition: namely, that there exists a typology of correspondences, according to which a statue of Hercules with imperial insignia on it is the *ante legem* equivalent to a sign of the pope's temporal power. Indeed, given that one legend of the stolen tiara's origin was that Constantine had given it to Pope Silvester, it could be argued that the unearthing of the imperial statue might rehearse or reconfirm the long since debunked Donation of Constantine.[168]

But it is, not surprisingly, the ancient corpse that raises for Pompilio the most interesting questions of interpretation. For all the thousands who come to see her, she is, of course, a text, and Pompilio's onlookers have a considerable range of texts at their disposal. Her age, the location where she is found, the care and expertise with which she is buried, produce a flurry of insertions into the major families of Roman history, as we have seen—not only Tulliola is suggested but also one of the Scipios or the daughter of Julius Caesar and wife of Pompey. But Pompilio introduces his friend the Spanish humanist Hieronymus Pau (whom no other chronicler mentions) as an arbiter of truth who speaks directly to the hypothesizing crowds:

> Who would dare to claim whose body this might have been? Besides, all guesses are blind: there is no clear indicator made manifest to us, nothing unique, unless you wish the indicator to be the very fact that there is no inscription here to be read. By this it is almost possible to guess that it was that deadly woman Poppea Sabina, the wife of Nero. For I remember reading in Tacitus that she died by the accident of her husband's wrath. The body was not burnt in sacrifice, according to the Roman usage, but rather following foreign habits stuffed, dressed with herbs, and placed in the mound of the Julii. So speaks Tacitus. It might be that the coffin of this very same Poppea was carried out into the fields on account of Nero's hatred. Such a far-fetched conjecture can be made by me since no truth at all seems to come to light here.[169]

Pau uses his erudition—he quotes verbatim from Tacitus—not to fix the girl's identity but to unfix it.[170] He turns the problem from the body that is being watched to the body doing the watching and makes it a story about acts of interpretation undertaken in the presence of an outsider who cannot be easily read. In this encounter that defines history while also collapsing historical distance, this may be the most historicist reading of all.

Yet in the end, there is another kind of reaction to the corpse on the Appian Way that collapses history even more. When Pallas's body was supposedly discovered back in 1065, its truth was rendered corporeal by the still visible gigantic wound that Turnus had administered. What Virgil had written about could now be confirmed, more or less literally, in the flesh. The mark on Tulliola's body, on the other hand, is her extraordinary beauty, rendered by countless of the eyewitnesses as a poetic blazon of perfections: her hair, her eyes, her nose, her cheeks, her lips, her tongue, her teeth.[171] By seeing a great antique beauty as deathless, Renaissance viewers are realizing the culture's erotic dreams in their most absolute classical and humanistic form. They are also comprehending the fact that the reception of beauty is a transhistorical form of encounter, whether that reception is to be understood as erotic or aesthetic—if, indeed, we wish to make the distinction. Which, once again, takes us back from bodies to statues. The sculpture that is emerging so miraculously from the ground (like Pompilio's Hercules) is also the dead that can be raised; it is also antiquity that needs to be named and placed in a diachronic narrative; it is also work of corporeal perfection that can be received as unmediated beauty.

On the subject of ancient statues and ancient people, I conclude with a retrospective from later in the sixteenth century. Pirro Ligorio, himself making a palimpsest of what he takes to be a Plinian metaphor,[172] tells us that the number of statues in ancient Rome was so considerable that Pliny describes Rome as having

> two populations, the one of living men and the other of marble statues, these last being all placed in their homes, palaces, theatres and amphitheatres, arches, piazzas, and baths; so that, just like living Romans, as well as foreigners, these were transported from all the various parts of the world, not sparing even that the gods and heroes be moved from their native places to install them among all the cities of the world. It is to be noted the greatness of spirit of such a people that it did not scorn to hold in high esteem even a statue of Hannibal, implacable enemy of the name of Rome, such was the value among them of *virtù*, which they still respected among their enemies. But what would Pliny have said, seeing such a large population of statues in the time of the emperor Vespasian if he had been able to observe the many emperors who succeeded, who brought an infinite number of statues to Rome commemorating innumerable gods, emperors, prefects, consuls, tribunes, and other great men without number, as well as those which they dedicated to their gods in public and private ex votos? I am sure he would have said that in Rome there was one population of living men and ten of marble statues.[173]

Rome contained a whole population in marble, complete with its own residences (presumably made of matching marble) and even its own immigrants, paralleling the peripatetic real inhabitants of the empire. The explicit difference between the two groups—as witness the case of Hannibal, who would be hateful in himself but honored as a statue—is that the marble population is the ideal form of the flesh-and-blood creatures it represents. In 1485, when the girl is found on the Appian Way, or in 1506, when the *Laocoön* is dug up on the Esquiline, the authentic life of antiquity is emerging from the ground, demanding that the moderns hear its voice and respond with a voice of their own.

2.1. After Myron, *Discobolus*, marble, Roman copy of fifth-century B.C. original, Vatican Museums, Rome

CHAPTER 2

HISTORIES

Before the images of ancient sculpture reappear, there exists already a body of verbal lore concerning the world in which they once lived. That body is large, consisting of all the documents of ancient culture, which had been avidly read since antiquity almost without interruption. We have so far focused on what might be called the tradition of ignorance: the effort to imagine Rome (in the literal sense) with the smallest recourse to hard facts and the largest recourse to the faculty of symbolization. But this symbolization of the art of Rome is not merely a tissue of imaginings, whether of ancients who look beyond the structures they really see or of medievals who must invent structures out of ruins. Many widely preserved classical texts offered early Renaissance observers an account in words of the world of ancient images.

Some of the most important of these texts were not meant to be documents in art history at all. The celebrated Horatian "ut pictura poesis" is merely the most widely diffused, if also the most unspecific, formulation in an ancient tradition by which poetry is defined, defended, or attacked by analogy to the visual arts.[1] Characteristically, painting or sculpture is thought to offer a simpler case in the speaker's rhetorical gambit; once the point about poetry is made by analogy, the speaker does not go back to clean up the matter of the differences between the verbal and the visual arts.[2] As viewed retrospectively in the early Renaissance, this analogical tradition enforces the sisterhood of the arts while rendering the terms of similarity and difference between them highly ambiguous. So far as the rediscovery of ancient art objects is concerned, ut pictura poesis and its progeny teach very little about what to see in ancient art. Yet these pronouncements generate and validate the belief that the history of textual thinking, with its greater documentation and respectability, can be applied quite directly to a newly reconceived history of images, even if there is no consensus on how to apply it.

Closer to the phenomena of ancient art itself is the oratorical tradition going back to Cicero and Quintilian, according to which rhetoric is taught by reference to well-known works of art or even to the theory of the visual arts. In part this is merely a special example of ut pictura poesis, with all the ambiguously totalizing qualities of that analogy, but it is something more as well. An influential passage in Quintilian, for instance, uses the mannered qualities of Myron's *Discobolus* (fig. 2.1) to justify verbal *figura*, equating an upright body with literal speech and an artistically arranged body with elegant rhetorical variation.[3] Another important description, of a painting depicting the Sacrifice of Iphigenia, suggests that the artist Timanthes renders grief most vividly by covering the face of the suffering Agamemnon. Once again, this exemplum makes a rhetorical point, here concerned with the persuasive power of silence. It appears in both Cicero and Quintilian, and, significantly, it is repeated by Alberti in *De Pictura* and emerges visually in borrowings by both Donatello and Ghiberti from a relief version (fig. 2.2), known by the early fifteenth century, of the same subject with the same iconography.[4] Besides enforcing the analogy between words and images, this textual tradition describes some important works of art. More important, it establishes the rhetoricity of images and instructs Renaissance viewers in a rhetorical mode of ekphrasis.

We shall have occasion to return to these readings and ways of reading. But my present concern is with a textual tradition that is fully and explicitly concerned with the history of art rather than with *sententiae* about images that are excerptable from other discourses. When modern archaeology attempts to reconstruct ancient art, it can rely upon Lucian and the Philostratuses for imaginative accounts or Pausanias and Apollodorus for documentary accounts, though these texts were scarcely available in the early Renaissance. Vitruvius was extensively read, largely in the attempt to reconstruct architecture.[5] But it is from three late books of Pliny's *Natural History*, well preserved and widely read at least from the time of John of Salisbury, that the moderns had reason to suppose they knew what to expect of ancient art.

THE *NATURAL HISTORY* OF ART

It is the destiny of a text like the *Natural History*, encyclopedic and discursive, to be read for facts, Pliny's books on art more than most because they document a world of objects largely lost.[6] A historian of ancient art, whether in 1490 or 1990, has a vested interest in *not* deconstructing Pliny, in not raising too many questions concerning his limitations, his prejudices, and above all his imagination. Modern scholars, armed with other contemporary documents and with a great many of the art objects themselves, tend to believe (or even assume) that they can filter out Pliny's idiosyncrasies so that he can serve the purpose of helping to reconstruct the history of ancient art. Perhaps this is true; perhaps the idiosyncrasies are inseparable from the encyclopedic material; or perhaps the idiosyncrasies themselves would be a better guide to ancient art than the encyclopedic material. These are questions in twentieth-century method. In the fifteenth and sixteenth centuries the constellation of facts and imagination within the orbit of the *Natural History* is quite different. I propose to consider Pliny as the central grounding text of the rediscovery of ancient art. Our subject, in other words, is situated at an intersection between the long-canonized account of art history to be found in Pliny and the new phenomenon of the unearthing of art objects as well as a revised viewing of ancient objects long since above ground. Pliny's text, known widely from at least the twelfth century onward, will come to define both art objects and aesthetics in the Renaissance. To understand the fifteenth and sixteenth centuries we must read the first century carefully.

Pliny creates the History of Art by carving out a small territory from the space long occupied by two other, better-established Histories: Natural History and the History of Rome. The first is his explicit subject. Pliny sets out to organize the natural universe, to provide a record of its diverse manifestations, and to organize them into a taxonomy. This turns out to be anything but a value-free enterprise, a dry scientific record, because it is motivated by a powerful sense that the story of nature has been eclipsed and threatened by sophisticated civilization. One can scarcely find a page of this long work that does not contain a lament about the corruption of nature by human beings. It would be wrong to ascribe to Pliny the mid-twentieth-century idea of corruption within a holistic ecosystem; yet his purpose is to memorialize a nature that is being distorted, misused, or ruined. The History of Rome is the inescapable other context for the History of Art. Pliny writes in what we might call the first great twilight of Roman civilization, close to the memory of the Augustan age but closer to the times of Tiberius, Caligula, and Nero. The decay of nature becomes a newly powerful subject for Pliny and his audience not because of a sudden increase in technology or pollution but because the state of political power in the first century inspires an awareness of universal decay, of the falling off from some better age in the past—which has generally been associated with a purer state of nature than that of the present moment. When he concludes the whole work with the proposition that "pulcherrima omnium est iis rebus quae merito principatum naturae optinent Italia" ("there is no land so well endowed with all that wins Nature's crown as Italy" [37.201]), he is knitting together the national and the natural in a tone of melancholy retrospective.

The History of Art is born of these other histories for reasons that are quite obvious: first, works of art are made out of natural materials; second, they are defined both in origin and in use by their place in public life. But in what sense do these associations of art objects give art a *history?* Natural history, to begin with, gives art a taxonomy, a kind of vertical system, as the field of art comes to be structured by the materals out of which it is made. The developments of the various arts are understood as taking place within a given medium. Art objects come to be defined by all the material hierarchies that govern the natural world: works made of clay, for instance, are given relatively short shrift near the end of book 35, though they are praised precisely because of Pliny's reverse snobbism in regard to humble objects. Art, furthermore, becomes the crowning case of human beings' developmental relation to their natural environment, granting it a technological model for progress—and, given Pliny's pessimistic view, for regress as well. On the side of progress, there is Pliny's account of early times when Phidias *aperuisse* statue making while Polycleitus *consummasse hanc scientiam* (34.54, 34.56). In the present age, on the other hand, certain elements of technologi-

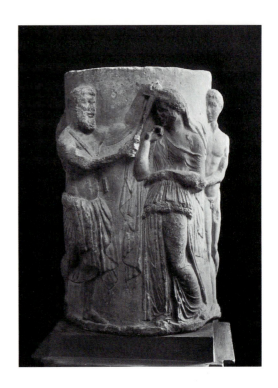

2.2. *Iphigenia Prepared for Sacrifice, Agamemnon with Covered Head*, two views from the *Ara of Cleomenes*, Roman marble, first century B.C., after Greek original attributed to Cleomenes, Galleria degli Uffizi, Florence

cal progress have been lost precisely because the moderns have developed corrupted notions about natural materials: so bronze casting has fallen on evil days because Nero was interested only in gold and silver. In other cases technology has become *too* good, as in the use of multiple exotic pigments or of wall painting in fresco, which were unknown and unnecessary in the great past time of Apelles.[7]

If natural history offers one axis for art, political history offers the other. The chronology of history itself is tightly bound up with the birth and flowering of the visual arts. Marble sculpture, which Pliny describes as the earliest of the arts, has its origins in the time of the first Olympiad, with the representation of the human likeness at first consecrated to Olympic winners (34.16). This is more than a chance conjunction, since the Olympics form the basis for Pliny's calendar, which he then uses as a kind of matrix for the development of the arts: "cessavit deinde [olympiade CXXI] ars ac rursus olimpiade CLVI revixit" ("after that the art languished, and it revived again in the 156th Olympiad" [34.52]). In Rome's history as well, the origins of society and of art are closely related. Pliny dates the early flowering of Greek painting with the time of Romulus (35.55) and describes the Hercules statue in the Forum Boarium as having a great ritual significance in the time of Evander (34.33), another founding figure in the myths of Roman origins. Within modern times, the history of art is partly the history of its promotion by a succession of Roman rulers. Particularly in the case of painting, Pliny writes one version of his history as the progress of the art's respectability, as encouraged, in a stepwise manner, from the early time of Messala, who made painting respectable by using it to commemorate a victory in the Punic

Wars; through Julius Caesar, who dedicated mythological paintings in important public spaces; to Augustus, who decorated the Forum with paintings; to the patronage of Tiberius, whose very promotion of art, Pliny implies, had a regressive effect on its respectability, given the emperor's own perverse values.[8]

Insofar as art is at the nexus of nature and public power, it may come in conflict with them. Although Pliny may ultimately validate the notion that art triumphs over these constitutive realms, there is also considerable grounding in the *Natural History* for the anxiety that art can become as corrupted as the natural world, and for the same reasons. Julius Caesar made painting respectable by promoting public subjects in public spaces, whereas artists like Apelles and Protogenes proved their worth by not executing private commissions. But generations of patrons, plunderers, and collectors have made art into a private business or a matter of private enjoyment.[9] Whole categories of artistic endeavor—categories, as it happens, of great prominence in the Renaissance—are seen as intrinsically corrupted. Fresco painting Pliny declares to be a decadent modern practice because he associates it with privatization and property. Color is itself damned by association with imperialism. The overuse and trivialization of the color purple, says Pliny, can be traced to the exploitation of the resources of India: "omnia ergo meliora tunc fuere, cum minor copia" ("everything in fact was superior in the days when resources were scantier" [35.50]). The history of marble sculpture, though it rises to great heights of appreciation, is introduced as "praecipua morum insania" ("the prime folly in our behaviour" [36.1]), because the quarrying of materials destroys nature and bestows no benefit on humankind.

These nostalgic reflections on the making of art objects begin to suggest that art is not only the victim but also the medium of corruption in its relations to nature and power. Nor is this an accident of art's material basis or its imperial promotion. Its very communicative impulses are corruptible. Once upon a time, the *Apoxyomenos*, Lysippus's beautiful statue of a boy scraping his body, was displayed publicly outside the Baths of Agrippa; Tiberius, however, fell so in love with the statue that he removed it to his own bedroom, until finally the people were so outraged that they demanded its return to public view (34.62). Which is the truer message of the *Apoxyomenos*: the literal signification of a boy who is cleansing himself as a fittingly accessible emblem in front of the public baths or the erotic signification of a beautiful youth reserved for the emperor's private delight? Pliny has no doubts, particularly since Tiberius is famous for his perversity. But one does not forget, as in the old joke about the Rorschach blots and the dirty-minded patient, that it is Lysippus who is drawing the dirty pictures; the "love" that Tiberius feels for the statue ("apoxyomenos . . . quamquam adamatum") slides all too easily between lust and art appreciation.

Another Lysippean statue, of the young Alexander, is appropriated by a different hated emperor, Nero, who is so enchanted by the work that he orders it to be plated with gold. This, as Pliny explains, so reduces the statue's value that the plating must eventually be removed; its worth is only partially restored, however, since the process leaves serious "wounds" (34.63). Once again it is a tale of imperial decadence. Nero, notorious for orientalizing the shows of power, appropriates the image of Alexander in both literal and figurative senses, covering it with gold as part of his self-aggrandizement and his indulgence in luxury.[10] Like Tiberius, he takes too much pleasure in the statue—the word here, *delectatus*, like *adamatum*, has ironic appropriateness to the context of connoisseurship—and like Tiberius he perverts the statue as a result. But what Nero responds to is not the erotic so much as the totemic significance of the statue, and he perverts it not by privatizing it but by imposing on it values determined in the material world, which is the basis (but only the basis) for art objects themselves. Nero, like his predecessor, fails to understand the true value of art, and in so doing fails to understand the real value of Alexander—or rather the distance that separates him from Alexander. In the paradoxical discovery that the statue is worth more (*pretiosior*) without the external augmentation of its value (*pretium*) lies one of Pliny's deepest presuppositions: namely, that the work of art, however entangled with the value systems of power and of the material world as valorized by power, determines its own value independently.

The Alexander statue is not merely marble or gold and not merely a representation of Alexander; the *Apoxyomenos* is not merely a beautiful boy and not merely a symbol of cleanliness; nor in either case can the emperor be trusted to make the determinations. Behind this account lies a sense of tension in the triad of nature, art, and power that animates much of Pliny's text and will continue to reverberate powerfully in the Renaissance. At issue are conflicting determinations of value. The normative histories, natural and political, bestow values based either on materials or on subject matter: in the first case, gold makes a statue valuable, and in the second, the representation of Alexander makes a statue valuable. Both kinds of value are further enhanced by their association with powerful patronage, which determines what subjects are valuable and sets the going rate for precious materials. But the very presence of these alternatives describes another basis for value. Pliny criticizes as "foolish" Cato's decision to sell all the statues he finds when he conquers Cyprus, except for one, which is that of the philosopher Zeno. It is the subject matter—and Cato is proverbial for his philo-philosophy—that enchants the general, of whom Pliny says, "Non aere captus nec arte" ("it was not the bronze nor the artistry that attracted him" [34.92]).

The alternative of artistry itself is the crucial missing term in Pliny's jeremiads against his own contemporaries. So long as the history of art is inseparable from the histories of nature and the state, Pliny's account can only be highly ambivalent. Pliny introduces an apparently enthusiastic history of artistic achievement as the crowning term in his history of the natural world. But it turns out that art and its natural materials are at war with each other, as a consequence of which art perverts the natural world. A developmental model of the human being in nature bestows upon Pliny's history of art the model of technological progress. At the same time, technological progress is precisely what has led art away from authentic public use and into realms that are perverse, private, and sybaritic. Yet this whole argument is couched in a narrative whose central purpose is to celebrate artistic genius and artistic achievement. That narrative can emerge only when art is granted its own history.

The intersection of artistry and history is, for Pliny, the awareness that artistic objects are subject to decay and loss. To understand artistic loss as significant is already to presuppose that the individual object is unique for its artistry: in other words, not replaceable by another object made of the same material or depicting the same subject. Often this decay is physical. The Colossus of Rhodes, for instance, is grandiose even in ruined condition. What was a human body, admittedly of gigantic proportions, is now a collection of corporeal fragments: "Pauci pollicem eius amplectuntur, maiores sunt digiti quam pleraeque statuae" ("Few people can make their arms meet round the thumb of the figure, and the fingers are larger than most statues" [34.41]). This dissolution of the corporeal architectonic makes it possible to compare arms to fingers, fingers to statues, and trunk to caves, since all the body parts are now reformed at the lowly level of modern, normal-sized individuals rather than high off the ground on the scale of the mythic ancients who produced such colossi and were depicted in them. The modern observer on the ground substitutes for the lost original a new set of imaginative shapes that constitute the heritage of the ancients.

Another form of decay engages Pliny even more. The Colossus of Rhodes, though ancient and crumbling, can be ascribed to Chares of Lindus, whose artistic origins go back to the primal figure of Lysippus. But there are statues in mint condition, newly installed in Pliny's own time, that lack an identity:

Romae quidem multitudo operum et iam obliteratio ac magis officiorum nego-
tiorumque acervi omnes a contemplatione tamen abducunt, quoniam otioso-
rum et in magno loci silentio talis admiratio est. qua de causa ignoratur artifex
eius quoque Veneris quam Vespasianus imperator in operibus Pacis suae dicavit
antiquorum dignam fama.   [36.27]

At Rome, indeed, the great number of works of art and again their consequent
effacement from our memory, and, even more, the multitude of official functions and business activities must, after all, deter anyone from serious study,
since the appreciation involved needs leisure and deep silence in our surroundings. Hence we do not know the maker even of the Venus dedicated by the
emperor Vespasian in the precincts of his temple of Peace, although it deserves
to rank with the old masters.

The Venus in Vespasian's temple is a victim of *obliteratio*, a term whose physical meaning of erasure is being transferred to a metaphorical meaning of loss of fame. Pliny's
underlying model—of constant importance in his account of art, though it lies too
deep to be directly confronted—is that of the Roman statue-cum-inscription.[11] In perfect condition, such a statue presents an image and a set of words that may reveal both
the subject and the name of the artist. The loss of letters—*obliteratio*—is as devastating a form of decay as is the loss of body shape to the Colossus of Rhodes. Equally significant is the implied cause of this obliteratio, which is the public life of Rome itself.
Statues become *obliteratae* because there are too many of them, related to too many
public functions, crowding the contemplative space of Rome. What is needed is the
reinscription of letters.

These *litterae* are, in fact, art history. The physical decay or disappearance of
an important work is parallel to—indeed, virtually synonymous with—the loss of
information as to the identity of the artist. Complete works are not only perfect in all
their parts; they also have pedigrees that include the names of the artists as well as
their bloodlines—that is, their placement in a narrative sequence demonstrating the
development of the art. The uniqueness of the individual object is therefore identified
with the person of the artist who produced the work: name, life, character, the rest of
the artist's oeuvre. Inhering in this nexus of assumptions are both the principles of art
history and the definition of the historian's task as we continue to understand them.
Just as those who contemplate the Colossus of Rhodes re-create the statue, the art historian re-creates the space of Rome, producing a kind of museum of history in which
the contemplative function is restored at the same time as the works and their pedigrees are put back together. Thus, according to Pliny's model, as with the statue and
its inscription, art itself depends on words for both existence and meaning. The historian, who provides and preserves names and bloodlines, becomes an essential term in
the completion of the work.

What those words are about is the memorializing of fame. Pliny's search for historiographic principles generally begins with a history of the medium's technology until it reaches maturity; then he proceeds through a sequence of great men. The sequence itself comes to be determined by the relations among great men, sometimes of a personal kind, as in the case of Apelles and Protogenes, but more often through the medium of discipleship, rivalry, and influence. In either case, the determining factors in the nature of an artist's work are the individual personality and the fabric of what we would call the artistic community. Even Lysippus, whom Pliny immortalizes as denying artistic parentage ("negat ullius discipulum fuisse" [34. 61]), is soon placed in a complicated family tree of descendants—both biological and aesthetic—who make up the *secta Lysippi*, a term for philosophical schools, here transferred to artists and thence immortalized on the walls of every modern museum.[12]

Pliny valorizes this system of relations by conceiving his account in terms of the famous. The chronology of the history of bronzes, for instance, is based on the most famous names. Pliny then goes on to explain that he will proceed quickly through an account of the most famous (though there is nothing "raptim" about the thirty paragraphs he devotes to this section), "reliqua multitudine passim dispersa" ("throwing in the rest of the throng here and there under various heads" [34.53]). *Passim dispersa*, indeed: the lesser artists in this medium are consigned to lists in alphabetical order! The account of painting enjoys a wider range of principles, but the most space is devoted to "celebres in ea arte." The history of marble sculpture is almost entirely devoted to the famous and to the subject of their fame. The earliest known sculptors *inclaruerunt*; Phidias is "clarissimum . . . per omnes gentes quae Iovis Olympii famam intelligunt" ("the most famous sculptor among all peoples who appreciate the fame of his Olympian Jupiter" [36.18])—a construction that equates the sculptor's renown with Jupiter's. The *Laocoön*, though it is referred to as greater than any painting or bronze, is introduced as an example not of excellence but of collaborative art, which poses special problems, as Pliny sees it, for the development and maintenance of individual fame.[13] Similarly, the Mausoleum, though it receives proper praise as being one of the wonders of the world, mostly interests Pliny as a problem in multiple authorship and glory (36.30–31). Four sculptors worked on the structure—one on each of the four walls. It was intended as a memorial to King Mausolus, but the queen who commissioned it died before it was completed, whereupon the artists agreed to continue working, thereby creating, according to Pliny, a monument to themselves and art more than, presumably, to either the subject or the patroness who commissioned it.

I spoke of the memorializing of fame, which implies a prior condition merely transcribed by the historian; yet it should already be clear that the *litterae* the historian provides make for a more dynamic relation between fame as it exists in the ambient culture and fame as it is canonized in the historian's text. We might say that these terms existed in a never-ending circle were it not for the fact that the point of entry to this circle is made quite clear. In his history of bronze sculpture, Pliny offers an etiology for canon formation:

venere autem et in certamen laudatissimi, quamquam diversis aetatibus geniti, quoniam fecerant Amazonas, quae cum in templo Dianae Ephesiae dicarentur, placuit eligi probatissimam ipsorum artificum, qui praesentis erant, iudicio, cum apparuit eam esse, quam omnes secundam a sua quisque iudicassent. haec est Policliti, proxima ab ea Phidiae, tertia Cresilae, quarta Cydonis, quinta Phradmonis.   [34. 53]

The most celebrated have also come into competition with each other, although born at different periods, because they had made statues of Amazons; when these were dedicated in the Temple of Artemis of Ephesus, it was agreed that the best one should be selected by the vote of the artists themselves who were present; and it then became evident that the best was the one which all the artists judged to be the next best after their own: this is the Amazon by Polycleitus, while next to it came that of Pheidias, third Cresilas's, fourth Cydon's, and fifth Phradmon's.

Fame is construed fundamentally as a competition, and the fact of a synchronic contest among artists living and dead judged by artists themselves speaks to a kind of transhistorical community of artists, who exist (as we have seen in connection with the history of progeny and influence) largely in relation to one another.[14] It is this community that Pliny presents as the ultimate place of judgment. But it is also presumed that every artist judges himself number one: indeed, the rules of the contest have to be changed so as to correct for this ego. And once fame has been so determined, Pliny accepts the competitive verdict. Polycleitus and Phidias receive a great deal of Pliny's attention; Cresilas gets a brief moment of praise; Cydon and Phradmon are scarcely mentioned elsewhere.

Fame, in other words, begins as a story that artists tell about themselves, nearly always in a highly competitive arena. Examples are many. The obscure Spartan sculptors Sauras and Batrachus have reason to fear that they will be thought of not as the creators of the temples at the Porticoes of Octavia but merely as rich philistines who paid for them in the hopes of gaining an immortalizing inscription; so they create their own figural inscription by sculpting their names in rebus form as a lizard and a frog (36.42). The sons of Archermus go these sculptors one better. They are engaged in a war with the satirical poet Hipponax, who attempts to achieve a *condemnatio memoriae* on them (partly successful, since even Pliny identifies them as having lived "Hipponactis poetae aetate"). But they respond by crossing into the realm of words, indeed of the historian, by producing an authoritative verbal inscription with the self-fulfilling assertion of their fame: "quibus [simulacris] subiecerunt carmen non vitibus tantum censeri Chion, sed et operibus Archermi filiorum" ("to their pedestals they attached verses to the effect that 'Chios is esteemed not merely for its vines, but also for the works of the sons of Archermus'" [36.12]).

The ego that had to be corrected for in Ephesus comes to be the hallmark of the myth of the artist that is at the heart of the Plinian inheritance:

[Zeuxis] opes quoque tantas adquisivit, ut in ostentatione earum Olympiae aureis litteris in palliorum tesseris intextum nomen suum ostentaret. postea donare opera sua instituit, quod nullo pretio satis digno permutari posse diceret. . . . [Fecit athletam] adeoque in illo sibi placuit, ut versum subscriberet celebrem ex eo, in visurum aliquem facilius quam imitaturum.   [35.62–63]

Also [Zeuxis] acquired such great wealth that he advertised it at Olympia by displaying his own name embroidered in gold lettering on the checked pattern of his robes. Afterwards he set about giving away his works as presents, saying that it was impossible for them to be sold at any price adequate to their value. . . . [He made an Athlete], in the latter case being so pleased with his own work that he wrote below it a line of verse which has hence become famous, to the effect that it would be easier for someone to carp at him than to copy him.

[Parrhasius] fecundus artifex, sed quo nemo insolentius usus sit gloria artis, namque et cognomina usurpavit habrodiaetum se appellando aliisque versibus principem artis et eam ab se consummatam, super omnia Apollinis se radice ortum et Herculeum, qui est Lindi, talem a se pictum, qualem saepe in quiete vidisset.   [35.71]

Parrhasius was a prolific artist, but one who enjoyed the glory of his art with unparalleled arrogance, for he actually adopted certain surnames, calling himself the 'Bon Viveur,' and in some other verses 'Prince of Painters,' who had brought the art to perfection, and above all saying he was sprung from the lineage of Apollo and that his picture of Heracles at Lindos presented the hero as he had often appeared to him in his dreams.

Countless traits of the artist-myth are launched and elaborated in these descriptions of the two famous painters. Works by geniuses are immensely expensive but at the same time beyond price; great works of art, however subject to the quibbles of critics, remain unique and unrepeatable, especially by critics; artists exist under the special patronage of the gods, which links them to a supernatural world of inspiration as well as to the very heroes of the past age whom they represent in their works.

Most important in all these etiologies of fame is the artist's self-immortalization and the logocentric nature of fame that brings artist and historian together. Parrhasius creates himself in verbal narrative, living the good life and making himself famous for it, inventing exalted rank on this earth and exalted ancestry beyond it, declaring himself in communication with the gods. Zeuxis, on the other hand, creates himself in the visual medium, but even this must be grounded in inscription. He writes himself a laudatory caption; he also appears at Olympia—once again, the symbolic point of origin of the arts—as his own work of art with his own signature upon himself. The historian's engagement in this mythmaking remains as involuted as his whole relation to artistic fame. The tone is a bit critical, for Pliny (like many writers on art in later periods) proceeds from an inscribed assumption, often denied, that artists are not meant to be rich and powerful. Yet in the end Pliny collaborates as ever in the project of assuring the fame of the artist, both by recounting these self-created myths and by validating them in regard to the works these artists created.

It is not only the greatness of the works that valorizes the myth of the artist: the art object and the personality exist in a complicated circular relationship, as a consequence of which the life can be read in the work and the work in the life. Thus in the heritage of Plinian historiography, biography and critical analysis are completely interwoven; and given Pliny's emphasis on the artist's self-invention and self-communication, the presence of the personality in the work is no accident but rather a kind of perpetual self-portraiture. Parrhasius paints some dirty pictures, which Pliny describes as a bit of spare-time recreation, but it is ambiguous whether the recreation consists in the painting or in the erotic activity upon which the painting was modelled (35.72). Praxiteles sculpts his Merry Courtesan with an autobiographical significance: "hanc putant Phrynen fuisse deprehenduntque in ea amorem artificis et mercedem in vultu meretricis" ("connoisseurs detect in the figure the artist's love of her and the reward promised him by the expression on the courtesan's face" [34.70]). Once again, the passage is ambiguous. It is not specified whether the reward visible in her face is the pleasure she will grant him or the gift (perhaps the statue itself) that he will grant her. The underlying ambiguity in all these cases is that of artistic self-representation, of the artist's capacity both to mirror and to re-create himself.

Not all these autobiographies are sexual; indeed, the most important and most frequently cited mythic materials are concerned with the artist's relation to art itself. We learn, for instance, of the frenzied artist Apollodorus, "inter cunctos diligentissimum artis et iniquum sui iudicem, crebro perfecta signa frangentem, dum satiari cupiditate artis non quit, ideoque insanum cognominatum" ("of quite unrivalled devotion to the art and a severe critic of his own work, who often broke his statues in pieces after he had finished them, his intense passion for his art making him unable to be satisfied, and consequently he was given the surname of the Madman" [34.81]). The elements of the myth, along with their many reverberations in later history, are clear enough: artistic frenzy is insatiable, indeed is a form of madness that leads to *non finito* and self-destruction. As it happens, this is a piece of metahistory, since Pliny is here speaking of Apollodorus not in person but as the subject of a statue by Silanion. Artistic frenzy turns out to be contagious: "hoc [cognomen, i.e., insanum] in eo expressit, nec hominem ex aere fecit, sed iracundiam" ("this quality he brought out in his statue, the Madman, which represented in bronze not a human being but anger personified" [34.82]). Who *expressit* madness so well? Presumably Silanion, but given that his subject is another sculptor, the confusion is all too easy; and at the very least the statue becomes a kind of compensation for all those works of Apollodorus lost through his artistic rage at the same time as it is analogously reduced to that very quality. The two sculptors together end up collaborating in a paradoxical image of self-expression and self-destruction.

The same terms—artistic frenzy, self-representation, metamorphic reduction—generate an aesthetic in one of Pliny's most interesting stories, concerning Protogenes, who also fulfills the myth of the eccentric artist similarly self-created—"quis eum docuerit, non putant constare" ("Who his teacher was is believed to be unrecorded" [35.101]). The anecdote concerns a painting of Ialysus in the Temple of Peace in Rome:

> est in ea canis mire factus, ut quem pariter ars et casus pinxerit. non iudicabit se in eo exprimere spumam anhelantis, cum in reliqua parte omni, quod difficillimum erat, sibi ipse satisfecisset. displicebat autem ars ipsa. . . . spumaque pingi, non ex ore nasci. anxio animi cruciatu, cum in pictura verum esse, non verisimile vellet, absterserat saepius mutaveratque penicillum, nullo modo sibi adprobans. postremo iratus arti, quod intellegeretur, spongeam inpegit inviso loco tabulae. et illa reposuit ablatos colores qualiter cura optaverat, fecitque in pictura fortuna naturam. [35. 102–3]

> In the picture there is a dog marvelously executed, so as to appear to have been painted by art and good fortune jointly: the artist's own opinion was that he did not fully show in it the foam of the panting dog, although in all the remaining details he had satisfied himself, which was very difficult. But the actual art displayed displeased him. . . . The foam appeared to be painted, not to be the natural product of the animal's mouth; vexed and tormented, as he wanted his picture to contain the truth and not merely a near-truth, he had several times rubbed off the paint and used another brush, quite unable to satisfy himself. Finally he fell into a rage with his art because it was perceptible, and dashed a sponge against the place in the picture that offended him, and the sponge restored the colours he had removed, in the way that his anxiety had wished them to appear, and chance produced the effect of nature in the picture!

Like Apollodorus, Protogenes is an insatiable perfectionist, nearly driving himself mad over what must be an unimportant detail in a heroic picture concerning the founder of a city.[15] So extreme is his frustration that he risks destroying the picture (much as Apollodorus smashed the statues that displeased him); but through a kind of miracle the fit of anger solves the problem. Throwing in the sponge (so to speak) is not—for all Pliny's references to *casus* and *fortuna*—in the least random. The sponge is the locus of all Protogenes' colors; and hurled at the picture, it does not *introduce* colors but *reponuit*, that is, puts them back. In fact, it is a story of metamorphosis, with Protogenes' art concentrated in the sponge, producing a work of art—the dog foaming at the mouth—that is the image of the raging painter himself. More than the Silanion anecdote, however, this story describes an aesthetic. *Displicebat ars; verum esse, non verisimile vellet*: for the painter in a frenzy of creation, art and verisimilitude are shams; he insists upon the thing itself. The thing itself turns out to be the painter's own passion, which is transmitted to the canvas not by a sequence of well-articulated brushes but by the random throwing of a sponge (which is presumably intended to *remove* colors). For that throw Pliny uses the verb *impingere*—hurl against, drive— which turns the action into an alternative type of *pingere*, or painting. The artist becomes not only the affective subject of his work but also the measure of its authenticity as reality rather than representation.

Given the political world in which Pliny writes and in which he was read, both originally and fifteen hundred years later, the most telling index of the artist's importance is not fame per se, nor eros, nor the frenzy of inspiration, so much as it is the artist's independence from public power and authority as embodied in the sovereign. Part of Pliny's account of this relationship is, roughly speaking, historical. Throughout these books of the *Natural History*, there are countless references to the high cost in money and effort that powerful individuals are willing to expend for the sake of works of art; it is also clear that art was an important pawn in the exercise of power, as evidenced by the many references to plunder, collecting, and privateering.[16] But Pliny's stories of personal relations between artist and sovereign are mythic rather than historical—examples not of some authenticatable patronage relations but of some persistent idea as to how artists' lives might be lived. Whether these ideas are concerned with eros, egotism, inspiration, or politics, the codification and transmission of such stories inspires, in contemporary or later times, the belief that such roles for the artist have existed. This in turn becomes an important standard for measuring the present or the recent past; canonized by Pliny, by antiquity, and by humanism, this body of tales provides a standard to be imitated.

In one of the most widely disseminated of these stories, Alexander, we are told, often visited Apelles' studio (a detail that turns up in narratives of other artists employed by monarchs). These visits occasion a considerable shift of power as the monarch attempts to discuss painting and is ridiculed even by the boys who help Apelles mix his colors. Pliny could hardly have embarrassed Alexander more than by making the *pueri*, his young assistants, into the emperor's superiors in the realm of art. The principal force of these political narratives is to establish art as its own independent realm, in which (in this case) Apelles is so much more the emperor than Alexander that even his lowliest helpers rank higher. It is not enough, of course, to assert this independent power of the artist; the story must demonstrate that Alexander recognizes it—since, after all, it is the emperor's power that authorizes other powers. So by decreeing that only Apelles may paint his portrait, Alexander creates an emperor of painting and selects Apelles for the job.

The relationship turns more subversive when the emperor gives over his favorite concubine in marriage to Apelles, once the artist has fallen in love with her after painting her in the nude. The exposure of Pancaspe to the artist is another of Alexander's extraordinary recognitions of Apelles; that the painter should fall in love with her follows both from the beauty she must possess to have won the emperor's heart and from the well-established eroticism of visual representation and the artist. It is not even surprising, given the emperor's other recognitions of the artist's "equality," that he should grant her to Apelles. But it is the gloss upon Alexander's gift that most strikingly demonstrates the power of the artist: "magnus animo, maior imperio sui nec minor hoc facto quam victoria alia, quia ipse se vicit" ("great-minded as he was and still greater owing to his control of himself, and of a greatness proved by this action as much as by any other victory" [35.86–87]). Pliny takes the truism that the conquest of one's own desire is greater than the conquest of a kingdom and makes Apelles into the agent by which Alexander achieves his greatest victory—a victory of art, love, and self-control.

The story of Protogenes and King Demetrius dramatizes the same contest of powers. The king wishes to lay waste the very territory in which the artist's studio is located. When he fails to persuade Protogenes to leave the battle zone, he abandons his plans for conquest. The result is a victory for art and a defeat for Demetrius's ambitions against the Rhodians; and just as Alexander's power is necessary to confirm Lysippus', so Demetrius must accept—even enthusiastically—that it is better for him to visit the artist in his studio than to win a military victory: "relictisque victoriae suae votis . . . spectavit artificem" ("quitting his aspirations for his own victory, . . . [he] looked on at the work of an artist" [35.105]). But the payoff of this anecdote is not so much about power as about art:

> sequiturque tabulam illius temporis haec fama, quod eam Protogenes sub gladio pinxerit: Satyrus hic est, quem anapauomenon vocant, ne quid desit temporis eius securitati, tenentem tibias.

> Fecit et Cydippen et Tlepolemum, Philiscum tragoediarum scriptorem meditantem, et athletam et Antigonum regem, matrem Aristotelis philosophi, qui ei suadebat, ut Alexandri Magni opera pingeret propter aeternitatem rerum; impetus animi et quaedam artis libido in haec potius eum tulere.   [35.105–6]

> And even to this day the story is attached to a picture of that date that Protogenes painted it with a sword hanging over him. The picture is the one of a Satyr, called the Satyr Reposing, and to give a final touch to the sense of security felt at the time, the figure holds a pair of flutes.

> Other works of Protogenes were a Cydippe, a Tlepolemus, a Philiscus the Tragic Poet in Meditation, an Athlete, a portrait of King Antigonus, and one of the Mother of Aristotle the philosopher. Aristotle used to advise the artist to paint the achievements of Alexander the Great, as belonging to history for all time. The impulse of his mind and a certain artistic capriciousness led him rather to the subjects mentioned.

So far is Protogenes from representing the dramatic experience of public life, in which he is himself an important participant, that he creates a masterpiece of bucolic relaxation. The sword hanging over him, whether literal or figurative, appears in the picture only by absolute negation, by being transformed, if not into a ploughshare, then into the instrument of rustic music making. Nor is it a coincidence that Pliny chooses this moment to contrast Protogenes' genius with Aristotle's practical notion of art. The philosopher presumes that the immortality of art is a function of the immortality of its subject matter. Protogenes does not limit himself to the private or the pastoral, but we have already seen him concentrate his attention upon the detail of a barking dog in a picture that was supposed to celebrate the founder of Rhodes. The list of subjects offered here is notably independent from royal patronage, and to the extent that it rides on the coattails of public fame, that fame is of a poetic and imaginative kind. The effect of Pliny's narration is to place "impetus animi et quaedam artis libido" in a highly privileged position. The ultimate significance of a history of art defined by artists—their personalities, their interrelations, their particular genius—is to grant an independent reality to the works that they produce. The paradox of Pliny's account, which so embeds art in the contexts of politics and matter, is that those contexts make it possible to offer art a magna carta and a declaration of independence.

MIMETIC NARRATIVES

Pliny's great-man theory is only one aspect of his history of art. By our standards it is scarcely history at all, since the stories of individual fame stand as a set of ahistorical, excerptible anecdotes with no necessary placement in an evolutionary narrative.[17] Yet there is definitely such a narrative in the *Natural History*. Indeed Pliny's establishment of art as an independent discourse may have less to do with the anecdotes of powerful or self-absorbed artists than with his depiction of growth and change in the history of representation—for it is in relation to the *signified* that art as *signifier* will ultimely declare its most vital independence:

> est et equus eius [Apellis], sive fuit, pictus in certamine, quo iudicium ad mutas quadripedes provocavit ab hominibus. namque ambitu praevalere aemulos sentiens singulorum picturas inductis equis ostendit: Apellis tantum equo adhinnivere, idque et postea semper evenit, ut experimentum artis illud ostentaretur. [35. 95]

> There is, or was, a picture of a Horse by him [Apelles], painted in a competition, by which he carried his appeal for judgement from mankind to the dumb quadripeds; for perceiving that his rivals were getting the better of him by intrigue, he had some horses brought and showed them their pictures one by one; and the horses only began to neigh when they saw the horse painted by Apelles; and this always happened subsequently, showing it to be a sound test of artistic skill.

in foro fuit et illa pastoris senis cum baculo, de qua Teutonorum legatus
respondit interrogatus, quantine eum aestimaret, donari sibi nolle talem vivum
verumque.   [35.25]

It was also in the forum that there was the picture of the Old Shepherd with his
Staff, about which the Teuton envoy when asked what he thought was the value
of it said that he would rather not have even the living original as a gift!

These anecdotes about paintings, at least one of which is meant to be a joke, describe
two extreme attitudes toward the nature of pictorial representation. The first is an
example of perhaps the most famous of all topoi in the visual arts, clearly something of
a cliché already in Pliny's time, since he tends to manipulate it in witty and unexpected
ways. The story, in all its dozens of forms, praises an artistic image by declaring that it
is absolutely indistinguishable from the thing it was meant to represent. The critic
who makes this determination of equivalence is nearly always an animal. As it develops, the belief in absolute equivalence between representation and thing represented
must generally be ascribed to a naïf, even though that ascription need not undercut the
praise for the work of art that represents reality so faithfully. The other story also
depends upon a naïf—the ambassador from the barbarian North. It further depends
upon a crucial fact of Hellenistic art about which we shall have more to say: that is, the
great fashion in Rome and elsewhere for humble and even disagreeable subject matter
in art. The Teuton is ridiculed for having the most unsophisticated theory of representation: namely, that a thing is always better than a representation of a thing, and since
the ambassador does not wish to possess an old shepherd, he is still less interested in
a picture of an old shepherd. What the sophisticated listeners perceive from this story
is that the value of a picture of an old shepherd is completely unrelated to the value of
an old shepherd; indeed, that representation and thing represented occupy different
planes of reality.

Both Apelles' horses and the anonymous old shepherd are understood to be
great works, but they are praised for nearly opposite reasons. These are not isolated
examples, for almost every one of Pliny's stories about a work of art is concerned
either with one of these two extreme positions or with the problematic of their opposition. Nor do these provide merely alternative categories for understanding the artistic
impulse itself; rather they become the key to a developmental history. In a familiar
model that parallels ontogeny and phylogeny, the early history of art is representation-
ally naive. True to his ambivalence about civilization, Pliny does not ridicule the archaic period. Indeed, however foolish the Teuton ambassador may seem in the present
age of Vespasian, Pliny expresses a fervent nostalgia for a time when art objects and
the things they represented could be measured against one another in clear and simple ways. The principal example is the portrait, which originated, according to Pliny,
at the Olympic games, the first occasion on which human achievement was sufficiently great to allow that mortals—rather than gods—might be represented. Once again,

the Olympic Games form the terminus a quo for the history of art. As a further tribute, those who were victorious three times received the award in their statues of perfect mimesis—*similitudo expressa*, thus establishing a parallel between the equivalence of representation and the equivalence of lofty actions and suitable recompense.

For Pliny, the accurate representation of the human figure lies at the heart of precisely that social and cosmic order which is disappearing in the modern world.

> Imaginum quidem pictura, qua maxime similes in aevum propagabantur figurae, in totum exolevit. . . . statuarum capita permutantur. . . . adeo materiam conspici malunt omnes quam se nosci, et inter haec pinacothecas veteribus tabulis consuunt alienasque effigient colunt, ipsi honorem non nisi in pretio ducentes. . . . itaque nullius effigie vivente imagines pecuniae, non suas, relinquunt. iidem palastrae athletarum imaginibus et ceromata sua exornant, Epicuri voltus per cubicula gestant ac circumferunt secum. . . . artes desidia perdidit, et quoniam animorum imagines non sunt, negleguntur etiam corporum.
> [35.4–5]

> The painting of portraits, used to transmit through the ages extremely correct likenesses of persons, has entirely gone out. . . . Heads of statues are exchanged for others. . . . So universally is a display of material preferred to a recognizable likeness of one's own self. And in the midst of all this, people tapestry the walls of their picture-galleries with old pictures, and they prize likenesses of strangers, while as for themselves they imagine that the honour only consists in the price. . . . Consequently nobody's likeness lives and they leave behind them portraits that represent their money, not themselves. The same people decorate even their own anointing-rooms with portraits of athletes of the wrestling-ring, and display all round their bedrooms and carry about with them likenesses of Epicurus. . . . Indolence has destroyed the arts, and since our minds cannot be portrayed, our bodily features are also neglected.

The principle of mimetic likeness is first of all associated with orderly relations in families, which also express their regularity by means of resemblance. Mimesis becomes for Pliny equivalent to respect for one's ancestors. Its decay is accompanied by a perversion in regard to Pliny's other basis for valuing an artistic object: fetishizing the material and developing a connoisseur's attitude toward the thing itself. The death of mimesis also destroys the possibility of uniting animus and corpus in a work of art—or indeed, of portraying either accurately. By ascribing this state of affairs to Epicureanism, Pliny associates the death of portrait painting with theories that the universe is ultimately random.

Between the similitudo expressa of the Olympic portraits and the randomness of the present day, Pliny sees a progressive decadence from this mimetic ideal. In the golden age a grateful populace erected statues to the greatest heroes. Later, lesser men were memorialized, sometimes at their own behest, and usually with falsifications in the representation made necessary by the undeserving nature of the individual represented. Inscriptions—viewed negatively from the perspective of early history—became necessary to bridge the gap between the fame the individual subjects really deserved and the propaganda that was being disseminated about them. Closely parallel are the living inscriptions provided by those who erect statues of themselves and then give speeches in front of the statues advertising their own heroic actions.[18]

Not only inscriptions but, more seriously, art itself comes to be used to distort accurate representation. The simple toga is replaced with cloaks or with self-aggrandizing costumes; a short poet erects a statue of himself (among the Muses, no less) in which he is tall. In particular the staging of the human figure distorts its authentic value. The first equestrian statues were (parallel to the first exact portrait likenesses) reserved for winners of horseback-riding contests; hence the subjects were accurately represented in this posture. But now nonequestrians appear exalted on horseback, and the fashion gives itself further airs with chariots drawn by two, four, or even six horses. Pliny attaches the same criticism to the placing of statues at great heights: "Columnarum ratio erat attolli super ceteros mortales, quod et arcus significant novicio invento" ("The purport of placing statues of men on columns was to elevate them above all other mortals; which is also the meaning conveyed by the new invention of arches" [34.27]). The argument is ultimately a mimetic one: real-life mortals spend their time on the ground and thus should be represented at that level. By extension, the triumphal arch—though not directly mimetic—is understood as an oversized extension of the triumphator's person. Portrait representation, even without frills, is a potentially dangerous exaltation; and the fact that the honorees for this exaggerated standing have not always been well chosen—that they include tyrants, women clad in togas, Hannibal, and the prefect of markets Lucius Minucius—attests to a decay in the authenticity, both mimetic and political, of representation.

Yet Pliny's ambivalences about art—its connection with civilization, its connection with decadence—turn this nostalgic account of archaic mimesis into the first stage of an evolutionary argument that celebrates a development away from perfect likeness and toward more complicated forms of representation. The origins of figurative sculpture and painting turn out to be quite similar:

> [filia Butadis] capta amore iuvenis, abeunte illo peregre, umbram ex facie eius ad lucernam in pariete lineis circumscripsit, quibus pater eius inpressa argilla typum fecit et cum ceteris fictilibus induratum igni proposuit.   [35.151]

> [The daughter of Butadis] was in love with a young man; and she, when he was going abroad, drew in outline on the wall the shadow of his face thrown by a lamp. Her father pressed clay on this and made a relief, which he hardened by exposure to the fire with the rest of his pottery.

De pictura initiis incerta nec instituti operis quaestio est. . . . omnes umbra hominis lineis circumducta, itaque primum talem. [35.15]

The question as to the origin of the art of painting is uncertain and it does not belong to the plan of this work. . . . All agree that it began with tracing an outline round a man's shadow and consequently that pictures were originally done in this way.

The artistic image is taken directly off reality. Although representation and the thing represented are not identical (as they are to the whinnying horses of Apelles), the act of representation completely subordinates itself to the real. That this subordination is by means of the shadow relegates representation both to a verisimilar and to an inferior position.

The early history of improvements upon this primitive verisimilitude tends explicitly to increase the exactitude of mimesis: various sculptors are praised for more accurate renditions of sinews, veins, or hair. Implicitly, however, representation is already developing in other dimensions. Myron, we learn in a telling phrase, "primus. . . multiplicasse veritatem videtur" ("is the first sculptor who appears to have enlarged the scope of realism" [34.58]). *Multiplicare veritatem* is an appropriately ambiguous notion. Sometimes it seems to involve what we would call conventions of representation, like the invention of different skin colors to distinguish male from female. At other times it is concerned with the showing of emotion or with elegant decoration of hair or drapery. Most often, however, progress is defined in terms of *symmetria*, a term one translates at one's peril, given the fact that, as Pliny says, "non habet Latinum nomen" (it has no Latin name).[19] In concrete terms, this quality seems to be expressed most essentially in the proportions of the human body. Lysippus "quadratas veterum staturas permutando," "capita minora faciendo quam antiqui, corpora graciliora siccioraque, per quae proceritas signorum maior videretur" ("modifying the squareness of the figure of the old sculptors," "by making his heads smaller than the old sculptors used to do, and his bodies more slender and firm, to give his statues the appearance of greater height" [34.65]). Already in Pliny, real bodies—especially ones from the past—are understood as blockish, while the mission of a more sophisticated art is to produce grace and stylishness as defined in what the sixteenth century would think of as mannerist terms.

This canon becomes explicitly antiverisimilar when Pliny shifts to the same evolutionary history in painting. In this case, Zeuxis offers a counterexample:

reprehenditur tamen ceu grandior in capitibus articulisque, alioqui tantus diligentia, ut Agragantinis facturus tabulam, . . . inspexerit virgines eorum nudas et quinque elegerit, ut quod in quaque laudatissimum esset pictura redderet. [35.64]

Nevertheless Zeuxis is criticized for making the heads and joints of his figures too large in proportion, albeit he was so scrupulously careful that when he was going to produce a picture for the city of Girgenti, . . . he held an inspection of maidens of the place paraded naked and chose five, for the purpose of reproducing in the picture the most admirable points in the form of each.[20]

It is no accident that Pliny juxtaposes the overlarge features with the classic anecdote that derives female beauty from the imitation of multiple sources. Zeuxis (whom Pliny often damns with faint praise) produces unaesthetic works precisely because he places himself within the limits of the real. The Girgenti painting has questionable prospects both because five women's beauties cannot be proportionally combined and because the work will be the result not of the artist's genius but rather of his (misguided) attempt at multiple mimesis. Zeuxis, it should be remembered, will lose the contest with Parrhasius because of a similarly "unenlarged" notion of verisimilitude.

The persistence in these descriptions of *videri*—seeming in the context of seeing—points to what is for Pliny the high point of technical evolution in art: not reality or even verisimilitude but something like the illusion of verisimilitude. Painting in particular lends itself to this distinction, since, as Pliny is well aware, two-dimensional art always operates on illusion; and he gives special praise to the rare work that can suggest figures beyond what is visible, such as one by Parrhasius, which "ostendat etiam quae occultat" ("disclose[s] even what it hides" [35.68]). As he goes on to describe the practice,

> extrema corporum facere et desinentis picturae modum includere rarum in successu artis invenitur. ambire enim se ipsa debet extremitas et sic desinere, ut promittat alia et post se ostendatque etiam quae occultat.   [35.67–68]

> To give the contour of the figures, and make a satisfactory boundary where the painting within finishes, is rarely attained in successful artistry. For the contour ought to round itself off and so terminate as to suggest the presence of other parts behind it also, and disclose even what it hides.

Even more famous and influential is the etiology of foreshortening:

> [Pausias] eam primus invenit picturam, quam postea imitati sunt multi, aequavit nemo. ante omnia, cum longitudinem bovis ostendi vellet, adversum eum pinxit, non traversum, et abunde intellegitur amplitudo. dein, cum omnes, quae volunt eminentia videri, candicanti faciant colore, quae condunt, nigro, hic totum bovem atri coloris fecit umbraeque corpus ex ipsa dedit, magna prorsus arte in aequo extantia ostendente et in confracto solida omnia. [35.126–27]

> [Pausias] first invented a method of painting which has afterwards been copied

by many people but equalled by no one; the chief point was that although he wanted to show the long body of an ox he painted the animal facing the spectator and not standing sideways, and its great size is fully conveyed. Next, whereas all painters ordinarily execute in light colour the parts they wish to appear prominent and in dark those they wish to keep less obvious, this artist has made the whole ox of a black colour and has given substance to the shadow from the shadow itself with quite remarkable skill that shows the shapes standing out on a level surface and a uniform solidity on a broken ground.

It is a celebration of deception, a trick to make an ox seem large or to cause the spectator looking in the margins of the lines to imagine forms that are not really there. But it is the sculptor Lysippus who is characterized as having made the quintessential breakthrough in the evolution of representation: "vulgoque dicebat ab illis [sculptoris veteribus] factos quales essent homines, a se quales viderentur esse" ("he used commonly to say that whereas his predecessors had made men as they really were, he made them as they appeared to be" [34.65]). Lysippus, it should be remembered, is something of an enfant terrible, given to extravagant boasts about his originality and his skill. That he should praise himself so boldly for *not* making men as they are; that Pliny should place Lysippus as a milestone in the progress of art for his rejection of *esse* and embrace of *videri* is the most powerful of signals that art is not the servant of reality but rather the master of its own reality.

The establishment of value in terms of artistry rather than of mimesis speaks to particular choices of subject matter. In early times only the truly worthy were honored by representation. The devaluation of this mark of esteem via the elevation of the trivial and the self-glorification of the ambitious correspondingly brings honor to works of art that represent matters not apparently connected to power. The three-time Olympic winners of ancient days were of apolitical significance; in more modern times, Protogenes is implicitly praised for not following Aristotle's advice to glorify Alexander. Pliny's tastes for a disinterested art and for personal style converge upon works that represent apparently insignificant or even unpleasant matters. Such works cannot derive their value from the sponsorship of the parties represented nor from the nobility of the narrative conception; what is left is the contribution of the artist. In this, as we have suggested, Pliny reflects the practice of Hellenistic art, in which such genre subjects were popular for parallel reasons—that is, the development of private but powerful connoisseurship. Pliny, however, goes beyond the recognition of this state of affairs by placing his praise for these works in the context of the alternative (and less valued) aesthetic of power and significance. He tells us, for instance, that a statue of a dog licking its wounds is so valuable that the only insurance policy worthy of it is a death sentence upon its guardians, should it ever come to grief (34. 38). Pliny places it at a pivotal spot in the development of the nobility of art as an example of *audacia*, presumably because of the boldness of the subject matter—the more so since the piece is housed in the shrine of Juno on the Capitol. Pliny is often correspondingly unimpressed with self-important subject matters. He passes over the likeness of Theodorus's self-portrait in bronze to dwell upon the "magna suptilitate" of the tiny figures—presumably images of works of art themselves—held in the figure's hands (34.83). Similarly in his account of Phidias, he mentions, but does not praise, the vast size of works like the Jupiter or the Minerva, while he concentrates on the impressive quantity of detail carved into small spaces (36.18).

The logical endpoint of this movement away from the thing represented and toward the method of representation is that a work of art have no subject at all. This extreme might appear radically anachronistic were it not for two of the most often retold stories in the *Natural History*. Both involve the quintessential Plinian arena of competition between two geniuses. It seems that Apelles, who is the very prototype of the famous and worldly artist, wishes to pay a call upon Protogenes, for his part the prototype of the troublesome hermit artist. Not finding him at home, Apelles leaves as his calling card neither his name nor an image but an extremely fine line which he paints on a handy canvas. Protogenes returns, recognizes the "hand" of Apelles at once, draws an even finer line in a different color on top of the first line as an identification of himself when Apelles should once again return. Whereupon Apelles draws yet a third and finer line; Protogenes admits defeat and seeks the real person of his adversary in the town. The story places ultimate value upon pure technique—not even the technique of producing similitudo or of making human features more elegant than they really are—but of the most fundamental and nonrepresentational basis of draughtsmanship. In this basic act, the anecdote suggests, is the quintessential signature of the artist (as perhaps only equal or near-equal geniuses can read it), the more perfect as a means of identification because it is not blurred by reference to external reality. Yet though completely nonrepresentational, it is a work of art: "spectatam nobis ante, spatiose nihil aliud continentem quam lineas visum effugientes, inter egregia multorum opera inani similem et eo ipso allicientem omnique opere nobiliorem" ("It had been previously much admired by us, on its vast surface containing nothing else than the almost invisible lines, so that among the outstanding works of many artists it looked like a blank space, and by that very fact attracted attention and was more esteemed than any masterpiece" [35.83]). Once again, the judgment of value is on the side of artistry: a perfectly executed blank space is preferred to *egregia opera*.

The competition between the painters Zeuxis and Parrhasius turns more directly upon the question of representation. Zeuxis depends for his contest entry upon the traditional animal test of realism, painting grapes so real that birds try to peck at them:

[Parrhasius] detulisse linteum pictum ita veritate repraesentata, ut Zeuxis alitum iudicio tumens flagitaret tandem remoto linteo ostendi picturam atque intellecto errore concederet palmam ingenuo pudore, quoniam ipse volucres fefellisset, Parrhasius autem se artificem. [35.65]

Parrhasius himself produced such a realistic picture of a curtain that Zeuxis, proud of the verdict of the birds, requested that the curtain should now be drawn and the picture displayed; and when he realized his mistake, with a modesty that did him honour he yielded up the prize, saying that whereas he had deceived birds Parrhasius had deceived him, an artist.

We have already seen that Zeuxis is something of a mimetic literalist, and he will continue to be so even after this concession to Parrhasius, since in the next anecdote he criticizes his own painting of a child carrying grapes, because the birds that (once again) swarm about it prove that the image of the boy must be less realistic than that of the grapes if it fails to deter the birds. In the contest with Parrhasius, literal mimesis as defined in this tradition is exploded, or at least relegated to a realm many phyla below that of art and artists. But the reading that Zeuxis offers in regard to his own defeat does not sufficiently take into account the nature of Parrhasius's image. The painting of a curtain offers a kind of ultimate step in the *audacia* that for Pliny characterizes nontraditional subjects for representation. Well beyond the realm of dogs licking wounds and boys playing dice, a curtain is another type of that *nothing* toward which images like the fine lines of Protogenes and Apelles were tending. More than that, however, a curtain is a nothing that makes the viewer think of represented images, that seems to promise a real image underneath. To be fooled in this way is to respond precisely to the aesthetic of representational illusion. It was Parrhasius, we should recall, who was praised for an art that "ostendat etiam quae occultat." The curtain with an invisible picture behind it—an image that a fellow artist believed in—is the ultimate case of revealing what it hides.

Both in the technique that Pliny praises and in the painting of the curtain, Parrhasius is, in fact, painting the invisible, for the ultimate way to "multiplicare veritatem" is to capture in an image that which cannot be seen. This step beyond representation has its own history, viewed by Pliny as contrasting with the evolution of grace and *symmetria*. Myron, credited as the first to "complicate truth," is said to have been unable to depict the invisible ("animi sensus non expressisse" [34.58]), as though artistic refinement were incompatible with revelation of inward values, while painters who succeed in communicating the spirit of their subjects are often criticized for their maladroit proportion or colors. The nature of this interiority for Pliny is both moral and affective: that is to say, it consists in rendering the invisible spiritual values of its (presumably human) subjects; but it also offers a dramatic representation of the psyche, which is similarly invisible in literalist terms. Thus Aristides, for instance, was "omnium primus animum pinxit et sensus hominis expressit, quae vocant Graece ἤθη item perturbationes" ("the first of all painters who depicted the mind and expressed the feelings of a human being, what the Greeks term *ethe* [character], and also the emotions" [35.98]).

But there is another, perhaps more significant invisibility in the greatest artistic images as Pliny understands them—that is, the genius of the artist: "in unius huius [Timanthis] operibus intelligitur plus semper quam pingitur et, cum sit ars summa, ingenium tamen ultra artem est" ("Indeed Timanthes is the only artist in whose works more is always implied than is depicted, and whose execution, though consummate, is always surpassed by his genius" [35.74]). Timanthes, it will be remembered, veiled the face of Agamemnon. In his work, as Pliny sees it, inwardness is preferred to artfulness, for the *summa ars* that is surpassed in this oeuvre is surely gracefulness, technique, and symmetria. But the inwardness here is not merely ethe, which has reference to the subject, but also the invisible idea of the artist that inspires the work. Pliny's aesthetic reveals itself most vividly when he relates the ontogeny of individual painters to the phylogeny of the history of art, here speaking about the conclusion of both histories:

> illud vero perquam rarum ac memoria dignum est, suprema opera artificum inperfectasque tabulas, sicut [opera Aristidis, Nicomachi, Timomachi et Apellis] in maiore admiratione esse quam perfecta, quippe in iis liniamenta reliqua ipsaeque cogitationes artificum spectantur, atque in lenocinio commendationis dolor est manus, cum id ageret, exstinctae.   [35.145]

> It is also a very unusual and memorable fact that the last works of artists and their unfinished pictures such as [he cites works by Aristides, Nicomachus, Timomachus, and Apelles] are more admired than those which they finished, because in them are seen the preliminary drawings left visible and the artists' actual thoughts, and in the midst of approval's beguilement we feel regret that the artist's hand while engaged in the work was removed by death.

The unmistakable Plinian ambivalence must not go unnoticed: the strategy of the sentence suggests that the connoisseur's pleasure at these works is virtually purchased at the expense of an early death for the artistic genius. Yet the ringing tones of the aesthetic are not muted for this sadness. What is most important in the artistic image is not the material from which it is constructed, not the memorialization of the subject, not even artfulness or beauty, nor yet the memorialized life of the artist; it is rather the artist's idea that inspired the work. In this claim, which is almost more Vasarian than Vasari, Pliny turns the work of art into a representation of its own unique idea.

ART IN THE KEY OF MYTH

"More Vasarian than Vasari": my immediate reference is to a much quoted passage from the *Life of Michelangelo* concerning the *Medici Madonna*: "Although the figure is not equal in every part, and it was left rough and showing the marks of the gradine, yet with all its imperfections there may be recognized in it the full perfection of the work."[21] I am not initiating a full-scale comparison between the two inventors of art history. Rather I conclude my discussion of the *Natural History* by admitting the extent to which it has been a reading across time—specifically, from the perspective of the Renaissance. I make no apology for this. Pliny's text, like any grandly ambitious and culture-summing work that is widely accessible for many centuries, is open to more than one reading that focuses legitimately on its actual contents. The focal points of the preceding analysis—loss, inscription, fame, representation—do not consist of a complete account either of Pliny or of the Renaissance; but they do describe a grand area of overlap between the two. Wholly other readings of these books are possible, which would probably reveal much about the Renaissance by negation.[22] I shall sum these differences up in a single issue, which could stand as an almost universal principle for what gets omitted from diachronic readings.

A Renaissance reading of Pliny, by building into itself—however tacitly—the historical distance between imperial Rome and early modern Italy, is bound to flatten all the historical distances written into the original text. To be specific: the *Natural History*, and especially its books on art, enact a complicated and by no means explicit structuring of history, not to mention geography. To talk in his own place and time about art, Pliny must juggle Greece and Rome, classical and Hellenistic (our terms, not his); he must show an awareness of the world of difference that separates, say, the *Doryphoros*, the *Laocoön*, and the Corinthian bronzes that Cicero valued.[23] He must deal with the paradox of Roman chauvinism versus an assumption such as was expressed by Virgil's Anchises that the arts are definitionally other to the *pax Romana*,[24] and along the same lines he must integrate the triumph of Rome with his disposition to claim that things were better in the past. He must construct a calendar that somehow relates ancient mythic time to the chronology of the modern Caesars. While he tells the legendary stories about the distant past of Phidias and Zeuxis, he also must reflect such realities as the downgraded native arts of Italy and the Roman fashion for assembling ostentatious collections of not always authentic imported work.[25]

All these layers of time and place are present in Pliny's world and, after a fashion, in his book. They can be teased out by modern scholarship, and that process may reveal much about first-century attitudes toward art and history. But Pliny is not writing modern scholarship, and he does not share our historicity nor our structure of categories. In short, Pliny's history of art already gives permission to readers to collapse historical and geographical distinctions. A reading such as I have offered in the previous pages abundantly takes that permission. The result is not, I would argue, ahistorical, but it is a history of art in the key of myth—that is, grounded in a set of ancient stories and large structures that seem to swallow up and account for the events of more recent times. If Pliny is already writing such a history, then his Renaissance readers are, like myself, all too glad to comply by treating the *Natural History* as more a flat map than a relief.

Material from books 34, 35, and 36 of the *Natural History* is cited, borrowed, alluded to, plagiarized, and reinvented whenever there is talk about art from the fourteenth to the sixteenth centuries; indeed, Pliny forms the core—the repeated and familiar set of cultural données—upon which any new aesthetic or historical claims are constructed.[26] But its very ubiquity renders a historical account difficult. The *Natural History* was not discovered or rediscovered during the Renaissance: it was simply present as a constant, a source of largely unimpeachable lore. Petrarch, to whose example we shall return, creates no self-regarding romance of rebirth surrounding this particular text, as he does with other works to which he accords a greater imaginative prestige—though he does lament the loss of Pliny's *History of Rome*, which he uses as an example of the unbridgeable distance that separates his age from antiquity.[27] As for the *Natural History*, he does possess a manuscript that he lavishly annotates, and he borrows from it in a wide range of ways in *De Remediis utriusque fortunae*, among other places. Indeed the history of ancient art is plagiarized from Pliny more or less verbatim and without much change from Ghiberti's *Commentari* in the 1440s to the prefatory letter by Giovanni Battista Adriani that is intended to fill in the ancient background to the revised edition of Vasari's *Lives* published in 1567. As for individual excerpts—typically, narrative anecdotes—their presence is to be noted from the days of Boccaccio and Petrarch to the age of the learned academies and treatises upon art that close the sixteenth century.

As a way of mapping this monolith, let us concern ourselves with the modalities by which the *Natural History* enters and shapes the Renaissance discourse of art. Alberti must be the logical, if not the chronological, starting point:

> Sunt qui referant Phyloclem quendam Aegyptium et Cleantem nescio quem inter primos huius artis [picturae] repertores fuisse. Aegyptii affirmant sex millibus annorum apud se picturam in usu fuisse prius quam in Graeciam esset translata. E Graecia vero in Italiam dicunt nostri venisse picturam post Marcelli victorias ex Sicilia. Sed non multum interest aut primos pictores aut picturae inventores tenuisse, quando quidem non historiam picturae ut Plinius sed artem novissime recenseamus.[28]

> Some say that one Philocles, an Egyptian, and a certain Cleanthes were among the first to practice this art [of painting]. The Egyptians declare that painting was practiced in their country some six thousand years before it was brought over to Greece. They say that the art was brought from Greece over to us in Italy after the victories of Marcellus in Sicily. But we do not care all that much to make claims about who the first painters or the inventors of painting were, since we are not recounting *historiam picturae* like Pliny but rather surveying this art in an entirely new way.

The ambiguities of the passage cluster about the phrase *historia picturae*, which is the activity ascribed to Pliny and against which Alberti designates his own, new approach. In fact, Alberti borrows not only the information from Pliny but also the gesture of *praeteritio*, that is, of offering an opinion while pretending to dismiss the subject. Pliny had said of his own etiology of painting, "De pictura initiis incerta nec instituti operis quaestio est" ("The question of the origin of the art of painting is uncertain and it does not belong to the plan of this work" [35.15]). But what exactly is this supposedly rejected historia picturae? *Historia* is both *history* and *story*. An account of painting that begins with its earliest Egyptian origins is a history; an account that focuses on *a certain* Philocles and *some* Cleanthes *or other* is a set of stories.[29] Alberti places himself outside either of these activities in order to define a third alternative, which appears to be a phenomenological account of the way that perception and representation actually function. By modern—or even later Quattrocento—standards, Alberti's account may be whimsical and unscientific, but that should not dim the force of his reaction to Pliny as bearer of the prevailing methodology.

Alberti is of course correct about Pliny in his punning description: Pliny writes a developmental history largely through the medium of anecdotes. And Alberti, no less than any other writer on the history of art in the Middle Ages and the Renaissance, depends considerably on Pliny's history of anecdotes. Indeed his somewhat disingenuous rejection of the Plinian model becomes even more complicated when we recollect that for him the very highest achievement of the visual arts is a kind of narrative image to which he gives the ambiguous name *historia*. These much praised *historiae* are sometimes classical, like Timanthes' painting of Iphigenia, which we mentioned earlier, and sometimes modern, like Giotto's *Navicella*. In one passage Alberti declares that no ancient artist knew how to compose a historia; yet he implies throughout that ancient artists invented and defined this model. Pliny's history will in effect turn the culture of art itself into just such a historia as those Alberti praises in the practice of art: that is, a narrative of complex parts.

In Alberti's (partial) rejection of this kind of historia for himself, we can understand both the Plinian tradition and the new attitude promoted in *De Pictura*. Alberti's humanist project looks upon the conjunction of anecdote and history as part of an old-fashioned and exploded tradition of commonplaces. Compared to a set of physical rules for perception or representation, the endlessly repeated stories of birds being fooled by painted grapes or of artists being deferred to by emperors emerge essentially as fantasies about nonexistent things. But we should not be as quick to condemn the persistent industry of Plinian tales. As Ernst Kris and Otto Kurz demonstrated brilliantly half a century ago, the traditional stories of art and the artist—for which no document in the Western tradition is more significant than Pliny's—are not just a series of commonplaces but also a set of encoded beliefs that affect the ways art is perceived and (one would add from a late twentieth-century perspective) the ways artists design their lives and work.[30] To discard as empty cliché in the history of aesthetic writing, say, the repeated claim that an artistic image is so real that it almost speaks, is to compose a progressivist history whose advances are judged entirely by some reified form of modern scientific discourse.[31]

We are essentially dealing with another classical mythology, which comes to the Renaissance in close association with the corpus of tales about the pagan gods and which will be submitted to similar processes of reading. There are tales of origins—of painting, sculpture, and so on—whose model is Ovidian etiology. There are countless instances of multiply retold narratives—like King Demetrius's terminating his war rather than harming Protogenes' studio, or the contest of verisimilitude between Zeuxis's grapes and Parrhasius's curtain—which become the fundamental myths of art. And there are the towering individuals, like Lysippus, Zeuxis, and Apelles, who turn into the gods or epic heroes of this material, collocating not only sequences of anecdotes but also sets of characterizations and personality traits.

Examples of this procedure of mythmaking ought properly to begin with the *Natural History* itself. Pliny reports, for instance, that Apelles never let a day go by without drawing at least one line. Shortly thereafter he tells the story of the shoemaker who properly corrects the same artist's rendition of a sandal but then, puffed up with critical pride, goes on to fault the shape of the leg; to this Apelles indignantly replies that shoemakers should not surpass their fields of expertise (34.84–85). Both of these stories, Pliny announces, have issued in proverbs—"nulla dies sine linea" and "ne sutor ultra crepidam" (the latter continues in our language as "shoemaker, stick to your last"). Roman readers were doubtless familiar with the proverbs and could see them coming as the anecdotes unfolded. Petrarch, for his part, glossed both these punch lines by writing *Proverbium* in the margin of his manuscript, though it is unclear whether he was recording something he already knew or discovering and thereby disseminating an old proverb afresh.[32] Whether in the first or the fourteenth century, the biography of an artist attains an originary function in determining the very language as it is spoken in the culturally definitive realm of the proverb. Pliny's direct reference to this operation will encourage later readers to proverbialize many more narratives of ancient art in their attempt to speak the language of antiquity and naturalize themselves within it.

As it happens, the Renaissance has powerful and venerable models for naturalizing ancient stories into its own culture. We may take the example of Ghiberti, who in a more or less exact translation tells the story of Apelles and Protogenes drawing ever finer lines on a panel (N.H. 35.81–83). At the conclusion he adds his own view:

> Tengo che questo che Prinio scrive veramente può essere vero, ma molto mi meraviglio sencio in costoro tanta profondità [di scientia] d'arte e con tutte le parti del pittore [et di geometria] et dello scultore, mi pare certamente una debile dimonstratione e'ssì fatto auctore questo recita la pruova di costoro, parlo come scultore et certo credo dovere essere così. . . . Appelle compuose et publicò libri continenti dell'arte della pictura, essendo ito a Rodi a casa Protogine trouando la tauola apparechiata et uolendo mostrare Appelle la nobiltà dell'arte della pictura et quanto egli era egregio in essa, tolse il pennello et compuose una conclusione in prospettiua appartenente all'arte della pictura.[33]

> I maintain that that which Pliny writes could actually be true. But I am much amazed, finding in those people such depth of knowledge about art including all aspects of the painter and of geometry, as well as sculpture, that it seems to

me a weak demonstration if this story is supposed to prove that, I speak as a sculptor and assuredly believe it has to be so. . . . Apelles wrote and published books about the art of painting, having gone to Rhodes to the house of Protogenes and finding the table set, and he wanting to demonstrate the nobility of the art of painting and to what extent he was himself exceptional in it, he took his brush and composed a problem in perspective relative to the art of painting.

He goes on to detail each of the finer lines as increasingly learned and perfect solutions to the problem of perspective. Ghiberti swerves from Pliny by locating in the ancient story a validating etiology for the most up-to-date and advanced development in the science of art. That is not so surprising, given Ghiberti's wish to establish Apelles as a theoretician and to identify himself with that activity.[34]

What is perhaps more interesting is the *mode* of Ghiberti's thinking, for his relation to Pliny's anecdote is precisely that of a modern mythographer to ancient myth. He narrates the event straight and declares that it *might* be true, but only if understood by means of a specialized hermeneutic system. In place of biblical exegesis, which qualifies mythographers for their task, Ghiberti offers his experience as sculptor and theoretician, enabling him to traverse Pliny's ignorance (or secrecy) and unlock the truth hidden in the ancient story, known specially by himself and Apelles. Pliny, in fact, may offer the original grounding for the special exegetical role that Ghiberti assigns himself: the panel with the lines was later considered extremely valuable, as Ghiberti translates it, "spetialmente da' pictori et dagli statuarij et da quelli erano periti" (especially by painters, sculptors, and experts).[35]

Whatever the particular utilities of the Apelles-Protogenes anecdote—and they turn out to be great—this exegetical process demonstrates that the artist legends tend to have one of the crucial requisites for both myth and mythography: a core of meaning that is elliptical, empty, or mysterious. The panel with the lines, as both Pliny and Ghiberti tell us, was burned in a fire: we will never know what it really looked like. And even if we could see it, its nonrepresentational subject would render it especially unrevealing. But equally elliptical is Parrhasius' curtain or the Helen that Zeuxis makes up out of five separate women or (perhaps most notoriously) the canon of measurement that is credited to Polyclitus. All these stories inspire mythological hermeneutics because they demand completion; and in their various ways, Renaissance writers on art and Renaissance artists (quite often the same people) feel the need to enter the stories by way of completing them.

In another instance, more than one Renaissance individual enters a Plinian anecdote:

He is not universal who does not love equally all the elements in painting, as when one who does not like landscapes holds them to be a subject for cursory and straightforward investigation—just as our Botticelli said such study was of no use because by merely throwing a sponge soaked in a variety of colours at a wall there would be left on the wall a stain in which could be seen a beautiful landscape. He was indeed right that in such a stain various inventions are to be seen. I say that a man may seek out in such a stain heads of men, various animals, battles, rocks, seas, clouds, woods and other similar things. It is like the sound of bells which can mean whatever you want it to. But although these stains may supply inventions they do not teach you how to finish any detail. And the painter in question makes very sorry landscapes.[36]

The writer is Leonardo, and the reference is to Pliny's anecdotes about Protogenes and Nealces (N.H. 35.103–4), who overcome difficulties of artifice in representing animals by the accident of hurling their painting sponges at the panel they are working on. Once again, the swerve from Pliny is itself interesting. Pliny's artists are depicting the foam that issues from the mouths of beasts. It is therefore quite natural that a randomly thrown sponge might leave the appropriate impression, because foam is itself variegated and formless and because the anger of the artist who throws the sponge (at least in Protogenes' case) replicates the mood of the foaming beast. None of this is true of landscape painting. As with Ghiberti's exegesis of the Apelles story, the Renaissance here goes the ancient text one better on its own terms. Pliny had introduced the subject of the sponge as an example of fortune intruding upon the world of artistic skill. Leonardo expands the role of fortune into a much larger principle—a sort of Gombrichian "beholder's share," that is, the way perceivers create the images they perceive.[37] Not surprisingly, Leonardo finds this possibility disturbing; and though he cannot deny it on the part of the viewer, he scorns it in regard to the education of the artist.

But once again, it is the system of translation from ancient story to modern artist that is particularly revealing—all the more so when two modern artists are involved. Neither Leonardo nor Botticelli makes any reference to Pliny, though there are elsewhere abundant clues testifying to Leonardo's familiarity with the *Natural History*.[38] Botticelli's comment, whatever its authenticity and its missing context, speaks to a domestication of the Plinian anecdote: the myth has been detached from its ancient past and become a transhistorical proof or demonstration of an artistic principle. Botticelli and his contemporaries may enter the narrative at will and displace Protogenes or Nealces. The myth has also become an evident commonplace in the conversation of artists at the same time as it retains vestiges of ancient and incontrovertible truth. It is this latter quality that troubles Leonardo, who must go to considerable lengths to dislodge its authority. If the Plinian myths are universalized and made anonymous, they are also reinvented and transferred to specific modern artists. To continue for a moment with the sponge story, Vasari reports of Piero di Cosimo that "he would sometimes stop to gaze at a wall against which sick people had been for a long time discharging their spittle, and from this he would picture to himself battles of horsemen, and the most fantastic cities and widest landscapes that were ever seen; and he did the same with the clouds in the sky."[39]

From Protogenes to Botticelli to Piero (or Pliny to Leonardo to Vasari) this story is increasingly attaching itself to the eccentric painter. On another mythic front, the number of artists whose work, like that of Zeuxis, deceives animals (and occasionally human beings) is legion.[40] A somewhat smaller number (e.g., Titian, Michelangelo) have experiences with emperors and popes that resemble those of Apelles with Alexander.[41] A somewhat less famous story concerning Apelles deals with his success in restoring himself to the good graces of Ptolemy by drawing a perfect likeness of the scoundrel who had slandered him to the emperor (35.89). Several derivative treatises on art from the middle of the sixteenth century narrate this tale in its original Plinian form. But it then appears in Armenini's *De' veri precetti della pittura* as a lengthy narrative from the life of Il Sodoma, who is insulted by a Spanish soldier in the garrison at Siena and succeeds not only in perfectly identifying his assailant in a drawing but also in ingratiating himself with the Spanish prince as a result of the talents he thereby exhibits. Vasari, incidentally, does not tell this story in his biography of Il Sodoma but offers a variant of it in the life of Filippo Lippi, who is captured by Moorish pirates and endears himself to their captain by drawing his portrait—an art, Vasari tells us, unknown to the Moors.[42]

The familiarity (not to say banality) of this procedure, common to myths of many different types in many different cultures, should not lead us to overlook its significance. Those who tell stories about Titian or Il Sodoma that are identical to stories Pliny told about Apelles are undoubtedly aware of the earlier versions, since their familiarity with the *Natural History* is beyond dispute, as is that of many members of their audience. To us, the doubling casts doubt on the veracity of both ancient and modern narratives, and by way of explanation we are moved to leave history behind in favor of psychology, sociology, or anthropology. Renaissance habits of mind, on the other hand, seem to find in the repetition something more like a confirmation. Once again, we are observing what happens when the materials of art history become mythology: that is, they come to be understood typologically. The recurrence of these events—even if we cannot understand it as the working out of a divine plan such as that which links Old and New Testaments or pagan and Christian narratives—tends to confirm both their accuracy and their enduring importance. More specifically, this recurrence validates the modern artist at the same time as it helps to construct an unbroken tradition.

If the Plinian heritage is narrative or mythological, it is also (like many other such traditions, including mythology) *rhetorical* in its later appropriation. Michael Baxandall has demonstrated the complexity and significance of rhetoric in the development of the visual arts and their languages during the early Renaissance, but it is worth restating and extending his valuable observations in regard to the *Natural History* in particular.[43] The ways Pliny will be used rhetorically are themselves written into the original work. Even in its own terms and time, the *Natural History* is an act of persuasion: not only the celebration and canonization of a list of great artists but also a polemic concerning the glories of nature and tradition as they are threatened by modern decadence. If the material is *ab ovo* rhetoricized, it will certainly not turn "straight" in the Renaissance: that is why Plinian lore is less often repeated as a complete history in itself and more frequently cannibalized to furnish *exempla* for other histories and other acts of persuasion. Along these lines the *Natural History* will provide for the Renaissance a storehouse of instances upon which an epideictic rhetoric is built, whether the thing being praised is art, a particular artist, humanism, or the example of antiquity.

This praise can often be a matter of some ambiguity. In Pliny's own work we have also seen how complicated, not to say self-contradicting, the polemic can be, when praise for great artistry gets tangled up with denunciations of high technology and aesthetic hedonism. In similar ways—though the particular issues may vary—Plinian materials will find themselves in Renaissance contexts where different rhetorical stances contradict one another. There are many instances of individual stories that function in multiple ways—like the sponge throwing that seems to support quite opposite aesthetic opinions as refracted through Botticelli and Leonardo. But this is a matter best viewed in terms of the entire project of praising ancient aesthetics rather than individual stories.

This project may be best observed in a dialogue from Petrarch's *De Remediis utriusque fortunae* between Gaudium and Ratio, which provides one of the first extensive redactions (perhaps *the* first) of material from Pliny's history of art in modern writing, including information concerning the origins of the arts and their place in Rome's public culture, a description of the patronage circle surrounding Alexander the Great, comparisons of various artistic media, and a discussion of the relation between materials and artistry. Most of what Petrarch reproduces from the *Natural History* are claims for the importance of the visual arts. Pliny is credited by name with declaring painting to be the basis of the liberal arts. He is credited indirectly with demonstrating the high value that Augustus, Vespasian, and other emperors and nobles had placed upon the arts, as well as "the great fame of the artists, based not on the babble of the crowd or on the silent works themselves, but loudly proclaimed and celebrated in the works of established authors."[44] Petrarch also repeats Plinian assertions concerning the antiquity of the arts, the high educational standing of practitioners, the power of artistic verisimilitude, and the specially humble nobility of modeling in clay.

What is not evident from this summary is that all these *exempla* of praise are woven into an argument that condemns the practice and, especially, the appreciation of art. The context is Reason's attack on Pleasure, in which the larger rhetorical claim—fundamentally Platonic—declares that aesthetic pleasure, specifically *visual* aesthetic pleasure, is fetishistic; that is, it substitutes for the pleasure that comes with contemplating God's real creation and may act as an obstacle to that activity. (The text does at one point wrestle with the possibility that artistic images might, in the Platonic way, facilitate our love of God's creation, but it then finesses the whole argument by sliding over to the biblical injunction against graven images.) Petrarch, we might surmise, finds something uncanny and irreligious in all those stories of deceitful representations—grapes that fool birds, curtains that fool artists—which Pliny adduces in praise of their makers. One might further see in this reaction early signs of the Renaissance paragone. After all, Petrarch's own medium cannot be said to substitute for God's reality, while the fact that the visual arts in comparison with the verbal seem to have a more direct appeal to a single bodily sense makes them a convenient target for charges of unregenerate hedonism.

But I am less interested in decoding Petrarch's message than in observing the process of his rhetoric:

> You take delight in the pencil strokes and colors which please because of price and skillfulness—their variety and artistic composition. And you are fascinated by the lifelike gestures, the movement in these inanimate and immobile pictures, the faces jutting out of posts, and the portraits that seem about to breathe and make you think that they might utter words. The danger here lies in the fact that great minds, in particular, are captivated by these things—and what a peasant will pass off with brief enjoyment, a man of intellect may continue to venerate with sighs of admiration. This is a complicated matter, and our task here is not to inquire into the origins of art and its development, nor the wonders of its works, the dedication of the artists, the mad extravagance of princes, and the enormity of the prices which brought paintings from far across the oceans to Rome and hung them in the temples of the gods, the bedrooms of the emperors, on public avenues, and in galleries. Nor was this sufficient. The Romans themselves had to apply their right hands, as well as their minds, which should have been applied to greater tasks, to the pursuit of painting. This the most eminent philosophers of Greece had done long before. As a result, you regard painting as more closely related to nature's creations, above all other handicrafts, and, if you can believe Pliny, the Greeks even assigned it to the front rank of the liberal arts.
>
> But I pass by these things, because, in a way, they are contrary to my intent to be brief and to my present purpose; they might, in fact, seem to contribute to the very illness I promised to cure, and to excuse the lunacy of connoisseurs by the sheer beauty of the artifacts described.[45]

Nearly all of Pliny's grounds for celebrating the visual arts are packed into this gigantic parenthesis—or what is declared at the end to have been a parenthesis—in, once again, a gesture of praeteritio, pretending to silence on a subject about which some decisive opinions have been uttered. Pliny faced the same problem, for instance, when he introduced marble sculpture as the "praecipua morum insania" ("the prime folly in our behaviour") and proceeded to wax rapturous over masterpieces like the Laocoön.

For both authors, and many later ones, the exemplarity offered by the ancient artists turns out to be easily overwhelmed by the things themselves—for Pliny the actual art objects, for Petrarch and the Renaissance the stories about them. To give Petrarch his due, he knows that his rhetoric has got out of hand, that the attempt to frame each article of Pliny's praise in pejorative terms fails to suppress the wonderment of the original. This may, of course, be no failure at all: Petrarch may have a more complicated strategy. Or else, as is yet more likely, his own cultural attitudes may be too deeply self-contradictory to result in a clean strategy at all. After all, in this dialogue Gaudium, the art lover who speaks only in one-sentence banalities that refer to unreflective enjoyment, has certainly not read Pliny; it is left to Ratio both to celebrate and to condemn the power of art. Later writers will not always feel as guilty about artistic pleasures, or as competitive. But that will not prevent them from finding in Plinian materials a rhetoric that inevitably threatens to get out of hand—that is, to menace the established superiority of the Christian over the pagan or the verbal over the visual. Material that is always rhetoricized always threatens to take on a life of its own.

What we have been observing so far is rhetoric turned on itself. More fundamental and more universal is the way rhetoric turns on other things. To declare the uses of Plinian material rhetorical, in other words, is to say that it furnishes a set of exempla that may be transferred from their original context to other arguments or discourses. Whatever Pliny's original strategies of praise may have been, the Renaissance epideictic project that exploits the *Natural History* attempts to translate ancient history to modern analogy. Citing the high prices that Pliny quotes for works of art alongside the story of Demetrius' abandoning his attempt to conquer Rhodes, Alberti declares that "Pliny collected many other such things in which you can see that good painters have always been greatly honoured by all."[46] Lodovico Dolce, at the other end of the Renaissance, has Aretino praise Raphael over Michelangelo by reference to Pliny's account of Apelles, who bested his rivals through the unique qualities of his art.[47] In the operations of rhetoric and exemplarity between these instances, there is considerable divergence. Alberti offers a barrage of ritually repeated anecdotes all proving a simple and stable point about the importance of art. Dolce, on the other hand, captures the subtle rhetoricity of the original text, which locates Apelles in competition with contemporary rivals (like Raphael in regard to Michelangelo); he goes on to worry the very quality that sets him apart, referring to it first as *venustas*, then as *venus* (a complicated name and abstraction, to be sure), and finally as the Greek *charis*—all rendered as though in the voice of Apelles himself. It is therefore no surprise that Dolce ends up having to call this quality "la venustà, che è quel non so che, che tanto suole aggradire, così ne' pittori come ne' poeti, in guisa che empie l'animo d'altrui d'infinito diletto, non sapendo da qual parte esca quello che a noi tanto piace" (that loveliness, namely, that certain something which has a way of being so pleasing, among both the painters and the poets, to the extent that it fills the souls of other people with infinite pleasure, without our being able to know whence comes that which pleases us so); as a way out of all this je ne sais quoi, Dolce refers the reader to Petrarch's description of Laura (*Rime* 215) for clarification—itself endowing her beauty, specifically her eyes, with a *non so che* that can scarcely set the matter on firm ground.[48]

This kind of epideictic gesture moves quickly beyond the rhetoric of persuasion into the rhetoric of figural language and, more than that, into a self-consciousness about language. The *Natural History* itself shows the way. Throughout his account of ancient art, Pliny lays explicit stress on the problems of terminology; and the passages in which he invents terms or calls attention to them, or throws up his hands and slides over to a Greek word, are frequently repeated in the Renaissance.[49] Plinian praise, in other words, comes down to the moderns already embodied in a language that calls attention to its own limitations—that is, of words attempting to capture images—as well as to the paragone that exists among different languages and different discourses. Apelles' venustas, as interpreted by Dolce, ends up invoking a different language in the most literal sense; then it slides from the world of images to that of poetry. This is no isolated example. As a massive verbal construction, the *Natural History* is by its very nature likely to feed into the problematics of differing discourses.

Pliny's text also becomes the art-historical term in a set of interrelations with other, more explicitly rhetorical works from antiquity that make use of the same narratives. An especially noteworthy instance is that most widely diffused rhetorical exemplum of all, the tale of Zeuxis and the painting of Helen commissioned by the citizens of Croton, a narrative found in the *Natural History* but more fully rendered in Cicero's *De inventione*.[50] The story of the painter who creates a single work of art by composing five separate but partial real-life models becomes a central paradigm for Renaissance accounts of some quite divergent activities in divergent disciplines. Cicero, who tells the story first and at greatest length, uses it as what seems a disproportionately bulky justification for a rather simple point about his own use of multiple sources rather than a single model. That turns out to be a methodological issue of almost obsessional interest to all sorts of Renaissance humanists, as witness the much discussed use of the analogy to the bee, who creates honey by mixing the pollen from many flowers.[51] Petrarch's bee—itself a grain of pollen plucked from Seneca—may be wholly logocentric, and Cicero may himself have had no notions of visual theory when he made a similar point by reference to the Crotonian painting. Yet the attachment of the name Zeuxis to this argument in rhetoric renders it a living piece of the history, theory, and practice of the visual arts. From Alberti to Raphael to Vasari (not to mention the inevitable Dolce), Zeuxis' painting of Helen will be used to define and complicate the nature of visual representation, the sources of artistic inspiration, and the means by which painters form their individual styles. It maintains this position of authority in part because it is woven into a Plinian narrative concerning both the specific qualities of Zeuxis and a larger historical argument about the place of verisimilitude in the development of a visual aesthetic. Yet the story also remains attached to its origins in the history of verbal discourse. It thus maintains a constant double utility, providing intellectual authority to writers on visual subjects and representational authority to writers on verbal subjects.

All these modalities—narrative, myth, rhetoric—apply themselves to the Plinian *story*, whereas a different set of approaches in the Renaissance is concerned with the Plinian *history*. It has been widely observed that the historical narrative offered in the *Natural History* exercised great influence. A teleological account that moves from primitive attempts at mimesis to marvelously successful replication to aesthetic distinctiveness that transcends mere copying—each of these moves associated with particular break-through geniuses—this plot seems all but inevitable post-Pliny. But is it *propter* Pliny? Rather than hypothesize alternative histories, it seems appropriate to understand the structural nature of this history, for which I turn to a widely read contemporary of Pliny's, the rhetorician Quintilian, who draws frequent analogies to the visual arts in his *Institutio oratoria*, as we saw in connection with Myron's *Discobolus*. Toward the end of his lengthy account of oratory, Quintilian turns to the problem he calls *genus orationis*, which H. E. Butler renders as the "kind of style."[52] It is reasonable enough that the translator places quotation marks around his own phrase, because style is a problematic concept here and not to be taken for granted as the English equivalent of whatever Quintilian is talking about.

In fact, the whole point of the passage is to define, describe, or invent the category under consideration:

> The question of the "kind of style" to be adopted remains to be discussed. This was described in my original division of my subject as forming its third portion: for I promised that I would speak of the art, the artist and the work. But since oratory is the work both of rhetoric and of the orator, and since it has many forms, as I shall show, the art and the artist are involved in the consideration of all these forms. But they differ greatly from one another, and not merely in *species*, as statue differs from statue, picture from picture, and speech from speech, but in *genus* as well, as, for example Etruscan statues differ from Greek and Asiatic orators from Attic.[53]

Quintilian is recording the breakdown of his own *divisio*—especially significant, since his very purpose is to make tight logical distinctions. In this quandary, he turns first to the long-established distinction between genus and species and then—at some length—to the record of painting and sculpture as practiced by the famous Greek artists of the past. This body of traditional material offers Quintilian a great scheme of differences: Zeuxis knew how to represent light and shade, while Parrhasius was the master of the line; Polyclitus triumphed in gracefulness, Phidias in grandeur.

Crucial to this set of distinctions is that they are not purely hierarchical. The varying genera are not understood as simply better or worse; rather, they legitimize a free play of alternatives. Separate kinds of work have "their own following of admirers, with the result that the perfect orator has not yet been found, a statement which perhaps may be extended to all arts, not merely because some qualities are more evident in some artists than in others, but because one single form will not satisfy all critics, a fact which is due in part to conditions of time or place, in part to the taste and ideals of individuals."[54] This last set of determinants is vital to the structuring of the argument and will take us finally back to Pliny. Quintilian does not design his claims as historical: as a rhetorician, he is far more concerned with taxonomies than with teleologies. Yet when he comes to enumerate the varieties of visual style, many of his assertions are based in chronology. Early work is relatively coarse and stiff (though he does not dismiss it), and only when one arrives at the high point in artistic development is difference rendered largely without value judgment. The model of evolutionary development through time is all but inescapably joined to the more synchronic model of legitimate difference among artistic practitioners; the two together depend on a narrative in which great individuals appear in a generational pattern of their own. We can call these three structures art history, art criticism, and the lives of the artists.[55] Or we can be more cautious and say that however we define the various modern discourses of the visual arts, their origins are written in the first century and subsequently reread and rewritten.

Some of the most influential arguments about the conceptual origins of the artistic Renaissance have observed how Pliny's (or Quintilian's) narrative is retold in the fourteenth and fifteenth centuries.[56] By the 1380s, when Filippo Villani composes an originary catalogue of great Florentines, including artists from Cimabue to Taddeo Gaddi, there exists already in nuce an account of the progressive improvements wrought by Giotto.[57] The Dante version—subjected to much commentary over the half century following the appearance of the Commedia—has Giotto eclipsing the once great fame of Cimabue:

> Credette Cimabue ne la pintura
> > tener lo campo, e ora ha Giotto il grido,
> > sì che la fama di colui è scura.

> Cimabue thought to hold the field in painting,
> > and now Giotto has the cry,
> > so that the other's fame is dim.

The Boccaccio version refers only to Giotto, "avendo egli quella arte ritornata in luce, che molti secoli sotto gli error d'alcuni, che più a dilettar gli occhi degl'ignoranti che a compiacere allo 'nteletto de' savi dipigneano, era stata sepulta" ("who has brought back to the light this art, which had for many an age lain buried under the errors of certain folk, who painted more to divert the eyes of the ignorant than to please the understanding of the judicious").[58] It is noteworthy that both these loci classici place the arts on a time line without specifying which aesthetic developments count as progress. They may be said to be implicit in the Decameron story, where Giotto is praised in traditional fashion for creating images that can be mistaken for the real thing. The pattern starts to emerge as explicitly Plinian when Villani prefixes his Florentine history of painters with an uncommented-upon sequence of ancient artists. A century later, in his similarly patriotic project of writing a preface to Dante's *Commedia*, Cristoforo Landino (who had translated the *Natural History*) goes the final step. He begins with the earliest progressive developments in Pliny's narrative—tracing a shadow; using a limited number of colors—and segues to a detailed account of Florentine art based on the familiar mix of functional differentiation, chronological progress, and great-man theory.[59]

Both Ghiberti and Landino recount the progressive details of the origins of the arts; but, when arriving at the sequence of the most famous ancient names, they tend to imitate Pliny the catalogue rather than Pliny the teleologue. The antique narrative serves as a model, but the moment of progress is displaced onto Cimabue and Giotto. The modern history of art begins with the demise of this classical magnificence in the Middle Ages and on its rebirth—a concept that is also Plinian, as witness the often quoted "cessavit deinde ars ac rursus olimpiade CLVI revixit" ("after that the art languished, and it revived again in the 156th Olympiad" [34.52]).[60] The terms of the rebirth are drawn from a Plinian history that is far more extended and technical in the way it distributes the gradual improvements in verisimilitude and style.

It is not so clear, as it has sometimes been claimed, that the fifteenth-century writers convert the developmental account in the *Natural History* into a full-scale history of art in their own time. Villani's Cimabue "antiquatam picturam . . . arte et ingenio revocavit" ("summoned back with skill and talent the decayed art of painting"), while Ghiberti's Giotto "fu inventore e trovatore di tanta doctrina la quale era stata sepulta circa d'anni 600" ("was inventor and discoverer of so much learning that had been buried some six hundred years"). But once both writers get past the Cimabue-Giotto nexus, they offer a synchronic description of difference rather than a time line of progress. Villani, for instance, has Maso di Banco as master of beauty and then the famously apocryphal Stefano as master of verisimilitude—precisely the Plinian opposition but rendered as rhetorical alternatives and not as chronology (if anything, the chronology is backward).[61] The same holds for Ghiberti, who adds many details to the varying skills of artists but does not place them in a progressive relation. Landino is yet more schematic, granting each painter or sculptor a distinctive talent without reference to any teleology: Andrea del Castagno is a draughtsman, Uccello a perspectivist, Fra Angelico a master of gracefulness, Pesellino a miniaturist. Rarely before the time of Vasari, in other words, can we detect a full-scale historical or evolutionary narrative.[62]

For the fourteenth and fifteenth centuries, then, art history may resemble an evolutionary account but is more likely to consist of a one-time developmental big bang, wrought by a great man (occasionally with the help of a precursor) and leading to a period of artistic production differentiated less by linear improvements than by a series of legitimized alternative skills or styles. The reigning model is not a grand continuum of history but a set of individual encounters across a single great divide. In a

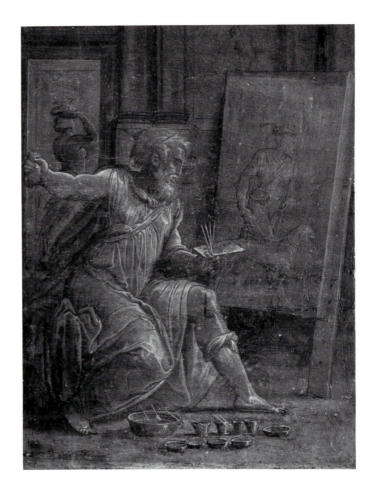

sense, this is the inevitable paradox of historicism. If the moderns are living under the influence of an ancient originary text—in this case, Pliny—does that text merely structure their own history, or does it also equip them to observe how their history swerves from the past example?[63] When Ghiberti organizes the calendar of art history by Olympiads, which are appropriate to Pliny but have no reference in Quattrocento Florence, or when the pseudonymous Prospettivo Milanese, writing about a visit to Rome in 1500, describes the Domus Aurea grotteschi as painted by "Cimabuba Apelle Giotte," it is clear enough that ancient example has produced an unhistoricist history.[64] Yet the issue becomes less risible when we recognize how much of this history is being composed by artists themselves. At the beginning of the Renaissance Petrarch will write "Nota tu, Francisce," or some other encouraging message, to himself at several points in the margins of his *Natural History* manuscript where Pliny offers pithy *sententiae* of use to an artist. At the end of this period, Vasari will decorate his house with scenes from Pliny (figs. 2.3, 2.4) as a kind of identification and inspiration.[65] Modern artists (and some of the humanists who write about them) place themselves in a Plinian framework as part of a project of self-definition and self-promotion that, to

be sure, depends on history but also acts to erase some of what we would consider historical distance. Pliny's stories, his history, and his historiography are all susceptible to being objects of an unmediated, and therefore, by our standards, naive, face-to-face encounter between past art and present artists.

"CERTAIN ANTIQUITIES CITED BY PLINY"

Finally, Pliny is also the great enabler of that more literal encounter with sculpture. It should be said at once that this is no simple or straightforward relation. In the pages of the *Natural History* so extensively analyzed above, not only does Pliny fail to mention the rediscovered statues by name (with the exception of the *Laocoön*), but his most salient and most often repeated assertions about art, whether historical, theoretical, or biographical, generally have little direct reference to the kinds of objects that the Renaissance excavated. Marble sculpture in general gets a relatively small share of Pliny's attention. More is devoted to bronzes, of which the moderns saw few, and more still to painting, of which they saw nothing. Nor is the matter merely statistical. As we

2.5. *Farnese Bull,* Roman marble, second century A.D., Museo Nazionale, Naples

have already seen, marble brings out Pliny's greatest moral qualms about the arts as luxury goods. Bronze interests him because it is more technological as well as less pretentious than marble, while painting occupies the greatest spotlight (and these proportions increase in the postclassical reception), because it raises the most complex questions concerning representation. One can note these facts and argue that they render Pliny irrelevant to the subject of this book. But given that the theory and practice of the arts during the Renaissance embraces all the media, I would suggest rather a kind of hourglass-shaped model, according to which the complete range of the visual arts in antiquity stands in parallel to the complete range produced by the moderns, with the meeting point being that small subset of ancient art that is still visible and consisting mostly of marble fragments. It is the *Natural History* that fills in the empty spaces.

In fact, we are in a position to draw quite a few interesting lines of connection between objects rediscovered in the Renaissance and passages in Pliny, though it is noteworthy how rarely such links were made before the later years of the sixteenth century. Eventually it becomes almost commonplace. The Niobid hoard unearthed in 1583 is identified with the statue that Pliny declares to be an example of uncertain authorship ("par haesitatio est in templo Apollinis Sosiani, Niobae liberos morientes Scopas an Praxiteles fecerit"; "equally there is doubt as to whether the Dying Children

of Niobe in the temple of the Sosian Apollo was the work of Scopas or Praxiteles"
[36.28]), and this conjunction initiates a centuries-long quixotic debate as to whether
the artist is Praxiteles or Scopas.[66] The *Farnese Bull* (fig. 2.5), found in 1545 at the Baths
of Caracalla, is at first given various, usually Hercules-related, titles; but by the time of
its extensive restoration in the 1580s, it has clearly been correlated with Pliny's
description of a work by Tauriscus and Apollonius of Rhodes, "Dirce et taurus vincu-
lumque ex eodem lapide" ("Dirce and the bull with its rope, all carved from the same
block of stone" [36.34]).[67] Not that Pliny was without authenticating value before this
time. Francesco Albertini (1510) looked at some Vatican fragments and identified them
as coming from Polyclitus's *Astragalizontes.* Ulisse Aldrovandi (1550), enthusing about a
Pan and Apollo (fig. 2.6) in the Cesi sculpture garden, declares, "This is one of those
most beautiful works that one sees in Rome. And perhaps it is one of the three Satyrs
which Pliny celebrates so much," thus responding to a Plinian passage (36.29) that is
confusing about the nature and number of statues but not about their fame and value.[68]

  That these somewhat improbable identifications could be proposed renders
all the more surprising those Plinian references that are *not* associated with new discoveries, as, for instance:

2.7. *Hercules Standing*, colossal gilt bronze, Roman copy of Lysippean original, second century B.C., Palazzo dei Conservatori, Rome

Fuisse autem statuariam artem familiarem Italiae quoque et vetustam, indicant
Hercules ab Euandro sacratus, ut produnt, in foro boario, qui triumphalis
vocatur atque per triumphos vestitur habitu triumphali.   [34.33]

That the art of statuary was familiar to Italy also and of long standing there is
indicated by the statue of Hercules in the Cattle Market said to have been dedicated by Evander, which is called "Hercules Triumphant," and on the occasion
of triumphal processions is arrayed in triumphal vestments.[69]

More even than that of the *Laocoön*, this Plinian description would seem tailor-made
for the construction of a modern myth. In fact, during the pontificate of Sixtus IV a
beautiful bronze Hercules (fig. 2.7) is discovered in none other than the Forum
Boarium. This work, which is soon moved to the Conservators' Palace, appears in
exceptionally fine condition and receives wide attention, notably from both Aldrovandi
and Albertini. Aldrovandi even mentions the discovery location, but that interests
him only insofar as to propose a connection between the Cattle of Geryon and the
origins of the Forum Boarium.[70] None of the commentators seems to have made the
connection.

There are many other such instances of what we must call lost opportunities.
Who could resist applying Pliny's phrase "the second most famous *symplegma* in the
world" ("alterum in terris symplegma nobile" [36.35]) to those many statues of two
men in erotic or athletic postures, such as that noticed by Aldrovandi in the Cesi garden?[71] Did no one try to link any of the innumerable rediscovered satyr statues to
Pliny's account of the Praxitelean work (N.H. 34.69), which was called "periboëton,"
or famous? As for the *River God Nile* (fig. 2.8), with its many fragmentary putti, discovered around 1512–13, there is clearly some disposition to allegorize the figures,[72]
though no connection is drawn to Pliny's *Nile* in the Templum Pacis, about which he
says that the sixteen children denoted the height in cubits of the river at flood stage.
Nor does the etiology of foreshortening, which Pliny invokes to praise Pausias's
Immolatio Boum, get applied to the Suovetaurilia relief, which was well known and
widely imitated before the end of the fifteenth century.[73] Perhaps the most surprising
instance of all is the so-called *Cleomenes Altar* depicting Iphigenia's sacrifice (see fig.
2.2). As was suggested earlier, there existed a powerful verbal tradition, both in antiquity and in the Renaissance, devoted to the painter Timanthes, whose version of this
subject was said to have reached the highest levels of emotional representation by covering rather than revealing the suffering face of Agamemnon. It appears as a rhetorical
topos for Cicero and Quintilian, and gets repeated as such by Alberti, and the image
itself is quoted by both of Alberti's most distinguished contemporaries, Ghiberti and
Donatello. Yet the realms remain separate, at least until Vasari, late in his life, chooses
as one of the Pliny stories with which he decorates his house the scene of Timanthes
painting the Iphigenia (see fig. 2.4), where the painting-within-a-painting may be a
version of the altar.[74]

There is, of course, a limit to how much historical capital we can make out of what *doesn't* happen or what *isn't* written down. Most such identifications between Plinian descriptions and the rediscovered works would be shaky if attempted. Nor can one be sure that no such claims were made in documents that have not survived or that I haven't noticed. At all events, it is easy enough to pinpoint the precise meeting place of Pliny's text and the rediscovery of ancient statues in two texts that have been, and will continue to be, at the center of this book. First, Francesco da Sangallo's retrospective report on the 1506 discovery of the *Laocoön*, which declares that the statue was identified by reference to the laudatory account in the *Natural History*: "Questo è il Laocoonte, di cui fa mentione Plinio."[75] And second (though it was in fact written earlier), the pivotal moment in Vasari's developmental version of art history. He offers a three-stage account of the development of modern art, beginning with the stiff and clumsy (though laudable) efforts of Giotto and Cimabue, then turning to the fifteenth-century artists, who had better style and drawing ability but lacked delicacy, refinement, and supreme grace. Then he turns toward his own age:

> That finish, and that certain something which they lacked, they could not achieve so readily, seeing that study, when it is used in that way to obtain finish, gives dryness to the manner.

> After them, indeed, their successors were enabled to attain it through seeing excavated out of the earth certain antiquities cited by Pliny as among the most famous, such as the Laocoon, the Hercules, the Great Torso of the Belvedere, and likewise the Venus, the Cleopatra, the Apollo, and an endless number of others, which, both with their sweetness and their severity, with their fleshy roundness copied from the greatest beauties of nature, and with certain attitudes which involve no distortion of the whole figure but only a movement of certain parts, and are revealed with a most perfect grace, brought about the disappearance of a certain dryness, hardness, and sharpness of manner.[76]

For the discoverers of the *Laocoön* in 1506, the *Natural History* is an authenticating guidebook; when they come upon a statue in the appropriate place and fitting the Plinian description, the statue and the book gain a mutual and interdependent authority. Through this conjunction, the whole of Pliny's text gains a truth value and renders itself eligible for transfer to the modern age as readily as does the marble of the statue. Vasari's citation of Pliny signals the completeness of that transfer. It is not just that this climactic stage of aesthetic achievement corresponds to the highest accomplishments recognized in the *Natural History*—that is, gracefulness rather than pedantry. But in addition these are shown to be the direct result of, first, the excavation of ancient sculpture and, second, the canonization of a list of rediscovered masterpieces by Pliny. Vasari summons into being a kind of humanistic triangle trade: the authoritative words of Pliny, the statues that come out of the ground and get shipped to the Belvedere, the making of artistic geniuses of the order of Michelangelo.

2.8. *River God Nile*, colossal Roman marble, second century A.D., Vatican Museums, Rome

As may have already become clear, such an account is, and is not, the thesis of this book. That ancient texts, excavated art objects, and Renaissance aesthetic theory and practice are bound together is fundamental. That it is possible to specify the workings of these relationships and to see them as so efficiently productive is, on the other hand, open to question. While we read Pliny as the text that accompanies the rediscovery of ancient sculpture, we must simultaneously observe the difficulties of such a reading. Those difficulties begin in the Renaissance itself—indeed, they show up in the two texts I have just cited. The case of Vasari is quite simple: apart from the *Laocoön*, the statues he lists are anything but "citate da Plinio."[77] What he is really enumerating are the principal attractions on view in the Belvedere. Moreover, he is partaking in a widely shared sixteenth-century cultural fantasy that these are the same as the work of the canonized masters celebrated in the *Natural History*.

As for the *Laocoön* itself, although it seems likely that here Pliny and the discovery are on the same track,[78] it is clear, as I have suggested already, that some Renaissance observers at least were perceptive enough to notice divergences between what they read and what they saw. I have quoted Cesare Trivulzio's letter of 1506 before, but it is worth reviewing more fully:

> Questa statua, che insieme co' figliuoli, Plinio dice esser d'un pezzo, Giovanangelo romano, e Michel Cristofano fiorentino, che sono i primi scultori di Roma, negano ch'ella sia d'un sol marmo, e mostrano circa a quattro commettiture; ma congiunte in luogo tanto nascoso [sic], e tanto bene saldate e ristuccate, che non si

possono conoscere facilmente se non da persone peritissime di quest'arte. Però dicono che Plinio s'ingannò, o volle ingannare altri, per render l'opera più ammirabile. . . . L'autorità di Plinio è grande, ma i nostri artefici hanno le sue ragioni, nè si dee disprezzare quell'antico detto: *Foelices fore artes si de iis soli artifices iudicarent*; onde non so dire a qual parere io mi appigli. Comunque sia la cosa, le statue sono eccellentissime, e degne d'ogni lode.[79]

This statue, which together with the sons, Pliny declares to be of one piece, the Roman Giovanangelo and the Florentine Michel Cristofano [Michelangelo], who are the leading sculptors in Rome, deny to be of a single block of marble; and they point to approximately four junction points but fused in such hidden places and so well consolidated and plastered together that only the greatest experts in this art can readily recognize them. They say that Pliny was deceived, or wished to deceive others, in order to render the work more impressive. . . . The authority of Pliny is great, but our artists can also be right; nor should one undervalue that ancient saying: *how fortunate the arts would be if they were judged solely by artists*. From all of which I can't say which opinion to support. However it may be, the statues are of the greatest excellence, and worthy of the highest praise.

This document testifies to the same lively conversation among artists that was implied in the more often cited Sangallo letter about the *Laocoön*. But the link with Pliny—also clearly part of an ongoing conversation—produces here, at least, a remarkable awareness of the distance between text and discovered object. It is not just that they contradict each other; rather, this difference opens the door to the possibility of a much more indeterminate hermeneutic. If Pliny is mistaken about the *Laocoön*, then he may be fallible on grounds of misinformation. Or he may be intentionally deceitful because he is engaging in a specifically rhetorical project of overpraising the statue. Or he may be ignorant because he is a writer and not an artist. In any of these cases, the moderns, who have the object in front of them, who are (supposedly) speaking uninflated truth, and who include artists capable of seeing the work through expert eyes, have the advantage over the fifteen-hundred-year-old text. Despite Trivulzio's cautious impartiality, his true preference is perhaps signaled by his adoption of the plural when he refers to the *Laocoön*. I raised the question earlier whether Pliny's authority equipped his Renaissance readers to swerve from that very authority: this is one of the cases in which that seems to have taken place.

With all due respect to the case of the *Laocoön*, then, the real place to look for Pliny and the rediscovery of ancient art is neither in the way they coincide nor in the way they contradict each other but in the space between them. Perhaps this can be best summed up through two citations, one verbal and the other visual, that long pre-date the discovery year of 1506. The first takes us back to *De Pictura*. We saw how Alberti rejects a Plinian "historia picturae" while embracing the notion of historia for what he considers the highest achievement of visual art. He introduces historia by distinguishing it from another term: "Amplissimum pictoris opus non colossus sed historia. Maior enim est ingenii laus in historia quam in colosso" ("The great work of the painter is not a colossus but a 'historia', for there is far more merit in a 'historia' than in a colossus").[80] The opposition between "historia" and "colossus" is hardly self-explanatory until we realize that Alberti is once again positioning himself in relation to the *Natural History*. Pliny introduces the colossal statue (and, in one instance, painting; see N.H. 34.39–46, 35.51) as a generic category with his characteristic mixture of awe for grandiose achievement and contempt for human overreaching. When Alberti opposes it to historia, the colossus comes to include not only the massive works that Pliny had in mind—some of which were, of course, visible throughout the Middle Ages—but also all the other kinds of monumental Plinian works of art that, in 1435 at least, Alberti can read about but not see. His historia, on the other hand, is imagined on the basis of ancient narrative paintings described by Pliny along with the similarly discursive sarcophagi that are widely visible in modern times but not mentioned in the *Natural History*. "Non colossus sed historia" becomes Alberti's way of creating a modern aesthetic devoted to story, discourse, and an honest, human-sized imitation of nature, in contrast to a grandiosity that Pliny chronicles but also (half-heartedly) censures.[81] Alberti derives this aesthetic under Pliny's influence at the same time as it expresses itself in opposition to Pliny and by reference to the distance that separates Pliny's text from the currently visible arts of antiquity. It is a position that will become far more difficult by the end of the fifteenth century, when so much rediscovered monumental sculpture will have captured the visual imagination and rendered a preference for the less aesthetically ambitious narrative reliefs more problematic.[82]

If Alberti is attempting to force a distance between the ancients and the moderns, my other citation is attempting to force them together. From late antiquity until their installation was radically altered in 1589, the massive *Horse-Tamers* of the Quirinal Hill were placed on pedestals inscribed "Opus Fidiae" under the left-hand pair of figures and "Opus Praxitelis" under the right-hand pair (fig. 2.9).[83] In the upcoming chapter I shall have more to say about the role of error, uncertainty, and fragmentariness in our subject, and I shall return to these inscriptions. For the moment, let us say there is something curious in ascribing these virtually identical statues to two great Greek sculptors who, even by Plinian account, lived thirty Olympiads apart (according to our information, more like 150 years). It is, of course, more surprising that such attributions could be convincingly made in late imperial Rome than that they would be believed by the moderns. We have no records with which to reconstruct the fifth-century logic of this claim, but we have considerable information about postclassical responses. Medieval viewers had no idea who Phidias and Praxiteles were; because they were unable to identify the subjects, it was not surprising that they dreamed up an elaborate story in which the names belong to two philosophers.

Whatever the questions about the statues' narrative, by the fourteenth century it is clear enough who Phidias and Praxiteles were. Petrarch's pithy account of the works probably stands as the truest reading of this long-accepted attribution: "Hoc

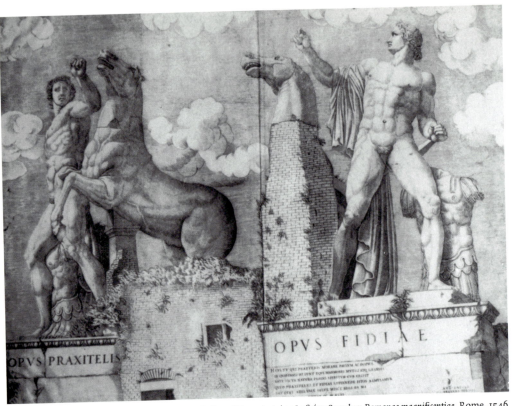

2.9. Nicolas Beatrizet, engraving of *Dioscuri* from Antoine Lafréry, *Speculum Romanae magnificentiae*, Rome, 1546

Praxitelis Phidiaeque extans in lapide tot iam seculis de ingenio et arte certamen" ("On these stones still survives after so many centuries the great rivalry in talent and skill between Praxiteles and Phidias").[84] Yet again, a swerve from the *Natural History* that is very much in keeping with it. Petrarch, seeing the works themselves as almost literally a horse race, uses the Plinian term for artistic competition (cf. N.H. 34.53, 35.95, cited above) and applies it to a pair of artists who had not been characterized as rivals. Whether later Renaissance viewers were as quick to read the pair of statues as a monument to emulation is hard to say, but they did continue to ascribe them to the two sculptors, in a remarkably persistent act of attribution.[85] The names inscribed on the two *Dioscuri* therefore stand for a barely tenable dream that the ground of the modern city might contain not just the imports, copies, and lesser works that constitute late imperial Roman collection but the works of the great mythic artists themselves. There are some noteworthy indications that the idea of these attributions does not survive the fifteenth century.[86] But when Flavio Biondo writes in the 1440s that these are "opera sane tantis opificibus digna"[87] ("works wholly worthy of such great artists"), no real Phidiases and Praxiteleses are available to act as benchmarks for recognizing what it meant to be "worthy" of them. There were only the words of Pliny and, almost as enduring, the sculpted inscriptions, which stand as a link between the *Natural History* and the material remains of the ancients as well as a measure of the great distance that separates them. Viewers of this installation were, until the end of the sixteenth century, invited to make the statues into the embodiment of Pliny's heroic version of art history.

In effect, then, the *Natural History* steps into a crucial lacuna at the center of the rediscovery of ancient art. These masses of newly unearthed glorious fragments appear as the work of geniuses. What they are missing is their corporeal wholeness and, more important, the inscriptions or the verbal history that will announce who the geniuses were. Fourteenth-century writers had already begun to transfer the model of literary fame, indeed of mythic fame, to certain artists. Dante uses the names of celebrated painters to problematize fame—the new success of Giotto has eclipsed the once mighty fame of Cimabue—but the writers of the next generations, including Boccaccio, Petrarch, and Filippo Villani, owing perhaps to greater self-consciousness or to greater Florentine chauvinism, begin to produce canonical myths about figures like Giotto and Simone Martini in a tradition that had generally been reserved for writers like themselves.

The aspiration for (or the achievement of) great fame in the visual arts is, in other words, nothing new in the early Renaissance. But the appetite for this fame goes unfulfilled in regard to these massive mute discoveries in marble and bronze. Pliny provides exactly what he seems to have intended to provide: a verbal account of fame and the famous that can stand alongside the material history that the objects themselves silently imply. As it will develop, this "standing alongside" is quite problematic in the first or the fifteenth century, because the *Dioscuri* are not by Phidias and Praxiteles, the *Bed of Polyclitus* is not by Polyclitus, the trio of *Laocoön* sculptors are nobodies, and the signer of the *Torso Belvedere* is not even mentioned in the *Natural History*. The troublesome equation of late Roman imports with legendary Greek masterpieces creates a will to identify Hellenistic sculpture—intricate, decadent, self-referential, and "baroque"—with the words appropriate to a high classicism produced centuries earlier and commented upon through a first-century veil of nostalgia that is itself part of what the Renaissance imports.

In the end it may not be so much a question of coincidences, or failures of coincidence, between the *Natural History* and the phenomenon of discovery as it is of elective affinity between Pliny and the Renaissance. The ancient writer himself derived his role as a historian from a recognition that the visual arts have a special capacity to sink into oblivion. The *Natural History* already inscribes the sense of ruin that will be manifest in the experience of the modern observer of these arts; and it invests with meaning the phenomenon of art perceived through decay. These first-century reflections on art, fame, and the written word thus form an extraordinarily meaningful time capsule for the fifteenth and sixteenth centuries. Pliny projects a sense that works of art have fallen into a decay that is both material and memorial; he writes in order to reconstruct the objects and their fame. For the Renaissance, those losses are not projections but a part of visible experience. As soon as a modern sense of history starts to develop—that is, once ancient works of art begin to appear afresh and once they are understood as products of a continuous past rather than as ahistorical marvels—Pliny's task of reconstruction comes to be understood as both possible and necessary. Indeed, the role that Pliny envisages for himself as a historian, along with his allusions to others who memorialize visual works in words, cannot be truly perceived until fourteen hundred years after he writes his history. Only then does Pliny's prophecy fulfill itself. Above all, this prophecy declares the indispensability of the written word in the history of art. What Pliny describes in the Hellenistic period—the competition and cooperation of writers and artists, the wide transmission of personal fame—he himself helps to enact in the Renaissance.

Even this elective affinity is part of the *Natural History*'s own internal logic. Gian Biagio Conte, Pliny's most sensitive reader in our time, has said, "An encyclopedia is essentially a text whose author cannot—and must not—foresee the totality of its possible uses, an 'open' totality of mechanisms that can be disassembled and rearranged differently according to the reader's needs."[88] This is a particularly telling description coming from a scholar who has perceived so subtly the ways in which texts exercise strong control over their eventual reading.[89] Applied to the *Natural History*, these notions do not contradict one another; rather they point to a particularly active or paradoxical interpretive destiny, one that is torn between authorial control and the inevitable openness of the medium. Pliny begins his work with an epistle to the emperor that is explicitly concerned with his own place in a history of reading and of being read. He composes a whole theory of imitation, influence, and plagiarism, comparing his own practices to those of Virgil, Cicero, and other writers (N.H., preface, 21–23), and he explains to the emperor exactly how the book can be read. These directive strategies are true of the whole encyclopedia: the elaborate table of contents, the lists of numbers of facts, the references to sources are all part of a bid for authority.

Yet in the same preface Pliny recognizes a different approach to intertextuality:

Et ne in totum videar Graecos insectari, ex illis nos velim intellegi pingendi fingendique conditoribus quos in libellis his invenies absoluta opera, et illa quoque quae mirando non satiamur, pendenti titulo inscripsisse, ut *Apelles faciebat* aut *Polyclitus*, tamquam inchoata semper arte et inperfecta, ut contra iudicorum varietates superesset artifici regressus ad veniam, velut emendaturo quicquid desideraretur si non esset interceptus.   [preface, 26]

And so as not to seem a downright adversary of the Greeks, I should like to be accepted on the lines of those founders of painting and sculpture who, as you will find in these volumes, used to inscribe their finished works, even the masterpieces which we can never be tired of admiring, with a provisional title such as *Worked on by Apelles* or *Polyclitus*, as though art was always a thing in process and not completed, so that when faced by the vagaries of criticism the artist might have left him a line of retreat to indulgence, by implying that he intended, if not interrupted, to correct any defect noted.

At the same time that Pliny is describing how he wishes to be read, he is defining a kind of indeterminacy in the process, producing an etiology and justification for the existence of future readings as integral to the text itself.[90] It is a sort of manifesto of reader response avant la lettre. What is especially significant for us is that his comparative term for the place of his text in history is the practice of just those visual artists that he will become so famous for chronicling. The analogy to the practice and tradition of painters, here and elsewhere, signals an importation into discursive thinking of the flexible, the labile, the multivalent—in this case, specifically, the open-ended futures of a text's reading. It is a powerful historical coincidence—yet not a coincidence—that the liveliest of all the intertextualities to which Pliny will be subjected is precisely the entry of material art objects and later art history into the reading of the *Natural History*. Apelles, Polyclitus, and the others, more than anything else, will end up leaving Pliny's history in the imperfect tense.

3.1. Henry Fuseli, *The Artist Overwhelmed by the Grandeur of Antique Ruins*, chalk and sepia wash, 1778–79, Kunsthaus, Zurich

FRAGMENTS

What is it about a fragment? If one looks at Piranesi or Winckelmann, the fragment appears to be the very defining visual trope of neoclassicism. A reading of Benjamin or Kracauer turns the fragment into an index to twentieth-century sensibility. Coleridge and Schumann stamp the fragment as quintessentially Romantic. The pursuit of Barthes and Derrida may lead one to find the fragment at the heart of the postmodern condition.[1] Granted, fragment does not mean the same thing in all these cases: sometimes it is language, sometimes image; sometimes it is a human construction, sometimes a human body. But whatever the ultimate validity of each of these visions, it seems as though anything that is uncompleted or that has been robbed of its completeness by time, both fascinates us and offers us the special vantage point from which the salient characteristics of moments in history are divulged. Or perhaps the fragment reveals one of *our* salient characteristics: the wish to enter historical moments via their breaks or discontinuities.

I am inspired by an essay in which Linda Nochlin convincingly argues for the fragment as the legacy bestowed on modernism by the French Revolution.[2] Her subject, however, is neither the Renaissance nor antiquity; she begins with the Fuseli drawing of *The Artist Overwhelmed by the Grandeur of Antique Ruins* (fig. 3.1) and proceeds to detail the post-1789 industry in corporeal fragments that was produced by such circumstances as the iconoclastic demolition of monarchist public sculpture, the artistic recording of the excesses of the revolutionary period and, above all, the real-life activity of the guillotine. The years around 1500 offer neither organized iconoclasm nor organized execution (though both enterprises flourished well enough); but in Rome, at least, they do present a landscape as littered with artistic body parts and truncated objects as any scene of aesthetic and social carnage attendant upon whatever revolution or counterrevolution.

According to Nochlin's argument, a sequence of associations, if not of direct causality, proceeds from the guillotine to Van Gogh's ear. But it is the intermediate steps that tell her story most eloquently: the representation of historical scenes of bloodletting, including pileups of corpses or studies of detached limbs; more innocently, or aesthetically, the truncation of bodies in large pictorial compositions, usually at the edges; the use of fragmentary sculptural studies of human anatomy in the midst of lush still lifes; and the exposure of parts of bodies (especially female bodies)

3.2 Marten van Heemskerck, courtyard of Palazzo Medici-Madama, ca. 1532–36, sketchbook, II.48, Staatliche Museen, Berlin

in the expectation of fetishistic viewing. In my terms, these phenomena are simply what happens when mutilation is crossed with artistic representation—that is, when cultural circumstances bring to explicitness the underlying connections between the contingent or recombinable anatomies designed by artists and the fragile conditions of material bodies, whether of flesh or stone. If Van Gogh, the artist visiting mutilation upon himself, is one unmediated endpoint of the process, then another, I would argue, is the Renaissance discovery of ancient sculpture, in which art itself appears to be born as a set of fragments.

NOT A HISTORY BUT AN AUTOPSY

There is nothing more obvious or more important about rediscovered sculpture than the fact that it is nearly always broken. The works that emerge from the ground complete in all their parts could probably be counted on the fingers of one hand (so to speak); missing pieces, in other words, are the fundamental condition of the vast classical museum that is Renaissance Rome. How broken the art objects are varies greatly, of course. Many of the most famous works, e.g., the *Apollo Belvedere* and the *Laocoön*, are nearly complete, but others, like the *Torso Belvedere* and the *Pasquino*, are radically fragmentary. And famous or not, hundreds or even thousands of richly sculpted body parts—heads, feet, and torsos—become highly valued collectibles, recorded with honor in inventories and depicted with great care in sketchbooks.

A brief glimpse at one important collection will demonstrate to what extent this fragmentariness imposed itself on Renaissance eyes. We have relatively consistent accounts of the Medici-Madama collection in sketchbook drawings and in a prose inventory. The artist Maarten van Heemskerck (fig. 3.2), who viewed the collection in the 1530s, reveals a massive courtyard whose columns, vaulting, and fountain nearly dwarf a dozen or so monumental marble statues. All are single human forms, arrayed rather casually around the bases of the columns. All the standing figures are missing heads, and barely any have a complete set of arms or legs.[3] Ulisse Aldrovandi, some fifteen years later, records similar data in his description of the Palazzo Madama holdings:

> There is another quite beautiful nude Bacchus, but he has no head or arms. There is a trunk with grapes and a serpent wound around it, and with that another smaller nude statue without head or arms, and missing one leg—all out of one piece of marble.
>
> There is a female nude from the thighs down, but without head or arms.
>
> There is a seated nude Venus, in a position of reclining downward, who seems to be covering herself in front with her hands, but she has neither hands nor head.
>
> There is an extremely beautiful statue on a base made of the same marble with arms in a strained position, but its legs and head are missing.[4]

While the mutilations in this pair of accounts may be a bit more concentrated than usual, there is nothing exceptional in the possession of a highly valuable collection whose pieces are all broken. Both Heemskerck and Aldrovandi demonstrate that fragmentariness was understood to be the natural condition of rediscovered ancient statues. The owners of the collection, and in turn those who record it for posterity, display these mutilated works with no shame or apology, recognizing them as beautiful despite the carefully catalogued missing parts that under other circumstances might cause them to be considered monstrosities. There is, clearly, some sort of premium on greater completeness: the Belvedere collection, for instance, contains rather complete objects. But fragments—whether they consist of bodies missing only an arm or of arms missing the whole body—are capable of receiving passionate attention and validation from the Middle Ages onward.

Exactly what Renaissance viewers see, and do not see, when confronted with fragmentary art objects must remain a difficult question. How, for that matter, does a culture respond to *anything* that is broken—a table, a loom, a lyre, a roof? The question is neither far-fetched nor irrelevant considering that, as we saw in Chapter 1, many of these classical survivals became fragments in the first place because they were used as modular objects, already broken and further breakable so that they could be repaired or reconfigured in a utilitarian manner. To declare of a fragment instead that it has a value independent of any potential for being made whole again is to engage in a category shift. In place of usefulness and raw materials as determinants—my terms follow arguments from the discussion of Pliny in the previous chapter—value comes to be related to some qualities immanent in the object as it originally existed, qualities that may be diminished by fragmentation but not wholly erased. Perhaps holy relics are more appropriate as analogies to sculpture than practical or technological objects. The sacred potential of a saint's bone is not proportional to its size, even though churches may struggle to obtain a complete set. It consists in some invisible qualities that are all-in-all. To be sure, no facile equation should be made between the miraculous afterlife of a saint and the transmission of aesthetic or cultural power from a classical fragment to a modern viewer; yet in both cases there is an immaterial essence contained in the part, and it becomes a whole through the acts of beholding and contemplation.

By the 1530s, when Heemskerck is sketching stray body parts with exquisite accuracy, or the 1550s, when Aldrovandi is including detailed enumerations of sculpted heads in his inventory, even though "non si sa di chi fusse" (142), it is probably not surprising that a fragment would have distinctive value. Yet this phenomenon is not born in the world of high Renaissance aesthetics and private collection; rather, it dates back to some of the earliest displays of antique survivals, in particular the bronze head and hand (fig. 3.3) that formed part of the Lateran collection by the middle of the twelfth century. Unlike the majority of later fragments, these body parts are gigantically oversized—some six times larger than life—but in common with all the other classical sculpture known through the Middle Ages, they are subject to the lively imaginations of centuries of uninformed viewers. They are, at various early times, assimilated to the Colossus built by Nero, which was understood as an idol representing the sun god or as an icon of Rome; they are said to form part of a statue of Samson, whose name means "Sun man"; their origins are located in the seven wonders of the world; they are said to have been dismantled by one or another of the early popes, but with bits left intact so as to provide a warning concerning the power of paganism or the dangers of idolatry.[5] (Only in the fifteenth century do viewers give these body parts historical names, e.g., Nero, Commodus, various members of the Constantine family.)[6]

Whatever the particular reasons or plausibilities behind these claims, all of them end up granting a special significance to the figures' fragmentariness. It renders them that much more powerful as objects of worship, while also emphasizing the skill of the artist (Magister Gregorius: "Although of horrific size, one can nonetheless admire in them the great skill of their maker, and indeed nothing of the perfect beauty of the human head or hand is lacking in any part").[7] Finally, through the story of how the statue came to be mutilated—since no aspect of the history can be left unmoralized—both the attractiveness and the danger of the original work are kept alive. In fact, one could say that the colossal fragment is the precise meeting place between a divinity that is anathematized but by no means discountable and the signs of artistic

3.3. Colossal bronze head and hand, fourth century A.D., Palazzo dei Conservatori, Rome

genius whose transcendent worth needs no apology. The beautiful fragment becomes a place where pagan worship is turned into the religion of art.

The giant bronze remains from the Lateran collection are in many ways a special case. Not all fragments are anatomical—a broken frieze or sarcophagus is a ruined body only metaphorically—and not all anatomical fragments are colossal in size. Yet the paradoxical mix of larger-than-life and corporeally mutilated will mark the whole field of rediscovered ancient sculpture, defining an antiquity that is as magnificent as it is ruined, as mythical as it is immediate to the modern viewer's experience. As in so many other ways, Pliny had already written the script for this kind of encounter with the past. Speaking of the Colossus of Rhodes, he writes: "Even lying on the ground it is a marvel. Few people can make their arms meet round the thumb of the figure, and the fingers are larger than most statues."[8] It is that direct tactile relation between the puny living arms and the gigantic ruined thumb that tell the story of antiquity's greatness and decline.

In the postclassical world, the note is struck as early as the twelfth century by Hildebert of Lavardin:

Par tibi, Roma, nihil, cum sis prope tota ruina;
quam magni fueris integra fracta doces.[9]

Nothing, Rome, is equal to you; even when you are nearly all in ruins, you teach us how great you would be if your fragments were whole.

The elegy is almost obsessionally in the comparative mode: ruined Rome versus Rome at its height; ancient gods versus mortals; statues versus living beings; and finally—since this praise for the ancients is paired with another elegy elevating the pope over Caesar—pagan versus Christian. It is a rhyme whose essential message, often rephrased as "Roma quanta fuit ipsa ruina docet," echoes throughout the early modern period.[10] What is distinctive in this very persistent mentality, however, is not the flat comparison but the ratio, or what we might term exponential thinking: however ruined Rome is now, by that much more do we need to multiply the once living city in our imaginations. From this perspective, the fragment, far from containing a diminished immanence, points to a greater wholeness than would any complete works. The more ruined, the more it inscribes; the more it inscribes, the more it invokes the modern imagination. Broken antiquities thus contribute to a living text of epic similes whereby that which is seen becomes aggrandized through a ratio of comparisons to that which cannot be seen.[11]

The case must not be overstated, however: the experience of the fragment has at least as much to do with minuses as with pluses. Early moderns are likelier to look at these objects in terms of what is missing rather than to be impressed by the remote wholenesses inherent in them; and any complete record of what the Renaissance sees in sculptural remains must inevitably chart the interplay of positive and negative in the experience of looking at a fragment. To understand that, we must remind ourselves that mutilated limbs represent only the most literal type of fragmentation. Let the *Laocoön* story count yet once more as paradigm and antiparadigm. The exclamation that greets the unearthing of the statue— "questo è il Laoconte, di cui fa mentione Plinio"—records an epiphany that could very rarely be repeated.[12] Moments of discovery were almost never so dramatic or so impressively witnessed, and, more to the point, identification of the works that were found was not often so easy, even when they retained their most important pieces. Works that are complete in all their parts become fragments if they brandish an identity without fully revealing it, and to viewers of ancient sculpture from the twelfth to the sixteenth centuries, a great many identities are unreadable.

These difficulties of reading are easiest to establish with a catalogue of howlers, some of which have already been discussed here. We saw at the end of the last chapter how the *Horse-Tamers* (fig. 3.4; cf. fig. 2.9) of the Quirinal bore for many centuries the inscriptions "Opus Fidiae" and "Opus Praxitelis." Medieval viewers, unfamiliar with the history of Greek sculpture, read these expressions as captions rather than as attributions, and they invented various historical fables in which the men were visionaries and the horses were allegories of their vision. One sixteenth-century proposal is the historical account of the Armenian king Tiridates who sent horses to Nero (according to this, the men are reduced to being horse tamers who came along for the ride). More widely accepted is the argument that the statues represent Alexander and his famous horse Bucephalus; the improbability of *two* Alexanders and

3.4. *Dioscuri*, colossal marble pair, second century A.D., Piazza del Quirinale, Rome

two Bucephaluses is resolved by a reversion to Petrarch's idea that the statues were competition pieces by Phidias and Praxiteles, who unfortunately were not contemporaries of each other or of Alexander.[13] There has also been reference in these pages— who could resist?—to Magister Gregorius's identification of the delicate, almost epicene *Thorn Puller* as "Priapus," owing to his mistakenly alleged "genitals of extraordinary size."[14] The list of bad guesses could go on at length, and it need not be confined to the benighted medievals. The pseudonymous "Prospettivo Milanese," who has the disadvantage of composing his verse account of Roman antiquities half a century before Aldrovandi, sees a nymph who is probably bending over to adjust her sandal as "more bowed with care than Judas."[15] Another long visible statue, the *Marforio* (fig. 3.5), goes through identification as many different bodies of water, as Mars, and as Neptune, not to mention the fact that the plump rocks upon which the recumbent figure is resting give rise to the theory (solemnly debunked by Flavio Biondo in 1446) that he is *Jupiter the Baker*, stretched out, presumably, on a display of loaves.[16]

Renaissance learning, in short, offers no guarantee that statues will be consistently or correctly named, though there is a shift from allegory and myth toward history, as is evident when the colossal head and hand stop being thought of as pagan idols and start being passed around among specific Roman emperors or when similar changes come about in identifying the *Marcus Aurelius* (see fig. 1.16).[17] In particular, one can trace to Andrea Fulvio, Raphael's colleague in the 1520s, a sequence of more empirical observations that somewhat change the direction of the naming processes.

3.5. *River God Marforio*, colossal marble statue, second century A.D., Museo Capitolino, Rome

It is he who studies the clues on the various river god statues, who relates the *Farnese Captives* to a passage concerning caryatids in Vitruvius, and who compares faces on statues to the physiognomies on ancient coins.[18] Yet by no means does this slow down the flow of guesses as to the identities of figures represented in ancient sculpture: works discovered in the late Renaissance and beyond, such as the so-called *Idolino*, or the *Gaul and his Wife*, or the female and male pair now generally called *Papirius and His Mother*, are all subject to an enormous range of identifications.[19] Even today, in many cases, we are not certain exactly whom we are looking at.

It is, in sum, not easy to name the names on sculpture that was created fifteen hundred or two thousand years ago. We have mostly been discussing the monumental freestanding works that have always been the most valued of these objects: it is their very independence that often deprives them of the iconographic attributes that would identify them—even when the statues are not actually broken. The case of two-dimensional sculpture, including reliefs, sarcophagi, and the occasional carved gem—as a group, far more numerous among classical survivals—is somewhat different. In principle these ought to have been more decipherable than individual figures because they represent complete narrative scenes that establish dynamic relations among the participants. Although they were as mutilated as any other category of ancient sculpture, many more of them survived and there were many similarities evident among them, owing to the almost mechanical system of reproduction in which they were fabricated during the later Roman empire. Yet these works are extremely difficult to read, and as a

3.6. Marsyas, Apollo, and Olympus,
gem attributed to Dioscourides,
first century B.C.,
Museo Nazionale, Naples

result historians of Roman art even now cannot identify all of them with certainty. It is instructive to watch Ghiberti struggling with the action on two sculpted gems. He sees Diomedes abducting the Palladium as a youth threatening an idol with a knife, and on a carnelian (fig. 3.6) depicting Marsyas, Apollo, and a somewhat miniature Olympus, he misidentifies the last of these figures as a child and therefore reads the story as the Three Ages of Man.[20] But even well into the sixteenth century misreadings abound. Vasari, who introduces Nicola Pisano with a long account of the inspiration the artist drew from a sarcophagus in the Cathedral of Pisa, mistakes Hippolytus and Phaedra for Meleager. Pentheus being killed by Maenads is taken for Orpheus being killed by Maenads, the Rape of the Sabines is mixed up with the Rape of the Leucippids. Orpheus and Medea, certainly well-known figures in the Renaissance, go unrecognized on their respective sarcophagi when the literary source is Euripides rather than Ovid.[21]

Thus some of the most influential artworks of all furnished the pictures for a text of antiquity that was not necessarily recognizable in the fifteenth and early sixteenth centuries. Representations that are fragmentary in any of the many possible ways demand completion, whether in the mind, on drawing paper, in the marble itself, or between the covers of scholarly books. It is easy to view this fragmentary condition as something of an embarrassment, a set of obstacles in the way of the Renaissance desire to reexperience antiquity, many of which subsequent scholars have been able to sweep away. But that sort of teleology overlooks the terms in which the Renaissance itself viewed this material: that is, as a set of enigmas with multiple answers or no answers. We may not want to locate the origins of radical indeterminacy in the Quattrocento, and it is certainly true that Renaissance observers generally believed in the existence of one true completion of fragmentary bodies and of one true answer to iconographic enigmas. What we must not forget, however, is that they were faced with the near impossibility of realizing these true completions and of choosing among a plurality of iconographic claims.

In all these cases of uncertainty, the sheer plurality of possibilities recognized in the Renaissance even by those who argue fervently for a single solution should be enough to demonstrate that statues were places of disputed and disputable signification. An account of these objects in the Renaissance must respect this state of uncertainty: that is, it must do justice both to the efforts at resolution and to the space for imaginative speculation that thrives in the absence of resolution. It will come as no surprise that the present account is more committed to ambiguity than to certainty. But the process by which Renaissance viewers attempted to resolve the fragmentation of the objects or their own ignorance has much to reveal about the conditions of signifying in which the works of art and their viewers lived.

That a found artwork has missing parts or that beholders do not have the books or the wit to identify its subject—these factors can account for only part of the experience of viewing it, since in either case they are fundamentally extrinsic to the thing itself. It is equally true that the sculpture being rediscovered in the years around 1500 possessed, from its origins, qualities that were in themselves enigmatic and that could only become more so with time. In the previous chapter, we observed how the heritage of the *Natural History* was prefigured within it. This is true not only in the sense that the Renaissance came to share aspects of Pliny's aesthetics but also in the sense that the very matter of historical distance—with the accompanying awareness of loss, uncertainty, and nostalgia—seems to have been already written into this originary account. An analogous set of forces operates in the transmission of the objects themselves. Renaissance viewers are estranged from the rediscovered antiquities in and around Rome, but many of these artworks are strange to begin with. I mean this not as a casual value judgment but as a shorthand for characterizing the entire cultural field of the Late Antique. This is not the place to write that history again,[22] but it is worth repeating that the objects available for rediscovery, whether art history calls them Roman or Hellenistic, reflect a milieu with some very particular aesthetics, systems of representation, and relations to history.

The Romanness of the visual arts, to take these designations one at a time, is a troubled subject for Pliny just as it continues to be when Otto Brendel writes his indispensable *Prolegomena to a Book on Roman Art* in the 1950s.[23] Rome enters Pliny's account as a historical and social field in which art is more used than produced. Telling the story in that way involves certain deliberate silences and a cultural disposition (like that signaled by Virgil's Anchises in his underworld prophecy of Roman glory)[24] to view the aesthetic sphere as essentially other; it also may come closer to reflecting the reality of first-century Rome than it would two hundred years later. Whatever Pliny's purposes or presuppositions, it is a fact that the visual arts in Rome are—one might use the term almost literally—*alienated*, first in the sense that they are produced in a variety of foreign places with cultures that differ from one another and from that of the imperial center, and second in the sense that many of the works have been appropriated by conquest. This alienation, based in estrangement and theft, leaves a stamp on whatever art will be rediscovered.

Art, as Pliny demonstrates, is a valuable commodity in the exercise of Roman imperialism; and if Greece is the homeland of its production, then many art objects first appear in Rome when they are pillaged from the Hellenistic world. Accounts by Livy and others covering the early periods of Roman expansionism detail the massive collections of spoils coming from Greek cities like Syracuse and Tarentum. Generally measured in weight and number, these art objects and other valuables are often chronicled as a hodgepodge. Nor is it always clear to their new owners whether they are sacred or profane and how the foreign divinities they represent may square with Roman religion.[25] The tide turns by the time of Cicero, who composes one of his most abusive legal attacks on Gaius Verres, the plundering praetor of Sicily in the 70s B.C.; the orator's portrait of this malefactor becomes a classic account of the Philistine, who is motivated by avarice rather than by aesthetic taste and who thinks nothing of reworking the objects he has collected.[26] As these activities of pillage start to become politically unacceptable and as the opportunities diminish owing to the emptying out of the Greek cities, Roman taste turns to purchase and collecting. Public displays of imported statues and paintings are installed in such locations as the Portico of Metellus and its successor, the Portico of Octavia, while individuals like Asinius Pollio and Cicero himself spend great sums on their private museums. But these undertakings can be as decontextualizing as those of pillage since, once again, they are based not on the indigenous cultural significance of the art but on its usefulness when recombined in a new culture.[27]

Greek art, then, is already orphaned in a second home when it is amassed by the Romans; what happens from there can only continue to play out variations on the same destiny. To observers of this phenomenon, whether in antiquity or later, the ruling image of this uprootedness is that procession of spoils which signals the first appearance of this art in the city. After all, some of the most important and most enduring *Roman* monuments precisely record the triumphal scene in which art objects, together with arms, valuables, and captives, are brought to the city as disconnected collections. Such images are characteristic of the imperial commemorative arches that were visible throughout postclassical times, the most famous example being the procession of spoils from the Temple of Jerusalem that appeared on the Arch of Titus (fig. 3.7), which were widely reproduced in drawings throughout the Renaissance. In any of these images the art objects are a random collection unified only by their placement in the Roman triumph.[28]

3.7. Booty relief from Arch of Titus, first century A.D., Forum, Rome

Josephus describes these events much as the Arch of Titus depicts them, while emphasizing the randomness of the collection: "The rest of the spoils were borne along in random heaps. The most interesting of all were the spoils seized from the Temple of Jerusalem: a gold table weighing many talents, and a lampstand also made of gold."[29] Flavio Biondo writing in the 1450s draws the connection between this text and the sculpted version of the arch, which he much prefers.[30] But it is from an earlier eyewitness, the Greek scholar Manuel Chrysoloras, who visited Rome around 1411, that we glean the sharpest awareness of what it means to look at these objects as part of a procession of spoils:

> On these [triumphal arches] are carved in relief their battles and captives and spoils, fortresses taken by storm; and also sacrifices and victims, altars and offerings. . . . Herodotus and some other writers of history are thought to have done something of great value when they describe these things; but in these sculptures one can *see* all that existed in those days among the different races, so that it is a complete and accurate history—or rather not a history so much as an exhibition, so to speak, and manifestation of everything that existed anywhere at that time. Truly the skill of these representations equals and rivals Nature herself, so that one seems to see a real man, horse, city, or army, breastplate, sword, or armour, and real people captured or fleeing, laughing, weeping, excited or angry.[31]

3.8. Sacrificial instruments from frieze of Roman temple, Republican period, Museo Capitolino, Rome

It is not surprising that both Renaissance viewers gravitate so directly to the mode of competition between the art and the verbal descriptions; nor is it a surprise that the sculpture is preferred to Josephus and Herodotus. The sight of this aggregate of things inspires thoughts of history books (not to mention inspiring the verbal syntax of the series), but it also transcends the history book. Most telling of all is Chrysoloras's change of terminology for what he is seeing. "Μᾶλλον δὲ οὐχ ἱστορίαν, ἀλλ᾽ ἵν᾽ οὕτως εἴπω, αὐτοψίαν" ("not a history so much as an exhibition"), for which, irresistibly, the Greek term is *autopsia*: perhaps it took a Greek, whose origins were in the far less historically alienated city of Constantinople, to perceive the fundamental difference between objects in their own context and objects that have been appropriated.

That opposition between a discursively organized history and a decontextualized exhibition hangs over the fate of these statues in ancient Rome, in the Renaissance, in the Napoleonic appropriations at the end of the eighteenth century, and in the modern museum. Whether individuals in the Renaissance perceive it or not, the broken and disconnected art objects that they see emerging from the soil were in some ways culturally fragmentary to begin with. If individuals in 1500 are unable or unwilling to invent "archaeology"—the systematic discipline of recovering an organized civilization underground—that is in part because the original placement of the objects, which we might call museological, did not always obey the laws of an indigenous culture.[32] In that sense, the disconnectedness that characterizes Roman art,

3.9. Trophy pillars, marble, first or second century A.D., Galleria degli Uffizi, Florence

while rendering it more complex as philology or historiography, will bestow on it a surprising kind of sympathy or familiarity in the early modern world. The means of discovery in the Renaissance, as well as the eventual nature of the display, actually re-create the original decontextualized context of these works in Rome. In other words, modern Italians are experiencing the antiquities out of their own past in very much the way ancient Romans experienced them as plunder and show.[33] After all, the term *spo-lia*, or spoils, is used continuously to describe imperial objects of pillage and the reuse of earlier art in Christian building projects from the early Middle Ages.[34]

This is not only a story about display, however. The disconnected aggregation of foreign art objects moving along in processions or stationary in public display spaces corresponds with a set of decontextualized fashions in the production of new art. The representation of *things*—that is, objects lovingly and independently depicted apparently for their own sake—is one of the hallmarks of Roman art. This has been described and explained in many different ways. Alois Riegl, among the first to attempt an independent definition of Roman art at the beginning of the twentieth century, took as his paradigm the minor arts—hence his title *Spätrömische Kunstindustrie*—from which he determined that the salient quality of Roman representation was of the individual form isolated from contextual space.[35] A somewhat more concrete view would focus on the narrative relief as a central form in Roman art. At least from the time of Augustus, and increasingly with the proliferation of funereal and triumphal monuments in the later empire, these reliefs tend to be filled with highly particularized detail, often involving the mundane aspects of life, whether military, like those on Trajan's Column, or domestic, like the friezes that commemorate the lives and professions of ordinary citizens.[36]

The depiction of common objects is not necessarily decontextualized—it's hard to think of Trajan's Column as lacking in a centralized conception—but there is a growing tendency in later antiquity to decorate the Roman public space with reliefs and friezes depicting sequences of individual items strung (or unstrung) together. In some respects these might be considered quintessential survival pieces. When they were first made, these works were almost invisible, owing both to their physical distance from observers and to their aesthetic status as "mere" ornament. But as antique remains during the Middle Ages and the Renaissance, they are at ground level, and their (literal) detachment from original structures serves to objectify the disconnectedness of their own representations. For example, a six-part frieze depicting what appear to be nautical and sacrificial emblems (fig. 3.8) was visible perhaps as early as the Middle Ages in the walls of San Lorenzo fuori le Mura and transferred to the Capitoline in the sixteenth century; in addition, a pair of four-sided pillars covered in military trophies was known on the Aventine at least from the late Quattrocento (fig. 3.9). Both are remarkable for the quantity and particularity of their *things*. The frieze contains nineteen items—anchors, prows, cattle skulls, knives, axes—several of them repeated, sometimes with variations. The pillars have been tallied to include 800 pieces of military gear broken down among 106 categories.[37]

If representations such as these emerge as enigmatic (and they do), the primary enigma is whether or not they were meant to be enigmas. Are they simply a collection of things stylishly and artfully designed together, or is their very multiplicity and particularity a sign that they mean something, secretly, in the aggregate? Renaissance response to works like these follows those alternative paths quite precisely. For those sketching ancient remains, such as Aspertini and Heemskerck, or for those re-creating design all'antica, such as Mantegna and Raphael, these are the per-

3.10. *Trophies of Marius*, freestanding marble trophies, first century A.D., Capitol, Rome.

fect detachable and recombinable images. They can be faithfully copied singly or in groups; they can be turned and revised with all the facility available in a modern computer program; they can be rendered seriously as decorations on fictive ancient buildings.[38] For the learned observers, on the other hand—and this applies particularly to the sacrificial frieze—these images are the materials of secret knowledge. Alberti, in his discussion of secular architectural ornament, refers to these kinds of representations, significantly, in his chapter on inscriptions, which, he says, "should be either written—these are called epigraphs—or composed of reliefs and emblems."[39] For him, apparently, words, rebuses, and the figural decoration of triumphal arches are all part of the same artistic and commemorative activity. Francesco Colonna, not surprisingly, will use some elements from the Capitoline frieze as part of a hieroglyph in the *Hypnerotomachia*. And Flavio Biondo will perform a grand work of discursive philology in making sense of the sacrificial objects as part of Roman religious practice.[40]

But it may be a different, and far more monumental, work that most fully illustrates the power and the problematic of an art of (in this case, literally) disembodied things as it reads across a gap of fifteen hundred years. The massive pair of works known as the *Trophies of Marius* (fig. 3.10), probably constructed to commemorate a first-century victory under the emperor Domitian, were in later antiquity used to decorate a nymphaeum on the Esquiline, where they remained until they became part of Giacomo della Porta's design of the Capitoline in the 1590s. Each is a fifteen-foot-high display of the spoils of war—shields, armor, prisoners—piled up anthropomorphically so that it

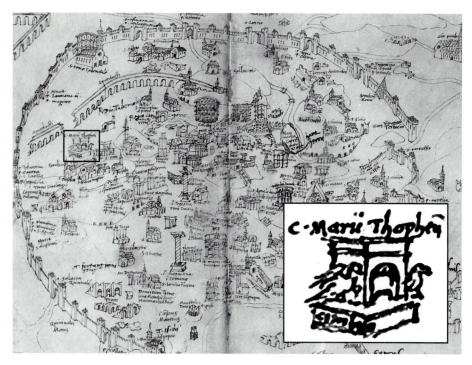

3.11. Alessandro Strozzi, map of Rome, 1474, Biblioteca Laurenziana, Florence (inset: note birdlike shapes flanking monument labeled "c. marii tropheum")

appears to be a giant triumphator decked out in all the victorious trappings but lacking a body inside. Then or now one might attempt to domesticate this peculiar conception: we characterize it as a fixed genre of ancient victory art, while from the time of the *Mirabilia* and later it was associated with a description in Plutarch and Suetonius of Marius's victory over the Cimbri. In any event, it remains, to say the least, a perceptual enigma, challenging fundamental notions of verisimilitude and representation.[41]

Anyone attempting to provide these figures with an identity will have to struggle with the question of what constitutes sculpted personhood. Beginning in the fifteenth century these works were linked to a story about the proverbially unruly geese whose timely honking saved the Capitol from a barbarian invasion. Indeed, the pair come to be known as the *oche armate*, or armed geese—a more imaginative name than the *Trophies of Marius*, if equally erroneous—and in a late fifteenth-century illustrated map of the city the nymphaeum on the Esquiline is signaled by the presence of two tiny fowl, which make no effort to simulate the statues (fig. 3.11).[42] Considering how little the *Trophies* resemble poultry, this identification has less to do with narrative plausibility than with an imaginative freedom bestowed on the viewer by their strange mix of reality and fantasy.

This set of qualities emerges most vividly in the sketchbooks. While verbally or historically oriented viewers try to attach these works to a Capitoline beast fable, artistically minded viewers must come to terms with objects that are Arcimboldesque avant la lettre—anamorphic double images that are, and are not, representations of

3.12. Francisco de Hollanda, drawing
after *Trophies of Marius*, 1538–40, sketchbook
fol. 15, Escorial, Madrid

the human body. In a drawing by Francisco de Hollanda and in other drawings from
the so-called Ripanda Sketchbook (figs. 3.12, 3.13), the trophies are "restored" into an
exquisite completeness, every boss on the shields and every lappet on the armor having been perfectly finished.[43] But in each case the body is left as blank as it is in the
ruined originals, preserving exactly the status of these works as human representations that are empty of the human. In postclassical times that piece of archaeological
correctness takes on additional meaning unsuspected when the *Trophies* were first
imagined, though implicit in their design. The absence of a body inside these works
assimilates them closely to those many statues that were once whole but are now
missing body parts. So the *Trophies of Marius* become an occasion in which rediscovered ancient art is in a sense pre-ruined; they demonstrate the fine line that divides
artistic fragments from works that complicate the conventions of representation,
while they question the possibilities of naming and identifying that inevitably accom-
pany these idiomatic conventions.

MARGINAL BODIES

A historiography that keeps looking backward, like that being practiced here, tends to
defer its chain of causalities into an ever receding past. But, at least up to a point, that
movement may be necessary. It is not enough to say that Roman art decontextualizes
its predecessors if such a claim presumes that the predecessors were themselves

3.13. Drawings after *Trophies of Marius*, from sketchbook attributed to Jacopo Ripanda, fols. 37, 62, early sixteenth century, Ashmolean Museum, Oxford

uncomplicated models of order. In fact, neither trophies nor processions of booty begin with the Romans; and if art exhibited in this manner is amoral, commodified, and culturally disconnected, the source must be traced back to Hellenism itself—that is, to the geographical and stylistic broadening of culture that follows the classical age of fifth- and fourth-century Greece. Once again, we cannot write a complete history of the antique but can only try to see it through the vantage point of those who come later. Renaissance viewers, as I have already suggested, approach the antiquities with heroic notions of classicism and order, but much of what they actually see is—to select some terms from what might be a much longer list—decadent, exotic, playful, self-parodic, antiheroic, fin de siècle, hermetic. Persistent expressions like "Hellenistic Rococo" testify both to the difficulties of defining this period style and to the habit of identifying it across time.[44]

However precisely or imprecisely one might define these aspects of Late Antique taste, they produce a gap of expectation that renders certain art objects difficult for the Renaissance to read—in effect, fragmentary. One way to describe this gap is to constitute a group of rediscovered statues with one or more of the following attributes: the figures depicted are uncanonical—that is, foreigners, barbarians, or children; the figures depicted are, whether the Renaissance knew it or not, minor players in some larger narrative; the figures are posed in an awkward or nonheroic posture.

To begin with some simple instances, an enormous class of objects represents children, especially boys, or putti. There is nothing intrinsically strange about

3.14. Amoretti with attributes of Neptune (this page), marble frieze from first-century B.C. altar, San Vitale, Ravenna; (facing page) amoretti with attributes of Saturn, Museo Archeologico, Venice

these figures—usually represented sleeping, cavorting, in an amorous situation, or in the company of small animals—except their relation to what might be perceived as normative subjects for art. As these works are originally conceived, they hover between narrative and decoration, between mock-heroic and domestic naturalism. Some, representing Cupid and Psyche or the infant Hercules, tell real stories; most (apparently) do not. They, along with their avatars found passim in Renaissance art, come to be called Cupids, Amoretti, Amorini, Erotes, and the like, as though these were fixed mythological categories, when in truth both the art and the poetry of Late Antiquity imagines such beings quite unsystematically. Among the rediscovered works, for instance, a notable subset consists of boys with geese, which even now are difficult to read: are they a kitschy conceit or a naturalistic record of domestic life?[45] In some cases the boy is strangling the goose, in others he cuddles it, and it is sometimes hard to tell the difference. Renaissance viewers may reference such an image via Pliny, who speaks of Boethos producing "infans eximium anserem strangulat" ("an exceptional [statue of] a child who is strangling a goose"), or, as Pirro Ligorio does, via a Plutarch story concerning a boy who falls in love with a goose.[46] The difference in the end has less to do with what the boy is doing than with the choice of contextualizing it by reference to the history of narratives or to the history of art objects.

Such are the perils of a learned approach to decoding these works. A different process can be observed in relation to an influential set of reliefs that were already visible in Ravenna by the late Middle Ages (fig. 3.14). These depict empty thrones in front of which groups of putti play with attributes belonging to the various Olympian divini-

ties. Observers from early times accord these works enormous value, not for their narrative or their iconography but for their artistic perfection. They are attributed to Praxiteles and Polyclitus; they appear in 1335 on Oliviero Forzetta's itemized shopping list of antiquities; one part of the series is immured as a sort of relic in the choir of San Vitale.[47] And in the *Hypnerotomachia Poliphili*, they are granted paradigmatic status as the standard against which the success of a fictional artwork must be measured: "Da l'uno et l'altro extremo dilla tabella aenea erano dui retinenti fanciulli overo spirituli alati, perfectamente formati per sì facto modo, che il diligente statuario degli celebri fanciulli geruli dilla ravennata cochlea tale exemplare non vide" ("From the one and the other side of the bronze tablet there were two tenacious boys, or winged little genii, perfectly formed in such a way that even the painstaking sculptor of the famous standard-bearing boys with the shells in Ravenna never saw such a fine example").[48] In fact, none of these references identifies or characterizes the iconographic principle that relates these figures to their respective gods. But the works are voraciously copied and adapted from at least the Quattrocento onward.[49] And in some sense it is this artistic heritage that performs the best philology, contributing to an uncannily accurate sense of the works as Hellenistic parodies of the gods' awful majesty. When the same conceit turns up, for instance, in the decorative programs designed by Raphael and executed by Giulio Romano, it should demonstrate that Renaissance art was susceptible to the Late Antique aesthetic, whether the scholars knew it or not.[50]

A quite different class of objects can be grouped, roughly, by body position, which one might describe variously as bending, crouching, or stooping. In these cases

3.15. *Nymph "alla Spina,"* marble, Roman copy of second-century B.C. original, Galleria degli Uffizi, Florence

3.16. *Venus Binding Her Sandal,* Hellenistic bronze statuette, British Museum, London

3.17. *Venus Crouching,* Roman copy of third-century B.C. Hellenistic statue, British Museum, London

it must be admitted that the uncanonical had long since started to become a canon of its own. Quintilian's use of Myron's *Discobolus* (see fig. 2.1), with its tortured yet balanced posture, as an analogy to justify figurative—as distinct from literal—speech becomes the centerpiece of a Renaissance aesthetics grounded in the discipline of rhetoric.[51] It is no coincidence that by the sixteenth century the body in torsion, which will be described by terms like *contrapposto* and *figura serpentinata*, has come to be a defining feature of art theory, with important citations in the writings of Leonardo, the table talk of Michelangelo, and the fuller expositions of Lomazzo's *Trattato dell'arte della pittura*.[52] But there is a concomitant path toward the institutionalizing of this figure by which a set of influential statues allows viewers to observe the body in torsion not only as a rhetorical idea but as a set of problems in narrative and artistic practice. Among these is a group of female figures, all understood as Venuses or nymphs, including the seated *Nymph "alla Spina"* (fig. 3.15), which belonged to the Caffarelli family before 1500; the bending *Venus Binding her Sandal* (fig. 3.16), of which we have a number of drawings and imitations but no specific locatable example known to the Renaissance; and the *Venus Crouching* (fig. 3.17), several versions of which were visible in Italy by the early years of the sixteenth century.[53] In terms of their Hellenistic origins, these works arise out of a taste for sensual play of the body that pretends at the same time to a certain naturalism; in addition, like the putti, they probably relate to literary fashions for a proliferation of submythological erotic personages or new subplots in the lives of the major Olympians.

Renaissance taste is certainly receptive to these attractions. But what more

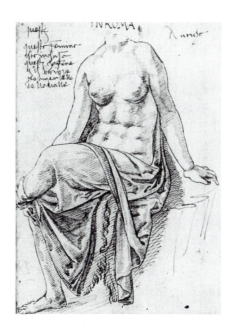

3.18. Drawing after *Nymph "alla Spina,"* ca. 1490s, Holkham Album, fol. 34 (detail), Holkham Hall, Norfolk, England

3.19. "Invitation to the Dance," marble, Roman copies of second-century B.C. originals, as reconstructed by Wilhelm Klein

fundamentally identifies these as a group is that the unusual body position becomes an alluring enigma, partly because the works are literally fragmentary, often missing just those extremities that would render the posture logical. The title *Nymph alla Spina*, for instance, which Bober and Rubinstein apply without historical explanation, works by analogy to the *Spinario*. That he is removing a thorn from his foot is obvious both because the gesture is explicit and because the bronze remained in perfect condition. The Caffarelli-Uffizi marble, on the other hand, was missing the head, the right hand, and the right foot. Because the whole focus of the figure appears to be something that the right hand is doing to the left foot while the face watches, the omissions almost perfectly frustrate the viewer. Or is that focus largely a result of modern, philologically informed restorations? In 1500, with only the mutilated figure to read, Prospettivo Milanese sees no foot action but rather a "seated nude with head bowed from care seemingly more penitent than Judas." And the draughtsman from the Holkham album (fig. 3.18), contemporaneous with Prospettivo though less imaginatively extravagant, renders the figure scrupulously (including a caption, "this woman is in the house of those Caffarelli opposite Messer Lelio della Valle") by allowing no room on the sheet for the missing body parts; as a consequence, the figure, far from being oriented toward its right foot, seems merely to be seated in a relaxed position—indeed, hardly bending forward at all.[54]

A series of miniature bronzes from the beginning of the sixteenth century offers a further anthology of positions for the hand—extended in mid-air, folded in the lap, and holding an apple branch, presumably to create some identity as Venus.[55]

The figure has an equally lively career in the modern imagination. Wilhelm Klein, who saw her as the very paradigm of Hellenistic Rococo, persuasively demonstrated that she belongs with the separate statue of a cymbal-wielding faun; he constituted them together as a group now known as the *Invitation to the Dance* (fig. 3.19). Curiously, the faun in question was also well known in late fifteenth-century Rome and has ended up, like the *Nymph*, in the Uffizi.[56] Although we have no direct evidence that this grouping was imagined by Renaissance viewers, it does appear from some of the bronze statuettes that the Nymph was meant to be in dialogue with another figure, an argument that in turn depends on the position of her head—once again uncertain, given the mutilated state of the original.[57] In short, a figure in an uncanonical posture wanting some extremities can only tease the observer with the possibilities that she is extracting a thorn, attaching (removing?) a shoe, holding an iconographic attribute, being invited to dance, or acting as penitent as Judas.

The *Venus Crouching*, given its more compact shape, seems to have been in better condition than the *Nymph*, possibly perfect, but is more likely missing parts of its arms. Whatever her condition, she is quite capable of generating enigmas. Her very pedigree depends on a manuscript crux. Pliny, listing marble statues in the Portico of Octavia, refers to a Bathing Venus, but the text is corrupt and lends itself to radically alternative readings: "Venerem lavantem sesededalsa stantem Polycharmus" (N.H. 36.35). Depending on how one emends "sesededalsa," one may arrive at a Bathing Venus by an otherwise uncited sculptor whom art historical posterity has given a name ("Doidalsas") as well as a whole genealogy, ethnic background, and oeuvre—this work implicitly seated or crouching since it is contrasted to a *Venerem stantem* by Polycharmus.[58] Or one may identify a single work by Polycharmus located in a *sede alia* or *alta*, and evidently washing herself while standing—in which case the reference is not to this statue at all. These are for the most part modern quandaries, to be sure. What is significant for the Renaissance is that Pliny—whether or not he is actually describing this statue—tells readers what the figure is doing and justifies the belief that she is in a crouch.

Despite the helpful gloss, the exact logic of the position remains ambiguous. If she is at the bath, it may be that she is crouching because a Cupid behind her is pouring water over her back, as is demonstrated by a relief known in the Renaissance (fig. 3.20) that places her in a very similar position;[59] or it may be that she is bent over to dry her hair. Alternatively, she may not be bathing at all but may be newly born from the sea, which might depend on some close readings of the object she is crouching upon. Nor are the alternatives merely semantic; as Ridgway has persuasively argued, even the extent of the body's torsion is an impression created by the head and arms; and these might or might not be present in any given Renaissance find.[60] All these possibilities revert to the historically self-referential qualities of Late Antique art, since this statue, whatever she may be doing, clearly performs a witty pastiche on some high classical standing paradigm like the *Venus Pudica* or *Anadyomene*. (Not to mention relations to completely different subjects, including the bathing Artemis, or to figures

3.20. *Venus Crouching at Her Bath* (detail), marble, Roman funerary relief, British Museum, London

pulling a bow.) And as with the Nymph, these ambiguities of posture contribute to a variety of Renaissance identities: Aldrovandi looks at a similar work, possibly related to the Venus and Cupid relief but clearly three-dimensional, sees apples in her hand, and calls the female figure Leda, while in the seventeenth century she is captioned as Helen of Troy.[61]

These inventories of uncertainty tell the story negatively—that is, from the perspective of the Renaissance viewer passively attempting to decode an ancient enigma. But let us return to the unmutilated form of the *Venus Crouching* that has her, *Anadyomene*-like, pulling her long dripping tresses away from her head. There is no sign that the Renaissance had—or could have—an example so perfectly preserved as to include the fine filigree work in the head, hair, and hands.[62] Yet in the Vatican Logge an iconographically original and philologically sophisticated version of *David and Bathsheba* (fig. 3.21) renders the temptress exactly as a seated version of the *Venus Crouching*, with her right arm stretching out as she dries her hair in full view of the army.[63] It is certainly possible that Raphael or some member of his workshop had seen a complete version of this image that has eluded us—possibly on a relief, where it could be more easily preserved. But it is equally possible that the artist arrived at this accidental piece of philological correctness simply by playing with the anatomical possibilities of the incomplete sculptural examples he had before him.

In the face of all these corporeal and iconographical uncertainties, it is that *play* which might be considered the positive version of the story. The counters in this artistic game are, first, those ellipses that result from the fragmentary state of the work

3.21. Perino del Vaga (attributed),
David and Bathsheba, fresco (detail),
ca. 1520, Vatican Logge, Rome

and, second, the uncanonical posture, which manages both to deny a single classic way of completing the body and to challenge artists into an exercise of skill. The various positions of the hands that we observed in the statuette forms of the *Nymph alla Spina* may be viewed not only as confusions or errors but also as signs of a permission to invent. One sign of that permission is the development of a whole subgenre of drawings after the antique, generally post-1500, in which the work is reproduced more than once from different angles. They include two contemporary examples (ca. the 1530s) from the statues under consideration: Heemskerck's pen-and-ink drawing after the *Venus Binding Her Sandal* (fig. 3.22) and a Florentine black-chalk drawing in the Fogg after the *Crouching Venus* (fig. 3.23).[64] These compositions respond to what we might call a 360-degree interest excited by these figures, just as they respond to the problematic of capturing three dimensions in two—in effect, the *paragone* between sculpture and painting. And these *are* compositions, not simply two or three images joined on a single sheet but unitary works that turn the disadvantage of two-dimensionality into a celebration of simultaneous multiples created by the artist and not replaceable by any viewer's real experience of moving around a statue.[65]

It is no coincidence that works like the *Nymph* and the *Venus* should be sketched iteratively. Figures in heroic postures tend to dictate a single preferred vantage point, whereas bodies that are bending, crouching, and turning become as ambiguous in the way they place the viewer as in what they tell the viewer about their actions. In addition, figures that are missing body parts also invite artistic response, as we saw in the case of the *Laocoön*. The artist of the Fogg drawing, by repeating the

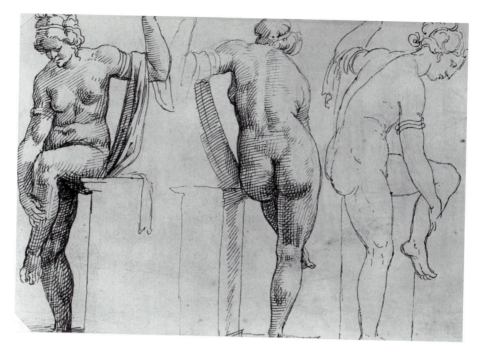

3.22. Marten van Heemskerck, drawing after *Venus Binding Her Sandal*, ca. 1532–36, sketchbook, I.25v, Staatliche Museen, Berlin

3.23. Circle of Fra Bartolommeo, drawing after *Crouching Venus*, black chalk and black crayon, ca. 1525–35, Fogg Art Museum, Cambridge, Massachusetts

figure, follows—and exaggerates—the circular motion of the original work. Such a focus also emphasizes the fleshy corporeality of the midsection; what has been called a Michelangelesque quality in this drawing is in effect a modern (Mannerist) realization of the original Hellenistic conceit by which a graceful Praxitelean Aphrodite is rendered more naturalistic.[66] At the same time, the double image becomes a way of experimenting with alternative positions for the right arm, most likely owing to the fact that it was already broken off on the original. Heemskerck, on the other hand, tends not to restore missing parts. As he moves around his statue, he keeps as a constant the absent left forearm; indeed, he designs his composition in part so that each left hand can, as it were, fall off the paper. Meanwhile, the alternative points of view are in part a pretext for exploring differences in technique of drawing. One might read the representations as a sequence moving from sketchy to complete (right to left) or from surface to deep structure (left to right); but I would argue that the play of difference is more significant than its directionality. At all events, what is revealed by both Heemskerck's polished sketchbook practice and the more casual work of the Florentine drawing is that the qualities of the statues both liberate and determine the artistic exploration they inspire.

To turn from these bending and crouching females to the similarly posed *Spinario* and *Arrotino* is to move from some relatively minor players in the rediscovery of antiquities to a pair of the most celebrated statues of all. (Even the existence of the two Italian nicknames is a sign of their fame.) By way of explaining this difference it should be pointed out that these two works are unique (at least in the Renaissance), while the others exist in many interchangeable versions; they are also in nearly perfect condition, while the others tend to be broken. Gender counts as well, but through some complicated mediations. Observers of enigmatic female representations try to make sense of their body positions or at most to give them a generalized iconographic attribute; observers of male figures want to locate them rather in specific narratives that will offer a master explanation. Precisely because these works are corporeally complete, the focus is not so much on what they might be doing as on why they are doing it—a question that demands fuller narrative response. The fame and influence of the *Spinario* and the *Arrotino* therefore depend to a considerable extent on the relation between a distinctive pose artistically realized and a narrative enigma that teases viewers but does not readily resolve itself.

The *Arrotino* (fig. 3.24) is, at least by my taxonomy, the perfect Hellenistic representation.[67] He crouches in an unheroic posture, his features identify him as a barbarian, and his function turns out to be as a minor (if pivotal) player in a larger narrative. This ensemble of qualities enables us to map quite fully what does and does not get transmitted from the Late Antique into the Early Modern. The *Arrotino*, we know now, was part of a sculptural group—that is, a staged installation of freestanding works. These came to define the taste for drama and pathos characteristic of the second century B.C.—an advance in these respects on the dramatic possibilities of multiple-figure reliefs, like the Pergamon frieze, or even of single statues depicting more than

one individual, like the *Pasquino*. We have already made reference to another contemporary group, the Nymph and Satyr who have been dubbed *Invitation to the Dance*. The *Arrotino* group—to judge from a much later Alexandrian coin recording the entire staging—probably consisted of three figures representing the *Flaying of Marsyas*: on the left, Apollo with his lyre; in the center, a crouching Scythian preparing his knife for the grisly operation; on the right, Marsyas tied and strung to a tree.[68] The story may have been little more than an excuse for representing dramatic pathos; but in characteristic Late Antique fashion the pathos is decidedly aesthetic—that is, it offers an excuse to display artistic technique. Each figure is a distinct sculptural exercise: the classic, relaxed body of Apollo is poised against the horrific and distended representation of a Marsyas who is about to be, as it were, unsculptured, while the Knife Grinder occupies a middle ground between tension and relaxation, between a canonical and an invented posture.

The Renaissance easily recognizes the *Arrotino*'s marginalized racial identity. Cosimo de' Medici, trying to get Vasari to bargain the price below eight hundred scudi, refers to the work in 1567 as "il villano che arrota il coltello" (a peasant sharpening his knife).[69] What no one perceives, at least until the seventeenth century, is the story, which is rather surprising, especially in a Medicean context. Not only is the narrative well known from Ovid's *Metamorphoses*, but the apposite Marsyas figure (or ones very like it) had been readily identified and had formed a significant part of the Medici collection early in the fifteenth century, as Vasari declares at length in his lives of Donatello and Verrocchio.[70] In fact, the Medici carnelian (see fig. 3.6), which Ghiberti describes

3.25. Domenico Ghirlandaio, *Baptism of Christ* (detail), fresco, 1490, Santa Maria Novella, Florence

in his *Commentari*, is nothing other than a variant on the Hellenistic three-statue installation; and, as it will be recalled, the artist identifies its subject as the Ages of Man.

The failure to name the *Arrotino* has something to do with a Renaissance assumption that no statue so artful, original, and suggestive could be devoted to a minor player, even if he is clearly a *villano*. The question is significant even without reference to the Renaissance, because genre figures are a major feature of Late Antique art and because Pliny, as we have seen, offers complicated opinions about what sorts of persons are worthy of sculptural representation. When Renaissance viewers do attempt to narratize the *Arrotino*, they seek stories in which lowly persons perform heroic acts, like Attius Navius, the soothsayer who effectively opposed Tarquin (in fact, mentioned by Pliny as the subject of an early Roman statue), or like Marcus Manlius, who helped save Rome when he was awakened by the Capitoline geese.[71] But even if these viewers cannot name him, they do understand that he is an exercise of art. The Knife Grinder's posture is sketched and copied, more precisely than freely, perhaps owing to the fact that it lacks the erotic charge of the crouching females—and not just for reasons of gender. And when he gets introduced into larger compositions, like the bending nude in Ghirlandaio's *Baptism of Christ* (fig. 3.25), he is, in fact, reinserted into the role of a minor character who seizes visual attention not for narrative reasons but as a display of artistic skill.[72] By which act the Renaissance has reinvented a crucial aspect of Hellenistic aesthetics.

But it is the *Spinario* (fig. 3.26) that truly fulfills this destiny—in fact, all the destinies of the classical fragment that reinserts itself into a modern culture and helps

3.26. *Spinario*, bronze, first-century B.C., Palazzo dei Conservatori, Rome

3.27. *Thornpuller,* terra cotta from Priene,
second century B.C., Staatliche Museen, Berlin

remake that culture. Not that the *Spinario* was literally fragmentary: no ancient statue
made it through the millennia in better condition (apart from missing eyeballs), nor
does it ever seem to have been underground at all. What renders it fragmentary is
rather the mystery of the boy's identity. Figures like the *Arrotino* or the sculpted heads
catalogued by Aldrovandi clearly had names and stories, whether the Renaissance
could recognize them or not. But eight hundred years of philology applying itself to
the problem seem to suggest that the *Spinario* is just a Boy with a Thorn. Efforts in the
nineteenth and early twentieth centuries to locate textual sources in pastoral or patriotic literature do not appear much more definitive than the medieval conjectures, a few
of which have already been exposed to ridicule in these pages. Some of these come in
the form of allegory, like Priapus or the Month of March, others in the form of mythological narratives, like Battus, Absolom, or the Roman boy who ran to bring a crucial
message to the Senate; at no time in the history of these hypotheses has there been a
universal consensus.[73]

The temptation to conjecture, balanced against the difficulties of getting the
answer right, is perhaps stronger here than in almost any other instance of classical
sculpture, possibly because the boy's action is so very precise while its larger purpose is
so murky. Faced with this uncertainty, modern scholarship must be content with some
such designation as "Hellenistic Genre Figure." But that very paradigm points to further
enigmas that are built in to the original composition. This is a class of statues usually
defined under the term *realism:* the figures, often performing some action understood to
be typical, include the lower classes, foreigners, and persons who are aged, drunk, or

engaged in a menial occupation (or combinations of the above). What defines them as a group is, fundamentally, that they are physically ugly. Why there should have been a fashion for expensive and important artworks depicting such individuals—whether they are to be construed as documents of daily life, as objects of pathos, or as perverse bits of elite class humor—is the subject of lively modern debate, with much depending on conjectures about viewer response in late antiquity. Children may also figure in this group, once again if they are of alien feature or performing lowly actions.[74]

Representations of this kind do not seem to have the elegance of artistry and grace of feature that belong to the Capitoline statue—until we discover (post-Renaissance) a whole class of Hellenistic *Spinarios* (fig. 3.27) that are roughly muscled, of apparently foreign race, and engaged in their surgical effort with grim naturalism.[75] The canonical Thorn Puller, though he stands alone in the Middle Ages and the Renaissance, therefore comes out of a complex tradition in which a motif from the gritty end of Hellenistic taste is being transformed into a work of high refinement. The same uneasy combination expresses itself in the contrast between the roughness of the stump on which the boy sits and the extraordinary polish of the body. Even more to the point is the fact that the boy's head is of a completely distinct period of artistic taste: a physiognomy of classic fifth-century restraint has been fused—literally, in the opinion of some scholars, but that hardly matters to us—to a highly expressive Hellenistic body.[76] The statue thus incorporates the whole transhistorical problematic of a Renaissance that is attempting to define a single, classic antiquity.

The *Spinario*, then, is more Proteus than Priapus, one of the classic Rorschach tests in the history of art, with not only different identities but different *kinds* of identity, embodying not only the otherness of the past but also the diachrony of different pasts. He is no less multivalent as a physical image than as a historical subject. Looking back through the grand industry of Renaissance *Spinarios*, including a myriad of sketches in single or multiple form, the quotation and reinterpretation of the figure in painting and relief from Giotto to Rubens, and (not surprisingly) the notable production of humanist-inspired statuettes, one sees first of all to what extent the *Spinario* demands and repays 360-degree interest. More than that: we would need a three-dimensional geometry to calculate points of view in regard to this work, since its placement on a column of uncertain height seems to have added altitude to the possibilities of artistic response.[77]

More than almost any other work, the *Spinario* develops a radically different footprint when viewed from alternative perspectives. Quotations of the statue inside narrative paintings illustrate the range of possibilities from frontal to profile.[78] The Quattrocento frescoes in the Sistine Chapel, as we shall see, actually include two versions facing in opposite directions. The sketchbooks manipulate point of view even more radically. The Holkham Album (fig. 3.28) offers the familiar double viewpoint on a single sheet; both sketches are drawn from behind and below, with the cross lines indicating an alternative play of light as the statue is viewed from left and right. Placed as the centerpiece among fragmentary antiquities in a beautiful finished draw-

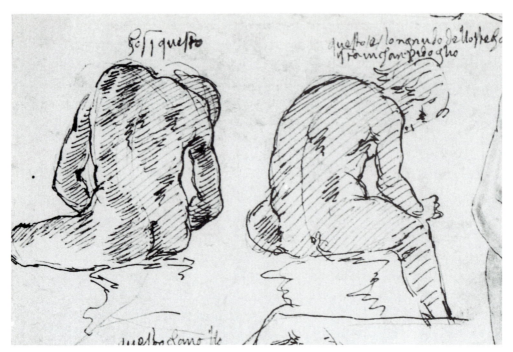

3.28. Drawing after *Spinario*, ca. 1490s, Holkham Album, fol. 34v (detail), Holkham Hall, Norfolk, England

ing by Jan Gossaert (fig. 3.29), who was in Rome around 1508, the *Spinario* is seen three-quarters frontally but from below, and in such a manner as to render him anything but a slender boy. And an extraordinary drawing in Oxford by Heemskerck (fig. 3.30) also takes the vantage point from below and behind, producing an emphasis on the weight-bearing buttocks and a distension of upper and lower body that almost turns the boy into an abstract form.[79]

Drawings such as these raise one of the most important issues in the response to ancient statues—and one of the most difficult to pin down. Works like the *Spinario* are sexy, and the artistic play they inspire is itself a sign and an exercise of this eroticism. The corporeality of these sculptures, the qualities that make them "Rome's other population" (to quote Pirro Ligorio again), speak to their fictive reality not only as historical persons but also as objects of desire. It should hardly come as a surprise that a 360-degree statue of a nude boy viewed from below that allows frontal perspective on the genitals and rear perspective on the buttocks might inspire erotically charged drawings. Magister Gregorius, looking from beneath at the *Spinario* elevated on a high column, may not have been so far off the mark with the name Priapus and the reference to oversized genitals. Such a vantage point would, after all, produce a quite dramatic view of the pubic region. Centuries later Bishop Ludovico Gonzaga writes that he is relieved to ship off a bronze pendant to the *Spinario* to his sister Isabella d'Este because the servant women in his house are becoming too interested in it.[80] Nor is it, in my view, a coincidence that works inspiring imaginative artistic liberty should also be erotic paradigms—but that is the subject of a later chapter.

3.29. Jan Gossaert, called Mabuse, drawing after *Spinario*, ca. 1508–9, Welcker Collection, Bibliotheek van de Rijksuniversiteit, Leiden

3.30. Marten van Heemskerck, drawing after *Spinario*, ca. 1530s, Ashmolean Museum, Oxford

There is one more related quality to the *Spinario*, which may seem more psychological than aesthetic; in fact, it is connected both to artistic enablement and to erotic attractiveness. The *Venus Crouching*, the *Nymph alla Spina*, and the *Arrotino* are directed outward; their own actions, whether definable or not, appear to refer to events in some larger space. The *Spinario*, by contrast, one might describe as a narcissistic composition. The intense self-concentration of the boy is not only a question of narrative—suggesting a purposefulness that requires but also obscures explanation; it also endows the figure with a kind of fungible, or recombinable, utility in artistic composition. The *Spinario* icon, in other words, can be used almost anywhere but remains blithely independent of the context in which he is placed. In truth, all the qualities of the statue—the almost infinite variability of viewpoints with which to see it, the potential for aesthetic and erotic display, and the dramatic self-sufficiency of the figure—are in some sense part of the boy's enigma, at once eluding certainty and liberating the viewer's imagination. And the same qualities combine to make of the *Spinario* the paradigm of what the Germans call the *Nebenfigur*, that is, the personage who is extraneous to story and iconography but who exists in narrative compositions as an exercise of beauty, of technical skill, of artistic liberty, of classical erudition, in short of sublime irrelevance.

It is almost too good to be true that this recombinable *Spinario* looms so large as one of Abraham's two servants in Brunelleschi's competition piece for the Florentine Baptistry doors (fig. 3.31). The story of the contest in which seven sculptors were given a year to produce samples of their best work on the theme of the *Sacrifice of Isaac* is, after all, a kind of foundational narrative for the emergence of the Renaissance

3.31. Filippo Brunelleschi,
Sacrifice of Isaac (competition
panel), bronze relief,
1402, Museo dell'Opera
del Duomo, Florence

artist as a self-asserting personage. As Vasari tells the story, the particular biblical
theme was chosen because it imposed specific artistic and technical demands, including the rendering of landscape, the depiction of persons clothed and nude, and the
varying techniques of relief carving. Further, the commissioners seem to have
specified the inclusion of all the players in the Genesis narrative—not only Abraham,
Isaac, the angel, and the ram, who are necessary to the plot, but also the ass and the
two servants, who exist in the story as placeholders, innocently waiting in the low-
lands while Abraham proceeds secretively up the mountain.[81]

Ghiberti, in his winning entry (fig. 3.32), handles the priorities between the
two groups of characters with what can only be described as a proto-Albertian sense of
the *historia*: the triad of servants and animal in the lower left are clearly designed to
separate the quotidian space from the miraculous and, at the same time, to point
the viewer's attention toward the significant action at the center of the panel. The
artist thereby demonstrates his ability to integrate a narrative into unitary space.
Brunelleschi's panel, on the other hand, has been seen as conservative, diffuse, and
medievalizing even in its borrowings from antiquity.[82] But the two supernumerary
figures in the foreground may offer the key to a different view of his plan, one less
dependent on our knowledge that he lost the contest. Brunelleschi's lowland characters
include an elegant quotation of the *Spinario*, clothed and somewhat more upright than
the original, alongside another bending figure who has been associated loosely with
various ancient relief representations but who could also be described as a version of

3.32. Lorenzo Ghiberti, *Sacrifice of Isaac* (competition panel), bronze relief, 1402, Museo dell'Opera del Duomo, Florence

the *Spinario*, though more crouched and seen from a higher vantage point. (The gesture toward the lower leg has quite a bit in common with the so-called *Nymph alla Spina*.)

Brunelleschi's choice of the famous classical bronze for this part of the assignment can only have the effect of disintegrating the narrative, as the statue that so perfectly embodies aesthetic beauty, manipulability, and self-absorption cannot serve to center the whole composition. The success of which can perhaps be witnessed by Vasari, who seems to remember only the supernumeraries from Brunelleschi's panel: "He had represented Abraham sacrificing Isaac; and in that scene a slave who is drawing a thorn from his foot, while he is awaiting Abraham and the ass is browsing, deserves no little praise."[83] In short, Brunelleschi gambled that the commissioners were more interested in the presentation of the artist than in the story. It was a reasonable strategy given the atmosphere of Florentine individualism and self-promotion that radiates from the whole episode of the contest. And even if Brunelleschi lost this battle, the war continues throughout the High Renaissance between the Albertian *historia*, which places narratives in perspective space, and the boldly independent artistic self-presentation, which produces larger than life figures with their own relations to the colossal works of antiquity. In the end, whatever the Operai or Brunelleschi had in mind, destiny forges a link between the supplementary figures in a visual narrative and the artfully realized allusions to ancient sculpture—a link that will continue to disintegrate the organic structures of narrative, perspective, and iconography.

The *Spinario*, then, becomes the paradigm of the supernumerary figure who

3.33. Pinturicchio-Perugino, *Baptism of Christ*, fresco, 1480s, Sistine Chapel, Rome

exits from the pictorial composition into the world of art itself. If the Baptistry represents one locus classicus for the Renaissance artist, another is the Sistine Chapel. Among the fifteenth-century frescoes, one *Spinario* equivalent appears in the Perugino-Pinturicchio *Baptism of Christ* (fig. 3.33) as a nameless young man awaiting baptism and about to remove the last bit of clothing from his leg, while in the Signorelli *Last Days of Moses* (fig. 3.34) a seated youth, identity similarly unspecified, also takes the form of the ancient bronze. In both cases the quoted figure is completely extraneous to the narrative while seizing a disproportionate (one might almost say heretical) amount of attention within the composition. The young man on the verge of baptism is almost a double of Christ and is the only other nude figure on a crowded panel. The seated individual at almost the dead center foreground of Signorelli's *Last Days of Moses* is even more of a scene-stealer; in a composition where everyone is clothed and engaged in active conversation, he sits alone in glorious nude physique, once again fulfilling the *Spinario*'s combination of destinies.[84]

These qualities, and their influence on the future, can perhaps best be isolated in another work by Signorelli, his remarkable Munich tondo depicting the *Madonna with Child in a Landscape*, from about 1495 (fig. 3.35). This is one of a series of tondi—possibly the last—in which the artist introduces classically inspired male nudes in the edges of the circular space surrounding the holy pair.[85] In the Uffizi painting (fig. 3.36) there are several such individuals in elaborately varying all'antica attitudes, possibly representing the shepherds, though there are no sheep and only some rather stagy athletic interactions; they are, however, in roughly logical perspective relation to

3.34. Luca Signorelli, *Last Days of Moses*, fresco, 1483, Sistine Chapel, Rome

the Madonna and Child. In the Munich tondo, however, there is only one figure, a precise quotation of the *Spinario*. He is outsized for the landscape background, he is elaborately muscled, and he is, in familiar fashion, completely self-absorbed and unconnected to the central figures of the composition.

The combination of the Sistine fresco and the Munich tondo inevitably points to that artist who, as a painter, so often reveals the influence of Signorelli. Michelangelo in his *Doni Tondo* (fig. 3.37) takes over the curious double composition involving a foreground scene of the Holy Family and a classicizing background with nude males who, like the quoted *Spinario*, are narratively irrelevant but rich with suggestions of antiquity and artfulness.[86] By placing a wall between the two scenes, Michelangelo gives them a spatial logic that at once separates and unites the pagan and Christian worlds. It is as though Michelangelo has taken Signorelli's conceit (in both senses of the word) in the showy quotation of ancient sculpture and given it a structure that is theological and at the same time art historical. Yet the gesture of artistic ostentation is no less bold for the presence of an iconographic program. Vasari claims that Michelangelo included the nudes "per mostrare arte sua essere grandissima" ("the better to show how great was his art").[87] From there it is a short step to the *ignudi* of the Sistine ceiling, who almost literally break out of the spatial composition and can be integrated to no larger agenda of story or iconography than that of *l'arte sua grandissima*, though by that time there are more spectacular ancient statues to appropriate, like the *Laocoön* and the *Torso Belvedere*, and a yet bolder artistic self-assertion in creating variations upon them. So the *Nebenfigur* remains a site of classicism and artfulness, whether it is a wholly invent-

3.35. Luca Signorelli, *Madonna with Child in Landscape*, oil on panel, 1490s, Alte Pinakothek, Munich

3.36. Luca Signorelli, *Madonna with Child* (detail), oil on panel, 1490s, Galleria degli Uffizi, Florence

ed personage like those of the various tondi or a barely integrated bystander, like those of the Sistine narratives. Vasari will not be the last viewer to be distracted and decentered by these exercises of art, though the twentieth-century imagination may wander yet further off-center: one thinks of W. H. Auden's "Musée des Beaux-Arts," in which the speaker's eyes move away from the martyrdom of the saint to

> some untidy spot
> Where the dogs go on with their doggy life and the torturer's horse
> Scratches its innocent behind on a tree.[88]

IMPERSONATIONS

The enigmas we have been considering here, while definable in terms of period styles like Roman and Hellenistic, essentially concern the *what* of representation: who is the peasant with the knife? why is Venus crouching? what does the string of nautical and sacrificial objects add up to? Another approach focuses on the *how* of representation. It ought to be obvious that the two approaches cannot be definitively separated. The questions raised by the *Trophies of Marius*, for instance, concern both the distanced historical circumstances of what is being represented and the curiosities that arise from depicting the space of a human body without the body inside. If one whole set of Renaissance questions has to do with identifying the objects of representation, another set focuses on works that by their very nature challenge what viewers expect of representation, often in

3.37. Michelangelo, *Doni Tondo*,
oil on panel, 1503–4, Galleria
degli Uffizi, Florence

such a way that they knew they were being challenged. Perhaps the simplest form of the
paradigm is the statue that is itself an impersonation or a disguise. Modern historians of
Roman art recognize, for instance, a significant subset of post-Augustan portraiture in
which real people, usually of imperial rank, are represented with the dress and attributes
of gods.[89] But what was easily readable propaganda in the second century could become
a mimetic conundrum in the fifteenth, since a visual impersonation has little hope of
being penetrated when the cues are exclusively visual. (It's rather like Mark Twain's quip
about Wagner's music not being as bad as it sounds.) The *Venus Felix* (fig. 3.38), for
instance, which was prominently displayed in the Belvedere courtyard from early in the
pontificate of Julius II, appears clearly to modern art historians as a portrait of some
princess from the Antonine imperial family tricked out in the guise of Praxiteles' *Cnidian
Aphrodite*.[90] Sixteenth-century viewers, however, were not sufficiently familiar with the
relevant real-life physiognomies and coiffures to make this determination. Nor, though
they copied it faithfully, did they get much help from the inscription,

> VENERI FELICI   SACRVM
> SALLVSTIA   HELPIDVS D D

since it records not the subject of the portrait but the patrons, Sallustia and Helpidus,
who dedicated the statue to her. In fact, I can find no one who tries to decode the
inscription at all, which suggests that viewers have no sense of an enigma in the representation that might be resolved by consulting the text. Here, then, is a case where

Renaissance viewers are unable to recognize that they are looking at a double image—as we might expect, given both the historical and the conceptual difficulties of arriving at such a perception.

Yet another statue belonging to Julius II, which is now known as *Hercules and Telephus* (fig. 3.39) and not considered to be an impersonation, tells a different story. This more than lifesize figure with a lion's skin over his shoulder and some part of a club in his right hand is not in himself difficult to name. The identity of the infant whom Hercules is holding was less obvious: some early viewers found him perplexing in the heroic context of the subject, while others knew enough to propose Hylas, Hercules' favorite who was abducted by water nymphs. Even with this uncertainty, the main figure's identity would seem so obvious as to close speculation. But in the very letter that first announces the discovery—Giorgio di Negroponte writing to Isabella d'Este in May 1507—an additional level of representation is proposed: "Fedra dice che non è Ercole ma Comodo."[91] The authority cited here is Tommaso Inghirami (1470–1516), the immensely learned Vatican librarian, papal courtier, and stager of humanist pageants, who bore the lifelong nickname "Fedra" because he had so memorably performed the leading female role in a production of Seneca's *Hippolytus* when he was sixteen.[92]

What Inghirami is understood to have meant is that this statue represents the emperor Commodus *as* Hercules, a reading that is clear from Albertini's inventory, ca. 1510, where the work is described as "Comodi imperatoris, imitantis Herculem." It is tempting to speculate that it was Inghirami's theatrical interests which stimulated him

3.39. *Hercules and Telephus* ("Hercules-Commodus"), marble, Roman copy of fourth-century B.C. Greek statue, Vatican Museums, Rome

to see beyond the "character" Hercules to the "actor" Commodus. And it was surely his erudition which made him aware that Commodus was fond of impersonation, that according to Dio Cassius he had a statue's head cut off, replaced it with his own, and added Herculean attributes. This identification of the statue becomes almost universal at the papal court, doubtless owing to Inghirami's authority and influence: even in account books recording its installation in the Belvedere, it comes to be known as "Commodo Imperatore."[93] Doubtless it is the political significance of this object—absent from the *Venus Felix*—that made it possible to see the work as an impersonation, since the notion of a monarch dressed in mythological trappings was already quite familiar. But however it came to be, the double identification of a statue that stood at the very entrance to the Belvedere, decorated with the famous inscription *procul este prophani*, demonstrates the extent to which Renaissance viewers were aware of the complexities of naming the representations they collected and displayed.[94]

But there is a kind of master trope of "dress up" that becomes the fundamental or even defining instance of representational disguise and visual enigma. We may take as the most immediately relevant instance a much observed sarcophagus of *Achilles on Scyros* (fig. 3.40), now at Woburn Abbey, which was publicly visible from the fourteenth century, when it was immured in the Aracoeli stairway. The subject, widely diffused in ancient narrative art, is narrated by Statius.[95] Achilles, who has been dressed in women's clothes by his mother so that he will escape military service, is surrounded by similarly attired real maidens, but, in response to Odysseus's ruse of hurling military gear among the supposed girls, he has instinctively grabbed a lance

3.40. *Achilles on Scyros*, Roman sarcophagus relief, ca. third century A.D., Woburn Abbey, Bedfordshire, England

and thus revealed his true identity. The double image, in other words, is of a man made to resemble a woman; and, like Commodus made to resemble Hercules, the object inevitably complicates mimesis since the same visual medium must represent two contradictory things at once. In practice, this is not so difficult: in the Aracoeli sarcophagus Achilles is parallel in clothing and stance to the maidens but allowed to show some virile musculature, while in other examples not known to the Renaissance the representational game is all but abandoned, with the Achilles figure showing his flat chest or even his genitals.[96]

Yet however artists may "cheat" in practice, the *idea* of simultaneous cross-gender representation takes on the status of mimetic paradigm. Philostratus the Younger had already moralized a painting of the same subject in these terms:

> To the other girls he seems to be a girl, but one of them, the eldest, he has known in secret love, and her time is approaching when she will bring forth Pyrrhus. But this is not in the picture. . . . All are surpassingly beautiful, but while the others incline to a strictly feminine beauty, proving indisputably their feminine nature by the frank glances of their eyes and the bloom of their cheeks and their vivacity in all they do, yet yonder girl who is tossing back her tresses, grim of aspect along with delicate grace, will soon have her sex betrayed, and slipping off the character she has been forced to assume will reveal Achilles.[97]

The key to the whole method of the *Imagines* is the phrase "this is not in the picture" (Άλλ' οὐκ ἐυταυθα ταυτα): these ekphrases are based on a play between what is materially visible in the (fictive) painting and what can be imagined by the learned and

3.41. *Hermaphrodite Discovered by Eros in the Presence of Venus*, cameo, first century A.D., Museo Nazionale, Naples

3.42. *Reclining Hermaphrodite with Three Putti*, cameo, probably fifteenth-century copy of first-century A.D. original, Museo Nazionale, Naples

rhetorically gifted observer—hence the choice of a version of the story that offers few visible clues to decipher Achilles' sex. Ambiguity of gender comes to define ambiguity of representation. Achilles is both male and female, both concealing and revealing. In fact, there is, as Philostratus cleverly realizes, a double game of perceptual gender bending, since the ability to read the ambiguous representation is an issue inside the narrative as well as in the experience of the observer.

When Pirro Ligorio looks at the Aracoeli sarcophagus in the mid-sixteenth century, he sees the impersonation and transvestism as triumphs of the sculptor's art. The real maidens exhibit the artist's skill in the thinness of their garments, which renders them almost nude. But Achilles inspires a fuller aesthetic appreciation: "What proves that it is Achilles is that he doesn't have the form of a woman like the others; in that matter the sculptor exhibited a lovely sense of taste. For he fashioned him with a partly uncovered chest, which exposes something of his masculinity. Then also what betrays him is the clothing which he is holding stretched out on his side, which reveals part of the masculine thigh, along with his whole rather muscular leg, such that he differs from the rest of his female companions."[98] Rendering the hero in drag becomes a study in the pleasurable illusions of artistic representation. In effect, Pirro revisits the concept of elegant variation in responding to a multiple group of girls, one of whose variations is more than merely elegant.

It is noteworthy that this is the same work that leads Aby Warburg to enunciate a whole theory of historic transmission. In the billowing and dancelike dress of these heterogeneous maidens, Warburg saw the motif of "bewegtes Beiwerk," that is, accessories in motion, which would become for him the touchstone for the influence

3.43. *Standing Hermaphrodite*, marble, Roman copy of Hellenistic statue, Villa Doria Pamphili, Rome

of antiquity on the Quattrocento.[99] I would argue that there is more than a chance connection between the refinements of art and the cross-gender subject. The elaborately graceful play of sameness and difference in the depiction of these maidens—and the ability to notice it—has much to do with the fact that one of them is no maiden. The very terms of the narrative force viewers into a careful reading of what might seem like merely decorative accessories; in the process, what starts as ambiguous gender representation emerges as the "bella discrettione" of artistic skill and refined aesthetics.

There is a much more famous subject in the classical repertoire that focuses aesthetic work on the delineation of gender—indeed, it may be the paradigm for the gendering by art rather than nature. The *Hermaphrodite* was known to the Renaissance in a remarkable variety of shapes. The Medici gem collection contained two different versions of this figure, one seated with Venus and Cupid, the other reclining and surrounded by putti (figs. 3.41, 3.42). Even more significant are two marble statues (each probably known in more than one version), one standing and encircled with a billowing drape, the other—most famous of all—sleeping in almost prone position (figs. 3.43, 3.44).[100] We have already cited Ghiberti on a version of this last type, but he is worth repeating:

> I saw in Rome . . . an hermaphrodite, the size of a thirteen-year-old girl, which had been made with admirable skill. . . . It is impossible for the tongue to tell the perfection and the knowledge, art and skill of that statue. The figure was on spaded earth over which a linen cloth was thrown. The figure was on the linen

3.44. *Sleeping Hermaphrodite*, marble, Roman copy of late Hellenistic statue, Villa Borghese, Rome

cloth and was turned in a way to show both the masculine and the feminine characteristics. . . . One of the legs was stretched out and the large toe had caught the
cloth, and the pulling of the cloth was shown with wonderful skill. The statue
was without a head but nothing else was missing. In this state were the greatest
refinements. The eye perceived nothing if the hand had not found it by touch.[101]

Ghiberti catches what will be the central set of conceits in both the making of the
Hermaphrodite figures and in the viewers' responses: that is, refinements of artistry
deserving high praise, the doubleness of gender, and—perhaps most important of
all—the exquisite rendering of the draperies. In the case of the *Sleeping Hermaphrodite*,
the drapes are under the figure and do not conceal its sex; but it is no coincidence that
Ghiberti notices them, given a subject that is often precisely *about* the position of the
cloth. In one of the Medici gems, Cupid is removing the drape and thereby revealing
the figure's male genitals to Venus, though it does not seem to have revealed them to
the compiler of Lorenzo's 1492 inventory, who records merely "uno chammeo . . . con
2 femine meze nude."[102]

The standing marble statue is, appropriately enough, derived from the *Venus
Pudica*, another subject whose central action is the veiling of genitals; but the conceit
of the *Hermaphrodite*, perhaps playing on the more familiar *Venus*, is that the flowing
cloth almost covers the genitals but not quite. Although post-sixteenth-century
restoration of the Doria Pamphili statue has completed the transition to *Venus Pudica* by
extending the drapes, Renaissance viewers were fully aware of the play on cloth and

3.45. Drawing after *Standing Hermaphrodite*, northern Italian, ca. 1503, British Museum, London

3.46. *Camillus-Zingara*, bronze, first century A.D., Palazzo dei Conservatori, Rome

genitals.[103] Aldrovandi notes semirevealing clothing among several statues (indeed, he may have imagined some straightforwardly gendered figures to be hermaphrodites simply because they were suggestively covered) and comments on even some headless figures that one could tell had "chiome lunghe da donna" (women's long hair). Prospettivo Milanese singles out the "Hermaphrodita . . . e parte un sottil velo ha circuita" ("partially enveloped by a veil").[104] And an early sixteenth-century drawing of the standing statue (fig. 3.45) not only depicts the veil as framing the genitals but also places next to this figure a version of the *Crouching Venus* who is staring wide-eyed at the Hermaphrodite's exposed—if somewhat defaced—male organs.[105]

All this play on artistry, veils, and sexual organs takes us back to the Achilles sarcophagus and the responses of Pirro Ligorio and Warburg. The ability to render drapery with beauty, subtlety, and verisimilitude is one of the touchstones of great art in the whole classical tradition—both in sculpture and painting, both in Northern Europe and in Italy. But this seemingly technical achievement is inseparable from two other significances of the veil: first, that it conceals and reveals gender; and second, that it stands for the covering and uncovering of the truth—indeed, for the whole discourse of interpretation.[106] This tradition of ancient images that play explicitly on sexual ambiguity turns into more than a chance expression of these issues: they define a nexus of eros, art, and the problematics of interpretation.

The Scyros story and the Hermaphrodite are designed around an explicit enigma of gender that must be recognized through visual clues. But many other rediscovered sculptural objects became ambiguous even though their original sexual identity was perfectly clear. A remarkable range of three-dimensional and relief works appeared to viewers in the fifteenth and sixteenth centuries without clear gender characteristics, sometimes because they were fragments and sometimes because the moderns could not read ancient conventions in representing male and female. The operative word is "convention." Pliny had already included the rendering of sexual difference, in painting at least, as one of the stages in the historical progress of technical innovation. When he says that Eumarus "primus in pictura marem a femina discreverit" ("[was] the earliest artist to distinguish the male from the female sex in painting"), he is not suggesting the actual representation of genital organs but referring to the fact that different colors were used semiotically to signal sex.[107] Although sculpted figures might well have unmistakable sexual characteristics, the representation of gender remains an aspect at once of individual artistic choice and of contemporary social conventions. Neither of these communicates easily across millennia. As we have seen in other contexts, the fragmentary and unreadable qualities of many of these works highlight the enigmas already intrinsic to them.

An impressive full-length bronze, probably part of the original group of Lateran antiquities transferred to the Capitoline in 1471, offers a notable example of this gender conundrum. This work was not intended to be sexually ambiguous, nor was it mutilated by the passage of time—indeed, it is probably the most perfectly preserved of any ancient statue. It has been known since the late seventeenth century as the *Camillus* (fig. 3.46), in reference to the class of noble Roman boys who assisted at sacrificial rites.[108] For the Renaissance, however, this was a female, specifically, *La Zingara*. Before addressing the question of what viewers see in this statue when they call it the Gypsy Woman, let it be noted that what they are *not* seeing is any definitive sexual characteristics, whether primary or secondary. Musculature, stance, facial features, clothing—all turn out to be curiously enigmatic. The long hair probably read as female, while the short tunic suggested the status of gypsy (Aldrovandi says she is called *La Zingara* "per quello habito, che tiene" [274]), though, as it happens, both are characteristics of camilli. Renaissance viewers were sensitive to the marks of hierarchy, but a noble boy acting out a temporarily subservient position is, in the absence of full information about classical paedeia and Roman religious practice, almost as unreadable as an impersonation like the *Venus Felix*. To see in this statue a Gypsy Woman is to render its status more logical on grounds of both sex and social standing. In fact, caste may be even more definitive than gender, since Andrea Fulvio, as always philologically ahead of his time, recognizes the figure as male but still a servant.[109]

Yet this historical (or erroneously historical) reading would be no more than philological curiosity were it not that the statue's affect can be made to confirm it. This is a figure whose enigmas are not limited to gender. The contrapposto-like stance and the outstretched right hand are potentially powerful signifiers. When he is a camillus, they place him in the role of pious acolyte holding a libation bowl; when she is *La Zingara*, they speak as they did to Prospettivo Milanese, who saw the statue in 1499:

3.47. *Icarius Relief*, marble, Roman copy after Greek original, first century B.C., British Museum, London

> Propinquallui [i.e., the Spinario] a una circata dochio
> a una zingra di magior varizia
> che non son quelle che fecel verochio.[110]

> Nearby within eye range there is a gypsy showing greater greediness
> than those modelled by Verrocchio.

It has been several centuries since Magister Gregorius predetermined that the adjacent *Spinario* was a Priapus and therefore had to see gigantic genitals. But the process remains similar: to see this figure as female and a gypsy depends on and legitimizes what we might consider a willful reading of the physical evidence. The extended hand becomes a sign of extraordinary greed, with the result that this figure is almost as much gendered by its arm as the *Spinario* was by its penis. It should be noted that there is some controversy concerning Prospettivo's lines. Tilmann Buddensieg understands the *varizia* not as *avaritia* but as *varietà*—in other words, as a tribute to the artfulness with which the sculptor has rendered clothing and attitude.[111] Perhaps this is the same kind of gendered variety that Pirro Ligorio saw in the ambiguously represented maidens of Scyros. But whether this response concerns the identity of the subject or the talent of the artist, it is clear that in a state of fragmentary knowledge, the observer creates his or her own narrative, in effect, assimilating the *Camillus* either into the class of female gypsies or into the class of great artworks.

Of course, Prospettivo Milanese is the very model of fragmentary knowledge,

3.48. *Mithras Slaying a Bull,* marble, Roman relief, third century A.D., Louvre, Paris

as witness his possible implication that Verrocchio was famous for sculpting gypsy women or other figures of exceptional greediness. But the complications of the proverbial little learning only intensify as one moves higher up in philological difficulty. A camillus is only by accident a hermaphrodite. His problem is that he forms part of a particular set of religious practices that were too little known for the philology of the early Renaissance to decipher. As we have seen, Fulvio, in the 1520s, begins to get an inkling of the historical truth. Perhaps it is significant that Aldrovandi, writing twenty years later and still offering nothing but the traditional label for the figure, names the statue by saying, "la chiamano *volgarmente* La Zingara."[112] In that act of distancing, he is recognizing an uncertainty. More specifically, he is pointing to the familiar gap between humanist and popular conceptions of ancient objects—even if in this case he can propose nothing better than the statue's common name. As it happens, this gender confusion—specifically the switch from male to female—often appears when Renaissance viewers are struggling with the more arcane aspects of classical culture. While learned observers attempt to find the texts that will adequately label these narratives, others assimilate them into a story of male and female.

These issues emerge more fully in two elaborate narrative tableaux than in the solitary *Camillus.* A work generally known as the *Icarius Relief* (fig. 3.47) depicts Dionysus, accompanied by his retinue of Silenus, satyrs, and maenads, approaching a recumbent figure on a couch in the midst of elaborate scenic trappings.[113] Another object centers on Mithras slaying a bull and surrounded by appropriate cult icons including various animals and representations of heavenly bodies (fig. 3.48). Both these works are known to the Renaissance in multiple versions; both are influential, as is evident from numerous replicas in sketchbooks after the antique and from adaptations in contemporary narrative art. Given the presence of multiple figures in significative patterns (the Mithras relief has in addition some rather elliptical inscriptions, but even "deo soli invicto mitrhe" goes undeciphered)[114], viewers had to know that they were looking at specific sets of historical materials. But the textual keys to identify these assemblages were very slow in coming, since neither Mithras nor these particular epicycles of Dionysiac legend occupied the mainstream of the classical heritage.

A multiplicity of unreadable signs produces a special philological allure, and both these works become the sites for a learned cottage industry beginning in the first half of the sixteenth century. On Mithras, scholarship makes notable progress: the object is, from the beginning, located in a Mithraeum on the Capitoline hill. The cave was certainly not identifiable in those terms, but even in the time of Cola di Rienzo it was known under the ethnically appropriate name of "Lo Perso." Much later, antiquarians like Pirro Ligorio and Lorenzo Pignoria begin to decipher the objects and develop a strong interest in Mithraic iconography and religion. Indeed, the variety of figures on this relief offers a whole matrix of interpretive possibilities to Renaissance antiquarian scholarship, which will delight in its exoticism and its potential for allegory.[115]

The *Icarius Relief* has a quite different career. Even today there is no unanimity in naming the subject of this piece, though countless examples full of iconographic detail have been brought to light. When Bober and Rubinstein call it "Bacchus Visiting the Poet Icarius," they are conflating two possibilities: first, a story told most fully by Nonnos, in which Icarius receives from Dionysus the gift of wine but is murdered by those with whom he shares it; and second, a generic allegory of the god inspiring the poet, which is based on no specific literary source but grounded on the presence of theatrical masks and a possible muse visible on the relief.[116] The titles are neither altogether satisfying in themselves nor mutually compatible, since Icarius was an agriculturist and not a poet; but none of these possibilities was readily manifest to the Renaissance. Still, the Bacchic personages were easily recognized, and philological study concentrated on the relief's generous quantities of detail suggestive of the domestic, social, and theatrical milieus in which the Romans lived. The work was read as a representation of the *triclinium*, or the room in which three dining couches were set out.[117]

I set out all these circumstances of reception because in both cases there is a considerable tradition of understanding the central figure as a woman. The alternative versions of the *Icarius Relief*, whatever their many differences of detail, offer no variety in the rendering of the recumbent Icarius—no physical reason, in other words, to supplement or resolve an ambiguous sign by changing its sex. Yet Amico Aspertini, in the Codex Wolfegg, endows her with female breasts (fig. 3.49), as does the artist of the Ripanda sketchbook. The drapery covering the rest of the body (again, that veil!) can be read equally in the conventions of male heroism or of female modesty; the inviting gesture can be read as a salutation to the god or as a sexual invitation; and the entire narra-

3.49. Amico Aspertini, drawing after *Icarius Relief*, ca. 1500–03, Codex Wolfegg, fols. 46v–47 (detail), Schloss Wolfegg

tive can metamorphose from the inspiration of the poet to some erotic encounter under the aegis of the god Dionysus. Perhaps it is significant that both artists appear to be more interested in the god than in the individual on the bed, which is less true in other versions where the figure remains a man. Without knowledge of a particular sexual narrative, they downgrade *him* as they produce *her*, and they render the woman as something like another attribute of Dionysus. On the other hand, when the early sixteenth-century Veronese artist Giovanni Maria Falconetto chooses to represent a female on the bed (fig. 3.50), he not only depicts her in unmistakably gendered terms—protruding breasts, long hair, diaphanous clothing—but also invents a Bacchic-Hymeneal ritual. The *kline* is now a marriage bed, the god's retinue is now a group of musical celebrants, and an added satyr on the left holds the wedding torch.

Granted that in this game of the Lady or the Poet, not very much may have been at stake, since no one could offer a historically accurate substitute for the erotic narrative of a female character inviting a visit to her bedchamber. The alternatives are sharper in the case of the *Mithras*. Not only is the subject abundantly clear, but that subject is also—theoretically—as resistant to eroticizing or to a sex change as it is possible to be. Mithraism, famously the leading adversary to Christianity in the first centuries of the common era, was above all the soldiers' religion.[118] It depended on Manichaean-style oppositions of good and evil and elemental allegories of nature; it was far less concerned with humanized narratives than its Galilean rival religion (not to mention its pagan predecessors). When the sixteenth-century antiquarians get hold of Mithraic materials, including the Capitoline relief, they may be unable to name the god, but their

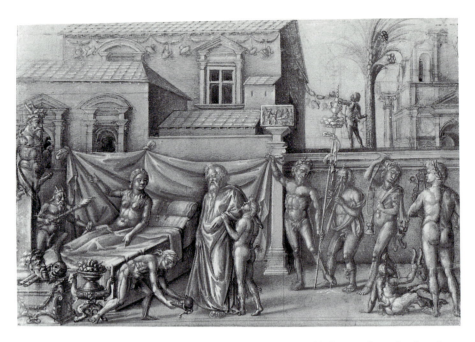

3.50. Giovanni Maria Falconetto, drawing after *Icarius Relief*, ca. 1500, Graphische Sammlung Albertina, Vienna

intuitions about the symbolic significance of the attributes, suggesting the struggles between light and dark or the origins of agriculture, are very much on the mark.

Modern scholarship, with good reason, continues to place the Mithras icon at the center of what we might call the heroic mainstream of classical survivals—even if it is always cited as an example of imperfect survival. Panofsky sees it as the paradigm for his theory concerning the Renaissance triumph over a medieval inability to put the right ancient image together with the appropriate classical text. (Hence the appearance of the image on a twelfth-century capital at Monreale demonstrates the discursively unsophisticated transmission of an icon deprived of its own meaning.) Fritz Saxl, Panofsky's original collaborator in the making of the theory, devotes yet more of his scholarly time to Mithras.[119] For him, the man overpowering a bull becomes the pivotal instance not of random and uninformed icon copying but of a principle that elevates images to a primary status in historical transmission: "Images with a meaning peculiar to their own time and place, once created, have a magnetic power to attract other ideas into their sphere; . . . they can suddenly be forgotten and remembered again after centuries of oblivion."[120] Following such a trajectory, this image begins as a nameless allegory of the taming of the bull, with suggestions of the heroic invention of culture and agriculture. It then develops a decisive form in early Greek versions that are similarly non-narrative, but it comes to be exploited as a representation of various Herculean struggles. All of this is preparation for the climax of the history, the union of this icon with the fully articulated Mithraic religion and cosmology. "The old image now has a new metaphysical meaning" (20), as Saxl describes it; there is now a decisive icon of the hero who brings civilization, which subsequent culture—specifically Christian culture—can incorporate and retextualize.

Much as one agrees with this formulation, both as a theoretical principle in the history of images and as an account of one in particular, its omissions must also be noted. A couple of Renaissance observers who knew nothing about Mithras read the Capitoline relief differently. First, Prospettivo Milanese:

> Di marmuna nympha amazun toro
> sacrata al degnio cesari Romano
> che sparsel sangue sopral drapo doro.[121]

> A nymph slaying a bull made of marble consecrated to the esteemed Roman Caesar who spilled blood upon a golden drape.

Then, a half-century later, with much scholarship under the bridge, a reminiscence by Flaminio Vacca: "I remember to have seen in my childhood a hole, like a chasm, in the Piazza del Campidoglio; and those who dared to enter it said that there was a woman sitting on a bull. I happened to mention the subject one day to my master, Vincenzo de' Rossi, and he said he had seen the place; that it contained a bas-relief set into the rock in a cave which cut through the hill from the Arch of Severus to the steps of the Aracoeli; and that the bas-relief represented the Rape of Europa."[122] This is not just another mistake, like mixing up Hercules and Mithras. It represents a category shift that should make us aware of the existence of the categories, however we precisely choose to name them: heroic versus erotic, public versus private, male versus female. That the sculptor Vincenzo de' Rossi, a younger colleague of Bandinelli who worked extensively on pagan subjects, should see this work as a Rape of Europa is all too logical in a mid-century moment when Ovidian classicizing icons have enjoyed such aesthetic privilege. That neither Saxl nor Panofsky includes this possible swerve of the bull image serves to remind us what is invested, from a gender-perspective, in the notions of taming nature, inventing civilization, and perfecting classical scholarship. Prospettivo Milanese, for his part, seems to waver between the two categories: she is a nymph, but she is also sacred to the Caesars, which is appropriate enough to the Capitoline setting. Perhaps it is significant that both these wayward and sex-changing observers are artists rather than antiquarians. At all events, the question of gender remains—like the poetics of the veil—fundamental to the science of interpretation, whether practiced in the fifteenth or the twentieth century.

STATUES FIXED AND UNFIXED

If the fragmentary nature of rediscovered sculpture complicates and challenges the act of representation—that is, if a statue is enigmatic partly because it is missing head or limbs or attributes—then there is one time-honored way to resolve the problem.

3.51. *Standing Juno*, marble, Greek statue mounted in first-century B.C. relief, Villa Medici, Rome

3.52. Amico Aspertini, drawing after *Standing Juno*, 1530s, London sketchbook, I, fol. 7, British Museum, London

Restore the statue and put back the pieces that you think are missing. Some pieces of sculpture are the sites for a particularly free play of possibilities. A headless and armless draped female figure (fig. 3.51), probably a Juno to begin with, is in one instance restored as Ceres; another more widely observed version of the same work is given a head and cemented into a relief depicting the Temple of Mars Ultor; it is in turn reextracted on paper by Amico Aspertini (fig. 3.52), who inserts her as a figure of mourning taking part in a dramatic scene drawn from an unrelated Meleager sarcophagus that nevertheless shows some compositional affinities to the statue.[123] Real restoration is practiced upon statues themselves, permanently altering their appearance and fixing their significations. But in analogous ways works can be restored when they appear in drawings, when they are copied, when they are fused with other antiquities or installed in groups, or when artists quote them inside other works of art. The practice of restoration is so out of fashion nowadays that we are liable to dismiss it as a harmful error of the past that has further separated us from the accurate experience of antiquities. That may be true, but it is also the case that we cannot fully understand the status of fragmentary antiquities in the Renaissance if we do not appreciate how changeable these material conditions were.

Yet before we can even do that, we must remind ourselves of the role that centuries of restorations have played in what we ourselves see when we look at antiquities. Just how contingent the whole process becomes can be demonstrated by two statues that were displayed in the courtyard of the Palazzo Medici-Madama by the beginning of

3.53. *Tyrannicides* ("Aristogeiton" [left] and "Harmodius"), marble, Roman copies of Greek bronze statues from fifth century B.C., Museo Nazionale, Naples

the sixteenth century and restored only much later. We call them the *Tyrannicides* (fig. 3.53) and classify them as Roman copies of the well-documented fifth-century statues by Kritios and Nesiotes depicting two heroes who killed the tyrant Hipparchus and sought thereby to liberate Athens from despotism. In the form that we see these works, they are a matched pair; both individuals stand on boldly striding legs, the elder, Aristogeiton, proceeding nobly forward with his cloak over his left arm, and the younger, Harmodius, threatening aggressively as he lifts his (fragmentary) sword above his head. There is every reason to credit the scholarly work that has identified this subject; but it is post-Renaissance and could not be deduced from texts or images available in the sixteenth century. What the Renaissance saw were two separate objects, one of which ("Aristogeiton") had neither head nor arms, while the other was probably nothing but a torso with perhaps just the stumps of a pair of jutting legs.[124] In the palazzo's inventory, and wherever else these works are securely identified, they were known as "Gladiatori."[125] But it is clear from the testimony of both verbal description and drawings that, at least in the case of the Aristogeiton, what most powerfully impressed viewers was not the identity of the figure but the nearly 180-degree spread of the legs. Aldrovandi speaks of "una bellissima statua sopra la basi del marmo istesso, con un'atto di gambe sforzato" (a very beautiful statue atop a base of the same marble, with a forced position of the legs), while Heemskerck makes three sketches in different postures that concentrate on the figure's midsection, culminating in the truncated but stretched-out limbs (figs. 3.54, 3.55). Aspertini restores this figure on paper (fig. 3.56),

3.54. Marten van Heemskerck, drawing after *Gladiators* and *Marcus Aurelius*, ca. 1532–36, sketchbook, I.44v, Staatliche Museen, Berlin

3.55. Marten van Heemskerck, drawing after *Gladiators* and other fragments, sketchbook, I.57v, Staatliche Museen, Berlin

as he will many others: the legs are exaggeratedly splayed, and the artist has invented a strange, widely stretched pair of arms to go with them.[126]

Apart from the "atto di gambe sforzato," however, all the significant qualities of the modern *Tyrannicides*—their existence as a pair, their names, their distinctive faces and gestures, as well as their placement in the stylistic history of Greek sculpture—are the product of modern restoration. Although this work is philologically correct, it also responded to a kind of historical necessity. According to Pliny, the original statues of the Tyrannicides were, after all, the first instance of Athenians honoring their real-life contemporaries at public expense, while Pausanias reports that Xerxes carried the statues away as spoils, presumably in revenge for their anti-Persian message.[127] We are therefore looking at works—or copies after copies of works—that were themselves significant in the history of both art and Athenian public life, rendering their specific identification and reconstruction all the more essential. But for a historically correct Renaissance view, we must try to know less about them than the restoration tells us.

This plea on behalf of lesser knowledge is perhaps all too easy to make, especially when discussing statues that were restored in post-Renaissance times. The *Tyrannicides* are only one example of what we might call a philological back-formation. Many pieces of sculpture that remained broken and unretouched through the sixteenth century were restored in later times (correctly, it is generally to be assumed), owing to the possibility of collating them with an ever-increasing database of works

3.56. Amico Aspertini, drawing after "Aristogeiton," from *Tyrannicides*, 1530s, London sketchbook, II, fol. 3, British Museum, London

and texts—that is, of corroborating contemporary documents and of related art objects in different states of preservation. It is the amassing and interpreting of this database, whether correctly or incorrectly, whether in 1500 or 2000, whether proposed on paper or realized in stone, that underlies the remaking of ancient objects.

Muses, for instance, could be identified by being in groups of nine, but only with later restoration were they each given their appropriate attribute (not always accurately); a single Muse from Cardinal Riario's collection was called Minerva or Ops during the Renaissance and only later got a large tragic mask placed in her right hand so as to leave no doubt that she was Melpomene (fig. 3.57).[128] An Uffizi statue (fig. 3.58) now carries a club, some fruit, and a winesack as he reaches up toward a bunch of grapes while a panther gnaws at the vine growing on a tree stump behind him. But everything from the shoulders up represents a modern decision to make him a *Satyr*, while all the props, even if they already formed part of the fragmentary statue, are confusingly rendered, if at all, in Renaissance drawings.[129] A heavily clothed female figure, made famous as the classical source for Lorenzetto's Madonna at Raphael's tomb, in her Vatican version stares fixedly at a Cupid whom she is holding in her left hand (fig. 3.59). Modern scholarship has linked her, along with a whole series of female statues known in the sixteenth century under different names, to Scopas's *Aphrodite of Capua*. Yet in the Renaissance she lacked a head, most of her arms, and the fully formed Cupid that sits on the end of her arm. Consequently, the Skopian pose itself was in effect invisible, as was her identity as Venus, particularly since in another

3.57. *Muse Melpomene*, marble, colossal Roman copy after Greek statue, Paris, Louvre

3.58. *Satyr Holding Up Grapes with Panther*, Roman copy after Greek statue, ca. A.D. 300, Galleria degli Uffizi, Florence

3.59. *Female in Pose of Venus of Capua*, marble, Roman copy of Hellenistic statue, Vatican Museums, Rome

version she was called Hygeia and eventually given a snake while being installed alongside a statue of Aesculapius.[130]

The difficulties of reading these statues emerge via hindsight—or, more precisely, the removal of hindsight. But it is the various attempts to complete fragmentary works *during* the Renaissance period that offer a glimpse at the relations between identifying sculptural representations and altering them. Many of these completions, like those of later times, are simply designed to round out an iconography that is understood to be already evident, though even in these cases there may be disagreement as to what is evident. A colossal armed torso (fig. 3.60) that is totally fragmentary when drawn by Heemskerck in the 1530s—it looks rather like a sculpted turkey with its neck cavity gaping—will gradually get more and more of an armed body on its way to becoming a *Pyrrhus*, though we call it *Mars* (fig. 3.61).[131] A *Dead Amazon* (figs. 3.62, 3.63) seems to have had a child added to its breast (though there is no trace of it now), perhaps to conform to Pliny's account of the sculptor Epigonos, who was famed as a copier of other artists' works (*nomen est omen*), except in the case of his *Weeping Infant Caressing Its Murdered Mother*.[132] River gods are particularly prone to this kind of touching up. The *Marforio* (see fig. 3.5) gets identified with various bodies of water and is only fixed as "Oceanus" (probably incorrectly) when a pseudo-Michelangelo seashell is placed in its hand at the end of the sixteenth century. The pair of *Tiber* (fig. 3.64) and *Nile* (see fig. 2.8) that is discovered near Santa Maria sopra Minerva in 1512–13 already teems with unmistakable iconographic specificity, but another pair, long exhibited on

3.60. Marten van Heemskerck, antiquities from Galli Garden, including *Mars in Cuirass*, ca. 1532–36, sketchbook, I.27, Staatliche Museen, Berlin

the Quirinal (see fig. 1.17), gets passed around among various gods (including Neptune) before being identified with a succession of different rivers.[133] Although a sphinx identifies one of the pair clearly as the *Nile*, the other, now called the *Tigris*, will have its effaced tiger misread as a crocodile by Prospettivo Milanese and restored into a wolf suckling Romulus and Remus so that it can be patriotically identified as the Tiber.[134]

But these are relatively simple cases of movement toward a predetermined iconographic goal. Many works are too fragmentary, or too ambiguous, to receive this kind of completion; and it is those that demonstrate both the uncertainty and the flexibility of the material conditions in which antiquities found themselves. Let us take as examples three statues of a seated human figure, all with one leg forward and the other back and with drapery artistically arranged over the knees. One, made of porphyry, lacked hands, feet, and possibly part of its head when it was first recorded in the Sassi collection at the beginning of the sixteenth century (fig. 3.65). Another, which eventually decorated Ippolito d'Este's Roman villa, was made of marble but minus head, parts of both arms, and one foot when drawn by Marcantonio around 1516 (figs. 3.66, 3.67). The third, which includes part of a throne on which the figure is seated, consists in its modern form merely of the lower body, and it appeared in the same way to most of the early sixteenth-century viewers (fig. 3.68); but from the time of Heemskerck at least until Hubert Robert's visit to Rome in the 1750s, it was a nearly complete human figure with torso, head, and parts of both arms.

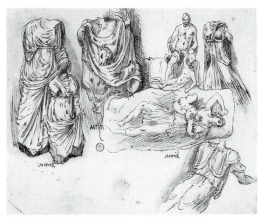

3.61. *Mars in Cuirass*, marble,
first century A.D.,
Museo Capitolino, Rome

3.62. Frans Floris workshop,
drawing after *Dead Amazon*,
1540s, Basel sketchbook,
fol. 19, Kunstmuseum, Basel

This last work, now referred to as the *Jupiter Enthroned* or the *Jupiter Ciampolini*, after the first collection in which it is recorded, is never given a name in the Renaissance.[135] But drawings of it appear frequently, both truncated and complete, as do quotations of it, whole, in paintings. It is tempting to conclude that the fuller form of the work represents a restoration that took place, say, in the 1520s, which then became canonical; but this is probably not the case, especially considering that drawings show the upper body itself to have been fragmentary. Perhaps it was not restored but joined to the broken half of a different statue, from which it was eventually separated again. These questions further complicate the unmistakable efforts at restoration that appear in drawings and paintings after the statue. The statue clearly helped inspire Raphael's Christs in the Perugia *Trinity* and in the Vatican *Disputa* (fig. 3.69), both likely to have been produced before the upper and lower halves were joined, while a similar influence can be seen in a Giulio Romano fresco of *Jupiter Enthroned*, which could only have been painted subsequent to that time (fig. 3.70).[136] These are more than pesky questions of chronology, since the differing forms of the Ciampolini statue help define whether Raphael is recording, elaborating, or proposing a completion for the work (as well as defining the complex nature of his influence on Giulio Romano). But perhaps the most telling attempt to see it as a whole comes from Aspertini's Wolfegg sketchbook (fig. 3.71), which almost certainly dates from the period when it consisted of a lower body only. There, in shadowy form (next to his gender-bending version of the *Icarius Relief*), appears a completed form of the statue, but as a woman holding a mirror out in her right hand.[137]

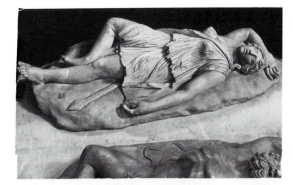

3.63. *Dead Amazon*, marble, Roman copy of second-century B.C. Pergamene original, Museo Nazionale, Naples

3.64. *River God Tiber*, marble, colossal Roman statue, Louvre, Paris

The seated and draped body of the Este statue was probably a nymph to begin with, cognate to some of the stooping and bending figures discussed above, but all projects for the work's completion construe her as a Venus.[138] Furthermore, though the surviving Marcantonio drawing of the fragmentary statue suggests no evidence of any accompanying figure, she is never left by herself when hypothetically or actually restored. It may, once again, be the influence of Raphael, whose designs for the *stufetta* of Cardinal Bibbiena amount to a little anthology after the antique.[139] In that composition (fig. 3.72), a naked Cupid is attached to the Venus's bended knee. Half a century later, once the statue is installed in the Este collection (fig. 3.73), it is restored in a somewhat different design but with two Cupids, which Cavalieri will engrave with labels as Eros and Anteros. The process moves steadily toward greater iconographic specification, though not necessarily greater accuracy. In its modern form, minus the two Cupids and with an entirely different completion of the upper body, the figure is once again fixed as a Venus, only now with a love arrow in her left hand and an apple in her right. Just to confuse matters further, judging from the torso and the musculature of the limbs, neither the original statue nor the Raimondi drawing of it in unrestored form need necessarily be female at all.

If this suspicion of mistaken gender seems too far-fetched, since no Renaissance viewer seems to have imagined the fragment to be male, let us consider a more explicit tangle of identities and sexualities, beginning with the third seated figure, the porphyry statue from the Sassi collection.[140] As the object now presents itself in the Museo Nazionale of Naples, its body has been elaborately completed in white marble,

3.65. *Apollo Draped and Seated*, porphyry and marble, colossal Roman statue, second century A.D., Museo Nazionale, Naples

3.66. *Venus Seated*, marble, Roman copy after Hellenistic type, Vatican Museums, Rome

contrasting dramatically with the original porphyry parts; in addition to the restored anatomy, it has been furnished with laurel wreath and large lyre, so as to be rendered unmistakably as an Apollo. That last iconographic touch provokes comparison with another even more widely diffused statue type, the *Apollo Citharoedos*, one example of which—in basalt rather than porphyry—was, as it happens, also in the Sassi collection (fig. 3.74).[141] (Indeed, the works appear together in drawings by both Heemskerck and Aspertini, without any sign that they were thought to have similar subject matter.) To complicate matters further, the *Citharoedos* was known in several versions that were fragmented in different ways. If we correlate the two Sassi statues and a widely viewed *Citharoedos* from the Della Valle collection, we have apparently three certifiable Apollos, each with a lyre. But these similarities are the product of restoration. On its discovery, the Della Valle statue was, judging from a beautiful Raphaelesque drawing at the Ashmolean (fig. 3.75), lacking head, arms, and right shoulder; but a letter written by Giovanni da Tolentino in 1490 refers to it as "Apollo Cythara modulans carmen,"[142] from which we must conclude that something of a musical instrument was visible, though not rendered in the drawing as we have it.[143] By the time both Heemskerck and Hollanda draw the Della Valle antiquities and Aldrovandi describes them, this work has been restored into a complete identity as Apollo, with a right arm circling its head and a fully formed lyre supporting its left hand.

The Sassi *Citharoedos*, retaining most of its right arm but nothing of its left shoulder, is, on the other hand, never known as Apollo in the Renaissance. Aldrovandi

3.67. Marcantonio Raimondi (attributed), drawing after *Venus Seated*, ca. 1516, Graphische Sammlung Albertina, Vienna

3.68. *Jupiter Enthroned*, marble, fragment from colossal Roman statue of Hellenistic type, Museo Nazionale, Naples

mentions a musical instrument, though it is more or less invisible in the drawings from the Heemskerck sketchbook, while Aspertini restores the left side but with no reference to any Apollonian attribute. Whether the lyre could be seen or not, it clearly made no iconographic impression, because this statue, though originally all but identical to the Della Valle *Apollo*, is always known as the *Hermaphrodite*. That name does more than signal an assignment to the wrong iconographic database. Clearly this fragmentary body, despite its unmistakable male genitals, was being read as female; only by reference to the double-sexed mythological figure could the incongruity be rationalized. That it awaited restoration until more modern times when it could be identified as Apollo may testify to the ultimately unconvincing quality of the identification or to a cultural bashfulness in reconstructing a genitally unorthodox figure. In this respect it would resemble the Pamphili standing *Hermaphrodite* discussed above, which, though missing many body parts, retained all the evidence of its two genders; it would await later restoration as a *Venus Pudica*, with additional drapery covering the problematic genital region.

From Apollo to Hermaphrodite, one more step beckons. The porphyry statue, for its part, sports modern white-marble restorations of head, hands, and feet that are a fuller replacement for a set of bronze prostheses that seem to have been added around the time the work passed from the Sassi to the Farnese.[144] Although it carries an outsized lyre in its present form, neither the rediscovered fragment nor the sixteenth-century completion was so equipped. Not only does the Renaissance never see

3.69. Raphael, detail of Christ from *Disputa*, fresco, 1508–9, Vatican Museums, Rome

3.70. Giulio Romano, *Jupiter Enthroned*, fresco, ca. 1545, Casa di Giulio Romano, Mantua

3.71. Amico Aspertını, drawing after *Jupiter Enthroned*, ca. 1500–03, Codex Wolfegg, fol. 46 (detail), Schloss Wolfegg

this statue as Apollo, but whenever the statue is described, sketched, restored, or used as a model for new works, it is invariably female. A veritable network of interrelated Roman imitations of this statue, for instance, begins around 1518 with Jacopo Sansovino's *Madonna* in San Agostino (fig. 3.76), as well as the Raphael figure of *Justice* in the Stanza della Segnatura; these exerted a retrospective influence on Aspertini's drawing of the ancient statue (fig. 3.77), which he "restored" by reference to the modern imitations; and the whole minitradition culminates in Heemskerck's canvas of *Saint Luke Painting the Virgin* at Rennes (fig. 3.78), dated around 1553, in which Mary is modeled after the Sansovino *Madonna*, itself based on the classical statue, while the entire scene is played out in front of the Sassi collection of antiquities, with both basalt and porphyry Apollos readily in evidence.[145] At no point in this declension of imitations is the statue ever male.

By the eighteenth century the one-time *Apollo* is *Cleopatra* or a *Muse*. Earlier, she is Vesta or, in the words of Aldrovandi, "un bellissimo simulacro di una Roma trionfante assisa." What really fascinates Aldrovandi is the mix of materials, the fact that the marble statue "has head, feet, and hands with a bit of the arms in bronze, which almost has the color of brass; but the rest is porphyry, all made with marvelous artistry."[146] He does not seem to know that he is looking at a restored work, though he proves capable of this perception in other cases. In effect, that *meraviglioso artificio* is the recompleted art object as it appears across time—partly ancient, partly modern, partly marble, partly bronze. And like other triumphs of ancient artfulness as perceived in the Renaissance, it defines the open-endedness of its identity by switching genders as it is reviewed and remade.

3.72. Giulio Romano, drawing after *Venus Seated*, ca. 1515, Windsor Castle, The Royal Collection

3.73. Restored version of *Venus Seated*, from Giovanni Battista Cavalieri, *Antiquarum statuarum urbis Romae*, ca. 1574

In effect, then, the changes wrought upon fragmentary sculptural objects represent attempts to fix their shape and their identity. Yet observed diachronically, with the antique original placed alongside Renaissance and post-Renaissance attempts to repair it, the process suggests just the opposite—that is, how persistently unfixable these works prove to be. At the same time, the historicist approach raises another kind of question, perhaps more fundamental than those concerning a statue's gender or its name: What are the forces that give a culture permission to restore these works at all, and what are the resistances to that permission? In truth, it is difficult to credit the early modern period with a consistent and definable set of answers to the question.[147] We operate here in a cacophony of possible mentalities, both theirs and ours. A disposition to alter fragmentary works clearly depends on the cultural value that they are assigned, and the whole present volume ought to have demonstrated just how ambiguous that can be. From the Middle Ages onward, the remains of antiquity can be viewed as the most fungible of building blocks, subject to reconfigurations that ignore their original value; but they are also by turns feared, respected, scorned, and admired as traces of eclipsed divinity and lost artistic skill. Works like the colossal bronze head and hand, for instance, which receive the various attentions of Gregory the Great, medieval travelers, and humanists and artists who witness their move in 1471 from the Lateran to the Capitol, are never restored—though what combination of Christian distaste, artistic bashfulness, and technological impossibility underlies this circumstance we cannot say. Alternatively, the case of the *Laocoön*, which exemplifies the High Renaissance attitude on these matters, is, as we have seen, quite conflicted:

3.74. *Apollo Citharoedos*, marble, Roman copy after Hellenistic type, from Sassi Collection, Museo Nazionale, Naples

3.75. School of Raphael,
drawing after *Apollo Citharoedos,*
early sixteenth century,
Ashmolean Museum,
Oxford

3.76. Jacopo Sansovino,
Madonna and Child
("Madonna del Parto"),
marble, 1518–21,
San Agostino, Rome

3.77. Amico Aspertini,
drawing after *Apollo Draped
and Seated,* 1530s, London
sketchbook, I, fol. 41,
British Museum, London

this work, highly valued in its own historical and aesthetic terms, is at various times respectfully untouched, expertly completed, and audaciously mutilated.

Meanwhile we must investigate our own predispositions on this subject. In our times, when Renaissance art rarely hogs the headlines, one of the most persistent cultural news stories has been the cleaning of the Sistine Chapel frescoes.[148] At the center of this public debate was the question whether modern knowledge—both historical and technological—could be allowed to impinge physically upon revered artworks of the past. That in turn depends on asking whether the work of art is more real in its original form or in the form in which we are accustomed to seeing it. The terms are quite similar to arguments about restoration at any time, and no simple resolution could be reached. The golden age of restoring antiquities, from the late seventeenth to the early nineteenth century, depended on a belief that progress in classical studies, combined with what we would call a neoclassical aesthetic, ought to express itself in rendering ancient objects precisely as they were when they were made. This mentality was succeeded by a positivism that could simultaneously believe in the absolute possibility of arriving at the original form of these works and also refuse to lay a finger on them. Only with the next turning of the episteme has it been possible to realize how inevitably paradoxical all these attitudes are; to appreciate, in other words, the differing privileges of works that remain in their original pristine condition, of works that have a long and familiar history in some altered state, and of works that are technologically returned to some earlier condition that we can only guess at.

3.78. Marten van Heemskerck, *Saint Luke Painting the Virgin*, oil on panel, ca. 1560, Musée des Beaux-Arts, Rennes

All of which is to say that Renaissance restoration is something of a minefield. Rather than defining a set of contemporary attitudes toward this activity, it is better to ask what signs there are of any cultural conversation on this topic. In explicit terms there is very little. Individual episodes, like those surrounding the *Laocoön* or the various projects of Giovanni Montorsoli, who became a kind of Belvedere restorer-in-chief, excite little general discussion of principles;[149] and moments when such artists as Donatello, Tullio Lombardo, Bandinelli, or Cellini do work of this kind either pass without any theorizing or else form part of a local polemic that cannot be generalized. The clearest statement of all, which turns out to be pro-restoration, appears in Vasari's life of Lorenzetto, the same artist who rendered the fragmentary *Venus of Capua* as a Madonna for Raphael's tomb. Vasari is speaking of Lorenzetto's architectural work for the Della Valle family, which included a great many restorations of antique fragments:

> Higher up, below some large niches, he made another frieze with fragments of ancient works, and above this, in those niches, he placed some statues, likewise ancient and of marble, which, although they were not entire—some being without the head, some without arms, others without legs, and every one, in short, with something missing—nevertheless he arranged to the best advantage having caused all that was lacking to be restored by good sculptors. This was the reason that other lords have since done the same thing and have restored many ancient works; as for example, Cardinals Cesis, Ferrara, and

Farnese, and, in a word, all Rome. And, in truth, antiquities restored in this way have more grace than those mutilated trunks, members without heads, or figures in any other way maimed and defective.[150]

Like many of Vasari's judgments, this cannot be taken precisely at face value. It is true, judging from a very detailed engraving after Heemskerck, that the niche sculptures in the upper story of the Della Valle garden are complete. It is less clear from visual or textual evidence that the collections Vasari enumerates in this passage are largely devoted to restored works. And it is very much to be doubted that "tutta Roma" was gripped in a mania of restoration. On the other hand, Vasari is surely describing an authentic cultural predisposition and offering a sincere opinion about it. In fact, he is operating in the familiar mode of epideictic rhetoric, where he praises a thing for its own particular excellence. The excellence in question here is that of princely decoration, the universe of *grazia* and *maniera*, in which broken objects would be read as too severe, too learned, and too demanding upon the viewer.

But there are alternative excellences, even for Vasari himself. The opposing argument will not have so direct or so ringing an endorsement at the time, but its influence will be deeper and longer lasting. To understand this, we must turn to those antiquities that were never restored, and to one in particular that was never restored *on purpose*. The *Torso Belvedere* (fig. 3.79), which consists of a massive body segment from shoulder to knee dramatically rotated at the waist, will be one of those canonical works that define antiquity for the modern world. Although it was obviously in a far more fragmentary condition than its famous neighbors, the *Laocoön* and the *Apollo Belvedere*, alone of the three it was never subject to any restorer's hand. To understand this circumstance, along with its enduringly untouchable status as a fragment, is to see into a world far different from that of Lorenzetto's Della Valle decor. But how does this particular fragment acquire such unique status? To a modern viewer that may appear self-evident. We cannot fail to see the *Torso* as a magnificent piece of heroic art: tensive, muscular, a kind of emblem for all the tragic power that the Greek aesthetic could claim for itself. It is almost too obvious to point out that the work attains this kind of power not *despite* but *because of* its fragmentary condition.

On this subject Winckelmann's judgment remains eloquent and persuasive:

> It seems inconceivable that one could depict the power of thinking in any other part [of the body] than the head; yet witness here how the hand of a creating master has the capacity to render material into spirit. I have the sensation as though the statue's back, bent over by lofty acts of contemplation, manages to create for me the image of a head which is busied with happy recollection of its extraordinary deeds. And just as this head, so full of majesty and wisdom, rises before my eyes, so the other missing limbs start to form themselves in my thoughts. Out of the present condition of the work a new creation assembles itself, producing, as it were, a sudden complete restoration.[151]

3.79. *Torso Belvedere*, first-century B.C. marble signed by Apollonios, son of Nestor, Vatican Museums, Rome

3.80. Amico Aspertini, drawing after *Torso Belvedere*, ca. 1500–03, from Codex Wolfegg, fol. 42, Schloss Wolfegg

This is a work, then, which would be a sacrilege to restore in marble, because it achieves its magic by enabling viewers to restore it in their imaginations. It is all but impossible to disagree with this assessment; the question is how to situate it historically. Shall one say, as Winckelmann implies, that this is a universal and transhistorical description of the *Torso*; or shall we declare it to be based on a uniquely Romantic and post-Romantic aesthetic of which the Renaissance could not have the slightest inkling? Does this particular marble fragment ineluctably declare itself a masterpiece; or is it a mere blank slate overwritten by a particular *Rezeptionsgeschichte*?

The truth is more complicated than any one of these possibilities, as the Renaissance career of the *Torso Belvedere* will make clear.[152] The work certainly makes no enormous impact upon its discovery. We happen to be able to identify it above ground as early as the 1430s not because it is so preeminent an art object but because it contains an inscription (of which more below) that will be recorded by an epigrapher. At this point the statue is to be found on the Quirinal, probably in the possession of the Colonna family. But it receives little or no attention for the first seventy years of its reappearance. It does not even make its way to the Vatican during the formative period of the papal collection, but only in the 1530s, well after it has gained its own fame. The *Laocoön* took two months from unearthing to Belvedere canonization; the *Torso* took a hundred years.

Nor does the fragmentary condition of the work have any very lively or widely publicized relation to hypothetical narratives, such as we have seen with a number of statues in this chapter. For those in the Renaissance who talk about the statue in these

3.81. Marten van Heemskerck, two views
of *Torso Belvedere*, ca. 1532–36, sketchbook,
I.63, I.73, Staatliche Museen, Berlin

terms, it is, without much dispute or discussion, Hercules *tout court*. He is, after all, of heroic proportions, and he sits on an animal skin that partly covers what there is of his right leg. Only in the seventeenth and eighteenth centuries will viewers attempt to narratize the subject more dynamically by locating Hercules at some particular moment in his saga, while much more recently the subject been moved elsewhere, with the pelt proving to belong to a panther rather than to a lion and with missing pieces being ascribed to other suffering figures like Philoctetes and Marsyas. But even once the *Torso* has become a famous Renaissance masterpiece, iconography is generally not at the center of conversation about it; in fact, it will more often be referred to by its shape than by its name.

The visual record of the *Torso*'s early years may be seen in a leaf from Amico Aspertini's Wolfegg Sketchbook (fig. 3.80). Produced in the very first years of the sixteenth century, these drawings generally take narrative relief sculptures and render them complete, while removing the individual figures sufficiently from their backgrounds so that the images appear almost as living narratives rather than as sketches after the antique.[153] All missing parts of the original sculptures are restored in the drawings, which further maintains the illusion of life. The *Torso Belvedere* appears at the center of a single half sheet that breaks all these rules, displaying some six torsos, four busts, one entire figure, and miscellaneous other fragmentary bits. None of it is narrative; all is three-dimensional and obviously sculpture rather than life. At this moment, then, at least for an artist who will continue to be more interested in complete works than in broken pieces, the *Torso* is being consigned to a ghetto of fragments, though given preeminent position.

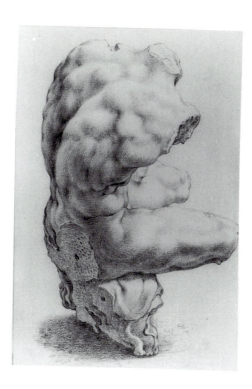

3.82. Hendrik Goltzius, drawing after *Torso Belvedere*, ca. 1590, Teylers Museum, Haarlem

From preeminent, the *Torso* moves toward unique, becoming one of the favorite subjects for careful, finished artistic rendering.[154] Much will be made of its musculature, which often summons up elaborate techniques of draftsmanship not yet available to Aspertini. Like other 360-degree pieces of sculpture, it will often be drawn from varying perspectives, sometimes on the same sheet. Heemskerck (fig. 3.81), who can always be counted on for dramatic points of view, renders it once seated in the normal position (though without base) and once lying on its back with the forelegs up in the air and staged next to a fragmentary obelisk, which may serve to imply enormous size. What characterizes all of these remarkable drawings, from an Umbrian sketchbook leaf dated around 1500 to the time of Goltzius in the seventeenth century (fig. 3.82), is an unfailing fascination with its fragmentariness. No one sketching the *Torso* ever seems to shy away from its gaping neck or the rough edges where the arms and lower legs ought to be or the strange flat edge of the buttock.[155]

This view of the *Torso* seems to me confirmed rather than challenged by a curious set of early sixteenth-century images in which it is quoted. A group portrait of the artist Arrigo Licinio's family (fig. 3.83), painted by his brother in the 1520s, places a marble miniature of the *Torso* in the hands of the eldest son, while the father looks on approvingly from the other side of the canvas. The boy is staged in an exaggeratedly demonstrative posture holding the piece of sculpture so that it stands out from the nine live portraits. Oddly, the miniature statue is *partly* restored—that is, it is given a complete right leg and foot while its fragmentariness is rendered accurately in every other way. As it happens, the earlier sixteenth century sees a small industry of what

3.83. Bernardo Licinio, family portrait with *Torso Belvedere*, oil on wood, 1524, Galleria Borghese, Rome

one would take to be documentary versions of the *Torso*—not quotations or completions—that are nevertheless semirestored, including bronze miniatures representing the work precisely as in the Licinio painting and a somewhat earlier engraving by Giovanni Antonio da Brescia presenting the statue as complete from the waist down (fig. 3.84).[156] These *jeux d'esprit* depict a *Torso* that is more strangely fragmented than the real one; they speak, in other words, not to the restorability of the work but to its iconic—and mutable—status as broken. To insert this anomalous creation so stagily into the family portrait is to use it as an icon for the boy's future as an artist. At some point in the first twenty years of the century, the *Torso* that is not yet *Belvedere* has become the special property of artists, and its fragmentary labile status appears as its primary qualification for this role.

It is, to be sure, not easy to define historical cause and effect in these events, to point to the precise origins of an association between artist and fragment or to demonstrate why this particular torso should link them. We can adduce one—admittedly rather equivocal—physical detail, a fact that is (so far as I know) unique among all the rediscovered antiquities: the artist's signature. Prominently displayed on the front of the base are the words

ΑΠΟΛΛΩΝΙΟΣ ΝΕΣΤΟΡΟΣ ΑΘΗΝΑΙΟΣ ΕΠΟΙΕΙ
Apollonios of Athens, son of Nestor, made [this work]

Some statues, like the *Venus Felix*, had original inscriptions that were clearly not the

3.84. Giovanni Antonio da Brescia, engraving after *Torso Belvedere*, ca. 1515, British Museum, London

makers' names; others, like the *Laocoön*, could be attributed by reference to Pliny. The *Horse-Tamers*, it will be remembered, came with labels referring to Phidias and Praxiteles, but even if one believed the attribution, it was in the mode of third-person documentation rather than of authorial self-proclamation. In the case of the *Torso*, on the other hand, there is the magic verb ποιεὶυ that signifies artistic creation. Having said all that, one must report that there is little evidence of a lively conversation arising out of this remarkable fact. The words do get recorded in the Renaissance—indeed we are aware of the *Torso*'s first appearance above ground because Ciriaco d'Ancona records the inscription, along with an aside concerning the statue ("singularissima figura, quae dicitur Herculis" [a most singular figure, said to be Hercules]).[157] The simple Greek formula will continue to be transcribed, and some drawings after the *Torso* will include it on the base, though most do not.[158] Part of the problem is doubtless that "Apollonios of Athens, son of Nestor" appears nowhere else in the entire ancient corpus of art objects and texts; only Doidalsas is less traceable. Consequently, the attribution could not be placed on any Plinian historical grid—except perhaps to create stupefaction in a viewer who reasoned that if this magnificent work was done by a completely unknown artist, then the true masterpieces of Phidias and Lysippus must have been beyond imagining.[159] At all events, the signature remains a tantalizing detail: given its uniqueness and given the particularly artist-centered destiny of the work, it is difficult to dismiss its importance; on the other hand, there is little we can prove about it.

One other datum pointing toward the canonization of the *Torso*, perhaps no more definitive than the signature, is its apparent provenance after the dissolution of

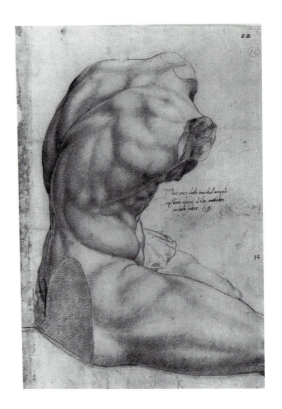

3.85. Drawing after *Torso Belvedere*, red chalk, mid-sixteenth century, Cambridge sketchbook, fol. 22, Trinity College, Cambridge

the Colonna collection but well before its entry into the Belvedere. There are a number of testimonies to the fact that around 1500 the statue belonged to the sculptor Andrea Bregno, who had assembled a notable collection of antiquities.[160] Although the ownership of antiquities by artists goes back at least to the time of Ghiberti, it is worth pointing out that all the great Roman collections of important works during the early sixteenth century are in the hands of the pope or the rich princely families and not in the hands of even the most famous and successful artists. Bregno's stewardship of the piece—necessarily brief, since he died in 1503—may have contributed to its status as an object of special interest to artists, in a theme that goes back to Pliny's tablet of fine lines contributed by Apelles and Protogenes. It is likely that Aspertini got to see the statue through personal connections to his fellow artist; and it is certainly the case that he sketched other works in Bregno's collection. The Umbrian sketch mentioned earlier labels the *Torso* as "de m Andrea da Milano." Yet more revealing, however, is the first verbal reference to the fragment since the time of Ciriacus, which comes from Prospettivo Milanese, who visited Rome in 1500:

> Poscia in casa dun certo mastrandrea
> ve un nudo corpo senza braze collo
> che mai visto non ho miglior diprea [= di pietra].[161]

Then in the house of a certain Master Andrea there is a nude torso without arms or neck the equal of which I have never seen in stone.

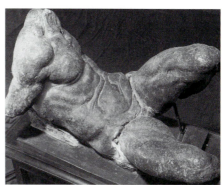

3.86. Michelangelo,
Ignudo over Jeremiah,
fresco, 1511–12,
Sistine Chapel, Rome

3.87. Michelangelo,
model for *River God*,
wax, ca. 1524–26,
Accademia, Florence

It must be remembered that the author of these lines, a self-proclaimed associate of Bramante and Da Vinci, was very much in touch with artistic thinking at this particular fin de siècle, even if he betrays considerable naïveté and a limited imagination. In the whole of his poetic catalogue, there are many formulas of praise like that extended to the *Torso*, but there is very little reference to the fragmentation of the works he admiringly describes. Even the radically effaced *Pasquino* passes as a Hercules and Antaeus without comment on its condition. Only here does he declare with such conviction that a work is fragmentary and magnificent at once.[162] That will become the key to the great value placed on the *Torso*, as well as to its success at resisting the restorer's hand.

In the long run, however, neither Andrea Bregno nor the Milanese perspectivist with the great Quattrocento artists behind him are sufficient to endow the *Torso* with this status. Perhaps the clearest message on this subject is to be found in a leaf from the Trinity College Cambridge Sketchbook, executed around 1550 (fig. 3.85), where a beautiful drawing of the *Torso*, the base all but erased, the musculature and the broken parts of right shoulder and buttock lovingly rendered, is captioned "This pees doth michelangel exstem above all the anttickes in belle fidere."[163] The canonization of the *Torso Belvedere*—as masterpiece, as representing art itself, as iconic of a particular aesthetic vision of the human body, indeed as defining the category "torso" as fundamental to the exercise of visual representation—is unimaginable without the career of Michelangelo. And perhaps vice versa.

One way to tell this story is to follow the *Torso* as it reveals its influence

3.88. Michelangelo, *Victory*, marble, ca. 1527–30, Palazzo Vecchio, Florence

throughout the course of the artist's career. The beginnings can be dated quite precisely to the later stages of the Sistine Ceiling frescoes. The right-side *Ignudo* above the Prophet Jeremiah (fig. 3.86) is a relatively exact completion of the fragmentary Belvedere body, even to the extent that the necessary additions below the knees are rendered somewhat awkwardly and in shadow. The *Torso* then turns up as a basis for sculptural work in the Medici tombs, revealing its strongest influence on the recumbent *Day*, and perhaps an even clearer connection to the projected River Gods, which we know only from a wax model that exhibits the *Torso*'s distinctive turn at the waist as well as a similar state of fragmentation (fig. 3.87). From a still later period, the *Victory* in the Palazzo Vecchio (fig. 3.88) demonstrates some affinities in its torsion and its musculature, particularly when seen in the light of a British Museum drawing (fig. 3.89) that stands midway between the Belvedere work and Michelangelo's; it is, once again, truncated in a similar way. Still later the influence of the *Torso* has been widely noticed in at least two prominent figures of the *Last Judgment*, the pivotal judging Christ (fig. 3.90) and the tormented Bartholomew (fig. 3.91) holding his own skin.

This is, of course, a highly selective list; and that process of selection may begin to reveal the limitations of studying this influence merely by tallying up works with the most precise physical similarities. Which of the ignudi—particularly those from the second phase of the Sistine painting—do *not* appear to be influenced by the *Torso* (see fig. 1.10)? All of them are prominently muscular and sharply turned at the waist. Indeed the whole rather curious conception of figures who can exhibit titanic

power while sitting down must owe either its origins or its elaborations to the Belvedere fragment. Subsets of these physical traits and postures show themselves passim in Michelangelo's work, whether in two or three dimensions, from the *Battle of Cascina* (several years prior to the Sistine Ceiling) to the various *Slaves* and *Prisoners* of the Julius II projects to the Pauline Chapel frescoes and the Florentine *Pietà*. Which is not to say that the *Torso Belvedere* is the key and unifying source for Michelangelo's genius. We must rather opt for a more complex account of imitation and invention: certain forms and structures of the human body carry imaginative power for the artist, and these qualities—aesthetic, formalistic, affective—are reified and enforced by their appearance in antiquities. Nor does one antiquity explain everything by itself, as we saw in Chapter 1. Virtually all the works listed here need to be tallied up again under the influence of the *Laocoön*. In truth, the archetypal Renaissance or Michelangelo torso is an amalgam of the two celebrated Belvedere pieces.

There is another way to tell the story about Michelangelo and the *Torso*, however. The Cambridge sketchbook drawing, with its caption citing Michelangelo's predilection, speaks less about the influence of the work on the artist than about the *belief* in that influence. The two possibilities do not necessarily contradict—nor, for that matter, confirm—each other. But it is worth noting that the data linking Michelangelo to the Belvedere fragment are for the most part a series of widely repeated, and embellished, anecdotes. One can take this body of material to mean that the link is historically dubious—von Salis, for instance, persuasively argues that

3.90. Michelangelo,
Christ from the *Last Judgment*,
fresco, 1534–41,
Sistine Chapel, Rome

Donatello had already furnished a *Torso*-like model for the later sculptor avant la let-tre[164]—or one may note that, whatever the true origins of Michelangelo's inspiration, his contemporaries loved to imagine him in close proximity to the work.

The volume of these imaginings, beginning around the middle of the century, is considerable. Contemporary with the Cambridge sketchbook is Aldrovandi's com-ment that "E stato questo busto singularmente lodato da Michel' Angelo,"[165] but this needs to be placed in the context of a volume that seems to use Michelangelo as a seal of approval almost promiscuously, for example, regarding the *Juno Cesi* (122), the Capitoline *Lion Attacking a Horse* (270), a miniature *Laocoön* (267), and an unidentifiable bust in the Santacroce collection (239). The tradition gathers steam in the second half of the century, with Lomazzo citing the *Torso* as paradigm for the limits of Michelangelo's ability to surpass the ancients: "Michelangelo . . . was never able to add anything to the beauty of the Torso of Hercules by Apollonios of Athens, which is located in the Belvedere in Rome, and which he unceasingly pursued. In the same way, Daniele da Volterra, Perino del Vaga and others who pursued the *maniera* of the same Michelangelo, could never equal him."[166] In the transitive relations from the *Torso* to Michelangelo and from Michelangelo to his imitators, Lomazzo outlines a whole the-ory of influence, which maps out a kind of Vasarian history of art. From that point onward, there are stories in which Michelangelo declares the *Torso* his chief teacher, in which he is discovered kneeling before it, in which he asserts that "questa è l'opera d'un uomo che ha saputo più della natura" ("this is the work of a man who knew more than nature"), and in which he produces a beautiful wax model after it.[167]

3.91. Michelangelo,
Saint Bartholomew
from the *Last Judgment*,
fresco, 1534–41,
Sistine Chapel, Rome

If these stories of Michelangelo's attachment to the *Torso* seem to belong to subsequent periods of art history and mythmaking, it is nevertheless true that much of the contemporary lore surrounding the artist turns on closely related issues. In one of the celebrated anecdotes from Michelangelo's youth, he sculpts a perfect replica of an antique faun's head in order to please Lorenzo de' Medici and is instructed by the Magnifico that old people never retain all their teeth, whereupon the boy extracts one of the teeth and bores a hole in the gum. In an equally famous story from the artist's adolescence, he produces a sleeping Cupid and is advised that it will fetch a higher price if it is believed to be an antique; in response, he defaces it in such a way that it seems to have been buried in the ground.[168] Not only do these stories pay Michelangelo the compliment of identifying him with the greatness of the ancients, but, more specifically, they achieve this identification by having him recast his own works in the mutilated form that signals antiquity. In effect, both the Faun and the Cupid are better when they are broken.

These mythic terms take on a curious sort of reality with yet another work of the artist's youth—the only one of these that still exists—the *Bacchus* (fig. 3.92), which he produced around 1496 for Cardinal Raffaele Riario. This is a work that seems to have been both imagined and received as a faux antiquity, attempting not simply to pass as an ancient statue but rather to tease the viewer with uncertainty as to whether it was ancient or modern. Michelangelo's protégé Francisco de Hollanda will later recount his own cleverness at guessing that the apparently classical statue was in fact contemporary; his interlocutors will inform him that "it was a work that Michelangelo had completed a long time ago for the purpose of fooling the Romans and the pope

3.92. Michelangelo, *Bacchus*, marble, 1496–97, Bargello, Florence

3.93. Marten van Heemskerck, Galli Garden, ca. 1532–36, sketchbook, I.72, Staatliche Museen, Berlin

with its antique style." And Aldrovandi, who includes the work in his catalogue of ancient sculpture in Roman collections, describes it at some length before revealing that it is "opera moderna."[169] In fact, its placement in these collections clearly contributes to the is-it-or-isn't-it? game. Cardinal Riario was an ambitious collector of ancient sculpture, who seems to have either wished to mix imitation antiquities with the real ones or else to have been the victim of false claims. (He is the purchaser, according to one version of the story, of Michelangelo's faux Sleeping Cupid.) Subsequently, when the *Bacchus* passes to the larger collection of the Galli family nearby, it is even more seamlessly inserted in a context of real antiquities.

Only one thing is lacking in the *Bacchus* to complete the impersonation, and this is provided in the 1530s, when the statue is represented with its right hand broken off. Thus in Heemskerck's drawing of the Galli collection (fig. 3.93) it appears as a starring fragment in the foreground while real antiquities in yet more mutilated condition surround it. It is difficult to determine the when and why of this break. There is no sign that the work was unfinished or mutilated when it was first made—Condivi describes the hand and cup in detail—nor do we have a record of the circumstances under which it was broken and subsequently reattached. After 1550 it is never again represented as broken. Whatever these events may have been, by the middle of the century the statue has been assimilated into legends of antiquity and fragmentation:

the ever-informative Cambridge sketchbook (fig. 3.94) captions it "Scoltur de Michelangeli the which was buried in the grownd and fond for antick," conflating this work with the falsely buried Sleeping Cupid but also identifying it with all the real antiquities that were mutilated owing to their sojourn underground.[170]

All these stories of modern works that can be "antiqued" by being mutilated—which may be compared with the equally whimsical possibility of *half*-restoring the *Torso*—are less about the assigning of fixed values to fragmentariness, wholeness, and restoration than they are about the potential openness of the categories. After all, Michelangelo, whose authority has always been cited as the reason why the *Torso* remained untouched, provided a similar legendary chartering function for the restoration of antiquities. We have already followed what may have been his aggressive involvement in the completions of the *Laocoön*.[171] We know for a fact that he sponsored Giovannangelo Montorsoli for work of restoration on the *Apollo Belvedere* and the *Hercules-Commodus* as well as the *Laocoön*. He was certainly engaged in the installation of both Capitoline and Belvedere antiquities; and in some cases, especially the *Tiber-Tigris* and possibly the *Farnese Bull*, there is some chance that he provided replacement parts for the statues themselves. Countless other restorations were ascribed to him, particularly in the seventeenth and eighteenth centuries; they include works like the Capitoline *Dying Gladiator* and various Uffizi favorites including a *Hermaphrodite*, a *Dancing Faun*, and a *Venus Pudica*, all of which were first discovered many decades after his death.[172]

These attributions may be mere tourist hype. But there is a considerable conversation beginning within Michelangelo's lifetime that focuses on the restorations that he is said to have undertaken, or at least approved of. Already in the *Poetics* of Lodovico Castelvetro, Michelangelo's supposed work on the *Tigris* becomes a topos for the paragone between the ancient and the modern, and it will continue to be repeated as an argument for the superiority of the ancients. Contrariwise, in another often retailed anecdote, Guglielmo della Porta (also promoted for the job by Michelangelo) has provided new marble legs for the *Hercules Farnese*; when the originals are rediscovered, Michelangelo is said to offer the opinion that the restorations are so masterful that they ought not to be removed, in order to show that "le opere della scultura moderna potevano stare al paragone de' lavori antichi" ("the works of modern sculpture can stand on a par with the ancients").[173] The formula is precisely that which Vasari introduces as the moral of the story about the Sleeping Cupid as a pretended antiquity: "Modern works, if only they be excellent, are as good as the ancient."[174]

If Michelangelo is the legendary figure who authorizes both the restoration of ancient fragments and the refusal to restore, if the modern and complete *Bacchus*, which will after all turn out to be one of the few statues Michelangelo finishes, can be rendered as a fragment while the proverbially fragmentary *Torso* can be represented as partially restored, that is because the culture in which these works find themselves is radically undecided about the relative merits of ancient and modern, of fragmentary and complete, and because it is sentenced to remain on the cusp rather than to decide.

3.94. Drawing after Michelangelo *Bacchus*, red chalk, mid-sixteenth century, Cambridge sketchbook, fol. 14, Trinity College, Cambridge

Each fragment may be completed, imagined as completed, recombined, or left alone. Every modern work that is under the influence of antiquity may be imaginatively (and, once in a while, literally) taken apart and returned to the fragmentary condition of the art objects that inspired it. Every one of these exercises is implicitly a *querelle des anciens et des modernes*, but the continuing appeal of all this play arises from the fact that the battle can never be definitively won or lost.

I conclude with three interrelated propositions, all of which speak to the status of the fragment. First, the Renaissance found beauty in ruins; that is, individuals responded to vistas of ancient remains as satisfying in themselves. Second, fragmentary works like the *Torso Belvedere* were allowed to remain as such not by inadvertence or uncertainty or disagreement in respect to how they might be restored but because they were understood as beautiful (perhaps *more* beautiful) in their effaced condition.

Third, Michelangelo's celebrated habit of abandoning, not finishing, or even mutilating his sculptures formed a real part of his aesthetic, whether consciously or otherwise, and was not a biographical happenstance later elevated into a principle of art.

These are, needless to say, highly controversial notions. They all smack of romanticism, in both the psychological and chronological sense: that is, they seem to take for granted a sort of transhistorical emotional response that ignores the categorical rigors we ascribe to the early modern worldview. And there is no shortage of scholarly arguments, well informed and historically contextualized, that would declare such ideas impossible in the Renaissance mind.[175] I am hesitant in principle to declare ideas impossible in any given period (there is such a thing as *too much* historicism), and in any event, there are signs in regard to all three of these propositions that they could well have been entertained in the period of the rediscovery of ancient sculpture. As early as Petrarch's famous strolls through Rome or Pius II's search for a region of peaceful contemplation amid the ruins of Hadrian's Villa, it was possible to look upon a landscape or cityscape of ruins not merely as an absence but as something that could be imaginatively filled up in ways that were and were not simple replications of what used to be there.[176] And from at least the fifteenth century onward, many artists, whether their primary purpose was to sketch ancient objects or to set their religious subjects in classical surroundings, took evident pleasure in representing an antiquity that was as beautiful for its decay as for its absent grandeur. As for the right of sculptural fragments to remain unrestored, I leave this whole chapter as evidence for the possibility. It is not merely a question of the *Torso Belvedere* remaining untouched; rather, all the possibilities of modern artists and viewers in regard to fragments—whether the works were literally restored, imagined as restored, or quoted complete in new art works—result in a validation of the fragment, whether contemporary art theory explicitly articulates that value or not.

The third of my propositions, having to do with Michelangelo and the so-called *non finito*, probably opens the most frightening Pandora's box of all.[177] It is a fact that Michelangelo finished almost none of his sculptural projects after the *David* in 1504 and also that he left many individual statues—those involved in the Medici and Julius tombs—at the very least unpolished and at the most barely roughed out. He was not alone in having this kind of career. As the famous example of Leonardo and the somewhat less famous example of Baccio Bandinelli will attest, unfulfilled artistic promises may have been all but unavoidable given a new combination of circumstances in the Renaissance, including the operations of patronage and commissions, the arrangements of labor in the studio, and the value placed on the solitary creative genius. Still, Michelangelo stands out even in his own time for his persistence in not finishing things and (perhaps this is more to the point) for the value that was placed on them even when unfinished.

Precisely what kind of value, or where it came from, is not easy to say. If we look at the radically incomplete *Slaves* or *Prisoners* and imagine that an exercise of the artist's intentionality is sending these into the world as inchoate works of genius, we are clearly stepping outside sixteenth-century modes of thought. But if we take as an example Vasari's remarks about the Medici Madonna (which is not nearly so "unfinished" as the *Slaves* or *Prisoners*) that "ancora che non siano finite le parti sue, si conosce nell'essere rimasta abozzata e gradinata, nella imperfezione della bozza, la perfezione dell'opera" ("although the figure is not equal in every part, and it was left rough and showing the marks of the gradine, yet with all its imperfections there may be recognized in it the full perfection of the work"), we begin to see that there exists already a philosophy of artistic creation—let's place it under the rubric Platonic— which might value the abstract inspiration underlying a work as one sort of perfection and the completeness of its surface polish as a different, even lesser, perfection.[178] Nor can it be argued that this is a merely Vasarian idea irrelevant to Michelangelo, since echoes of such notions are to be found throughout in the artist's poetry and since Vasari might be said to have no ideas that were not generated from his experience of Michelangelo as person and artist.[179] Suffice it to say that a variety of practices within and around the career of Michelangelo—unfinished works, great attention paid both by artist and connoisseur to even the most casual sketches, a celebrated mania of perfectionism, a well-documented tendency to destroy work that is unsatisfying—all suggest that the non finito is not a mere romantic anachronism but a real expression of early modern artistic culture.

But my real purpose here is not to settle any of these difficult questions; it is rather to observe how closely they are related to one another. To place broken sculpture at the center of Renaissance culture is to declare that it carried a great value within itself, a value that depended on—but was not limited to—its reference to some past or future condition in which it was *not* a fragment. If the *Torso Belvedere* is the paradigm of ancient sculpture and Michelangelo is the tragic hero of the fragment, that is because he based his career in part on what could be imagined and not seen or because he appeared so often to be unable to produce statues more complete than the fragments that inspired him. Yet neither the landscapes full of ruins nor the statues with missing parts nor the unfinished works of Michelangelo are really deficient at all. Rather we should say that they are *open*; in other words, they admit the historical imagination as a genuinely collaborative force. It is therefore no coincidence that this topic should raise questions concerning historicism. After all, the ancient fragment that is open to completion after fifteen hundred years manages by its very nature both to exemplify and to challenge the otherness of the past. It is not surprising that the problems it raises might render us uncertain whether we *can* look at these works through our own eyes or whether we are sentenced as well to look at them through the eyes of others—of Vasari, of Winckelmann, or, for that matter, of Rodin.

4.1. *Pasquino*, Hellenistic marble, second century B.C., Piazza del Pasquino, Rome

CHAPTER 4

RECONSTRUCTIONS

The whole phenomenon of classical survival—disjointed, challenging to read, open, seeming to solicit modern response—makes it difficult to separate fragmentation from reconstruction. Even if we leave aside the literal restoration of broken statues, every aspect of fragmentariness contains within it, at least implicitly, a positive response. The whole project of making art in response to broken bodies—whether those bodies are mutilated statues or guillotined persons—is, in however limited a way, an activity of reconstruction. The same can be said for a wide range of more specific Renaissance projects: for instance, collecting and displaying whole gardens full of fragments, even when no individual restoration takes place; imagining ancient Rome from mutilated residues; naming the persons represented in uncaptioned statues and arguing about a variety of names; making narrative or physiological sense out of unorthodox body positions and taking up the artistic challenge of repeating or rationalizing them; reusing attractive but mysterious figures as decorative motifs in larger narrative works; being enabled to consider the gender of a represented figure as subject to philological or artistic redefinition; understanding literal drapery or the hermeneutic veil as provoking rather than foreclosing interpretation. All of these are reconstructions. Even *not* reconstructing antiquities is an activity of reconstruction: it merely transfers the arena of possibilities from the material realm to the imagination.

One way to avoid the repetitiveness of simply transposing the last chapter from minor to major would be to move away from the antiquities per se and to provide a history of Renaissance art that was created in response to the remains of antiquity. That is not exactly what follows in the remaining pages of this book, though elements of it are woven in everywhere. For one thing, that history has been written before, and with great authority. In addition, as will become increasingly clear, I am troubled by what is sometimes tendentiously referred to as the "triumphalist" rhetoric of such accounts.[1] That there were great works and ancient influences seems beyond dispute; still, when the connection between these circumstances is taken for granted, there is not enough sense of the process of mediations that made it all possible. In this chapter I shall attempt to fill in that space from the perspective of the antiquities themselves—that is, by telling the story of three objects, each notably fragmentary and, more to the point, each the basis for a distinctive Renaissance activity of cultural, intellectual, and aesthetic recuperation.

Rather than locating the argument's dividing line with fragmentation on one side and reconstruction on the other, it may be better to distinguish between the *material* and the *discursive*. The chapter on fragments, though it ranged over many kinds of significant absences in the ancient sculptural objects that emerged in the Renaissance, focused the problem on that which was missing—as well as on the means for recuperating these absences. Not only does the current chapter slide from absence to presence; it also shifts from a material account to an investigation of the ways early moderns reconstructed these objects as places of discourse. Or, put in plainer language, how these objects became occasions to tell verbal stories that were new and original but at the same time could be seen as fulfillments of a history that began in the hallowed time when the ancient art was made. The pieces of sculpture that will be considered here, whatever their physical condition (severely fragmentary in one instance, nearly perfect in the other two), were reconstructed in words. And the different kinds of words will describe a range of possibilities in which ancient art could give rise to modern languages.

If these are works reconstructed in discourse, then the names by which we know them are the first and clearest signs of the languages they are made to speak. The ordinary semantics of titles—let the *Laocoön* stand as normative one more time— simply records that which is by common agreement the subject represented in the statue. Once Sangallo has said, "Questo è il Laocoonte, di cui fa mentione Plinio," an uncomplicated equivalence has been established between the word and the thing.[2] We shall see no such simplicity among the objects to be discussed here, however. The first of these works, the *Pasquino*, is named neither for the person depicted nor for any other aspect of its narrative; rather Pasquino is an imaginary character, indeterminately associated with the material object—essentially the possessor of a voice made to emanate from the object. The second of these works, a reclining female figure found in the Vatican collections, is named quite determinately for the person represented; but its sixteenth-century history demonstrates no agreement among the candidates for this title or even between the kinds of narrative that the names signaled. The final work reveals no such dispute as to title. Unanimously known as the *Bed of Polyclitus*, this piece of relief sculpture is named not after its voice or its story but after its presumed maker, but that presumption is wildly off the mark. The three objects, then, signal three different units of discourse: voice, narrative, history of art.

PASQUINO DISFIGURED AND REDRESSED

Many pages ago I attributed some of the origins of the present volume to a deconstructionist interest in voice—the sense that poetic language was in its essence derived from a need to make inanimate things speak and thereby to attain personhood. Such an approach Paul de Man describes (with a relevance to our subject that is as uncanny as it is unintentional) as dealing "with the giving and taking away of faces, with face and deface, *figure*, figuration, and disfiguration."[3] It is precisely in relation to the disfigured condition of ancient sculptural representations that voices reverberate around them. According to the deconstructionist model, the trope of personification is made up on the one hand of *apostrophe*, that is, speech that is addressed to an inanimate object, and on the other of *prosopopoeia*, the object's reply. To which one might add that one of the ways this process conceals and naturalizes itself is by seeming to be reversed, as when the inanimate object initiates the conversation. "Voice," says de Man, "assumes mouth, eye, and finally face" (76). In the present case, we are dealing not with metaphorical objects but with real ones—indeed, real ones whose literal possession of mouth, eye, and face may be quite problematic. In addition, we are dealing with objects set in specific and separable time frames. The result is a more complex interplay of tropes and realities, of rhetoric and history. The voices that reconstruct ancient art objects will turn into dialogues; whoever is speaking, the conversation will be both historical and transhistorical.

The *Pasquino* (fig. 4.1) deserves a place of honor among the grand enigmas of rediscovered sculpture. None of the famous rediscovered antiquities was more radically mutilated. The statue, little changed from the Renaissance to the present time, consists merely of the remains of two joined bodies: one is limited to a turbaned or helmeted head and muscular upper torso and forelegs; the other is merely a slice of torso from below the breast to the upper edge of the pubic hair. Nor has any statue been christened with more names. The Renaissance cast its net among some of the usual designations for large heroic subjects lacking clear iconographic cues, including *Hercules, Alexander the Great*, and *Gladiator*. Nineteenth-century scholarship fixed the true identity as *Menelaus with the Body of Patroclus*; and restorations of some similar works helped confirm this idea (fig. 4.2).[4] But the best scholarship of our own time has reopened the question, citing additional Iliadic narratives in which one individual supports the dead body of another; and the many examples of physically similar statues that have come to light (at least thirteen by now) have tended to confuse rather than to clarify the identification, since these may turn out to be different narrative subjects imitating each other rather than different versions of the same subject.[5] Finally, this fragment, unlike the analogously mutilated *Torso Belvedere*, never became a significant artistic icon. It was not copied widely in artists' sketches nor inserted into larger pictorial compositions. Occasionally it was said to be beautiful, and Bernini seems to have taken credit for launching it as the greatest antique in Rome.[6] On the whole, however, the *Pasquino* as an object in itself must have looked as truncated, perplexing, and even unaesthetic during the sixteenth century as it now appears in the streets of modern Rome.

We cannot precisely reconstruct the circumstances of the *Pasquino*'s first appearance above ground. A late sixteenth-century reminiscence by Flaminio Vacca places the work near the Stadium of Domitian "doue è hoggi la torre de gl' Orsini"— that is, very close to where it was eventually displayed; and if he means that it was discovered while the tower was being built, then it would have been visible as early as the

4.2. *Pasquino*, restored in the seventeenth century by Lodovico Salvetti as *Menelaus with the Body of Patroclus*, Loggia dei Lanzi, Florence

1430s.[7] The exact date is conjectural, but it is clear that by the time of the first explicit references to the statue, which begin in earnest around 1500, it has been above ground for many years "truncated, with arms, legs, and nose broken off . . . neglected and covered with dirt."[8] The object was rescued from this oblivion by the occupant of the same Palazzo Orsini, Cardinal Oliviero Carafa, cardinal-protector of the Dominican Order, éminence grise behind Innocent VIII, admiral of a papal crusading fleet, and famously stern follower of Saint Thomas Aquinas.[9] The cardinal placed it in front of his residence (near where it is today, though the modern installation dates from 1791) with an inscription in the voice of the statue that read "Oliverii Carafae beneficio hic sum, anno salutatis M.D.I."

Despite the fact that this statue could make no extraordinary claims for its dramatic narrative, its physical condition, its early history, or its artistic excellence, it would attain the status of internationally famous paradigm.[10] The *Pasquino*, in countless modern languages, is the eponymous originator of a genre or mode of satire in which powerful figures in authority are attacked in some public way, often scurrilously or even obscenely, by individuals who operate under the cloak of anonymity. Like senates, statute miles, and public buildings with banks of columns in front of them, the pasquinade is one of those pan-European institutions that traces its lineage back to an ancient Rome that was filtered through the Renaissance. The historical conjunction between a luridly corrupt imperial court in the century after the emperor Augustus and a flourishing school of witty but vicious satirists including Juvenal, Perseus, and Martial establishes a set of origins for this mode of public expression. For its part, papal Rome not only provides juicy materials for satire but also functions as a polity in which there are enough conflicting sources of authority so that even the most subversive utterances can find some sort of protection and (generally) avoid being silenced.

The pasquinade will become an all but official medium for obstreperous forms of public debate throughout the sixteenth century. What begins as an arena of parochial dispute among segments of the Roman people or the Curia will be exported north of the Alps by the more radically contrarian purposes of the Reformation.[11] Meanwhile back in Rome, the two hotly disputed papal conclaves of the early 1520s, both of which center on the strong candidacy of Giulio de' Medici, who has to wait for the second election to emerge as Clement VII, turn the pasquinade into an instrument of public propaganda all too familiar in our own times.[12] The next pope, Paul III Farnese (1534–49)—his sister the mistress of Alexander VI, his son Pierluigi an alleged sodomite, his grandson Ottavio said to be impotent—provides more than his share of material.[13] In the succeeding decades, the Counter-Reformation will further polarize a Rome torn between license and repression, to the time in 1570 when the satirist Nicolò Franco will be condemned to death by Pius V, probably for having attached to the newly built Vatican privies the celebratory lines

> Papa Pius Quintus, ventres miseratus onustos,
> hocce cacatorium nobile fecit opus.

> Pope Pius V, taking pity on our loaded bellies,
> created, o noble work, this shithouse.[14]

Nor does the story—or the term *pasquinade*—stop here. At least until the French Revolution, when citizens develop more vivid and more widely exportable models for public protest, the pasquinade will continue as the name and the formula by which western Europeans attack authority. And even beyond this period in Rome itself, there long remains that combination of satirical raw material and a liberty to indulge in it that is not to be found in more effectively ruled principalities.

But this is the pasquinade without *Pasquino*. Anonymous verses will have a career throughout Europe and among individuals who have never seen or heard of the object that Oliviero Carafa set up in front of his palace. But the tradition begins sometime in the very last years of the fifteenth century when the statue begins to be called "Pasquino" and when Roman citizens publish their verses by attaching them to it, as is later represented in Lafréry's *Speculum* (fig. 4.3). In fact, the name and the affixed verses are born—or at least imagined—together. A considerable literature about the "real" Pasquino begins as early as 1509, all of which consigns him to a shadowy mythic past, even though no more than ten to thirty years would have elapsed since he had supposedly given his name to the statue. In one set of explanatory narratives, Pasquino was a tradesman, variously shoemaker, workman, innkeeper, barber. Lodovico Castelvetro, writing in 1560, remembers being told by Antonio Tebaldi (1463–1537)

4.3. *Pasquino*, from engraving for Antoine Lafréry's *Speculum Romanae magnificentiae*, Rome, 1546

that Pasquino was a successful tailor in the neighborhood of Parione, with a large staff of apprentices and considerable clientele among papal courtiers:

> [Pasquino and his assistants] spoke openly and in safety censuring the deeds of the popes and the cardinals, as well as the other prelates of the church and the lords of the court. The loutish speech of these people, coming from lowborn and base individuals, was not taken seriously, nor did they suffer any penalties or ill will. And so anyone noble, religious, or otherwise respectable who wanted to recount something ill of someone in power, would—in order to avoid the hatred of that person, who might consider himself offended by these words and do harm against the speaker—make a shield for himself of the person of Pasquino, along with his assistants, naming them as the authors of this gossip. Thus in the course of time it passed into common use and became almost a proverb of the people to attribute to Master Pasquino that which came into the mind of whatever kind of person who wished to defame the ecclesiastical and secular lords of the court.[15]

After the tailor's death, the statue was dug up in front of his shop and was moved inside so as to protect it from harm: "The shrewd courtiers and cautious poets of Rome, not wanting to put aside the already time-honored custom of attacking the faults of great men, as they had been revealed by Master Pasquino, credited to the statue the opinions they had in their minds when they wanted, or still want, to assert those things which they could not, or cannot, speak or write without obvious danger, were they to admit their own authorship of them."[16] It is a notable account of Roman social interchange, in effect a sequence of mediations. Ordinary people are free to express their (presumably disapproving) opinions of those in authority. Courtiers, who have no such freedom, escape punishment by displacing the authorship of their subversive opinions onto the lowly tailor. In Tebaldi's haunting phrase "si faceva scudo della persona di maestro Pasquino," they make a shield for themselves out of the persona of Pasquino. All of the tailor's immunity from prosecution is thereby transferred to the art object that has assumed his name and social function.

The story of the tailor shop may be mythical, but its principles appear to be borne out by the first satirical verse we hear about as specifically attached to the *Pasquino*. In his diary entry for 13 August 1501, Giovanni Burckard records a pasquinade written à propos of the possible absence of Pope Alexander VI from Rome:

> Predixi tibi papa bos quod esses.
> Predico: Moriere, si hinc abibis;
> succedet Rota consequens Bubulcum.[17]

> I predicted you pope, ox, what you are.
> I predict: You will die if you go away from here.
> The wheel will be the next successor to the ox-man.

Like many future pasquinades, these verses operate in the mode of anonymous gossip and threat that seems to emanate from the voice of the Roman populace. In truth, however, they have unmistakably courtly origins. The opening line is a sophisticated game of Latin triple meanings based on the Borgia emblem of the *bos*: "I predicted that as a pope, you would be an ox"; "I said beforehand, O Pope, that you were an ox"; "I foretold your becoming pope, ox that you are." The enigma of the final line, which gets deciphered by Agostino Vespucci in a letter to no less a student of current events than Machiavelli, refers to threats against the pope from the Cardinal of Lisbon, whose emblem was the wheel.[18] The whole production strongly suggests that, despite the public display of these verses, their origins are internal to the Curia, where such predictions would carry the greatest force and be best remembered. Indeed, the Vespucci letter details a kind of collective composition of these lines by highly placed churchmen; it also points out that the pope decided to heed the warning and stay put. To borrow Tebaldi's metaphor, the statue has become an offensive shield.

Giacomo Mazzocchi, who begins in 1509 to publish annual volumes of the pasquinades, tells a different tale of origins for the person and the ritual. Pasquino in this version is a humble grammarian or school teacher who happened to live in front of the place where Cardinal Carafa located the statue. Owing to the proximity of the grammar school as well as of the church of San Lorenzo in Damaso, whose priests traditionally had literary inclinations, the statue begins to be covered with verses that are in effect Latin grammar exercises. Whether the schoolmaster existed or not, there is much about the pasquinades that emerges from the early Renaissance culture of classical pedagogy. Many of the Latin lyrics from the beginning resonate with the life of young scholars—and, correspondingly, many Italian pasquinades will consist of bitter attacks on "Pedanti." Notable among the expressions of goliardic high spirits are poems attacking the foibles and physical peculiarities of teachers, especially one "Donato"—which may be a real name or else a reference to the author of the canonical Latin grammar—himself apparently the arbiter of all this poetic production.[19]

An even larger number of school-based pasquinades are concerned with the sexual implications of humanist instruction—that is, the tendency of *paedeia* to be accompanied by pederasty. A verse of possibly elaborate double meanings from 1521 emphasizes the need to have Latin instruction in the passive voice. And there are many indications that the occasion of affixing verses to the statue itself was understood as a time when participants practiced sexual as well as verbal license, for example,

> Formosum puerum qui semper ardet in Urbe
> advocat hunc votis terque quaterque diem.[20]

Whoever in the city is hot for pretty boys can't stop longing for that day to come.

Even more explicitly, Giano Parrasio, who had been prosecuted for sodomy, suggests that pupils whose Latin versifying abilities were wanting could get help from their teachers on a quid pro quo basis:

> Namque rudes pueri tecum dum ludere cultis
> gaudent versiculis quos sua musa negat,
> pro modulis rigido, proh dolor, saepe pedanti
> prostituunt sese turgidulasque nates.[21]

> For the inexperienced boys, while they delight in playing at learned verses with
> you which their muse denies them, in exchange for the rhymes—oh, sorrow—
> often prostitute their distended buttocks to the rigid pedant.

Mazzocchi, silent on this subject, nevertheless responds to the teacher caricatures. In the 1510 volume he confesses that he has been constrained to include some verses directed against himself—perhaps the pseudonymous "Donato"—characterized as boring, physically repellent, and pompous. Mazzocchi declares these verses to be full of errors, though not, he assures the reader, because of their disagreeable subject matter. In general Mazzocchi plays the role of grammar police. He recollects (or invents) the schoolmaster origins of the pasquinade because he is himself promoting the verses as part of a larger educational project to replace bastardized medieval Latin with a revived pure classical language. In his prefaces to the first two annual volumes he speaks of his efforts at encouraging the students by improving the correctness of their grammar and prosody. He looks forward to "next year [when] the most erudite men, more than this year, will offer their verses, and I hope that these people, competitively and with all manner of verse, will take part in and help outfit this spectacle, which has been from the beginning held in such contempt and derision by them."[22] The defensive tone tells us much about the project, born from a naïve desire to identify with antiquity and subject to ridicule by those who pursue this goal in a more erudite manner, scorning schoolboys' exercises and their ephemeral system of dissemination.

The enigmatic pair of figures erected in front of the Carafa palace is far more than a mere backdrop to all this verbal production. As Mazzocchi himself explains, there had been a long tradition of decorating the area around the statue on the feast day of Saint Mark (25 April). Beginning around 1500, the statue became the centerpiece for the festival. Each year it was dressed up for twenty-four hours as a different mythological figure. Once that choice was made known—only on the day itself—poets and poetasters vied with one another to compose rhymes they could attach to the display. Many of these were conceits based upon the mythological dress; most referred to current events. By the next day the whole ensemble of costume and text had disappeared, but, beginning with Mazzocchi's 1509 volume and continuing at least until the mid-1530s, the rhymes were published under the direction of a series of humanists connected to the Curia. These volumes advertise themselves with titles alluding to the *Pasquino* while bearing frontispieces depicting the annual mythological personage in a classic iconography that generally makes no reference to the shape of the statue.[23]

Despite the claims for a popular origin via Pasquino the tailor or Pasquino the schoolmaster, the management of this annual event seems to have been in the hands of powerful and well-connected cardinals or even, in some cases, the pope himself.[24] The choice of themes, however variously they might get interpreted, was in the hands of these managers or their humanistic advisers; and—at least in historical hindsight—they seem to allude to current political situations in such a way as to support the pope. Prefatory material in the 1510 edition refers to a history of the earliest costumings of the statue—Saturn, Mars, Minerva, Astraea, Venus, Ceres, Genius, Phoebus, Jupiter, and Harpocrates—but lacking the texts, we can only guess how these were meant to be interpreted. With the publication of the annual volumes we are on surer ground. The choice of Janus in 1509 coincides with the outbreak of war between the papacy and the Venetian Republic, since it was the Temple of Janus whose doors were opened in time of war; the following year's theme, of Hercules destroying the Hydra, alludes to the same conflict, perhaps emphasizing the multiple territories in Romagna that the papacy wished to reconquer. The death of Oliviero Carafa in 1511 is memorialized in the personage of *Lutto*, or Mourning (fig. 4.4). Mars, the theme of 1512, once again refers to war, in this case against France. Apollo in 1513 and Orpheus in 1515 (fig. 4.5) provide compliments for Leo X on the prospects for a golden age of the arts, while the choice of Mercury in 1514 bestows a parallel compliment on behalf of the prospects for commerce.

In sum, the pasquinade—a mediated outlet for social dissatisfaction, an exercise in philology and goliardic high spirits, an annual day of license sanctioned and manipulated by the Curia—is one of those overdetermined cultural events that has too many causes. What is probably most true about the origins of the festival is that they are collective and that several independent strands go into the creation: revived ancient festivals of misrule; activities of local churches and schools; the celebration of Easter—after all, neither the April date nor the verbal coincidence of *Pasqua* and *Pasquino* can be accidental; and the recently revived *Paliliae*, or birthday of Rome, which fell on 20 April.[25]

As the pivotal object in all these social interactions, the statue qualifies impeccably. The history of the *Pasquino* is the history of a very special form of reconstruction. The statue is being completed—in effect, restored—both with the words that surround it and with the identities in which it is dressed. In effect, what the statue possesses, and what it does not possess, become together the mold upon which the object can be reconstructed and the citizens of Rome can represent and express themselves. The statue is classical—that is, it forms part of the highly valued collection of antiquities that underlie modern Rome's claims for authority, thus giving it oracular presence. It is sufficiently mutilated—that is, in a ruined form of the human body—that it barely encourages any specific guesses about its "true" identity and therefore invites a liberal range of completions. Further, the statue is on the street, placed there officially in a self-memorializing gesture by a powerful member of the Roman ruling

CARMINA
Appoſita Paſquillo An.M.D.Xv.

4.5. Title page, *Carmina apposita Pasquillo,* 1515: *Orpheus*

class but apparently belonging to the people in a way that few other pieces of ancient sculpture did. In effect, the revival of correct Latin and the circulation of Roman public opinion, which are variously credited to the historical Pasquino, can be turned into a single triumph poised between ancient and modern, just as the conjunction of costume and language creates a less mediated relationship between image and word.

This happy mix of qualities generates many verses, particularly in the early years, that are not devoted to aggressive political praise and blame but to the wonders of the Pasquino ritual itself:

> Come ciascun romano anticamente
> per le aquistate glorie triunfava
> in Roma un giorno solo, poi tornava
> come era prima, miser e dolente;
> cosí son io, qual universalmente
> la pioggia, l'acqua, il vento sempre grava
> per tutto l'anno ed un giorno ne cava,
> che mi fa onorar da tanta gente.
> Variate forme in aspetto divino
> spesso rasembro e poi, consunto un giorno,
> pur mi ritorno a l'usato Pasquino.
> Ed in tal grado, benché io pata scorno,
> per tempo assai mi chiamo piú felice
> che molti, ch'a veder mi stan d'intorno.[26]

[84, 1515]

As each Roman in ancient times triumphed with acquired glories in Rome for one single day, then returned as he was before, wretched and suffering, so am I, burdened on all sides constantly by rain, water, and wind throughout the year; but for one day I manage my way out and am honored by so many people. I frequently take on diverse forms with a godly aspect and then, one day being past, I return again to being the ordinary Pasquino. And under those conditions, even though I suffer scorn, for a little time I consider myself happier than many who stand around looking at me.

Pasquino is the object of an ancient triumph who is at the same time an enduring ruin; his festival is the fitting revival of antiquity; he is at once a figure of divine visage and the familiar ordinary citizen with the diminutive name; he suffers scorn but lives perpetually to turn the tables on any fellow citizens who look down on him while they are looking up at him.

Viewed in this light, Pasquino offers a structure upon which antiquity can be revived and revised; in fact, by reclothing and verbalizing the statue, modern Romans can stage a citizens' version of those elite games in which humanists reenacted ancient rituals pretending they were classical philosophers and poets.[27] Yet even as the statue is classic, inviting, and accessible, it is also highly disturbing: broken, alien, monstrous. And suggestive: as we have seen so often in other contexts, it is the sexualizing of the object that signals the most unsettling aspects of its power. Insofar as the original statue can be deciphered at all, it consists of two men of epic proportions in close physical proximity and posed in what has to be considered a physically ambiguous interrelation, imaging forth some aspects of ancient *virtù* that were most troubling to early modern Christians, connecting the heroic, the sexual, and the homoerotic. Sixteenth-century viewers may not have had the art-historical expertise to place this statue in the problematic category of the symplegma—that is, pairs of male figures who may be fighting or may be having sex, or some combination of the two;[28] but they certainly could not fail to notice the relatively good preservation of both sets of genitals or the physical conjunction of the two bodies.

Countless pasquinades respond to the power or the fragmentariness or the enigmatic qualities of the *Pasquino* by concentrating on its genitals. He has big testicles: "commovet ingentes testiculosque suos" (he sets his huge testicles in motion [15, 1510]);[29] he orders the designers of his regalia to add testicles:

Dicite, pictori, postquam me pinxit ad unguem,
addat item geminos ut mihi testiculos.   [26, 1515]

After the painter has perfectly represented me, tell him to add a pair of testicles.

His testicles are harder than rock and, though they are hidden, he offers to take them out and show them to girls passing by:

haec tangite, monstro quae libenter
vobis inguina, duriora saxo,
quae sub veste latent, habent superbum
ac rubrum caput: usque quod placebit.   [74, 1525]

Touch this groin, harder than rock, which I am happy to show you; it is under
my clothing and has a noble red head. Go for it as much as you like.

Or he figures his bad physical condition as a problem of genital endowment:

Cum robustos erat penis mihi, amabar ubique;
nunc sortem ridet turba fututa meam.   [39, 1518]

When my penis was vigorous I was loved everywhere; now the fucking crowd
ridicules my fate.

Further, the utility of pasquinades for attacking public figures by accusing
them of sodomy is not accidental. In a year when the statue is costumed as Hercules,
one poet regrets that Pasquino has been hidden behind the disguise and wonders why
Hercules has not brought his boyfriend along (perhaps a reference to the hidden second figure in the original statue):

Ercule . . .
Hai nascosto Pasquin sotto le carte:
non piaceria a Iove un simil fatto.
Perché non hai portato in queste parte
teco Ila?   [19, 1510]

Hercules, . . . you have hidden Pasquino under the paper; Jupiter wouldn't like
such a thing. Why didn't you bring Hylas with you?

In the year of Argus, another poet sees the multiple eyes of the peacock as so many
anuses and offers a sodomitical map of the Curia:

Ognun in cortesia
se fotte l'un con l'altro cardinale.   [356, 1526]

Each and every one of the cardinals, out of politeness, is fucking around with
each other.

Most acutely, in an extravagant attack on the sexual mores of Pierluigi
Farnese, an interlocutor curious to compare the pleasures of sex with girls or boys
approaches the statue as though to seek legal advice from a learned professional:

vorrei saper da te, come colui
che sei ne l'utriusque molto esperto,
qual miglior robba parti d'ambidui.
E per dir chiar, a cui
t'attaccaresti con maggior diletto,
o alla vitella o al tenerin capretto?
Perché so ch'in effetto
a' preti spuzza di chiavar in potta,
ma danno drieto a tutti a tutta botta.   [450, ca. 1539]

I'd like to know from you, as someone who is very expert in the utriusque, what seems to you the best of the two. So to speak plainly, which would you tuck into with greater pleasure, the young heifer, or the tender billy-goat? Because I know that in fact priests wouldn't be caught dead screwing in the usual place, but they go in the back way with each thrust to everybody.

That expertise in utriusque—in effect, in going both ways—points to many forms of doubleness. The premise of the joke is that Pasquino is an expert in utriusque iuris—both civil and canon law. In addition, the lurid context makes of utriusque a sort of euphemistic shorthand for sexual versatility, recollecting Ovid's gender-changing Tiresias, to whom "Venus . . . erat utraque nota."[30] Dropping the Latin word in the midst of the Italian only serves to emphasize these oppositions. Religious versus secular; male versus female; homosexual versus heterosexual; Latin versus Italian; ancient versus modern: Pasquino covers the territory of binary oppositions.

But there is another, perhaps more significant reference in the utriusque. In the practice of rhetoric, the ability to change shape—that is, to take both sides—had been canonically described by Cicero as the ability to speak "in utramquem partem."[31] The poet who addresses Pasquino as an expert in utriusque is recognizing something more powerful and disturbing than the object's ambiguous sexuality, that is, its ability to generate many kinds of speech. Uniting all the Pasquino materials, both the mythical and the historical, are these operations of civic discourse. The statue in front of the Palazzo Orsini is an object that can speak and be spoken to. Even more, it is an object through which voices can be diffused, dissembled, redirected, ventriloquized. The story of the tailor, after all, is one in which voice is transferred and reassigned among the social classes; and the story of the grammarian is one in which modern Romans attempt to transfer classical Latin into modern speech. In fact, perhaps the most reliable account of the pasquinade's historical origins relates it to the Parione neighborhood itself, which we would call the communications center of Rome, frequented in the fifteenth century by copyists and stationers, and, in post-Gutenbergian times, by printers.[32] It is probably no coincidence that Saint Mark, celebrated on 25 April, was the patron of these groups. In addition, the fact that the adjacent Via dei Banchi housed money changers also contributed to the transfer of information—or gossip—

4.6. *Marforio*, from engraving for Antoine Lafréry's *Speculum Romanae magnificentiae*, Rome, 1546

not only among Romans but also with foreigners. This is, in short, a place where relatively unfettered public conversation can occur and be diffused; *Pasquino* lives as the sign, the representation, and the mechanism for all that talk.

In particular, the *Pasquino* embodies talk *in utramque partem*—not only on both sides of questions but so as to complicate the matter of individual voice in the public arena. The sheer range of social impulses behind the ritual and the variety of qualities in the statue that were thus exploited produced a Pasquino with a complex voice allowing for no simple determination of who is speaking. In the most fundamental way Pasquino is dialogic. He speaks to the viewers, and the viewers speak to him. In addition, he engages in question and answer games or competitions with other oracles. The Capitoline *Marforio* (fig. 4.6; cf. 3.5), Pasquino's steadiest companion, is in every way a more stable structure, less mutilated and more classically rooted in its place.[33] Probably for that reason, *Marforio* tends to play the straight man to his crosstown comrade, asking for the truth about current events, like the cause of Leo X's death (*Pasquino*'s response: "per fotter troppo in cul un suo ragazo"—for fucking the asshole of one of his boys too often [286,1521]), or for an exegesis of the annual disguise or else to understand better the whole business of allegorical representation. (It is, in fact, Marforio who asks Pasquino's advice about the sexual merits of boys versus girls.) Relations are far more strained with Luca Grillo, who appears in 1521 and 1526. He is not a statue but merely a fictional one-eyed barber whose utterances seem to have been more insistently proletarian than those of Pasquino. And one finds a host of other speaking objects around town, including the *Bocca della Verità*, whose legend of truth telling goes back at least to the Middle Ages, and "Madonna Lucrezia," a classical statue exhibited in the courtyard of San Marco, who was sometimes said to be Pasquino's wife.[34]

But it is not the number or variety of alternative speakers that renders Pasquino multivalent; it is the many identities he can assume all by himself. Who is supposed to be speaking when Pasquino speaks? Often it is the mythological personage in whose image he is reconstructed: "Sono el bifronte Ian" (I am the two-fronted Janus [3, 1509]); "Figliolo io sono del tonante Iove," (as Hercules: I am the son of thundering Jupiter [8, 1510]); "Son lutto, pianto e duol e gran mestizia" (I am mourning, plaint, sorrow, and great sadness [28, 1511]); "Son io Marte; sí sono" (I am Mars, yes I am [57, 1512]); "Orfeo son, con mia squillante lira" (I am Orpheus, with my sounding lyre [89, 1515]); "I' son l'Occasione (I am Occasion [408, 1535]). But sometimes this is precisely what he denies:

> Argo non sono, o populo romano,
> né d'argo furno mai questi occhi cento.   [354, 1526]

> I am not Argus, o Roman people,
> nor did these hundred eyes ever belong to Argus.

> Chi desia vedere Argo perfetto
> non se afatichi in me, ch'io son Pasquino.   [371, 1526]

> Whoever would like to see Argus perfectly,
> don't waste your time with me, I am Pasquino.

> Che mirate con bocca aperta, o pedanti?
> Son pur Pasquil, com'era innanti.   [15, 1510]

> [As Hercules] What are you looking at with open mouths,
> you pedants. I am still Pasquino, as I was before.[35]

Sometimes he is stuck between identities:

> Pasquillo mihi nomen erat, nunc Orphea dicunt
> et mihi nescio quis plectra luramque dedit.   [24, 1515]

> My name was Pasquino, now they call me Orpheus, and I don't know who gave me this plectrum and lyre.

Sometimes Pasquino's disguise is itself multiple, like Janus :

Dimostrami qui Italia con due teste,
una di gioventú, l'altra vechieza.   [3, 1509]

I show here an Italy with two heads,
one youthful, the other aged.

Or Proteus:

De Pasquillo in Proteo son trasformato,
sí come già Proteo s'è convertito
in orso, o leon, o tigre ardito.   [106, 1516]

From Pasquino into Proteus
I am transformed, just as Proteus converted himself
into bear, lion, or bold tiger.

Sometimes the disguise seems to him not part of an endless cycle but rather a
culmination:

Ogni mia forma e mio modo diverso,
ch'in varie guise io fui già trasformato,
se determina or qui mio scuro stato.   [39, 1511]

[As Mourning] Every one of my forms and varying modes,
which in differing guises have transformed me,
concludes itself now in this dark condition.

Sometimes it is neither Pasquino nor the annual personage who speaks, but a third
party: "Non Ercol, non, anzi Marco mi appello" (as Mars: Not Hercules, no, rather my
name is Mark [20, 1512]). Or else,

Italia son, che me ralegro alquanto
che 'l furibondo Marte ha l'arme in mano.   [61, 1512]

[As Mars] I am Italy, and I rejoice considerably
when the raging Mars has weapons in his hand.

Sometimes he speaks as the statue underneath the disguise:

Quis deformis eram vili de marmore truncus,
Persei miraris esse modo ora mihi?

I who was a deformed trunk of lowly marble;
now are you amazed that I have become Perseus?[36]

And sometimes there is no stability at all because even the statue form is taken to be
the result of ancient metamorphosis:

> Non dolme già d'esser tanto mutabile,
> né che m'avesse el natal destinato
> a cangiar de mia forma el primo stato,
> qual fu de omo, in pietra dura e stabile. [109, 1516]

> [As Proteus] I do not suffer any longer for being so changeable,
> nor that I had the innate destiny to change
> in my form from the original condition,
> which was that of a man, to become hard and solid rock.

These are the voices of the strong Pasquino—the larger-than-life, classical,
articulate, oracular monument, so rich in potential significations as to take on a
wealth of varying identities. But the celebration of Pasquino, and the voices that reverberate around him, may finally depend more on what he is lacking than on what he
has got. Verses are frequently devoted to Pasquino's ruined condition: he tauntingly
asks his viewers why they are laughing at him:

> An laceras nares, mutilataque labra, manusque
> Et nihil integri quod mea forma tenet? [Mary-Lafon, 128, ca. 1536]

> Is it because of my nose, my mutilated lips and hands,
> and that I do not retain any of my complete form?

While in another poem he composes his last will and testament, including the gift of
"i piè, el naso e le braccia" (my feet, my nose, and my arms [105, 1516])—none of
which, of course, he possesses. Or he is viewed as a monstrosity:

> col volto tuo orrendo e dispietato
> tu faresti paura allo elefante. [124, 1516]

> With your terrifying and merciless face,
> you would frighten an elephant.

Rarely do we hear of the statue's ruined condition without hearing of that fear.
Perhaps nothing is more revealing in the conduct of the annual rite than its conclusion. In one of the earliest published pasquinades, the statue refers to himself as

> adorato per la solita vesta
> volendomi per devozione,
> l'altro tempo rotto con molesta. [2, 1509]

Worshiped simply on account of my garments,
they desire me for adoration,
but the rest of the time I am attacked with ruin.

The events are more explicitly recounted in a later prose pasquinade addressed to the statue: "The boys then stripped you, who were so gaudily decorated moments earlier; and scarcely had the sun completed its course into the ocean when you were rendered as mutilated and deprived as you had been in the first place. . . . And I worry lest some terrible great ill be done to me by the boys since I see them now surrounding me, armed with both rocks and stones and bent on your destruction."[37] The fascination of the object partly inheres in its terrible condition; and the power that it exerts on the ritual day must be violently exorcised even as it is confirmed.

The heart of what is both powerful and missing in the *Pasquino* is precisely its voice. The statue is silent both by definition and by virtue of its historical distance; but it speaks with uncanny force. This fearfully articulate silence is often figured as power:

> Non homo me melior Romae est: ego nil peto ab ullo,
> non sum verbosus, heic sedeo et taceo.   [19, 1511]

> There's no better man in Rome than I. I ask nothing of anyone,
> I am not talkative. I sit here and keep silent.

And the power in question stands in paradoxical relation to the blockish ruin that possesses it:

> Sì come di stupor restò conquiso
> il gran Pigmalion vedendo il sasso
> converso in donna quale amava, ahi lasso,
> ch'ancor di quel mirar so' anch'io diviso,
> che in me pensando e poi guardando fiso
> che un mostro orrendo, d'ogni senso casso,
> adorna e fa immortal che è vile e basso
> e fa soi versi degni in paradiso.   [148, 1518]

> Just as the great Pygmalion remained overcome in amazement when he saw the
> stone transformed into the woman he loved, so, alas, I too am struck in two
> by that wonderment, that thinking to myself and then watching fixedly how a
> horrid monstrosity void of any sense decorates and renders immortal that
> which is vile and base and makes his verses worthy of paradise.

The silent statue produces voice in those who stand in front of it, just as the other qualities that are wanting in the *Pasquino* bring about attempts at reconstruction from among the onlookers.

In one particularly memorable pasquinade the statue declares,

Pasquillo son, formato in pietra dura,
chi la razon d'ognun ascolto e tazo.

I am Pasquino, made out of hard stone.
I listen to everyone's talk, and I keep silent.

He offers, in other words, no reasons of his own but merely waits in silence to review the guesses hazarded by his viewers. On Saint Mark's Day,

posso senza paura
di fatti d'altri pigliarmi solazo,
in versi, o in prosa, o in sublime rima:
tutti i dittati al mio nome s'imprima.   [118, 1516]

I can without fear
take comfort from the doings of others,
in verse, in prose, or in high rhyme—let all those things
which are composed be stamped with my name.

It is that *imprima*/*imprimatur* that perhaps best characterizes the voice of Pasquino. In blunt political terms, the statue is—as it was for the noble clientele of Pasquino the tailor—a device to evade responsibility. But it is also a means of publication. What the statue can do, given greater evocative power, is to enable the voice to be both transferred in its origins and diffused in its destination. By creating the ritual of the pasquinade, sixteenth-century Romans are inventing and investigating all the paradoxes of publication. In the early years, the statue declares himself "maestro d'ogni citra" (master of every instrument), who, despite his own stony roughness gives out

pumicato metro e stesa prosa
in latin ed in vulgar chiosa

polished meter and extended prose,
whether in Latin or in the vulgar language

as though he had created it himself—"com di mia testa" (as though they came from my head [2, 1509]). Later, Pasquino hesitates to call himself author, though he understands that such a role is being ascribed to him, and instead characterizes himself as

pastore,
avendo per armento ogni scrittore.   [119, 1516]

a shepherd
who has every writer as a member of his flock.

Still later, Marforio asks how his colleague can tolerate all the terrible and shameful verses that are pinned up on him, to which Pasquino replies,

Sai pur che meco ogni penna si stanca,
. . . .
        Cosí sempre sta franca
la mia persona, e perché mi sia dato
o laude o disonor, non cangio stato.
        Ma chi mi ha mal trattato,
dove viver credea mille anni o piúe,
appen pur vive dieci ore e due.
        E quelle carte sue,
ch'esso sperava fossero immortali,
le vede comparar da li speziali.
        E suoi versi cotali,
che disonoran la poltronaria,
durano quanto fa la testa mia.
        Io pur torno qual pria:
essi, dover eran prima reputati
uomini, son poi bestie diventati.   [395, 1533]

You know as well that every pen tires itself out on me. . . . So always my own person remains free, and whether I am praised or dishonored, I do not change condition. But whoever treats me badly, though he may believe he lives a thousand years or more, barely stays alive for twelve hours. And those pieces of paper of his, which he hoped would attain immortality, get bought up by the grocers. And such verses, which dishonor the big shots, last just as long as my costumed head. I moreover return as I was before; they, on the other hand, once thought to be men, have become beasts.

All the pasquinades on these themes chronicle the shifts of power, of authority, of presence, and of durability in the ritual of the statue, its reclothing, and its ascribed speech.

But as the voice of this late pasquinade suggests, the statue remains: it facilitates or embodies or symbolizes the production and distribution of a social voice, but it refuses to be wholly instrumentalized and surrender its own indefinable qualities. Like other art objects, the *Pasquino* neither rises above politics, nor does it act as a ventriloquist's dummy for the expression of a political power that is wholly independent of it. Some of the most revealing pasquinades are those that recognize the impossibility of defining the force of the statue and the power of its voice. For instance:

Herculis haec statua est tota notissima in urbe
quam Carrapha pius cardineus posuit;
in varias formas mutari sueta quotannis,
perdidit hoc anno non decus ipse suum.
Tu, mendax Pasquille, tace; non est tua imago!
Personam alterius parce tibi induere.
Forte tamen dices: "Populus me sponte vocavit
ex hebeti ingenio saxeus ut fierem."   [8, 1510]

This statue of Hercules, installed by the pious Cardinal Carafa, is well known in
the whole city. Having the habit of being transformed annually, it has not lost
that honor this year. You, lying Pasquino, be silent; this is not your imago. Stop
assuming the persona of someone else. Still, perhaps you are saying, "The people have spontaneously summoned me to become stone owing to the weakness
of my intelligence."

The speaker is frustrated by the elusiveness of *mendax Pasquille*, his capacity to operate
as a persona; but his stoniness offers a troubling and insistent sense that he is that
other undefinable category—vox populi.

Or, in an even more subtle reading,

Le tue tante, Pasquin, forme che muti
coprendo il tuo coroso, antico sasso,
fa cosí dir a chi te fece: "Oh lasso,
son questi colpi di scarpel perduti."
O plebe ignara e poco antiveduti,
ingegni ottusi, equali al babuasso,
che con carton, bitume e cole al basso,
cosí vilmente par che te trasmuti;
ch'una sí altera e viva forma,
che forse fu de Prasitele o Fidia,
sia fatta, a questa età de sarti, forma.
Gli crudel mastri d'ignoranza e invidia
Pasquin te dice, e ogni anno te disforma
Alcide, alor bel simulacro a Roma.   [III, 1516]

Those many forms of yours into which you change, Pasquino, covering your
rusted ancient stone, are as if to say to whoever made you, "Oh, alas, these are
so many blows of the chisel lost." O populace unknowing and wanting in
vision, obtuse intelligences, tantamount to blockheads, who with paper, coal,
and glue on the pedestal so vilely, it seems, have transformed you, that a form
so different and lively, which was perhaps made by Praxiteles or Phidias, could
be made a dummy in this age of tailors. The cruel masters of ignorance and
envy call you Pasquino, and every year they deform you, Alcides, once a beautiful likeness in Rome.

The statue is at once a masterpiece of Praxiteles or Phidias and a pathetic ruin. The poet confirms the year's costuming of Pasquino as Proteus while not speaking the name but instead associating that identity with the ignorance of the crowd and a dismal sense that the world has deteriorated from the age of the Greeks to the age of tailors—like the historical Pasquino himself. In the process, the poem both gives and takes away the name Pasquino in a way that mirrors the work's complicated identity as the ruin of something great now ineptly, but inevitably, redressed. The punchline offers what might be a more stable name for the statue—its supposed original identity as Hercules—but that possibility serves only to emphasize the Pasquino's continual disformation. In the end, we might call Pasquino one of the crucial founding figures of *le travesti*, or drag. He dresses up in borrowed clothes, and he speaks in travesties. The borrowed clothes are not just the annual costumes of the April ritual but also the whole condition of the ruined classical statue that is living again in modern times. The travesties are not only nasty slurs but also witty language games all'antica. The phenomenon is as complexly circular as that earliest of pasquinades on the subject of Alexander VI. The statue is *en travesti* because it is a great work pretending to be a ruin and because it is a ruin pretending to be a great work; it is also *en travesti* because it is a stone that has a voice.

NARRATIVE AND THE EYE OF THE BEHOLDER

If language and voice are the fundamental systems of recuperation for fragmentary ancient sculpture and ekphrasis and prosopopoeia the fundamental tropes, then the *Pasquino* deserves to stand as paradigm for a cultural encounter in which art object and observer reconstruct each other in a kind of mutual conversation. But in another significant respect the statue in front of Palazzo Orsini is an anomaly. The name "Pasquino," as has already been suggested, was never thought to identify anyone or anything that was depicted in the statue. Correspondingly, the notion of an authentic name and narrative that would recuperate the representational function of the fragmentary ancient work is almost completely eclipsed by the bestowing of contemporary voices on the object. But for most pieces of ancient sculpture that are widely known and influential, the act of modern reconstruction consists in rediscovering the story. In these cases, the voices that reverberate between the object and the modern viewer are conditioned by the attempt to determine the figures' identities and to enter into the world of their narrative.

The world of their narrative has certain distinguishing characteristics. First of all, it is visual. Throughout the densely populated territory theorizing relations between words and images perhaps no area has been covered so fully as that which interrogates the possibilities of the visual medium in telling verbal stories. In the literature both of and about ekphrasis from Philostratus to Murray Krieger, in the work of speculative aestheticians from Gotthold Ephraim Lessing to Nelson Goodman, it is remarkable to observe the number of changes that can be rung on a single point: verbal narrative takes place in the fullness of time, while visual narrative must be represented in unitary instants.[38] What has not so frequently been pointed out—though Lessing knew it—is that the difference between verbal and visual narrative is best defined in terms of reception. If the norm of narrative is the logical sequence of events in time, then it becomes a fictive representation of individual experience recounted from a position of full knowledge. But if the model for narrative were not my telling my own story but rather my decipherment of *your* story—my recognition of you at some individual moment in your story along with my own efforts to make sense of that moment—then visual narrative, lacking firm sequence and causality, would become something much more like the norm.[39] Despite all the careful taxonomies that distinguish among visual narratives in multiple panels, in prolepsis, in individual pregnant moments, or even those that are scarcely stories but rather single actions or simple identifications, all representational images invite or even demand narrative decipherment.[40] Any of these kinds of image may operate as one of those pregnant moments that Lessing identified as paradigmatic of visual narrative for—among other things—the close involvement of the beholder's imagination.[41]

In the sculptural narratives that are the subject of this book, there is another issue of reception. As we saw throughout the previous chapter, fragmentary antiques engage the beholder's imagination for reasons of historical distance. When Gregory the Great near the beginning of the Middle Ages makes his famous anti-iconoclastic formulation—"For a picture is displayed in churches on this account, in order that those who do not know letters may at least read by seeing on the walls what they are unable to read in books"—he appears to be untroubled by the difficulties involved in reading the walls or in making precise equations between the visual material and that which the literate may read.[42] Perhaps he is loath to consider any space for ambiguity in the Christian story, whatever its medium of transmission. A thousand years later, however, when Alberti attempts to create a new humanistic visual culture out of classical materials, his quintessential pictorial medium is the historia—both history and narration—and the central activity that the viewer engages in and which the artist is urged to inspire is that of decipherment: "I like there to be someone in the 'historia' who tells the spectators what is going on, and either beckons them with his hand to look, or with ferocious expression and forbidding glance challenges them not to come near, as if he wished their business to be secret, or points to some danger or remarkable thing in the picture, or by his gestures invites you to laugh or weep with them. Everything the people in the painting do among themselves, or perform in relation to the spectators, must fit together to represent and explain the 'historia.'"[43] Alberti's hermeneutic model for the visual narrative is one that both facilitates and obstructs decipherment. And it is no coincidence that his examples of visual narratives are almost exclusively antique: among dozens of classical references only Giotto's Navicella comes from the modern Christian tradition. The classical sample and the emphasis on decipherment are closely related. There is a simple sense in which pagan materials, free of doctrinal absolutes, offer greater latitude for the activity of decoding. More important, though, is the fact that Alberti grows up in a humanistic tradition that sees the antique as the historical Other. Ancient stories rendered in visual form require decipherment because their language is different; and that difference defines the gaps of history.

So the interpretive operation that Alberti promotes is both rhetorical and historical. The rhetorical or ekphrastic tradition, which predates the experience of seeing large numbers of classical artworks, comes to be validated by the new Renaissance sense of history; at the same time, the necessary practice of deciphering classical images helps to define the activity of decipherment as central to all visual experience, even where the material is well known and doctrinally fixed. Alberti, a non-Roman writing in the 1430s, forms part of a generation of artist-humanists (including Donatello, Brunelleschi, and Ghiberti) whose actual experience of ancient art objects is rather limited. But it is precisely the scarcity of such objects and their consequent desirability that makes it possible for these individuals to establish the theories by which ancient art will be assimilated into modern aesthetic experience during the High Renaissance. When viewers of ancient statues are attempting to master the works that are being unearthed in 1500, they are wrestling with both the rhetorical and the historical difficulties of naming the names of individuals who are represented and of deciphering their stories. In the process, they are inventing or reinventing both antiquity and narrative. They are discovering (or making up) new classical narratives and interrelating them; they are also composing the narrative of their own experience of beholding.

The massive reclining female figure in the Vatican collections that I take to be the paradigm for these operations is first recorded near the beginning of the sixteenth century in the extensive collection of the Maffei family in Rome (fig. 4.7).[44] It was acquired in 1512 by Julius II for the Belvedere courtyard, where it was given an elaborately designed fountain setting and where its neighbors included the *Laocoön* and the *Apollo Belvedere*. Although this work is not as estranged or mutilated as some that have been considered in these pages, its identification in the Renaissance was still far from obvious. In the history of this work from 1512 until now, three principal captions, or narrative ascriptions, hover around it. Its official Renaissance name, from the first we ever hear of it, is *Cleopatra*. She is called Cleopatra because a snake is represented on her upper arm; judging from the early descriptions, that is the primary means of identification, but some viewers take the next logical step and decide from her body position and closed eyes that she is in the process of dying from the snakebite.[45]

The second Renaissance caption is, if possible, an even less direct response to the denotative clues of the statue itself. From at least the late fifteenth century onward, a widely circulated report described a statue of a sleeping nymph that was the centerpiece of a beautiful fountain somewhere on the banks of the Danube; it quoted a supposedly classical inscription referring to the sleep and the fountain (fig. 4.8).[46] Henceforth, sculpted reclining female figures, classical inscriptions, and foun-

4.7. *Cleopatra-Ariadne*, marble, second-century A.D. copy after Hellenistic original, Vatican Museums, Rome

tains became a tradition in Renaissance garden design. Because the inscription was repeated by humanists close to the papal court, sometimes alongside drawings resembling the work, and because the Vatican statue was installed into a fountain setting there, we can be certain that the caption of *Sleeping Nymph* is as much a part of its Renaissance history as is the more directly cited caption of *Cleopatra*.[47]

Historians of ancient art in our own time no longer call this statue "Cleopatra" or "Sleeping Nymph." At the end of the eighteenth century, parallels were observed between the position of this figure and that of Ariadne, abandoned by Theseus and/or discovered by Bacchus, as she appears on a number of sarcophagi whose other details leave no room for doubt as to the story being narrated.[48] Some of these sarcophagi, as it happens, were known, reproduced, and accurately identified in the Renaissance, but they do not seem to have led anyone to associate the Vatican statue explicitly with their subject matter.[49] Here, then, the third identity, *Ariadne*, generally understood nowadays as the thing signified by the person or persons who made the original work.

The very multiplicity of these identities ought to suggest the difficulty of naming the figure. In case it is necessary to make the point, the iconology of the statue does not conform very fully to the narrative of Cleopatra's death, which was well known in 1512.[50] The object on her upper arm, which is the only tie to Cleopatra, resembles bracelet much more than snake, and in any event it is tiny and barely three-dimensional. There are, of course, other utilities in bestowing this name.

HVIVS NYM PHA DOCI BACRI CVSTODIA FONTIS
DORMIO DVM BLANDAE SENTIO MVRMVR AQVAE
PARCE MEVM QVISQVIS TANGIS CAVA MARMORA SOMNV
RVMPERE SIVE BIBAS SIVE LAVERE TACE.

4.8. Fountain nymph from Colocci Garden, Rome, engraving from Jean-Jacques Boissard, *Romanae urbis topographiae*, Frankfurt, 1600

Considerable documentation, principally from poets and humanists of the courts of Julius II and Leo X, testifies to the constructing of imperial propaganda around this statue, whose papal ownership is parallel to the relations of either Julius Caesar or Octavius Caesar to the real-life Egyptian queen. There is much to be said about this aspect of the statue's reception, to which we shall return; for the moment, suffice it to note that "Cleopatra" was an attractive identification because it could be turned into immediate political significance in a way that, say, "Ariadne" or "Reclining Female Figure" could not. And whatever the cause of the identification as Cleopatra, the effect is certainly that the statue becomes instrumental in establishing the papal revival and protection of antiquity as a sign of Roman continuity, from the first imperial Julius to Julius II, or between their respective great successors, Augustus and Leo X.

Nor does the name "Ariadne," which was first given to the statue around the time it was captured by Napoleon, resolve all questions about the figure's identity. As scholars of a more scientific bent, we might be expected to resist the temptation to make a whole identification out of a tiny bracelet. Rather than fix on an external verbal narrative reflected in the art object, we consider the history of art objects themselves, a field that has greatly expanded since 1512. Yet we tie this history together by means of a small and ambiguous sculptural gesture. We call her Ariadne because she has her arm around her head and because in a sizable number of ancient sarcophagi Ariadne sleeps in that position. Indeed the gesture does appear to be an icon for sleep, but is it an icon for Ariadne? On another set of sarcophagi, the same gesture belongs to Rhea

4.9. *Mars and Rhea Silvia* (detail), marble sarcophagus, second century A.D., Vatican Museums, Rome

Silvia, who is sleeping while she is approached by Mars, on his way to impregnating her with Romulus and Remus (fig. 4.9). And on yet another series, the gesture belongs to Endymion, who is sleeping when Selene falls in love with him (fig. 4.10).[51] In other words, all we have really proved is that the figure is probably sleeping rather than dead and probably to be construed in some erotic sense. These discoveries, of course, were as manifest to early modern intuition as to twentieth-century iconographic science.

What is perhaps most instructive in considering these past and present acts of naming is not the gradual attainment of philological accuracy but the way the name conditions the experience of seeing the work. Sixteenth-century viewers saw a woman whose defining trait was an asp. As for us, I quote the description from the indispensable work of Bober and Rubinstein:

> Ariadne lies in uneasy slumber on a rocky support. . . . The sculptor has managed to capture both the pathos of her situation, exhausted and abandoned by Theseus on the island of Naxos, and the salvation that awaits her, awakening to the epiphany of Bacchus (Dionysus), who will take her as his bride. Although a thin under-*chiton*, girdled high beneath the breasts, sensuously unveils her left breast and part of her abdomen, it seems by its tattered quality to testify to the rigours of the sea-passage from Crete. . . . The majestic thighs and legs, calmly disposed and wrapped in grandiose folds that recall sculptures in the Parthenon pediments, seem to speak of the divine honours to come.[52]

4.10. *Diana and Endymion* (detail), marble sarcophagus, third century A.D., Galleria Doria Pamphili, Rome

Absent the name "Ariadne," I am not sure the slumber would seem so uneasy or the garment so tattered. Nor is it clear in what part of the body or the clothing we are to find the figure's psychological condition, her recent travels, or her future marriage prospects. Do "majestic thighs and legs" really speak, and, if so, do they say the same thing to everybody, or do they not rather give viewers the opportunity to exercise their own narrative and imaginative skills?[53] We have, in short, a great deal in common with sixteenth-century viewers.

There is, to be sure, nothing misguided or quixotic about the quest of modern art historians to recover a name for this sleeping individual that the Hellenistic artist and viewer alike might have agreed upon—so long as they bear in mind that a rhetorical gap separated the object even from its contemporary viewer and that both rhetorical and historical gaps separate it from any later viewer. When we fail to place these contingencies at the center of the story, we are not taking crucial factors into account. Some of these speak to the particulars of the Renaissance, that is, the evolving and uncertain nature of information about antiquity. Some speak to larger historical considerations, which include differences in the conventions of verbal and visual narrative. And some have no cultural limits at all: they are concerned rather with the waywardness of the human gaze.

Let us begin to reacquaint ourselves with these rhetorical and historical gaps by means of the other caption for this statue, in its own way improbable enough. The "Sleeping Nymph" finds her origin in a report that dates from the 1480s:

On the banks of the Danube there is sculpted a sleeping nymph at a beautiful fountain. Under the figure is this epigram:

Nymph of the grot, these sacred Springs I keep,
And to the Murmur of these Waters sleep;
Ah spare my Slumbers, gently tread the Cave!
And drink in silence, or in silence lave![54]

The antiquity of the inscription—which is the point of the report, since it appears in a manuscript offering newly discovered ancient epigraphy—is dubious, though some have attempted to trace it to the eastward travels of Ciriaco d'Ancona, himself no infallible guarantor of authenticity. The statue is surely as incapable of being authenticated as the inscription; and even if someone once saw it, none of those in western Europe who re-created it ever claimed to have seen it.[55]

The identification of the Vatican statue with this reported fountain-sculpture is clearly different in kind from such titles as "Cleopatra" or "Ariadne." "Sleeping Nymph" is not a story in itself, though some viewers then and now have sought to impose on the work particular tales in the course of which nymphs (Ariadne among them) go to sleep. The enormous diffusion of this Danube statue sighting—including the requotation of the inscription, the repeated drawing and painting of reclining female figures at fountains with and without the inscription, and the use of the words and the image in actual landscape design—testifies to the deep satisfactions produced by this particular representation of ancient culture.[56] The topos alluded to here, so widely known in the Renaissance, is the *locus amoenus*, which, in its many appearances in classical literature, turns from static image to dynamic narrative when it is destroyed through some immoral or tragic action.[57] Thus the proverbial milieu of the sleeping nymph becomes a sacred garden materially lost in the mists of time and geography but captured in words which themselves can guide the reconstruction of present-day paradisiacal gardens with their own verbal inscriptions, which in turn generate more material constructions, and so on. So the temporality of an ancient myth—whichever ancient myth—is rendered in part transhistorical. In reimagining and reconstructing the locus amoenus, the Renaissance takes it out of the past and is empowered to design a sixteenth-century paradise now. After all, Julius's Belvedere itself is only the most famous of the collections of ancient sculpture that are conceived simultaneously as timeless pleasure gardens and as authentic re-creations of a particular ancient villa.[58] The "Sleeping Nymph," and other such classical ornaments in a landscape, therefore begins to take part both in timelessness and in varying forms of narrative time.

Which brings us back to the Vatican statue. The report from the Danube did not come with pictures; the Vatican statue was not discovered in the company of a fountain or an inscription. But an elective affinity brings them together, making the sometime Cleopatra into the principal model for the realization of the *locus amoenus* as well as

for the various narratives of sleeping nymphs.[59] Nor are they related merely by collateral similarity and *Zeitgeist*. Almost immediately upon its arrival at the Belvedere the statue was installed as a fountain, as a drawing by Francisco de Hollanda attests (fig. 4.11). The verbal evidence of 1512 and the visual evidence from the late 1530s presumably refer to the same installation, in which the statue sits in front of a moist grotto and is surrounded by jets of water that flow into a sarcophagus placed underneath.[60] Clearly the terms of the Danube report relating nymph and water were realized in an especially unmediated way. The literary observer, Giovanni Francesco Pico della Mirandola, like his more famous uncle a Savonarolan, found himself interrupted in the serious pursuit of active public business with Pope Julius ("causa negotiorum et vel pacem vel arma tractandi"; for the purpose of negotiating both peace and war) and instead forced into a paganizing contemplative life among the statues of the Belvedere garden, which acted as a sort of antechamber. The experience led him to compose a moralistic satire entitled *De Venere et Cupidine expellendis* (inspired especially by the *Venus Felix*), which, along with an accompanying letter to L. G. Giraldi, demonstrates that Pico is an accomplished classical scholar and poet despite his ardent fundamentalism.

Of the fountain-statue Pico says, "And in another corner one can see the image of Cleopatra bitten by the asp. A fountain trickles down almost from her very breasts in the manner of the ancient aqueducts; it is then caught in an antique marble sarcophagus on which some of the deeds of the Emperor Trajan are depicted."[61] In the Hollanda drawing the water is definitely not flowing from the statue's breasts; nor is it at all clear that the sarcophagus in question (which is still in the Vatican collection, though not currently part of this installation) depicts Trajan. To be sure, words like *quasi* and *quaepiam* make it apparent that Pico is a bit anxious about these assertions. But he offers no such distancing devices when he makes the more curious claim that the flow of the water resembles ancient aqueducts. Most likely the analogy is to the fountains associated with the emperor Agrippa's plumbing projects, but why should this particular fountain make Pico think of them?[62] What I think Pico is recognizing in his highly disapproving way is the great distance that separates the ancient Rome of high imperial deeds and engineering miracles—the world of *negotium* that the popes had been appropriating at least from the time of Sixtus IV[63]—from the new reconstructed ancient Rome of *otium* as epitomized in the Belvedere garden and in a statue of Cleopatra, once a spoil of imperial war but now an erotically represented fountain whose trickle of water mocks the antique aqueducts.

Pico may not have been familiar with the Danube inscription that helped to authorize the rendering of this statue as a fountain nymph. For that reason he stands as all the more powerful a witness to the transvaluation that is taking place. Even if Cleopatra and Roman propaganda are not forgotten, and even if the Danubian inscription is not included in the monument, the statue has definitely been assimilated into the world of paganized nature, as is abundantly clear from the elaborate illusionistic details of landscape in the Hollanda drawing. The illusion that the Belvedere garden seeks to create is that it can stop time—a prospect all too obvious to Pico, who is sentenced to use it as a waiting room—and it therefore depends on a different kind of narrative time, even though it is also a place where the pope advertizes his ability to control everyday time.

These conflicts in temporality are rooted in conflicts over different narratives and different kinds of narrative. Too many possible captions, such as in the case of this statue, turn out to be something like too few captions, as in the case of the *Spinario*. They destabilize a fixed link between the sign and the thing signified; that is, between the sculpture and its cognitive referent. (One of the words for statue in Latin is, after all, *signum*.)[64] And they produce a contagion among quite separate narratives that happen to converge in the enigmatic space of the signum-statue. Evangelista Maddaleni Capodiferro, a humanist in the Belvedere milieu of whom we have heard before, composed a number of verses in response to the Vatican statue.[65] All are speeches by the statue-figure herself rather than descriptions of the work or of the viewer's response to the work. But the alternative captions combine to produce a single composite voice. The identity of Sleeping Nymph—whose very attribution is prosopopoeic—gives the Egyptian queen a voice, which is, significantly, that of Cleopatra at a fountain. There is certainly a historical and political narrative in these verses: the first Julius subjugated Egypt while Augustus defeated Cleopatra; now Julius II ("second only in respect to years") has placed her as the defeated guardian of his fountain. But there are other matters separable from this story, for instance:

> *Quantum me, vivam, Caesar mundi arbiter, arsit*
> *Marmoream tantum Iulius alter amat.*

> As much as Caesar, ruler of the world, burned for me when I was alive, so much
> the other Julius loves me in marble.

The passionate desire of the first Julius for the living Cleopatra is compared with—
or transformed into—the aesthetic love that the second Julius derives from his art
collection.

Referring more directly to the Danubian inscription, a hypothetical (masculine) intruder is told to drink and wash in silence and not to disturb the queen's sleep;
but with the historical narrative comes a *reason* why she so badly needs sleep—that is,
to suffer through the great sorrow of her fall and loss:

> *Accedas et abi tacitusque lavere bibasque*
> *Infaelix somno dum Cleopatra fruor*
> *Iulius invicta nulli pietate secundus*
> *Quam duxit statuit me bene propter aquam*
> *Nam veluti fluit ista fluunt mortalia regna.*

> Approach and depart, drink and wash in silence, while I, wretched Cleopatra,
> take pleasure in sleep. Julius II placed me here, though unconquered by any
> sense of duty, up against the fountain; for just as the water flows, so flow mortal
> realms.

The queen herself tends not to be dying from the venomous snake-bracelet but sleeping, like the Danubian nymph, and similarly demanding something of the viewers. Not
only are they to be silent, but they are also required to take part in her own historical
meditation, itself ambiguously poised between the conflated imperial-papal triumph
and the misery of her defeat. The nymph's undisturbed sleep becomes a figure for the
long time span between Juliuses, which not only separates ancient and modern Rome
but also distinguishes one set of desires (both libidinous and imperial), requiring a living, subservient Cleopatra, from another set (aesthetic) that is satisfied with—or even
prefers—a Cleopatra in marble. What is being added to the history of the Egyptian
queen is not a new episode in which the dying Cleopatra escapes with snake from her
palace into a Danubian wilderness but instead an enforced meditation on what the
queen feels about her own tragic life and an inscribed set of responses for the viewer.

But if these prosopopoeic voices constitute a historical and personal dialogue, it is nevertheless also true, as Paul de Man suggested in his discussion of this
trope, that they arise from and reveal the poet-viewer's fear of being silenced.[66]
Alberti, it will be recalled, had offered as one of the possible "explanatory" effects in a
historia the figure who "with ferocious expression and forbidding glance challenges

[the viewers] not to come near, as if he wished their business to be secret."[67] One of the ways in which the image unfolds itself, in other words, is to challenge or exclude the viewer's involvement. So that force of deanimation which de Man diagnoses as the poet's latent fear may be more like the natural condition of those who observe powerful but enigmatic visual representations. This is essentially the burden of the prosopopoeic Sleeping Nymph inscription, which I quote once again:

> Huius nymphae loci, sacri custodia fontis,
> Dormio, dum blandae sentio murmur aquae.
> Parce meum, quisquis tangis cava marmora, somnum
> Rumpere. Sive bibas sive lavere tace.

> Nymph of this place, custodian of the sacred fountain,
> I sleep while I hear the murmuring of the smooth-sounding water.
> Spare me, whoever touches upon this marble cave, do not
> Interrupt my sleep. Whether you drink or wash, be silent.

It is a speech that cancels speech, thereby introducing a maze of linguistic paradoxes. An object that is inanimate but for a representational illusion "speaks," only to establish that it is in a condition (i.e., sleep) that forbids speech. In the process it demands silence of the observer, who, unlike the statue, is both awake and animate and therefore quite capable of speaking. While the statue identifies itself as possessing a consciousness, it reveals little of itself—only that it *could* reveal something if it chose. What the inscription inscribes is the observer; that is, it turns the statue into a work that knows it is being watched and defines the terms for the watching. According to these terms, the observer, intruding on sacred ground, becomes a hostile and even destructive force. That is in itself no surprise within a locus amoenus, whose very definition depends on a contrast between timelessness, equivalent to the immobility of the statue, and threats from the external world of action, equivalent to the observer. The imaginary Danube setting and its realization in the Belvedere implicitly criticize the teleological world of time and history, represented by the wayfarer-addressee of the inscription who is basically told to wash up, drink up, shut up, and leave. So, to the extent that sixteenth-century viewers see the statue as Sleeping Nymph—and this is much abetted by staging it as a fountain in a garden—they are creating their own narrative experience in a perpetually present temporality that is independent and critical of history and even of language. To the extent that they see it as Cleopatra—abetted by many verbal and visual cues—they are entering a world of both stories and histories, which tie the observers directly to the Roman Empire.

This is more than a struggle between aesthetic timelessness and the linearity of public history. The inscription defines itself and the work as a paradigm of the artistic experience. The caption that tells viewers to be silent is bound to make them aware of what it is that they would say if they were permitted to speak. It forces them into a

4.12. Michelangelo, *Night*, marble, 1520s, Medici Tombs, Florence

dynamic relation with the work even as it seems to disallow such a relation and to declare that the work is sufficient unto itself. What the sculpted figure contributes to this reading—after all, she doesn't offer much—is her somnolence. Sleep, particularly as it is filtered through the Danube inscription, is definitive of the condition of the work of art: alive yet immobile, capable of psychic activity but not of speech, existing in an alternative but parallel world to that of the real-life daylight observer. The sleeping work of art is thus paradigmatic of that most ancient and universal article of praise for representational images: that they are so real they could almost come to life. To wake up would be to come to life. The barrier between sleep and waking becomes the experiential equivalent of that between art and life.

The same problematic is illustrated in one of the most famous poetic responses to a work of art from this period. The subject is Michelangelo's *Night*, in the Medici Chapel (fig. 4.12), and the first quatrain is the response of a viewer who is evidently not silenced:

> La Notte, che tu vedi in sì dolci atti
> Dormire, fu da un Angelo scolpita
> In questo sasso: e, perchè dorme, ha vita:
> Destala, se no 'l credi, e parleratti.

> Night, which you see sleeping in such a lovely position, was sculpted by an Angel [i.e., Michelangelo] in this stone; and because she sleeps, she lives. Disturb her, if you don't believe it, and she will speak to you.

To which the sculptor responded, in the voice of his creation:

> Grato mi è il sonno, e più l'esser di sasso:
> Mentre che il danno e la vergogna dura,
> Non veder, non sentir, m'è gran ventura;
> Però non mi destar; deh parla basso![68]

> Sleep is pleasing to me, and being made of stone is more so, while injury and
> shame endure. Not to see, not to feel are my good fortune; therefore, don't dis-
> turb me, please, speak softly.

Both poets are clearly familiar with the Danube inscription, or at least its genre. Giovanni Battista Strozzi, the poet-viewer, understands that her being-as-art consists in her sleeping, but he is willing to throw it away rather blithely just to prove how real she is. Michelangelo uses the occasion for a comment on the restored Medici, but he also makes the point that the sleep of the statue is equivalent to its artistic perfection and to its independence from the changeable (and politicized) real world of the observer.

There are many different ways for figures in artistic representation to be sleeping, not all of which would promote the claim that the observer might be danger-ous to their sleep or their existence. The gaze that is identified and described by the Danube caption is not merely aesthetic; it is erotic. What the wayfarer is really being told is *noli me tangere*. Do not, in other words, intrude on the sacred fountain space with a sexuality that is at least voyeuristic and that might become carnal. And just as the inscription's injunction to silence inspires the wish to speak, so the injunction against a sexual gaze is bound to bring voyeurism into conscious play. But this is one voyeurism that is not merely in the eye of the beholder; nor is it merely invented by the caption. The beautiful woman asleep with a notable promise of nudity is in herself a perfect object for the voyeur—an object that may be watched with impunity. In this sense, one could say that the inscription is generated precisely as a guilty response to this pleasure, that is, as a means of contradicting the supposition that the work of art may be viewed as merely a passive pornographic object that is unaware of being watched. It is therefore no coincidence that our statue's gesture has so much in com-mon with sarcophagal representations of Ariadne or Rhea Silvia, for they, too, are figures who inspire erotic passion while they sleep. As does Endymion. This class of figure is not limited to females. The beautiful boy has an equally long history as passive sex object; he is represented in this posture not only by the beloved of Selene but also, for those who might respond to an even more passive object, by the dying Adonis.

The aesthetic experience rendered and defined as voyeurism and the dramatic situation of an intrusion upon the locus amoenus are in their nature quite separate. Indeed, nothing about the Vatican figure requires us to imagine her outdoors, let alone in the wilderness. That the Renaissance imagination places such a well-dressed and, *pace* Bober and Rubinstein, peacefully sleeping individual in that setting is another of the paradoxes that surround the experience of seeing her. The fact that the Vatican statue was imaginatively dragged to the far-off Danube is prophetic of a fundamental indoor-outdoor problematic in all the countless painted figures in landscapes that come to be a ruling icon in sixteenth-century, and later, art. The genre of the beautiful woman reclining in a landscape, from Giorgione to Titian and onward, has been contextualized in the iconographic universe of classical mythology, often with the assumption that high levels of exegesis were meant to be applied to the works.[69] But all such stories and allegories coexist with the visual narrative of the viewers who come upon an enigmatic beauty exhibiting herself passively before their gaze. It is the incongruity of an elegant female relaxing in the wilderness that creates the dramatic illusion of surprise, turning the viewer into the protagonist of a narrative, like those of the bathing Diana and Susanna, so popular in the Renaissance—except that here the performance of voyeurism has no mythological mediators like Actaeon or the Elders, and it takes place in the ever-present time of the beholder.

That which the viewer-voyeur comes upon in the wilderness is not only a beautiful woman but also a beautiful work of art. The context of the Danube report, after all, places the statue in the history of works of art rather than the history of empires or gods; the anonymous traveler to the East reported seeing not a nymph but a statue. The art object thus becomes not so much a secondary re-presentation of an unrecoverable history as it is the primary event itself. As it turns out, the diachronic Cleopatra narrative can also be focused on the material object. From a number of sources, the Renaissance knew well the story of the queen's death, which centered on the secrecy and exoticism of her means of suicide.[70] Through the stratagem of the asp she outwitted Octavius Caesar and prevented herself from being taken alive and from enduring the humiliation of appearing in a Roman triumphal procession as one of the spoils of war. But according to Dio Cassius, one of many sources on this story known to the Renaissance, the strategy is only partly successful: "On the second day [of the triumphs in Rome] the naval victory at Actium was commemorated, and on the third the subjugation of Egypt. . . . The Egyptian celebration surpassed them all in costliness and magnificence. Among other features, an effigy of Cleopatra upon a couch was carried by, so that in a way she, too, together with the other captives and with her children, Alexander, called also Helios, and Cleopatra, called also Selene, was a part of the spectacle and a trophy in the procession."[71] The flesh-and-blood historical Cleopatra, in other words, already exists in a complicated relation of exchange with her sculptural representation. Dio Cassius is declaring that the queen was, in effect, present in the effigy, comparable to the way her children were literally present in the procession. The force of such a claim in this case is as a comment on the great final struggle of Cleopatra's life, which was to avoid being exhibited in Rome, a goal she accomplished by killing herself. Indeed so valuable was this prize of Cleopatra dead in Egypt rather than alive in Rome that her achieving it represents a significant victory over the otherwise all-powerful Octavius. But all the tropes that celebrate visual art objects—their verisimilitude, their ability to breathe or to speak—are precisely what defeat the queen's purpose by rendering her, in effect, alive to her humiliation in Rome.

And, come the Renaissance, she *is* being exhibited in Rome. Not surprisingly, a number of responses to the Vatican statue suggest that viewers at least entertained the hypothesis that this was the very effigy carried in the post-Actium triumphs. There is nothing so fanciful in this belief. Renaissance Roman celebrations, such as the *possesso* of Leo X in 1513,[72] made use of the newly discovered ancient statues, while the narrative of the ancient triumph gives the recently discovered work a perfectly credible provenance. When the work is viewed with this possibility in mind, its very ontology changes and multiplies. It becomes a real part of history in a basic touristic sense. What that means is, once again, that it is not a re-presentation but the thing itself; thus it focuses the viewer's gaze not so much on the remote events that the statue represents as on the thing that is performing the representation. This is particularly the case in that the triumphal effigy has a problematized history *as* representation. But it also inserts the viewer into a kind of transhistorical position, in which the experience of seeing Cleopatra—erotic, aesthetic, political—is perpetually played out with all the ambiguities it possessed back in the days of the post-Actium triumphal procession.

The statue-Cleopatra is thus both a piece of history and a piece of art that collapses or substitutes for historical time, a fact perhaps best understood by Castiglione in the monologue that he wrote for the object:

> Quod licuisse mihi indignatus perfidus hostis
> saevitiae insanis stimulus exarsit et ira;
> namque triumphali invectus Capitolia curru
> insignes inter titulos gentesque subactas
> exstinctae infelix simulacrum duxit, et amens
> spectaculo explevit crudelia lumina inani.
> Neu longaeva vetustas facti famam aboleret
> aut seris mea sors ignota nepotibus esset,
> effigiem excudi spiranti e marmore iussit
> testari, et casus fatum miserabile nostri.[73]

> My treacherous enemy, outraged that it was permitted to me to die in Egypt, burned with anger and the mad goadings of rage, for, in his triumphal chariot on the Capitol among the famous captives with their labelled titles, he was so unlucky as to have only a simulacrum of me dead to lead in his procession. In his frenzy he had to satisfy his cruel desire for glory with an empty spectacle. Yet all the ages of the future will not cancel the fame of my deeds, nor will my fortune go unknown among my later descendants. This statue that he ordered to be hammered out of living, breathing marble will bear witness both to my fall and to my miserable fate.

It is ventriloquism on the scale of Pasquino: is this Cleopatra or the statue who is speaking? Cleopatra attempts to cancel the humiliation of being exhibited in Rome by declaring that the emptiness of a mere statue-representation signifies a defeat for Augustus. But she transvalues the image of the statue so that it is not a pale substitute for her own self but a positive force for the memorialization of her personal history. By having the voice both of the queen and of the statue, this speaker effects a transformation from *infelix simulacrum* to *effigiem spiranti e marmore* and thus moves from instrument of imperial propaganda to an independent work of art that is judged not by its representational utility but by its affective verisimilitude. Castiglione is returning the viewer's gaze both to the beauty of the object and to the person of Cleopatra. A dead queen, a sleeping statue, a living and speaking narrative of history.

Different narratives, different kinds of narrative; one might add, challenges to narrative. The re-viewing of a statue like the Vatican *Reclining Female* is perhaps best summed up in the ambiguities that surround Alberti's *historia*. History consists of many different stories, one or more of which may be reflected in the mute material relic from ancient times. But given that these same works may be endowed with voices or the ability to respond to voices, they also tell the story of viewership itself, which telescopes history. At the same time, the reappearance of these objects is a historical, and not just a transhistorical, event. In that sense, the unexpected sight of a sleeping beauty, a work of art that is also an erotic object, is the paradigmatic story of rediscovering ancient sculpture, where all the drama and anxiety of awakening becomes the narrative equivalent to the present threshold moment in history. As with the voices of Pasquino, the histories and stories of *Ariadne-Cleopatra* find their point of convergence in the art object itself. It is therefore fitting that the final category of reconstruction be that history which is explicitly focused on such objects: the history of art.

IN BED WITH POLYCLITUS

Even more than the *Pasquino* or the *Ariadne-Cleopatra*, the *Bed of Polyclitus* (figs. 4.13, 4.14) reveals everything and nothing in its name. But the emphasis, at least to begin with, needs to be more on the nothing than on the everything. What one can say for certain is, first, that unlike almost every other highly significant piece of rediscovered sculpture, this is not a single work but a family of similar objects. That it existed in multiples is appropriate to its genre of relief sculpture, which was often mass-produced to begin with, though it is noteworthy that relatively few such works, whether unique or not, garnered such fame as this one. It is also easy enough to describe what is represented in the work, notably, the upper half of a male figure, eyes closed, reclining in a position of extreme relaxation on a bed, balanced by a complete and elaborately turned nude female figure, partly recumbent on the same bed while she lifts the coverings to reveal the male figure; and, finally, a tiny crouching figure at the foot of the bed.

I offer the description in this clinical manner, first, because it appears that

4.13. *Bed of Polyclitus*, marble, Roman relief after Hellenistic figure types, Palazzo Maffei, Rome

this precise configuration—nothing more, nothing less—was common to all the works that went under the name and, second, because none of this pileup of detail has produced any very clear possibility of identifying the subject matter. Here the case is different from the two other pieces of sculpture considered in this chapter: this relief is not mutilated like the *Pasquino*, nor does it consist of a solitary figure deprived of narrative context, like the Vatican female. Further, the very frequency and uniformity of its representations ought to point to some obvious story that could be easily recognized, at least in late antiquity. Nevertheless, no one in postclassical times has ever been very certain what this is a picture of. The prevailing opinion is that this is Psyche uncovering Cupid while he sleeps.[74] The episode comes from the widely read and depicted story by Apuleius, in which Psyche is allowed to be the wife of an unknown but immensely rich and loving husband only so long as she remains, literally, in the dark as to who he is. But she breaks the rules and brings a candle to observe him. The candle wax drips, and the bargain comes undone. Whether this is the correct caption or not, it appears only in the seventeenth century when this composition is imitated in depicting the Apuleian story afresh. Pirro Ligorio in the mid-sixteenth century offers a different (and, in my view, more plausible) suggestion, namely, that the relief depicts the moment in book 8 of the *Aeneid*, when Venus approaches her sleeping husband, Vulcan, with the offer of sexual favors so that he will forge a shield for the hero.[75]

What is probably more significant than the debate on possible captions is how little the Renaissance seems to have asked the question. In a considerable field of

4.14. *Bed of Polyclitus*, Renaissance copy of Roman relief, location unknown

references to this object from the fifteenth and sixteenth centuries, Pirro Ligorio is the only observer who ever mentions a story at all. Even in this account, the narrative occupies much less space than two other matters that, by this time, are already the defining features of this work. The first is the precise disposition of the bodies: Ligorio describes the exact placement of each limb of both Vulcan and Venus. The second matter interests him even more:

> Polyclitus was a most illustrious sculptor from Thasia, who sculpted . . . [a list of briefly described works, then] a Venus flirting with Vulcan while he is reclining on a bed. One finds many copies in small format of this work in middle relief, one of which was discovered in Rome near the Temple of Peace, now in the possession of Monsignor Pietro Bembo cardinal of Padua. Another similar one was discovered around Trajan's Baths, on that side where the vineyard of Monsignor Giovanni Gaddi, cleric in the Camera Apostolica had his vineyard. After the death of this gentleman it passed into the hands of Rodolfo Pio, Cardinal Carpense; subsequently it was presented by his brother to his serene highness Duke Alfonso II of Ferrara, and he has placed it among his extraordinarily beautiful collection of antiquities, where . . . [a Greek inscription] declares that the work is without any doubt from the studio of Polyclitus of Thasia, that it is entirely the work of that sculptor, a relief made in the form of a bed or pallet worthy of praise, and that it is a thing not to be harmed or mutilated, indeed to be held in awe.[76]

All the usual caveats about Ligorio's scholarly reliability apply: the catalogue of Polyclitus's oeuvre is whimsical, even by the standards of sixteenth-century art history; the provenances are open to question; the Greek inscription is of dubious authenticity, and even if it is genuine, it gets incorrectly interpreted.77 No matter: this text is the complete Renaissance retrospective on the *Bed*, and in it the work's most important characteristic is the definitive ascription of authorship to Polyclitus, by no means original to Ligorio but contained in every reference to the object, back to at least the early fifteenth century. The passage further outlines all the significant issues that surround such a claim. Many avatars of the work were made, have been unearthed, and are circulating among collectors; there is, however, a true and authentic original defined by the hand of the ancient master; that original, confirmed textually by antique epigraphy, earns the status of an artistic relic, to be revered and kept from the kind of harm that has evidently been visited on so many remains of ancient sculpture.

In case it needs to be said, this attribution, even by information that the Renaissance possessed, is nonsensical. It depends, as we will see, on Pliny, but neither the list of works nor any of the generic or stylistic indicators in the *Natural History* gives the least encouragement to it. In fact, almost any other rediscovered statue discussed in this book would make more sense as part of this artist's oeuvre. This particular act of reconstruction, then, consists in choosing an object, notable for many things but certainly *not* for any specific or lofty authorship, and electing to put the name Polyclitus to it. Who is responsible, what it is about the work that encourages such an attribution (or indeed *any* attribution), what the consequences of this belief are in Renaissance artistic culture—these interlocking issues will define a notable strand in the recuperating and reimagining of antiquity and antiquities.

The matter of attribution in general has arisen at a number of points in this book. Few objects resurfaced with unimpeachable evidence of their authorship, and none of those presented impressive credentials. The *Torso Belvedere* is signed, though by an artist with no other record of his existence, and the *Laocoön* is ascribed by Pliny to three sculptors who are not very important. Attributing unsigned works long after the fact is a quite different (and time-honored) practice. The late antique inscriptions on the two *Dioscuri*, which read "Opus Praxitelis" and "Opus Fidiae," suggest the most basic motives for the attachment of such names: commerce and prestige.78 Rich individuals with private collections and monarchs engaging in self-aggrandizing public display, whether they live in imperial Rome or in Medicean Florence, are happy to inflate the pedigree of art objects in their care. But with regard to the rediscovered antiquities, such strategies are not, on the whole, effective. One might indeed ask, negatively, why the Renaissance does so little to link up the statues they are looking at with the legendary names that they read about: the answer would have to do with a gap between textual antiquity and material antiquity, such as was discussed above in Chapter 2. It is nevertheless true that the famous names plucked from Pliny's history do sometimes hover about these objects. When the Ravenna thrones or a Venus fragment in the collection of Gentile Bellini are declared to be the work of Praxiteles, when the horses of San Marco are ascribed to Lysippus, when Cencio da Rustici declares that he would "pay more for a small marble figure by Phidias or Praxiteles than for a living and breathing image of the man who turns the statues of those glorious men into dust or gravel," when the *Pasquino* is said to be "forse de Prassitele o Fidia," it is part wishful thinking, part ostentatious erudition.[79] The underlying force, however, is the capacity of Pliny's text to be read as a document of rhetorical praise and, especially, to inspire a sense that certain artists' names were exemplary and even proverbial.

In spite of the real and legendary merits of the sculptors mentioned in these references, the proverbial Name of the Artist par excellence was Polyclitus. For the Renaissance his canonization is assured by important citations in both Dante and Petrarch. The context in the *Commedia* is a set of narrative reliefs carved at the entrance to Purgatory:

> Là sù non eran mossi i piè nostri anco,
> quand'io conobbi quella ripa intorno
> che, dritta, di salita aveva manco,
> esser di marmo candido e addorno
> d'intagli sì, che non pur Policreto,
> ma la natura lì avrebbe scorno.[80]   [10.28–33]

Not yet had we moved our feet on it when I perceived that the encircling bank (which, being vertical, lacked means of ascent) was of pure white marble, and was adorned with such carvings that not only Polycletus but Nature herself would there be put to shame.

In the *Rime* the subject is Laura's beauty and a portrait of her executed by Simone Martini:

> Per mirar Policleto a prova fiso
> con gli altri ch'ebber fama di quell'arte,
> mill'anni non vedrian la minor parte
> della beltà che m'àve il cor conquisto.[81]   [77.1–4]

Even though Polyclitus should for a thousand years compete in looking with all the others who were famous in that art, they would never see the smallest part of the beauty that has conquered my heart.

Polyclitus stands for greatest human artist, even when the immediate referent is not sculpture but painting.[82] The context for such a judgment is the Platonic hierarchy of God, nature, and humanity, each of which can be understood as having its own ability to produce forms. In this scheme the artist exists as a rhetorical placeholder designed to be exponentially outdone by more transcendent types of creation. It is, nevertheless,

4.15. After Polyclitus, *Doryphoros*, marble,
Roman copy after fifth-century B.C. original,
Minneapolis Institute of Arts

a highly honorable defeat, which Polyclitus earns owing to his appearance in a passage from the *Nichomachean Ethics* that is repeated and commented on by Aquinas. Aristotle is moving from a discussion of individual categories of wisdom (σοφία) toward a more universal notion of the concept: "We use the term 'wisdom' to designate certain specific arts [τέχναιζ], designating those who are most perfect at each of them. So we call Phidias a wise stonecutter [λιθουγὸν] and Polycleitus a wise statue-maker [ἀνδριαντοποιόν]. In this case, wisdom simply refers to the particular excellence of their art."[83] As we have seen before, the history of art serves an exemplary function in the making of logical distinctions, especially when they are meant to be functional rather than hierarchical differences.[84] This may indeed be the ur-instance, since the subject is that quintessentially Aristotelean idea of things working out their own individual perfections. The philosophical notion soon becomes a linguistic one, given that the point needs to be made by the use of highly refined distinctions in terminology. The expression *sculptor*, in other words, has to be broken down into subcomponents one might not ordinarily recognize as separable.

      None of these references, of course, is sensitive to the actual work of the two artists: for Aristotle they are rhetorical exempla, while for Aquinas and the poets they are merely legends and textual residues. Still, the marriage of Aristotelean perfections and Platonic ladders has a remarkable intertextual force by the fourteenth century; and the discourse of the visual arts serves both to ground a philosophical account of difference and to embody all the paradoxes of being and representation that join theology with poetics. Yet it seems as though Aristotle is in the long run defeated by his own rhetorical examples. He may have wished to define equal but separate perfections; later readers confronted with one stonecutter and one statue maker, however, are bound to place the laurel on the *statuificus* Polyclitus. Hence his proverbial standing for the poets.

But it is a wholly different textual Polyclitus that grounds his significance for art theory and practice—that very text of Pliny which seems to render it so unlikely that he could have produced the *Bed*:

> Polyclitus Sicyonius, Hageladae discipulus, . . . fecit . . . idem et doryphorum viriliter puerum. fecit et quem canona artifices vocant liniamenta artis ex eo petentes veluti a lege quadam, solusque hominum artem ipsam fecisse artis opere iudicatur. fecit et destringentem se et nudum telo incessentem duosque pueros item nudos, talis ludentes, qui vocantur astragalizontes et sunt in Titi imperatoris atrio—quo opere nullum absolutus plerique iudicant. . . . hic consummasse hanc scientiam iudicatur et toreuticen sic erudisse, ut Phidias aperuisse.[85]

> Polyclitus of Sicyon, pupil of Hageladas, made . . . the *Doryphoros* [the spear bearer], an image of a boy already manly. He was also the creator of the statue that artists call the *Canon*, which they turn to as a sort of standard for the rules of their art; alone among human beings he is judged to have created art itself out of a work of art. He also made the statue of the Man using a Body-scraper and, in the nude, the Man Attacking with a Spear, and the Two Boys Playing Dice, also in the nude, known by the Greek name of Astragalizontes and now standing in the fore-court of the Emperor Titus—this is generally considered to be the most perfect work of art in existence. . . . He is said to have carried art to its highest point, and, if Phidias is the inventor of sculpture, Polyclitus may be said to have perfected it.

Pliny seems to be unaware that the *Doryphoros* (fig. 4.15) and the *Canon* are one and the same (or this may be a textual problem, since it all rests on one simple *et*).[86] For all that, however, his account is precisely focused on the mirror relations between theory and practice, between making art objects and establishing the rules by which they should be made. We know that Polyclitus also wrote a theoretical treatise in which he expounded his theories. But either Pliny was unaware of this (which, considering the number of ancient references to the work, seems unlikely) or else he deliberately wished to present the sculptor as having transcended the distinction between theory and practice.

Such seems to be the burden of Pliny's remarkable claim that "solusque hominum artem ipsam fecisse artis opere iudicatur" ("alone among human beings he is judged to have created art itself out of a work of art"). Pliny is telling his readers that Art as an abstract universal category (with a capital A, as we would say) was created—and therefore can be seen—in a work of art. He is also (though very elliptically) characterizing this Art. It is a statue that is also a "rule," and Pliny has to have recourse to Greek for the word Κανών which he seems for the first time here to be domesticating into Latin. This collective object belongs to artists themselves ("quem canona artifices vocant"). And it is transitive; that is, artists use this work of art to go on to make other works of art—a fact confirmed by accounts of the Polyclitan canon in both Cicero and Quintilian.

So far as the details of the system are concerned, all accounts are tantalizingly ambiguous. Indeed it is something of a comfort that we know hardly any more than the Renaissance did about the actual system of measurement that Polyclitus promulgated. A few pronouncements emerge in citations, for example, "perfection comes about little by little through many numbers" and "the work is hardest when the clay comes to the fingernail," which seem to refer to complex and minute proportions. Galen makes a passing allusion to the Canon in an argument that distinguishes between a system of flexible ratios and a system based on a corporeal unit, like the head or foot, that is used rigidly and repeatedly as a measurement.[87] In a number of sources the Canon is associated with the term *symmetria*.[88] Pliny, once again, is responsible for domesticating this word into Latin; only this time he leaves no doubt about what he is doing: "non habet Latinum nomen symmetria." But Pliny is not talking of Polyclitus here—at least not explicitly. In his progressive model for the history of sculpture, which runs Polyclitus-Myron-Lysippus, Myron is "more careful" than Polyclitus in his symmetria, while Lysippus manages to follow the rules of symmetria most diligently at the same time as he paradoxically creates a new system of proportions that renders figures more attractive to look at.[89] So the system of symmetria, whether it belongs to Polyclitus or to Lysippus or to their collaboration, is grounded in numerical proportions but also transcends their particularity.

In postclassical times the notion of a canon of proportions for the human body, perhaps because of the imprecision with which it was recorded, covers the entire range of discourse from practical information for artists to the most abstruse speculations on universal order.[90] For the later Middle Ages and the Renaissance the corporeal canon is a vital link in the chain of cosmologies that begins with the *Timaeus* and ends with those familiar microcosmic readings in the doctrines of universal harmony and analogy, like Leonardo's Vitruvian man. What is particularly significant is that systems of analogy like these offer some common ground between the ideological work of theologians, cosmologists, or poets and the practical achievements of visual artists. In fact, it may be the art objects themselves that produce the most reliable means of transmission for the theory. Modern art-historical research has identified many copies after the canonical *Doryphoros*, and in them we recognize not a succession of numbers or ratios but rather a complex form of corporeal complementarity: straight versus flexed, weight-bearing versus relaxed, face front versus turned, stationary versus moving. No one in the Renaissance seems to have made such an identification, even though many a rediscovered "Antinous" or "Satyr" (the titles are hardly dependable) was, in fact, based on the canon statue.[91]

But one means of identification was signaled in Pliny: "Proprium eius est, uno crure ut insisterent signa, excogitasse, quadrata tamen esse ea ait Varro et paene ad exemplum" ("A discovery that was entirely [Polyclitus's] own is the art of making statues throwing their weight on one leg, although Varro says these figures are of a square build and almost all made on one model" [34.56]). This claim, though complicated by modern readings of Pliny and Polyclitus,[92] still resounds as the etiology for one of the most salient tropes of the rediscovery of antiquity, namely, the *contrapposto*. And the Varronian criticism would only serve to emphasize the foundational quality of Polyclitus's role in this invention, since it was an article of faith that great enterprises had primitive beginnings. ("Nothing, they say, can be newborn and perfected at the same time," says Alberti, paraphrasing Cicero as he concludes the *De pictura*.)[93] Although none of the possible systems of proportion requires a specific bodily posture, it is in fact through the stance of the contrapposto that the Polyclitan canon is made visible to the Renaissance and replicated in a number of its greatest artistic works, beginning with Michelangelo's *David*.

So the struggles to realize, or specify, the canon that arise out of the (inevitable) generality of Pliny and the other ancient texts become arenas for certain crucial intellectual activities. First, there is the correlation of theory to practice—that is, the perpetual motion between abstract systems and either empirical measurement of the body or a "scientific" account of the mediations by which viewers perceive represented bodies. Second, there is a constant refinement of terminology, or distinction making, that generates a whole lexicon of expressions, like *concinnitas*, *lineamenta*, *dimensio*, *finitio*, with the result that, like Pliny's *symmetria* "for which there is no Latin word," the subject of the canon inspires an awareness of the role that language plays in shaping, and limiting, thought.[94] Finally, the pivotal role of Polyclitus as exemplar for Platonic hierarchy and Aristotelean perfectibility as well as practical guide to the making of art objects and inventor of the contrapposto guarantees the talismanic qualities of his name and its viability as a metonym for Art.

It is, of course, the appropriation of that name that concerns us here. If this account of art theory and practice has taken us far from the *Bed of Polyclitus*, that is because it is far. The attribution that becomes the very name of this object depends not on how much it resembles the supposed work of the Greek sculptor but on how grand a bridge was being constructed between what the early moderns could imagine of antiquity and what they could see with their own eyes, between a theory decoded from the past and a practice experienced in the present. Although we do not have a smoking gun, it is quite likely that the individual who forged this bridge, who owned and entitled the work, was none other than Lorenzo Ghiberti. At the very least, he appears as the terminus a quo for the object and its name. Vasari, joining the artist's own production with his collection, tells us that "besides the works by his own hand, [Ghiberti] bequeathed to his heirs many antiquities both in marble and in bronze, such as the bed of Polycletus, which was something very rare."[95] He does not discuss the work in his *Commentari*, but, following on Dante and Petrarch, he does use "Polyclitus" as a sort of synonym for artistic greatness, while the earliest report on his collection speaks of works by Polyclitus but does not mention the *Bed*. At all events, many of those who seek this object will associate it with the Ghiberti family, suggesting that there is at least a family tradition of ascribing it to Polyclitus.[96] Ghiberti's fame as artist, writer, and antiquarian provides a pedigree, and the cluster of associations among him, Polyclitus, and this relief prevails for at least 150 years after it first appears. By the time of the so-called Anonimo Magliabecchiano (some point in the first half of the sixteenth century), the account of Polyclitus, inevitably plagiarized from Pliny, now includes not only the *Diadomenos*, the *Doryphoros*, the *Dice-Players*, and references to the contrapposto and the rules of art but also such statements as "even in our own time one can see the work in bronze from his very hand, the bed with marvelous figures on it . . . which was among the possessions of Lorenzo Ghiberti."[97]

In effect, it is Ghiberti himself—in reality or in reputation—who fulfills and embodies everything that the name Polyclitus stood for. In his *Commentari* he, too, composed art history, art theory, and a canon of corporeal proportion. Unlike the parallel (and relevant) case of Alberti, Ghiberti was above all a practicing artist, so that his verbal project is undisguisedly an attempt to appropriate humanist respectability for those who practice the plastic arts. When Ghiberti undertakes to write a history of ancient art, it is clear that he has read his Pliny. Of Polyclitus, for instance, he tells us exactly what the *Natural History* reported, only it is apparent that Ghiberti has a corrupt text and that he has certainly not seen with his own eyes the works Pliny mentions. In the manuscript that Ghiberti read, the *Doryphoros* must have been a *Dorophoros*, since Ghiberti describes the statue as a "Young Man Bearing Gifts." But the most important thing about Polyclitus he has right: "fece regole e liniamenti dell'arte." Nor is the word "liniamenti" accidental, since Alberti, establishing it as the topic for the first of his books on architecture, would make it the fundamental term for art theory as distinct from practice and, specifically, for a theory based on the analogy to the human body.[98]

The very title *Commentari* not only signals a bid for high humanist status but also associates Ghiberti with those many ancient artists (including Polyclitus) who, according to Pliny, composed theoretical treatises as well as artistic masterpieces.[99] Ghiberti draws this connection as he concludes his first book, which is a history of ancient art:

> In questo abbiamo racconti gl'antichi et egregij statuarij et pictori, ancora l'opere
> che per loro furono prodotte con grande studio et disciplina et ingegno, uen-
> nero a tanta excellentia d'arte, furon si periti essi fecerono comentarij et infiniti
> uilumi di libri i quali dieron grandissimo lume a quelli che uennero poi.[100]

In this book we have told the story of the great ancient sculptors and painters as well as of the works they produced with such great study and discipline and genius. They arrived at so high an excellence of artistry and were so skilled that they produced commentaries and innumerable volumes of books that gave brilliant illumination to those who came after.

In these volumes, he goes on to say, they "ridusseron l'arte con quella misura che porge la natura": they "reduced"—presumably without negative connotation, that is, they *concentrated* or *abstracted*—art by means of that system of measurement that nature offers. Clearly Ghiberti's commentary is an attempt to compensate for the loss of these innumerable volumes.

Statues—as well as libraries—have volumes, and Ghiberti's self-appointment as a commentator provokes the same question as did Pliny's account of Polyclitus: what is the relation between theory and practice? One fragment of that answer emerges with Ghiberti's account of the canon of human proportions, in which he repeats the traditional harmonistic clichés, largely drawn from Vitruvius and Alberti, concerning symmetry, the fractional relations of the parts of the body, and the geometric shapes into which the human body can be inscribed. But there is one crucial difference. Ghiberti's model is not the human body: it is the human body of ancient sculpture:

> Non è da partirsi dalla forma de' nobili antichi statuarij nè dalla inuentione et forme data del cerchio de' pictori i quali ànno con nobili mesure et nobilissime simetrie et con grandissima arte et ingegnio . . . et seguiremo la forma come per loro è stata ordinata della misura del cierchio et porremo in esso la statua uirile come essi ànno fatto gli antichi statuarij et seguiremo in gran parte loro. [1.228]

> One must not depart from the form given by the great ancient sculptors nor from the inventiveness and the forms given by the circle of painters with their noble measurements and lofty symmetries and superlative artistry and genius. . . . So let us follow form as they ordained it from the measurement of the circle; and let us propose for this the male statue as the ancient sculptors made it; and let us for the most part follow their example.

He even imagines the scene of the ancients describing the corporeal circle not upon a living person but upon the "statua virile supina" (231). Ghiberti, then, whether through naïveté or owing to the insufficiencies of his learning or merely because he is an artist first and humanist second, elides the step between nature and the ancients. That is, he imagines ancient works of art as being—literally—the measure not only for modern works of art but also for works of nature.

At least as an observer, Ghiberti fulfills Pliny's terms for Polyclitus: "He is judged to have created art itself out of a work of art." For later readers that is an extra-

4.16. Lorenzo Ghiberti, detail from *Resurrection* panel on North Baptistry doors, bronze relief, ca. 1405–15, Florence

ordinarily haunting assertion, and it can stand as the motto for the whole history of art that the *Bed of Polyclitus* will narrate. For the history and theory of art, it is the canon of Polyclitus, and not the numbers of the *Timaeus*, that measures microcosm and macrocosm. So the choice of Polyclitus as the author of this object, as well as the persistence of this belief, exists in a climate where Polyclitus is associated with a harmonistic theory of the human body that depends upon a system of proportions that governs the body and relates it to the cosmos and in which such valuable property belongs to artists. Yet, to return at last to the work that Polyclitus did *not* make, in which one figure is completely limp and the other gyrated 180 degrees, it should at once be clear that a paradoxical relation exists between the sculptor's reputation as exemplary anatomist of harmony and a work in which the human body seems to be made of silly putty.

To understand the force of this problem, we must consider the work itself. The sheer quantity of correspondence in the sixteenth century concerning objects referred to as "The Bed of Polyclitus" is daunting, and it touches upon an extraordinary number of major names in the world of art and collecting. Vasari's assertion that a *Bed of Polyclitus* was owned by Ghiberti bears particular weight because of other, earlier testimonies and because Vasari was close to Ghiberti's descendants. Many decades after the sculptor's death we hear of an attempt by Alfonso d'Este to secure this work on the enthusiastic recommendation of none other than Raphael; the go-between in this affair fails but urges the purchase of a similar work in Rome. Still further into the

4.17. Michelangelo, drawing including male figure on *Bed of Polyclitus*, pen and red chalk, 1517–18(?), Windsor Castle, The Royal Collection

4.18. Baccio Bandinelli, drawing after male figure on *Bed of Polyclitus*, Département des arts graphiques, Louvre, Paris

century, as we have seen, Pirro Ligorio cites two discoveries of *Beds of Polyclitus* in Rome. One is owned by Giovanni Gaddi—whom Vasari describes as the inheritor of Ghiberti's copy, which means that either Pirro is mistaken about the origins of this item or else Gaddi owned two of them. The other Roman *Bed of Polyclitus* is in the collection of no less a figure than Cardinal Bembo. Later in the century we hear that the longtime eagerness of Rudolf II to possess this object is rewarded twice over—one copy comes via a French connection (this might just be the Ghibertian ur-bed), the other via Alfonso d'Este II, successor of the Ferrarese duke who had (probably) failed to get any version of the work.[101]

This account of the art market reveals more than the high value placed upon this object and more even than the great diffusion of its fame; it suggests what we might call a currency model for artistic value. That a work exists explicitly under the name of its maker, that its (supposed) maker is the individual who made art out of art itself means that this work is transitive: that is, artists will use it to make more art. Pirro Ligorio explains the possibility of multiple discoveries of the work in Rome by asserting that there was a Polyclitan original, of which many "memorie di picciola forma" were made, presumably in antiquity. It should be recollected that Pirro himself was not only a discoverer and recorder of authentic archaeological finds but also a restorer, forger, and, as one might say, antiquer of works with less certain pedigree. Consequently, his claim concerning multiple ancient copies reflects and gives permis-

4.19. Circle of Gentile da Fabriano or Pisanello, drawing after Rhea Silvia and Orestes sarcophagi, pen and silverpoint, mid-fifteenth century, Biblioteca Ambrosiana, Milan

sion to a more flexible system of production, both ancient and modern, which should come as no surprise considering that the examples we possess are themselves probably Renaissance replicas. This alternative system of value, which makes it worthwhile to have two *Beds of Polyclitus* in one collection, is based on the idea that works of art define their worth from their position in a continuing sequence of artistic inspiration. In this sense, the kinds of uncertainties that surround these rediscovered objects may enhance, rather than detract from, their value in the aesthetic realm. Multiple so-called originals, alternative media and dimensions, confusing stemmata of origin and ownership: all of these contribute to what we might refer to as aesthetic liberation. They empower artists and viewers to enter and shape the tradition at the same time as they may destabilize distinctions between finding and inventing, between original and copy, and between collector and artist.

The material evidence of all this empowerment is, of course, the persistent reuse of the image in Renaissance artworks; and if I do not offer an exhaustive catalogue of this prodigious phenomenon, it is because that story has been well told.[102] The male figure provides inspiration in the work of Ghiberti himself, in one of the soldiers on the *Resurrection* panel on the north Baptistry doors (fig. 4.16); he appears as well in drawings by Michelangelo and Bandinelli (fig. 4.17, 4.18) and becomes almost a trope for the dead Christ among mannerist artists.[103] The female figure (of whom we shall hear more) is almost a signature piece in the work of Raphael's studio, especially that of Giulio Romano. As is clear from this brief catalogue, the afterlife of the *Bed of Polyclitus* is, for the most part, modular.[104] Just as there is very little verbal speculation in the Renaissance on the narrative in which these people are joined, there are remarkably few attempts to reproduce the image as a whole. This is all the more striking in view of the fact that this relation, at least in iconological terms, is so rich with potential interest. A nude female figure uncovers—though not very fully—a nude male figure. The roles in countless famous stories of voyeurism widely realized in visual terms are reversed. What remains constant from those various Dianas, Susannas, and Antiopes, however, is that our experience of seeing is itself replicated in the image, except that here it is the represented voyeur who lies exposed to our eyes and not the voyeur's object. There is, of course, the story of Cupid and Psyche, and many of the Raphael and Giulio Romano versions of the female figure appear in visual cycles telling that very story. But these quotations *never* take place in the scene devoted to Psyche's unveiling of her sleeping lover. In fact, the nonidentification (whether it would be correct or incorrect) of this scene as Cupid and Psyche until the seventeenth century must be taken as the strongest indication that Renaissance viewers refused to see this image as a whole.[105]

This is the career of the metonymic art object. Among the myriad misread and unread narratives of ancient art as they appeared in the Renaissance, a widely agreed upon narrative identification of a group of figures focuses the experience of the observer centripetally, producing a response that is oriented toward the referentiality of the images and their interrelations; the failure to agree on (or even propose) an identification focuses the experience of the observer on individual forms—and on form itself. Or, one can approach it from the opposite direction: in these ancient images brought to life in the Renaissance, the power of individual forms, whatever it consists in, when it is particularly intense, suppresses the referentiality of the image as a whole and produces misreadings or nonreadings of that image.

There exists, in other words, a set of attractions in the art object that constitute alternatives to narrative, referentiality, and wholeness. By way of clarification let us consider a sketch attributed variously to Gentile da Fabriano or Pisanello or some member of their classicizing circle in the early fifteenth century (fig. 4.19).[106] The principal source is a sarcophagus depicting the meeting of Mars and Rhea Silvia, which probably formed part of the Lateran collection (see fig. 4.9). It is a highly decorative object with many figures that are not intrinsic to the narrative handed down from Livy or Ovid, including Oceanus and Tellus, Venus and Vulcan, the Seasons, and innumerable Amoretti. Indeed it has required the assiduity and ingenuity of those who produced the great nineteenth- and twentieth-century German inventory of sarcophagi to decipher all the figures, an achievement surely beyond the capacities of Quattrocento artists, even if the main plot was theoretically accessible to them.[107]

In fact, the artist does not "see" the oversized striding figure of Mars, who seems disproportionally prominent, at least to a viewer who is looking for dramatic relations. Instead what is produced is an elegant and complicated pattern of reclining figures: one female, the other male, one facing toward us, the other away, one decorated with the grace note of a leaning Amoretto, the other with that of a standing Amoretto. In all these cases we may understand visual patterning as the contrary of narrative: on the one hand, the abstract balance of complementarity; on the other, a dynamic and teleological force that operates in one direction only and insists upon choosing one from any pair of alternatives. The artist here further demonstrates a lack of interest in Mars's teleology by adding a reclining figure imitated after another widely known work, the dying Clytemnestra from an enormously influential (and equally modular) Orestes sarcophagus (fig. 4.20).[108] The identification of the story in this latter work remained unknown as late as the end of the seventeenth century; and just as its narrative was never identified, so, too, it was rarely reproduced in toto. As for the drawing, this added figure further complicates the patterns of body and draperies by providing a drooping mirror image to the upright reclining figure of the female above it. The organic wholeness of the work does not depend on the wholeness of either of the sarcophagi but is recomposed as an image without a narrative.

So the alternative to narrative, referentiality, and wholeness is, in effect, art itself. We are back in the semantic field of Aby Warburg's *bewegtes Beiwerk*, those accessories in motion that signaled to him a rediscovery of antiquity that was something other than a progressivistic movement toward the "accurate" depiction of human beings and nature.[109] If we consider objects of the kind that inspired Warburg, such as some Louvre friezes (figs. 4.21, 4.22) depicting women in motion (not cited specifically by him), it should not surprise us that Renaissance artists from Botticelli onward should be struck by the flowing forms of hair and drapery rather than by anything more substantial about these figures, because these representations are fundamentally decorative to begin with.[110] But there is a further stage of desubstantialization. One of these reliefs explicitly depicts a dance, presumably involving a movement of the women to the left and to the right. Their garments are billowing as a logical consequence of these movements. In the other, the figures are placing offerings on a candelabrum in front of a temple. Their garments are even more actively aloft, but there is no sign, apart from the garments themselves, of any movement to justify all this billowing. In this particular manifestation of Hellenistic taste, billowing garments, by existing as a property of artistic style, are independent not only of narrative but also of physics.

The drawing after the Rhea Silvia sarcophagus reminds us that, at least to the early Renaissance, all classical relief representations were fundamentally the raw material for this kind of decorative independence. The ability, or privilege, to make fragmentary works of art more fragmentary—that is, to ignore their story, to excerpt them, to change them, to recombine them—is itself granted by the fragmentation of the originals, by the disjunctive circumstances of their rediscovery, by the unrecognizability of their "serious" meaning, as well as by their often frolicsome style. But there is more involved here than playfulness with the human body. First, as is particularly

4.20. *Orestes*, marble sarcophagus, second century A.D., Palazzo Giustiniani, Rome

4.21. *Dancing Maidens*, marble, Roman relief, first century B.C.– first century A.D., Louvre, Paris

clear from this example, the body is becoming an abstract form—not that it is losing its representational significance, but its position is being directed by the demands of geometric pattern. Second, to create these patterns, the body must be rendered in ways that defy our phenomenological experience of it. That is, it faces in two ways at the same time.

Which takes us back to the *Bed of Polyclitus*. The extraordinarily turned female figure—180 degrees, as Gombrich puts it, from nose to toes—is more than a random pattern-book module;[111] it is the very paradigm of what an artist can do to the human body independent of semantic signification. Viewers can narratize the gesture of uncovering the other figure—as, for instance, by entitling this work "Cupid and Psyche"—but they cannot name any real-life situations that would necessitate this extraordinary posture. Rather, what is signified is artistic style. The ascription to Polyclitus goes along with the non-natural artfulness of the posture to make the object a valuable aesthetic export. This figure, whose career ranges from a tiny piece of stucco decoration in the Vatican Logge to larger and freer versions in a whole repertoire of turned bodies in the work of Giulio Romano and others (figs. 4.23, 4.24), may be called Mannerist; it may also be called art being made of art itself.[112]

And art itself seems to be what this is a picture *of*. If this figure comes from

4.22. *Maidens Decorating a Candelabrum*, marble, Roman relief, first century B.C.–first century A.D., Louvre, Paris

no narrative necessity, neither does she get plugged into any new narrative necessity. The nonreferentiality of this posture is of a piece with the impossibility of realizing it in the studio. It is an artist's fantasy of something that can be done to the human body. Art historians who grew up in the shadow of Kant and Cassirer are quick to speak of images as symbolic forms; I would say that the great leap forward that begins with the earliest revival of antique images is the ability to consider the human body as an unsymbolic form. Those who see and are inspired by these images are overcoming the intractability of the human body, defying its symbolization as identity, soul, and biography, its sacred God-given otherness, indeed (though they may not have formulated it this way) defying its physical laws.

That raises once again the problem of the Canon and the Bed. In the end there is no resolving the paradox that joins Polyclitus the exemplar of cosmic harmony to the image of bodies denaturalized by art and artifice. On the contrary, it works because it is a paradox, because the Renaissance fantasy of artistic possibilities is both to embody the perfect canon of natural proportion *and* to enjoy complete imaginative freedom—a mix that is historically grounded in an antiquity that contains the archaic, the High Classical, and the Hellenistic as though emerging from a single unified aesthetic. This is, in other words, not an either/or; it is a both/and opposition. The mannerist attacks on the rule of mathematical proportion that Panofsky records in his *Idea* also betray a great longing for numerical clarity.[113] The claim for aesthetic autonomy is, at base, *both* Ghiberti's claim that the world can be measured by the perfect proportions of ancient sculpture *and* the claim that artists produce another nature. It is of a piece with other oppositions: that, for instance, between the Platonic-Vitruvian tradition of the perfect cosmic body and the Ovidian-Dantesque tradition of changed and warped bodies. After all, the punishment meted out in Dante's hell to the false divin-

ers sounds remarkably like the position of the female figure on the *Bed of Polyclitus*. As Virgil describes to Dante the Theban augur Amphiaraus,

> Mira c'ha fatto petto de le spalle;
> perché volse veder troppo davante,
> di retro guarda e fa retroso calle.

> Look how he has made a breast of his shoulders;
> because he would see too far ahead,
> he looks behind and makes his way backwards.[114]

What would be torture in the world of phenomena is beauty in the world of artistic representation. The difference, when there is one, is in the eye of the beholder, who is cued to see the image neither as muscular distress nor as moral deformity but as a representation of artistry. That cue emanates precisely from the way the work itself is made into a document in the history of art.

In the case of the *Bed of Polyclitus*, the consciousness of this history is stimulated by the particular distortion of the body. If this figure is not an icon of physical torment, that is because its posture is not only an impossibility but also in part an artistic abstraction. What the frieze of the Dancing Maidens or the Quattrocento drawing accomplished by juxtaposing multiple bodies, the *Bed of Polyclitus* image achieves in a single body—which is to say, forming its own mirror opposite by making a complete half-turn. In the process it achieves balance, complementarity, indeed a kind of *symmetria* not so foreign to Plinian art history. The turned figure—however little it has to do with Polyclitus—defies mathematical exactitude while rendering the body symmetrical in an entirely new way, that is, around a circular axis of torsion rather

4.24. Giulio Romano, *Hercules and Deianira*, fresco, from Sala dei Cavalli, 1525–26, Museo Civico di Palazzo Te, Mantua

than merely along the vertical line that divides a standing figure from head to toe. It thus manages to inscribe itself in the Polyclitan canon while defying the rules of the harmonic rendering of the body—it is, in fact, a new *symmetria* invented by an artist.

Yet it is insufficient to leave these figures completely in the realm of non-signification, as there are some decidedly semantic cues generated by the image and its many descendants. No less than the *Pasquino* or the *Ariadne-Cleopatra*, the *Bed of Polyclitus* generates its affect in part owing to its potential for an erotic response. The work is allusively sexual, like many pictures that animate the Renaissance imagination. It *refers* to sexual intercourse but does not depict it. Still, however disconnectedly, the elements are there: a bed, a nude female, an act of voyeurism, the lifting of the veil, an exhausted, possibly postcoital man à la Botticelli's *Venus and Mars*. It may be precisely this decomposition of the familiar elements that offers permission for all the modular reconstructions of the work. Perhaps it is not surprising, then, that Titian (fig. 4.25), without transcribing the work as a whole, composes all his *Venus and Adonis* pairs as recombined versions from the relief, Adonis as a semi-upright version of the sleeping figure (a remarkable Uffizi drawing [fig. 4.26] attests to the painter's careful sketching of this position), and Venus in the floating 180-degree posture of the female figure.[115] It has been argued that the boy's unmistakably limp arm, which reflects not only the *Bed* but also the many Depositions and Pietàs that imitate it, signals his imminent death.[116] Perhaps more fundamental, however, is that the pairing of the two postures signals the sexual relationship that is interrupted by the boy's death. Indeed, if it

is true that Titian was radically altering Ovid's narrative and creating a more problematic sexual story, then the elliptical and ambiguous motifs offered by the *Bed of Polyclitus* become especially appropriate.

Nor is the erotic field always so elliptical. The principal exporter of the female figure on the *Bed of Polyclitus* was Giulio Romano, who, while still in Rome, produced a series of drawings illustrating sixteen positions of sexual intercourse.[117] With Giulio's consent, Marcantonio Raimondi produced etchings. Later Aretino wrote *Sonetti lussuriosi* to be published along with them, and among the consequences of this whole episode was the imprisonment of Marcantonio. None of the women's postures in the *Modi* directly resembles that on the *Bed of Polyclitus*, though ancient relief sculpture offers source material for many of them. In a number of cases (as one might expect, given premodern sexual politics) the man appears in a comfortable, even canonical posture and the woman in some elaborate contortion that may alternatively signify pain or pleasure, beauty or ugliness depending on one's point of view and tastes (fig. 4.27). As it turns out, the impossibly turned body, in addition to its potential as an icon of hellish torture or aesthetic beauty, may also represent a highly explicit, even pornographic, rendering of sexual intercourse. All these works become, in effect, an erotic repertoire of the *figura serpentinata*. The modular art of recombinable ancient sculptural motifs is analogous to the equally modular possibilities of moving nudes—especially female nudes—through sixteen sexual positions. It may be recollected that Titian sent the *Venus and Adonis* to Philip II with a letter in which he advertised the variety

4.26. Titian(?), drawing including male figure from *Bed of Polyclitus*, late sixteenth century, Galleria degli Uffizi, Florence

of viewpoints on the female anatomy that could be seen among the mythological can-
vases he was offering the king.[118] Those different points of view are at the same time an
erotic code and a demonstration of painterly skill. In similar fashion, the *Bed of Polyclitus*
derives no small part of its force from its ability to enfold both art and eros.

In his story of Protogenes, who chose to paint mythological and pastoral subjects rather than political ones, Pliny recounts how Aristotle urged the artist to concen-

4.27. Woodcut after
Marcantonio Raimondi,
after Giulio Romano,
position eleven from
I modi, Graphische
Sammlung Albertina,
Vienna

trate on the deeds of Alexander the Great "on account of their immortality," which
would presumably bring the painter along on their coattails. But Protogenes refuses,
owing to "impetus animi et quaedam artis libido" (the impulse of his mind and a certain libido of his art [N.H. 35.106]). In some fundamental ways, these cultural reconstructions after the antique represent further skirmishes in that war. On the side of
Aristotle and Alexander are all the ways in which the rediscovered ancient objects
serve—and serve decisively—as instruments in the shaping of public power, in the
making of propaganda concerning a glorious history reborn in the present moment.
The argument here, however, has been on the side of Protogenes. The sequence of
sculptural objects considered in this chapter is no accident. The *Pasquino*, one might
say, allowing for a certain amount of leeway in cultural analysis, belonged to the Curia
and the Roman people, the *Ariadne-Cleopatra* to the pope and the humanists, the *Bed of
Polyclitus* to the artists and the collectors. That ordering deliberately moves in the
direction of the aesthetic. To be sure, all these works—and many others as well—are
places of struggle. If I give pride of place to art, that is because history (and historiography) so often do not. These accounts of reconstruction, then, unashamedly chronicle the attempts of art, artists, and art objects to have their own history, their own phenomenology, their own discourse. Insofar as art separates itself from its materiality, its
social utility, and even its mimetic function, then the external ground on which it
reposes is desire: the desire of the artist, the desire perceived in the bodies of the
figures represented, the desire experienced by the beholder. All that these desiring
subjects have to work with is the fundamental intractability of the art objects themselves—their silence, their ambiguities, their contradictions, the unmanageably erotic
quality of their aesthetics.

5.1. Baccio Bandinelli, *Orpheus*, marble, ca. 1519, Palazzo Medici Ricciardi, Florence

CHAPTER 5

ARTISTS

It seems, and has always seemed, to me that Tasso is in his inventions stingy, poor, and wretched; while on the contrary Ariosto is magnificent, rich, and marvelous. When I force myself to consider Tasso's knights with their actions and experiences, as with all the other little episodes of his poem, I feel as though I am entering the tiny private study of some curious little man who has taken pleasure in decorating his room with things that because of age or rarity or some other reason have some interest for the credulous but which are in fact bits of trash—including, let's say, a petrified crab, a dried chamaeleon, a fly and a spider preserved in gelatine or amber, some of those earthen puppets that are said to have come from ancient Egyptian tombs; plus the picture collection—some little sketch by Baccio Bandinelli or Parmigianino among countless other pieces of rubbish. But on the other hand, when I enter the Furioso, I see opening before me a treasure cabinet, a museum, a princely gallery decorated with a hundred ancient statues by the most famous sculptors, along with complete narrative works, as well as pictures by the best and most famous painters, a large number of vases; crystal, agate, lapis lazuli, as well as other jewels, all the cabinets filled with rare, precious, marvelous things of the greatest excellence.
— GALILEO GALILEI

Looking back from the end of the century, Galileo sees the cultural adventure of humanist aesthetics almost as fully as he saw into the heavens. It's all there: the interrelations of poetry and the visual arts; the revival and re-creation of antiquity; the archaeological passion alongside the mania for curiosities; the canonization of ancient sculpture and sculptors; the making of a modern culture out of the reordered fragments of past culture. But from all these gems I wish to examine one tiny nugget only. It would be fair to say that Baccio Bandinelli was more famous in his own time than he is now, though not if that expression is taken, as in the usual way, to mean that his work was more respected or loved in his own time than it is now. Bandinelli, who was born in 1488 and died in 1560, was an enormously prominent figure during much of the first half of the sixteenth century: monumental sculptor, renowned draughtsman, would-be painter and architect, pivotal figure in Medici politics and patronage, an individual extensively chronicled both in his own words and by numerous contemporary observers.[1] One could call him Michelangelo's evil twin. Like his greater contemporary, responsible for countless grandiose but unfinished projects; an artist who ventured into all the media, including the written word; possessor of a personality famous for its *terribilità*; above all, the subject (and object) of a large quantity of literature concerning sculpture, painting, poetry, and aesthetics. Whereas in the case of Michelangelo, even the failures were viewed as triumphs, for Baccio even the triumphs were chronicled as failures; and since the observers and chroniclers who hated him included Michelangelo, Vasari, and Cellini, the art-history deck is pretty heavily stacked against him.

But I do not disinter Bandinelli in order to seek new justice for him. When Galileo places Bandinelli in his imaginary Tassonian collection of oddities, it may be for all sorts of motives. A simple slur it is not: both Bandinelli and Parmigianino were highly prized for their drawings, and the association of the two may suggest—as it did to Panofsky—that the key is Mannerism, which, via this passage, can be shown to embrace Bandinelli, Parmigianino, *and* Tasso, while it excludes Ariosto and all the artists and art objects that Galileo imagines in the alternative, and grander, museum.[2] Some of this is doubtless true, even if the division into opposing schools correlates far too neatly with post-Wölfflinian periodization. Leaving Parmigianino aside, what interests me here is the way that Bandinelli is positioned in regard to artistic master-pieces, antiquity, and upper-end art collecting. High humanist aesthetics is a magnificent gallery of famous ancient statues, unmutilated narrative reliefs, and beau-tiful paintings (presumably modern, assuming that Galileo isn't being *too* utopian), which coexist alongside *objets* valuable both for their materials and their artistry. Bandinelli, on the other hand, belongs among the curiosities, those things that seem to possess the requisites for entry into the museum—rarity and antiquity—but that are missing the far less definable characteristics that signal real value. Instead they become the sort of sham relic that can be palmed off on credulous pilgrims who try to master the marvelous by carrying pieces of it away with them.[3]

This attack is devastating (even as it is so full of *sprezzatura*, in every sense of the term) precisely because Bandinelli spent his whole career wanting to be in the oth-er museum and because all his contemporaries knew this and many pilloried him for his failure. The most frustrating of failures at that: so near and yet so far, as is clear even from Galileo's binary division. Bandinelli may stand as the artist who lives in the overwhelming immediacy of the unearthed ancient art objects and the voluminous cultural discourse that surrounds them. Granted that in some ways Bandinelli is a typ-ical example and in other ways unique. But the issues he raises are, for this cultural milieu, universal. Here is an artist whose career is shaped, both from the inside and from the outside, by the power and influence of rediscovered antiquity; at the same time, here is an artist extraordinarily interconnected with other artists, with writers—often the same people—and with those who commission, pay for, and help set the val-ue of art and aesthetics. Bandinelli will offer us a window on both the individual artist and the cultural community forged by the presence of antiquity. To end this book with Baccio is to declare that not all the histories of revival are composed in a fugue of glorious antiquity, great genius, and originality produced by passionate engagement with the past. That is the story of Michelangelo; this is the story of Bandinelli.

As a framework, let us begin with some glimpsed moments in Bandinelli's career where he stands in explicit relation to ancient sculpture. The first snapshot is of the artist's childhood. Baccio's father was a famous goldsmith who wished the boy to continue in his footsteps, as Vasari tells us in a suitably formulaic account, but instead Baccio rebels by bending his efforts toward painting and sculpture. He hangs around the studio of an unimportant painter called Girolamo del Buda, who, on the occasion of a big snowstorm, says to the boy as a joke,

> "Baccio, if this snow were marble, could we not carve a fine giant out of it, such as a Marforio lying down?" "We could so," answered Baccio, "and I suggest that we should act as if it were marble." And immediately, throwing off his cloak, he set his hands to the snow, and, assisted by other boys, taking away the snow where there was too much, and adding some in other places, he made a rough figure of Marforio lying down, eight braccia in length. Whereupon the painter and all the others stood marvelling, not so much at what he had done as at the spirit with which he had set his hand to a work so vast, and he so young and so small.[4]

The story is two folktales spliced together: the statue constructed of snow and the adult who makes a joke that the child artist takes seriously. Both motifs appear in the life of Michelangelo, who mutilated his own bust of a faun in response to some banter from Lorenzo de' Medici and, after the Magnifico's death, is said to have been summoned by Piero (himself a youngster) to produce a statue of snow in the palace courtyard.[5] As for the object in question, the *Marforio* (see figs. 3.5, 4.6), one of the famous Roman antiquities visible and widely known throughout the Middle Ages, helps set the pattern for sculptural *giganti*, both those that were rediscovered, like the various River Gods, and those that were newly made, like Michelangelo's *David* and Bandinelli's own *Hercules and Cacus*.[6] The word *gigante* itself takes on considerable significance as both a technical term and an honorific for large marble sculptures.

Vasari is already playing on Baccio's complicated relation to his ancient predecessors. To make a new *Marforio* out of snow is to achieve the impossible, and the lad unexpectedly proceeds to do just that, with the familiar but controversial combination of sculptural activities—adding and subtracting. Snow is a suitable practice medium, much easier to come by than marble and lending itself more readily to being *scemato*, not the last time this slightly disparaging word will be used in characterizing Baccio's relation to his medium. The "giant" quality of the new *Marforio* refers only to quantity, and even that is notably short-lived. Vasari's conclusion separates the artist's

5.2. *Apollo Belvedere*, marble, Roman copy, second century A.D., after Hellenistic original, Vatican Museums, Rome

animo—his spirit, his guts, his will—from his actual achievement. In the end, Baccio's triumph is not that he did it well but that he did it at all—"it" being the replicating of an ancient masterpiece. Shades of Galileo's two museums, one containing the real *Marforio*, the other, presumably, a soggy floor.

As epilogue to Vasari's version, it is worth noting a reference by the artist himself in an autobiographical document called the *Memoriale*, which he wrote toward the end of his life with the prime purpose of establishing the nobility of his family and heritage. There, Baccio is an irrepressible little draughtsman and an unstoppable baby sculptor, who works even with snow and dirt; and it is this frenzy of activity that induces his father to begin instruction in drawing.[7] What is for Vasari a story about replicating an antique model is for Baccio a story of the artist's natural impulses bursting to get out, representing the originating moment for both his talent and his training. Whichever account we choose to believe, it is clear that the battle is joined between an artistic inspiration that comes from naive but direct observation of nature and one that is formed by copying ancient masterpieces in a devalued and perishable medium.

Passing on to early works in a less perishable medium, around 1519 Bandinelli, with help from Leo X, secured a commission in Rome to do some work for the courtyard of the Medici palace in Florence. The result is an *Orpheus*, who appears to be fresh from pacifying Cerberus with his music (fig. 5.1). The subject has undoubted significance as political iconography, representing the travails of the Medici as attempts to keep hell at bay. But there is an iconography of artistic form here as well: Bandinelli modeled the *Orpheus* closely on the *Apollo Belvedere* (fig. 5.2), in a manner that seems to have been manifest to his contemporary viewers. Part of the significance may well have rested upon the many iconographical relations between the two mythological figures in themselves and in their collective relation to the Florentine cultural environment. In addition, the Apollo reference undoubtedly complimented the territorial ambitions of the Medici by bringing the famous masterpiece from the collection of Leo X in Rome to the temporal seat of the family in Florence, where it was actually ordered by Cardinal Giulio de' Medici, who would soon become Clement VII.

Yet this form of direct and unmistakable influence from one ancient to one modern statue is, perhaps surprisingly, rather unusual. This is not the kind of source-relation that transforms and subsumes its original—say, like the relation of Michelangelo's ignudi to the *Torso Belvedere*. Nor is it a case of plagiarism such as comes to be leveled at Baccio's version of the *Laocoön*. It may signal the poverty of Bandinelli's imagination; it may signal the importance of registering in no uncertain terms among Florentine beholders the conquest of Rome.[8] But it is something quite different from either of these that interests Vasari: "He imitated in this work the Apollo of the Belvedere at Rome, and it was very highly praised, and rightly, because, although the Orpheus of Baccio is not in the attitude of the Apollo Belvedere, nevertheless it reproduces very successfully the manner of the torso and of all the members."[9] There is a direct relation between Vasari's praise and the source-relationship that he locates in this statue. Vasari approves a practice of imitation that keeps the viewer aware of the gap between an ancient original and a modern work. What the presence of this gap reveals is *maniera*—Bandinelli "immita molto propiamente la *maniera*" of the Apollo—or, more precisely, the difference between the actual placement of torso and limbs and some more ineffable stylistic quality that derives from the practice of an artistic tradition and emerges in the special vision and talent of an individual practitioner.

In fact, the expressions of this maniera in the *Orpheus* are quite cautious. Bandinelli imitates certain archetypally all'antica elements of the predecessor work closely, including the topknot of the hair and the contrapposto, while he confines his more original touches to the places where the Vatican statue was missing its parts—

5.3. Donatello, *David*, bronze, ca. 1440, Bargello, Florence

particularly, the left arm. Further, he is working in careful relation to the Donatello *David* (fig. 5.3), which had previously been displayed in exactly the same spot.[10] Perhaps what Vasari sees in the Bandinelli statue is a respectful and noncompetitive form of imitation, a dutiful if gently innovative self-insertion by the artist into the traditions of both ancient and modern sculptural representation. Such a response may well be generated by other, less formal aspects of the *Apollo*; that is, the very qualities of harmony and repose in the original work may tend to dictate a certain approach to imitating it. Given the affective nature of the antiquities themselves, in other words, it is no coincidence that Baccio is understood to be in harmony with the *Apollo Belvedere* and in tension with the *Laocoön*.

The next event in this story is the most important for establishing Bandinelli as a classicizing artist, both in his own time and for us. It is a story that has occupied, and will continue to occupy, us in many contexts;[11] for the moment, let us concentrate on Bandinelli's part in it. The ambassadors from Francis I are being received in the Belvedere by Cardinal Giulio de' Medici (once again) and Cardinal Bibbiena, himself recently returned from France. There is talk of a gift to the king, and the ambassadors pointedly lavish praise on the *Laocoön* (fig. 5.4), declaring that of course it would be *too* great a gift. "Then the Cardinal said to them: 'There shall be sent to his Majesty either this one or one so like it that there shall be no difference.' And, having resolved to have another made in imitation of it, he remembered Baccio, whom he sent for and asked whether he had the courage to make a Laocoon equal to the original. Baccio

answered that he was confident that he could make one not merely equal to it, but even surpassing it in perfection."[12] Vasari goes on to describe how Bandinelli first made a wax model ("molto lodato") and afterward a full-scale drawing; then, with the arrival of the marble, he was installed in a shed in the Belvedere itself where he proceeded to make a copy of the larger boy, so that "all those who were good judges were satisfied, because between his work and the ancient there was scarcely any difference to be seen" (6:146; deVere, 2:273). The work is interrupted by the inopportune papacy of Adrian VI. But upon the accession of Giulio as Clement VII, Bandinelli returns to the Belvedere and within two years has completed the work "with the greatest excellence that he ever achieved" (fig. 5.5).

   This is a crucial moment in the making of Renaissance culture out of the ancients: the creation of an official replica. It has a transfer value that is determined by kings and popes but is also dependent on artistic talent and aesthetic values that can be furnished only by sculptors and validated by humanists. These relations will be further complicated by the punchline of Vasari's account—that is, that Giulio-Clement eventually likes the statue too much to let it go to France, instead sending it home to Florence. It is a choice that can be read as a triumph of aesthetic over political power or as a switch from ceremonial international politics to Medicean image making back home. Bandinelli's appearance at the birth of this project further amplifies the twists of his status as a modern artist in relation to antiquity. "Risolutosi di farne far un altro [Laoconte] a immitazione di quello, si ricordò di Baccio": Vasari, writing this life for

5.5. Bandinelli, *Laocoön*, marble, 1525, Galleria degli Uffizi, Florence

the first time in the 1568 edition, narrates this story with the hindsight of Baccio's career; in 1520, however, the task of making such a copy is itself new and strange, which renders it somewhat unlikely that the choice of Bandinelli would be such a reflex action as Vasari's words suggest. What is already characteristic of the young man's career is a particular sort of devotion to Medici patronage—a force that will only increase as time goes on and that also contributes to Vasari's hindsight. The *Orpheus*, which, as Vasari indicates, is clearly not a copy of the *Apollo Belvedere*, nevertheless gives Bandinelli a reputation as a classicizing sculptor and a great young talent who can export the Belvedere. Already in the artist's early work, certain imitative relations to antiquity are becoming identified with certain political purposes. After all, both imitation and patronage operate on a continuum between self-effacement and competitiveness.

Not that it is altogether clear where to place Bandinelli on this continuum. Vasari thought the *Orpheus* balanced originality and imitation. He compliments the *Laocoön* more lavishly but mostly marvels at how indistinguishable Bandinelli's work is from the original. As a basis for high praise, this does not seem to square with our own post-Romantic aesthetic or, for that matter, with Vasari's. Nor is it altogether clear to twentieth-century eyes that Bandinelli's work is identical to its predecessor. Allowing for some difficulties in making the comparison, it seems safe to say that the ancient *Laocoön* possesses a noticeably tenser form of musculature and that Bandinelli's work is characterized more by the continuities of its surface layer than by an internal corporeal logic. If we attempt to write these differences into an account of Bandinelli's personal style, the results are somewhat perplexing: it is true that the *Orpheus* is also somewhat flaccid (in part owing to its original); yet on the other hand Bandinelli will soon become associated with classicizing projects—including many drawings and the *Hercules and Cacus*—where the musculature of the male body tends to be wildly exaggerated. Perhaps this is another of those Bandinellian extremes, like self-effacement and competitiveness.

But Vasari, who would almost certainly never have seen the two works together, does not observe such differences at all. He transfers the problem to another realm, celebrating Baccio for his achievement in verbatim imitation but deriding him for his attitude—that is, by attributing to the artist the confident claim that he had the guts not only to make a *Laocoön* equal to the original but in fact to surpass it. Other observers also ridiculed Bandinelli in this spirit, though the sculptor's own self-congratulations in the *Memoriale* are never at the expense of the ancient work. Whether Bandinelli ever made this bold claim or not, it clearly points to a problem in the ongoing definition of the artist's relation to great antique models, forming, as it were, another side of the coin from the praise for the *Orpheus*, which suggested that there was such a thing as an original approach to imitation.

Our next snapshot, which dates from the late 1540s, depends on a chronicler who is less trustworthy than Vasari. According to his own account, Benvenuto Cellini, while attending upon Cosimo de' Medici, witnesses the delivery of a small ancient

5.6. Benvenuto Cellini, *Ganymede,*
marble, 1545–46, Bargello, Florence

5.7. Bandinelli, *Hercules and Cacus,*
marble, 1527–34, Piazza della Signoria,
Florence

marble fragment, understood to be the torso of a boy. Cellini immediately conceives
the plan to rework this torso into a Ganymede (fig. 5.6). And he proceeds to a discourse about the fragmentary piece: "So then, as far as I could, I did my best to make
the Duke appreciate such beauty, and the fine intelligence and rare style that it contained. I held forth on these things for a long time, all the more willingly as I knew
how much his Excellency enjoyed my doing so." Whereupon Bandinelli enters the
room, looks at the torso, shakes his head, and speaks, "My lord, here you have one of
those things I have so often mentioned to you. You see, those ancients knew nothing
about anatomy, and as a result their works are full of errors."[13] The position here
ascribed to Bandinelli is apparently at odds with the usual way in which he is represented (or caricatured)—that is, as excessively beholden to the ancients. Whether
these things were ever said or not, Cellini is here constructing a simplified version of
Vasari's paradox concerning Bandinelli the imitator. Cellini dramatizes Baccio's by
now ludicrous claim to prevail over the ancients, but he does not deliver the other side
of the attack—namely, that Bandinelli's own work is merely a replica of the ancients
he boasts to excel.

Whatever was really said in this scene, it is clear from both speakers that
there is a highly developed and habitual discourse between artist and patron that is
devoted to the evaluating and explicating of the rediscovered ancient art objects—an
impression confirmed by several references in Vasari's life of Bandinelli.[14] And there is
an all but inevitable flow within this cultural milieu from abstract discussions of antiquities to highly particularized debates over modern works:

5.8. Michelangelo, *David*, and Bandinelli, *Hercules and Cacus*, in front of
Palazzo Vecchio, Florence

> "My lord," [Bandinelli] said, "when I uncovered my Hercules and Cacus I am sure
> that more than a hundred wretched sonnets were written about me, containing
> the worst abuse one could possibly imagine this rabble capable of."
>> Replying to this, I said: "My lord, when our Michelangelo Buonarroti
> revealed his Sacristy, where there are so many fine statues to be seen, our splendid,
> talented Florentine artists, the friends of truth and excellence, wrote more than a
> hundred sonnets, every man competing to give the highest praise."[15]   [336]

Cellini has in his usual way touched all the bases, seemingly unaware of their
significance. It is unlikely that Bandinelli would himself bring up the *Hercules and Cacus*
debacle (fig. 5.7). But the subject is a natural one, probably nudged by Cellini himself,
above all because one's taste in antiquities exists in an intimate and perpetually circular relation to one's own talents. Baccio's claim that the ancients knew nothing about
anatomy is rendered absurd by the incompetent way he represents the body in his own
work. Furthermore, in Cellini's account these truths depend not on the pronouncements of experts—and certainly not on his *personal* opinion—but on the "virtuosa
Scuola" of public opinion, which produced sonnets in favor of Michelangelo and
which instead declared of the *Hercules and Cacus* that it had the shoulders of a jackass, a
face that was a cross between a lion and an ox, a torso that looked like a sack full of
pumpkins, and so forth.

If the ancient torso fragment quickly becomes a kind of cover for discussing
Bandinelli's recent work, it also—inevitably—introduces and disguises the subject of

5.9. Bandinelli, *Adam and Eve*, marble, 1548–50, Bargello, Florence

Michelangelo. He is the individual who embodies that perfect union between taste in antiquity and supreme personal talent. And just as the whole scene revolves in part around the not so hidden agenda of jockeying for Medici patronage, it also reveals a desire to identify with the cultural prestige of Michelangelo, himself in the very last years of his life when Cellini is writing. Bandinelli is, once again, the perfect antagonist. After all, the *Hercules*, though compared by Cellini with the Medici Tombs in the New Sacristy, is in real life the pendant to the *David* (fig. 5.8). That comparison Vasari will make at some length and with careful justice to Bandinelli, declaring that the later work is well studied and adapted to its site but that it suffers from the nearness of "il più bel gigante che mai sia stato fatto" ("the most beautiful colossal figure that has ever been made") while "la maniera di Baccio è tutta diversa" ("the manner of Baccio is entirely different" [6:160; deVere, 2:283]).

But it is Bandinelli himself who has begun the sequence of these comparisons in a long history of entanglement with the *David*. Back in 1515 on the occasion of a visit to Florence by Leo X, the young Bandinelli had constructed a different Hercules out of stucco for the Loggia dei Lanzi: "From the premature words of Baccio men expected that it would surpass the David of Buonarroti, which stood there near it; but the act did not correspond to the word, nor the work to the boast, and it robbed Baccio of much of the estimation in which he had previously been held by the craftsmen and by the whole city" (6:141–42; deVere, 2:270).[16] The *David*, in other words, forms the primal case of Baccio's self-destructive acts of boastful competitiveness, defining the distance between *dire* and *fare* and between *opera* and *vanto*. And Bandinelli will contin-

5.10. Bandinelli, *Dead Christ Held by an Angel*, marble, 1552, Santa Croce, Florence

ue in this mode when he creates the *Hercules and Cacus*, once again declaring his capacity "di passare il Davitte di Michelagnolo" (6:149). Not that Bandinelli is solely responsible for this atmosphere of rivalry. As we shall have more occasion to discuss later, Vasari tells us that the long-suffering marble out of which Bandinelli's statue will eventually be made was originally promised to Michelangelo, who himself had planned to produce a Hercules and Cacus. The argument that sways the pope to make this transfer is that "through the emulation of two men so eminent his Holiness would be served better and with more diligence and promptitude, rivalry stimulating both the one and the other in his work" (6:149; deVere, 2:275). Emulation becomes an instrument of state designed to produce the best results.

Finally, Cellini's evocation of these comparisons-competitions is anything but disinterested. He is, after all, on the point of placing another sculptural contestant in the arena of the Piazza. The *Perseus*, whose production forms the climactic episode of the *Autobiography*, acts in its own way to disdain Bandinelli's *Hercules* and enter into a more direct struggle with the *David*.[17] Indeed, the placement in eternity of these works in such visible juxtaposition—unaffected by the substitution of a replica *David* in the nineteenth century—remains the most enduring nail in the coffin of Bandinelli's reputation. It is still his very success at gaining publicity—that is, his exposure in so visible a spot among such illustrious colleagues—that undoes him. Whether his rival is the *Laocoön* or Michelangelo, whether his strategy is to produce an exact replica or a sharply contrasting original art object, Bandinelli becomes known by his boasts to excel his predecessors more than by his actual work.

5.11. Bandinelli, *God the Father*, marble, 1550s, Santa Croce, Florence

In the last snapshot we may observe the long, sad, final phase of Bandinelli's Medici service when he was in constant danger (both imagined and real) of being supplanted by figures like Cellini, Vasari, and Ammannati. Among a number of sculptural and architectural projects during this time, our concern is principally with the interlocking plans for aggrandizing the Brunelleschian choir in the Florentine Duomo and for creating an elaborate sculptural environment on and around the altar.[18] The story, which begins around 1540 and continues beyond Bandinelli's lifetime, is not unusual and certainly would contain no surprises for those who have followed Michelangelo's sculptural projects. Bandinelli was clearly a practiced draughtsman and salesman, able to persuade Cosimo to spend the whole budget of the Opera del Duomo on an elaborate pair of projects that required countless statues, reliefs, bronzes, architectural forms, and the like, as well as the collaboration of many different artists, not all of whom were famous for their adaptability or their efficiency. Of all that was planned, only a handful of statues were realized, notably an *Adam and Eve* (each in two versions; fig. 5.9), a *Dead Christ held by an Angel* (fig. 5.10), and a *God the Father* (fig. 5.11). Apart from a couple of small reliefs on the (truncated) choir walls, none of this work remains in the Duomo and only a few pieces ever got there.

This project forms what might be called the climax of Bandinelli's fatal destiny. He has finally arrived at the sanctum sanctorum, at once achieving the high point of Medici patronage and occupying the most visible center of Florentine religious worship. Previous secular projects like the *Orpheus* and the *Hercules* had received good enough exposure; on the other hand, Baccio's sacred works, including his own tomb and the tombs for the Medici popes, have been and will continue to be shunted from one place to another. Under these circumstances it is not surprising that the plans would be overly ambitious. He needs to seal his triumph by creating works of a special monumentality, but their very modes of grandeur and self-promotion will ultimately disqualify them from becoming monuments. When we look at these works through the eyes of his contemporaries, we observe a great paper trail of unfriendly responses to this monumentality, often ascribing their failure to the fact that they look too much like classical statues. Like many attacks on Bandinelli, this could easily be leveled against other artists who, then and now, have been praised for their adaptation of classical forms in sacred contexts—not only the Michelangelo of the *Risen Christ* in Santa Maria sopra Minerva or the painted Christ figure in the *Last Judgment* but also Quattrocento artists like Donatello and Ghiberti. Whether or not there is an ulterior motive in the storm of abuse on Bandinelli, these claims are asserted with special force, and they respond to significant imperatives in the works themselves.

> Chi dice: e' sembra il Tebro, Arno, o Mugnone;
> altri un gigante che posto si sia
> stracco a dormir per qualche gran fazione.
> O ladro micidiale,
> ch'ammazzi i marmi, e rubi altrui l'honore
> guastando pur Santa Maria del Fiore.
> Che 'n su l'altar maggiore
> Dio padre, e 'l figlio, Eva, e Adamo hai fatti,
> Quattro birboni storpiati, e rattrati.   [Antonfrancesco Grazzini detto Il Lasca]

Some say he seems like a Tiber, an Arno, or a Mugnone; others call him a giant who is worn out and is sleeping after some big skirmish. O, murdering thief, you destroy pieces of marble and steal from others the honor, even ruining Santa Maria del Fiore, now that right there on the high altar you have placed God the Father, the son, Adam, and Eve, looking like four crippled and maimed rascals.

> Bandinello, ha' tu fatto quel gigante
> ch'à prosteso là in su l'altare,
> che par ch'egli stia là a 'chattare
> a guisa di uno svaligiato fante?
> O tu, se ben d'ogni altro più 'gnoriante
> 'stà hai voluto Christo figurare?
> fa' a miei modi, là fallo levare
> chè e' non uniscie tra le cose sante.
> Per l'avvenire, intendi Bandinello,
> copia de' Bacchi e fa delli Euconti,
> e in ciò usa la subbia e 'l martello.[19]   [Alfonso de' Pazzi]

Bandinelli, did you make that giant who is stretched out there on the altar, the one who seems as though he is lying there in the shape of a down-at-the-heels serving boy? You, stupider than anyone else, this is the way you decided to represent Christ? Do what I tell you, have it removed and not joined together among holy things. In the future, listen to me, Bandinelli, copy your Bacchuses and make those Laocoöns—that's what you should use your hammer and chisel for.

The writers of satirical verse have a field day with the *Dead Christ*: he is more like a classical athlete, a "giovan stanco afflitto," or one of the River Gods in the Belvedere than like the crucified Jesus; he resembles an epic hero (one correspondent sees no sign of the physical suffering endured during the forty days in the desert); he is a stone gigante, that is, a pagan marble and not the son of God. The verdict: Bandinelli should stick to Bacchuses and imitation Laocoöns; his Adam and Eve should be chased out of the paradise of the Duomo.[20]

In part we are witnessing Counter-Reformation-style piety—de' Pazzi elsewhere speaks of giving the Lutherans material to attack, and another anonymous response singles out the *Adam and Eve* in the hopes that God will smite all this idolatry.[21] But that this particular engine should strike Bandinelli, and not Ammannati or Cellini or Sansovino—let alone Michelangelo—has to do with the kind of classicizing career he has pursued, or been thought to pursue. In certain respects, say, features of anatomy and modes of rhetorical presentation, the Duomo statues speak more of the Quattrocento or the early Michelangelo than they do of Belvedere antiquities; and Bandinelli, himself discussing the *Eve*, enthuses about her lifelikeness and the conquest of difficulty in having her stand up with so little support. It is all but inevitable, however, that these works be savaged for their classicism. Adam and Eve, monumental and naked, *are* extraordinary figures to surround a cathedral altar—explicable perhaps by reference to ekphrastic descriptions of ancient temples, though certainly not to anything the sculptor would have seen.

In Bandinelli's own words, high ambition is defined by reference to antiquities: "io ho disposto conseguire in quest' opera [the *Eve*], e al secolo di sua eccellenza, di quelli nobili effetti de' valentissimi Greci nè mi voglio risparmiare a nessuna estrema fatica" (I have arranged in this work and for the benefit of Your Excellency, the noble achievements of those supremely capable Greeks, nor have I had any desire to spare myself the extremest hard work).[22] Indeed that "estrema fatica" ends up in the production of laborious prior attempts on both Adam and Eve; and the first versions of the two were with little ado transformed, respectively, into Bacchus and Ceres. There was also a rejected version of God the Father, which Vasari describes as "mezzo ignudo a uso di Giove"—that is, resembling many of the newly discovered monumental, half-clad Jupiter figures, in the event it actually *became* a Jupiter in the Boboli Gardens. We are at the limiting case of the typology that celebrates the parallels of Christian and pagan, and equally the limiting case of the aesthetic power that ancient statues can exercise in Christian art.

One could say that Bandinelli lives at the extreme edge of a precipice inhabited at greater and lesser distance by all his contemporaries in the arts and in humanistic culture. The precipice may be defined as any or all of the paradoxical claims that are put forward at the beginning of the Renaissance, the most important of which for us goes back to Petrarch who, in both theory and practice, essentially propounds the claim that the more he imitates his classical predecessors, the more original he is. This is already a slippery slope in 1350. From Petrarch onward, this artistic process is approachable through a series of metaphors—bees, apes, digestion, portrait painting, procreation—which inevitably arrive at mystification when it comes time to explain exactly what happens when material goes in ancient and comes out modern. In this paradox, the revolutionary claims are about originality, not imitation—namely, that there is such a thing as originality, that it is tied to an individual defined as a subject, and that it constitutes a transverse history of subjects with an alternative calendar and complex interrelations.

Vasari, in an important passage we have already noted, will exploit the paradox most directly when he defines the third, or modern, phase of the Renaissance; and we must return to that very revealing passage. The second period of art history—roughly the Quattrocento—excels by achieving the authenticity of representation that the early Renaissance lacked, but the artists of that time are doomed by too much diligence and too little *gagliardezza*—vigor, boldness, guts.

> That finish, and that certain something which they lacked, they could not achieve so readily, seeing that study, when it is used in that way to obtain finish, gives dryness to the manner.
>
> After them, indeed, their successors were enabled to attain it through seeing excavated out of the earth certain antiquities cited by Pliny as amongst the most famous, such as the Laocoon, the Hercules, the Great Torso of the Belvedere, and likewise the Venus, the Cleopatra, the Apollo, and an endless number of others, which, both with their sweetness and their severity, with their fleshy roundness copied from the greatest beauties of nature, and with certain attitudes which involve no distortion of the whole figure but only a movement of certain parts, and are revealed with a most perfect grace, brought about the disappearance of a certain dryness, hardness, and sharpness of manner, which had been left to our art by the excessive study of Piero della Francesca [and there follows a list of a dozen or so Quattrocento artists].[23]

The realist disposition of the Quattrocento has been understood as artificial, studied, and inauthentic, while the exposure to the Plinian canon of ancient sculpture in the later period bestows upon High Renaissance art the qualities of motion, vivacity, and grace—in short, life—which Vasari ascribes paradoxically to the excavated art objects.

Two problems remain unspoken. First, the illogic of the model: How can dead and buried works, themselves so long the subject of pedantic study, become the identifying marks of freedom, liveliness, and originality? The second problem is more historical, or perhaps diachronic. As Vasari tells the story, the rediscovery of ancient statues has inaugurated a golden age of artistic inspiration, whose very Zeitgeist grants to artists this seemingly contradictory capacity to become original via imitation. Yet the precise alchemy by which the process works must remain rigorously individual, since from Petrarch onward it has been based on the celebration of the individual. Reduced to absurdity, Vasari's assertion would be that after the rediscovery of ancient sculpture, every Cinquecento artist becomes a genius. That claim being untenable, the narrative of history demands the anointing of great geniuses, like Leonardo, Raphael, or Michelangelo (or the self-anointed Petrarch), whose means of translating imitation into originality are ineffable, while it leaves unresolved the question of how the spirit of the age expresses itself among artists and the community of the arts as a whole. And since the special anointments tend to be after the fact, the question of Zeitgeist versus individual genius remains wide open where any living artist is concerned.

Quite obviously, Bandinelli lived in that open space. The points of contact with ancient sculpture that I have described all depend on ways of gauging the relations between the inspiration offered by the ancients and the artistic payoffs provided by the modern artist. When Bandinelli is praised, it is for achieving something personal that transcends mere imitation (whatever that is); when he is blamed, it is for falling into one of the traditional traps—plagiarism, lack of individual vision, braggadoccio. I say "traditional" because the first thing to understand about Bandinelli's position is that it is a donnée, forming part of the ground for the claims that cultures have tended to make about themselves, whether it is Virgil, Cicero, or Varro in relation to the Greeks, Augustine in relation to the pagans, or Petrarch in relation to the ancients. The placement of Bandinelli in this role is made particularly clear by a witticism widely credited to Michelangelo by his contemporaries and almost certainly referring to Baccio. Vasari's version is the most complete: "Asked by a friend of his what he thought of someone who had replicated in marble the most famous antique artworks, the imitator all the while bragging that he had far exceeded the ancients, Michelangelo responded, 'A person who runs behind others never manages to pass them; and someone who doesn't know how to work well on his own cannot make good use of other people's work'" (7:279–80; deVere, 2:743). In Vasari's version: "Chi va dietro a altri, mai non li passa inanzi; e chi non sa far bene da sè, non può servirsi delle cose d'altri." Armenini quotes the witticism almost verbatim, while Varchi makes the Bandinelli identification clearer by referring directly to a *Laocoön* copy, though leaving the artist unnamed.[24] The joke about following and not passing is a very old play on a traditional metaphor for artistic imitation. Michelangelo has put his finger on the essential problem, which is the relation between self and external inspiration. The footrace metaphor is appropriate precisely because Bandinelli has boasted that he can "win" or surpass his model; the very terms of the relation are thus dictated by the model, and the imitative artist is doomed to coming in second on a linear course. Michelangelo's alternative is, on the other hand, circular, consisting in a continuous exchange between *saper fare bene da sè* and *servirsi delle cose d'altri*, since each of these is needed to define the other. As important as the theory, though, is the identity of the two personages. If this encounter did not really happen, it had to be invented, to establish the absolute distance that separates the genius from the mere mortal and to postulate a relation to antiquity—Michelangelo's—freed of historical dependency.

THE ARCHAEOLOGY OF THE ARTIST

In fact, however, the culture of Cinquecento art is not a binary system inhabited only by Bandinelli and antiquity or only by divine geniuses and hacks. It is a system of relations and exchanges in which artists of whatever category are made not only by their talent but also by their relations to other talents and by the terms in which their contemporaries are able to characterize them. In this system antiquity is not just an antagonist in a footrace or a source to be sublimed; it also defines the very terms in which such interconnections will be conceptualized. I return to Bandinelli, then, to see how the system of relations and exchanges actually operates, to ask what happens in the space between influence and inspiration, between ancient and modern, when an artist is not shrouded in the mystifications of divine genius but, rather, is mercilessly exposed by himself and his contemporaries.

The first, and perhaps most obvious, point of relation and exchange is the discourse of the artist's formation or education.[25] Ancient sculpture, while in some respects standing as the summit of an artistic achievement that is all but impossible to equal, is also the material that those learning their trade cut their teeth on. This paradox remains so ingrained in post-Renaissance notions of the artist's development that we tend not to notice that it is a paradox. It becomes another sign of the complications involved in any theory or practice of imitation. The activity of the beginner who "copies" canonical ancient masterpieces must be radically disjoined from the activity of the mature artist who "quotes" or "reshapes" or "contends with" the ancients; yet this very subliming of the imitative skill is part of what the beginner is being taught, along with the practical technique itself. The ancient art objects take part in a sort of ontogeny-recapitulates-phylogeny process that places them at the foundation level of every artist's formation. But as the story of Bandinelli and the *Marforio* suggests, there is often a built-in devaluation of the beginner's imitative activity. In that case it is the medium of the copy—snow. More often, it is the medium of the original: that is, beginners are represented as drawing their inspiration from unimportant or miniature or plaster versions of the ancient works. Nor is it merely a representation, of course. Pupils did work in the studios of masters who were hardly likely to own Belvedere-quality antiques; and the eventual dispersion of plaster replicas has the effect of both canonizing and trivializing the place of ancient sculpture in the formation of the artist in a way that mirrors the distance between the great classicizing work by the genius and the technical imitation by the beginner.

5.12. Agostino Veneziano, after Bandinelli, *Academia di Baccio Brandin. in Roma in Luogo detto Belvedere*, engraving, 1531, Davison Arts Center, Wesleyan University, Middletown, Connecticut

As it happens, Bandinelli will be central to the development of these rules. He seems to have been the first (beginning in the 1530s in Rome, a decade later in Florence) to hold organized instructional sessions for young artists in his home and, in particular, the first to name this place and these proceedings as an *accademia*.[26] Or at least so he asserts; so far as I can determine, we have no other evidence than Bandinelli's word (directly or indirectly) for the existence of this accademia. (Vasari, who is fairly obsessed with academies, never mentions it.) In the *Memoriale*, Bandinelli declares that he had his "own academy of Design."[27] He quite unashamedly establishes that his activity was one of publicity: as proof of the existence of the academy, he made a drawing, had it printed, and gave it a name that focuses upon himself and on his alleged aristocracy.

The images of the academy themselves—there are two engravings in existence, neither of which is captioned precisely as Bandinelli claims—are highly evocative (figs. 5.12, 5.13).[28] They will help inspire images not only of academies of design and painters' studios but also of art collections and assemblages of curiosa (Galileo strikes again). The rooms are filled with ancient art objects, both in the direct sight line of the pupils and, in even greater profusion, as incidental decoration of the space. The antiquities are all either miniature or fragmentary or both—they could easily be copies or casts—and in the later, Florentine image they are interspersed with bones and skulls (and a cat and a dog). The various activities of the individuals are somewhat enigmatic: some are drawing, others contemplate the art objects, yet others adopt

5.13. Enea Vico, after Bandinelli, *Bandinelli's Academy*, engraving, ca. 1550, Museum of Fine Arts, Boston

what we might call humanistic poses, that is, contemplating themselves or engaging in dialogue, vignettes taken roughly from Raphael's *School of Athens*. In one case, Bandinelli is himself drawing; in the other, he is a marginal observer indicated only by the noble order emblazoned on his garment. As striking as any of the semantic messages is the extraordinary emphasis on chiaroscuro, with very intense visible light sources, radiating (particularly in the Veneziano engraving) extreme, even ominous shadows.

The very richness of enigmatic interpretive possibilities would appear to be part of the publicity venture itself. Many remarkable things go on in the academy, not all of which can be understood by those on the outside. The abundance of antiquities, hardly surprising in itself, seems to square with all this funereal darkness. But it raises its own questions. It seems so natural to us that an art academy should be crammed with statues and statuettes that we may forget how the idea has its own particular history. The conceptual source for Bandinelli's academy is the garden of Lorenzo de' Medici,[29] celebrated by Vasari as an Edenic locale of humanism and the arts but destroyed, its contents sold off, after Lorenzo's death:

> [Torrigiano] in his youth was maintained by the elder Lorenzo de' Medici in the garden which that magnificent citizen possessed on the Piazza di S. Marco in Florence. This garden was in such wise filled with the best ancient statuary, that the loggia, the walks, and all the apartments were adorned with noble ancient

figures of marble, pictures, and other suchlike things, made by the hands of the best masters who ever lived in Italy or elsewhere. And all these works, in addition to the magnificence and adornment that they conferred on that garden, were as a school or academy for the young painters and sculptors, as well as for all others who were studying the arts of design, and particularly for the young nobles. [30]

Although the collection was doubtless real, Vasari's naming of this locus amoenus as an academy may be even more a case of wishful thinking than is Bandinelli's academy, and it almost certainly postdates Bandinelli. Despite these limitations, it is clear from the start that an academy is a classical institution—complete with the Plinian reference to young noblemen who are being instructed in the art of drawing—and that it will focus on the lessons taught by ancient sculpture. This focus is characteristic of Vasari's nostalgic retrospective upon the Quattrocento, but it is no less true in "academy" art of much later France and England, and no less true in the establishment of all the many national "academies" in Rome beginning in the eighteenth century, when the primary purpose of an artist's sojourn there was the viewing of, once again, ancient sculpture.

In Bandinelli's version, this activity is the only thing going on. Unlike the hypothetical Medici academy, these rooms contain no paintings and if there are any modern works of art, they are themselves copies after the antique; in addition, the atmosphere is anything but a sylvan locus amoenus. The dramatic lighting effects doubtless have something to do with creating a generally exotic atmosphere and may also be part of a pedagogical technique that uses artificial light to stress the contours of the sculptural objects. But the lighting also tends to seal off the room, so that the only relations of the student artist are either with the ancient statuette or with his own tablet. Indeed, apart from a couple of onlookers, every individual in these crowded spaces acts as though he were alone in the room. If there is a polemic here, it is not only a celebration of the value of ancient sculpture in forming young artists and not only a plea for high humanist status in this pedagogical activity. It is also a conspicuous exclusion of drawing from life, or indeed nature, which may have less to do with an antirealist aesthetic—since the argument of the classicizers is always that ancient sculpture is nature—than with claims for the quality of personal and individual inspiration that somehow travels from the ancient art objects to the modern artist.

In this process Bandinelli himself plays a strangely ill-defined role. In a sense, having advertised himself so boldly in these images (especially in the words written on them), he then has to retire from a very active place in the narrative because of the unresolvable dissonance between himself as source of inspiration and the ancient statues as sources of inspiration. The pupils are not doing one thing we know they did a great deal: copying their teacher's work. So Bandinelli's publicity aims to canonize a process of artistic formation by imitation that denies mere replication while promising—as in Vasari's claim about the third period of Renaissance artists—that inspiration via the ancients is available to everyone.

The *accademia Baccii* may be a phantom of self-promotion, but another set of contemporaneous documents leaves little doubt of the artist's practical interest in the whole institution of studio assistants or apprentices. Whenever Bandinelli writes to ask for more help in realizing his ambitious projects in the Duomo, it is clear that he is also defending himself, and his profession, from the charge that too many *garzoni* mean too little original work by the master. To refute this charge he writes a whole history of artistic education from antiquity to the present time. Without such relations, great projects could never have been completed, neither the Donatello altar in Padua nor the Ghiberti bronze doors nor—and in one of the letters this is the crowning instance—Trajan's Column. Arguing the same point negatively, Bandinelli becomes so bold as to criticize Michelangelo for not following this practice:

> E mi ricordo quando stavo con Papa Leone, sua Santità in Firenze mandò per Raffaello da Urbino e pel Bonarroto, e concluse la facciata di san Lorenzo, e si determinò che egli facesse i modelli delle statue e delle istorie grandi come li marmi, e sotto la sua guida si facessono lavorare a più giovani. E sappi vostra eccellenza, che la causa che 'e non ha mai fornito nessuna opera di marmo, è solo stato [sic], perchè non ha mai voluto aiuto di persona per non fare de' maestri.[31]

> And I remember when I was with Pope Leo in Florence that his Holiness sent for Raphael and Michelangelo to carry out the facade of San Lorenzo; he determined that Michelangelo should make models of the statues and of the larger marble narrative panels, and the Pope made him work with a number of young men under his guidance. Your Excellency should know that the reason why Michelangelo has never finished any of the marble work has been solely because he has refused the assistance of anyone in order not to make masters of them.

As that last phrase suggests, there is a virtue in all this necessity. The Baptistry doors demonstrate the values—and difficulties—of producing new generations of artists:

> Quando gli [a Ghiberti] furono allogate le porte, per suo aiuto prese giovani con ottimo disegno, e fece due beni, opera mirabile e valenti maestri; e 'l paragone apparisce nelle porte, che le storie da basso della porta dinanzi furono le prime bruttissime a comparazione dell'altre; ma nel fare li giovani si feciono tanto valenti, che l'uno fu Maso Finiguerra, l'altro fu Disiderio [da Settignano], Piero, e Antonio Pollaiuolo, e Andrea del Verrocchio, tutti valenti e pittori e iscultori.[32]

> When [Ghiberti] was commissioned to produce the Baptistry doors, he took on as helpers some young men with an excellent sense of design, thereby produc-

ing two good things—a remarkable work of art and a group of talented masters. And the comparison appears clearly on the doors, where the narratives on the bottom of the door in front, which were the first, seem quite poor by comparison with the others. But in the course of making these the young men realized their talents to such an extent that they became the likes of Maso Finiguerra, others including Desiderio [da Settignano], Piero and Antonio Pollaiuolo, as well as Andrea Verrocchio—all gifted painters and sculptors.

The formative and collaborative history of Trajan's Column, for its part, signals a whole theory of artistic relations:

> E in Roma le colonne istoriate, che ciascheduna è l'età di venti maestri; dove si vede chiaro che 'l disegno e la invenzione, che tiene il principato d'ogni eccellenza, viene da un solo ingegno; nientidimeno le figure, per essere infinita quantità, sono lavorate di molte maniere, e tutte buone e belle, perchè un valente disegnatore guidò tutti quelli maestri; in altro modo non si potrebbe mai fornire simili opere.[33]

> And in Rome there are the narrative columns, each the work of some twenty masters, in which one sees clearly that the *disegno* and the *invenzione*, which are the basis of every excellence, come from a single genius; nevertheless the figures, being of such vast quantity, were produced in many different *maniere*, all fine and beautiful because a talented *disegnatore* guided all those masters—otherwise, no such works could ever have been finished.

Bandinelli focuses on what would be within his milieu the two greatest narrative sculptural projects of all time—both, significantly, projects of *relief* sculpture—and he reads them as occasions when not only masterpieces were created but also masters. His strategies in making this argument are, as usual, highly self-interested. He makes himself the keeper of art's historical record, with scholarly knowledge of ancient practice and street awareness of modern practice. In the process, he establishes the category of *disegnatore*—more than what we mean by "designer"[34]—and assumes it for himself as the master-artist who possesses *disegno* and inspires the more manual work of the assistants, themselves on their way to becoming masters. He recognizes that the work of assistants may not be as good as that of the master—his Medici statues are recognizably his own, while the panels executed by apprentices on the Baptistry doors are recognizably less fine than those of Ghiberti himself. Yet he defends the practice on the grounds of education, which soon grounds artistic tradition, too: artists like Maso and Verrocchio could not have been produced without the risks of inferior work incurred by the apprenticeship system.

At the same time, the labor arrangements as Bandinelli describes them turn into an illustration of the classical relations between theory and practice, an expression of how disegno is actually performed. After all, the practical purpose of these letters to Cosimo or the members of his court is to beg for more and better garzoni to help in doing all the work of the Duomo choir and altar; he is trying to redefine the necessities of manual labor into the terms appropriate to a contemplative, theoretical paedeia. According to this theory, grounded on the example of Roman narrative columns, the single genius possesses disegno and invenzione, which in turn act as guides to the work of the many, itself characterized by *molte maniere*. The classical example is crucial: the system has its visible origins in the largest known piece of ancient sculpture, and it organizes the central terms of Renaissance art theory along the lines of an Aristotelean model of epistemology. At the same time, these studio arrangements represent the continuity of art history itself, an unbroken line of practical discipleship that goes back to the making of Trajan's Column.

The classical example has its problems as well. Baccio's reflections on garzoni are haunted by one aspect of master-pupil relations with classical antecedent:

> Sono stato sforzato cacciar via quel fanciullo, per non vedermi innanzi alli occhi tale scelleratezza; e so certo che a questi medesimi costumi avvezza i giovanetti della sua guardaroba, che sa sua eccellenza ch'io ho durato fatica a insegnar loro qualche virtù solo per potermene valere alle cose del bronzo, massime alle storie del Coro, e questo pessimo mostro di Natura del continuo li avvezza a stravizi, e va la notte fuora con arme, cose al tutto nocive a ogni virtù e onesto vivere; e come usa dire il Buonarroto, mai può stare il vizio con tanta eccelsa arte.[35]

> I was forced to get rid of that boy in order not to have to witness such villainy before my own eyes; and I know for a fact that the young men of his studio are brought up among those very same habits. As his excellency knows, I have endured much labor in teaching them any *virtù* at all, just to make them useful for some work on the bronzes or at most for some of the narrative panels on the Choir. And that dreadful monster of Nature keeps leading them into great vices, going out at night in arms, things wholly destructive to any kind of *virtù* and honest living. And as Michelangelo is always saying, vice can never accompany great art.

Virtù, Baccio reminds us, is poised between virtue and virtuosity; those who have passed through the hands of the monster Cellini are unable to be taught any great artistic skill because they have been trained in vices. The time-honored institution of discipleship, as I have discussed it elsewhere, is bound up with classical—specifically Socratic—notions concerning erotic relations between men and boys.[36] (Bandinelli, in the speeches attributed to him by Anton Francesco Doni, will say that Protogenes was the pupil of Apelles "ma virtuosamente, & con buona amicitia.")[37] When they clashed in the *Autobiography*, Bandinelli viciously addressed Cellini as "sodomitaccio," thus naming him as a lover of the antique in quite the wrong way. Cellini turned the accusation around so as to make a claim for his special relations to antiquity; here, in a complementary move, Bandinelli is struggling to define a modern virtù that is free from ancient vice.

But if the institution of apprenticeship becomes for Bandinelli a way of constituting the history of art, it also functions as an arena for the interaction of contemporaries, a critical place of exchange among living artists. Bandinelli threatens to fire apprentices who have been tainted by Cellini, but in another place he complains that Cellini has stolen away one of his apprentices.[38] Decades earlier, at the time of the *Laocoön* copy, a letter from Giovan Francesco Fattucci to Michelangelo reports on one Ceccone, "who once worked for Maestro Andrea of Fiesole and has recently been working here [in Rome] for Bandinelli; and since Baccio hasn't paid him, he wants to come work for you."[39] Apprentices were clearly being passed from hand to hand almost like mistresses. In Cellini's numerous narratives on the subject and in certain innuendos surrounding Michelangelo, the parallel is explicit.[40] Whatever the sexual implications, much is at stake here concerning the relations among the different masters as well as the creation of a family tree of disciples that will eventually become the Pliny-style begats of modern art.

As for Ceccone in particular, we do not have a response to Fattucci's proposal, and yet the entry of Michelangelo into the arena is noteworthy, if only by negation.[41] Although evidence to the contrary continues to mount, Michelangelo was widely viewed as the solitary worker who did not maintain a studio of apprentices.[42] Baccio's telling remark about the debacle of the San Lorenzo facade—"la causa che 'e non ha mai fornito nessuna opera di marmo, è solo stato, perchè non ha mai voluto aiuto di persona per non fare de' maestri"[43]—signals the most effective armament in competing with his rival; that is, Baccio exploits the image of a Michelangelo who is unproductive because he refuses to be connected to the means whereby past and future tradition are forged. Baccio, with his sense of the ancients, his academy, and his efforts to maintain a band of assistants, whether these individuals were in reality artistic disciples or chisel-sharpening gofers, sees himself as the alternative. But imitation and influence are always transitive: Bandinelli the teacher of imitation is very much Bandinelli the imitator. Perhaps he situated himself in this way because he knew he lacked a unique individual talent; perhaps he developed the notion of the disegnatore because he agreed with his critics that he was better at drafting projects than at bringing them to fruition with his own chisel. At all events, under the influence of ancient sculpture, an artist who represents himself as a master of imitation may be dooming himself to the limits of that role.

But this model of classicism is by no means limited to the pedagogue. When Bandinelli publicizes his academy, he is not only vaunting his abilities in forming young minds; he is also advertising himself as a certain kind of artist, a learned or archaeologizing artist. Now this is certainly not as much a cultural novelty as the academy itself, nor does Baccio occupy this space alone. But the archaeologist-artist is a figure in a significant process of cultural definition when Bandinelli begins to play the role so visibly. It has various hybrid origins. Poets—the ur-examples would be not only Petrarch but also Dante and Boccaccio—had long since been granted the right to be both learned and artistic, though it might be argued that this polymathic possibility was disappearing in the Cinquecento under the weight of specialization and professionalization. Still, if Ariosto abjures this kind of title, it is in the course of expressing fervent hope that someone else may be able to take it up in the next generation.[44] And whatever privileges poetry had declared for itself in the dawning of the Renaissance, the visual arts were sure to be demanding by 1500.

The history of visual aesthetics also contributes to the development of the learned artist. Beginning in the early Quattrocento, there is an enormous industry of archaeological humanists, from Ciriaco d'Ancona to Pirro Ligorio, many of whom are dabblers in the visual arts themselves—which is to say, their work is interspersed with drawings or closely related to known visual representations. There are countless draughtsmen like Amico Aspertini and Girolamo da Carpi—along with many more visiting non-Italians—whose most important achievements are the drawings of antiquities. There are Quattrocento artists like Pinturicchio and Mantegna whose work reveals careful research and historical sophistication.[45] And, again in the earlier period, Alberti and Ghiberti had acted as the progenitors of the whole movement, humanistic geniuses who wrote the script that would contextualize the rediscovery of ancient art objects fifty years before the material events had fully begun. But it is only in the decades after the turn of the century that it becomes fully possible for a practicing, visible, public artist to be understood as performing humanistic research in the exercise of his art. For this grand designation the true heir is Raphael, who, as we have seen, engaged in a massive project of mapping the urban space of ancient Rome and planning the reconstruction of its architecture at the same time as he was executing masterpieces of humanistic art in the Vatican.[46] Raphael died too young to fulfill this promise, but for other reasons as well he remains too grand and mysterious a genius to play this part as the culture may have needed it played.

Although they made no Raphael of him, the signs of Bandinelli's special relation to the antique are to be found everywhere in the making of his career. As Vasari recounts the story, the Laocoön commission—a pivotal event, as we have already seen—turns Baccio into a resident of the Belvedere. Meanwhile, the correspondence that surrounds Michelangelo in 1520 indicates that the world is watching Bandinelli at work. He shows a cartoon of the work to Sebastiano del Piombo, who reports back to Michelangelo that Baccio "non ha più paura di nessuno, se non di voi" (isn't afraid of anyone, unless it is of you); later the same year Baccio "che fa el Laoconte" is at the center of efforts at papal patronage in the aftermath of Raphael's death.[47] During the Medici exile from Florence, Bandinelli returns to Rome and takes refuge at Clement's court, "where he was given the rooms in the Belvedere, as before" (6:152; deVere,

5.14. Antonio Susini after Bandinelli, *Descent from the Cross*, bronze relief after 1529 original, Louvre, Paris

2:278). From here, appropriately, Baccio delivers a long string of classicizing statuettes, "many little figures . . . as of Hercules, Venus, Apollo, Leda, and other fantasies of his own" (6:153; deVere, 2:279); the multiples and the miniature size ("due terzi") may be Vasari's subtle slur, but in any event they represent part of a great industry of replicas, forming a bridge between the activity of the students such as we saw in the academy images and the activity of humanist collectors later in the century. In this case, the replicating productions have a special mark of authority, given their author's provenance in the Belvedere.

While the *Memoriale* dwells little on artistic production, it manages to foreground classical subjects:

> Quanto alle mie opere di scoltura e disegno, essendo apparenti in Francia, in Spagnia, in Germania, in Roma e particolarmente in Firenze a' tempi di Alessandro e di Cosimo, delle quali il Laocoonte fatto ad instanzie di Clemente, la Venere donata a Carlo Quinto, l'Ercole di piazza ed altre di bronzi e marmi, lascerò lodarli a l'altrui penne ed alle lettere che troverete scritte dalli eccellentissimi sig(no)ri duchi Cosimo e Leonora.[48]

> As for my works of sculpture and draughtsmanship, they are visible in France, Spain, Germany, Rome, and especially in Florence since the time of Alessandro and Cosimo, among which there are the *Laocoön* made at the request of Pope Clement, the *Venus* given to Charles V, the *Hercules* in the Piazza and other works in bronze and marble, which I will leave to be praised by other writers and in those letters which you will find written by their exalted Highnesses the Duke Cosimo and the Duchess Leonora.

The imperial *Venus*, despite the confident gesture of allowing others to celebrate it, is recorded by no one else and not apparently reflected in any drawings that we possess. According to Vasari, the work for Charles V, which resulted in Bandinelli's all-important knighthood, was a bronze relief of the *Descent from the Cross* (fig. 5.14), produced during the same Belvedere residency as the miniatures mentioned above. Although the original is lost, its existence and importance are attested to by many drawings, copies, and verbal references, including Vasari's own detailed and enthusiastic praise.[49] The *Memoriale* never mentions it. Could there have been two works for Charles V, one discussed only by Bandinelli and the other only by everybody else? Was the *Venus* in Bandinelli's real or imagined recollection really a Venus holding the dead Adonis and therefore reminiscent of certain aspects of a *Deposition?* (Certainly, the versions of the work we have look nothing like a Venus and Adonis; but we might recollect Bandinelli's casual transformations of an Adam into a Bacchus and an Eve into a Ceres, which are taking place around the time he is writing the *Memoriale*.) Suffice it to say that Bandinelli wishes to represent himself as an artist of antiquity even at the expense of celebrating one of his most successful commissions. And, as so often, the word evokes antiquity as effectively as the image, so Bandinelli devotes considerable space in the *Memoriale* to an account of his literary production—books on sculpture, disegno, architecture, and so on (all lost)—and to his extensive readings in ancient and Renaissance authors. The reputation sticks: as we shall see, when Antonio Doni wishes to introduce a voice of ancient authority into a dialogue on sculpture and painting, he brings Bandinelli on stage.

The role of the artist who speaks with the voice of a scholar and the scholar who has the eye of an artist—even if it is only an idea and far too grandiose for what

Bandinelli actually achieved—signals some important developments in aesthetic culture. Some of these are negative. When Bandinelli becomes an *artista studioso*, he may be being damned with faint praise. Post-Romantics like us will not miss the barb when Vasari ascribes to Baccio the thought that "by continual work he would surpass all others who had ever practised his art, and promising this result to himself as the reward of his incessant study and endless labour" (6:140; deVere, 2:269); such a reading links the competitive impulse with that of the drudge. But not all patrons, or critics, want each work to be conceived in a delirium of private inspiration, and one of the important features of Bandinelli's career, as is evident from the *Laocoön* project, is the developing taste for what we might call learned commissions—typically, secular monuments intended to associate powerful individuals with classical heroic virtues. The most visible instance in Baccio's life (concluding, like many of his other projects, unhappily) was the Genoese monument for Andrea Doria, "which was to be a Neptune in the likeness of Prince Doria, to be set up on the Piazza in memory of the virtues of that Prince."[50] We know much care went into the choice of a learned artist—followed by another such candidate, Montorsoli, when Bandinelli had faltered—in the continuing effort to make the monument authentic and classical.

But it is the artist more than the commission that interests us here. The learned artist represents himself, and is represented, as the keeper of the historical tradition—not just a practitioner whom others more learned can insert into the narrative of history but an individual who can design his works so as to write himself into that narrative. This appears most visibly in relations with patrons, where the traditional roles of artist and humanist are being fused. Bandinelli's praise for the second *Eve* statue, which we have already quoted—"io ho disposto conseguire in quest'opera . . . quelli nobili effetti de' valentissimi Greci, nè mi voglio risparmiare a nessuna estrema fatica"—marshals powerful scholarly resources at the same time as it conditions the Duke's eye with the highly valorized language of ancient art.[51] (It also suggests that the association of classicism and assiduousness was as present in Bandinelli's mind as in Vasari's.) And the artist is even more insistent when he addresses the duchess, reassuring her about the sculptural representation of her husband:

> Sarà chome vedere Otavio o Ponpeo Magno cho' quei beli ciufoleti e barba ritonda, cho queli richi adornamenti di coraza a l'uso romano, e 'l moto suo e che distende uno brachio alu(n)chando la mana da patifichare e popoli, ch'è 'l più celebrato ato che si faciesi fare agli antichi i(m)peratori.[52]

> It will be like seeing Octavius or Pompey the Great with those beautiful tufts of hair and rounded beard, with those richly decorated cuirasses in the Roman style, along with that typical gesture of extending an arm holding the hand in such a way as to bring peace to the peoples, which was the most famous attitude in which the ancient emperors had themselves represented.

It is a show of history and visual experience—Bandinelli has seen many ancient busts, he has seen the Capitoline *Marcus Aurelius*, and with an artist's eye—that is irrefutable. And it is quite different from having even the most enthusiastic humanist observer praise the artist's achievement after the fact, because here the classical authority appears to arise out of the very invention or inspiration that produced the work.

This authority is powerful because so many historical voices are being conglomerated in the newly articulate speech of the learned artist. The Bandinelli whom Anton Francesco Doni makes the ultimate judge in his dialogues on the paragone of painting and sculpture does not provide a very clear answer to the principal argument of the book.[53] Like many other Bandinelli projects, it's all windup and very little pitch. At the very end he does pronounce upon the question at hand—the difference between painting and sculpture, he declares, is equivalent to that between shadow and substance—but he only gets to this point after a much longer sequence of declarations of special authority. He renders himself as the artist who offers thanks to the institution of patronage by inserting moderns like the Medici and the emperor into a history dating back to Maecenas. He retells Plinian anecdotes about artistic representation and the esteem in which artists were held. He discourses on the theory of human proportions, on the science of physiognomy, and on the relative difficulty of rendering various parts of the body. His claims move smoothly between the historical and the transhistorical— that is, between matters of universal truth that only an artist can recognize and matters of particular truth grounded in a long tradition that the historian records.

The real Bandinelli is perhaps even more eloquent and more decisive. The (possibly imaginary) *Venus*, of which we have already spoken, becomes the occasion for a direct self-association with antiquity:

> Avendoli [Carlo V] fatto dono di una bellissima Venere stimata al pari di quella di Fidia, la quale mandò in Germania e che gli fu carissima, mi diede, e di sua propria mano, un nicchio tutto d'oro smaltato e incastrato con pietre preziose.[54]

> I made a gift to Charles V of an extremely beautiful Venus valued as the equal of Phidias', which was sent into Germany and was much loved by the emperor who gave me with his own hands a chain all of burnished gold and set with precious stones.

Imitatio Phidiae, plus the gratitude of the emperor borrowed from the life of Apelles. Bandinelli moves past self-congratulation via the conventional Plinian anecdotes to provide a long view—how the ancients did it; how Donatello, Ghiberti, and Michelangelo have done it—that situates these truths in the context of practical artistic experience.[55]

But all this self-conscious working within history is not merely a matter of representations and advertisements. An artist who declares himself simultaneously a scholar and archaeologist may have truth on his side. The crucial case, once again, is the *Laocoön*. Earlier I recounted the negative side of Vasari's narrative, including Bandinelli's boasts about surpassing the original and Vasari's own ambiguously poised claim that the copy was indistinguishable from the original. But his final evaluation is in no way equivocal: "He also restored the right arm of the ancient Laocoon, which had been broken off and never found, and Baccio made one of the full size in wax, which so resembled the ancient work in the muscles, in force, and in manner, and harmonized with it so well, that it showed how Baccio understood his art; and this model served him as a pattern for making the whole arm of his Laocoon."[56] To say that Baccio "intendeva dell'arte" is to pay him a powerful, if enigmatic, compliment. We cannot determine, either from Vasari's *Life* or from other forms of documentation, exactly whether the wax arm was ever attached to the Belvedere statue and therefore whether it was made for the purpose of physical restoration.[57] (If it was attached, it certainly had a brief career in situ, since Montorsoli's arm, which was definitely attached, dates from the 1530s; furthermore, none of the countless drawings from this period represents Laocoön with an arm like that of Bandinelli's copy.) As Vasari presents it—and he is our only source on its existence—the wax arm is itself a piece of artistic archaeology, a study of the maniera of the ancients as well as of the physical requirements of this particular represented body. That may be why he can lavish the praise on this fragment that he withholds from the completed copy. The project for an arm whose original was lost does not partake of the discourse of equaling or surpassing the ancient work; nor can it possibly be described as the other extreme, a sedulous imitation verging toward plagiarism. Rather it has a kind of unique median status, between originality and imitation, between scholarship and art. Also between the physical existence of the ancient work and that of the modern. The claim that the wax arm served as the origin for the arm of the complete copy suggests a process of imitative inspiration that unites the original and the copy by means of an archaeology only an artist could provide. And it may retrospectively demonstrate that Vasari's praise for the replica *Laocoön* is indeed sincere, reflecting his approval of the process that led from the invented arm to the completed copy. The whole project becomes much more like the *Orpheus*, which was praised for capturing so successfully the maniera of the ancients.

In one way, at least, Bandinelli's *Laocoön* differs visibly from the Belvedere statue: it is signed "BACCIVS. BANDINELLVS. FLORENTINVS. SANCTI. IACOBI. EQVES. FACIEBAT." And the *Orpheus*, whatever its similarities to the *Apollo Belvedere*, distinguishes itself by a similar signature-inscription, though minus the knighthood since it predates the conferring of that title. For Bandinelli the archaeologizing artist or the master of imitation, the other side of the coin—and once again, he is not alone in this—is a particularly strong and public emphasis on his own name, identity, and self. Signatures in general are a complicated novelty in the time of Bandinelli's formation as an artist, and signatures on sculpture are especially noteworthy. Among the rediscovered ancient works, the *Torso Belvedere*, with a signature that disturbingly names an artist nowhere else recorded, is almost a unique case. The signature on Michelangelo's Saint Peter's *Pietà* requires a special legend, in which the young artist hears the as-yet-unsigned work credited to a different sculptor, whereupon he decides to leave no room for doubt and place his name prominently; to this, Vasari adds that nowhere else did Michelangelo sign his work.[58]

Nor did Bandinelli sign indiscriminately. The fact that the *Orpheus* and the *Laocoön* are the principal examples—leaving aside the artist's own tomb, which includes both signature and self-portrait—may be explicable on the grounds that he could not so easily sign a religious work, even though Michelangelo did and even though Bandinelli was often accused of just that form of egotistical sacrilege.[59] More to the point, I think, is the complex connection between classical subject matter and the bold assertion of selfhood. Once again, these matters are linked in a complex chain that can be traced back to Petrarch. The antiquity that is refracted through humanistic culture validates individual heroism and self-assertion. The self-assertions made by the antiques themselves, on the other hand, are so confident that they make us feel small by comparison, even as they offer permission for us to advertise ourselves. So Bandinelli names his name publicly in precisely the contexts where the competition is greatest. Bandinelli was also a tireless self-portrait maker, as he himself announces:

> Per ultima impresa, la quale conservai e conserverò insino a morte, feci una torre da venti combattuta col motto: "*Né per soffiare de' venti*," il quale tolsi da Dante, dove dice:
> > Sta come torre ferma che non crolla
> > già mai la cima per soffiar de' venti
> e la feci gettare in bronzo, con la mia effigie da una parte con questo iscrizione nella circonferenzia: BACCHUS EQ. S. J. EX COM. BANDINELLIS, e nell'altra l'impresa.[60]

> As my final *impresa*, which I have preserved and will preserve until my death, I made a tower buffeted by winds with the motto "Not even by the gusting of wind," which is taken from Dante, who says, "He stays still like a tower which does not collapse even when the top is blowing in the wind." And I had it cast in bronze with my portrait on one side and with this inscription on the rim: BACCIO KNIGHT OF SAN JACOPO OF THE FAMILY OF THE COUNTS BANDINELLI.

The terms are almost identical to his account of the academy: he publicizes both the project and the project's extensive publicity. What also connects this activity to the academy—besides the inevitable presence of his self-portraits within those images—is the link between the antique material and the self-assertion.

Certain of the images themselves place Bandinelli in the context of his artistic oeuvre of a specifically classical kind. In a painting at the Isabella Stuart Gardner Museum (fig. 5.15), he is pointing histrionically to what appears to be a finished drawing (or painting?) of a *Hercules and Cacus* quite different from that work in its final form—perhaps as part of a polemic in favor of a version that he preferred. In an engraving (fig. 5.16) he is surrounded by classical miniatures, or imitations of classical miniatures. He clutches a Hercules-like figure in bold contrapposto while on the windowsill a miniature *Doryphoros* (not unlike the Michelangelo *David*) points upward to the artist's name.[61] Like the academy engravings, both of these images are set in a highly dramatic chiaroscuro. Both emphasize an art that is not in its finished state but rather in the process of its making—hence, too, the significance of pedagogy as a mode in which the artist identifies himself. Perhaps Bandinelli was himself reflecting the widespread opinion that he was better at preparing projects than at completing them. Whatever the motive, it is clear that, at least in the oeuvre of Bandinelli, to represent artistic process is to represent antiquities. If we cannot tell whether these are modern versions or the real thing, so much the better, since this artist represents himself as the master of that very nexus. If we then ask why—that is, why display oneself with a Hercules statue rather than with one of God the Father, or why claim it was a *Venus* that earned the knighthood rather than a *Deposition*—the answer must lie in the paradox of imitation and selfhood that plays itself out where Renaissance artists were beginning to declare themselves as originals.[62]

To be sure, in this instance the originality of selfhood is almost entirely negative. Bandinelli has a *terribile* personality in a far less ambiguous sense than was applied to Michelangelo. One might choose to take with a grain of salt some of Vasari's more extravagant accusations: that Bandinelli tore up Michelangelo's Cascina cartoon, that he tried to trick Andrea del Sarto into giving up the secrets of color, that he informed on fellow Florentines who had supported the republic, that he misused funds intended for the Medici tomb project, that he smashed to pieces statues he found in Michelangelo's studio, that he mistreated his son. It is less easy to dismiss the record of how universally Baccio was disliked, which is confirmed by much of the considerable documentation that surrounds his career. One might even say that Bandinelli's unpleasantness was his most famous artistic product. Except that it wasn't. There is a medium quite separate from the psyche in which his fame was universal; but that, too, might best be approached via the question of the artist's identity.

DISEGNO AND PARAGONE

There is another side to the selfhood of Bandinelli the artist, less heralded then and now. The assertion of an individual identity in the midst of the competition offered by all the imposing models for imitation involves artistic introspection as much as personal assertion. We have observed, and will continue to observe, the remarkable extent of Bandinelli's awareness of the processes by which an artistic object is made. For the most part, these are interpersonal processes: whether it involves pupils or patrons, colleagues or predecessors, Baccio is remarkably articulate. But he is also capable of an awareness of process that involves himself alone:

5.15. Bandinelli, *Self-Portrait*, oil on panel, ca. 1545, Isabella Stuart Gardner Museum, Boston

5.16. Niccolò della Casa, after Bandinelli, *Self-Portrait*, engraving, 1540s, Museum of Fine Arts, Boston

Io ho finito un altro disegno per farne la voglia di sua eccellenza, la quale supplico, che si degni udire la causa perchè al presente io non l'ho mandato; si è perchè io mi trovo molto disposto a trovar bellissime invenzioni, e di già ne ho cominciato un altro, e non resterò di seguitare e dar fine a tutti. Ma egli è necessario, se io voglio fare variate le invenzioni, che io mi vegga tutti i disegni, che io fo, innanzi agli occhi, perchè l'uno mi fa gran luce all'altro in conoscere la verità degli errori di ciascuno, perchè gli veggo al paragone, ed in questo modo varierò e migliorerò in modo che piaceranno a sua eccellenza, perchè i disegni non si fanno per altro che per vederli insieme a paragone.[63]

I have finished another drawing in order to satisfy his excellency, and I beg that he be willing to hear the reason why at present I have not sent it to him. Namely, that I feel myself disposed to find beautiful *invenzioni*, of which I have now begun yet another; and I do not wish to pause and finish them all. But it is necessary, if I wish to produce variation among the *invenzioni*, that I place all the designs in front of my own eyes, so that each of them illuminates the others helping me to see the truth of the errors in each, because I see by comparisons, and in this manner I will vary and improve my work so that it will please his excellency, since drawings are made for no other reason than to consider them in comparison to each other.

Once again, the context is apology and the making of excuses; once again, we see a Bandinelli who is immersed in *fatica* and who is more dedicated to preparing than to

finishing. But we are also afforded a view here of what occupies him in all this dilation—that is, himself as a source of inspiration. The ancient sculpture and all it represents have furnished examples of variety and invention, a set of interrelated models
that provide the grounds for aesthetic comparison. Here, looking at his own works
almost as though he were not their author, he will start to assimilate this body of
material to the same modalities as were operating between his own creative process
and the art of others, whether ancient or modern. He is a hoarder of antiquities, of
sources, and of himself. With his *disegno*, and his *disegni* in front of him, he has
become a Belvedere, or at least an object of *paragone*, for his own contemplation.

Bandinelli was right to contemplate his drawings, since they are at the center
of his life as an artist and of his relations to antiquity. And they are the one element in
his life and career that seems to have never been controversial:

> Ma perchè il suo disegnare, al che si vede che egli più che ad altro attese, fu tale
> e di tanta bontà, che supera ogni suo difetto di natura, e lo fa conoscere per
> uomo raro di questa arte: noi perciò non solamente lo annoveriamo tra i
> maggiori, ma sempre abbiamo avuto rispetto all'opere sue, e cerco abbiamo
> non di guastarle, ma di finirle, e di fare loro onore: imperocchè ci pare che
> Baccio veramente sia di quelli uno, che onorata lode meritono e fama eterna.
>
> [Vasari, *Vite*, 6:195]

> But since his drawing, to which it is evident that he gave his attention more
> than to any other thing, was of such a kind and such excellence that it atones
> for his every natural defect and makes him known as a rare master of our art,
> we therefore not only count him among the greatest craftsmen, but also have
> always paid respect to his works, and have sought not to destroy but to finish
> them and do them honour, for the reason that it appears to us that Baccio was
> in truth one of those who deserve honourable praise and everlasting fame.
>
> [deVere, 2:309]

> Tutto il mio intento era nel disegniare e nel quale, al giudizio di Michelagniolo,
> de' nostri préncipi e de' migliori, tanto prevalsi. Gran quantità ne hanno Loro
> Eccellenzie, altri mandati in Germania et altri in Francia, ed altri sparsi per
> l'Italia, alcuni dei quali so che si sono venduti sino a dugento scudi; . . . con tut-
> to ciò ve ne lascio quasi pieno un cassone, quali terrete come tante gioie, né ve
> li lasciate uscire di mano, poi che verrà tempo che varranno tesori; e Dio vi
> benedica; avvertendovi però di uno errore che nacque nella stampa di S.o
> Lorenzo, ove l'intagliatore, in cambio di intagliare *Band.*, intagliò *Brand.*, onde
> molti che non sapevano lo interpretavano per Brandi, Brandini e Brandinelli,
> onde io ne feci ristampare un'altra in più piccola e migliore forma, col nome
> finito Bandinelli.[64]   [*Memoriale*]

> All my efforts were in draughtsmanship, in which according to the judgment
> of Michelangelo, as well as of our princes and nobles, I prevailed. Their

Excellencies have a great many of my drawings, others have been sent to Germany and to France as well as distributed throughout Italy, some of which I know have been sold for as much as two hundred scudi. . . . Of all of these I leave you [his sons] almost a trunk full, which you should hold on to like so many jewels, nor should you let them out of your hands, since in the future they will be counted treasures, and God bless you. I must warn you, however, of an error that entered in the printing of the San Lorenzo, where the engraver instead of carving *Band.*, carved *Brand.*, as a result of which many who do not know better read it as Brandi, Brandini and Brandinelli. For this reason I had another made in a smaller and better form, with the complete name written out Bandinelli.

Se dal disegno, come da fonte, egli nasce la più rara bellezza, come non sarà credibile, che dalla mano del maggior disegnatore, che sia mai stato, come fu il Bandinello, non siano procedute opere rare, e singolari?[65]   [Bocchi, *Bellezze*]

If from *disegno*, as though from a source, the rarest beauty is born, then how could anyone believe that from the hand of the greatest draftsman who has ever lived—that is, Bandinelli—there would proceed works that were not rare and singular?

Blessing Baccio the draughtsman while damning him in other ways is more than a disinterested recognition of his talent. It involves a set of reciprocal definitions between this artist and the activity of drawing—its purposes, its meaning, its place in culture— all of which are notably in flux during this period.[66] In the artist's own words as cited above, drawings represent a medium of exchange, a literal currency—since in this memoir he is clearly proposing the stock of drawings as a set of investments likely to appreciate. But they are also a way of disseminating his personal talent all over Europe and of assuring the continuance of his name, if only it is correctly spelled.

Vasari's comment establishes the drawings not only as Bandinelli's greatest strengths but also as the completed works that anchor a whole career embracing many uncompleted, or less successful, works. The drawings that give Bandinelli eternal fame are understood not only as projects for these works but also as exhibiting a genius which requires that subsequent artists—notably Vasari himself—respect the talent that lies behind them, whatever the temptations to the contrary may be. Bocchi's comment is the most extravagant, touching upon a notable linguistic ambiguity: *disegno* means drawing, but it also means the principle of design. In famous contexts, both Michelangelo and Vasari (but many others before them, going back to Alberti and Ghiberti) had celebrated the principle of *disegno* as a kind of Platonic essence defining and exalting the practice of the visual arts.[67] It is noteworthy how Vasari in his life of Bandinelli tends to avoid using *disegno* in that transcendent sense— hence "il suo *disegniare*" in the passage quoted above. Bocchi, on the other hand, here speaking of the particularly maligned *Adam and Eve*, attempts to make the transfer from the universally praised Bandinellian *disegni* to the sublime condition of *disegno*;

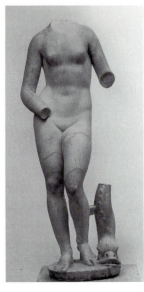

5.17. Bandinelli, *Nude Man Seated on a Grassy Bank*, red chalk, ca. 1525, Courtauld Gallery, London

5.18. Bandinelli, *Standing Female Nude (after the Antique)*, red chalk, ca. 1515, Private Collection

5.19. Venus of Cnidian type, Roman copy after Praxitelean original from fourth century B.C., Glyptothek, Munich

the very presence of the rhetorical question, however, reminds one of the difficulty in asserting that claim for Baccio.

Drawing is the the point of connection where the many practices of art and its cultural context converge. To say that Bandinelli is the greatest disegnatore there has ever been is to name him as the master of this convergence. Not surprisingly, antiquities are of central concern. In Francesco Sangallo's letter about the discovery of the *Laocoön*, he reports that as soon as the hole was widened sufficiently to extract the newly identified statue from the soil of the Esquiline such that it could be fully seen, "ci tornammo a desinare" (we started to draw).[68] Granted, there are other ways to react to ancient sculpture than to draw it; and there are certainly other things to draw than ancient sculpture. Yet the bond between antique statues and new work on paper is a special one, located at the crossroads of ancient and modern, of public display and private invention, of those who have seen the past with their own eyes and those who learn about it already mediated through publicity.

Bandinelli was, to be sure, not one of those professional sketchbook artists haunting Roman ruins.[69] Despite what we might imagine from all the various claims about his classicism or academicism, his oeuvre includes remarkably few verbatim sketches from the antique, though whether it is as low as the 2 percent figure offered by Roger Ward depends on the very slipperiness of this category.[70] A red-chalk drawing faithfully based on the *Torso Belvedere* (fig. 5.17) certainly fits this definition.[71] Probably an early work, perhaps related to the *Martyrdom of Saint Lawrence* materials from the mid-1520s, it appears in what might be considered an anomalous medium.

Massive three-dimensionality is usually translated into flat design by a sharp line; red chalk, which is Baccio's choice in many of these sketches after the antique, is sur- prising.[72] Yet this drawing is quite successful in rendering light and volume, in fact by an absence of chalk. Such incongruity already signals its transitional relationship to the sculptural original. In addition, the *Torso* is here given some arms, some more leg, and a head; but it is not fully completed as a person.[73] The stone base of the Belvedere statue is rationalized into a little hillock (as in many other Bandinelli drawings influenced by statues in a seated position), and the "landscape" is made minutely more substantial by a disproportionately small wisp of wild flowers. In the end, all these incomplete completions betray considerable ambiguity as to the very nature of what is being represented here. Is this the drawing of a (partly) completed statue, is this the representation of a (somewhat mutilated) living person in a landscape, or is this an imitation of the Belvedere *Torso* being prepared for transfer into another medi- um? In those alternatives we may already observe some of the different kinds of cross- roads at which Bandinelli, the draughtsman contemplating ancient sculpture, may find himself.

One way to elide these distinctions is to say that Bandinelli became intimately familiar with certain ancient images and *assimilated* them so that they became a set of themes on which he provided a lifelong fantasia of variations. Drawings from all peri- ods of Bandinelli's career (and he is not alone among his contemporaries) include a remarkable number of figures with midsections and turned waists like the Belvedere Torso, contrapposti and profile heads like the *Apollo Belvedere*, as well as other bodies and body positions that resemble River Gods, the *Laocoön*, and certain Venuses. In addition, many drawings of multiple figures suggest a close study and translation into his own idiom of the compositional structure associated with reliefs and sarcophagi. But this account is incomplete in precisely the way that the Petrarch-inspired theories of imitation are incomplete. "Assimilation" or "themes and variations" are metaphors covering a space of real-life exchanges that are, in fact, quite specifically recorded on these pieces of paper. Assimilation of ancient models comes about as the result of step-by-step procedures, including circumstances involved in seeing the originals (or copies of the originals), operations of memory or re-creation, and ways of using chalk, pencil, ink, and paper. And as these drawings emerge, they absorb all sorts of other contextual forces that bear upon the activities of seeing and drawing.

Occasionally it is possible, at least conjecturally, to watch the process of these forces at work, as in another drawing in red chalk of greater technical refinement, of a Standing Female Nude (fig. 5.18).[74] The departure point could be any of a number of Venuses known in Renaissance Rome that in turn owe their origins to the Cnidian stat- ue of Praxiteles (fig. 5.19), itself rendered immortal by an account in Pliny attesting to both its artistic and its erotic power.[75] The final destination in Bandinelli's work, or at least his fullest exploitation of this form, is the *Eve* done for the Duomo, notably in the final form now in the Bargello (see fig. 5.9), though the earlier version, now the *Ceres* of the Boboli Gardens, also reveals close similarities. These extremes of the itinerary

5.20. Bandinelli, *Birth of the Virgin*, marble relief, 1518–19, Basilica della Santa Casa, Loreto

already indicate something about the influence of the ancients. The rather bland quality of Bandinelli's female figures—Vasari quotes a lady viewer who diplomatically praises the *Eve* only for being of white and firm flesh, attributes of the marble, not the art[76]— can now be seen as the willed selection of a particular ancient canon for the female body that modern historians might refer to as neo-Attic, or itself deliberately archaizing, to which the medium of red chalk adds a further softening of line.

So far as the itinerary is concerned, in this image there is already some of the transitional work of the kind we observed in the *Torso Belvedere* drawing. We do not know exactly which statue Bandinelli was working from, but it would seem likely that the particular presence and absence of extremities in the drawing—the complete if sketchy head, the exceptionally well finished lower legs and feet, the arms truncated just below the shoulders—have more to do with the artist's purposes than with the exact state of the object he was sketching from. Most probably the more immediate destination of the drawing in question was not the first or second *Eve* but the relief figures in the Loreto *Birth of the Virgin* (fig. 5.20), a project that grows out of a great many drawings of female figures. In this regard a double-sided sheet in Turin (figs. 5.21, 5.22) documents the process with surprising exactness. On the recto there is an almost identical figure, also executed in red chalk, whose left arm is cropped by the edge of the paper but whose right arm has been completed and framed by part of a cloak.[77] It would be more correct to say that the arm has been *replaced* by a cloak that begins at the point of truncation and ends at a right hand that is more hastily sketched than any of the rest of the body itself. Similarly sketchy bits of cloak appear elsewhere around the figure, roughly conforming to the *pensieri* in the original sketch. The verso of

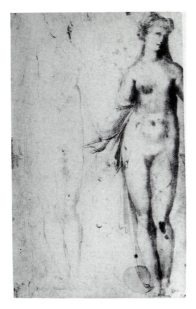 

5.21. Bandinelli, *Standing Female Nude*, red chalk, ca. 1518, Biblioteca Reale, Turin

5.22. Bandinelli, *Two Female Figures* (verso of fig. 5.21), pen and ink, ca. 1518, Biblioteca Reale, Turin

the sheet includes a pen drawing of the same figure, including some further play with the arm positions that the original statue left unspecified. But now the figure is completely—though quite diaphanously—clothed. She is no longer an independent statue but rendered as part of a dramatic scene with another sheerly clothed female figure. The statue figure on the verso is not traced from the red-chalk recto—indeed, she occupies precisely the other half of the sheet. As it happens, the nude body of the inked figure— that is, "under" the clothing—is drawn with a heavier line that bleeds through to the empty half of the recto in perfect mirror image of the chalk figure.

Figures are generated by left-right reversals, by changes in the medium of drawing that may be moving further from a statue being copied or closer to a statue being designed. Figures are also generated by the complementary relations between body parts that are missing and nudity that is being clothed. Pagan figures are by no means always naked, but they have a permission to be naked that is often denied to Christian figures (an issue that Bandinelli clearly struggled against in the very Adam and Eve toward which these drawings are pointing). Pagan figures are also mutilated in a way that, say, those assisting at the Birth of the Virgin ought not to be. In moving from the Cnidian Venus to the Loreto relief, Bandinelli is at the same time and by the same means clothing the naked and restoring their bodies. One could argue that the process of the drawings which occupy that intervening space is intended to insure that under all their drapery these females have Praxitelean bodies. (The Loreto relief as it stands would not support any such extravagantly classicizing claims, one of the many instances of the falling off between Bandinelli's drawings and his finished works.) In the end it is difficult to say whether the viewer is expected to see the secret Praxitelean

5.23. Bandinelli, *Two Nude Men Fighting, Watched by Three Others*, black chalk, ca. 1517, British Museum, London

5.24. Bandinelli, *Seated Male Nude Breaking a Rod with His Knee*, red chalk, ca. 1512, British Museum, London

under torsos in the final work or whether only God sees them. Either way, they exist as a by-product of a process of drawing that translates step by step from one work of sculpture to another, from an ancient pagan work to a modern Christian work.

But that triangular model of one ancient work, one modern work, one artist, which is established so appropriately by Vasari in regard to the *Orpheus*, tends to belie some of the resistances involved in translating antiquities into modern artistic practice. In Vasari's own account of Bandinelli's early work as a draughtsman, he moves from the young artist's imitation of Filippo Lippi to his father's placement of the boy in a studio where he might be noticed by Leonardo, who, in turn, recommends the example of Donatello, with the culminating result that the lad "set himself to copy in marble an antique head of a woman, of which he had shaped a model from one that is in the house of the Medici."[78] Copying the ancient marble, which appears as the destination of all this formative activity, is placed within a history of Baccio's draughtsmanship. The making of drawings is at the center of his relations to other artists. And the most fundamental activity of draughtsmanship, at least for the young artist, is in imitation of his masters, his older contemporaries, and his recent predecessors: "He stayed the whole day drawing in the Chapel of the Pieve from the work of Fra Filippo Lippi, and he did not cease until he had drawn it all, imitating the draperies of that master, who did them very well. And already he handled with great skill the style and the pen, and also chalk both red and black, which last is a soft stone that comes from the mountains of France, and with it, when cut to a point, drawings can be executed with great delicacy."[79] Drawing is a highly technical medium, and Vasari is careful to point out its particular demands, which are independent of those made by the media of the works the drawings imitate. To sketch from Filippo Lippi—to imitate him—is to master, among other things, lo stile, which is both Baccio's stylus and Fra Filippo's style.

If the drawings are produced by one set of artistic relations, they in turn produce another set. They become the medium by which the young artist is "discovered."

5.25. Bandinelli, *A Nude Man, Reclining on His Right Arm*, red chalk, ca. 1514,
British Museum, London

When Leonardo notices the work, he is able to direct the young man in several crucial ways that are all conditioned by the activity of drawing. He can select the proper medium, since disegno lies at the heart of all the media. In this respect Leonardo's choice is not only prophetic of the best later work, but, as we shall see, it also points to Baccio's great success in using drawing to simulate the experience of other artistic media, which is after all the very nature of this particular mentoring exercise. In addition, the drawings enable Leonardo to place the young man in an appropriate channel of discipleship—that is, to give him Donatello as a predecessor—which is also prophetic. And the ultimate result goes beyond drawings to the actual copy of an ancient statue—which is even more prophetic.

The relations of the modern artist to antiquity and to contemporary artists are thus mutually mediating; and the act of reproducing an ancient work is always partly informed by the system of relations, again based on draughtsmanship, that ties artists to their more immediate contemporaries. These mediations by draughtsmanship are decidedly multiple in their entanglements. More than many other artists of his time, Bandinelli has been seen as the dependent of the greatest geniuses among his contemporaries: not only Michelangelo but also Leonardo and Raphael.[80] When it comes to the most tangible evidences in graphic work, the connections generally come courtesy of a common relation to antiquities. Bandinelli's early efforts at the subject of Leda, though according to Vasari they may owe their origins to a desire to compete with Michelangelo, are indebted most visibly to Leonardo's enthusiastic embrace of the pagan subject as well as to the way the earlier artist redacted the classical standing female body, such as we have observed in the drawings associated with Bandinelli's *Birth of the Madonna*.[81] The head that Bandinelli attaches to such bodies owes a great deal to Leonardo's Leda head and turns up as a portrait without body in a number of Bandinelli drawings traditionally said to be depicting his wife.

The Raphael connection is generally cinched by the similarities between larg-

5.26. Bandinelli, *Nude Boy*, black chalk, Galleria degli Uffizi, Florence

5.27. Bandinelli, *Seated Woman Sewing with Two Children*, red chalk, ca. 1515, Département des arts graphiques, Louvre, Paris

er compositions of the two artists, often available only via engravings, such as two *Slaughters of the Innocents* (Raphael engraved by Marcantonio, Bandinelli by Dente) or the Raphael *Entellus and Dares*, echoed, for instance, in a British Museum drawing of nude men fighting (fig. 5.23).[82] But although there is no doubt that Bandinelli's work is mediated by the style of Raphael, especially in the Stanze, the material that is being transmitted in these cases is clearly that of figures from ancient sarcophagi—the individual bodies as well as those compositional principles that interrelate two- and three-dimensional spaces. In fact, the British Museum drawing resembles not only Raphael but also the Quattrocento style of drawings from reliefs associated with the School of Pisanello, in which figures are excerpted from more crowded compositions and translated into graceful, almost abstract patterns.[83] To complicate matters further, this drawing is preparatory for the figures behind the Leonardo-inspired and un-Michelangelesque *Leda*, in which the mysterious role they play seems to owe something to the latter artist's *Doni Tondo*.

Michelangelo is, of course, the principal mediator of antiquities. Vasari characterizes Bandinelli as the artist who surpassed all others in copying from the Cascina cartoon, a work that functioned both as a complete object and as a compendium of separable images (see fig. 5.33). In sketching from the cartoon, as well as from many individual parts of the Sistine Ceiling, Bandinelli rarely copied but frequently worked by quoting, excerpting, translating—precisely the way he worked from classical sources. But it is not so much the parallel between the operations of these sources as their interconnection that is significant. Baccio sees in the compositions of his older rival a mediated antiquity. Michelangelo provides versions of monumental and heroic

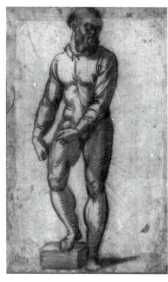

5.28. Bandinelli, *Man in Contemporary Dress, Kneeling in Profile to the Left*, black chalk, 1530s, Ashmolean Museum, Oxford

5.29. Bandinelli, *Standing Male Model*, black chalk, ca. 1515, Windsor Castle, The Royal Collection

human physiques, often in poses of complex torsion. In two early drawings (figs. 5.24, 5.25), one a seated man with his hands at his knees influenced by the Cascina composition and the other a reclining figure created compositely from the Sistine Ceiling, Baccio uses red chalk, as he often seems to do when he particularly wishes to translate an original into his own property.[84] Both images seize upon elements of classical sculpture, specifically relief figures, and turn the Michelangelesque imitations into sketches after the antique. In a large body of later work, Bandinelli runs the gamut of variations on the ancillary figures of the Sistine Ceiling: prophets and sibyls, ancestors of Christ, and, especially, the ignudi. In regard to these last, Bandinelli reinscribes the classical origins of the torsos (cf. fig. 1.10)—once again, from the most famous anthology pieces of the Belvedere. But he also reinstates their grandiose artfulness by inserting them back into monumental decorative poses—seated, bearing scrolls and tablets, or self-contained within a geometric form.

If the universe of the draughtsman consists solely in antiquities and in the work of contemporaries, then something—call it real life—would appear to be missing. Vasari, still on the subject of Baccio's early experience, has the boy drawing the naked laborers and livestock on his father's farm passionately ("con grande affetto"). Cellini, on the other hand, in one of his most scurrilous attacks on Bandinelli—part of his tirade against the *Hercules and Cacus*—takes up this very point: "Delle braccia dicono che le son tutt'a dua giù distese senza nessuna grazia, né vi si vede arte, come se mai voi non avessi visto degl'ignudi vivi" ("As for the arms, it's said that they both stick out gracelessly, nor does one see any artfulness in this, as though you had never laid eyes on any living nudes").[85] Cellini is implying that Bandinelli's art is in some fundamental sense neutered by the artist's own lack of physical engagement. It is noteworthy that this deprivation emerges for Cellini not as the statue's failure to look like an authentic living nude but as its failure to exhibit grace and artfulness. The real accusation has to do with Baccio's notorious attachment to ancient artistic examples. As Cellini encapsulates it, an aesthetic pedant like Bandinelli is necessarily deficient in firsthand observation, which deprives his work of beauty as well as of authenticity. It is precisely the opposite of Vasari's strategy in the preface to part 3 of the *Lives*, where the discovery of ancient statues comes to be understood as a force that liberates artists from the desiccated study of real-life examples into higher levels of artistic freedom and truth.

The answer may lie in a curious mediating practice of draughtsmanship. If Bandinelli's oeuvre includes relatively few perfectly faithful drawings after the antique or after Michelangelo, that is because many of the works most closely associated with these originals are essentially studio re-creations. Bandinelli, in other words, was in the habit of placing real-life models in the body positions of famous works of art, which he then sketched with assiduous faithfulness not only to the absent predecessor work but also to the quotidian and contemporary details that distinguished the staged version from the original. There are many examples, some from antiquity, most from Michelangelo. A boy, whose head is obviously inadequate to the rest of the body, is placed in the position of the Belvedere Torso (fig. 5.26). Figures from the lunettes and other decorative corners of the Sistine Chapel ceiling are rationalized as genre scenes in modern dress (fig. 5.27). Favorite images from the Cascina drawing are restaged by garzoni who are wearing ordinary clothes or are given different reasons for the specific distensions of their bodies (fig. 5.28; see fig. 5.24).[86]

It is as tempting as it is risky to reconstruct the full particulars of this practice. If there were sketches made in front of the originals that preceded these restagings, they have not by and large come down to us. This leads to the speculation that Bandinelli's imitations begin in something remembered rather than in something transcribed, just as the more faithful drawings after the antique, which are not explicitly restaged, are already in the process of modern transformation. This persistent restaging in the studio with obvious garzoni needs to be juxtaposed with the accademia engravings and the background drawings for them, in which the figures are not arrayed in famous artistic postures but are merely doing what they normally did in the studio, which was sketching. The studio, in other words, is a kind of theatrical space—one thinks of Alpers's profoundly suggestive work on analogous matters surrounding Rembrandt—where art becomes real life and real life becomes art.[87]

But it would be wrong to move too rapidly along this circle or to homogenize the various stages of progression. At all phases of his career as draughtsman—whether in an early and hasty sketch based on Michelangelo's *Saint Matthew* (fig. 5.29) or later finished drawings for the *Moses and the Tablets of the Law* painting (fig. 5.30),[88] Bandinelli is extremely careful with the contingent details of the studio posing—the clothing, for instance, or the inappropriate age of the model, details that differ from the imitated original and (where relevant) need to be once again suppressed when the

5.30. Bandinelli, *Study for the Figure of Moses*, 1550s, black chalk, Galleria degli Uffizi, Florence

composition is going to take final form in some new, more proprietary work of Bandinelli. A specially recurrent case has to do with figures who are seated. Michelangelo offers some rather divergent examples on the Sistine Ceiling: the prophets and sibyls are in seated postures, but it is not always clear what they are sitting on; the ignudi, on the other hand, are noticeably plumped on marble thrones, sometimes even with cushions. In many of Bandinelli's Michelangelesque drawings, considerable effort is made to rationalize classic seated postures in a similar way. The procedure begins in the studio with the practical details of arranging a pose, but the artist draws the studio props as carefully as the posture. So a young man holding a tablet (fig. 5.31) is quite obviously seated on the typical three-legged stool that we see in many of the academy drawings, while in the next stage of the idea (fig. 5.32) a prophetlike old man in the same position with the same tablet can now be seated in a much more abstract and monumental way.[89]

In at least one case we can follow this process with full documentation. The figure in the foreground at the far right of the Cascina cartoon (fig. 5.33) exercised considerable influence on Bandinelli (and others).[90] This is a clear instance of the antique being mediated through modern contemporaries, since several of the most famous and widely viewed ancient statues depicted individuals crouching or adjusting footgear. As we saw in Chapter 3, there is a significant body of important ancient sculpture positioned in this way—the so-called Doidalsas Venus, the *Nymph* "alla Spina," the *Arrotino,* the *Spinario.* These postures, once again, are more visually striking than they are narratively explainable. Deprived of such contexts (if they ever had them), these turned bodies appear as something like pure exercises of art. Yet one

5.31. Bandinelli, *Seated Young Man Pointing to a Tablet*, red chalk, ca. 1520, Kunsthalle, Hamburg

5.32. Bandinelli, *Seated Old Man in Pseudo-Antique Costume, Pointing to a Tablet*, pen and brown ink, 1520s, British Museum, London

might say that the whole fable of the Cascina cartoon—Michelangelo's choice of a moment in the war when the resting Florentine soldiers were surprised by a deliberately false alarm—provides a retrospective circumstantial logic to these artificial postures. The body position of the crouching man receives both a quotidian explanation (he is pulling on his leggings) and a heroic story line (the sudden alarm produces a new vigilance that will eventually defeat the Pisans).

Michelangelo's influential example validates the artfulness of the chosen antiquities in part by framing them in a narrative logic. When Baccio goes on to rework this figure, he begins by posing his models in the studio with highly particularized versions of this logic. The early red-chalk drawing of the *Man Breaking a Rod* (see fig. 5.24) relegates the base on which the figure is sitting to a few vaguely sketched lines, but it places great emphasis on the physical action and the stick itself. A later black-chalk Ashmolean drawing (see fig. 5.28) fully dresses the figure, sparing no detail of the costume so that the stage business of pulling on the boot emerges as logical and consistent. In what would appear to be a subsequent stage (fig. 5.34), a pen-and-ink drawing probably not done from an actual model, the figure has been rigorously removed from real life, stripped naked, greatly muscularized, and rendered in a more exaggerated physical position, while the gesture that ought to be the raison d'être of this position is so covered and abstracted that it becomes meaningless.[91] This figure finally emerges as a Bandinellian sculptural work in the upper part of one of the Clement VII tomb reliefs, the *Baptism of the Neophytes* at Santa Maria sopra Minerva (fig. 5.35): in this instance not

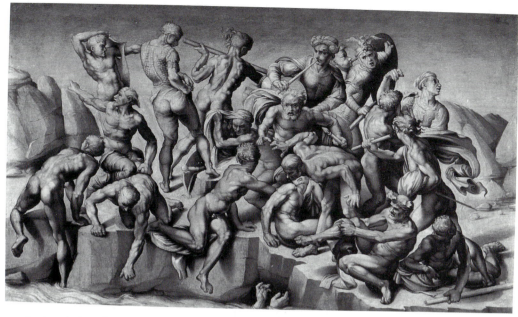

5.33. Bastiano da Sangallo (attributed), copy after Michelangelo, cartoon for *Battle of Cascina*, ca. 1542, Holkham Hall, Norfolk, England

only does the physical gesture have no logical explanation, but in fact the whole presence of the figure on the relief seems narratively gratuitous.

Whatever the quality of the results, we can observe in this process the building of at least one artist's notion of a complete representation of the human form. Just as the nude antiquity underlay the female figures in the Loreto *Birth of the Virgin*, or the three-legged stool underlay the seated posture of the prophet pointing to a tablet, here the clothed and logically arrayed studio models underlie the reconceived ancient nude. Cellini accused Baccio of never having seen a living body, but the truth is that he sketched carefully from life and did more: he interwove his life studies with imitations of great artistic examples. In so doing, he, no less than the ancients or Michelangelo, made quotidian reality part of the process of artistic authentication.

THE RHETORIC OF DRAUGHTSMANSHIP

Looking at the matter from outside rather than inside, drawing is central in the career of Bandinelli in part because, as we have seen, he is a propagandizer. He lives, of course, in a culture where drawings have begun to circulate. Here we are on familiar territory, mapped out by the Cascina cartoon at the beginning of Baccio's career and by his well-documented interest in exercising an educational influence on other artists. Michelangelo's project in the Palazzo Pubblico was not, of course, intended for the purpose of training artists. It was intended to be a completed fresco commemorat-

5.34. Bandinelli, *Nude Kneeling in Profile to the Left*, pen and ink, 1530s, Département des arts graphiques, Louvre, Paris

ing a great Florentine victory, and if the work had been finished (in fact, it was not even begun), the cartoon might well have been disposed of more quickly and the influence that the project exerted over artists would have been exercised in the Palazzo itself, probably in an attenuated way.[92] Instead it became the first great example of the non finito, canonizing for a whole epoch the relations between individual genius and perishable paper, while helping to establish a system of publication for these new products of the individual imagination. The diffusion and the destruction of the Cascina cartoon are of a piece, both testifying to the power of its example. And Vasari declares that Bandinelli was the number one student of the cartoon (which may well be true) as well as its destroyer (almost certainly false).[93]

The consequence for Bandinelli and others is that the large-scale drawing of a complex projected work develops a set of educational purposes, broadly construed, quite independent of its possibilities for actual realization. What was an accident in the case of the young Michelangelo gets institutionalized, in part owing to the culture of the academy in which Bandinelli played such an important role. In fact, some of these works may have had very doubtful prospects of realization, though the fiction of an eventual completed object of public display may have needed to be preserved. The examples in Bandinelli's career, many of them already cited, are numerous. There is a whole sequence of works, including the academy drawings themselves, a *Combat of the Gods*, and a drawing of *anatomie* cited by Vasari that we know were drawn specifically for the purpose of being published as engravings. And there are the famous instances

5.35. Bandinelli, *Baptism of the Neophytes*, from tomb of Leo X, marble relief, 1539–40, Santa Maria sopra Minerva, Rome

of the *Slaughter of the Innocents* (fig. 5.36) and the *Martyrdom of Saint Lawrence*—both drawings with little or no apparent evidence of realization. Vasari discusses both in detail; of the *Slaughter* he says, "This scene, which was filled by him with a quantity of nudes, both male and female, children living and dead, and women and soldiers in various attitudes, made known the fine draughtsmanship that he showed in figures and his knowledge of muscles and of all the members, and it won him great fame all over Europe."[94] The purpose of the image is clearly to teach *buon disegno* by example, and its success is evidenced by the fame it brings to the artist, a fame that can be conferred by fellow artists. Vasari's ekphrasis takes only brief note of the content or meaning of the image and sees it instead as a collection of model figures, a sort of pattern book divided by sex, age, and condition of life.[95] As usual, Vasari is right. The image as engraved by Marco Dente is a sort of display case of classical sculptural bodies in a studiously chosen set of variations—one thinks of Baccio's emphasis on *variazione* in the letter about the drawings. The rigors of the perspective design focus the image absolutely outward toward the viewer and help to deprive it of internal dramatic reality. Like the reduction of three-dimensional statues into relief compositions, this self-consciously artistic address of Bandinelli's images contributes to a sense that in his work the antique tradition is being not so much assimilated as *advertised*.

But the most important student in the school of disegno is the patron, for whom a drawing is the promise of a completed work that requires the commitment of large sums of money. Bandinelli was proverbial for his virtuosity in making deals with patrons, and much of his career, especially from the middle phase onward, is devoted to this activity. The *Hercules and Cacus*, the Andrea Doria monument, the tombs of the Medici popes, and the work in the Florentine Duomo are all accompanied by long stories of negotiations and many accounts of sketches and models. Vasari is particularly eloquent about one phase of the Duomo project: "This model was shown to the Duke, and also a double series of designs made by Baccio, which, both from their variety and their number, and likewise from their beauty—for the reason that Baccio worked boldly in wax and drew very well—pleased his Excellency, and he ordained that the masonry work should be straightway taken in hand, devoting to it all the expenditure administered by the Office of Works, and giving orders that a great quantity of marble should be brought from Carrara."[96] *Varietà* and *quantità* are the operative terms. The very practice that Bandinelli described as his own system of invention—the contemplation of multiple, varying drawings of a single subject—turns out also to be his means of address to his patron. "E che sia il vero, Sua Eccellenza non mi ha mai avuto a sollecitare, e per ogni invenzione, o in disegni o in modelli, gnen'ho fatti assai più che non m'ha ricerco" (And if the truth be told, His Excellency has never had to coax me; for every *invenzione*, whether of drawings or models, I have always made quite a few more than he has asked for), he says, echoing his comments in the other letter about his inspiration.[97]

The system of inspiration, it should be noted, is also one of indecision. All those expensive public projects mentioned above drag on in part because the artist himself goes through endless changes of plans, as is evidenced by variations in drawings. Given the official nature of these commissions, there are certainly external reasons, having to do with changes in finances, political fortune, and public taste, why plans had to be scrapped. On the other hand, both the quantities of surviving drawings and the testimonies of his contemporaries make it clear that Bandinelli was, in a personal way, mercurial. Lucretia Salvati, the surviving sister of Leo X, complains that she wants to take away Bandinelli's pen so that he will not keep bothering her with new versions of the popes' tombs; and Baldassare Turini, the superintendent of the same project, laments to Cosimo, "I needed, and still need, to take on the personality of a Job in order to deal with that man's brain, which is as flighty as a leaf; every evening we would reach one conclusion, and in the morning he would come back with new ideas."[98] These worthies are up against what is rather a novel phenomenon (and very different from the forces that retard Michelangelo's production): that of an artist who is searching out and laboring over his own inspiration in public.

At the same time, Bandinelli is attempting to turn these uncertainties into selling points. We have already seen how his self-appointed role as *artista archeologizzante* involved him in humanist-style conversation. It is a sort of conditioning project in which the artist relentlessly associates ancient sculpture, perpetual glory, and his own capacity to immortalize Cosimo through artistic production. This set of promises and persuasions makes drawings into exercises in rhetoric. Bandinelli's drawings are figural or metaphoric versions of various three-dimensional realities, including the

5.36. Marco Dente, engraving after Bandinelli, *Slaughter of the Innocents*, ca. 1520, British Museum, London

work of other artists, ancient and modern, as well as his own anticipated production. The work on paper effects a transfer to a nonliteral realm whose fictions reveal some deeper truth about the literal term while they may also change that term. Rhetoric understood in this sense as *figura* is to be juxtaposed with rhetoric in the sense of persuasion. It should already be clear the extent to which Bandinelli used drawing as a form of oratorical argument, whether the audience consisted of fellow artists or Medici patrons (or even the artist himself). The drawing is a sales pitch on behalf of that familiar collocation involving rediscovered ancient culture, the artist's power of mediation, and the immortal glories promised to the patron. The *figurae* of drawings—indeed their whole status as projects-projections—become the artist's means of oratorical exhortation; and drawing becomes a form of epideictic rhetoric.

We can catch a glimpse of this development in history through a Vasarian anecdote. Baccio had declared to a group of fellow sculptors that their older colleague Andrea Sansovino's work "non aveva disegno." But when "all that Baccio had said of Maestro Andrea came to his ears, he, like a wise man, answered him lovingly, saying that works are done with the hands and not with the tongue, that good design is to be looked for not in drawings but in the perfection of the work finished in stone."[99] A serious difference of opinion lurks under this *amorevole* exchange. In one sense, it is a simple face-off about words versus deeds: Sansovino is declaring that Baccio talks a good game but has no great productions in stone to prove his superiority (which is more or less true at this early stage of his career). This is already a significant accusation, since Bandinelli will remain a great talker, and he will be criticized both for the

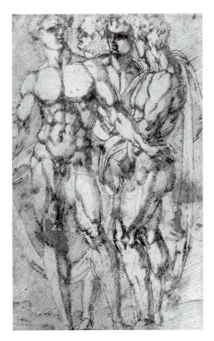

5.37. Bandinelli, *Group of Standing Male Nudes*, pen and brown ink, 1520s, Christ Church Picture Gallery, Oxford

5.38. Bandinelli, *Sacrifice of Noah*, pen and brown ink, 1546–48, Devonshire Collection, Chatsworth

quantity of his words and for their distance from his completed achievements. But Sansovino goes on to a broader field of attack. First, Baccio should use his tongue less and his hands more; then, real disegno lies not on pieces of paper but in the completed marble. The parallel is decisive: Baccio's loose tongue is the equivalent of his voluminous sheaf of drawings. Sansovino, an artist of the previous generation, opposes a "modern" practice that focuses on what we might call design theory—in other terms, all those discourses of speech and draughtsmanship that claim priority over the finished work. In his small way he is being represented as the antagonist of disegno in its Cinquecento transcendent senses; and Baccio is emerging as its representative in malo. Design is rhetoric, and stone is the real thing.

By the time Bandinelli has become the official Medici house sculptor and projector of grand designs, the connection between his tongue and his pen is no mere analogy. For the project of the Audience Hall, Giuliano di Baccio d'Angelo makes the plans and "with these [plans] in his hand Baccio spoke to the Duke" (6:172; deVere, 2:291): the combination does the trick. In regard to the choir for the Duomo, Baccio gives his accustomed lecture urging Cosimo to render the city that much more magnificent and to give the artist himself the chance to exert his powers on behalf of posterity and the Medici; "with these designs and these words Baccio so moved the Duke, that, consenting that such a structure should be erected, his Excellency commissioned him to make a model of the whole choir" (6:177; deVere, 2:295). "Disegni e parole"; "furono fatti disegni . . . e Baccio poi parlò": once again, the twin responses to the discovery of the *Laocoön*. The close association of these rhetorical operations in words and

5.39. Bandinelli, *Drunkenness of Noah*, pen and brown ink,
1547–48, British Museum, London

pictures turns the drawings themselves into a kind of language; essentially a written
language—that is, a set of signifiers whose signifieds are understood by convention.
Except that here the conventions are still being established, and the full reading of
these drawings—which is to say, their promise of a gloriously reevoked antiquity—
requires the accompaniment of the spoken language as enunciated by the artist.

The drawings themselves reflect these rhetorical impulses in a variety of
ways. In part, we are dealing with a matter of medium. Baccio, it should be remembered, finds himself at a difficult point of paragone, between relief sculpture and statues in the round. In a certain sense this is the opposition that lies closest to the heart
of the rediscovered antiquities. Alberti had read the antique tradition through this
dichotomy in his distinction between colossus and historia.[100] And we have already
observed Bandinelli write his own history of practice reaching back to Trajan's
Column but focusing on the Florentine Baptistry Doors, whose traditional importance
and great public display had canonized relief sculpture as a great modern medium.
But perhaps buried it as well. The age of sculptural discovery may bring out of the
earth many more sarcophagi than *Laocoöns*, and some of these sarcophagi become
valuable and influential; but there is no doubt that by the early sixteenth century statues in the round are the prestige items in the classical revival, and consequently in the
sphere of new artistic production. Relief operates in practice as mostly decorative,
while in theory it gets cited more honorifically as the meeting place of those two more
highly valorized media, painting and three-dimensional sculpture. But Bandinelli is
the great practical exponent of relief, its promoter as a medium for grand projects of

5.40. Bandinelli, *Nude Soldiers in Combat*, pen and brown ink, 1540s, Christ Church Picture Gallery, Oxford

artistic achievement. He thus develops a style of drawing individual figures after three-dimensional antiquities while placing them in groups that resemble relief compositions, like the Christ Church *Group of Standing Male Nudes* (fig. 5.37).[101] Like the whole of Bandinelli's relation to the separate artistic media, this becomes a kind of generic anomaly, as though he is reconstructing an ancient sculpture garden but trying to give it the consistent spatial arrangement of a narrative relief.

The drawings for Medici relief projects divide themselves neatly between finished *modelli* and hasty compositional drafts. Each group is stylistically consistent, and each speaks its own rhetorical language. In the former category, a superb group of Old Testament subjects—including *The Sacrifice of Noah* (fig. 5.38) and *The Drunkenness of Noah* (fig. 5.39)—reveals an extraordinary subtlety and variety of cross-hatchings.[102] Vasari, after all, had characterized Bandinelli in a memorable phrase as the most successful of all those who did drawings after Michelangelo's Cascina cartoon, because "egli dintornava e ombrava e finiva" ("he outlined, shaded, and finished them"; 6:137, deVere, 2:267). But this set of drawings demonstrates that cross-hatching is not just a representational technique but also a way of advertising varying depths of relief while rendering a two-dimensional subject more readable than it could be in bronze or marble. Essentially Bandinelli is promising the substantiality of sculpture in a mode that appears to possess the clarity of painting. Further, the use of multiple forms of cross-hatching sets off individual figures like Cain or the drunken Noah as though they were freestanding statues, and, not coincidentally, statues of a specifically classical type.

The compositional sketches seek to persuade in a different way, not by offer-

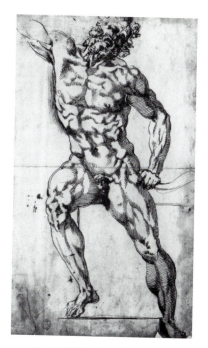

5.41. Bandinelli, drawing after the *Laocoön*, 1520s, black chalk, Galleria degli Uffizi, Florence

5.42. Bandinelli, drawing after the *Laocoön*, 1520s, pen and ink, Galleria degli Uffizi, Florence

ing a heightened version of the final work but by illustrating the fecundity of the artist's imagination. In a letter from 1540, Bandinelli reminds Cosimo of "una istoria di molti che combattono, la quale invenzione tanto piacque a V[ostra]. E[ccellenza] che me la fece fare di marmo" (a narrative of many men fighting, whose *invenzione* so pleased Your Excellency that he ordered me to produce it in marble);[103] he now proposes to complete that work as part of the tomb for Cosimo's father. The process already demonstrates how the drawing acts as bait for the duke to support the artist's finished work. If we look at the Christ Church *Nude Soldiers in Combat* (fig. 5.40), which Simon Ward has associated with this *invenzione*, we see a highly elliptical work that almost aspires to the condition of pure artistic design.[104] The artist may use the term *istoria*, but the work in question is less a narrative than a riot of varied corporeal shapes. The ancestry is both ancient and modern—battle sarcophagi along with the Anghiari and Cascina projects for the Palazzo Pubblico—all of which testify to the inventiveness of the gifted artist.

All these projects of relief sculpture are multiple compositions, Albertian historiae; a quite different form of rhetoricism is involved when we consider the drafting of the individual figure. Many of Bandinelli's works on paper—and not only on paper—depict hyperbolic (usually male) bodies possessing what we must call extravagant musculature. The canonical Belvedere sculptures are at the heart of this form of representation. On several occasions (fig. 5.41), Bandinelli rendered Laocoön as a mass of heavily shadowed brawniness; one of these (fig. 5.42) is almost *écorché*-like in its exposure of muscles from neck to toes. There are freer replicas from the *Apollo*

5.43. Bandinelli, drawing for a bronze *Hercules*, pen and ink, ca. 1530, Graphische Sammlung Albertina, Vienna

Belvedere or the *Torso Belvedere*; and a remarkable drawing, probably related to a bronze *Hercules* in the Victoria and Albert Museum (fig. 5.43), places the *Apollo* and the *Torso* on the same sheet, if not in the same space: all of these, once again, put exaggerated emphasis on the varying contours of the body. Yet other drawings, even when they do not replicate specific antiquities, represent highly muscular figures in sculptural attitudes—that is, borrowing elements of torso or limb from Belvedere figures and often truncated in a similar way (cf. fig. 5.17).[105] Bandinelli takes the heavily articulated bodies of ancient statues and places the individuals in positions of dynamic tension, quite impossible for three-dimensional sculpture but designed to emphasize the muscular consequences of various forms of motion. In effect, the body is rendered as a display, which may explain the close connection between this style of drawing and the most up-to-date forms of anatomical representation. So the explicitly muscular body, in whatever context it is represented, becomes a sign and a reference to the colossal works of freestanding sculpture that had recently been unearthed at the same time that it celebrates the "perfect" natural body of artistic and scientific representation.

These associations are hardly surprising. We have already mentioned how draughtsmanship was taught by viewing classical statues under extreme conditions of oblique light: the result would tend to be a linear exaggeration of the planar effects that signify three-dimensional musculature. Nor is it a mere matter of technique. The famous works of ancient sculpture were understood as spiritually larger than life, even when they were not physically so; an inflated style of drawing becomes a way to insure that the physical form of these works corresponds to their cultural status.

5.44. Bandinelli, *Standing Male Nude Turned in Profile to the Right*, red chalk, 1540s, British Museum, London

5.45. Bandinelli, *Two Nude Men Facing Each Other*, pen and ink, Museo Horne, Florence

In fact, Bandinelli's practice of the hyperbolic body begins not only in the sculpture collection but also in the studio. Just as he stages his studio models in the postures of statues, he muscularizes the garzoni in his sketches. Drawings of male nudes that give evidence of being studio sketches, based on their poses, often involve physiques difficult to imagine as normative for the boys in the *bottega* (fig. 5.44).[106] Almost from inception, it seems, Bandinelli's figures are defined in corporeally inflated terms, translated at the same time into bodybuilders and into statues. In fact, the recto of a drawing whose verso includes three robust garzoni (fig. 5.45) seems almost to acknowledge this problematic with its pose of a highly muscular figure who is almost a statue facing a more or less normal individual in the position of the sculptor—normal, that is, except for being heroically in the nude. (Of course, these visions are of an antiquity heavily mediated through the work of Michelangelo, especially the ignudi of the Sistine Ceiling; he, too, had depicted himself as creating art while in the nude.)[107]

In a certain sense, the hyperbole of the individual body is at odds with the rhetoricity of compositional *invenzione*. What may most sharply identify Bandinelli's style—and his limitations—is the transfer of these grandiose figures into dramatic groups, whether in drawings or in projects for sculptural reliefs. Granted that Bandinelli is not very successful with large-scale dramatic compositions that involve multiple figures. He does not handle perspective skillfully, and he is almost never comfortable with the spatial or dramatic relations between any two figures (even those of his colossal freestanding works like the *Pietà* or the *Adam and Eve*). But one must also recognize in these compositional awkwardnesses Bandinelli's insistence on a rhetoricalized body. He is torn between the demands of the colossal freestanding figure and those of the dramatic scene. To put it another way, he could not let go of the aura that surrounded Belvedere antiquities sufficiently so as to allow them to live in the world. In some respects this is merely the mark of the sculptor. The heavily muscular body in the midst of a two-dimensional composition is a sign to the viewer or the artist himself of a projected three-dimensional work. The patron is enabled to imagine a finished product. As for the artist, we have already observed how a drawing of what looks like a bodybuilder intervenes between a studio sketch depicting a model of quite ordinary physique and a relatively high relief nude figure on the Leo tomb who is somewhat massive but hardly of exaggerated muscular proportions. The artist records life in its own authentic shape; he then produces an extreme pen-and-ink *invenzione*; and, as we saw in the case of the female figures who end up in the *Birth of the Virgin* relief, he concludes with a quite decorous figure who has been authenticated in a classicizing way by the intervening composition of his body, now rendered implicit.

But all those qualities that are inflated by the techniques of draughtsmanship are never quite implicit enough in Bandinelli's larger compositions: the authenticating power of antiquity, of Michelangelo, of anatomy lessons, is simply too desirable to permit any viewer the possibility of forgetting that it is there. Which in the end may help explain what many viewers have really been observing when they have declared that there is a falling off between Bandinelli's drawings and the finished products: his images do a far better job of promising significances than of delivering them. That is why they appear so rhetorical. And on certain notable occasions—say, the ever visible *Hercules and Cacus*—the problem is that the finished work looks too much like a drawing that attempted to promise monumentality by overusing the trope of hyperbole. As a result of which, Bandinelli seems destined to be always read as a sculptor of rhetorical style, and his drawings always seem better than his finished work.

GOOD MARBLE, BAD MARBLE

That finished work is constructed in a medium that takes us full circle back to the rediscovered antiquities. Drawings are the conceptual realm in which ancient aesthetic culture is transformed into modern and communicated to moderns; marble is the material realm in which both ancient and modern art objects actually live. If the *Hercules and Cacus* (see fig. 5.7) has its origins in an overblown conception of draughtsmanship, it is also visible in the Piazza as a hyperbolic use of marble. The very massiveness of its forms acts as a reminder of the grandeur and expense of the material from which it is made, as though its author were less interested in conveying the finesse of his artistry than in demonstrating the extent of his personal privilege in being granted such a fine block to work in. At the same time—to be fair to him—the statue also advertises the difficulties of the medium in articulating multiple forms and the special capacity of the medium to offer full views in the round. It clearly establishes that Bandinelli is to be as completely (or obsessively) identified with the chisel as with the pen.

Within this classicizing milieu, stories about marble itself are legion. An olympian career is launched in the famous tale of the gigante, a block of marble eighteen feet high, which had been mutilated by earlier sculptural efforts and was about to be offered to Da Vinci and Andrea Sansovino, when the young Michelangelo returns from Rome in 1502 to turn it into the *David*.[108] As for Bandinelli, we have already heard about the snow *Marforio* that Baccio constructs as a child. Its medium is, appropriately enough, pseudo-marble, allowing the boy to practice in a material that permits him to add and subtract, though it may also sentence him to a second-rate career as a sculptor who models in masses rather than carving his way to the conception inside the stone, as canonized by his grander rival. Real marble also forms a crucial part of Bandinelli's artistic formation. Leonardo, as we have seen, leads the young man through disegno to working on a marble bust after the antique. Baccio's father orders some small pieces from Carrara out of which the sculptor produces—of all things—a Hercules holding the dead Cacus between his legs on the ground, thereby prophesying the work that will advertise most visibly his mastery of marble.[109]

As a mature artist, Bandinelli expresses all the worst sides of his personality in relation to marble—at least as Vasari tells it. In frustration over successes of his rivals, he gets Cosimo to permit him access to Michelangelo's storehouse of slabs; and despite the fact that the master had already begun work on some of them, he "hacked and broke to pieces everything that he could find, thinking that by so doing he was avenging himself on Michelagnolo and causing him displeasure" (6:168; deVere, 2:289). Later in his life Baccio gains control over a gigantic piece of marble in Carrara, pays a deposit on it, and bombards Cosimo with plans for a massive fountain to be constructed from it. But years go by without Baccio paying the owner, while in the meantime Cellini and Ammanati also hear about the promising piece of stone and demand their chance to compete for it. Cosimo is, as usual, happy to inspire productive competition among his artists. But Baccio does an end run via the duchess, goes off to Carrara on his own, and "had the marble so reduced in size—as he had planned to do—that he made it a sorry thing, and robbed both himself and the others of a noble opportunity and of the hope of ever making from it a beautiful and magnificent work."[110] Bandinelli (or at least Vasari's Bandinelli) in a nutshell. He is the master of disegno, but his design has more to do with triumphing over his rivals than with making great works of art. As for his sculpting, it is once again *scemare* and *ridurre*—the techniques he learned on the snow *Marforio* and continues to exercise at the end of his life.

What these—and many more—stories are telling us is not only that marble is a valuable material and a medium requiring the development of great technical virtuosity but also that it is, more than drawings, more than apprentices, more (perhaps) even than the goodwill of patrons, the much contested and central point of contact among artists and within the community of the arts. Marble is, after all, the medium that links living artists with their ancient predecessors. Antique works in marble had, from the Middle Ages onward, been recycled as building blocks, as spolia decorating grand edifices, even as newly Christianized tombs. Renaissance artists generally seem

5.46. Benvenuto Cellini, Crucifix, marble, 1562, Escorial, Madrid

INRI

to have sought virgin marble from Carrara rather than carve new works of art out of fragments of the old.[111] Yet that quarrying itself, described time and again in heroic terms, is remarkably similar to the miraculous discovery of marble statues. In addition, many artists were engaged in restoring antique sculpture, which involved direct material contact between the modern and the ancient artist—as is evident from the involvement of both Bandinelli and Michelangelo in the ongoing material conditions of the *Laocoön*. And the whole sequence of events that Cellini narrates concerning his fight with Bandinelli is set in motion because of the appearance of an antique torso that inspires Cellini to create a kind of collage Ganymede out of different pieces of ancient marble. (Of course, Bandinelli and Cellini can fight over bronze just as easily as over marble. Cellini refuses to get involved in producing bronze reliefs for the Duomo choir because he thinks they will be placed too low so no one will see them and they will become "un pisciatoi da cani.")[112]

If marble links moderns to ancients, it links moderns to one another even more directly. The best way to tell this story is to write a couple of brief biographies of pieces of stone, each of which is passed around, and each of which touches upon Bandinelli. "Era fino al tempo di Leone X stato cavato a Carrara . . ." ("As far back as the time of Leo X there had been quarried at Carrara . . ."), begins Vasari, in one particularly juicy narrative. It is nine and a half *braccia* in height (i.e., a foot taller than the *David* piece); since it is found while stones are being collected for the San Lorenzo facade, it belongs by rights to Michelangelo: "With this block of marble Michelagnolo Buonarroti had thought of making a giant in the person of Hercules slaying Cacus, intending to place it in the Piazza beside the colossal figure of David formerly made by him, since both the one and the other, David and Hercules, were emblems of the palace."[113] Vasari skirts the political issue—in fact, the sense in which David and Hercules acted as "insegna del palazzo" were as republican, not to say anti-Medicean, emblems—but he establishes that there is a Michelangelo concept of this subject well in advance of Bandinelli's. Or at least in advance of the statue that Bandinelli finally exhibited in this spot, though predated by his practice version of *Hercules and Cacus* and contemporaneous with his stucco Hercules exhibited nearby for the entry of Pope Leo in 1515.

In short, Michelangelo has a kind of artistic primacy in the conception, as well as place of installation, for this marble block. But the Florentine Republic does not have primacy, nor do the negotiations surrounding Michelangelo's San Lorenzo facade do him much political credit, with the result that the marble "da fare il gigante" is transferred to Baccio, who sets about to produce his version of the same subject. The stone has, however, not yet left Carrara. In the course of its travel down the Arno, it sinks in the river: "Tempted by this accident to the marble, certain persons wrote verses, both Tuscan and Latin, ingeniously ridiculing Baccio . . . saying that the marble, after having been approved by the genius of Michelagnolo, learning that it was to be mangled by the hands of Baccio, had thrown itself into the river out of despair at such an evil fate."[114] In the event, the suicidal marble is rescued by dint of laborious engineering work only to elude Bandinelli in a new way—that is, by proving to be neither high enough nor wide enough to accommodate the artist's elaborate plans as exhibited in a wax model. This time Baccio makes a life-size wax model that fits the marble but, as Vasari tells us, remains inferior to the first work he had conceived.

Neither the political nor the lapidary tale is at an end, however. The Medici are overthrown in 1527, and Michelangelo, while working on the Florentine fortifications, is once more shown the stone "che Baccio aveva *scemato*," along with the wax model of Hercules and Cacus, "the intention being that if the marble had not been cut away too much Michelagnolo should take it and carve from it two figures after his own design. Michelagnolo, having examined the block, thought of a different subject; and, abandoning the Hercules and Cacus, he chose the subject of Samson holding beneath him two Philistines whom he had cast down" (6:155; deVere, 2:279).[115] While Baccio had taken over Michelangelo's concept for the block, Michelangelo will certainly not take it back once the material has been sullied by an inferior hand. The republic falls again; Hercules and Cacus are reinstated; Baccio spends his time informing on fellow citizens; and they retaliate with a virulent reaction to the statue when it is finally installed in 1534. Cellini reports (with who knows what accuracy) that he spoke up to Cosimo about the whole fracas, comparing Michelangelo's plan for Samson with *four* figures (the number has escalated) to the work as it actually stands: "il vostro Bandinello ne cavò dua figure sole, mal fatte e tutte rattoppate" ("Your Bandinello got only two figures out of it, badly made and hopelessly contorted").[116] A whole aesthetic, political, and interpersonal culture is being lived out in the fortunes of an excavated piece of marble.

I am going to close with one final tale, which also turns on marble. The story comes in many parallel phases taking place over many years; but as we concluded the last story with Cellini, let us begin with his part in this one. He is, as usual, wrangling with Cosimo and Eleonora over a valuable piece of marble, in this case the fountain piece that Baccio would eventually spoil for anyone else (at least in Vasari's version; Cellini says nothing of this) and that Ammanati finally realized as a Neptune.[117] Cellini engages in protracted courtiership trying to convince both duke and duchess that he should be permitted to submit a model in contestation with Bandinelli. Despite the frequently reiterated claim that more competition means better art for Florence, Cellini does not get very far, especially with the duchess, whom he characterizes as prejudiced in Bandinelli's favor. His final tactic with her is diversionary. If she is willing not to stand in the way of his claim, he will make for her another work of even greater marmoreal distinction—a full-sized figure of the crucified Christ made from pure white marble affixed to a cross of blackest marble (fig. 5.46). Cellini does not record her response but goes on to describe in detail his work on the crucifix, his intentions that it decorate his own tomb, and his invitation to place the work and his own remains in the Santissima Annunziata in Florence.

Which is where Bandinelli comes in. Cellini suggests that the news of his own planned crucifix prompts Bandinelli to go back to work on a Pietà of his own, which was to decorate his tomb and was already destined for the Santissima Annunziata (where, unlike the Cellini work, it was eventually installed; fig. 5.47). Cellini, who fears that Bandinelli might beat him to the finish, furthermore stipulates in his will that should he die without completing the crucifix, no descendants of Bandinelli will be engaged to finish it. Despite the implication that Bandinelli's statue was created largely in reponse to Cellini himself, in fact it has a history of its own that originates not with Baccio but with his son, Clemente, who was said to be enormously gifted but who died young after escaping from his father's milieu. According to Vasari, Clemente left unfinished a Dead Christ supported by Nicodemus; it appears that Clemente had completed the Nicodemus figure and that his father went on to work on the Christ.

The choice of Nicodemus can hardly fail to summon up the presence of another sculptor and another work. Vasari makes the connection explicit, when he offers in place of Cellini's a different competitive reason why Bandinelli takes up the Pietà statue at this moment: "For he had heard that Buonarroti was finishing one in Rome that he had begun to carve from a large block of marble, containing five figures, which was to be placed on his tomb in S. Maria Maggiore" (6:189; deVere, 2:304).[118] The work in question is, of course, the Florentine Pietà (containing four rather than five figures; fig. 5.48), notable for the inclusion of Nicodemus, perhaps iconographically doubled with Joseph of Arimathea as the individual who offers his own tomb as the earthly housing for the newly crucified Christ. If one adds the traditional identification of Nicodemus as sculptor, then the choice of the artist presenting this figure as presiding over his own tomb is all but overdetermined—as though perhaps he and Christ were to be climbing in together.[119]

5.47. Bandinelli, *Pietà* or *Nicodemus with Dead Christ*, marble, 1558–59, SS. Annunziata, Florence

In this context Bandinelli's decision to return to his own Nicodemus *Pietà* appears as the ultimate and most perverse act of imitation. Perhaps the history is more complicated, however. Decades earlier, at the time of the struggle with Michelangelo over the *Hercules and Cacus* marble, Baccio began working on not one but two Nicodemus paintings, one with the dead Christ, Mary, and other figures, and the other with "Christ taken down from the Cross and held in the arms of Nicodemus, with His Mother, who was standing, weeping for Him, and an Angel" (6:151; deVere, 2:277). Vasari goes on to detail Michelangelo's visit to see this latter cartoon, which was exhibited in the Mercato Nuovo. The elder artist "marvelled that so good a draughtsman as Baccio should allow a picture so crude and wanting in grace to leave his hands, that he had seen the most feeble painters executing their works in a better manner, and that this was no art for Baccio."[120] Michelangelo invokes against Baccio the oft repeated for-

5.48. Michelangelo, *Pietà* marble, 1547–55, Museo dell'Opera del Duomo, Florence

mula concerning his own diffidence in regard to painting. We cannot say whether or not Michelangelo was also storing up visual and iconographic ideas that he would turn to a quarter-century later. Nicodemus is far from a commonplace figure in painting or sculpture; yet he seems to abound in the competitive space between these two artists. Clearly there is more at work in both men than pure individual inspiration. Michelangelo's Hercules and Cacus, we are certain, becomes Bandinelli's as if by marble contagion, though it cannot go back to its originator when the marble does. Was Michelangelo enabled to return the favor by the fact that the "original" Nicodemus was not made of marble but glimpsed in an inferior medium as produced by his lesser rival?

So Bandinelli's *Pietà*, like much of his output, is poised between the works of others, between Michelangelo and Cellini. All three works have in common important elements that we have only touched upon. Notably—and here I am building on the work of Irving Lavin—all three are calculated exercises in the possibility of constructing articulated monumental works out of a single block of marble.[121] From Pliny onward, this stood as the great *difficulté vaincue* of the mastery of marble. We saw many pages ago that the *Laocoön* was identified by the paradoxical fact that it had three sculptors but only one piece of marble. That would be an extraordinary feat given the filigreed nature of this work, and Renaissance viewers seemed to have no trouble realizing that the claim was untrue. The determination was made notably by Michelangelo himself, who, along with his colleague Giancristoforo Romano is reported to have observed that the *Laocoön* is in four parts, "but joined together in such hidden places and so well joined and mended that only persons extremely expert in this art could readily recognize it. But they say that Pliny was fooled, or wanted to fool others, so as to render the work more amazing."[122] Pliny's claim, in other words, defines the supreme goal for marble working at the same time as the real experience of the unearthed antiquities demonstrates that this goal has been left to the moderns to achieve.

Every one of these sculptors, then, is engaged in imitating and surpassing the paradigmatic ancient masterpiece. Michelangelo actually does carve a closely knit group of figures out of a single block: "a rare achievement in a single stone and truly inspired," says Vasari. Or he nearly does so. First of all, of course, he doesn't finish the work—hardly surprising in the context of his career. More to the point, right around the time when Bandinelli is reverting to his *Pietà*, Michelangelo smashes his own single block into pieces, thereby occasioning for Vasari the fullest account of Michelangelo's non finito—that is, his passion for abstract perfection which makes it impossible for him to allow any work to be materially completed. As a result, Vasari tells us, "I know not what new pieces" need to be added when the *Pietà* is finished by lesser artists.[123] Cellini, for his part, concentrates on the difficulty of producing a complete Christ in the round out of marble—not surprising, given that he is a relative novice especially eager to make his way in the medium, "solo per mostrare se con la forza dell'arte mia io potevo trapassare i mia maggiori, i quali non si erano mai provati a tale impresa" (solely to show whether I could with the power of my art surpass my predecessors, who had never attempted such a challenge).[124]

Bandinelli, finally, as the notorious incompetent, is identified by his inability to work in grand single blocks. Back in the 1520s, gossips had pointed out to Michelangelo that Baccio was doing the *Laocoön* "a pezzi."[125] And Vasari attacks him on these grounds through his whole career: "It was a custom of Baccio's to add pieces of marble both small and large to the statues that he executed, feeling no annoyance in doing this, and making light of it. He did this with one of the heads of Cerberus in the group of Orpheus; in the S. Peter that is in S. Maria del Fiore he let in a piece of drapery; in the case of the Giant of the Piazza, as may be seen, he joined two pieces—a shoulder and a leg to the Cacus—and in many other works he did the same, holding to such ways as generally damn a sculptor completely."[126] Baccio may have laughed about this breach in sculptural decorum—Vasari seems particularly galled by such indifference—

thus confirming the shallowness of his respect for antiquity. Yet his *Pietà* does indeed appear to be boldly fashioned from a single piece; at the very least it involves the most daring effects within this sphere of difficulty in that it is full of open spaces between the figures and within the anatomy of the Christ.[127] And, great identifying mark of Bandinelli that it is, the material is commemorated by the presence at the base of Christ's body of a miniature block on which Bandinelli signs his name. The unmet challenge of the ancient *Laocoön*—equally unmet by the copy—is finally realized in this work.

The final element that all these works have in common is the extent to which they are intimately identified with their makers. Each artist makes this work as a tomb for himself. Cellini speaks extensively—if disingenuously—of the fact that his crucifix is not made under the influence of patronage or for profit. In the case of the other two sculptors, the relations are even more intimate. Michelangelo's Nicodemus is a self-portrait: he is the sculptor who himself places Christ into his own tomb, which is also the altar, out of which Christ is perpetually risen. The lifelong struggle of the aged, wrinkled self and the beautiful young man—the *Victory* also involves a self-portrait—is laid to rest along with the artist's own body. The case of Bandinelli is yet more intricate. We must recollect that despite his *Pietà*'s being of one block it is (once again) *imitatio Laocoontis*—that is, a collaboration, if only of two sculptors. The young Clemente sculpted the old Nicodemus, Vasari tells us, as a portrait of his father; the elderly Baccio, we must assume, was left to sculpt the young Christ in memory, at least, of his own son who had died in Rome some years before. And Baccio, not alone in the world like Michelangelo, intended for this tomb to encompass both his son and his father. Indeed, Vasari reports that Baccio died from exertions involved in the transport of his father's bones to this tomb.

Many years earlier, in a gesture that Cellini himself has trouble understanding, Baccio offered him a piece of marble to work on. It turns out to be the beginning of both the rivalry between the two artists and the career of Cellini as a classicizing sculptor in marble. At the time, Cellini says to Bandinelli's boy apprentice, "Digli che io l'accetto; e potria essere il mal marmo per lui" ("Tell him I accept, and let it be the bad marble for him").[128] The bad marble is, of course, the marble of the tomb. We may sum up all the unearthed past chronicled in this volume by tracing one simple cultural declension: antique funerary monuments are everywhere visible; notable living persons are constructing their own tombs; ancient art emerges from the ground; modern art places human beings back in the ground. Dust must return to dust; but the art that emerges when the dust settles may hope for more enduring life.

INTRODUCTION:

Epigraph: Michel Foucault, *L'archéologie du savoir* (Paris, 1969), 61. Translation mine.

1. This project has issued in the indispensable *Renaissance Artists and Antique Sculpture: A Handbook of Sources*, by Phyllis Bober and Ruth Rubinstein (London, 1986). For an earlier statement concerning the project itself, see Phyllis Bober, "The Census of Antique Works Known to Renaissance Artists," in *The Renaissance and Mannerism: Acts of the Twentieth International Congress of the History of Art* (Princeton, 1963), 82–89.

2. Michel Foucault, *The Archaeology of Knowledge*, trans. A. M. Sheridan (New York, 1972), 131.

3. Ibid., 123.

4. The relevant bibliography is considerable. I am thinking particularly of J. Hillis Miller, *Versions of Pygmalion* (Cambridge, Mass., 1990), *The Ethics of Reading: Kant, de Man, Eliot, Trollope, James, and Benjamin* (New York, 1987), and *The Linguistic Moment: From Wordsworth to Stevens* (Princeton, 1985); and Paul de Man, *The Rhetoric of Romanticism* (New York, 1984), and *Allegories of Reading: Figural Language in Rousseau, Nietzsche, Rilke, and Proust* (New Haven, 1979).

5. De Man, *Rhetoric of Romanticism*, 75–76.

6. The Wordsworth citation is to *Wordsworth's Literary Criticism*, ed. W. J. B. Owen (London, 1974), 133. For the Milton, see *The Poems of John Milton*, ed. J. Carey and A. Fowler (Harlow, 1968).

7. Citations are to *The Complete Signet Classic Shakespeare*, ed. S. Barnet (New York, 1972).

8. For a graceful turning of this argument, see Peter Platt, *Reason Diminished: Shakespeare and the Marvelous* (Lincoln, Neb., 1997), 167–68.

9. "If painters were capable of praising their work in words, as poets have done, I do not believe that painting would have been given such a bad name. Painting does not speak, but is self-evident through its finished product, while poetry ends in words, with which it vigorously praises itself" (*Leonardo on Painting*, ed. M. Kemp and M. Walker [New Haven, 1989], 46).

10. Ludovico Ariosto, *Orlando Furioso*, 33.1, ed. E. Bigi (Milan, 1982).

11. Citations are to Joachim du Bellay, *Antiquitez de Rome* translated by Edmund Spenser as *Ruines of Rome*, ed. M. C. Smith (Binghamton, N.Y., 1994). Translation in this instance is mine; in all other instances, it is by Spenser.

12. I am much indebted to the discussions of du Bellay by Thomas Greene, *The Light in Troy: Imitation and Discovery in Renaissance Poetry* (New Haven, 1982), 220–41; and Margaret Ferguson, *Trials of Desire: Renaissance Defenses of Poetry* (New Haven, 1983), 18–53.

13. On this letter, 6.2 of the *Letters on Familiar Matters*, see below, Chap. 1 and n. 61.

14. On the region of Pompey's Theater and the sources by which it can be reimagined, see L. Richardson, Jr., *A New Topographical Dictionary of Ancient Rome* (Baltimore, 1992), 383–85. For the Coponius sculptures, see Pliny *Natural History* 36.41.

15. The story is told in Vasari's *Life of Brunelleschi*, for which see *Le vite de' più eccellenti pittori scultori ed architettori*, ed. G. Milanesi (Florence, 1906), 2:339–40.

16. For a discussion of this letter, see below, Chap. 1.

CHAPTER 1: DISCOVERIES

Epigraph: Francesco Petrarca, *Letters on Familiar Matters*, 18.8, trans. A. S. Bernardo (Baltimore, 1985), 3.57.

1. The principal source for all the rediscovery materials is Phyllis Pray Bober and Ruth Rubinstein,

Renaissance Artists and Antique Sculpture: a Handbook of Sources (London, 1986), itself based on "The Census of Ancient Works Known to Ancient Artists," which is discussed in the Introduction. Similarly indispensable to my research is Francis Haskell and Nicholas Penny, *Taste and the Antique* (New Haven, 1981). Less definitive but learned and wide-ranging are Arnold von Salis, *Antike und Renaissance: Über Nachleben und Weiterwirken der alten in der neueren Kunst* (Zurich, 1947), and Heinz Ladendorf, *Antikenstudium und Antikenkopie* (Berlin, 1958). As for the cases cited here, the *Apollo* is visible as early as the 1490s in the collection of Giuliano della Rovere (who would become Julius II). See Walther Amelung, *Die Sculpturen des vaticanischen Museums* (Berlin, 1903), 1:264–69; Adolf Michaelis, "Geschichte des Statuenhofes im vatikanischen Belvedere," *Jahrbuch des deutschen archäologischen Instituts* 5 (1890): 10–11; Bober and Rubinstein, *Renaissance Artists*, 71–73; and Phyllis Pray Bober, *Drawings after the Antique by Amico Aspertini* (London, 1957), 59. For attempts by Pirro Ligorio and others to create a narrative of discovery after the fact, see Hans Henrik Brummer, *The Statue Court in the Vatican Belvedere* (Stockholm, 1970), 44. For the Filippo Strozzi letter on the Pergamene statues, see Giovanni Gaye, *Carteggio inedito d'artisti dei secoli XIV, XV, XVI* (Florence, 1839–40), 2:139. On the Tiber's first discovery—if it is the *Tiber*—see Poggio Bracciolini, *De varietate fortunae*, in R. Valentini and G. Zucchetti, eds., *Codice topografico della città di Roma* (Rome, 1953), 4:235. For the Grossino letter on the second discovery, see Brummer, *Statue Court*, 191–92.

2. The closest we can come to a terminus a quo for the reappearance of the *Torso* is a comment on it by Ciriaco d'Ancona, who saw it in the Colonna collection sometime in the 1430s. It may have been owned by the sculptor Andrea Bregno at the beginning of the fifteenth century, but it attains real prominence only when it is "discovered" by Michelangelo. This affinity, first mentioned by Ulisse Aldrovandi in *Delle statue antiche* (Venice, 1556), reprinted in Lucio Mauro, *Le antichità della città di Roma* (Venice, 1557), 120, turns into a chestnut of later sixteenth-century art theory; see Giorgio Vasari, *La vita di Michelangelo nelle redazioni del 1550 e del 1568*, ed. P. Barocchi (Milan, 1962), 4:2100–103. For a fuller discussion of this subject, see Chap. 3, this vol. For documentary and other materials on the *Torso Belvedere*, see Bober and Rubinstein, *Renaissance Artists*, 166–68, Haskell and Penny, *Taste*, 311–14, and Brummer, *Statue Court*, 143–52.

3. The *Laocoön* bibliography is extensive enough to make *Hamlet* look like a victim of scholarly neglect. Citations on more specific subjects will follow in later notes; for general materials, see Bober and Rubinstein, *Renaissance Artists*, 151–55; Haskell and Penny, *Taste*, 243–47; Brummer, *Statue Court*, 74–119; C. C. van Essen, "La découverte du Laocoon," *Mededelingen der Koninklijke Nederlandse Akademie van Wetenschappen*, afd. Letterkunde 18 (1955): 291–308; Margarete Bieber, *Laocoön: The Influence of the Group since Its Rediscovery* (New York, 1942); Adriano Prandi, "La fortuna del Laocoonte dalla sua scoperta nelle terme di Tito," *Rivista dell' istituto nazionale d'archeologia e storia dell'arte*, n.s., 3 (1954): 78–107; and, perhaps most instructive of all, Matthias Winner, "Zum Nachleben des Laokoon in der Renaissance," *Jahrbuch der Berliner Museen* 16 (1974): 83–121.

4. On the making of the place of display in the Belvedere, see Brummer, *Statue Court*, 75–76, who cites a letter from Cesare Trivulzio (Giovanni Bottari and Stefano Ticozzi, *Raccolta di lettere sulla pittura, scultura ed architettura* [Milan, 1822; rpt. 1979]), 3:475) suggesting that the existing structures of the space were already adaptable to the niche that would display the *Laocoön*.

5. The letter about the "fauns," dated 13 February 1488, is by Luigi di Andrea Lotti; it is reprinted in Gaye, *Carteggio inedito*, 1:285. See Aby Warburg's treatment of this subject in his lecture "Der Eintritt des antikisierenden Idealstils in die Malerei der Frührenaissance": "I no longer fear to be misunderstood if I say that, as for the sculptural group depicting the sufferings of Laocoön, if the Renaissance had not discovered it, they would have had to invent it" (*La rinascita del paganesimo antico* [Florence, 1966], 307).

6. In the years following 1796, nearly one hundred masterpieces of Italian art (almost all classical) were transported to the Louvre; most—but not all—were returned after the Congress of Vienna. On this fascinating episode in the history of art and politics, see Haskell and Penny, *Taste*, 108–16. For a fuller account, including reprints of documents, see M.-L. Blumer, "La commission pour la recherche des objets de sciences et arts en Italie (1796–1797)," *Révolution Française* 87 (1934): 62–88, 124–50, 222–59; and Henri Grégoire, "Rapport sur le vandalisme, 14 fructidos, an II," in *Oeuvres de l'Abbé Grégoire* (Liechtenstein, 1947), 2:257–78.

7. The phrase can be found in Johann Winckelmann, "Gedanken über die Nachahmung der griechischen Werke in der Malerei und Bildhauerkunst," published in 1754. For the English version, see below, n. 29. For his writings on the *Apollo* itself, see his *Geschichte der Kunst des Alterthums* (New York, 1969), esp. chap. 3. See also the interesting treatment by Alex Potts, *Flesh and the Ideal: Winckelmann and the Origins of Art History* (New Haven, 1994), 118–32.

8. Nathaniel Hawthorne visited Rome in 1858 and recorded his very enthusiastic impressions of classical sculpture in his *Passages from the French and Italian Notebooks*, first published in 1883. His novel *The Marble Faun* was published in 1860, and, to quote Haskell and Penny (*Taste*, 210), "the fame of the statue soon became world-wide, as the theme of the novel was taken up (in ways that would have surprised Hawthorne) by generations of writers, painters and photographers who flocked to Italy to admire the beauty of uninhibited pagan youths."

9. The episode appears in chap. 19 of *Middlemarch*, which was first published in 1871–72. George Eliot visited Rome frequently during the 1860s. For a reading of this scene, see Leonard Barkan, "The Beholder's Tale: Ancient Sculpture, Renaissance Narratives," *Representations* 44 (1993): 157–58; and Abigail S. Rischin, "Beside the Reclining Statue: Ekphrasis, Narrative, and Desire in *Middlemarch*," *PMLA* 111 (1996): 1121–32.

10. The poem, dating from 1908, is entitled "Archaischer Torso Apollos." Rilke's conceit is that the fragmentary nature of the work—specifically, the absence of a head—transfers to the body itself all the communicative powers of a face: glowing, smiling, and finally seeing. "Denn da ist keine Stelle, / die dich nicht sieht. /Du mubt dein Leben ändern" (*New Poems*, trans. J. B. Leishman [London, 1964], 164).

11. The passage appears at *Aeneid* 2.199–233.

12. For an interesting treatment of the relations between the Lippi fresco and the statue, see Winner, "Zum Nachleben," 83–102. See also P. Halm, "Das unvollendete Fresko des Filippino Lippi in Poggio a Caiano," *Mitteilungen des Kunsthistorischen Instituts in Florenz* 3 (1931): 393–427; and A. Scharf, "Zum Laokoon des Filippino Lippi," *Mitteilungen des Kunsthistorischen Instituts in Florenz* 3 (1932): 530–33.

13. "Io era di pochi anni la prima volta ch'io fui a Roma, che fu detto al papa, che in una vigna presso a S. Maria Maggiore s'era trovato certe statue molto belle. Il papa commandò a un palafreniere: va, e dì a Giuliano da S. Gallo, che subito le vada a vedere. E così subito s'andò. E perchè Michelangelo Bonaroti si trovava continuamente in casa, che mio padre l'aveva fatto venire, e gli aveva allogata la sepoltura del papa; volle, che ancor lui andasse; ed io così in groppa a mio padre, e andammo. Scesi dove erano le statue: subito mio padre disse: questo è Laocoonte, di cui fa menzione Plinio. Si fece crescere la buca, per poterlo tirare fuori; e visto, ci tornammo a desinare: e sempre si ragionò delle cose antiche, discorrendo ancora di quelle di Fiorenza." The letter was first published in Carlo Fea, *Miscellanea filologica, critica e antiquaria* (Rome, 1790), 1:329.

14. See Chap. 2 for a full discussion of the *Natural History* and its influence in the Renaissance.

15. "Sia come si voglia: ella [l'invenzione] è espressa così bene, che potrebbe venire in dubbio se

Rafaello l'avesse tolta da' libri di Luciano o Luciano dalle pitture di Rafaello; se non fosse che Luciano nacque più secoli avanti. Ma che è perciò? Anco Virgilio discrisse il suo Laocoonte tale quale l'aveva prima veduto nella statua di mano dei tre artefici rodiani, la quale con istupor di tutti oggidì ancora si vede in Roma. Et è cosa iscambievole che i pittori cavino spesso le loro invenzioni dai poeti, et i poeti dai pittori" (Lodovico Dolce, "Dialogo della pittura," in P. Barocchi, ed., *Trattati d'arte del '500* [Bari, 1960], 1:192). Modern scholarship dates the *Laocoön* statue well after the composition of the *Aeneid*, which may suggest yet another turning on Dolce's account of bidirectional influence.

16. Ekphrasis is becoming one of the liveliest topics in current humanistic study. Among the primary texts from antiquity are the EikóueV, generally Latinized as *Imagines*, by the Elder and Younger Philostratuses and by Callistratus (for which see the Loeb edition, trans. Arthur Fairbanks [Cambridge, Mass., 1979]); certain passages of Achilles Tatius's *Adventures of Leucippe and Clitophon* (e.g., a Europa painting at 1.1 and a diptych of Andromeda and Prometheus at 3.7–8), the Shield of Achilles in bk.18 of the *Iliad*, many of the Dialogues of Lucian (e.g., the famous description of Apelles' painting of Calumny in "On Calumny," 5), and many of the lyrics in the *Greek Anthology* (e.g., countless epigrams in bk. 9 concerning artworks, including a long series devoted to Myron's statue of a heifer). For recent theoretical work on ekphrasis, see Murray Krieger, *Ekphrasis: The Illusion of the Natural Sign* (Baltimore, 1992); W. J. T. Mitchell, *Picture Theory* (Chicago, 1994), 151–81; David Carrier, *Principles of Art History Writing* (University Park, Penn., 1991), 101–19; François Rigolot, "Ekphrasis and the Fantastic: Genesis of an Aberration," *Comparative Literature* 49 (1997): 97–112; Perrine Galand-Hallyn, *Le reflet des fleurs: Description et métalangage poétique à la Renaissance* (Geneva, 1994); Michael Ann Holly, *Past Looking: Historical Imagination and the Rhetoric of the Image* (Ithaca, 1996), 1–28; and Grant F. Scott, "The Rhetoric of Dilation: Ekphrasis and Ideology," *Word and Image* 7 (1991): 301–10. On ekphrasis in literary and artistic practice, see Svetlana Leontief Alpers, "Ekphrasis and Aesthetic Attitudes in Vasari's *Lives*," *Journal of the Warburg and Courtauld Institutes* 23 (1960): 190–215; Leonard Barkan, *The Gods Made Flesh: Metamorphosis and the Pursuit of Paganism* (New Haven, 1986), 8–12, and *Transuming Passion: Ganymede and the Erotics of Humanism* (Stanford, 1991), 76–78; Michela J. Marek, *Ekphrasis und Herrscherallegorie: Antike Bildbeschreibungen im Werk Tizians und Leonardos* (Worms, 1985); and Froma Zeitlin, "The Artful Eye: Vision, Ecphrasis, and Spectacle in Euripidean Theatre," in S. Goldhill and R. Osborne, eds., *Art and Text in Ancient Greek Culture* (Cambridge, Eng., 1994).

17. All Pliny texts and translations are drawn from the Loeb Classical Library edition, trans. H. Rackham and D. E. Eichholz (Cambridge, Mass., 1962).

18. For a discussion of exactly what this cross-generic praise might mean, see Chap. 2, n. 13.

19. For a compilation of the relevant Leonardo writings, see *Leonardo on Painting*, trans. M. Kemp and M. Walter (New Haven, 1989), esp. 20–46. On the tensions among different arts in Michelangelo's career, both contemporary biographies recount the beginnings of the Sistine Chapel project as nefarious attempts to divert the artist from sculpture and force him into painting, where he was supposedly less gifted: see Ascanio Condivi, *Life of Michelangelo* in *Michelangelo, Life, Letters and Poetry*, trans. G. Bull (Oxford, 1987), 32–33; and Giorgio Vasari, *Le vite de' più eccellenti pittori, scultori ed architettori*, ed. G. Milanesi (Florence, 1906), 7:172–74, translated as *Lives of the Painters, Sculptors and Architects*, trans. G. duC. deVere (New York, 1996), 2:664–66. Michelangelo expresses similar concerns during the work, in a letter to his father (*The Letters of Michelangelo*, ed. E. H. Ramsden [Stanford, 1963], 1:48) and in a comic poem addressed to his friend Giovanni da Pistoia: "La mia pittura morta / difendi orma', Giovanni, e 'l mio onore, / non sendo in loco bon, né io pittore" (*The Poetry of Michelangelo*, trans. James Saslow [New Haven,

1991], no. 5). At the same time as Michelangelo is understood to struggle among the arts, he is also understood to triumph in all of them; see, for instance, the opening paragraph of Vasari's life, in which he is praised for different skills in painting, sculpture, and architecture. On the general subject of the paragone, two valuable recent works are Claire J. Farago, *Leonardo da Vinci's Paragone: A Critical Interpretation* (New York, 1992), and Leatrice Mendelsohn, *Paragoni: Benedetto Varchi's Due Lezzioni and Cinquecento Art Theory* (Ann Arbor, 1982).

20. For a general review of contemporary responses, see Norman E. Land, *The Viewer as Poet* (University Park, Penn., 1994), 72–75.

21. The text is printed in its entirety in Bottari and Ticozzi, *Raccolta*, 3:474–77. See Chap. 2, this vol., and notes for a fuller treatment of this letter, including the original text.

22. John Sparrow and Alessandro Perosa, *Renaissance Latin Verse* (London, 1979), 185–86.

23. The poem, which is found in Vat. lat. 10377, fol. 75v, Vat. lat. 3351, and Vat. lat. 3419, fol. 149r, is printed in Brummer, *Statue Court*, 118. For another version and material on the author, see Hubert Janitschek, "Ein Hofpoet Leo's X. über Künstler und Kunstwerke," *Repertorium für Kunstwissenschaft* 3 (1880): 52–60.

24. Vat. lat. 2874, fol. 3r, transcribed in Brummer, *Statue Court*, 119.

25. Bottari and Ticozzi, *Raccolta*, 3:476.

26. Gotthold Ephraim Lessing, *Laocoön: An Essay on the Limits of Painting and Poetry*, ed. E. A. McCormick (Baltimore, 1984), 178.

27. See L. D. Ettlinger, "Exemplum Doloris: Reflections on the Laocoön Group," in D. Meiss, ed., *De Artibus Opuscula XL: Essays in Honor of Erwin Panofsky* (New York, 1961), 1:121–26. Michael and Renate Hertl, in *Laokoon: Ausdruck des Schmerzes durch zwei Jahrtausende* (Munich, 1968), 42–47, reproduce photographs from some remarkable experiments undertaken in the 1850s by the French neurologist G. B. Duchenne, who used electrical stimulation of the forehead so as to produce the "Laocoön brow," defined as the physiognomic sign of tragic pain.

28. *Aeneid* 2.222: "clamores horrendos ad sidera tollis"; Sadoleto, l. 54: "paene audimus gemitus," in Sparrow and Perosa, *Renaissance Latin Verse*.

29. See Johann Winckelmann, "On the Imitation of the Painting and Sculpture of the Greeks" in G. Schiff, ed., *German Essays on Art History* (New York, 1988), 12: "He pierces not heaven, like the Laocoon of Virgil; his mouth is rather opened to discharge an anxious overloaded groan, as Sadoleto says; the struggling body and the supporting mind exert themselves with equal strength, nay balance all the frame." Lessing quotes the whole passage in the first chapter of *Laocoön*.

30. "The scream had to be softened to a sigh, not because screaming betrays an ignoble soul, but because it distorts the features in a disgusting manner" (Lessing, *Laocoön*, 17). "There is nothing to compel the poet to compress his picture into a single moment. . . . Each variation [of actions] which would cost the artist a separate work costs the poet but a single stroke; and if the result of this pen stroke, viewed by itself, should offend the hearer's imagination, it was either anticipated by what has preceded or is so softened and compensated by what follows that it loses its individual impression and in combination achieves the best effect in the world" (23–24).

31. On the staging of the *Laocoön* and the relations between the discovery site and the design of its Belvedere niche, see Brummer, *Statue Court*, 114; von Salis, *Antike*, 54, 136–41; and Seymour Howard, "On the Reconstruction of the Vatican Laocoon Group," *American Journal of Archaeology* 63 (1959): 365–69. A number of the early engravings of the statue seek to place it in what is probably an imaginative version of its place of discovery; see, for instance, Marco Dente (reproduced in Brummer, fig. 61) and Hendrik van Schoel (Brummer, 85). In another print (Adam

Bartsch, *Le peintre graveur* [Würzburg, 1920], 14, no. 353), the statue is returned to the walls of Troy, the site of its events.

32. On the statue's physical condition at the time of discovery, see Brummer, *Statue Court*, 78–83, who cites a report from January 1506: "Queste figure sono fragmentate, che al patre mancha uno braco in quo habebat telum, ad uno deli figliuoli mancha uno braco similiter, del resto sono assai integre et sane" (These figures are fragmented, since the father is lacking an arm in which he held a weapon, and similarly one of the sons is lacking an arm; everything else is relatively whole and in good condition). The fullest modern study of the work's condition was done by Filippo Magi, who was in charge of its restoration in the 1950s; see "Il ripristino del Laocoonte," *Atti della Ponteficia Accademia Romana di Archeologia*, ser. 3, 9 (1960): 5–117. See also Peter Henrich von Blanckenhagen, "Laokoon, Sperlonga und Vergil," *Archäologischer Anzeiger* 74 (1969): 256–75, for a discussion of the composite nature of the statue in relation to earlier versions of the subject.

33. For the general question of Greek art in Rome, see Brunilde Sismondo Ridgway, *Roman Copies of Greek Sculpture: The Problem of the Originals* (Ann Arbor, 1984); and Paul Zanker, "Griechische Skulptur in der Römerzeit," in *Entretiens Fondation Hardt* 25 (1979): 283–314, and *Klassizistische Statuen: Studien zur Veränderung des Kunstgeschmacks in der römischen Kaiserzeit* (Mainz, 1974). On the Laocoön in particular, see Ridgway, 23; F. Brein, "Zum Laokoon," in *Classica et Provincialia* (Graz, 1978), 33–38; G. P. Warden, "The Domus Aurea Reconsidered," *Journal of the Society of Ancient Historians* 40 (1981): 271–78, esp. 277 and n. 40; and von Blanckenhagen, cited in previous note. This subject is taken up again in Chap. 2, below.

34. Phidias and Praxiteles come into play because the *Dioscuri*, located throughout the Middle Ages and beyond on the Quirinal Hill, bore the inscriptions "Opus Fidiae" and "Opus Praxitelis"; see below, Chaps. 2 and 3.

35. For surveys of this restoration history, see Prandi, "La fortuna del Laocoonte"; Brummer, *Statue Court*, 87–110; and Haskell and Penny, *Taste*, 246–47. The early twentieth-century find was by Ludwig Pollak; on this subject, see his "Der rechte Arm des Laokoon," *Mitteilungen des deutschen archäologischen Instituts, Römische Abteilung* 20 (1905): 277–82. The drawing that prefigures the Laocoön's modern position is by Amico Aspertini, who was in Rome just before the discovery of the statue and again in the 1530s; see Bober, *Drawings*, 61–62, fig. 49. Even earlier, and with a similar arm position, is Antonio Lombardo's *Vulcan's Forge* (fig. 1.12), for which see below.

36. For this story, see Vasari, *Vite*, ed. Milanesi, 7:489.

37. Ibid., 6:145; *Lives*, trans. deVere, 2:272–73. I return to this subject at some length in the final chapter.

38. On Francis I and antiquities, see Haskell and Penny, *Taste*, 1–6. For Cellini's version, in which Primaticcio organizes the project of casting classical statues in an unsuccessful attempt to eclipse Cellini's own reputation at the French court, see Benvenuto Cellini, *La Vita*, ed. G. D. Bonino (Turin, 1982), bk. 2, chaps. 37 and 41, pp. 357, 364–66; trans. G. Bull (Harmondsworth, 1956), 291, 297–99.

39. For Montorsoli's restorations of the *Laocoön* and the *Commodus as Hercules*, as well as his close associations with Michelangelo, see Vasari's *Life of Montorsoli*, ed. Milanesi, 6:633–34.

40. See G. P. Lomazzo, *Scritti sulle arti*, ed. R. Ciardi (Florence, 1973), 2:381 for the classic statement about this reticence; this issue is discussed below, in Chap. 3.

41. For an account of this arm and speculations on Michelangelo as its author, see Magi, "Ripristino," 46–50. Georg Daltrop (*Die Laocoongruppe im Vatikan* [Konstanz, 1982], 18–19, 71–72) doubts that the arm could be by Michelangelo, given the artist's awe in the face of the *Torso*.

42. Ernst Gombrich offers an illuminating account of the origins of this approach in *Aby Warburg:*

An *Intellectual Biography* (Chicago, 1986), esp. 43–66. For Warburg's own work in this field, involving the impact of neo-Attic reliefs on early Renaissance artists, see "Sandro Botticellis Geburt der Venus und Frühling" in *Gesammelte Schriften* (Leipzig-Berlin, 1932), 6–22. Gombrich's views on these subjects are best seen in "The Renaissance Conception of Artistic Progress and Its Consequences" and "The Style *all'antica*: Imitation and Assimilation," both collected in *Norm and Form: Studies in the Art of the Renaissance* (London, 1971), 1–10, 122–28. Fritz Saxl's somewhat more flexible and subjective approach is exemplified by his essay "Continuity and Variation in the Meaning of Images" in *A Heritage of Images* (Harmondsworth, 1970), 13–26.

43. On Titian's encounters with antiquity and ancient art in general, see Harold E. Wethey, *The Paintings of Titian* (New York, 1969), vol. 3; Ludwig Curtius, "Zum Antikenstudium Tizians," *Archiv für Kulturgeschichte* 28 (1938): 235–38; Otto Brendel, "Borrowings from Ancient Art in Titian," *Art Bulletin* 37 (1955): 113–26; Erwin Panofsky, *Problems in Titian* (New York, 1969); and Marilyn Perry, "On Titian's 'Borrowings' from Ancient Art: A Cautionary Case," in *Tiziano e Venezia* (Vicenza, 1980), 187–91.

44. "A painting by the hand of Titian in which the Laocoön was depicted"; Wethey, *Titian*, 3:36 n.

45. The woodcut is credited to Niccolò Boldrini; the earliest authority for its origins in Titian is Carlo Ridolfi, *Le maraviglie dell'arte* (Venice, 1648; rpt. Berlin, 1914), 1:203. The major work on the subject is H. W. Janson, "Titian's Laocoön Caricature and the Vesalian-Galenist Controversy," *Art Bulletin* 28 (1946): 49–53. For arguments identifying other objects of satire in the work, see Hans Tietze and E. Tietze-Conrat, "Titian's Woodcuts," *Print Collector's Quarterly* 25 (1938): 349; von Salis, *Antike*, 142; and Oscar Fischel, *Amtliche Berichte königlicher Kunstsammlungen* 39 (1917): 60–63.

46. Cf. von Salis, *Antike*, 144–45, à propos of the Louvre *Slaves*: "Auf ein geflissentliches Studium seines Vorbildes durfte Michelangelo ohnehin verzichten; den Laokoon kannte er auswendig"; Daltrop, *Laocoongruppe*, 18, à propos of the San Lorenzo graffitti: "Dennoch lag ihm weniger am Kopieren und Nachahmen als an geistiger Durchdringung des Vorbildes." On the San Lorenzo drawings, see Marco Collareta, "Intorno di disegni murali della Sagrestia Nuova," in Craig Hugh Smyth, ed., *Michelangelo Drawings* (Washington, 1992), 163–77; and Caroline Elam, "The Mural Drawings in Michelangelo's New Sacristy," *Burlington Magazine* 123 (1981): 593–602.

47. These quotations of the *Laocoön* must be seen in the context of a vast set of relations to antique sculpture. Although it is not possible to offer a full bibliography on this theme, I would cite a few relevant works: Friedrich Kriegbaum, "Michelangelo und die Antike," *Münchener Jahrbuch der bildenden Kunst* 3–4 (1953–54): 10–66; G. Agosti and V. Farinella, eds., *Michelangelo e l'arte classica* (Florence, 1987); F. Wickhoff, "Die Antike im Bildungsgange Michelangelos," *Mitteilungen des Instituts für oesterreichische Geschichte* 2 (1882): 408–35; von Salis, *Antike*, passim, esp. 136–53, 177–89; Heinrich Weizsäcker, "Michelangelo im Statuenhof des Belvedere," *Jahrbuch der Preußischen Kunstsammlungen* 64 (1943): 45–58; and A. Hekler, "Michelangelo und die Antike," *Wiener Jahrbuch für Kunstgeschichte* 7 (1930): 201–23. For contemporary citations from Michelangelo's table talk concerning his love for various of the rediscovered antiquities, see Vasari, *Vita*, ed. Barocchi, 4:2100–103.

48. On Lombardo, see L. Planiscig, *Venezianische Bildhauer der Renaissance* (Vienna, 1921), 224–25, and Wendy Stedman Sheard, *Antiquity in the Renaissance* (Northampton, Mass., 1978), 61. On Moderno, see Planiscig, 247, and H. Beck and D. Blume, eds., *Natur und Antike in der Renaissance* (Frankfurt, 1985), 366–67.

49. On the altarpiece and its *Laocoön* connections, see Wethey, *Titian*, 1:126–28; Charles de Tolnay, *Michelangelo: The Tomb of Julius II* (Princeton, 1954), 97; and Hans Tietze, *Tizians Leben und Werk* (Vienna, 1936), 2:190–91.

50. The work in question is Aldrovandi, *Delle statue antiche*.

51. My terms are drawn from the magisterial work of Thomas Greene, *The Light in Troy: Imitation and Discovery in Renaissance Poetry* (New Haven, 1982). Greene understands the discipline of reading promoted by Petrarch as a kind of archaeological scrutiny; I am, in a sense, returning the metaphor to its literal origins. Another Greene-influenced project that has inspired my thinking is Margaret Ferguson, "'The Afflatus of Ruin': Meditations on Rome by DuBellay, Spenser, and Stevens," in A. Patterson, ed., *Roman Images: Selected Papers from the English Institute* (Baltimore, 1984), 23–50.

52. There is a considerable bibliography of fine work on Rome and mythmaking. In addition to the Patterson collection cited in the previous note, I would single out above all Charles L. Stinger, *The Renaissance in Rome* (Bloomington, 1985), esp. 1–5, 292–319, along with the many excellent essays in P. A. Ramsey, ed., *Rome in the Renaissance: The City and the Myth* (Binghamton, 1982), especially those by Thomas M. Greene, Charles T. Davis, Zachary Schiffman, Janet Smarr, and Charles Burroughs. A different approach to the issues is taken by Michel Serres, *Rome: The Book of Foundations*, trans. F. McCarren (Stanford, 1991).

53. *Aeneid* 6:847–53, ed. H. R. Fairclough, Loeb Classical Library (Cambridge, Mass., 1967); translation is mine.

54. See Chap. 2.

55. For this account of Rome in the later period, see Richard Krautheimer, *Rome: Profile of a City, 312–1308* (Princeton, 1980), 4–5, 38–42; and Peter Brown, *The World of Late Antiquity* (New York, 1971), 34–48.

56. For a particularly eloquent account of Roman tourism as palimpsest and showplace (including the equation between "Via Lata" and "Broadway"), see Krautheimer, *Rome*, 9–16.

57. On this situation, see Rodolfo Lanciani, *The Destruction of Ancient Rome* (London, 1903), esp. 28–46; and Krautheimer, *Rome*, 64–68. Procopius, writing in the sixth century, bears witness both to the remaining greatness of Roman public spaces and to the tenuous condition of the extant works of art (*Gothic Wars* 7.21.12–44). On the reuse of *spolia* in early Christian times, see F. W. Deichmann, "Die Spolien in der spätantiken Architektur," *Bayerische Akademie der Wissenschaften*, Phil.-Hist. Klasse 6 (1975): 1–101; Lucilla de Lachenal, *Spolia: Uso e reimpiego dell'antico dal III al XIV secolo* (Milan, 1995); and the essays in Joachim Poeschke, ed., *Antike Spolien in der Architektur des Mittelalters und der Renaissance* (Munich, 1996).

58. Ammianus Marcellinus, *Res Gestae*, trans. J. C. Rolfe, Loeb Classical Library (London, 1982), 16.10.13–17.

59. Cassiodorus, *Letters*, trans. Thomas Hodgkin, Loeb Classical Library (London, 1886), 3:30.

60. See *Aeneid* 8.185–275.

61. This much-commented-upon epistle is *Familiar Letters*, 6:2; for the English version, see Petrarca, *Letters*, trans. Bernardo, 1:290–95.

62. Petrarch actually reconstructs this Rome in a parallel passage from the eighth book (no coincidence) of the *Africa*, as Scipio is given a tour of the living city (8:862–951).

63. Erwin Panofsky and Fritz Saxl, "Classical Mythology in Medieval Art," *Metropolitan Museum Studies* 4 (1932–33): 228–80.

64. On Poggio, see below in the present chapter; on Nicola, see M. Seidel, "Studien zur Antikenrezeption Nicola Pisanos," *Mitteilungen des Kunsthistorischen Instituts in Florenz* 3 (1975): 307–92.

65. "On several occasions [Gilberte] surprised me a great deal. The first time was when she said to me: 'If you were not too hungry and if it was not so late, by taking that road to the left and then turning to the right, in less than a quarter of an hour we should be at Guermantes.' It was as

though she had said to me: 'Turn to the left, then bear right, and you will touch the intangible, you will reach the inaccessibly remote tracts of which one never knows anything on this earth except the direction.' . . . And the third occasion was when Gilberte said to me: 'If you like, we might after all go out one afternoon and then we can go to Guermantes, taking the road by Méséglise, which is the nicest way,' a sentence which upset all the ideas of my childhood by informing me that the two 'ways' were not as irreconcilable as I had supposed" (Marcel Proust, *In Search of Lost Time*, trans. Andreas Mayor and Terence Kilmartin [London, 1992], 6:3).

66. On Ovidian etiology, see Barkan, *Gods Made Flesh*, 34–37, 54–56.

67. Two classic statements concerning history and geography in the *Commedia* are Robert Durling, "Deceit and Digestion in the Belly of Hell," in S. J. Greenblatt, ed., *Allegory and Representation* (Baltimore, 1981), 61–93; and John Freccero, "Dante's Ulysses: From Epic to Novel," in R. Jacoff, ed., *Dante: The Poetics of Conversion* (Cambridge, Mass., 1986), 136–51.

68. Roberto Weiss, *The Renaissance Discovery of Antiquity*, 2d ed. (Oxford, 1988).

69. On inscriptions, in addition to Weiss (*Renaissance Discovery*, 145–66), see the excellent summation in Michael Greenhalgh, *The Survival of Roman Antiquities in the Middle Ages* (London, 1989), 172–82. See also Carlo Roberto Chiarlo, "'Gli fragmenti dilla sancta antiquitate': Studi antiquari e produzione delle imagini da Ciriaco d'Ancona a Francesco Colonna," in Salvatore Settis, ed., *Memoria dell'antico nell'arte italiana* (Turin, 1984), 1:271–97; I. Kajanto, *Classical and Christian: Studies in the Latin Epitaphs of Mediaeval and Renaissance Rome* (Helsinki, 1980); and Fritz Saxl, "The Classical Inscription in Renaissance Art and Politics," *Journal of the Warburg and Courtauld Institutes* 4 (1941): 19–46.

70. The text of Dondi's description of Rome is found in Valentini and Zucchetti, *Codice topografico*, 4:68–73. For more on Dondi and his response to antiquity, see below in the present chapter.

71. The text of Feliciano's journal is found in Laura Pratilli, "Felice Feliciano alla luce dei suoi codici," *Atti del Reale istituto Veneto di scienze, lettere ed arti* 99 (1939–40): 54. See also Charles Mitchell, "Archaeology and Romance in Renaissance Italy," in E. F. Jacob, ed., *Italian Renaissance Studies: A Tribute to the Late Cecilia M. Ady* (London, 1960), 455–83, as well as his "Felice Feliciano Antiquarius," *Proceedings of the British Academy* 47 (1961): 197–221.

72. The most eloquent account of Ciriaco's travels is found in Phyllis Williams Lehmann and Karl Lehmann, *Samothracian Reflections: Aspects of the Revival of the Antique* (Princeton, 1973), 2–56. On the Arch of Trajan, see Augusto Campana, "Giannozzo Manetti, Ciriaco e l'Arco di Traiano ad Ancona," *Italia Medioevale e Umanistica* 2 (1959): 483–504.

73. See Weiss, *Renaissance Discovery*, 152–53, and D. Bianchi, "L'opera letteraria e storica di Andrea Alciato," *Archivio Storico Lombardo*, ser. 4, 20 (1913): 47–57.

74. Cf. the closing words of Magister Gregorius's *Narracio*, à propos of the bronze tablet placed in front of the *Capitoline Wolf* containing (as we know it) the *Lex Vespasiani*: "On this tablet I read much but understood little, for they were aphorisms, and the reader has to supply most of the words" (*Narracio*, published in English as *The Marvels of Rome*, ed. and trans. John Osborne [Toronto, 1987], 36). A hundred years later the same tablet gave Odofredus problems (Weiss, *Renaissance Rediscovery*, 12). And around the same time Dondi, looking at the arch of Constantine, was finding "multae literae sculptae, sed difficiliter leguntur" (many letters carved, but to be read with difficulty; Valentini and Zuchetti, *Codice topografico*, 4:70). See I. Calabi Limentani, "Sul non saper leggere le epigrafi classiche nei secoli XII e XIII: Sulla scoperta graduale delle abbreviazioni," *Acme* 23 (1970): 253–82; see also Greenhalgh, *Survival*, 177–78, and the same author's "Ipse ruina docet," in Settis, *Memoria dell'antico*, 1:156–60.

75. On these specific debates and on the general matter of humanist conversation and debate concerning epigraphy, see Weiss, *Renaissance Discovery*, 160–66.

76. On this phenomenon in general, see Chiarlo, "Gli fragmenti"; and Mitchell, "Archaeology and Romance." For further discussion of Ciriaco, see P. and K. Lehmann, *Samothracian Reflections*, esp. 3–56. On Mansionario, see Weiss, *Renaissance Discovery*, 22–24. On Pisanello, see Anna Cavallaro and Enrico Parlato, *Da Pisanello alla nascita dei musei capitolini* (Milan, 1988), esp. 89–113. The definitive work on Mantegna in relation to epigraphy is by Millard Meiss, esp. *Andrea Mantegna as Illuminator: An Episode in Renaissance Art* (New York, 1957).

77. See Weiss, *Renaissance Discovery*, 157–60; Millard Meiss, "Towards a More Comprehensive Renaissance Palaeography," *Art Bulletin* 42 (1960): 97–112; and Emanuele Casamassima, *Trattati di scrittura del Cinquecento italiano* (Milan, 1966), 9–36. The highpoint of this development is reached in 1521 with the publication of Jacopo Mazzocchi's *Epigrammata antiquae urbis*, a human-ist visual record of epigraphy that, according to Armando Petrucci, "represents the conscious attempt of Renaissance culture to master the complex network of relationships existing among display writing and monument, architecture and inscription, lettering, sculpted mass, and empty space" (*Public Lettering: Script, Power, and Culture* [Chicago, 1993], 23).

78. Petrarca, *Letters*, 19:3, trans. Bernardo, 3.79.

79. Vasari recounts how Ghiberti "dilettossi anco di contraffare i conj delle medaglie antiche" (*Vite*, ed. Milanesi, 2:223). See Weiss, *Renaissance Discovery*, 172; and Cavallaro and Parlato, *Da Pisanello*, 80–83, 109–13.

80. A 1457 inventory of Pietro Barbo's extraordinary collections, including gold coins worth nearly fifteen hundred ducats, is included in Eugène Müntz, *Les arts à la cour des papes pendant le XVe et le XVIe siècle* (Paris, 1879), 181–287. See also Massimo Miglio, "Roma dopo Avignone: La rinascita politica dell'antico," in Settis, *Memoria dell'antico*, 1:91–93. For an anecdote about Barbo spiriting away some ancient coins that remained in Pisanello's studio after the artist's death, see Roberto Weiss, *Un umanista veneziano: Papa Paolo II* (Venice, 1958), 27–28. On Lorenzo's collecting, see Eugène Müntz, *Les collections des Médicis aux XVe siècle* (Paris, 1888), 79; and *Les arts*, 2.154–58.

81. This is published in Valentini and Zucchetti, *Codice topografico*, 2:163–207.

82. Reprinted in ibid., 3.143–67; published in English as *The Marvels of Rome*, trans. Osborne. See also G. M. Rushforth, "Magister Gregorius' De Mirabilibus Urbis Romae: A New Description of Rome in the Twelfth Century," *Journal of Roman Studies* 9 (1919): 14–58.

83. Reprinted in Valentini and Zucchetti, *Codice topografico*, 4:110–50. See the discussion in Weiss, *Renaissance Discovery*, 60–63.

84. The description of the Septizonium appears in Magister Gregorius, chap. 19; the accounts of the sibyl and of Virgil are taken from the anonymous *Mirabilia urbis Romae*, trans. F. M. Nichols (New York, 1986), 17–18 and 8, respectively. The original Latin version is reprinted in the *Codice topografico*, 3:3–65. So far as poetic ekphrasis and archaeological reality are concerned, compare Alberti's more practical view of two hundred years later: "It would be safer to entrust the doors of a temple to a pivot than to a system of pins, since, for the sake of durability, they must be of bronze, and consequently extremely heavy. Here I do not mean doors like those about which we read in historians and poets, so heavily weighted down with gold, ivory, and reliefs that they could be opened only by a team of men, and would give off a terrifying creak. I much prefer temple doors that are easy to open and close" (citations are to Leon Battista Alberti, *On the Art of Building in Ten Books*, trans. J. Rykwert, N. Leach, R. Tavernor [Cambridge, Mass., 1988], bk. 7, chap. 12, p. 226). From Magister Gregorius's undifferentiated assimilation of Ovid to Alberti's (intentionally droll?) revision of the poetical into the practical, we can observe the coming of the Renaissance.

85. On Poggio, see Philip Jacks, *The Antiquarian and the Myth of Antiquity: The Origins of Rome in*

Renaissance Thought (Cambridge, Eng., 1993), 95–99; Weiss, *Renaissance Discovery*, 63–66; and P. Castelli, ed., *Poggio Bracciolini, un toscano dell'400* (Arezzo, 1980). Poggio's principal work on the subject, the *De varietate fortunae*, is published in excerpted form in Valentini and Zucchetti, *Codice topografico*, 4:230–45.

86. See letters cited by Jacks, *Antiquarian*, 97, 99. In the first instance, Ambrogio Traversari complains to Niccolò Niccoli that Poggio has promised him a copy of Frontinus but refused to deliver it. The second letter, from Poggio himself, makes it clear that he is using Ammianus Marcellinus as a guidebook to the city.

87. Biondo's early work is *De verbis Romanae locutionis* of 1435, for which see Bartolommeo Nogara, *Scritti inediti e rari di Biondo Flavio* (Rome, 1927), 115–30. On Tortelli, see M. D. Rinaldi, "Fortuna e diffusione del 'De Orthographia' di Giovanni Tortelli," *Italia medioevale e umanistica* 16 (1973): 227–61.

88. Tortelli does a learned Greek derivation of the city's name (from ῥώμη meaning "red"), according to which the Latin name ought to be "Rhoma" rather than "Roma." See Jacks, *Antiquarian*, 154–57; and Weiss, *Renaissance Discovery*, 71.

89. Bernardo Rucellai, in *De urbe Roma*, is a particularly studious reader of inscriptions as a way of clearing up misinformation concerning the monuments of the city; see Valentini and Zucchetti, *Codice topografico*, 4:439, 445.

90. Dondi offers competing versions of measurements for the obelisk in front of Saint Peter's; see his *Iter romanum*, in Valentini and Zucchetti, *Codice topografico*, 1:68.

91. Alberti's map is reproduced in Valentini and Zucchetti, *Codice topografico*, 4:212–22. On Alberti's urbanistic enterprises, see Jacks, *Antiquarian*, 99–110; and Charles Burroughs, "Alberti e Roma," in J. Rykwert and A. Engel, eds., *Leon Battista Alberti* (Milan, 1994), 134–57.

92. Citations are to Alberti, *On the Art of Building*. Subsequent references are indicated in text. Two fine pieces of recent scholarship on the classical and intellectual contexts of Alberti's work are Christine Smith, *Architecture in the Culture of Early Humanism: Ethics, Aesthetics, and Eloquence, 1400-1470* (New York, 1992); and the same author's "Alberti, Vitruvio e Cicerone," in Rykwert and Engel, *Alberti*, 70–95.

93. See Weiss, *Renaissance Discovery*, 78. Rucellai cites *De re aedificatoria* in Valentini and Zucchetti, *Codice topografico*, 4:447, 456.

94. For a good selection of these responses, from Flavio Biondo and Alberti as well as Poggio, see Jacks, *Antiquarian*, 99–117.

95. The best recent accounts of these processes are Greenhalgh, *Survival*, 119–82; and Frugoni, "L'antichità," in Settis, *Memoria dell'antico*, 1:5–72.

96. See Frugoni, "L'antichità," in *Memoria*, 1:34–35.

97. On these practices, see Greenhalgh, *Survival*, passim, esp. 183–201; and the magisterial essay of Salvatore Settis, "Continuità, distanza, conoscenza: Tre usi dell'antico," in Settis, *Memoria dell'antico*, 3:375–486, esp. 399–410. Krautheimer, *Rome*, 65–66, gives a powerful account of despoiling and spolia in the early Middle Ages.

98. On Silvester, in relation to the Colosseum and the colossal bronze statue in front of it, see the *Mirabilia*, trans. Nichols, bk. 2, chap. 7, 28–29. A fuller account of this story is to be found below, in Chap. 3. Other medieval accounts credit this destruction to Gregory I; on this, see Magister Gregorius, *Marvels*, 48–51. See the definitive treatment by Tilmann Buddensieg, "Gregory the Great, the Destroyer of Pagan Idols: The History of a Medieval Legend concerning the Decline of Ancient Art and Literature," *Journal of the Warburg and Courtauld Institutes* 28 (1965): 44–65.

99. See John of Salisbury, *Historiae Pontificalis quae supersunt*, ed. R. L. Poole (Oxford, 1927), 81–82.

100. See Alain De Bouard, "Gli antichi marmi di Roma nel medio evo," *Archivio della Società Romana di storia patria* 34 (1911): 239–45.

101. "Eh bien! tous ces monuments décrits, inventoriés avec tant d'amour par des lettrés de toutes les nations, ces thermes, ces amphithéâtres, ces temples, tombèrent sous le pic des démolisseurs de Nicolas V. En même temps qu'il inaugurait le règne de la Renaissance, qu'il sauvait de l'oubli tant d'autres classiques, il porta une main téméraire sur ces ruines augustes et détruisit des édifices respectés par les Barbares. . . . Aura-t-on le courage, en face des services vraiment exceptionnels rendus par Paul II à l'antiquité classique, d'insister sur un acte de vandalisme tout à fait isolé: l'extraction de blocs de marbre et de travertine du Colisée? . . . Réservons notre sévérité pour ceux qui, à une époque plus éclairée, ont détruit, en quelque sorte de gaieté de coeur, les plus beaux monuments de Rome: pour Sixte V, qui fit démolir, en plein seizième siècle, le Septizonium de Sévère; pour Paul V, qui employa les marbres du forum de Nerva à la construction de la chapelle Pauline à Sainte-Marie-Majeure et à celle de la fontaine du même nom; pour Alexandre VII, qui renversa, en 1662, l'arc de triomphe de Marc-Aurèle! La responsabilité de Paul II est bien légère en comparaison de la leur" (Müntz, *Les arts*, 1.106, 2.7).

102. Weiss, *Renaissance Discovery*, 104; see also Lanciani, *Destruction*, esp. 203–13.

103. On this pivotal figure, see, for instance, George Holmes, *The Florentine Enlightenment, 1400–1450* (Oxford, 2d ed., 1992), 15–18, 56–63, who classifies Vergerio as part of the "Humanist avantgarde." On the civic humanism connection, see Hans Baron, *The Crisis of the Early Italian Renaissance* (Princeton, 2d ed., 1966), 126–34; and David Robey, "P. P. Vergerio the Elder: Republicanism and Civic Values in the Work of an Early Humanist," *Past and Present* 58 (1973): 3–15. Vergerio's letter concerning the decay of Rome, cited below, is published in Valentini and Zucchetti, *Codice topografico*, 4:93–100.

104. See, for instance, the jeremiad by Cencio da Rustici cited in the next note.

105. I quote the translation from *Two Renaissance Book Hunters*, trans. P. W. R. Gordan (New York, 1974), 189–90. For the original text, see L. Bertalot, "Cincius Romanus und seine Briefe," *Quellen und Forschungen aus italienischen Archiven und Bibliotheken* 21 (1929–30): 222–25. See also Miglio, "Roma dopo Avignone," in Settis, *Memoria dell'antico*, 1:88–91.

106. The best contexualized account of this intersection between urbanism and theology is Stinger, *Renaissance in Rome*, 170–84; see also Jacks, *Antiquarian*, 113–21.

107. Albertini writes what is essentially a popular guidebook to the city (and it *was* popular, as witness a lively publication history in the years following 1510). Its title, *Opusculum de mirabilibus novae et veteris urbis Romae*, makes it clear that it comprehends both ancient Rome and that of the newly ambitious papacy. Albertini takes care to distinguish the old and new eras into two separate parts of his volume. It is reprinted in Valentini and Zuchetti, *Codice topografico*, 4:462–546.

108. See Müntz, *Les arts*, 3.177–78.

109. The poem is transcribed by Müntz, *Les arts*, 3.133. For more on Capodiferro, see above, n. 23.

110. See the entry under 14 December 1471 in Rodolfo Lanciani, *Storia degli scavi di Roma* (Rome, 1989), 1.93, which cites Müntz, *Les arts*, 3.15.

111. See Stinger, *Renaissance in Rome*, 32.

112. The invaluable source for all the primary documents is V. Golzio, *Raffaello nei documenti* (Vatican City, 1936), 33–34, 78–92. On this project, see Lanciani, *Storia*, 1.223–24; Jacks, *Antiquarian*, 183–91; and Ingrid D. Rowland, "Raphael, Angelo Colocci, and the Genesis of the Architectural Orders," *Art Bulletin* 76 (1994): 81–104.

113. Golzio, *Raffaello*, 33. Serlio, however, refers to Raphael as "pittore, et ancho intelligente ne l'Architectura" (Golzio, 34).

114. The translation is quoted from R. Klein and H. Zerner, *Italian Art, 1500–1600* (Englewood Cliffs, N.J., 1966), 45; for the original text, see Golzio, *Raffaello*, 39–40.

115. For the complicated case of Gabriel de Rossi's marble statues and other antiquities, see Lanciani, *Storia*, 1.223; the texts are found in Golzio, *Raffaello*, 72–73. The account by Jacks (*Antiquarian*, 336n65) appears to be at variance with the sources cited.

116. On the twelfth-century decree, see above, n. 100. On the papal bulls, see Müntz, *Les arts*, 1.105, 3.12–53; and Lanciani, *Storia*, 1.83, 97.

117. It should be noted that Vasari says little about Raphael's architectural work and nothing about any studies of antiquity; see the editor's surprise over this omission in *Vite*, ed. Milanesi, 4:379–81 n.

118. On Raphael's team of artist-collaborators, see Vasari, *Vite*, ed. Milanesi, 4:362–63.

119. Golzio, *Raffaello*, 282.

120. For a good recent summary of the editorial and attributional problems, see Ettore Camesasca, ed., *Raffaello gli scritti* (Milan, 1993), 257–61. As with other Raphael-connected texts, citations here are from Golzio. Translations are taken from E. G. Holt, ed., *A Documentary History of Art* (Princeton, 1981), 289–96.

121. Golzio, *Raffaello*, 31. Translation is from Klein and Zerner, *Italian Art*, 32–33.

122. For a convincing attempt to unravel the enigma of the nonexistent Publius Victor, see Jacks, *Antiquarian*, 158–59.

123. Ibid., 186. On the earlier efforts in this vein, see P. Gustaf Hamberg, "Vitruvius, Fra Giocondo and the City Plan of Naples," *Acta archaeologica* 36 (1965): 118–19; and J. Richter and C. Pedretti, *The Literary Works of Leonardo da Vinci* (London, 1977), 2:192–94.

124. "Perchè di tre maniere di edificii solamente si ritrovano in Roma, delle quali la una è di que' boni antichi, che durarono dalli primi imperatori sino al tempo che Roma fu ruinata et guasta dalli Gotti et da altri barbari, l'altra durò tanto che Roma fu dominata dai Gotti et anchora cento anni di poi; l'altra da quel tempo sino alli tempi nostri" (Golzio, *Raffaello*, 85; "For there are only three styles of building to be found in Rome: the first is that of the good antique, which lasted from the first Emperors until the time when Rome was ruined and despoiled by the Goths and other barbarians; the second is what prevailed from that time until the Gothic domination of Rome and for one hundred years afterwards; the third is from that age until our own" [trans. Holt, *Documentary*]). On Ghiberti's and Vasari's versions of this history, see Chap. 2., this vol.

125. E.g., "Et aciochè più chiaramente anchora si intenda, havemo posto qui da sotto in disegno un solo edificio" (Golzio, *Raffaelo*, 90; And in order that this be understood even more clearly, I have placed beneath this a drawing of a single building).

126. On the loss of Raphael as a loss of the chance to renew ancient Rome, see the poetic epitaphs by Castiglione, Caio Silvano Germanico, and Capodiferro, reprinted in Golzio, *Raffaello*, 79–80.

127. On all these developments, see Frugoni, "L'antichità," in Settis, *Memoria dell'antico*, 1:6–8, 21–53. For the Einsiedeln itinerary, see Valentini and Zucchetti, *Codice topografico*, 2:163–207. On the iconoclastic early popes, see above in the present chapter.

128. For which see Luciano Gargan, *Cultura e arte nel veneto al tempo del Petrarca* (Padua, 1978), 34–65. The list itself (36–39) includes everything from chess pieces to heads made of bronze, marble, or wax, to texts by Seneca, Aquinas, and Averroes, to parts of animal bodies (sculpted or real: scholars disagree), to the Amoretti from the Ravenna Thrones, for which see Bober and Rubinstein, *Renaissance Artists*, 90.

129. "Non era aitri che esso, che sapessi leiere li antiqui pataffii. Tutte scritture antiche vulgarizzava. Queste figure de marmo iustamente interpretava" (Anonimo Romano, *Vita di Cola di Rienzo*, ed.

G. Porta [Rome, 1981], 104–5; There was no one like him for knowing how to read ancient inscriptions. He could translate all ancient writing into the vulgar language. These marble figures he could interpret correctly).

130. For the theory and practice of justice in relation to the animal group, see A. Michaelis, "Storia della collezione capitolina di antichità fino all'inaugurazione del Museo (1734)," *Mitteilungen des deutschen archäologischen Instituts* 6 (1891): 3–66; and C. Franzoni, "Inter Christianorum sacra statua Herculis," *Annale della Scuola Normale di Pisa*, Classe di Lettere e di Filosofia, ser. 3, 16 (1986): 725–41.

131. For citations to Latin and English versions, see above, n. 82.

132. Valentini and Zucchetti, *Codice topografico*, chap. 12; Gregorius, *Marvels*, 26.

133. See *Codice*, chaps. 4, 5, 7; *Marvels*, 19–23.

134. *Codice*, chap. 4.; *Marvels*, 20.

135. On Ovid and the Septizonium, see *Codice*, chap. 19; *Marvels*, 29; on Virgil and the Antony and Cleopatra story, see chap. 22, p. 30.

136. Neal W. Gilbert, "A Letter of Giovanni Dondi dall'Orologio to Fra' Guglielmo Centueri: A Fourteenth-Century Episode in the Quarrel of the Ancients and the Moderns," *Viator: Medieval and Renaissance Studies* 8 (1977): 341.

137. "This nonvisual, evocative approach to antiquity among the learned has dominated nearly all humanist thought down to recent times. To this day the literary outlook survives among historians, philologists, and educated sightseers. . . . The prevalence of the literary point of view has thus obliterated the fact that once a different, indeed, a diametrically opposed approach to antiquity existed among men who did not live by their pens, men who were artists for the most part" (Richard Krautheimer and Trude Krautheimer, *Lorenzo Ghiberti* [Princeton, 1970], 296.)

138. On the topography of the Quirinal, see L. Richardson, Jr., *A New Topographical Dictionary of Ancient Rome* (Baltimore, 1992), 324–26.

139. For these early histories, see Adolf Michaelis, "Monte Cavallo," *Mitteilungen des deutschen archäologischen Instituts, Römische Abteilung* 13 (1898): 248–74; Michaelis, "Storia della collezione," 25–30; and Thuri Lorenz, "Ein Nymphäum auf dem Quirinal," *Mededeelingen van het Nederlands Historisch Instituut te Rome* 41, n.s. 6 (1979): 43–57.

140. On the ancient appearance of the Capitol, see Henri Jordan, *Topographie der Stadt Rom im Altertum* (Rome, 1970), 2.1–154; and Giuseppe Lugli, *Roma antica: Il centro monumentale* (Rome, 1946), 1–51. See also the useful summary and plan in Richardson, *New Topographical Dictionary*, 68–70. For an eloquent view of the Capitol over the long range of history, see Fritz Saxl, "The Capitol during the Renaissance: A Symbol of the Imperial Idea," in his *Lectures* (London, 1957), 200–14.

141. "When this auspice of permanence had been received, there followed another prodigy foretelling the grandeur of their [Roman] empire. A human head, its features intact, was found, so it is said, by the men who were digging for the foundations of the temple. This appearance plainly foretold that here was to be the citadel of the empire and the head of the world" (Loeb Classical Library, ed. B. O. Foster [Cambridge, Mass., 1988], 190).

142. See above and n. 130.

143. The Roman Forum, so much the central piece of the city's antiquity for us, is conspicuously less significant as an originary location in the earlier periods, possibly because of its remoteness from the medieval life of the city. Only two major sculptural works can be traced there. The colossal marble head of Constantine, part of a massive seated figure located in the Basilica of Constantine and found there in 1486, was brought shortly thereafter to the Conservators' Palace. There it was sketched, for instance, by Francisco de Hollanda on a sheet alongside the

more widely influential colossal marble head, which had been at the Lateran until its removal to the Capitoline in 1471. (See Wolfgang Helbig, *Führer durch die öffentlichen Sammlungen klassischer Altertümer in Rom* [Tübingen, 1966], 2.252–54.) The *Marforio*, cited as early as the Einsiedeln itinerary, remained on the Forum near the arch of Septimius Severus until it began its various travels in 1588.

144. See Bober and Rubinstein, *Renaissance Artists*, 220–21; and Christian Hülsen, "Der Cantharus von Alt-St. Peter und die antiken Pignen-Brunnen," *Mitteilungen des deutschen archäologischen Instituts, Römische Abteilung* 19 (1904): 87–116. Both reprint a text from Lafréry's *Speculum* of the 1570s, which includes a set of historical origins for the *Pigna*, beginning with its placement in Hadrian's tomb, its removal and transformation into a fountain by the fifth-century Pope Symmachus, and its relocation in Saint Peter's.

145. The Lateran location of the *Marcus Aurelius* is first mentioned in the *Liber pontificalis* in connection with the tenth-century popes John XIII and John XIV. The *She-Wolf* is identified with the Lateran in another pair of tenth-century texts, the *Chronicon* of Benedict of Mt. Soracte and the *De imperatoria potestate in urbe Roma libellus*. Reference to these origins can be found in Magister Gregorius, *Marvels of Rome*, who also points out that Charlemagne's decision to erect a similar statue in Aachen may well signal a presence of the *She-Wolf* at the Lateran as early as the eighth century. (See also Richard Krautheimer, "The Carolingian Revival of Early Christian Architecture," *Art Bulletin* 24 [1942]: 1–38.) The twelfth-century *Mirabilia* reports on the colossal head and hand being placed at the Lateran (1.7) but credits this removal—mythically, one presumes—to the fourth-century pope Silvester I. The *Spinario* is sighted at the Lateran by Benjamin of Tudela, who traveled to Rome in the 1160s, for which see P. Borchardt, "The Sculpture in Front of the Lateran as Described by Benjamin of Tudela and Magister Gregorius," *Journal of Roman Studies* 26 (1936): 68–70.

146. Tilmann Buddensieg, "Die Statuenstiftung Sixtus IV. im Jahre 1471," *Römisches Jahrbuch für Kunstgeschichte* 20 (1983): 33–73; W. S. Heckscher, *Sixtus IIII Aeneas Insignes Statuas Romano Popolo Restituendas Censuit* (The Hague, 1955). I am particularly taken with Heckscher's idea of the medieval formula "image + column = idol" (46). But see Richard Cocke, "Masaccio and the Spinario, Piero and the Pothos: Observations on the Reception of the Antique in Renaissance Painting," *Zeitschrift für Kunstgeschichte* 43 (1980): 21–32, for some cogent questions concerning the hypothesis that these statues were placed so remote from view.

147. On Benjamin, see above, n. 145; on Magister Gregorius, see above and n. 82.

148. On the medieval lives and interpretations of these two works, see, esp., Philip Fehl, "The Placement of the Equestrian Statue of Marcus Aurelius in the Middle Ages," *Journal of the Warburg and Courtauld Institutes* 38 (1974): 362–67; Adalbert Erler, *Lupa, Lex und Reiterstandbild im mittelalterlichen Rom* (Wiesbaden, 1972), 9–16; and Cecile Dulière, *Lupa Romana: Recherches d'iconographie et essai d'interprétation* (Brussels, 1979), 21–43.

149. Heckscher, *Sixtus IIII*, 46.

150. See Buddensieg, "Statuenstiftung," 53.

151. In this regard, cf. the eloquent pronouncement of Buddensieg (ibid.): "Voluptas wurde nun auch in statuis paganis entdeckt, als neue autonome Kategorie der Ästhetik: Die Bewunderung, der Genuß, die Augenlust, die delectatio und voluptas, an der künstlerischen Arbeitsleistung und dem Sinneseindruck der Schönheit als platonischem Weg der Erkenntnis des Göttlichen, unabhängig von ikonographischer Fixierung und geschichtlicher Rechtfertigung."

152. This is true of most of them. Although arguments about the *Spinario* often imply that it was brought down to ground level once it was moved to the Lateran—see, for instance,

Schweikhart's discussion of "künstlerische Annäherung" ("Von Priapus zu Coridon: Benennungen des Dornausziehers in Mittelalter und Neuzeit," *Würzburger Jahrbuch für Altertumswissenschaft*, n.s., 3 [1977]: 243–52)—there are many indications that it remained atop a column even there. Cf. drawings by Marten van Heemskerck (Oxford, Ashmolean; our fig. 3.30) and Francesco de Hollanda (Sketchbook, fol. 29v). See Heckscher, *Sixtus IIII*, 22, who calculates a seven-foot-high column and suggests that it remained in that installation until the seventeenth century. But see also Cocke, "Masaccio and the Spinario," cited above in n. 146. For more discussion of the *Spinario*, see Chap. 3.

153. *Lorenzo Ghibertis Denkwürdigkeiten (I commentari)*, ed. Julius von Schlosser (Berlin, 1912), 1:62.

154. Grossino, cited in Brummer, *Statue Court*, 191–92.

155. William of Malmesbury, *Chronicle of the Kings of England*, 2.13, trans. J. A. Giles (London, 1847), 234–35.

156. See Weiss, *Renaissance Discovery*, 18–19, 114–15. Note as well the ancient story (Livy *History of Rome* 1.55) of finding a perfectly preserved human head on what was to be the site of the Capitol, which foretells the longevity of the empire. See n. 141 of the present chapter.

157. The many contemporary accounts, most of them collected in Rodolfo Lanciani, *Pagan and Christian Rome* (New York, 1893), 295–301, include Stefano Infessura, *Diario della città di Roma*, ed. O. Tommasini (Turin, 1960); Notarius a Nantiporta, in *Codice Vaticano*, 6.823, fol. 250; Raffaele Maffei da Volterra, *Commentarii rerum urbanorum*, col. 954 of the Lyons ed., 1552; Bartolomeo Fonte, letter to Francesco Sassetto, published by H. Janitschek in *Gesellschaft der Renaissance* (Stuttgart, 1879), 120; letter from Laur Pehem, April 15, 1475, in the *Codice Munich*, 716 (among the papers collected by Hartmann Schedel); copy of letter from Daniele da San Sebastiano to Giacomo di Maffei, in the *Codice Marciano* (Venice), 14.267; Alexander ab Alexandro, *Genialium Dierum libri sex, varia ac eruditione* (Paris, 1565), 3.2; fragment of a diary of Antonio di Vaseli (1481–86) in the *Archives of the Vatican*, Armar. 15, fasc. 44; Anonym ap. Montfaucon, *Diarium Italicum*, n. 157; Francesco Matarazzo, *Cronaca della città di Perugia dal 1492 al 1503 di Francesco Matarazzo detto Maturanzio*, *Archivio storico Italiano*, ser. 1, 16, 2, p. 180. Cf. also Alessandro Cortesi and another anonymous chronicler in *Biblioteca Laurenziana*, Florence, MS Ashburnham, 1657, fols. 107v–109r, cited in Weiss, *Renaissance Discovery*, 102.

158. Among the classic treatments are Jacob Burckhardt, *The Civilization of the Renaissance in Italy* (New York, 1950), 183–84; Ludwig Pastor, *History of the Popes from the Close of the Middle Ages* (St. Louis, 1950), 5.330–33; and R. Lanciani, *Pagan and Christian*, 295–301. More recently, the anecdote has been used at the beginning of such books as von Salis, *Antike*, 13, and Vincenzo Farinella, *Archeologia e pittura a Roma tra Quattrocento e Cinquecento* (Turin, 1992), 3–19. Among other discussions of this event, see Henry Thode, "Die römische Leiche vom Jahre 1485," *Mittheilungen des Instituts für österreichische Geschichtsforschung* 4 (1883): 75–91; Christian Hülsen, "Die Auffindung der römischen Leiche vom Jahre 1485," *Mittheilungen des Instituts für österreichische Geschichtsforschung* 4 (1883): 433–49; Emmanuel Rodocanachi, *Le capitole romain antique et moderne* (Paris, 1904), 54–55; Saxl, "Classical Inscription," 26–27, 44–45; and Weiss, *Renaissance Discovery*, 102–3.

159. Translation from Lanciani, *Pagan and Christian*, 296–97; the original is transcribed in Hülsen, "Auffindung," 435–36.

160. On these interlocking families of humanists and courtiers, see John F. D'Amico, *Renaissance Humanism in Papal Rome* (Baltimore, 1983), esp. chaps. 3 and 4.

161. Thode, "Römische Leiche," 82.

162. On the epigraphic evidences, see Hülsen, "Auffindung," 438–44. He cites, for instance, Codex

716 of the Munich library from the papers of Hartmann Schedel: "Plurique Ciceronis filiam voluere Tulliolam. Namque monumentum illius, cuius epigramma vidi et legi eo loco, patris illic est in proximo loco: tum quod eo in loco, ubi humata illa erat, agros habuerit Cicero" (Many took it to be Tulliola, the daughter of Cicero. For her monument, whose inscription I saw and read, was in that place, and that of her father was right next to it; in addition, in that place where she was buried Cicero owned lands). But cf. Lanciani (*Pagan and Christian*, 300), who solemnly discounts these claims: "The body was of a young and tender girl, while Tulliola is known to have died in childbirth at the age of thirty-two. Moreover, there is no document to prove that Cicero had a family vault at the sixth milestone of the Appian Way."

163. The principal source on Pompilio in relation to the discovery of the corpse is Giovanni Mercati, "Paolo Pompilio e la scoperta del cadavere intatto sull'Appia nel 1485," in his *Opere minori* (Vatican City, 1937), 4.68–86. For general discussions of Pompilio, see Carlo Dionisotti, *Gli umanisti e il volgare fra Quattro e Cinquecento* (Florence, 1968), 33–36; and D'Amico, *Renaissance Humanism*, 158, 296–98.

164. No otherwise recorded event corresponds to this discovery: there are no major finds near the Vatican, nor were any Hercules-like figures that even remotely fit this description unearthed around 1485. But it is easy to imagine some relevant fragments coming to light and passing into the realm of general discussion at that time.

165. See *Institutio oratoria*, trans. H. E. Butler (Loeb Classical Library [Cambridge, 1977], 6.1.1, pp. 382–83): "Rerum repetitio et congregatio, quae Graece dicitur ἀνακεφαλαίωσιϛ a quibusdam Latinorum enumeratio, et memoriam iudicis reficit et totam simul causam ponit ante oculos."

166. On Roman burial practice, see F. Hinard, ed., *La mort, les morts et l'au-delà dans le monde romain* (Caen, 1987); Jocelyn Toynbee, *Death and Burial in the Roman World* (Ithaca, 1971); and John Ferguson, *The Religions of the Roman Empire* (London, 1970), 132–39.

167. On this matter, see Greenhalgh, *Survival*, esp. 84–85, 183–201, and, by the same author, "Ipsa ruina docet: L'uso dell'antico nel Medioevo," in Settis, *Memoria dell'antico*, 1:115–67.

168. For sources on the theft of the tiara—including the same Stefano Infessura who reports on the discovery of the corpse—see Mercati, "Paolo Pompilio," 277 n. The Donation of Constantine, which purported to give secular dominion to the church under Pope Silvester I, had been proved a forgery by Lorenzo Valla, in *De falso credita et ementita Constantini donatione*. See Mario Fois, S.J., *Il pensiero cristiano di Lorenzo Valla nel quadro storico-culturale del suo ambiente* (Rome, 1969); and Stinger, *Renaissance in Rome*, 248–54.

169. Original text to be found in Mercati, "Paolo Pompilio," 278–79.

170. See Tacitus, *Annals*, 16.6: "Fortuita mariti iracundia . . . corpus non igni abolitum, ut Romanus mos, sed regum externorum consuetudine differtum odoribus conditur tumuloque Iuliorum infertur" (E. Koestermann, ed., *Academia scientiarum germania berolinensis* [Berlin, 1965], 378–79).

171. Cf. a letter by Daniel da Sebastiano in Marciana MS 14.267, cited by Hülsen, "Auffindung," 436: "Si scoperse uno viso cossì grato accepto et venusto, che quantunque se conjectura sia de anni MCCCCC, zoè 1500, e più: parea fosse manchata quello giorno medesimo cum li suoi capilli collecti in capo more romano che pariano a hora pectinati cum li occhii et palpebre mobile, cum li orecchie et naso integro i quali togando se mouetino et tornavano a suo locho, et tocando la faza ho altroue la carne se machiava et reveniva, li labri et la lingua uno pocho aparenti, li denti eburnei, le mane e i piedi cum li articuli che sepiegavano per quella conserva. . . . In vero se hauesti veduto questo viso saresti non meno innamorato che maravelgiato [sic] e credo se tegnira sopra la terra tanto che ciascuno sara del veder satisfacto" (There was discovered a face so pleasing, lovely, and beautiful that even though it was conjectured that she was 1500 years old,

and more, it seemed as though she had died that very day. Her hair, gathered on her head in the Roman fashion, was newly combed, her eyes and eyelids still moving, her ears and nose complete, both of which moved and turned in their places when touched; and wherever you touched her face, the flesh colored and then returned; her lips and her tongue were clear; her teeth were ivory; her hands and feet with all their joints moving because of her state of preservation. . . . In truth if you had seen this face you would have fallen in love as well as marveled at it).

172. I can find it nowhere in the *Natural History*, but it does correspond roughly to a passage from Cassiodorus's *Variae*: "Si clausis domibus ac munitis insidiari solet nequissimum votum, quanto magis in Romana civitate videtur illici, qui in plateis pretiosum reperit quod possit auferri? nam quidam populus copiosissimus statuarum, greges etiam abundantissimi equorum, tali sunt cautela servandi, quali et cura videntur affixi, ubi, si esset humanis rebus ulla consideratio, Romanum pulchritudinem non vigiliae, sed sola deberet reverentia custodire" (*Monumentum Germaniae historica*, ed. T. Mommsen 12 [1961], 210). Alberti alludes to the same tradition in *De re aedificatoria* 7.16.

173. "[Plinio] dice che in Roma a suoi tempi eran' due populi, l'un d'huomini vivi, et l'altro di statue di marmo, queste erano tutte dedicate et masse nelle loro case, Palazzi, Theatri et Amphitheatri, Cerchi Archi, et piazze, et Therme così degli huomini Romani, come anchora di que forastieri, ch'essi da varia parti del mondo trasportarono nella patria, non perdonando Agli Dei et Heroi di moverli da luoghi loro per dedicarle nela città di tutto il mondo, ove è da notare la grandezza dell'animo di tanto populo quando non si segno [sdegnò?] di tenervi honoratamente la statua di Annibale eterno inimico del nome Romano, tanto fù di valore appresso di loro la virtù, che ancora negli nimici le honoravano. Mà che haverebbe detto Plinio, quando vide si gran populo di marmo, nel tempo di Vespasiano Imperadore, se egli fusse possuto trapassare a molti altri Imperadori che seguirono poi nel tempo di quelli furono condotte in Roma infenite altre statue, et infenite fattene ha honor degli Dei, del'Imperadori, di prefetti, de consoli, de Tribuni militari, et altri huomini grandi senza numero, altra a quelle che si dedicavano alli Dei per voti publici e privati; sono certo che egli haverebbe detto in Roma, esser un populo d'huomini et diece di statue di marmo." The passage, which appears in Naples MS 13. B.7., is cited from Erna Mandowsky and Charles Mitchell, *Pirro Ligorio's Roman Antiquities* (London, 1963), 49–50 n.

CHAPTER 2: HISTORIES

1. The source of the phrase is ll. 361–65 of the poem known officially as the "Epistle to the Pisones" but more commonly as the *Ars Poetica*. The best annotated edition in English is *Epistles Book II and Epistle to the Pisones*, ed. N. Rudd (Cambridge, Eng., 1989). The basic work on the tradition in the Renaissance is Rensselaer W. Lee, *Ut Pictura Poesis: The Humanist Theory of Painting* (New York, 1940). But much has been done more recently; for bibliographies on these themes, see Arno Dolders, "Ut Pictura Poesis: A Selective, Annotated Bibliography of Books and Articles, Published between 1900 and 1980, on the Interrelation of Literature and Painting from 1400 to 1800," *Yearbook of Comparative and General Literature* 32 (1983): 105–24; Clark Hulse, "Recent Studies of Literature and Painting in the English Renaissance," *English Literary Renaissance* 15 (1985): 122–40; and Leonard Barkan, "Making Pictures Speak: Renaissance Art, Elizabethan Literature, Modern Scholarship," *Renaissance Quarterly* 48 (1995): 326–51.

2. The ur-instance is Socrates, who uses the analogy between poets and painters to demonstrate that poets are mere imitators; he is much more evasive when it comes to the question of how poetic imitation might be different from painterly verisimilitude. See *Republic* 10.595–607.

3. "It is often expedient and occasionally becoming to make some modification in the time-

honoured order [of words]. We see the same thing in pictures and statues. Dress, expression and attitude are frequently varied. The body when held bolt upright has but little grace, for the face looks straight forward, the arms hang by the side, the feet are joined and the whole figure is stiff from top to toe. But that curve, I might almost call it motion, with which we are so familiar, gives an impression of action and animation. So, too, the hands will not always be represented in the same position, and the variety given to the expression will be infinite. Some figures are represented as running or rushing forward, others sit or recline, some are nude, others clothed, while some again are half-dressed, half-naked. Where can we find a more violent or elaborate attitude than that of the Discobolus of Myron? Yet the critic who disapproved of the figure because it was not upright, would merely show his utter failure to understand the sculptor's art, in which the very novelty and difficulty of execution is what most deserves our praise. A similar impression of grace and charm is produced by rhetorical figures, whether they be *figures of thought* or *figures of speech*. For they involve a certain departure from the straight line and have the merit of variation from the ordinary usage" (*Institutio oratoria* 2.13.8–10, trans. H. E. Butler, Loeb Classical Library [Cambridge, Mass., 1989], italics in original). The passage is noteworthy for the intricate conceptual punning that goes back and forth between rhetoric and sculpture, including plays on figura and on motion-emotion.

4. For Quintilian, see *Institutio oratoria* 2.13.12–13: "[Timanthes' painting] represented the sacrifice of Iphigenia, and the artist had depicted an expression of grief on the face of Calchas and of still greater grief on that of Ulysses, while he had given Menelaus an agony of sorrow beyond which his art could not go. Having exhausted his powers of emotional expression he was at a loss to portray the father's face as it deserved, and solved the problem by veiling his head and leaving his sorrow to the imagination of the spectator." For Cicero, see *Orator* 22.74, and also Valerius Maximus *Memorabilia* 8.1.6. In all cases, the rhetorical payoff is rather complicated, residing somewhere between the inability of the artist to achieve an endlessly rising emotional effect and the desirability of leaving matters to the imagination of the audience. Alberti, who repeats Quintilian virtually verbatim at *De Pictura*, par. 42, comes down clearly on the side of the viewer's imagination. The context for the exemplum is, however, enigmatic: Alberti seems to take Timanthes as an instance of helping to explain the historia to the viewer, an all-important subject in *De pictura*, on which see below in the present chapter; in fact, the slightly jagged relevance is appropriate, since Alberti treats explaining and hindering as ultimately parallel semantic activities. The Quattrocento imitations probably have more to do with the rediscovered sculptural object—a round altar depicting the Iphigenia story (Phyllis Bober and Ruth Rubinstein, *Renaissance Artists and Antique Sculpture* [London, 1986], cat. 105)—than with the rhetorical topos per se. Donatello veils the Mary Magdalen on his bronze pulpit at San Lorenzo, Florence, while Ghiberti adapts the Iphigenia figure, who is veiled but not covered, in his Rebecca from the Isaac panel on the east doors of the baptistry. On the persistence of the rhetorical-artistic topos, see Elizabeth McGrath, "The Painted Decoration of Rubens' House," *Journal of the Warburg and Courtauld Institutes* 41 (1978): 256–59; see also below in the present chapter.

5. On the Vitruvian connections, see Lucia Ciapponi, "Il 'De Architectura' di Vitruvio nel primo umanesimo," *Italia Medioevale e Umanistica* 3 (1960): 59–99; and Pier Nicola Pagliara, "Vitruvio da testo a canone," in Salvatore Settis, ed., *Memoria dell'antico nell' arte italiana* (Turin, 1984), 3:5–85.

6. The text and translation of Pliny used here are *Natural History*, bks. 33–35, trans. H. Rackham, Loeb Classical Library (Cambridge, Mass., 1984), and bks. 36–37, trans. D. E. Eichholz, Loeb Classical Library (Cambridge, Mass., 1971). But this study is indebted to two superbly annotated editions: Pline L'Ancien, *Histoire naturelle*, bk. 34, ed. H. le Bonniec, H. Gallet de Santerre (Paris,

1953), bk. 35, ed. Jean-Michel Croisille (Paris, 1983), bk. 36, ed. J. André, R. Bloch, A. Rouveret (Paris, 1978); and Plinio, *Storia naturale*, ed. Gian Biagio Conte, vol. 5, trans. A. Corso, R. Mugellesi, G. Rosati (Turin, 1988). Also highly useful are E. Sellers, ed., *The Elder Pliny's Chapters on the History of Art* (London, 1896); Adolphe Reinach, *Textes grecs et latins relatifs à l'histoire de la peinture ancienne* (Paris, 1921; rpt. Chicago, 1981); and H. S. Jones, ed., *Ancient Writers on Greek Sculpture* (Chicago, 1966). The best recent critical discussions of Pliny are Jacob Isager, *Pliny on Art and Society* (London, 1991); and Gian Biagio Conte, "The Inventory of the World: Form of Nature and Encyclopedic Project in the Work of Pliny the Elder," in *Genres and Readers*, trans. G. W. Most (Baltimore, 1994), 67–104. See as well Jaś Elsner, ed., *Art and Text in Roman Culture* (Cambridge, Eng., 1996), esp. Andrew Laird, "Vt figura poesis: Writing Art and the Art of Writing," 75–102, and Helen Morales, "The Torturer's Apprentice: Parrhasius and the Limits of Art," 182–209.

7. For Nero, see N.H. 34.46; for colorful pigments, see N.H. 35.50; for wall painting, see N.H. 35.118.

8. For this historical sequence, see N.H. 35.22–28.

9. The public-private axis—that is, public as good, private as bad—is central to Pliny's value judgments in regard to all the arts. He praises Agrippa, for instance, for urging that all paintings and statues be public property and not exiled to individual country houses (35.26). On the nexus of public-private with *luxuria*, see Isager, *Pliny.*

10. On these historical developments, and Pliny's relation to them, see J. E. Gotz Whitehorne, "Golden Statues in Greek and Latin Literature," *Greece and Rome* 22 (1975): 109–19; G. Lahusen, "Goldene und vergoldete römische Ehrenstatuen und Bildnisse," *Mitteilungen des deutschen archäologischen Instituts, römische Abteilung* 85 (1978): 385–95; and Ottavio Vittori, "Interpreting Pliny's Gilding: Archaeological Implications," *Rivista d'archeologia* 2 (1978): 71–81.

11. Isager (*Pliny*, 156) makes this point more judgmentally: "Pliny's basis for identifying works of art seems to have been signatures on the sculptures themselves. He never refers to artistic style or special characteristics." And Andrew Stewart (*Skopas of Paros* [Park Ridge, Ill., 1977], 2) is yet more severe: "The Roman critics depended on signatures on bases and were lost without them."

12. *Secta* used as equivalent to *schola* or *disciplina* seems to be uniquely post-Augustan; even then it is generally confined to philosophical, juridical, or religious groupings. See Lewis and Short, *A Latin Dictionary* (Oxford, 1951), s.v. "secta."

13. Bernard Andreae (*Plinius und der Laokoon* [Mainz, 1988], 12–14) has demonstrated persuasively that the claim about the superiority of the *Laocoön* is more ambiguous than it at first seems. The phrase is often construed as suggesting that it was better than all other painting and sculpture; a more cautious rendering would be that it was better than any painting or bronze sculpture; Andreae argues that the field is much narrower, i.e., that it is better than any version of the Laocoön subject in those other media.

14. On the taste for the contest as definitive of the history of art in antiquity (and the tendency of these to be legendary and ahistorical), see the useful note in *Histoire naturelle* 34.214–25. This kind of myth continues into postclassical times as, for instance, when the *Dioscuri* are understood (e.g., by Petrarch) to be competition pieces by Phidias and Praxiteles, for which see below in the present chapter and Chap. 3. The victory of Polyclitus in the Amazon competition will also have important postclassical repercussions in his canonization as ancient artist par excellence, for which see below, Chap. 4.

15. On this and other artist stories that point to specific aesthetic values, see V. L. Brüschweiler-Mooser, *Ausgewählte Künstleranekdoten: Eine Quellenuntersuchung* (Zurich, 1973), 84–135.

16. See, e.g., the accounts of Mummius, who sacked Corinth in 146 B.C. and shipped off statues and paintings to Rome, which Pliny discusses with specific attention to numbers and cost (34.12, 34.36, 35.24). See also the many references to Augustus's use of imported art for propaganda purposes, such as works of Apelles (35.27–28, 35.94). On the foreign aspect of this matter, see Paul Zanker, "Griechische Skulptur in der Römerzeit," in *Le classicisme à Rome aux 1ers siècles avant et après J.C.*, Entretiens, Fondation Hardt 25 (1979): 283–314. For more discussion of this aspect of Roman aesthetics, see Chap. 3.

17. See below in the present chapter for a discussion of Alberti's approach to these materials as history.

18. For a detailed historical account of these propagandistic and rhetorical uses of sculpture, see N.H. 34.15–32.

19. On symmetria, see the definitive discussion in J. J. Pollitt, *The Ancient View of Greek Art: Criticism, History, and Terminology* (New Haven, 1974), 14–22, 256–58; see also S. Ferri, "Note esegetiche ai giudizi d'arte di Plinio il Vecchio," *Annali della Scuola Normale di Pisa, Classe di lettere e filosofia* 11 (1942): 69–116. This matter is discussed more fully below in Chap. 4.

20. More than the *Natural History*, it is Cicero's *De Inventione* 2.1–4 that is the locus classicus for this story, which becomes central to discussions of rhetoric and the visual arts. For the heritage of this story, see below in the present chapter.

21. "Ancora che non siano finite le parti sue, si conosce nell'essere rimasta abozzata e gradinata, nella imperfezione della bozza, la perfezione dell'opera" (Giorgio Vasari, *Le vite de' più eccellenti pittori, scultori ed architetti*, ed. G. Milanesi [Florence, 1906], 7:195; trans. deVere, 2:681). For more on the *non finito*, see Vasari, *La vita di Michelangelo nelle redazioni del 1550 e del 1568*, ed. P. Barocchi (Milan, 1962), 228–37, 1645–70; also, see below, Chap. 3.

22. I would especially signal the careful reading by Isager, *Pliny*, which is strongest in eliciting all the issues in Roman history and politics that underlie Pliny's account of art. This analysis is revelatory of the tensions between a real practice of art in Rome and a more legendary version of art in much earlier Greece—tensions that are quite specifically elided in the Renaissance reading of the text. (For more on this point, see next note.) Other valuable readings include Giovanni Becatti, *Arte e gusto negli scrittori latini* (Florence, 1951), 215–44; W. D. E. Coulson, "The Reliability of Pliny's Chapters on Greek and Roman Sculpture," *Classical Weekly* 69 (1976): 361–72; and Silvio Ferri, *Plinio il Vecchio: Storia delle arti antiche* (Rome, 1946).

23. As suggested above, the best reading of Pliny's text in these terms is Isager. But on the general theme of these relations, see A. C. Moorhouse, "A Roman View of Greek Art," *Greece and Rome* 10 (1940): 29–35; A. Reiff, *Interpretatio, Imitatio, Aemulatio: Begriff und Vorstellung literarischer Abhängigkeit bei den Römern* (Bonn, 1959); D. E. Strong, "Roman Museums," in Strong, ed., *Archaeology, Theory and Practice: Essays Presented to W. F. Grimes* (London, 1973), 247–64; C. C. Vermeule, *Greek Sculpture and Roman Taste* (Ann Arbor, 1977); J. J. Pollitt, "The Impact of Greek Art on Rome," *Transactions of the American Philological Association* 108 (1978): 155–74; and Brunilde S. Ridgway, *Roman Copies of Greek Sculpture* (Ann Arbor, 1984).

24. The lines are *Aeneid* 6.847–53, for which see above, Chap. 1.

25. Some realities he refuses to reflect: there is nary a word about Roman relief sculpture, which is a significant omission from the perspective of the Renaissance. Isager (*Pliny*, 119, 167) suggests that the lack of reference to historical reliefs (or "State art," as he calls it) may be explained by its absence from the list of traditional genres. If that is true, which seems likely, then one must further note the ideological implications of a historical and generic system that ignores sculpture which is (a) native, (b) explicitly political, and (c) not freestanding. As in so many

other respects, these prejudices—if we can call them that—contribute neatly to an early modern aesthetic that cultivates the same preferences.

26. For a good overview of Pliny's influence on art history, see Isager, *Pliny*, 9–17. For more specific studies of his heritage, see Giovanni Becatti, "Plinio e Vasari," in *Studi di storia dell'arte in onore di Valerio Mariani* (Naples, 1972), 173–82; Marjorie Chibnall, "Pliny's 'Natural History' and the Middle Ages," in T. S. Dorey, ed., *Silver Latin II: Empire and Aftermath* (London, 1975), 57–78; C. G. Nauert, Jr., "Humanists, Scientists, and Pliny: Changing Approaches to a Classical Author," *American Historical Review* 84 (1979), 72–85; M. Schiavone, "Dall'editio princeps della Naturalis Historia ad opera di Giovanni di Spira all'edizione Lione 1561," in *Plinio e la natura* (Como, 1979), 95–108; Maurizio Bettini, "Tra Plinio e sant'Agostino: Francesco Petrarca sulle arti figurative," in Settis, *Memoria dell'antico*, 1:245–64; and A. Roncoroni, "L'eredità di Plinio nel passaggio dal medioevo all'età moderna," in *Plinio: I suoi luoghi, il suo tempo* (Como, 1984), 23–39.

27. See *Rerum memorandum libri* 1.19, in Petrarch, *Opere*, ed. G. Billanovich (Florence, 1926).

28. Citation is to Alberti, *On Painting and on Sculpture*, bk. 2, par. 26, ed. and trans. C. Grayson (London, 1972), though I deliberately leave one phrase untranslated. On Alberti in relation to ancient theory, see D. R. E. Wright, "Alberti's *De pictura*: Its Literary Structure and Purpose," *Journal of the Warburg and Courtauld Institutes* 47 (1984): 52–71; and Creighton Gilbert, "Antique Frameworks for Renaissance Art Theory: Alberti and Pino," *Marsyas* 3 (1943–45): 87–106.

29. The two modern English translations differ radically: Grayson (*On Painting and on Sculpture*, 63) speaks of "writing a history of painting like Pliny," while Spencer (*On Painting* [New Haven, 1966], 65) translates the phrase as "telling stories like Pliny."

30. Ernst Kris and Otto Kurz, *Legend, Myth, and Magic in the Image of the Artist* (New Haven, 1979).

31. Without meaning to question the brilliant arguments of Michael Baxandall in *Giotto and the Orators* (Oxford, 1971), I would suggest that his particular telos, i.e., Alberti and pictorial composition, requires that artist anecdotes be construed as primitive, commonplace, and nonscientific. See, e.g., his *divisio* (97) of the earlier humanist positions on art.

32. Petrarch's MS is Bibliothèque Nationale, Paris, MS lat. 6802. See Baxandall's excellent analysis of the annotations (*Giotto*, 62–63). See also Pierre de Nolhac, *Pétrarque et l'humanisme* (Paris, 1907), 1:70–71.

33. *Lorenzo Ghibertis Denkwürdigkeiten (I Commentari)*, ed. Julius von Schlosser (Berlin, 1912), 1:24–25. Bracketed phrases appear in the original.

34. For more on these relations, see below, Chap. 4.

35. Ghiberti, *Commentari*, ed. Schlosser, 25. Compare N.H. 35.83: "at Protogenes victum se confessus in portum devolavit hospitem quaerens, placuitque sic eam tabulam posteris tradi omnium quidem, sed artificum praecipuo miraculo" ("Hereupon Protogenes admitted he was defeated, and flew down to the harbour to look for the visitor; and he decided that the panel should be handed on to posterity as it was, to be admired as a marvel by everybody, but particularly by artists").

36. *Leonardo on Painting*, ed. Martin Kemp, trans. Martin Kemp and Margaret Walker (New Haven, 1969), 201–2: "Quello non fia universale che non ama equalmente tutte le cose che si contengono nella pittura; come se uno non li piace li paesi, esso stima quelli essere cosa di brieve e semplice investigazione, come disse il nostro Botticella, che tale studio era vano, perché col solo gittare d'una spunga piena di diversi colori in un muro, esso lasciava in esso una macchia, dove si vedeva un bel paese. Egli è ben vero che in tale macchia si vede varie invenzioni di ciò che l'om vole cercare in quella, cioè teste d'uomini, diversi animali, battaglie, scogli, mari, nuvoli e boschi e altri simili cose; e fa com'il sono delle campane, nelle quali si pò intendere quelle dire quel ch'a te pare. Ma ancora ch'esse macchie ti dieno invenzione, esse non t'insegnano finire nessuno

particulare. E questo tal pittore fece tristissimi paesi" (Codex Urbinas 33v–34r; Leonardo da Vinci, *Libro di pittura*, ed. C. Pedretti and C. Vecce [Florence, 1995], 1:174). On this theme, see H. W. Janson, "The 'Image Made by Chance' in Renaissance Thought," in M. Meiss, ed., *De Artibus Opuscula XL: Essays in Honor of Erwin Panofsky* (Zurich, 1960), 254–66.

37. For the "beholder's share," see Ernst H. Gombrich, *Art and Illusion* (Princeton, 1969), 181–287.

38. Pliny is not mentioned by name in the notebooks so far as I am aware, but examples of Plinian ideas include discussions of images that are taken for reality (*Leonardo on Painting*, ed. Kemp, 19, 34), references to the paradigm of Zeuxis and the maidens of Croton (36, 224), and the account of the origins of painting (193). On larger aspects of Leonardo's relation to Pliny, see Carlo Pedretti's commentary in J. P. Richter, *Literary Works of Leonardo da Vinci* (Berkeley, 1977), 1:138, 1:372, 2:297; and G. Fararo, "Plinio e Leonardo," in *Miscellanea Cermenati* (Bergamo, 1919), 133–38.

39. "Fermavasi talora a considerare un muro, dove lungamente fusse stato sputato da persone malate, e ne cavava le battaglie de' cavagli e le più fantastiche città e più gran paesi che si vedesse mai: simil faceva de' nuvoli dell'aria" (Vasari, *Vite*, ed. Milanesi, 4:34; trans. deVere, 1:62).

40. See the far-ranging list of instances, from Bramantino and Titian to Murillo and Millais, in Kris and Kurz, *Legend, Myth, and Magic*, 62–63.

41. Michelangelo's relations with Julius II, which tend to overturn the normal balance of power between patron and artist, are the stuff of popular legend from Vasari to Irving Stone and Charlton Heston. But all the stories of Michelangelo's relations with popes tend to make a similar point: they must pursue him, rather than the reverse. Leonardo, Vasari tells us (*Vite*, ed. Milanesi, 4:49), was honored by being allowed to expire in the arms of the king of France. In Carlo Ridolfi's seventeenth-century life of Titian (*Le maraviglie dell'arte* [Venice, 1648], 1:154–55), the painter's relations to Charles V are explicitly compared to Apelles' relations with Alexander.

42. For the treatises in which the story is told, see Paolo Pino, "Dialogo di pittura," 111, and Lodovico Dolce, "Dialogo della pittura," 158, both in *Trattati d'arte del Cinquecento*, ed. P. Barocchi (Bari, 1961). For Armenini, see *De' veri precetti della pittura*, ed. M. Gorreri (Turin, 1988), 42–43, translated as *On the True Precepts of the Art of Painting*, trans. E. J. Olszewski (New York, 1977), 100–101. The Vasari story about Filippo Lippi appears at *Vite*, ed. Milanesi, 2:614–15.

43. See Baxandall, *Giotto*; on anecdotes and their exploitation in rhetorical form, see esp. 35–44.

44. *Petrarch's Remedies for Fortune Fair and Foul*, trans. C. H. Rawski (Bloomington, 1991), 2:131. The original text is reprinted in Baxandall, *Giotto*, 140–43; an Italian translation appears in Bettini, "Tra Plinio," in *Memoria dell'antico*, ed. Settis, 1:265–67.

45. *Petrarch's Remedies*, trans. Rawski, 2:126–28.

46. *On Painting*, trans. Spencer, 65. The Latin version, vaguer and more expansive, does not name Pliny but alludes to many sources: "Multa praeterea huiusmodi a scriptoribus collecta sunt" (*On Painting*, ed. Grayson, 62).

47. See *Dialogo della pittura*, in *Trattati*, ed. Barocchi, 1:195–96.

48. "Amor s'è in lei con onestate aggiunto, / con beltà naturale, abito adorno / et un atto che parla con silenzio, / et non so che nelli occhi che 'n un punto / po far chiara la notte, oscuro il giorno, / e 'l mel amaro, et addolcir l'assenzio" (*Petrarch's Lyric Poems*, ed. Robert Durling [Cambridge, Mass., 1976], no. 215).

49. For more on these questions of terminology, see below, Chap. 4. Pliny's occasional self-conciousness about his language should be compared to another locus classicus for the subject, i.e., Quintilian's more theoretical discourse about the problem of Latin equivalents for canon-

ized Greek terms. See *Institutio oratoria* 2.14.1–4. So far as the Renaissance is concerned, there is to my knowledge no comprehensive account of terminological awareness equivalent to J. J. Pollitt's *Ancient View of Greek Art*; we await, however, work by Professor Philip Sohm on this topic. But see the usefully annotated glossaries in Alberti, *Ten Books on Architecture*, trans. Rykwert et al.; and in *Leonardo on Painting*, ed. Kemp; see also Roland LeMollé, *Georges Vasari et le vocabulaire de la critique d'art dans les "Vite"* (Grenoble, 1988).

50. The source, as cited above in n. 20, is Cicero's *De Inventione* 2.1–4. On the postclassical heritage of this story, see Panofsky, *Idea: A Concept in Art Theory*, trans. J. J. S. Peake (New York, 1968), 47–59; David Summers, *Michelangelo and the Language of Art* (Princeton, 1981), 186–99; and Leonard Barkan, "The Heritage of Zeuxis: Painting, Rhetoric, and History," in *Text and Image in the Renaissance*, ed. A. Payne, A. Kuttner, and R. Smick (Cambridge, Eng., 1999).

51. Much fine scholarly work has been focused on the bee analogy itself, including Hermann Gmelin, "Das Prinzip der Imitatio in den romanischen Literaturen der Renaissance," *Romanische Forschungen* 46 (1932): 83–360; and Jürgen von Stackelberg, "Das Bienengleichnis: Ein Beitrag zur Geschichte der literarischen Imitatio," *Romanische Forschungen* 68 (1956): 271–93. For its larger literary implications, see G. W. Pigman III, "Versions of Imitation in the Renaissance," *Renaissance Quarterly* 33 (1980): 1–32; and the definitive work of Thomas Greene, *The Light in Troy: Imitation and Discovery in Renaissance Poetry* (New Haven, 1982).

52. Quintilian *Institutio oratoria* 12.10.1.

53. "Superest ut dicam de genere orationis. Hic erat propositus a nobis in divisione prima locus tertius; nam ita promiseram me de arte, de artefice, de opere dicturum. Cum sit autem rhetorices atque oratoris opus oratio pluresque eius formae, sicut ostendam, in omnibus his et ars est et artifex. Plurimum tamen invicem differunt; nec solum specie, ut signum signo et tabula tabulae et actio actioni, sed genere ipso, ut Graecis Tuscanicae statuae, ut Asianus eloquens Attico" (*Institutio oratoria* 12.10.1).

54: "Ut auctores, sic etiam amatores habent; atque ideo nondum est perfectus orator ac nescio an ars ulla, non solum quia aliud in alio magis eminet, sed quod non una omnibus forma placuit, partim condicione vel temperum vel locorum, partim iudicio cuiusque proposito" (*Institutio oratoria* 12.10.2).

55. Cf. Baxandall's related set of categories for discussing these varieties of discourse on art, which he names as "priority, quality, stature, kind" (*Giotto*, 78).

56. Among the classic versions of this story are Erwin Panofsky, *Renaissance and Renascences in Western Art* (New York, 1969), 114–18; and Ernst Gombrich, "The Renaissance Conception of Artistic Progress and its Consequences," in *Norm and Form* (London, 1966), 1–10.

57. "Images formed by his brush agree so well with the lineaments of nature as to seem to the beholder to live and breathe; and his pictures appear to perform actions and movements so exactly as to see from a little way off actually speaking, weeping, rejoicing, and doing other things, not without pleasure for him who beholds and praises the talent and skill of the artist" (*De origine civitatis Florentie*, Vatican, MS Barb. lat. 2610, 71r; translated in Baxandall, *Giotto*, 70.)

58. The Dante citation, from *Purgatorio* 11.94–96, is to *The Divine Comedy*, trans. Charles S. Singleton (Princeton, 1973); the Boccaccio citation is to *Decameron* 6.5, ed. E. Bianchi, C. Salinari, and N. Sapegno (Milan, 1952), 440; trans. J. Payne, rev. C. Singleton (Berkeley, 1982), 459. To complete the circle, note Boccaccio's commentary on the Dante lines, for which see *Il comento alla Divina Commedia*, ed. D. Guerri (Bari, 1918), 3:82.

59. See the transcription of two versions of this passage, along with an excellent introduction, in Ottavio Morisani, "Art Historians and Art Critics—III," *Burlington Magazine* 95 (1953): 267–70;

excerpts of a translation can be found in Creighton Gilbert, ed., *Italian Art, 1400–1500: Sources and Documents* (Evanston, 1992), 191–92.

60. On this point, see also Gombrich, "Renaissance Conception," in *Norm and Form*, 138n21.

61. For Villani, see Baxandall, *Giotto*, 147 (translation, 70–71). For Ghiberti, see *Commentari*, ed. Schlosser, 1:36–37 and nn. at 2:123–26. On the problem of Stefano, see Roberto Longhi, "Stefano Fiorentino," *Paragone* 2 (1951): 18–40.

62. On the Landino text, see above, n. 57. Gombrich ("Renaissance Conception," in *Norm and Form*, 1–10) does argue for a pre-Vasarian conception of developmental history. But the claim depends on the apparently unique case of Alamanno Rinuccini (1473), who does differentiate between the time of Giotto and his own time but still uses an elegant variation of epithets for individual artists—"artificiosius," "admirabilius," "ornatius"—when it comes to contemporaries. Gombrich also tries to turn Ghiberti's history into something developmental on the basis of one vague detail, the fact that "Gusmin"'s figures were "un poco corte." I find more persuasive Baxandall's developmental model of "prophet-saviour-apostles" (*Giotto*, 75).

63. It should be noted that the question of freedom in relation to imitating glorious past examples is itself a concern of the Renaissance, as witness the arguments of Erasmus's *Ciceronianus*, which make powerful claims about historical specificity in response to the humanist fashion for guiding the future by reference to the past. On these questions, see G. W. Pigman III, "Imitation and the Renaissance Sense of the Past: The Reception of Erasmus' *Ciceronianus*," *Journal of Medieval and Renaissance Studies* 9 (1979): 155–77.

64. On Ghiberti and the Olympiads, see Richard Krautheimer and Trude Krautheimer, *Lorenzo Ghiberti* (Princeton, 1956), 353–58. For Prospettivo Milanese, see D. Fienga, "The *Antiquarie Prospettiche romane composte per Prospectivo Melanese Depictore*: A Document for the Study of the Relationship between Bramante and Leonardo da Vinci," Ph.D. diss. University of California, Los Angeles, 1970, st. 125: "son spelunche ruinate grotte / di stucco di rilievo altri colore / di man di cimabuba apelle giotte" ("they are skeletal ruins / with fragments of stucco reliefs and paintings / by the hand of Cimabue, Apelle, Giotto").

65. The Petrarch pep-talk annotations are especially on issues related to efficient artistic composition, like making exploratory sketches before composition (à propos of Pasiteles, N.H. 35.156) or knowing when to declare a work finished (à propos of Apelles, N.H. 35.80). On Vasari's paintings after Pliny, and the whole genre of the artist's house, see the definitive work by Elizabeth McGrath, "The Painted Decoration of Rubens's House," *Journal of the Warburg and Courtauld Institutes* 41 (1978): 245–77; on Vasari's case in particular, see A. Paolucci, A. M. Maetzke, *La casa del Vasari in Arezzo* (Florence, 1988), 67, 74; and Liana Cheney, *The Paintings of the Casa Vasari* (New York, 1985).

66. On this late Renaissance set of discoveries, see Erna Mandowsky, "Some Notes on the Early History of the Medicean 'Niobides,'" *Gazette des Beaux-Arts* 41 (1953): 251–64; Gabrielle Capecchi, "Una Niobide da Vigna Tommasini," *Rivista Istituto Nazionale d'Archeologia e Storia dell'Arte* 3 (1980): 5–16; and Francis Haskell and Nicholas Penny, *Taste and the Antique* (New Haven, 1981), 274–79. For other related figures that were known in the earlier period, see Bober and Rubinstein, *Renaissance Artists*, cats. 108, 109. On the authorship debate, Winckelmann at first believed them to be the work of Scopas, then decided some were by Scopas and others by Praxiteles (cited in Haskell and Penny, *Taste*, 274). More modern archaeological study has tended to resolve the matter by noting that these are, after all, copies after copies, so that placing the name of the maker on them is questionable—though the sequence of replicas tends to be traced back to Scopas rather than to Praxiteles. See Wilfred Geominy, *Die florentiner Niobiden* (Bonn,

1984); Stewart, *Skopas*, 119; and Ridgway, *Hellenistic Sculpture*, 82–84.

67. That single telltale block of stone brings this work into conjunction with the *Laocoön* on a subject that is discussed at several points in this book. It is noteworthy that Pliny makes this same point about two *collaborative* pieces of sculpture; and in the case of the *Dirce*, there is a yet more elaborate play on artistic relations: "parentem hi certamen de se fecere, Menecraten videri professi, sed esse naturalem Artemidorum" ("These two artists caused a dispute about their parentage, declaring that their putative father was Menecrates and their real father Artemidorus"[36.34]). Non-Plinian identifications of the subject include the lengthy description by Ulisse Aldrovandi (*Delle statue antiche*, reprinted in Lucio Mauro, *Le antichità della città di Roma* [Venice, 1557], 158–59) as "Hercole, e del toro Maratonio, che egli ammazzò" and by Vasari (*Vite*, ed. Milanesi, 7:224) as "Ercole, che sopra un monte teneva il toro per le corna." On the *Farnese Bull* and the history of naming its subject with and without Pliny, see Haskell and Penny, *Taste*, 165–67.

68. For Albertini, see R. Valentini and G. Zucchetti, eds., *Codice topografico della città di Roma* (Rome, 1953), 4:490; for Aldrovandi, see *Statue*, 129. On the problematics of the Pliny description, see *Histoire naturelle* 36.151.

69. It is generally doubted by modern archaeologists that this space was Rome's cattle market. See L. Richardson, Jr., *A New Topographical Dictionary of Ancient Rome* (Baltimore, 1992), 162–63. On this site and the *Hercules* found there, see also below in the present chapter.

70. For Albertini, see Valentini and Zucchetti, *Codice topografico*, 4:491; for Aldrovandi, see *Statue*, 273. The literary text that definitively places the worship of Hercules in the Forum Boarium is Propertius *Elegies* 4.9.

71. Aldrovandi, *Statue*, 129. For censuses of works in this category, see Bober and Rubinstein, *Renaissance Artists*, cat. 74, and Haskell and Penny, *Taste*, cat. 70. On the interrelations among such works in antiquity, see Pollitt, *Art in the Hellenistic Age*, 130–31. Aldrovandi does mention Pliny in this connection (see above, n. 68), but he refers to a different passage; he mentions a version of similar subject matter at *Statue*, 155.

72. See Bernardo Gamucci, *Libri quattro dell'antichità della città di Roma* (Venice, 1565), 199, reprinted in Brummer, *Statue Court*, 271: "misteriosamente l'ingegnoso architetto ha voluto inferire per li XVII figliuoli li XVII regni, che nell'Egitto ricevono dalle sue acque perpetuo nutrimento" (enigmatically the talented architect wished to signify with the seventeen children the seventeen kingdoms, which in Egypt receive perpetual nourishment from the river's waters).

73. The passage, N.H. 35.126, is discussed above in the present chapter. For the relief sculpture, see Bober and Rubinstein, *Renaissance Artists*, cat. 190. On this sculptural subject, see Otto Brendel, "Immolatio Boum," *Mitteilungen des deutschen archäologischen Instituts, römische Abteilung* 45 (1930): 196–226. As Elizabeth McGrath sensitively analyzes the matter ("Painted Decoration," 259–61), it becomes clear that only in Rubens's time was the heritage of this object joined with the question of painterly technique.

74. On the subject of Timanthes in art history and rhetoric, see above in the present chapter. For its use by Vasari and then Rubens, see McGrath, "Painted Decoration," 256–59.

75. For a discussion of this letter, see also above, Chap. 1.

76. "Quella fine e quel certo che, che ci mancava, non lo potevano mettere così presto in atto, avvenga che lo studio insecchisce la maniera, quando egli è preso per terminare i fini in quel modo. Bene lo trovaron poi dopo loro gli altri, nel veder cavar fuora di terra certe anticaglie citate da Plinio delle più famose; il Laocoonte, l'Ercole ed il Torso grosso di Belvedere; così la Venere, la Cleopatra, lo Apollo, ed infinite altre; le quali nella lor dolcezza e nelle lor asprezze, con termini carnosi e cavati dalle maggior bellezze del vivo, con certi atti che non in tutto si

storcono, ma si vanno in certe parti movendo, e si mostrano con una graziosissima grazia, e' furono cagione di levar via una certa maniera secca e cruda e tagliente" (Vasari, *Vite*, ed. Milanesi, 4:10; *Lives*, trans. deVere, 1:619). The larger implications of historical influence emerging from this passage are discussed below, in Chap. 5.

77. There is some possibility that the Hercules is the bronze statue from the Forum Boarium; more likely, however, Vasari means the *Hercules-Commodus*.

78. Even in this case, there are traditional (as well as modern) doubts that the Esquiline *Laocoön* is identical to the one that Pliny describes. See Haskell and Penny, *Taste*, 246.

79. Cited from Giovanni Bottari and Stefano Ticozzi, *Raccolta di lettere sulla pittura, scultura ed architettura* (Milan, 1822), 3:475–76. "Giovanangelo romano" is generally understood to be Gian Cristoforo Romano (1465[?]–1512), best known as a medalist who worked mostly in Milan and Mantua. At the time of the discovery of the *Laocoön*, however, he seems to have been in Rome, possibly acting as an agent for Isabella d'Este in the purchase of antiquities—which would lend him the authority that Trivulzio's letter suggests. See the editor's note at Vasari, *Vite*, ed. Milanesi, 2:650–51, and A. S. Norris, "Gian Cristoforo Romano: The Courtier as Medalist," *Studies in the History of Art* 21 (1987): 131–41.

80. *De Pictura*, ed. Grayson, par. 35.

81. When he goes on to say, "Parts of the 'historia' are the bodies, part of the body is the member, and part of the member is the surface" (par. 35), he is joining the two great strands of his argument—that is, optics and narrative.

82. This issue will arise in the career of Baccio Bandinelli, for which see below, Chap. 5.

83. The fullest treatments of this whole history, to which I am much indebted, are A. Michaelis, "Monte Cavallo," *Mitteilungen des deutschen archäologischen Instituts, römische Abteilung* 13 (1898): 248–74; and Tilmann Buddensieg, "Zum Statuenprogramm im Kapitolsplan Pauls III.," *Zeitschrift für Kunstgeschichte* 32 (1969): 177–228. See also Bober and Rubinstein, *Renaissance Artists*, 159–61; and Haskell and Penny, *Taste*, 136–41.

84. *Familiarium rerum liber*, 6.2., reprinted in Valentini and Zucchetti, *Codice topografico*, 4:9; translation is from *Letters on Familiar Matters*, trans. A. S. Bernardo (Baltimore, 1985), 1:293.

85. Adolf Furtwängler in 1893 is still attempting to designate one of them as a copy after Phidias and the other as the work of a different, and lesser, Praxiteles (*Masterpieces of Greek Sculpture* [London, 1895], 95–102).

86. Though a succession of writers from Poggio Bracciolini (*De varietate fortunae*, reprinted in Valentini and Zucchetti, *Codice topografico*, 4:241), to Aldrovandi (*Statue*, 310; cf. also Flavio Biondo, "Roma instaurata," 4:283, and Albertini, "Opusculum," 4:478, both in *Codice topografico*) proudly name Phidias and Praxiteles when identifying these figures, it is noteworthy that the ascriptions do not tend to infiltrate the various Pliny-inspired (or Pliny-plagiarized) histories of ancient art, including those by Ghiberti, the Anonimo Magliabecchiano, and G. B. Adriani, even when these do occasionally cite extant works in Rome as by famous masters from the High Classical age of Greece. (See Ghiberti, *Commentari*, ed. Schlosser, 1:14–15; *L'Anonimo Magliabecchiano*, ed. A. Ficarra [Florence, 1968], 8–9, 20–22; Adriani, in Vasari, *Vite*, ed. Milanesi, 1:57–59, 64–67.)

87. Valentini and Zucchetti, *Codice topografico*, 4:283.

88. Conte, *Genres and Readers*, 68.

89. "A literary text is a product whose interpretative destiny belongs to its own generative mechanism. Generating a text means activating a strategy that predicts the moves of others" (*The Rhetoric of Imitation: Genre and Poetic Memory in Virgil and Other Latin Poets*, trans. C. Segal [Ithaca,

1986], 30). Perhaps the best example of such a move in the Renaissance is the reinvented Plinian discourse employed by Francesco Colonna when describing the architectural and artistic dream landscape in the *Hypnerotomachia Poliphili*, which is populated by inventions that owe their origins to the aesthetic wonders described in the *Natural History* but also supersede them. See *Hypnerotomachia Poliphili*, ed. G. Pozzi and L. A. Ciapponi (Padua, 1980), 1:50–51; for a translation into modern Italian, see *Hypnerotomachia Poliphili*, ed. M. Ariani and M. Gabriele (Milan, 1998), 2:75–76.

90. It should be noted that Pliny is here describing Greek and not Latin usage. As Jacob Wackernagel (*Vorlesungen über Syntax, Erste Reihe* [Basel, 1926], 181) points out, both the aorist and the imperfect were, in fact, used. And Pliny's claim involving the imperfect was based on a misunderstanding of the distinction. In Wackernagel's formula, "wenn der Künstler das Imperfektum ἐποίει setzt, so erzählt er von seiner Arbeit; wenn den Aorist ποίησεν, so konstatiert er sie als Faktum." I am indebted to Professor Seth Benardete for this reference.

CHAPTER 3: FRAGMENTS

1. My thinking is stimulated by Philippe Lacoue-Labarthe and Jean-Luc Nancy, *The Literary Absolute* (Albany, 1988), esp. 39–78; for instance: "[The] very conception [of "the romantic organon"] is always given in fragments and therefore always, despite everything, as a sub-work. The organicity of the fragment also designates the fragmentation of the organon and, instead of a pure process of growth, the necessity of reconstituting as well as constituting organic individuality. The model—which perhaps never attains the status of a true model or prototype [Urbild]—remains here that of fragmented Antiquity, the landscape of ruins. The individual—Greek, Roman, romantic—must first be reconstructed" (48). On the moderns, see David Frisby's stimulating account in *Fragments of Modernity: Theories of Modernity in the Work of Simmel, Kracauer and Benjamin* (Cambridge, Mass., 1985). His emphasis on the urban scene—i.e., Berlin and Paris in the earlier twentieth century—as generative of fragment consciousness forms an interesting counterpart to early modern Rome as discussed here. On Romantics and pre-Romantics, see Marjorie Levinson, *The Romantic Fragment Poem: A Critique of a Form* (Chapel Hill, 1986); and Charles Rosen and Henri Zerner, *Romanticism and Realism: The Mythology of Nineteenth-Century Art* (New York, 1984), esp. 24–28.

2. Linda Nochlin, *The Body in Pieces: The Fragment as a Metaphor of Modernity* (London, 1994).

3. For a brief history of the collection, see Phyllis Bober and Ruth Rubinstein, *Renaissance Artists and Antique Sculpture* (London, 1986), 477. The image is II, fol. 48, in Heemskerck's Berlin Sketchbooks. The definitive edition is Christian Hülsen and Hermann Egger, *Die römischen Skizzenbücher von Marten van Heemskerck* (Berlin, 1913; rpt. 1975).

4. Ulisse Aldrovandi, *Delle statue antiche* (Venice, 1556), reprinted in Lucio Mauro, *Le antichità della città di Roma* (Venice, 1557), 181–82. The final statue described, with its "atto di gambe sforzato," is, in fact, one of the *Tyrannicides*, for which see below in the present chapter.

5. The story of the Colossus is to be found, with all suitable contempt, in Suetonius's *Life of Nero* 31; but Pliny's reference is probably decisive: "Having given sufficient proof of his artistic skill in Gaul, [Zenodorus] was summoned to Rome by Nero, and there made the colossal statue, 106 1/2 feet high, intended to represent that emperor but now, dedicated to the sun after the condemnation of that emperor's crimes, it is an object of awe" (*Natural History* 34.46, trans. H. Rackham, Loeb Classical Library [Cambridge, Mass., 1984]). For a summary of the medieval identifications, see the extremely helpful edition of Magister Gregorius, *The Marvels of Rome*, ed. J. Osborne (Toronto, 1987), 48–53. An excellent overview of the history of both head and hand

is to be found in Anna Cavallaro and Enrico Parlato, *Da Pisanello alla nascita dei Musei Capitolini* (Rome, 1988), 218–21.

6. On the development of this historical awareness, see below in the present chapter.

7. Gregorius, *Marvels*, 23.

8. Pliny N.H. 34.41; see above, Chap. 2, for a fuller discussion.

9. *Oxford Book of Medieval Latin Verse*, ed. F. J. E. Raby (Oxford, 1959), 220.

10. The expression appears on a Heemskerck drawing, II, fol. 87v and on one of the title pages of Sebastiano Serlio's *Sette libri dell'architettura* (Paris, 1547). The lines have been sensitively analyzed by Salvatore Settis, "Continuità, distanza, conoscenza: Tre usi dell'antico," in *Memoria dell'antico nell'arte italiana* (Turin, 1986), 3:375–78. See also Nicole Dacos, *Roma quanta fuit: Tre pittori fiamminghi nella Domus Aurea* (Rome, 1995), esp. 5–13. One of the most eloquent Renaissance statements of this principle is found in the *Hypnerotomachia Poliphili* of Francesco Colonna: "Si gli fragmenti dilla sancta antiquitate et rupture et ruinamento et quodammodo le scobe ne ducono in stupenda admiratione et ad tanto oblectamento di mirarle, quanto farebbe la sua integritate" (*Hypnerotomachia Poliphili*, ed. G. Pozzi and L. A. Ciapponi [Padua, 1980], 1:51; "If the fragments of sacred antiquity, the ruins, their crumblings, and even their splinters lead us to stupefied wonderment and, in contemplating them, into pleasure, what would have happened if they were whole?")

11. I discuss this notion of exponential similes in epic literature and relate it to the rhetorical trope of transumption in my *Transuming Passion: Ganymede and the Erotics of Humanism* (Stanford, 1991), 44–45.

12. See above, Chap. 1.

13. On the history of these statues and their various identifications, see Adolf Michaelis, "Monte Cavallo," *Mitteilungen des deutschen archäologischen Instituts, römische Abteilung* 13 (1898): 248–74; and Tilmann Buddensieg, "Zum Statuenprogramm im Kapitolsplan Pauls III," *Zeitschrift für Kunstgeschichte* 32 (1969): 177–228. See also Francis Haskell and Nicholas Penny, *Taste and the Antique* (New Haven, 1981), 136–41; Gregorius, *Marvels*, 59–60; and Bober and Rubinstein, *Renaissance Artists*, 159–61. For Petrarch's view, see above, Chap. 2.

14. Gregorius, *Marvels*, 23.

15. "I chafarell an una sisa nuda/che p[er] straccheze tien so capo chino/fero io del pentir piu dur de giuda." The text of Prospettivo Milanese is to be found in D. Fienga, "The *Antiquarie Prospettiche romane composte per Prospectivo Melanese Depictore*: A Document for the Study of the Relationship between Bramante and Leonardo da Vinci," Ph.D. diss., University of California, Los Angeles, 1970, st. 23.

16. On the *Marforio*, see Haskell and Penny, *Taste*, 258–59; and Bober and Rubinstein, *Renaissance Artists*, 99–101. For the story of how Jupiter protected the Romans from a Gaulish siege by arranging for the milling of grain and baking of bread, see Livy *History of Rome* 5.48–51, and Ovid *Fasti* 6.349–94. For Biondo's discussion of the idea, see his *Roma instaurata*, 3:56, reprinted in R. Valentini and G. Zucchetti, eds., *Codice topografico della città di Roma* (Rome, 1953), 4:312.

17. In regard to the colossal head, Flavio Biondo is the first to assign the historical name of Commodus, which he identifies by reference to ancient coins, though he suggests that the colossus had been a representation of Nero until Commodus removed the original head and substituted his own (*Roma instaurata*, 3:7, reprinted in Valentini and Zucchetti, *Codice topografico*, 4:311). See also H. Stuart Jones, *A Catalogue of Ancient Sculptures in the Municipal Collections of Rome* (Oxford, 1926), 2:171, 173–75; and Wolfgang Helbig, *Führer durch die öffentlichen Sammlungen klassischer Altertümer in Rom* (Tübingen, 1963–72), cat. 1578. On related readings of Commodus

as interposer of his own form, see below in the present chapter. As for the equestrian statue, medieval readings include one historical figure, the Christian emperor Constantine, but also various legendary Roman republican heroes. The modern identification of the figure as Marcus Aurelius appears first at the end of the fifteenth century in the work by Bartolommeo Platina (*Liber de vita Christi ac omnium pontificum*, ed. G. Gayda, in L. A. Muratori, *Rerum italicarum scriptores*, 3:1 [Città di Castello, 1913–32], 418), but other learned identifications from the same period included Septimus Severus, Commodus, and Antoninus Pius. See Roberto Weiss, *The Renaissance Discovery of Classical Antiquity* (Oxford, 1969), 80; Haskell and Penny, *Taste*, 252–55; and Bober and Rubinstein, *Renaissance Artists*, 175–77.

18. On the River Gods, see Fulvio, *Antiquitates urbis* (Rome, 1527), 31, 36, the latter passage reprinted in Hans Henrik Brummer, *The Statue Court in the Vatican Belvedere* (Stockholm, 1970), 267. The passage on the *Captives* is at 4:67v, and the comparison of the face on the equestrian statue to coins depicting Marcus Aurelius and Lucius Verus is at 4:79v.

19. These examples are drawn from Haskell and Penny, *Taste*, cats. 50, 68, 71.

20. *Lorenzo Ghibertis Denkwürdigkeiten (I commentari)*, ed. Julius von Schlosser (Berlin, 1912). On the Palladium: "una figura d'uno giouane aueua in mano uno coltello, era con uno piede quasi ginocchioni in su un'altare e·lla gamba dextra era a·ssede insull'altare et posaua il piè in terra el quale scorciaua con tanta arte et con tanto maesterio, era cosa marauigliosa a uederlo. Et nella mano sinistra aueua un pannicello el quale teneua con esso uno idoletto; pareua el giouane il minacciasse col coltello" (the figure of a young man who has in his hand a knife, almost kneeling upward on an altar; his right leg was placed on the altar, and his other foot on the ground was foreshortened with such artfulness and mastery that it was a marvelous thing to behold. In his left hand he had a piece of cloth in which he held a small idol. It seemed as though the young man was threatening it with a knife [1:64]). On the Marsyas, "Le figure erano in detta cornuola uno vechio a sedere in su uno scoglio era una pelle di leone e legato colle mani drieto a uno albero secco, a piedi di lui v'era uno infans ginochioni coll'uno piè e guardava uno giovane il quale aveva nella mano destra una carta et nella sinistra una citera, pareva lo infans addimandasse doctrina al giovane. Queste tre figure furon fatte per la nostra età. Furono certamente o di mano di Pirgotile o di Policreto: perfette erano quanto cose vedessi mai celate in cavo" (The figures in that carnelian were an old man sitting up on a rock with a lion skin and tied with his hands behind his back to a dead tree; at his feet there was a child kneeling on one knee looking at a young man who has in his right hand a paper and in his left a lyre; it seemed that the child was asking to be taught by the young man. These three figures were made to signify the ages of man. They were certainly by the hand of either Pyrgoteles or Polycretus: they were as perfect as anything I have ever seen carved in hollow relief [1:47]). For more discussion of Ghiberti in relation to antiquities, see below, Chap. 4.

21. For Nicola, see Giorgio Vasari, *Le vite de' più eccellenti pittori, scultori ed architettori*, ed. G. Milanesi (Florence, 1906), 1:293–95. Giovannantonio Dosio, in his Berlin Sketchbook (ca. 1560, fol. 48), reproduces a Campo Santo sarcophagus of Pentheus with the inscription "it is thought to be the death of Orpheus" (Bober and Rubinstein, *Renaissance Artists*, 121), where the iconography is drawn from the *Bacchae* rather than from the *Metamorphoses*. A similar problem arises with a Medea sarcophagus (Bober and Rubinstein, *Renaissance Arts*, cat. 110; see also Nicole Dacos, *Le logge di Raffaello* [Rome, 1986], 207–8), where a more familiar Ovidian text concerning Minos and the Cecropides takes precedence over the actual source, though in this instance Pirro Ligorio does make the correct identification.

22. See, e.g., John Onians, *Art and Thought in the Hellenistic Age* (London, 1979); J. J. Pollitt, *Art in the Hellenistic Age* (Cambridge, Eng., 1986); Glenn W. Bowersock, *Hellenism in Late Antiquity* (Ann

Arbor, 1990); and Peter Brown, *The World of Late Antiquity* (New York, 1971).

23. Otto Brendel's *Prolegomena to a Book on Roman Art* first appears in *Memoirs of the American Academy in Rome* 21 (1953): 9–73, and is then published, along with another essay, as *Prolegomena to the Study of Roman Art* (New Haven, 1979). His brilliant summary of the historiography of his subject focuses on the nineteenth-century development of a cultural, or even racial, understanding of what it meant to be Roman. Landmark studies in this tradition include F. Wickhoff, *Der Wiener Genesis* (Vienna, 1895), and Alois Riegl, *Die spätrömische Kunstindustrie* (Vienna, 1927).

24. *Aeneid* 6.847–53.

25. See the passages from Livy's *History* (e.g., 25.40.1–3, 26.34.12, 34.52.4–5) and Plutarch's *Lives* (e.g., *Life of Marcellus* 21; *Life of Aemilius Paullus* 32–33), reprinted in J. J. Pollitt, *The Art of Rome: Sources and Documents* (Cambridge, Eng., 1983), 32–33, 42–44.

26. See Cicero *Verrine Orations* 2.4.; sections are reprinted in Pollitt, *Rome*, 66–73.

27. Of course, one of the most persistent contemporary (and later) claims about this art is that it is decontextualized to begin with—that is, so given over to crass ostentation that it is, as one might say, always already lacking in any authentic or indigenous identity. See, for instance, the descriptions of massive and disorderly luxury in Athenaeus's account of festivals and processions at the court of Ptolemy II (*Deipnosophistae* 196a–209e; reprinted in Pollitt, *Rome*, 34–40).

28. See the valuable overview in Richard Brilliant, *Roman Art from the Republic to Constantine* (London, 1974), 85–128. In my understanding of this artistic culture, I am especially indebted to a lecture by Ann Kuttner at the Institute of Fine Arts of New York University in 1996.

29. Josephus, *History of the Jewish War* 7.5.148, reprinted in Pollitt, *Rome*, 159.

30. Flavio Biondo, *Roma triumphans*, trans. L. Mauro (Venice, 1544), 10; cited in Bober and Rubinstein, *Renaissance Artists*, 204.

31. The text is a letter that Chrysoloras wrote back to Constantinople, cited extensively in Baxandall, *Giotto and the Orators* (Oxford, 1971), 80–81 (translation) and 149–50 (original). See Baxandall's complex and nuanced argument about the ekphrasis of what he calls "generalized enumeration" and the influence of Aristotelean notions of visual pleasure.

32. There are, of course, exceptions, notably statues of the gods that were located in centers where they were worshiped. Perhaps the best documented example is the Bronze Hercules (Bober and Rubinstein, *Renaissance Artists*, cat. 129), which originally formed part of the Ara Maxima in the Forum Boarium, where there was a considerable representation of the Hercules cult; as mentioned above, it was documented on that location in Pliny (N.H. 34.33), but that connection does not seem to have been made when the statue was unearthed at the end of the fifteenth century.

33. There are notable parallels to the way Napoleon caused the antiquities to be experienced when they were removed to France; see above, Chap. 1, n. 6.

34. On spolia, see above, Chap. 1, n. 57.

35. See, e.g., *Spätrömische Kunstindustrie*, 7–8, 45–47.

36. On these tendencies, see Brilliant, *Roman Art*, 165–95; on the lives of ordinary people, see Diana E. E. Kleiner, *Roman Sculpture* (New Haven, 1992), 303–4.

37. The analysis appears in J. W. Crous, "Florentiner Waffenpfeiler und Armilustrium," *Mitteilungen des deutschen archäologischen Instituts, römische Abteilung* 48 (1933): 1–119. See also Rudolf Wittkower, "Hieroglyphics in the Early Renaissance," in *Allegory and the Migration of Symbols* (London, 1977), 113–28.

38. For the Aspertini drawing after the trophy pillars, see Codex Wolfegg, 38v–39, for which see Gunter Schweikhart, *Der Codex Wolfegg* (London, 1986), 91–92; for Raphael quoting the same work, see the throne in the tapestry cartoon *Conversion of the Proconsul* (London, Victoria & Albert). Mantegna loosely imitates the sacrificial frieze on a triumphal arch in *Triumph of Caesar*

IX (Hampton Court), while Heemskerck closely copies segments of the frieze in his Berlin Sketchbook, I. fol. 21.

39. Alberti, *On the Art of Building in Ten Books*, 8:4., trans. J. Rykwert, N. Leach, and R. Tavernor (Cambridge, Mass., 1988), 256.

40. For the *Hypnerotomachia*, see the edition by Pozzi and Ciapponi. The design appears at 1:33; in their notes (2:69), they question the traditional idea that the Capitoline frieze is its source. For Flavio Biondo, see *Roma triumphans*, 25.

41. On the history of the *Trophies*, see Giovanni Tedeschi Grisanti, "*I trofei di Mario*": *Il ninfeo dell'Acqua Giulia sull'Esquilino* (Rome, 1977); Schweikhart, *Codex Wolfegg*, 58–59; and Gilbert Charles-Picard, *Les trophées romains* (Paris, 1957), esp. 148–63. Unmentioned among these treatments is the extraordinary quotation of the *Trophies* by Filippino Lippi in his *Saint Philip Exorcizing the Dragon* in the Strozzi Chapel of Santa Maria Novella.

42. On this identification, see, e.g., Nikolaus Muffel, "Beschreibung der Stadt Rom," in Valentini and Zucchetti, *Codice topografico*, 4:364: "die zwen abtgotter di man den gensen gemacht hat di Rom behielten, do man eingrub under dem Capitolium" (the two effigies erected in honor of the geese that saved Rome when they burrowed under the Capitol); and Giovanni Rucellai, "Della bellezza e anticaglia di Roma" (ibid., 4:414): "L'archo trionphale di Mario, dove sono due figure di marmi che si chiamano l'oche armate" (the triumphal arch of Marius, where there are two marble figures that are called the armed geese).

43. On the whole range of drawings after the *Trophies*, see Schweikhart, *Codex Wolfegg*, 58–59; and Tedeschi Grisanti, *Trofei*, 49–60.

44. The classic origin for these historically transferred expressions is Wilhelm Klein, *Vom antiken Rokoko* (Vienna, 1921). For more recent overviews of these stylistic designations, see Margarete Bieber, *The Sculpture of the Hellenistic Age* (New York, 1961), 123–56; and Pollitt, *Hellenistic Age*, 127–63.

45. See Pollitt's witty investigation of the problem: "Geese were kept in antiquity, and hence it is possible that the chubby enthusiastic child [wrestling with a goose] was looked upon with the same affectionate, sentimental warmheartedness that would be applied directly today to the picture of a freckle-faced boy and his dogs in an advertisement for dog-biscuits" (*Hellenistic Age*, 128).

46. Both the text and the exact identification of Boethos are highly disputed, for which see *Histoire naturelle*, ed. H. Le Bonniec, H. Gallet de Santerre (Paris, 1953), 34:267–69; but the work is widely known and appears in many copies. (In this case the Latin text, which appears at N.H. 34.84, is cited from that edition; translation is my own.) For Renaissance reflections on this subject, see Erna Mandowsky and Charles Mitchell, *Pirro Ligorio's Roman Antiquities* (London, 1963), 84–85.

47. On these important works, see Corrado Ricci, "Marmi ravennati erratici," *Ausonia* 4 (1909): 247–89; Lucio Gargan, *Cultura e arte nel Veneto al tempo di Petrarca* (Padua, 1978), 42–43; and André Chastel, "Di mano dell'antico Prassitele," in his *Fables, formes, figures* (Paris, 1978), 2:9–16.

48. Colonna, *Hypnerotomachia*, ed. Pozzi and Ciapponi, 1.44. The "ravennata cochlea" presumably refers to the conch shells that form part of Neptune's attributes.

49. See Chastel's brief but highly enlightening treatment of the revival of the putto from Donatello's *cantoria* in the Duomo in Florence to Titian's *Saint Peter Martyr* ("Di mano dell'antico Prassitele," 2:12–15).

50. See, e.g., the program of the Loggia di Psiche in the Villa Farnesina, designed by Raphael and executed by Giulio and other assistants, ca. 1518–19.

51. See above, Chap. 2, as well as Baxandall's discussion of these rhetorical issues (*Giotto*, 18–20).

No version of the *Discobolus* was found before the end of the eighteenth century; thus, for all its fame both in antiquity and in modern times, it was not known in its material form during the Renaissance. See Haskell and Penny, *Taste*, 199–202.

52. See John Shearman, *Mannerism* (Baltimore, 1967), 81–91, and, esp., David Summers, "*Maniera* and Movement: The *Figura Serpentinata*," *Art Quarterly* 35 (1972): 269–301. The Lomazzo discussion is found in his *Trattato dell'arte della pittura* (Milan, 1584), 22–24.

53. Bober and Rubinstein, *Renaissance Artists*, cats. 61, 20, 18. For additional background on this group of works, see Reinhard Lullies, *Die kauernde Aphrodite* (Munich, 1954); Bieber, *Sculpture*, 82–83; and Selma Holo, "A Note on the Afterlife of the Crouching Aphrodite in the Renaissance," *J. Paul Getty Museum Journal* 6–7 (1978–79): 23–36.

54. Fienga, "Prospectivo Melanese," st. 23.

55. See H. Beck and D. Blume, eds., *Natur und Antike in der Renaissance* (Frankfurt, 1985), cats. 193–95, including bronzes by Severo da Ravenna or from his studio.

56. See Wilhelm Klein, "Die Aufforderung zum Tanz—eine wiedergewonnene Gruppe des antiken Rokoko," *Zeitschrift für bildende Kunst* 20 (1909): 101–8. On the *Faun*, see Haskell and Penny, *Taste*, 205–08.

57. See *Natur und Antike*, 487, in reference to a Severo da Ravenna bronze miniature, "Gestus und Blickrichtung dieses Exemplares lassen daran denken, daß es ursprünglich eine Figur gab, auf die sie bezog. Vielleicht hat es sich dabei um einen Satyr gehandelt."

58. The crux and the history of responses, both on a textual level and in regard to constituting a history of art objects, provides a fascinating study in itself of all the problematics involved in chronicling the distant past. Although some scholars remain true to the idea that there was a Doidalsas who sculpted the *Crouching Aphrodite* (e.g., *Storia naturale*, 5.585), the suggestion that he is simply a philological coinage, which seems to originate with Andreas Linfert ("Der Meister der 'Kauernden Aphrodite,'" *Mitteilungen der deutschen archäologischen Instituts, athenische Abteilung* 84 [1969]: 158–64), is generally accepted nowadays. What is most striking is the quantity of construction built on the hypothesis of his existence—style, nationality, related works, even, as one article's title signals, "La personalità di Doidalses di Bitinia" (Luciano Laurenzi, in *Annuario della scuola archeologica di Atene* 24–26 [1946–48]: 167–79). Bieber (*Sculpture*, 83) reports that the artist "undoubtedly agreed with the taste of his patron, who may have had some Oriental blood or inclination for sensuous and voluptuous forms in women." Also remarkable is the extent of uncertainty that accompanies the textual crux: to doubt that there is a Doidalsas in Pliny is to revise not only the authorship of the *Crouching Venus* but also its very existence, at least insofar as it is mentioned in the *Natural History*. The fullest and most measured treatment of the crux is Brunilde Sismondo Ridgway, *Hellenistic Sculpture I* (Madison, 1990), 230–32.

59. On this work, a funerary relief now in the British Museum but located at the church of Santa Trinità dei Monti from the Middle Ages, see Bober and Rubinstein, *Renaissance Artists*, cat. 19.

60. Ridgway, *Hellenistic Sculpture*, 231.

61. Aldrovandi (*Statue*, 130) is speaking of the Cesi collection: "una Leda ignuda, ch'esce dal bagno, e con la man sinistra tien la sua camicia, con la destra un pomo" (a nude Leda arising from her bath who holds her blouse in her left hand and an apple in her right hand). On the seventeenth-century drawing of sculpture at Whitehall that declares this work to be "elena di troia," see D. Chambers and J. Martineau, *Splendours of the Gonzaga* (Milan, 1981), cat. 246. See *Natur und Antike*, cats. 114, 115, 121, for bronze miniature reconstructions of the figure with varying attributes in the hand.

62. See, e.g., Bieber, *Sculpture*, 83, figs. 294–95. Bober and Rubinstein (*Renaissance Artists*, 63) in their

catalogue of other *Crouching Venuses* known in the Renaissance include a Prado version of the statue "with back and arms raised to hair." But these parts of the statue prove to have been modern restorations, for which see A. H. Allison, "Antique Sources of Leonardo's *Leda*," *Art Bulletin* 56 (1974): 375–84.

63. For a full account of this image, which Nicole Dacos attributes to Perino del Vaga, as well as its relations to the classical prototype and to other Renaissance designs, see her *Logge*, 197–99.

64. The Heemskerck *Nymph Binding* drawing is I, fol. 25v, in the Berlin sketchbook (for notes, see Hülsen and Egger, *Skizzenbücher*, 2:15; cf. another triple Heemskerck drawing in the next note). Other multiple sights of a single statue include the triple Marsyas (again in three different states of completeness as drawings, as well as three different points of view) in the Teylers Museum, for which see Bober and Rubinstein, *Renaissance Artists*, cat. 32b; and the double *Spinario* in the Holkham Album, fol. 34v, as part of a sheet with five different drawings after sculpture, for which see Annegrit Schmitt, "Römische Antikensammlungen im Spiegel eines Musterbuchs der Renaissance," *Münchener Jahrbuch der bildenden Kunst* 21 (1970), fig. 20. A triple *Torso Belvedere* in Christ Church is discussed below in the present chapter. The Fogg drawing, credited to Fra Bartolommeo, was published as cat. 20 in *Italian Drawings, 1330–1780*, ed. Ruth Kennedy, Smith College Museum of Art (Northampton, Mass., 1941); it is also cat. 43 in Wendy Stedman Sheard, *Antiquity in the Renaissance* (Northampton, Mass., 1978).

65. See the very illuminating discussion of these questions in Leatrice Mendelsohn, *Paragoni: Benedetto Varchi's Due Lezzioni and Cinquecento Art Theory* (Ann Arbor, 1982), 150–52, 287–88. The Heemskerck three-angled version of the *Crouching Venus* (Berlin Sketchbook, I, fol. 6v) employs a variety of cross-hatchings to suggest different distances from the observer, indicating how the image is to be understood as a single viewing experience. I am indebted to a stimulating talk by Rona Goffen at the Institute of Fine Arts, New York University, on related questions of painting versus sculpture; Professor Goffen focused not on the inferiority of two dimensions but on their superiority as offering the possibility of multiple points of view.

66. On these qualities in the drawing, see Kennedy, *Italian Drawings*, cat. 20, and Sheard, *Antiquity*, cat. 43. On the fleshliness of the original statue, which separates it from other representations of Aphrodite, see Ridgway, *Hellenistic Sculpture*, 231; and Pollitt, *Hellenistic Age*, 56–57.

67. On the postclassical history of the Arrotino in general, see Haskell and Penny, *Taste*, 154–57; and Bober and Rubinstein, *Renaissance Artists*, 75–76.

68. On the reconstructing of the group, see Pollitt, *Hellenistic Age*, 118–19; Bieber, *Sculpture*, 111; and Brunilde Ridgway, *The Severe Style in Greek Sculpture* (Princeton, 1970), 85–86.

69. Giovanni Gaye, *Carteggio inedito d'artisti dei secoli XIV, XV, XVI* (Florence, 1839), 3:240.

70. For the Donatello, see Vasari, *Vite*, ed. Milanesi, 2:407. The Verrocchio reference is to be found at 3:366: "Cosimo de' Medici . . . aveva . . . fatto porre un bellissimo Marsia di marmo bianco, impiccato a un tronco per dovere essere scorticato: perchè volendo Lorenzo suo nipote, al quale era venuto alle mani un torso con la testa d'un altro Marsia, antichissimo, e molto più bello che l'altro, e di pietra rossa, accompagnarlo col primo; non poteva ciò fare, essendo imperfettissimo. Onde datolo a finire ed acconciare ad Andrea [Verrocchio], egli fece le gambe, le cosce e le braccia che mancavano a questa figura, di pezzi di marmo rosso, tanto bene, che Lorenzo ne rimase sodisfattissimo, e la fece porre dirimpetto all'altra, dall'altra banda della porta. Il quale torso antico, fatto per un Marsia scorticato, fu con tale avvertenza e giudizio lavorato, che alcune vene bianche e sottili, che erano nella pietra rossa, vennero intagliate dall'artefice in luogo appunto che paiono alcuni piccoli nerbici che nelle figure naturali, quando sono scorticate, si veggiono. Il che doveva far parere quell'opera, quando aveva il suo primiero pulimento, cosa vivissima." Translated in *Lives*, deVere, 1:553: "Cosimo de' Medici . . . had caused to be set up . . . a very

beautiful Marsyas of white marble, bound to a tree-trunk and ready to be flayed; and his grandson Lorenzo, into whose hands there had come the torso and head of another Marsyas, made of red stone, very ancient, and much more beautiful than the first, wished to set it beside the other, but could not, because it was so imperfect. Thereupon he gave it to Andrea to be restored and completed, and he made the legs, thighs, and arms that were lacking in this figure out of pieces of red marble, so well that Lorenzo was highly satisfied and had it placed opposite to the other, on the other side of the door. This ancient torso, made to represent a flayed Marsyas, was wrought with such care and judgment that certain delicate white veins, which were in the red stone, were carved by the craftsman exactly in the right places, so as to appear to be little nerves, such as are seen in real bodies when they have been flayed; which must have given to that work, when it had its original finish, a most lifelike appearance." The passage offers a fascinating glimpse into the way in which antique sculpture was viewed as an interlocking triumph of art and nature.

71. The story of Attius Navius is found at Livy *History* 1.36; Pliny (N.H. 34.22) mentions the statue as among the very earliest pieces of sculpture to be found in Rome. On Marcus Manlius and the geese, see Livy 5.47. The same story is discussed above, in the present chapter, in connection with the *Trophies of Marius*.

72. On these drawings after the *Arrotino*, see Dacos, *Logge*, 164; and H. Egger, *Codex Escurialensis: Ein Skizzenbuch aus der Werkstatt Domenico Ghirlandaios* (Vienna, 1905), 25. See also the priest slaughtering a ram in front of *Noah's Sacrifice* in the Vatican Logge (Dacos, *Logge*, 164).

73. On the various narrative identifications of the figure, see Gunter Schweikhart, "Von Priapus zu Coridon: Benennungen des Dornausziehers in Mittelalter und Neuzeit," *Würzburger Jahrbuch für Altertumswissenschaft* 3 (1977): 243–52. For an excellent account of the statue in its own historical terms, see Werner Fuchs, in Helbig, *Führer*, 2:266–68; see also Paul Zanker, *Klassizistische Statuen: Studien zur Veränderung des Kunstgeschmacks in der römischen Kaiserzeit* (Mainz, 1974), 71–74. On the postclassical fortunes of the work, in addition to Bober and Rubinstein, *Renaissance Artists*, 235–36, and Haskell and Penny, *Taste*, 308–10, see Richard Cocke, "Masaccio and the Spinario, Piero and the Pothos: Observations on the Reception of the Antique in Renaissance Painting," *Zeitschrift für Kunstgeschichte* 43 (1980): 21–32; W. S. Heckscher, "Dornauszieher," in *Reallexicon zur deutschen Kunstgeschichte* (Stuttgart, 1958), 4:289–99; and Arnold von Salis, *Antike und Renaissance: Über Nachleben und Weiterwirken der alten in der neueren Kunst* (Zurich, 1947), 124–34.

74. For interesting discussions of these questions in taste, see Ridgway, *Hellenistic Sculpture*, 338; and Pollitt, *Hellenistic Age*, 142–44. Inevitably, hypotheses about the reasons for certain kinds of representation depend on hypotheses about the dating of individual objects, so that there is a considerable possibility of tautological arguments. On children in these forms of representation, see Ridgway, 338–40.

75. See von Salis, *Antike*, 132.

76. On the question of the head, see Helbig, *Führer*, 2:266. It is worth noting that the hair does not lie in a logical gravitational position relative to the direction in which the boy is leaning.

77. On the proliferation of Renaissance *Spinarios*, see von Salis, *Antike*, 252–54, as well as Heckscher, "Dornauszieher." The discussion about the height at which the statue was displayed is generally based on the viewpoints in various drawings. It is not always noted that drawings are problematic as documents, since artists may be enjoying the freedom to conceive of the work in some imaginary position.

78. E.g., from Cossa's *Miracle of Saint Hyacinth* in the Vatican Pinacoteca to Luini's *Bathing Nymph* in the Brera.

79. The Holkham drawing is on the same sheet as our fig. 3.18. The Gossaert drawing is in the Print

Room at the Rijksuniversiteit in Leiden (published in H. Pauwels et al., *Jan Gossaert genaamd Mabuse* [Rotterdam, 1965], cat. 45). For the Heemskerck drawing, see Bober and Rubinstein, *Renaissance Artists*, cat. 203a.

80. For Magister Gregorius, see *Marvels*, 23. As for the Gonzaga story, in 1499 Isabella d'Este had requested from the bronze sculptor Pier Jacopo Alari-Bonacolsi (called "Antico") a pendant to a version of the *Spinario* that he had already provided for her. It is not clear from the correspondence precisely what form this pendant would take, nor is there an extant work that can be definitely linked to the request. But a female satyr in the posture of a Thornpuller, currently in the Copenhagen Statens Museum for Kunst (I.N. 5530), published as cat. 52 of *Natur und Antike*, may signal the possibility that Isabella was interested in *Spinarios* of both genders—which would add a further refinement to the erotic qualities of the statue. Whatever the form of the pendant, it is clear from Ludovico's correspondence that the work in question created something of a sexy sensation. See also U. Rossi, "I Medaglisti del Rinascimento alla corte di Mantova," *Rivista italiana di numismatica* 1 (1888): 176–77. On this collecting milieu, see C. Malcolm Brown, "'Lo Insaciabile Desiderio Nostro de Cose Antique': New Documents on Isabella D'Este's Collection of Antiquities," in C. H. Clough, ed., *Cultural Aspects of the Italian Renaissance: Essays in Honour of Paul Oskar Kristeller* (Manchester, 1976): 325–53.

81. The principal sources on the contest are Ghiberti's *Commentari* (ed. Schlosser, 1:45–46); the *Life of Brunelleschi* generally ascribed to Antonio di Tuccio Manetti and written sometime between 1471 and 1497 (the appropriate section is reprinted in English in E. G. Holt, *A Documentary History of Art* (Garden City, N.Y., 1958), 1:173–76); the so-called Anonimo Magliabecchiano, datable to some time in the first half of the sixteenth century (ed. A. Ficarra [Florence, 1968], 76–77); and Vasari's lives of Brunelleschi and Ghiberti (*Vite*, ed. Milanesi, 2:223–27, 2:334–36). Krautheimer's account of the history and the documents (*Lorenzo Ghiberti* [Princeton, 1956], 33–49, 281–83) remains definitive.

82. "Brunelleschi, as a rule, sees the forms of antiquity through an overlay of medieval transpositions" (Krautheimer, *Ghiberti*, 281).

83. "La storia di Filippo nella quale aveva figurato un Abraam che sacrifica Isac; ed in quella un servo, che mentre aspetta Abraam e che l'asino pasce, si cava una spina di un piede; che merita lode assai" (Vasari, *Vite*, ed. Milanesi, 2:335; *Lives*, trans. deVere, 1:350).

84. On the connections between these images and the *Spinario*, see Colin Eisler, "The Athlete of Virtue: The Iconography of Asceticism," in *De Artibus Opuscula XL: Essays in Honor of Erwin Panofsky*, ed. M. Meiss (New York, 1961), 82–97; and Carol F. Lewine, *The Sistine Chapel Walls and the Roman Liturgy* (University Park, Penn., 1993), 91–92. Both of these discussions, and particularly the latter one, focus on iconographical connections between the statue and the presumed content of the Sistine paintings.

85. On the Signorelli tondi in relation to Michelangelo, see Charles de Tolnay, *The Youth of Michelangelo* (Princeton, 1969), 110, 165.

86. On the *Doni Tondo* and its connections to ancient sculpture (but including no discussion of the Signorelli or *Spinario* connections), see Antonio Natali, "Dating the *Doni Tondo* through Antique Sculpture and Sacred Texts," in Pierre Théberge, ed., *The Genius of the Sculptor in Michelangelo's Work* (Montreal, 1992), 307–21. For one rather ingenious attempt to read the enigma of the nudes in relation to Signorelli, see M. L. D'Ancona, "The *Doni Madonna* by Michelangelo," *Art Bulletin* 50 (1968): 43–50; see also Robert S. Liebert, *Michelangelo: A Psychoanalytic Study of his Life and Images* (New Haven, 1983), 74–95.

87. Vasari, *Vite*, ed. Milanesi, 7:159; *Lives*, trans. deVere, 2:656.

88. *The English Auden*, ed. E. Mendelson (New York, 1977), 237.

89. See, e.g., Paul Zanker, *The Power of Images in the Age of Augustus* (Ann Arbor, 1988), 230–38; and Kleiner, *Roman Sculpture*, 280–83.

90. See Max Wegner, *Die Herrscherbildnisse in antoninischer Zeit* (Berlin, 1939), 222; and Helbig, *Führer*, 1:186.

91. This is one of the few works which, like the *Laocoön*, has a specific discovery time and place— i.e., the Campo de' Fiori on 15 May 1507—as the Negroponte letter establishes. The text is cited from Rodolfo Lanciani, *Storia degli scavi di Roma* (Rome, 1989), 1:189. Judging from a drawing in the "Maarten de Vos" sketchbook, which includes both a front view and a side view, the figure lacked the right arm prior to its restoration but retained the lion skin and the baby. See M. M. L. Netto-Bol, *The So-Called Maarten de Vos Sketchbook of Drawings after the Antique* (The Hague, 1976), 26–27. On various early attempts to determine which episode in Hercules' life is depicted, see Haskell and Penny, *Taste*, 188–89.

92. On this interesting personage, see John F. D'Amico, *Renaissance Humanism in Papal Rome* (Baltimore, 1983), 36, 134; and Fabrizio Cruciani, "Il teatro dei Ciceroniani," *Forum italicum* 14 (1980): 356–77. The sobriquet of "Fedra" becomes even more charged after Inghirami's death, when Jacopo Sadoleto includes him as a speaker in a section of his dialogue *De laudibus philosophiae* entitled "Phaedra." See D'Amico, 185–86.

93. For Albertini, see Valentini and Zucchetti, *Codice topografico*, 4:491. For the account books, see James Ackerman, *The Cortile del Belvedere* (Vatican City, 1954), docs. 34a, 34b. On Commodus's habits of impersonation, see Dio Cassius (*Roman History* 72.22.3) and the *Historia Augusta* 9.2.; both are in Pollitt, *Art of Rome*, 185–86. It is not clear when the idea that this was an imperson- ation dropped out of favor, but in Helbig's guidebook (*Führer*, 1:243) the possibility does not even merit a mention.

94. "Nec obmittam aliam statuam paulo post inventam apud campum Florae, a plebe Hercules cum puero vocatam, quam tua Sanctitas in aedibus palatinis collocavit apud ianuam porticus super viridarium, cum epitaphio: PROCVL ESTE PROPHANI" (Albertini, in Valentini and Zucchetti, *Codice topografico*, 4:491). The phrase is spoken by the Cumaean Sibyl at *Aeneid* 6.258, where it signals the approach to divinity. Brummer (*Statue Court*, 232–41) makes the conjunction of Hercules and this inscription into the centerpiece of an argument for the Belvedere as a sacred garden, specifically alluding to the Hesperides. See also Ackerman, *Cortile*, and Ernst Gombrich, "Hypnerotomachiana," in *Symbolic Images: Studies in the Art of the Renaissance* (London, 1972), 102–8.

95. See the *Achilleid* 1.874. For examples on sarcophagi, see Hellmut Sichtermann and Guntram Koch, *Griechische Mythen auf römischen Sarkophagen* (Tübingen, 1975), cats. 1–3; and Anna Marguerite McCann, *Roman Sarcophagi in the Metropolitan Museum of Art* (New York, 1978), cat. 9.

96. See, e.g., Sichtermann and Koch, *Griechische Mythen*, cats. 1, 2.

97. Philostratus the Younger, *Imagines*, trans. Arthur Fairbanks, Loeb Classical Library (London, 1931), 289.

98. For the original, see H. Dessau, "Römische Reliefs beschrieben von Pirro Ligorio," *Sitzungsbericht der Berliner Akademie* 40 (1883): 1093.

99. Aby Warburg, *Ausgewählte Schriften und Würdigungen* (Baden-Baden, 1979), 15–31. See also Ernst Gombrich's illuminating discussion of these matters in *Aby Warburg: An Intellectual Biography* (London, 1970), 43–66.

100. For full descriptions of the gems, see Nicole Dacos et al., *Il tesoro di Lorenzo il Magnifico* (Florence, 1980), cats. 4, 12. For the statues, see Bober and Rubinstein, *Renaissance Artists*, cats. 98, 99.

101. For the original text, see Ghiberti, *Commentari*, ed. Schlosser, 1:61–62, and Chap. 1 of the present volume; translation is taken from Holt, *Documentary History*, 1:163–64.

102. Dacos et al., *Tesoro*, 41. Aldrovandi (*Statue*, 125) refers to a *Hermaphrodite* in the Cesi collection that may be related to this version of the statue: "un Hermafrodito maggiore del naturale: sta ignudo assiso supra un tronco, con la veste avolta sopra una coscia."

103. All Renaissance representations of this statue include at least some traces of male genitals above the veil. Friedrich Matz and F. von Duhn (*Antike Bildwerke in Rom* [Leipzig, 1881], cat. 845) name the work unproblematically as a *Hermaphrodite* and confirm the history of its restoration. Raissa Calza et al., in *Antichità di Villa Doria Pamphili* (Rome, 1977), cat. 75, refer to it as an *Aphrodite* and argue that the fragmentary male genitals are the work of an early restorer. This claim, involving a sex-changing restoration, subsequent effacement of the newly added genitals, and another restoration that covers the genitals with a veil, seems unnecessarily complicated.

104. For the "chiome lunghe," see Aldrovandi, *Statue*, 155, referring to a work in the Farnese collection; others with similar descriptions, also at the Palazzo Farnese, appear at 148, 150, and 152. For Prospettivo Milanese, see Fienga, "Prospectivo Melanese," st. 18.

105. Published in A. E. Popham and P. Pouncey, *Italian Drawings in the Department of Prints and Drawings in the British Museum: The Fourteenth and Fifteenth Centuries* (London, 1950), cat. 352v. The rendering of the *Apollo Belvedere* on the recto may suggest a date just before 1503. On this argument, see Matthias Winner, "Zum Apoll von Belvedere," *Jahrbuch der Berliner Museen* 10 (1968): 198.

106. The guiding topos of this subject is the often repeated story of Timanthes, who, in painting the *Sacrifice of Iphigenia*, reached the highest peak of emotional expression by covering, rather than revealing, the face of Agamemnon. As discussed in Chap. 2, above, it becomes a rhetorical exemplum, e.g., for Cicero and Quintilian, as well as a visual motif, imitated by both Donatello and Ghiberti; it figures also as one of the stories from the mythology of the painter that Vasari depicts in his house. I am indebted to my student Paolo Alei for his fine work on this subject.

107. Pliny N.H. 35.56; for a modern art historical discussion of gendering conventions, see John Boardman, *Athenian Black Figure Vases* (London, 1974), esp. 197–98.

108. On the *camillus* in general, see I. S. Ryberg, *Rites of the State Religion in Roman Art* (Rome, 1955). On the statue and its postclassical heritage, see Stuart Jones, *Catalogue of Ancient Sculptures*, 2:47–49.

109. Andrea Fulvio, *Antiquitates urbis* (Rome, 1527), 21.

110. Fienga, "Prospectivo Melanese," st. 63.

111. Buddensieg, "Zum Statuenprogramm," 181.

112. Aldrovandi, *Statue*, 274; italics mine.

113. There is a considerable bibliography on both the background and the Renaissance reuse of the *Icarius Relief*; see, esp., Carl Watzinger, "Theoxenia des Dionysos," *Jahrbuch des deutschen archäologischen Instituts* 61 (1946): 76–87; E. W. Handley, "The Poet Inspired?" *Journal of Hellenic Studies* 93 (1973): 104–8; and Dacos, *Logge*, 155.

114. On these misreadings, see Erwin Panofsky, *Renaissance and Renascences in Western Art* (New York, 1969), 97–98. The inscription was known to Ciriacus and appears in the *Corpus inscriptionum latinarum* (Berlin, 1893), 6:107.

115. For Ligorio's account of sculptures found in caves under almost all the seven hills of Rome, which he describes in minute iconographic detail without being able to identify the subject, see Mandowsky and Mitchell, *Pirro Ligorio*, 60 n. On philological developments concerning the Mithras material extending further back in time, see Lanciani, *Scavi*, 4:238.

116. This piece offers a nice example of the persistence of uncertainty in reading the narratives on ancient art objects. While scholars of reception history may refer to this work as though its title

were unproblematic, recent students of Hellenistic art per se tend to call it the *Icarius Relief* without committing themselves (cf. Ridgway, *Hellenistic Sculpture*, 91–92; Bieber, *Sculpture*, 154). The story of Icarius, which is found at *Dionysiaca* 47.35–160, depends on a young Dionysus—quite contrary to what we see here, although there is one version (Louvre; Bieber, fig. 655) in which the visitor is young and the person on the bed is old. Given the configuration of ages on most examples (old visitor, young visitee), scholars are forced into a complicated hypothesis that it is the god as conflated with Sabazius, an elderly divinity associated with beer making. (If one wanted to get really ingenious, one could relate this to J. E. Harrison's notions about tragedy and *Tragos*, or spelt, which was used in Athens to make beer; see her *Prolegomena to the Study of Greek Religion* [Cambridge, Eng., 1908], chap. 8). I am not certain why the elderly visitor must be understood as Dionysus at all; could he not be a Silenus, accompanied by the rest of the throng, possibly even visiting the young Dionysus? Interestingly, Aldrovandi finds himself asking a similar question about a larger-than-lifesize statue identified as either Silenus or Bacchus, "ma non si legge, che mai Bacco si dipingesse barbuto" (*Statue*, 194). At all events, the other line of thought, promoted especially by Gilbert Charles-Picard ("Observations sur la date et l'origine des reliefs dits de la 'Visite chez Ikarios,'" *American Journal of Archaeology* 38 [1934]: 137–52, and "Nouvelles archéologiques et correspondances: Dionysos chez le poète: Suites diverses d'un thème antique," *Revue archéologique*, ser. 3, 1–2 [1961]: 114–17), has its own difficulties. No real textual source for this event can be directly adduced, though there is plenty of material in Plato and elsewhere concerning the Dionysiac frenzy of poets, and there are other images evidently relating to the celebration of poetic or dramatic inspiration. As for the *Icarius Relief* in particular, its relation to the drama depends on a close reading of some masks that are sometimes located on a pedestal under the *kline* as well as on the resemblance of the whole scene to a dramatic *skenographia*. But it is one thing to say that this is a scene from the theater (which seems quite possible) and another to assume that it is a scene *about* the theater.

117. Cf. Lafréry, *Speculum*, fol. 322v: "Tricilinarium Lectorum tripedis Mensae . . . ex marmoreis tabulis graphica deformatio," in Christian Hülsen, "Das *Speculum Romanae Magnificentiae* des Antonio Lafreri," in *Collectanea variae doctrinae L. S. Olschki* (Munich, 1921). On the triclinium in general, see Anthony Blunt, "The Triclinium in Religious Art," *Journal of the Warburg and Courtauld Institutes* 2 (1939): 271–76.

118. See Robert Turcan, *Mithra et le mithriacisme* (Paris, 1993), 37–41; and Manfred Clauss, *Mithras: Kult und Mysterien* (Munich, 1990), 43–46.

119. Panofsky, *Renaissance and Renascences*, 96–99; Fritz Saxl, *Lectures* (London, 1957), 13–44.

120. Fritz Saxl, *A Heritage of Images* (Harmondsworth, 1970), 14.

121. Fienga, "Prospectivo Melanese," st. 131.

122. Rodolfo Lanciani, *New Tales of Old Rome* (London, 1901), 193–94; see also T. Schreiber, "Flaminio Vaccas Fundberichte," *Berichte über die Verhandlungen der königlichen sächsischen Gesellschaft der Wissenschaften zu Leipzig* 33 (1881), no. 19. On de' Rossi, see Vasari, *Vite*, ed. Milanesi, 7:626–27.

123. The statue restored as Ceres is in the Museo Archeologico of Florence; see the Heemskerck drawing in Christian Hülsen, "Unbekannte römische Zeichnungen von Marten van Heemskerck," *Mededeelingen van het Nederlands Historisch Instituut te Rome* 7 (1927), pl. 16a. The version restored into the Mars Ultor relief is Bober and Rubinstein, *Renaissance Artists*, cat. 7, for which see also M. Cagiano de Azevedo, *Le antichità di Villa Medici* (Rome, 1951), cat. 4. For the Aspertini drawing, see Phyllis Bober, *Drawings after the Antique by Amico Aspertini* (London, 1957), 54.

124. The fullest account of the confusing multiple versions and provenances is to be found in Store Brunnsåker, *The Tyrant Slayers of Kritios and Nesiotes: A Critical Study of the Sources and Restorations*

(Stockholm, 1971). For the original works and their place in the narrative of Greek sculpture, see Andrew Stewart, *Greek Sculpture: An Exploration* (New Haven, 1990), 135–36. Bober and Rubinstein (*Renaissance Artists*, cat. 127) mention an additional pair in the Boboli gardens; these, which correspond to Brunnsåker, cat. A2, were no more complete or recognizable as a pair than those that were in the Palazzo Medici-Madama.

125. Cited at Bober and Rubinstein, *Renaissance Artists*, 162.

126. Aldrovandi, *Statue*, 182. The Heemskerck drawings are all in the Berlin sketchbook: two versions of the torso are to be found in I. 44v and a third version in I. 57v. The statue as a whole appears in the drawings of the Palazzo Madama courtyard, I. 5r and II. 48r. For the Aspertini drawing, see Bober, *Aspertini*, fig. 110.

127. Pliny N.H. 34.17; Pausanias *Guide to Greece* 1.8.5.

128. See Bober and Rubinstein, *Renaissance Artists*, cat. 39. On the history of its restoration, see Wilhelm Froehner, *Notice de la sculpture antique du Musée du Louvre* (Paris, 1869), 357–58.

129. On this statue, which moved from the Maffei to the della Valle and eventually to the Villa Medici, see G. A. Mansuelli, *Galleria degli Uffizi: Le sculture* (Rome, 1958), 1: cat. 98; and Bober, *Aspertini*, 49–50.

130. For a full discussion of this work, see Tilmann Buddensieg, "Raffaels Grab," in T. Buddensieg and M. Winner, eds., *Munuscula Discipulorum* (Berlin, 1968), 45–70. On the different versions known in the Renaissance, see Bober and Rubinstein, *Renaissance Artists*, cat. 33. On the history of the type and questions of attribution, see Ridgway, *Hellenistic Sculpture*, 89–90.

131. On the work, see Helbig, *Führer*, 2:46–48; on the Heemskerck drawing and the identification of its source, see the useful note at Hülsen and Egger, *Skizzenbücher*, 1:16–17.

132. For the work and its occasion of discovery, see Bober and Rubinstein, *Renaissance Artists*, cat. 143. Among the extant sixteenth-century drawings, there is no consistency as to the presence or absence of an infant on the figure's breast; the complete modern restoration, *sans baby*, dates from the 1790s. The relevant passage from the *Natural History* appears at 34.88: "Epigonus omnia fere praedicta imitatus praecessit in tubicine et matri interfectae infante miserabiliter blandiente" ("Epigonus, who copied others in almost all the subjects already mentioned, took the lead with his Trumpet-player and his Weeping Infant pitifully caressing its Murdered Mother").

133. On the *Marforio* restorations, see Haskell and Penny, *Taste*, 258–59; Ermete Rossi, "Marforio in Campidoglio," *Roma* 6 (1928): 337–46, and the same author's "'Tazze,' 'conche' e 'fontane,'" *Roma* 7 (1929): 271–74. On the *Tiber* and *Nile*, see Herbert Siebenhüner, *Das Kapitol in Rom: Idee und Gestalt* (Munich, 1954), 46–53. For Andrea Fulvio's varying conjectures about the identity of the rivers, see Bober and Rubinstein, *Renaissance Artists*, 101.

134. See Fienga, "Prospectivo Melanese," st. 118: "Nudi ambendui in terra cosolumi / un cocodrillo sopra un corno copia." The wolf appears in restoration in the 1560s, possibly as a consequence of the Michelangelo installation of the whole scene. Restorations of this kind take place much earlier as well, e.g., the addition of bronze twin babies to the *Lupa Capitolina*, which are in place by 1510 and perhaps as early as the Capitoline installation (see Helbig, *Führer*, 2:277–81).

135. On this statue, see Bober and Rubinstein, *Renaissance Artists*, cat. 1; and Edith Pogàny-Balas, "Antique Sources of Draped Figures," *Acta Historiae Artium* (Budapest) 24 (1978): 189–94.

136. On the question of missing halves and junctions with other statues, notably the *Jupiter of Versailles* (Bober and Rubinstein, cat. 2), see Netto-Bol, *Maarten de Vos*, 45–46. On the Raphael connection, see John Shearman, "Raphael, Rome, and the Codex Escurialensis," *Master Drawings* 15 (1977): 130; and John Pope-Hennessy, *Raphael* (London, 1971), 65–68. For the Giulio Romano

Jupiter Enthroned in the Casa di Giulio Romano, see Frederick Hartt, *Giulio Romano* (New Haven, 1958), 236–41.

137. See Schweikhart, *Codex Wolfegg*, 109–11.

138. On the designation as nymph, and for a general discussion of the fortunes of this work, see W. Amelung, *Die Sculpturen des vatikanischen Museums* (Berlin, 1903), cat. 353; see also Bober and Rubinstein, *Renaissance Artists*, cat. 17.

139. On this work, see Dacos, *Logge*, 28; and Konrad Oberhuber, *Raphaels Zeichnungen IX: Entwürfe zu Werken Raphaels und seiner Schule im Vatikan* (Berlin, 1972), cat. 454.

140. For material on this work, see Bober and Rubinstein, *Renaissance Artists*, cat. 36; and Mary D. Garrard, "Jacopo Sansovino's Madonna in Sant'Agostino: An Antique Source Rediscovered," *Journal of the Warburg and Courtauld Institutes* 38 (1975): 333–38. The fullest account of the restorations is R. Delbrueck, *Antike Porphyrwerke* (Berlin-Leipzig, 1932), 62–66.

141. For the history of the Sassi *Citharoedos*, now in Naples, see Bober, *Aspertini*, 71. Another more widely diffused version, now at the Villa Poggio Imperiale near Florence, was in the della Valle collection by 1490, as recorded there in a letter from Giovanni da Tolentino (see next note) and in an engraving after Heemskerck (Hülsen and Egger, *Skizzenbücher*, 2: pl. 128). See Bober and Rubinstein, *Renaissance Artists*, cat. 35; and G. Capecchi, L. Lepore, and V. Saladino, *La villa del Poggio imperiale* (Rome, 1979), cat. 2. Finally, there is a Venetian *Citharoedos*, on which see Marilyn Perry, "Cardinal Domenico Grimani's Legacy of Ancient Art to Venice," *Journal of the Warburg and Courtauld Institutes* 41 (1978): 240.

142. R. Schofield, "Giovanni da Tolentino Goes to Rome: A Description of the Antiquities of Rome in 1490," *Journal of the Warburg and Courtauld Institutes* 43 (1980): 255.

143. It is even more complicated because a roughly contemporaneous imitation of the work by Peruzzi in the Sala di Galatea of the Farnesina places a lyre in the figure's right hand, as though the artist knew that there should be an instrument but did not know exactly where to put it.

144. Delbrueck, *Antike Porphyrwerke*, 62, argues that the bronze head that existed before the eighteenth-century restoration was original, though the other bronze extremities were modern.

145. On these relations, see Garrard, "Sansovino's Madonna." For the Heemskerck painting, see Hülsen and Egger, *Skizzenbücher*, 1:43–45.

146. Aldrovandi, *Statue*, 147.

147. A great deal of interesting work has been done on the restoration of fragmentary antiquities in the Renaissance. See Heinz Ladendorf, "Antikenstudium und Antikenkopie in der neueren Kunst," *Abhandlungen der sächsischen Akademie der Wissenschaften zu Leipzig* 46 (1958): 55–61; Werner Oechslin, "Il Laocoonte—o del restauro delle statue antiche," *Paragone* 297 (1974): 3–29; Jürgen Paul, "Antikenergänzung und Ent-Restaurierung," *Kunstchronik* 25, no. 4 (1972): 85–112; Debra Pincus, "Tullio Lombardo as a Restorer of Antiquities: An Aspect of Fifteenth Century Venetian Antiquarianism," *Arte Veneta* 33 (1979): 29–42; Orietta Rossi Pinelli, "Chirurgia della memoria: Scultura antica e restauri storici," in Settis, *Memoria dell'antico*, 3:181–250; and Antoinette Le Normand-Romain, ed., *Le corps en morceaux* (Paris, 1990).

148. For an overview of the controversy, see Waldemar Januszczak, *Sayonara, Michelangelo: The Sistine Chapel Restored and Repackaged* (Reading, Mass., 1990), 169–97.

149. Montorsoli's career as restorer is anchored in his promotion by Michelangelo, and it issues in a highly respectful account of the younger artist's abilities: "Intanto essendo Michelagnolo a Roma appresso papa Clemente . . . , gli chiese Sua Santità un giovane che restaurasse alcune statue antiche di Belvedere che erano rotte. Perchè ricordatosi il Buonarroto di Fra Giovann'Agnolo [Montorsoli], lo propose al papa. . . . Rifece il braccio sinistro che mancava

all'Apollo, ed il destro del Laoconte, che sono in quel luogo, e diede ordine di racconciare l'Ercole [the *Hercules-Commodus*] simmilmente. E perchè il papa quasi ogni mattina andava in Belvedere per suo spasso, e dicendo l'ufficio, il frate il ritrasse di marmo tanto bene, che gli fu l'opera molto lodata, e gli pose il papa grandissima affezione, e massimamente veggendolo studiosissimo nelle cose dell'arte, e che tutta la notte disegnava per avere ogni mattina nuove cose da mostrare al papa, che molto se ne dilettava" (Vasari, *Vite*, ed. Milanesi, 6:632–33); "Meanwhile, Michelagnolo, being in Rome with Pope Clement, . . . his Holiness asked him to find a young man who might restore some ancient statues in the Belvedere, which were broken. Whereupon Buonarroti, remembering Fra Giovanni Agnolo, proposed him to the Pope. . . . [He] restored the left arm that was wanting to the Apollo and the right arm of the Laocoon, which statues are in that place, and likewise gave directions for restoring the Hercules. And since the Pope went almost every morning to Belvedere for recreation and to say the office, the friar made his portrait in marble, and that so well that the work brought him much praise, and the Pope conceived a very great affection for him, particularly because he saw him to be very studious of the matters of art, and heard that he used to draw all night in order to have new things every morning to show to the Pope, who much delighted in them" (*Lives*, trans. deVere, 2: 535). See in this connection Giovanni Agosti and Vincenzo Farinella, *Michelangelo e l'arte classica* (Florence, 1987), 87–95. For an earlier episode of restoration chronicled by Vasari, Verrocchio's work on a red marble Marsyas for Cosimo de' Medici, see above in the present chapter and n. 70.

150. "E più alto fece sotto certe nicchione un altro fregio di rottami di cose antiche, e di sopra nelle dette nicchie pose alcune statue pur antiche e di marmo, le quali sebbene non erano intere per essere quale senza testa, quale senza braccia, ed alcuna senza gambe, ed insomma ciascuna con qualche cosa meno, l'accomodò nondimeno benissimo, avendo fatto rifare a buoni scultori tutto quello che mancava: la quale cosa fu cagione che altri signori hanno poi fatto il medesimo, e restaurato molte cose antiche; come il cardinale Cesis, Ferrara, Farnese, e, per dirlo in una parola, tutta Roma. E nel vero, hanno molto più grazia queste anticaglie in questa maniera restaurate, che non hanno que' tronchi imperfetti, e le membra senza capo, o in altro modo difettose e manche" (Vasari, *Vite*, ed. Milanesi, 4:579–80). This passage appears only in the second edition of Vasari, placing it even further from the scene in which these attitudes toward fragments are being developed.

151. For the original, see J. J. Winckelmann, *Kleine Schriften, Vorrede, Entwürfe*, ed. W. Rehm (Berlin, 1968), 172. See the interesting treatment of Winckelmann's changing views of the *Torso* in Alex Potts, *Flesh and the Ideal: Winckelmann and the Origins of Art History* (New Haven, 1994), 173–81.

152. There is, of course, an enormous bibliography on the *Torso* in relation to postclassical art. For a general survey, see C. Schwinn, *Die Bedeutung des Torso von Belvedere für Theorie und Praxis der bildenden Kunst vom 16. Jahrhundert bis Winckelmann* (Frankfurt, 1973). Of particular interest in the present connection is Gunter Schweikhart, "Torso: Zur Geschichte und Bedeutung zerstörter Antiken im Mittelalter und Neuzeit," in K. O. Blase, ed., *Torso als Prinzip* (Kassel, 1982), 10–33. Among other interesting interpretations of the heritage of the work are Ladendorf, *Antikenstudium*, 55–61; and von Salis, *Antike*, 165–89. For useful entries on the work, see Bober and Rubinstein, *Renaissance Artists*, 166–68, Haskell and Penny, *Taste*, 311–14, and Brummer, *Statue Court*, 143–52. On the thing itself, useful readings are offered by A. Andrén, "Il torso del Belvedere," *Opuscula archeologica* 7 (1952): 1–45; and G. Säflund, "The Belvedere Torso: An Interpretation," *Opuscula romana* 11 (1976): 63–84.

153. It should be noted that Aspertini produced different sketchbooks after the antique at a considerable distance of time, possibly as much as thirty years. London I and II probably date from the

1530s, while the Codex Wolfegg, in which this drawing of the *Torso* appears, originates around 1503. See Bober, *Aspertini*, 11–15, and Schweikhart, *Codex Wolfegg*, 27–28.

154. A late exception—that is, a representation in which the *Torso* takes its place among multiple fragments—is a Melchior Lorch drawing of ca. 1550, for which see *Torso als Prinzip*, fig. 10.

155. For the Umbrian sketch, see Schmitt, "Römische Antikensammlungen," fig. 2; I would exclude from this claim those finished works of art that quote the *Torso* in completed form, which seems to me a different matter.

156. On these works and their interrelations, see Uwe Geese, "Antike als Programm: Der Statuenhof des Belvedere im Vatikan," in *Natur und Antike*, 43–46; and Brummer, *Statue Court*, 146–52.

157. Cited in Brummer, *Statue Court*, 144.

158. A beautiful drawing with a triple point of view in Christ Church, Oxford, includes the inscription on the full frontal version of the statue, for which see J. Byam Shaw, *Drawings by Old Masters at Christ Church* (Oxford, 1976), cat. 521. There is one similar case of an inscription relative to another statue: a sixteenth-century drawing after the *Hercules Farnese* (Uffizi 14787F), attributed variously to Daniele da Volterra or the circle of Salviati, is inscribed ΓΛΥΚΩΝ ΑΘΗΝΑΙΟΣ ΕΠΟΙΕΙ; see Agosti and Farinella, *Michelangelo*, cat. 41.

159. Not that we have any record of such reasoning; but see Haskell and Penny, *Taste*, 313, who ascribe this logic to Ennio Quirino Visconti.

160. An excellent account of Bregno and the general provenance of the *Torso* is found in Schmitt, "Römische Antikensammlungen," 107–13. On his collection in general, see Hermann Egger, "Beiträge zur Andrea-Bregno-Forschungen," in A. Weixlgärtner and L. Planiscig, eds., *Festschrift für Julius Schlosser zum 60. Geburtstage* (Zurich, 1927), 122–36. Among the other antiquities Bregno owned were an Adonis sarcophagus now in Mantua (Bober and Rubinstein, *Renaissance Artists*, cat. 21) and some sacrifice reliefs now in the Vatican (Bober and Rubinstein, cat. 194): both are labeled with some version of Bregno's name when they are sketched by Aspertini. On artist-collectors in general, see Claudio Franzoni, "'Rimembranze d'infinite cose': Le collezioni rinascimentali di antichità," in Settis, *Memoria dell'antico*, 1:338–43.

161. *Prospectivo Melanese*, ed. Fienga, st. 13.

162. Prospettivo does mention that the *Lion Attacking a Horse* is *un tozze* (st. 64), and he praises some of the colossal body parts in the Capitoline collection, but his fervor on behalf of the *Torso* appears exceptional.

163. The fullest account of this set of drawings after ancient and modern artworks—though it is focused on a questionable attribution to Giambologna—is Elizabeth Dhanens, "De Romeinse ervaring van Giovanni Bologna," *Bulletin de l'institut historique belge de Rome* 35 (1963): 159–90. See also Maria Teresa Fiorio's excellent entry on the *Torso* drawing (fol. 20) in Théberge, *Genius of the Sculptor*, cat. 18.

164. Von Salis, *Antike und Renaissance*, 180. It has also been argued that the bound Marsyas on the famous Medici Carnelian is, in fact, the source for much of what is ascribed to the *Torso*. See Säflund, "Belvedere Torso," 75.

165. Aldrovandi, *Statue*, 120.

166. Original cited in R. P. Ciardi, ed., *Scritti sulle arti* (Florence, 1974), 2:381.

167. The indispensable source for all this table talk concerning the antiquities is *La vita di Michelangelo nelle redazioni del 1550 e il 1568*, ed. P. Barocchi (Milan, 1962), 2100–11.

168. Both stories appear in Condivi's *Life of Michelangelo* and then in the second edition of Vasari. For Condivi, see *The Life of Michelangelo*, trans. A. S. Wohl (Baton Rouge, 1976), 11–12, 19–23; the Vasari versions are in *Vite*, ed. Milanesi, 7.142–43, 7.147–49. For an interesting reading of the

Cupid story, see David Quint, *Origin and Originality in Renaissance Literature: Versions of the Source* (New Haven, 1983), 1–3.

169. For the Hollanda anecdote, see E. Tormo, ed., *De la pintura antigua* (Madrid, 1921), 76–77; it is cited in Italian in Agosti and Farinella, *Michelangelo*, 48. Note the high level of historical and stylistic awareness with which Hollanda identifies the *Bacchus* as nonclassical: "Its arms and hands were placed in an intermediate position outside the rules of ancient practice, as they were neither lowered all the way down nor raised up very high; and similarly, the movement and the pose of Bacchus's legs were at the same time slack and lacking in the stability of the ancient style, even though the formal refinements, the invention, the proportions, and the figure of the satyr with his basket did seem to me antique." For Aldrovandi, see *Statue*, 168.

170. For a generally cautious and authoritative account of the statue's condition, see de Tolnay, *Youth of Michelangelo*, 142. The only two representations of the *Bacchus* that show it with the right wrist broken off are Heemskerck, from the 1530s, and the Cambridge sketchbook, from the 1550s. A drawing by Girolamo da Carpi, approximately contemporaneous with that of the Cambridge artist (Norman W. Canedy, *The Roman Sketchbook of Girolamo da Carpi* [London, 1976], cat. R86), exhibits the complete right hand with cup. The fullest treatment of the questions surrounding the broken hand is to be found in Pinelli, "Chirugia della memoria," in Settis, *Memoria dell'antico*, 3:198–200. See also Paola Barocchi, *Il Bacco di Michelangelo* (Florence, 1982). Edgar Wind, in *Pagan Mysteries in the Renaissance* (New York, 1968), 177–86, makes a fascinating argument about the work no less carefully nuanced for the fact that the premises concerning the mutilation and reconstruction of the statue are questionable. In an anecdote recorded by Jean-Jacques Boissard (*Topographia urbis Romae* [Frankfurt, 1627], 2:18), Michelangelo, having finished the statue, broke off its arm on purpose and buried it on the property of someone who was about to build a house. Once the arm was discovered and taken for an antique, Michelangelo was able to reveal himself as the author of the fragment by demonstrating its perfect fit with the rest of the statue. Boissard adds that the intended butt of this demonstration was Raphael (who, in fact, had not yet arrived in Rome).

171. See above, Chap. 1.

172. On Michelangelo's involvement with the Capitoline installation, including the River Gods, see Vasari, *Vite*, ed. Milanesi, 7:222; on the *Farnese Bull*, see Vasari, 7:224. For Michelangelo's apocryphal restorations of other works discovered later, see Haskell and Penny, *Taste*, cats. 224, 235, 206, 321.

173. For Castelvetro, see *Poetica d'Aristotele vulgarizzata e sposta*, ed. W. Romani (Bari, 1978), 1:37–38. On these stories, see Agosti and Farinella, *Michelangelo*, 87; and Seymour Howard, "Pulling Herakles' Leg: Della Porta, Algardi and Others," in *Festschrift Ulrich Middeldorf* (Berlin, 1968), 402–7.

174. "Tanto son buone le moderne, quanto le antiche, pur che sieno eccellenti" (Vasari, *Vite*, ed. Milanesi, 7:148–49).

175. See, e.g., John Pope-Hennessy on the Accademia *Slaves*: "For some students they are among the most valuable figures by Michelangelo that we possess. Through them, as through no other works, we plumb the depths of his vast reservoir of creative vitality. . . . For others—a very small minority—they are figures blocked out from the master's models in the quarry or the studio, in which he himself had, manually speaking, scarcely any part. The realism of the second view is more acceptable than the romanticism of the first" (*Italian High Renaissance and Baroque Sculpture* [Princeton, 1970], 33).

176. On Pius II, see Enea Silvia Piccolomini, *I commentari*, trans. G. Bernetti (Siena, 1972), 5:27, 11:19.

177. For an invaluable compendium of responses to the non finito from Michelangelo's own time and after, see Vasari, *Vita*, ed. Barocchi, 1645–70, and the same author's "Finito e non-finito nella critica vasariana," *Arte antica e moderna* 1 (1958): 221–35. See also Renato Bonelli, "Michelangelo e il

non-finito," in *Atti del Convegno di studi Michelangioleschi* (Rome, 1966), 403–16; Jean-René Gaborit, "Michel-Ange entre fragment et inachevé," in Le Normand-Romain, *Corps en morceaux*, 85–93; and, especially useful in the argument of these pages, Maria Teresa Fiorio, "Broken Sculpture: Michelangelo and the Aesthetic of the Fragment," in Théberge, *Genius of the Sculptor*, 68–84.

178. Vasari, *Vite*, ed. Milanesi, 7:195. It must be admitted that Vasari's comments on unfinished work can be considerably more cautious than the often quoted lines about the Medici Madonna. In his more extended reflection on what Michelangelo did and did not bring to completion (7:243), Vasari ascribes the non finito to the artist's perfectionism; it was his *giudizio* that did not allow him to continue with work that had revealed flaws. Still another approach is apparent in regard to the *Saint Matthew*, the earliest statue to be conspicuously unfinished: "la quale statua così abbozzata mostra la sua perfezione, ed insegna agli scultori in che maniera si cavano le figure de' marmi, senza che veghino storpiate, per potere sempre guadagnare col giudizio, levando del marmo, ed avervi da potersi ritrarre e mutare qualcosa, come accade, se bisognasse" (7:157–58); "which statue, rough as it is, reveals its full perfection and teaches sculptors in what manner figures can be carved out of marble without their coming out misshapen, so that it may be possible to go on ever improving them by removing more of the marble with judgment, and also to draw back and change some part, according as the necessity may arise" (*Lives*, trans. deVere, 2:655–56). It is one thing to find the mark of genius, another to gain practical instruction from a genius: in a sense, these are opposing poles of Vasari's heuristic project in the *Lives*.

179. See *The Poetry of Michelangelo*, trans. James Saslow (New Haven, 1991), 34–35. Related ideas in his poetry range from notions of an ideal conception inside the marble ("Non ha l'ottimo artista alcun concetto" [151]) to metaphors based on sculpture as subtraction ("Si come per levar, donna, si pone" [152]) to a *memento mori* suggesting that only death is equivalent to a completed sculpture ("Negli anni molti e nelle molte pruove" [241]).

CHAPTER 4: RECONSTRUCTIONS

1. I use "triumphalist" with some irony, as it smacks of an overreaction to the claims for Renaissance exceptionalism that have been made from Petrarch to Vasari to Michelet, Burckhardt, and beyond. For some revisionary approaches that are measured and interesting, see the collection edited by Claire Farago, *Reframing the Renaissance: Visual Culture in Europe and Latin America, 1450–1650*, esp. the editor's introduction; Peter Burke, *The Italian Renaissance* (Princeton, 1986), 1–11; and the same author's "The Uses of Italy," in R. Porter and M. Teich, eds., *The Renaissance in National Context* (Cambridge, Eng., 1992), 6–20.

2. See above, Chap. 1, n. 13.

3. Paul de Man, *The Rhetoric of Romanticism* (New York, 1984), 76.

4. The fullest history of identities given to the statue, as well as an account of alternative examples known in the Renaissance, is found in Francis Haskell and Nicholas Penny, *Taste and the Antique* (New Haven, 1981), 291–96. The *Pasquino* itself was never restored, but other versions of what was apparently the same subject that did get completed in the seventeenth century, as with many cases discussed in the previous chapter, helped to fix the notion of what the original subject had been—though even in that instance there proved to be several homoerotic possibilities of older soldiers holding the lifeless bodies of younger lovers. The designation as *Menelaus* seems to date from the end of the eighteenth century, when Ennio Quirino Visconti used texts and a selection of recently discovered sculptural remains to make a definitive claim, for which see *Notizie delle due famose statue di un fiume e di Patroclo dette volgarmente di Marforio e di Pasquino* (Rome, 1789).

5. The standard treatment of the work is B. Schweitzer, *Das Original der sogennanten Pasquino-Gruppe* (Leipzig, 1936), but the most up-to-date account of the research, casting doubt on the Menelaus

identification and opting for Odysseus and Achilles, is Brunilde Sismondo Ridgway, *Hellenistic Sculpture I* (Madison, 1990), 275–81.

6. See Filippo Baldinucci, *Notizie dei professori del disegno* (Milan, 1812), 139–40: "Fu primo il Bernino, che mettesse questa statua in altissimo credito in Roma, e raccontasi, che essendogli una volta stato domandato da un Oltramontano qual fosse la più bella statua di quella città, e rispondendo, che il Pasquino, il forestiero, che si credette burlato, fu per venir con lui a cimento" (Bernini was the first to give this statue a place of highest regard in Rome. He told a story that having once been asked by a northerner which was the most beautiful statue in the city and having responded that it was the Pasquino, the foreigner, thinking he was being made fun of, practically came to blows with him). This opinion, clearly meant to be radical and surprising, is sometimes traced back to an unsubstantiated report that Michelangelo was fond of the work; that idea may be due to a confusion with the *Torso Belvedere*, with which, logically enough, Bernini groups it.

7. See Theodor Schreiber, "Flaminio Vaccas Fundberichte," *Berichte über die Verhandlungen der königlichen sächsischen Gesellschaft der Wissenschaften zu Leipzig* 33 (1881): 43–91. The recollection in question is no. 29, but Vacca mentions another version, presumably that which was restored and eventually found its way to the Loggia dei Lanzi in Florence, at no. 97. On the relation between the statue and the Orsini tower, see Cesare D'Onofrio, *Un popolo di statue racconta* (Rome, 1990), 40. For an alternative provenance that connects the finding of the statue with Bramante's construction of the cloister at Santa Maria della Pace (working under the same patron, Oliviero Carafa, who will display the *Pasquino*), see Rodolfo Lanciani, "Il codice Barberiniano XXX," *Archivio della società romana di storia patria* 6 (1883): 483.

8. *Carmina quae ad Pasquillum fuerunt posita in anno .MCCCCC.IX*, fol. 2v (Rome, 1509).

9. For an excellent account of Carafa and the early years of the pasquinade, see Anne Reynolds, "Cardinal Oliviero Carafa and the early Cinquecento Tradition of the Feast of Pasquino," *Humanistica Lovaniensia* 34 (1985): 178–208. A good summary of the cardinal's career is to be found in Charles L. Stinger, *The Renaissance in Rome* (Bloomington, 1985), 144–45. Carafa is represented in Filippino Lippi's *Triumph of Saint Thomas Aquinas* in the Carafa Chapel of Santa Maria sopra Minerva, on which see Gail Geiger, "Filippino Lippi's *Triumph of St. Thomas Aquinas*," in P. A. Ramsey, ed., *Rome in the Renaissance: The City and the Myth* (Binghamton, 1982), 223–36.

10. The discussion here is indebted to a number of historical and urbanistic accounts of the *Pasquino* phenomenon, notably the pioneering work of Domenico Gnoli, *La Roma di Leone X* (Milan, 1938), esp. 164–84, 300–308; D'Onoforio, *Un popolo*, cited above in n. 7, 26–56; and Claudio Rendina, *Pasquino statua parlante* (Rome, 1991); more up-to-date in historical method is the fine introduction in V. Marucci, ed., *Pasquinate del Cinque e Seicento* (Rome, 1988), 7–21. Among other works of some usefulness are Mario Dell'Arco, *Pasquino statua parlante* (Rome, 1967); and P. Romano, *Pasquino e la satira in Roma* (Rome, 1932).

11. See, e.g., *Pasquillorum tomi duo* (1544), the important collection of Reformation-connected pasquinades published in Basel by a Piedmontese Protestant, Celio Secondo Curione. For a good overview of the phenomenon outside Italy, see Rendina, *Statua parlante*, 76–89, e.g., "[Pasquino] diventa portavoce di Zwingli, Calvino e Lutero in terra tedesca. Non ha una statua alla quale appendere le sue invettive; ha solo bisogno di un tipografo che mandi in stampa le 'esilaranti' satire antipapiste" (82). It will be noted that Pasquino's Roman origins are also connected to the printing press, however. He makes his way as far as England, where Thomas Nashe, in the midst of the Martin Marprelate controversy writes a *Pasquille and Marforius* and where John Webster's *Duchess of Malfi* makes a disgenuous reference to scandal she has heard about herself, to which her brother replies, "Let me be ever deaf to it: / One of Pasquill's paper

bullets, court-calumny, / A pestilent air which princes' palaces are seldom purg'd of"
(*The Duchess of Malfi*, 3.1.48–51, ed. J. R. Brown [Cambridge, Mass., 1964]).

12. These are two of the longest conclaves in the whole period, the first lasting over a month, the
second over two months. They roughly coincide with an increasingly libelous tone in the
pasquinades (already in 1518 Marcello Paloni is having to apologize to Cardinal del Monte for
the subversive quality of the texts; see Gnoli, *Roma*, 300–301). At the time of the papal elections,
Pasquino mounts attacks on all the cardinals for their failure to elect a pope, on specific candidates, and, once he is elected, on Adrian VI, for his moral severity. The other ingredient in this
mix is the entry of Pietro Aretino into the scene of composing pasquinades. Because the focus
in these pages is on the anonymous and civic quality of the ritual, this important figure—who
becomes in the 1520s and 1530s almost synonymous with Pasquino—is slighted here. On this
aspect of the story, see Alessandro Luzio, "Pietro Aretino e Pasquino," *Nuova antologia* 28 (1890):
679–708, and Aretino, *Sonetti lussuriosi e pasquinate*, ed. M. B. Sirolesi (Rome, 1980). So far as
Giulio-Clement is concerned, the pasquinades follow what appears to have been the general
cultural shift—and a quite rapid one—from enthusiasm over his election to disappointment.
There is some evidence that he was using Aretino to "plant" pasquinades during the conclaves,
but if so, the pope and the poet did not enjoy an enduring partnership. See Marucci, *Pasquinate
del Cinque*, 9, 12.

13. See the lively account under the title "'Duo cazi' per il Fregnese" in Rendina, *Statua parlante*,
159–78. See also Carlo Capasso, "Pasquinate contro i Farnesi nei codici Ottoboniani
2811–2812," in *Studi in onore di Francesco Torraca* (Naples, 1912), 399–410.

14. See Marucci, *Pasquinate del Cinque*, 16.

15. Original cited in Rendina, *Statua parlante*, 22. This information emerges from one of those
drawn-out literary battles between humanists for which the later Renaissance is famous.
Annibale Caro, in response to an attack by Lodovico Castelvetro, appropriates the voice of
Pasquino; Castelvetro responds by narrating the "true" origins of the figure. The original
publications are Caro, *Apologia degli academici de' Banchi di Roma contra m. Lodovico Castelvetro da
Modena in forma di uno spaccio di Maestro Pasquino* (Parma, 1558), and Castelvetro, *Ragioni d'alcune
cose segnate nella canzone d'Annibal Caro "Venite a l'ombra de gran gigli d'oro"* (Venice, 1560).

16. Original cited in D'Onofrio, *Un popolo*, 30.

17. Burckard, *Liber notarum*, ed. E. Celani, in *Rerum italicum scriptores*, 2d ser., 32, 1 (Città di Castello,
1906), 2:296. The verses, Burckard tells us, were attached to the *Pasquino* (a procedure that he
does not seem to find novel) and then copied on other pieces of paper hung up around the city.

18. This document is reproduced in Pasquale Villari, *Nicolò Machiavelli e i suoi tempi* (Florence, 1877),
1:560–63.

19. Gnoli (*Roma*, 169–74) identifies this figure persuasively with one Donato Poli, a teacher of
rhetoric who flourished in Rome during the first two decades of the century, for which the
strongest evidence is the mention of a "Donato semipoeta, soprannominato segretario di
maestro Pasquino" in the diary of Paride Grassi (Gnoli, 171, who refers to G. Marini, *Il Ruolo dei
professori dell'Archiginnasio Romano per l'anno 1514* [Rome, 1797], 69). But the interconnections
between "Donato" and Mazzocchi himself, as well as the fact that the official textbook of Latin
was by the fourth-century Aelius Donatus, lead me to agree with D'Onofrio (*Un popolo*, 35–36)
that the name may well have been a fictional projection—like Pasquino himself.

20. Cited by Gnoli, *Roma*, 173, and Rendina, *Statua parlante*, 28. The "terque quaterque" is an allusion to *Aeneid* 1.94: "O terque quaterque beati, / quis ante ora patrum Troiae sub moenibus altis /
contigit oppetere" ("O thrice and four times blest, whose lot it was to meet death before their

fathers' eyes beneath the lofty walls of Troy"; trans. H. R. Fairclough, Loeb Classical Library (Cambridge, Mass., 1967).

21. Cited by Gnoli, *Roma*, 174, and Rendina, *Statua parlante*, 28.

22. *Carmina ad Pasquillum Herculem obtruncantem Hydram referentem posita Anno M. D. X.* (Rome, 1510), fol. 3v.

23. This sequence of publications goes on almost uninterruptedly from 1509 through the 1520's; the last appears to be in 1536. Only *Lutto* (mourning) in 1511 and *Hercules and Cacus* (our figure 4.4) in 1517 have frontispieces that refer directly to the statue; but many consist of postures drawn from classical iconography or sculpture, including the *Apollo* of 1513, which is closely modeled on the *Apollo Belvedere*.

24. The occupant of the Orsini palace seems to have continued as the protector of the event: first Carafa, then, after his death in 1511, Christopher Bainbridge, cardinal of York ("ignorante e rozzo," according to Gnoli), then from 1515 until his death in 1533, Antonio Maria Ciocchi del Monte, cardinal of San Vitale. In 1517, the year of Hercules and Cacus, Leo himself pays for the festival, thus adding the Medici arms to the title page of the annual volume.

25. One of the Latin verses in the 1510 volume (no. 48 in the collection cited in n. 26) announces, "It is Easter alone that has given me the immutable name of Pasquino, with which I am always known in the world, just as I have only one mind and one appearance, despite the fact that every spring they have the habit of renewing my appearance." On the relevance of the birthday of Rome, see D'Onofrio, *Un popolo*, 44–56; for a fuller account of the tradition, which does not mention Pasquino, see Philip Jacks, *The Antiquarian and the Myth of Antiquity* (Cambridge, Eng., 1993), 125–74.

26. Unless otherwise noted, all subsequent citations to Italian pasquinades are to the magisterial work by V. Marucci, A. Marzo, and A. Romano, eds., *Pasquinate romane del Cinquecento* (Rome, 1983), to whose text, bibliography, annotations, and introductions, I am much indebted. Poems cited in the text are referenced by their number in this edition and by the year of their appearance on the statue.

27. The most famous of these are the fifteenth-century adventures of the Florentine Neoplatonists as well as such individual stories as the trip on Lake Garda of Mantegna, etc., on which see Charles Mitchell, "Archaeology and Romance in Renaissance Italy," in E. F. Jacob, ed., *Italian Renaissance Studies: A Tribute to the Late Cecilia M. Ady* (London, 1960), 455–83, and the same author's "Felice Feliciano Antiquarius," *Proceedings of the British Academy* 47 (1961): 197–221.

28. Pliny uses the term *symplegma nobile* in reference to figures who are wrestling (e.g., N.H. 36.24, 36.35) in some way that may conflate the bellicose and the erotic. The participants may be both men, one man and one woman, or even one man and one hermaphrodite. See *Histoire naturelle*, ed. J. André, R. Bloch, and A. Rouveret (Paris, 1978), 36.146, for useful notes on the diffusion of the term in both art historical and philosophical literature.

29. Unless otherwise noted, Latin pasquinades from this point on are cited from Marucci, *Pasquinate del Cinque*.

30. "He knew both sides of Love"; Ovid, *Metamorphoses*, trans. F. J. Miller, Loeb Classical Library (Cambridge, Mass., 1966), 3.323.

31. The phrase itself appears frequently, e.g., in Cicero's *De officiis*, 2.19. See also Quintilian, *Institutio oratoria*, 3.11.1.

32. See D'Onofrio, *Un popolo*, 43.

33. On the complex history of the *Marforio*, quite apart from his involvement in the pasquinades, see above, Chap. 1; see also Phyllis Bober and Ruth Rubinstein, *Renaissance Artists and Antique Sculpture* (London, 1986), 99–101, and Haskell and Penny, *Taste*, 258–59.

34. On Pasquino's interlocutors and competitors in general, see Rendina, *Statua parlante*, 58–75. On the Bocca della Verità in particular, see D'Onofrio, *Un popolo*, 11–24.

35. Cf. a pasquinade of 1529, when the statue is dressed as Concordia, in which Pasquino attacks the pope by precisely denying the relevance of the propagandistic annual costume: "Guarda gran fizïon, mira discordia / dil tuo Clemente, indegno papa elletto: / quand'a Firenze sua senza rispetto / dava tormento, mi fecce Concordia" (381).

36. Cited from Jean Bernard Mary-Lafon, *Pasquino et Marforio: Les bouches de marbre de Rome* (Paris, 1877), 138.

37. *Pasquillorum tomi duo* (Basel, 1544), 333, 348, cited in Gnoli, *Roma*, 169.

38. While the *Imagines* of the two Philostratuses and of Callistratus (Loeb Classical Library, trans. Arthur Fairbanks [Cambridge, Mass., 1979]) do not make this distinction explicitly, their whole descriptive method depends on intuiting the complex narrative sequences that are implied in frozen images. For Murray Krieger, see *Ekphrasis: The Illusion of the Natural Sign* (Baltimore, 1992). G. E. Lessing's doctrine of the "single moment of time" is enunciated in *Laocoön*, Chap. 3. For Nelson Goodman, see "Twisted Tales; or Story, Study and Symphony," *Critical Inquiry* 7 (1980): 103–19. See also Wendy Steiner, *The Colors of Rhetoric: Problems in the Relation between Modern Literature and Painting* (Chicago, 1982), 41–48, as well as her *Pictures of Romance: Form against Context in Painting and Literature* (Chicago, 1988), 7–42. Perhaps the most nuanced account of all, which uses photography and cinema persuasively, is an unreprinted essay by Ernst Gombrich, "Moment and Movement in Art," *Journal of the Warburg and Courtauld Institutes* 27 (1964): 293–306. Important recent works on pictorial narration are Marilyn Aronberg Lavin, *The Place of Narrative: Mural Decoration in Italian Churches, 431–1600* (Chicago, 1990); and Lew Andrews, *Story and Space in Renaissance Art* (Cambridge, Eng., 1995).

39. The leading exponent of the logic of narrative is Gerald Prince; see, e.g., "Narrativity," in K. Menges and D. Rancour-Laferrière, eds., *Axia: Davis Symposium on Literary Evaluation* (Stuttgart, 1981), 61–86. Compare Roland Barthes's very suggestive comments in "An Introduction to the Structural Analysis of Narrative" (*New Literary History* 6 [1975]: 237–72) about the jagged narrative relations between the consecutive and the consequential (248). That essay also develops interestingly the notion of "my" story versus "yours," or the narrator versus the reader (260–64).

40. This territory is, of course, that of *Art and Illusion*. But it should be noted that in Gombrich's account the deciphering of narrative plays a decidedly minor role in comparison with the deciphering of rabbits and ducks—i.e., of forms. The felicitously named "beholder's share" is concerned far more with psychological effects of perception than with viewers' recognitions of pre-existing verbal narrative. In fact, as Gombrich historicizes the matter, it is the sophisticated nature of Greek literary narrative that brings pictorial realism into being—thus, in effect, leaving less to viewers' imaginations. On the other hand, Gombrich offers some telling arguments about one of the most fundamental constituents of verbal narrative, that is, the beholder's involvement in deciphering the emotional state of pictorially represented human figures.

41. "[Timomachus'] raving Ajax and his infanticide Medea were famous paintings, but from the descriptions we have of them it is clear that he thoroughly understood and was able to combine two things: that point or moment which the beholder not so much sees as adds in his imagination, and that appearance which does not seem so transitory as to become displeasing through its perpetuation in art" (Lessing, *Laocoön*, 20–21).

42. For the complete texts and translations of these important letters, see the superb treatment by Celia M. Chazelle, "Pictures, Books, and the Illiterate: Pope Gregory I's letters to Serenus of Marseilles," *Word and Image* 6 (1990): 138–52.

43. "Tum placet in historia adesse quempiam qui earum quae gerantur rerum spectatores

admoneat, aut manu ad visendum advocet, aut quasi id negotium secretum esse velit, vultu ne eo proficiscare truci et torvis oculis minitetur, aut periculum remve aliquam illic admirandam demonstret, aut ut una adrideas aut ut simil deplores suis te gestibus invitet. Denique et quae illi cum spectantibus et quae inter se picti exequentur, omnia ad agendam et docendam historiam congruant necesse est" (original and translation cited from Alberti, *On Painting and on Sculpture*, ed. and trans. Cecil Grayson [London, 1972], 80–83).

44. For general background on the statue, see Bober and Rubinstein, *Renaissance Artists*, 113–14; Haskell and Penny, *Taste*, 184–87; Wolfgang Helbig, *Führer durch die öffentlichen Sammlungen klassischer Altertümer in Rom* (Tübingen, 1963), 1:109–10; and Hans Henrik Brummer, *The Statue Court in the Vatican Belvedere* (Stockholm, 1970), 154–84, 220–22, 254–64. Also useful is Wilhelm Müller, "Zur schlafenden Ariadne des Vatikan," *Mitteilungen des deutschen archäologischen Instituts, römische Abteilung* 53 (1938): 164–74.

45. See, e.g., the description in Ulisse Aldrovandi, *Delle statue antiche* (Venice, 1556), reprinted in Lucio Mauro, *Le antichità della città di Roma* (Venice, 1557): "pare che tramortisca e venga meno" (117).

46. The first recorded mention of fountain and inscription is by Michele Ferrarini in a manuscript that has been dated ca. 1480: "Super ripam Danuvii in quo est sculpta nympha ad amoenum fontem dormiens, sub figura est hoc epigramma . . ." (Paris, Bibliothèque Nationale, lat. 6128, fol. 114r, and Reggio, comm. cod. C. 398, fol. 28r; On the banks of the Danube, where there is a statue of a nymph sleeping at a lovely fountain, under the figure there is this inscription . . .). In another early MS (Florence, Riccardiana, cod. 907, fol. 172r) by Bartolommeo Fonte, it is credited to Giovanni Antonio Campani, a papal humanist from the time of Pius II, but it is unclear whether Fonte is giving Campani credit for finding the inscription or for making it up ("Romae recens inventum. Campani est"). I deal with the inscription in detail below. See nn. 54, 55. For the history of its authentication and de-authentication, see *Corpus inscriptionum latinarum* (Berlin, 1863–1940), 6.5.3e. On this imagined work and its diffusion in literary, horticultural, and aesthetic production, see Otto Kurz, "Huius Nympha Loci: A Pseudo-Classical Inscription and a Drawing by Dürer," *Journal of the Warburg and Courtauld Institutes* 16 (1953): 171–77, and Elisabeth B. MacDougall, "The Sleeping Nymph: Origins of a Humanist Fountain Type," *Art Bulletin* 57 (1975): 357–65.

47. On the garden installations, see Christian Hülsen, *Römische Antikengärten des 16. Jahrhunderts* (*Abhandlungen der Heidelberger Akademie der Wissenschaften*, Phil.-Hist. Klasse 4 [1917]), 32, 58, and Walter Amelung, *Die Skulpturen des Vatikanischen Museums* (Berlin, 1903–8), 2:82. MacDougall ("Sleeping Nymph," 361–63) traces two particular gardens with a sleeping nymph statue and the Danubian inscription, one belonging to Angelo Colocci, the other to Hans Goritz. Both men were papal officials beginning in the time of Julius II, and both assembled "academies" of humanists devoted to the muses which met in these gardens. Kurz ("Nympha," 172–73) adds many other such humanist gardens with statue and inscription, not only in Rome but also in Aquileia, Messina, and Palermo.

48. The first conjecture seems to have been made by Augustin Legrand in a description of the antiquities that were ceded to the Louvre after Napoleon negotiated the Treaty of Tolentino in 1797. A fuller account is offered by Ennio Quirino Visconti in his guidebook *Museo Pio-Clementino* (Milan, 1819), after the antiquities had been returned there. He dismisses Cleopatra on the grounds that the snake is mere jewelry. He also dismisses Winckelmann's claim that she is a nymph on the grounds that she has too many clothes on and that her body is too dignified; nor does her melancholy expression suit a nymph (though he concedes that it might suit Cleopatra). Rather he offers the identification of Ariadne on Naxos, first for affective reasons—the nobility of her garments bespeaks a princess, her dignity conforms to the future apotheosis, her sadness

is appropriate to her abandonment, etc. (321). He then goes on to confirm this intuition by reference to a bas-relief depicting the arrival of Bacchus on Naxos and to a description of such a work in Pausanias, *Guide to Greece*, 1.20.

49. See, e.g., the grand oval sarcophagus, Bober and Rubinstein, *Renaissance Artists*, cat. 80, which includes all that is necessary for an identification of the love scene on Naxos—Bacchus, satyrs, maenads, and sleeping female figure, both of whose arms are in the same position as those of the Vatican statue. This work was sketched as early as 1480 and appears in many of the major drawings collections based on ancient sculpture. The closest we can come to a Renaissance identification of the Vatican sculpture as Ariadne appears in Titian's *Bacchanale of the Andrians*: the beautiful sleeping female figure in the lower right corner is clearly based on a rotated version of our statue; and she seems to have been known from quite early on as "Ariadne." The authority for this identification is admittedly convoluted, since there is no immediate relation between the daughter of Minos and the narrative of the island of Andros with its wine-filled river. Edgar Wind suggested a punning connection between ANDRIA and ARIADNE in Bellini's *Feast of the Gods* (Cambridge, Mass., 1948), 60.

50. For the particular sources of this story in Horace, Virgil, Plutarch, and Dio Cassius, see nn. 70, 71, below. As an example of viewers revising the statue to fit the history, consider Aldrovandi's guidebook of the 1550s, in which he both describes the art works and fills in something of the commonplace lore concerning their narratives: "Cleopatra was the queen of Egypt . . . . Having finally been conquered in battle along with her lover M. Antonio by Augustus Caesar, she caused herself to be bitten by an asp on her chest below the breast, and she died. And in this position this image of her was sculpted" (117–18). The most specific detail of this account—the asp's point of entry—is completely inaccurate.

51. Works involving both these subjects with the relevant gesture were known in the Renaissance. For Rhea Silvia see, e.g., the sarcophagus at Palazzo Mattei, documented in Hellmut Sichtermann and Guntram Koch, *Griechische Mythen auf römischen Sarkophagen* (Tübingen, 1975), cat. 71. For Endymion the examples are innumerable. See Bober and Rubinstein, *Renaissance Artists*, cat. 26, and Sichtermann and Koch, cats. 17, 18. For a further sampling, just in Rome, see Wolfgang Helbig, *Führer*, cats. 569, 1331, 1406. The two myths are brought together on a single sarcophagus (Helbig, cat. 1005), which is, however, too damaged to permit a clear reading of the sleepers' gestures.

52. Bober and Rubinstein, *Renaissance Artists*, 113–14.

53. In a useful iconographic essay ("Ariadne and Others: Images of Sleep in Greek and Early Roman Art," *Classical Antiquity* 4 [1985]: 152–92), Sheila McNally allows for some possibility of questioning the identity of the Vatican statue, only to deny the possibility: "No later Ariadne appears fully clothed in sleep; the heavy clothing might throw some doubt on the identification, but it is essential to this artist's interpretation" (172). Physical details that do not fit the predetermined narrative are pressed into service as "artist's interpretation."

54. See above, n. 46, on the sources of the report. The prose is my own translation. I give the inscription in Alexander Pope's version, which he included in a letter late in his life celebrating his grotto at Twickenham: "It wants nothing to complete it but a good statue with an inscription, like that beautiful antique one which you know I am so fond of" (cited in Kurz, "Nympha," 176–77).

55. Cyriacus began his tireless searches for classical remains as early as the 1420s; and though he specialized in Greek materials, he also produced the largest collection of Latin epigraphy known up to that time. Close connections have been demonstrated between Cyriacus and Bartolommeo Fonte, in whose MS (among others) the inscription appeared; and it has also

been shown that Ferrarini's work may be traceable directly to Cyriacus. For that argument, see Charles Mitchell, "Felice Feliciano Antiquarius." On the whole subject of Cyriacus, inscriptions, and their humanist or artistic uses, see Roberto Weiss, *The Renaissance Discovery of Antiquity* (Oxford, 1988), 137–57; and F. Saxl, "The Classical Inscription in Renaissance Art and Politics," *Journal of the Warburg and Courtauld Institutes* 4 (1944): 19–46.

56. On these fashions, see David Coffin, *Gardens and Gardening in Papal Rome* (Princeton, 1991), 33–39.

57. See the account in E. R. Curtius, *European Literature and the Latin Middle Ages* (New York, 1963), 190–200. Curtius traces the name of the topos to Virgil's repeated use of *amoenus* to describe the loveliness of nature (*Aeneid* 5.734, 6.638, 7.30), a term which Servius glossed as related to *amor*: *loci amoeni*, in other words, become not only beautiful places but also places suitable to making love. At the same time, the *locus amoenus* develops into a rhetorical set-piece of ekphrastic description, which in ancient pastoral lyric or in Virgil's Elysium may remain quite static and not necessarily threatened by destructive action. It is the Ovidian tradition that turns the set-piece into a backdrop for, generally, amorous violence at the same time as it maintains the sense of nature's beauty and lushness. As I shall suggest more fully below, the inscription implies the presence of an observer who does threaten this *locus amoenus*.

58. The range is clear from titles alone of two of the most important scholarly treatments of the Belvedere: E. H. Gombrich, "The Belvedere Garden as a Grove of Venus," in *Symbolic Images* (London, 1972), 104–8, and J. S. Ackerman, "The Belvedere as a Classical Villa," *Journal of the Warburg and Courtauld Institutes* 14 (1951): 70–91. The source for the former is Francesco Colonna's *Hypnerotomachia Poliphili*, and for the latter the letters of Pliny the Younger (2.17, 5.6) describing his villas in the country, along with the Domus Aurea and the Temple of Fortune at Praeneste. See also Brummer, *Statue Court*, 216–43, who adds further mythical gardens, including the Hesperides and the bank of the Ilissus, which forms the setting of Plato's *Phaedrus*.

59. This idea, developed less extensively than here, is first proposed by Brummer, *Statue Court*, 171–80. Other works, to be sure, play some part in this history of imagining. Another sleeping figure, which may have been known as early as the fifteenth century and which formed part of the Galli collection when Marten van Heemskerck did his drawings in the 1530s (see fig. 3.60) has a much greater claim on being a fountain nymph since she has a jug in horizontal position under her left arm; but she is not so widely known as the Belvedere statue. This we could ascribe to her less prominent place of display, but we must remember that the place of display is not random: theoretically, at least, Julius could as easily have bought this statue from the Galli as he bought the other one from the Maffei. But few would deny that the Maffei statue, with its greater articulation and intricacy, makes more demands on the viewer and provides a more complex set of potential verbalizations—including, notably, the ability to "speak" the proposed Danubian inscription. See Bober and Rubinstein, *Renaissance Artists*, cat. 62.

60. The drawing is by Francisco de Hollanda, a Portuguese artist and writer on art who was in Rome between 1538 and 1540 and found his way into the Michelangelo circle. According to the drawing, the sarcophagus—despite its center being obliterated by an inscription—has been identified as a work still in the Vatican collections (Helbig, *Führer*, cat. 239; Bober and Rubinstein, *Renaissance Artists*, cat. 160) depicting a victorious general dispensing clemency to the barbarians. For further details on the mechanics of the installation, see Brummer, *Statue Court*, 155–67, who suggests that the fountain was probably prepared in advance of the acquisition of the statue. If this conjecture (based on James S. Ackerman, *The Cortile del Belvedere* [Rome, 1954], 44) is true, that would further complicate the relations between the statue's identities.

61. Original text cited in Gombrich, *Symbolic Images*, 223n28. Pico is an interesting figure: despite his attachment to Savonarola he seems to have frequented the humanist circles of the Roman Academy; he is also noted for his debate with Bembo on the subject of imitation. In addition to Gombrich, 105–107, 176–78, see Harry Caplan, *Gianfrancesco Pico della Mirandola on the Imagination* (Ithaca, 1930). Brummer (*Statue Court*, 227–33) argues that Pico may have been less relentlessly anti-pagan, which accords well with the conflicting mix of humanism and fundamentalism in his response to the Belvedere. The letter to Giraldi was published along with the poem in Rome in 1513; a Strasbourg edition of the same year includes a different letter that mentions only the *Venus Felix*, which it dismisses in more conventional terms as one of those "imagines . . . truncae, fractae" (Gombrich, 223n33) that demonstrates the brokenness of pagan culture.

62. Judging from Guy Tervarent, "L'origine des fontaines anthropomorphes," *Académie royale de Belgique, Bulletin de la classe des Beaux-Arts* 38 (1956): 122–29, and Waldemar Deonna, "La femme aux seins jaillissants et l'enfant 'mingens,'" *Genava* n.s. 6 (1958): 239–96, the Renaissance loved to construct fountains of the female body as imitations of antique models, when in fact there is little evidence (apart from one disputed passage in Pausanias' *Guide to Greece* 9.34.4) that there were any such fountains in antiquity. For the connection to the aqueducts, see Pliny's extensive discussion (N.H. 36.121–23) of the system of pools, tanks, fountains, columns, and statues that Agrippa constructed when he joined the Aqua Virgine to the Aqua Appia. See also Coffin, *Gardens*, 28–57.

63. The best overview is Stinger, *Renaissance in Rome*, 235–91. On the Belvedere in particular, see Ackerman, *Cortile*, 121–38.

64. Ovid uses the word *signum* repeatedly, especially in metaphoric contexts, e.g., Narcissus, who is described as "e Pario formatum marmore signum" (*Metamorphoses* 3.419). It continues to figure in humanist Latin of the Renaissance, as in Lorenzo Valla's definitional example: "Dicuntur autem signa opera sculptilia, sive fusilia, sive caetera eiusmodi ad effigiem animalium fabricata"; "By *signa* is meant carved or cast works of art or any other such things made in the likeness of human beings" (*Elegentiarum libri VI* 4.115; rpt. in Michael Baxandall, *Giotto and the Orators* [Oxford, 1971], 173). The term is submitted to some elaborate theorizing by Pietro Bembo when he is asked to write an inscription upon Cardinal Grimani's bequest of his art collection to Venice. See Marilyn Perry, "Cardinal Domenico Grimani's Legacy of Ancient Art to Venice," *Journal of the Warburg and Courtauld Institutes* 41 (1978): 220–21.

65. For these I follow Brummer's transcriptions (*Statue Court*, 221–22) from Vat. lat. 10377, with some corrections. But see also Hubert Janitschek, "Ein Hofpoet Leo's X. über Künstler und Kunstwerke," *Repertorium für Kunstwissenschaft* 3 (1880): 52–60.

66. Paul de Man, *Rhetoric of Romanticism*, 78. I discuss this more fully above in the Introduction and earlier in the present chapter.

67. Alberti, *On Painting*, 83.

68. This exchange is first recorded by Vasari; see *Le vite de' più eccellenti pittori, scultori ed architettori*, ed. G. Milanesi (Florence, 1906), 7:197.

69. I am thinking of such works as the Dresden *Sleeping Venus*, credited to Giorgione and Titian, as well as of Titian's own *Venus of Urbino*, *Sacred and Profane Love*, and the various Venuses with musicians or Cupids. Among the enormous bibliography of iconographic studies, not necessarily concerned with the narrative of the beholder, I cite—for their canonical status— Erwin Panofsky, *Problems in Titian* (New York, 1969), 109–71, and Edgar Wind, *Pagan Mysteries in the Renaissance* (New York, 1968), 141–51.

70. The principal sources would have been Horace *Odes* 1.37, which celebrates the boldness and nobility of her suicide by snake poison; Plutarch's *Life of Antony*, which describes the death and subsequent events in Rome in great detail; Dio Cassius's *Roman History*, bk. 51; and Virgil, *Aeneid* 8.685–723, where the ekphrasis of the scenes on Aeneas's shield includes the Battle of Actium and the triumphs that follow.

71. *Dio's Roman History*, trans. Earnest Cary, Loeb Classical Library (Cambridge, Mass., 1955), 51.21. Plutarch similarly reports that the Egyptian triumph included "an image of Cleopatra herself with the asp clinging to her"; he goes on to say that in Egypt the statues of Antony were torn down after his death but that those of Cleopatra were allowed to remain standing (*Plutarch's Lives*, trans. Bernadotte Perrin [London, 1950], *Life of Antony* 76.3).

72. See the chronicle of this event by Giovanni Giacopo Penni, which records the triumphal arch erected by the della Valle family including the installation of some seven newly discovered ancient statues; reprinted in Phyllis Bober, *Drawings after the Antique by Amico Aspertini* (London, 1957), 48. See also Stinger, *Renaissance in Rome*, 55–57. See also the discussion in the previous chapter about the paradigmatic quality of the triumphal procession of plunder in establishing notions of ancient art.

73. Alessandro Perosa and John Sparrow, eds., *Renaissance Latin Verse* (Chapel Hill, 1975), 193–95.

74. This is given unproblematically by Bober and Rubinstein as the subject of the work (*Renaissance Artists*, 127), and the same assumption is made by David Rosand in "Titian and the 'Bed of Polyclitus,'" *Burlington Magazine* 117 (1975): 242–45. If the original purpose and meaning of this relief sculpture remain questionable even today, that is partly because it is a work of interest almost exclusively to students of the classical tradition and of almost no interest to students of antique sculpture per se—which renders the *Bed of Polyclitus* a kind of extreme case of all the work considered in this book. The fullest treatments of the work's heritage, in addition to Bober and Rubinstein, are Julius von Schlosser, *Leben und Meinungen des florentinischen Bildners Lorenzo Ghiberti* (Basel, 1941), 123–40; Nicole Dacos, *Le Logge di Rafaello* (Rome, 1986), 210–12; and, esp., Phyllis Pray Bober, "Polykles and Polykleitos in the Renaissance: The 'Letto di Policreto'" in W. G. Moon, ed., *Polykleitos, the Doryphoros, and Tradition* (Madison, 1995), 317–26.

75. The episode appears at *Aeneid* 8.370–415. As in many of the most interesting cases where the subject of an ancient art work is uncertain, Ligorio knows that the question remains open. Others, he says, are of the opinion that the relief represents the courtesan Laïs at the bed of her friend Pausanias of Thessaly. Ligorio goes on to say that she was as beautiful as her fellow-courtesan Phryne and that both of them had been the models for statues of Venus executed by Praxiteles, Polyclitus, and Phidias. The kernel of historical information on which he builds this story is Pliny's reference to Praxiteles' statue of the "meretricis gaudentis," thought to be modeled by Phryne (N.H. 34.70).

76. Cited in Schlosser, *Leben*, 126; the original is found in the *Libro di antichità di Pirro Ligorio*, vol. 14, in the State Archives, Turin.

77. On Ligorio's problems as an antiquarian, see Robert W. Gaston's introduction to his collection, *Pirro Ligorio Artist and Antiquarian* (Florence, 1988), 11–17; and Erna Mandowsky and Charles Mitchell, *Pirro Ligorio's Roman Antiquities* (London, 1963), 50–51.

78. See the discussion of these inscriptions above in the present chapter. It is worth noting a rather uncharacteristic instance of early skepticism in regard to these attributions—indeed, concerning Polyclitus, though not the *Bed*. The late fourteenth-century Dante commentator Benvenuto da Imola, glossing a reference to Polyclitus in the *Commedia*, speaks of having seen in a Florentine home a marble statue of Venus: "erat enim mulier speciosissima nuda, tenens manum sinis-

tram ad pudenda, dexteram vero ad mamillas, et dicebatur esse opus Polycleti, *quod non credo*";
it was a most beautiful nude woman, holding her left hand over her genitals, her right hand
in fact in front of her breasts, and it was said to be the work of Polyclitus, which I do not believe
(*Benvenuti de Rambaldis de Imola, commentum super Dantis Aldigherij Commoediam*, ed. J. Lacaita
[Florence, 1887], 3:280.)

79. A definitive statement on at least one aspect of this subject is André Chastel, "Di mano dell'
antico Prassitele," in his *Fables, Formes, Figures* (Paris, 1978), 2:9–16. The present argument owes
some of its conviction to this marvelous essay, e.g., "Il faut tenir compte de l'excitation produite
dans les esprits par la connaissance, même fragmentaire et hâtive, de certaines phrases de
Pline ou de Vitruve, aux définitions et aux suggestions capables d'enflammer des imaginations
impatientes" (15). On the Venus and the Ravenna thrones, see Schlosser, *Leben*, 135. (Francesco
Sansovino, in *Venetia città nobilissima* [Venice, 1561], 63, refers to them as by Praxiteles *or*
Polyclitus.) On the San Marco sculpture, see Pietro Giustinian as cited in Marilyn Perry, *The
Horses of San Marco* (London, 1979), 107. The Cencio da Rustici letter is discussed above, in Chap.
1. For the Pasquinade, see above in the present chapter.

80. Text and translation are cited from *The Divine Comedy*, ed. and trans. Charles S. Singleton
(Princeton, 1973).

81. Text and translation are cited from *Petrarch's Lyric Poems*, ed. and trans. Robert M. Durling
(Cambridge, Mass., 1976).

82. In fact, there is a considerable tradition of making Polyclitus do duty as a painter. The fateful letter
concerning the New World that Amerigo Vespucci wrote to Lorenzo di Pierfrancesco de' Medici
declares that "even such an accomplished painter as Polyclitus" could not represent the wonders
that had just been discovered. See Chastel, "Di mano," 2:9–11; and Bober, "Polykles," 324n1.

83. Aristotle *Nichomachean Ethics* 6.7.1141a. Aquinas's commentary is largely a verbatim translation
of Aristotle; he merely refines the description of Phidias ("laterum et lapidum incisorem") and
restates the conclusion. See *In decem libris ethicorum Aristotelis ad Nichomachum expositio*, ed. R. M.
Spiazzi (Turin, 1964), 321.

84. See above, Chap. 2.

85. Pliny N.H. 34.55–56, trans. H. Rackham, Loeb Classical Library (Cambridge, Mass., 1984).

86. Given the expression "Polyclitus . . . fecit . . . doryphorum . . . fecit et quem canona artifices
vocant," it requires only the removal of *et* to bring the statue and the canon closer together. That
is the editorial conclusion of Ludwig Urlichs, *Chrestomathia Pliniana* (Berlin, 1857), 318, but the
emendation has no textual authority other than a wish to clear Pliny of a mistake. See the note on
this subject at *Histoire naturelle*, ed. H. Le Bonniec and H. Gallet de Santerre (Paris, 1953), 34.218.
J. J. Pollitt ("The *Canon* of Polykleitos and Other Canons," in Moon, *Polykleitos*, 23) points out that
no ancient source explicitly declares the statue and the canon to have been identical.

87. The Galen passage is in his *De Placitis Hippocratis et Platonis* 5: "Beauty, he [Chrysippos] believes,
arises not in the commensurability of the constituent elements [of the body], but in the commensurability [*symmetria*] of the parts, such as that of finger to finger, and of all the fingers to
the palm and the wrist, and of these to the forearm, and of the forearm to the upper arm, and, in
fact, of everything to everything else, just as it is written in the *Canon* of Polykleitos. For having
taught us in that work all the proportions of the body, Polykleitos supported his treatise with a
work of art; that is, he made a statue according to the tenets of his treatise, and called the statue,
like the work, the 'Canon'" (reprinted in J. J. Pollitt, *The Art of Ancient Greece: Sources and Documents*
[Cambridge, Eng., 1990], 76. There is considerable bibliography, both ancient and modern,
on the Canon of Polyclitus and the *Doryphoros*. The most valuable recent discussions are Richard

Tobin, "The Canon of Polykleitos," *American Journal of Archaeology* 79 (1975): 307–21; Andrew Stewart, "The Canon of Polykleitos: A Question of Evidence," *Journal of Hellenic Studies* 98 (1978): 122–31; and Stewart, *Greek Sculpture* (New Haven, 1990), 160–63, 264–66; J. J. Pollitt, *The Ancient View of Greek Art* (New Haven, 1974), 14–22; and Pollitt, "The *Canon* of Polykleitos and Other Canons," in Moon, *Polykleitos*, 19–24. The fragmentary quotation about numbers comes from Philo Mechanicus *Syntaxis* 4.1.49.20, while that about the fingernail appears in two versions within Plutarch's *Moralia* 86a and 636c. On the perplexities of *whose* fingernail—that is, the artist's or the subject's—see T. Visser-Choitz, "Zu Polyklets Kanon," in *Kanon: Festschrift Ernst Berger* (Basel, 1988), 127–33.

88. E.g., Galen, for which see note above. On the relations to symmetria, see Jeffrey M. Hurwit, "The Doryphoros: Looking Backward," in Moon, *Polykleitos*, 3–18, esp. 10–11. The matter is closely bound up with the relations between Polyclitus and Pythagoras, which in turn is bound up with Pythagoras of Samos the philosopher versus Pythagoras of Samos the sculptor, of whom (just to confuse matters) Diogenes Laertius said "he was the first to aim at *rhythmos* and *symmetria*" (Pollitt, *Art of Ancient Greece*, 44). On these various connections, see Hurwit cited above; J. E. Raven, "Polyclitus and Pythagoreanism," *Classical Quarterly* 45 (1951): 147–52; and Stewart, *Greek Sculpture*, 139–40.

89. That Myron should be "in symmetria diligentior" (N.H. 34.58) than the author of the Canon, who is so closely connected with symmetria, has contributed to some uncertainty about the meaning of the term for Pliny (or possibly about corruption in the text). Both the Loeb and the Budé editions, for instance, translate *symmetria* as "proportions" when it refers to Myron, but as "symmetry" (in quotation marks) or "*symmetria*" (italicized) when it refers to Lysippus. See the note on 34.58 in *Histoire Naturelle* 34.226, and Ernest Gardner, "Two Archaeological Notes," *Classical Review* 8 (1894): 69–70.

90. The definitive essay is Erwin Panofsky, "The History of the Theory of Human Proportions as a Reflection of the History of Styles," in *Meaning in the Visual Arts* (Garden City, NY, 1955), 55–107. See also Leonard Barkan, *Nature's Work of Art: The Human Body as Image of the World* (New Haven, 1975), 116–24.

91. Cf. the standing male nude which found its way to the Farnese collection by 1520 (Bober and Rubinstein, *Renaissance Artists*, cat. 128) and the *Bacchus/Satyr* first described by Prospettivo Milanese in the Santacroce Collection (Bober and Rubinstein, 107–08): both are in the tradition of the *Doryphoros*, as are statues designated with different names, e.g., the so-called *Idolino*, which was found in 1530 and placed in Francesco Maria della Rovere's Villa Imperiale near Pesaro (Haskell and Penny, *Taste*, 240–41). Even the *Camillus*, discussed above in Chap. 3, could be seen as a clothed *Doryphoros*.

92. See the interrelated notes on this passage and on Polyclitus's *nudum telo incessentem* in *Histoire naturelle* 34.219, 222.

93. "Simul enim ortum atque perfectum nihil esse aiunt" (Alberti, *On Painting*, 106, translation mine). The source passage, from Cicero's *Brutus* (18.71), is "Nihil est enim simul et inventum et perfectum."

94. For sources on terminology, see above, Chap. 2, n. 49.

95. Vasari, *Vite*, ed. Milanesi, 2:245; *Lives*, trans. deVere, 1:305.

96. Of the figures on the Medici carnelian, for instance (discussed above in Chap. 3), Ghiberti says, "Furono certamente o di mano di Pirgotile o di Policreto" (*Lorenzo Ghibertis Denkwürdigkeiten* [*I commentari*], ed. Julius von Schlosser [Berlin, 1912], 47). Bober ("Polykles," 323–24), in an intriguing argument that is different from mine but not really incompatible with it, sees this

passage as explaining Ghiberti's attribution of the *Bed* to Polyclitus—that is, by reference to this gem, which can be seen to have qualities in common with the relief sculpture, though not with the real work of Polyclitus. The pre-Vasarian description of Ghiberti's collection, which dates from 1510, is by Francesco Albertini: "Non fo menzione di quelle excellentissime [sculture] per mano di Policleto antiquo, sono in casa de' Ghiberti, dove ho visto uno grande vaso marmoreo intagliato bellissimo, il quale Lorenzo Ghiberti fece portare di Grecia, cosa bellissimo" (cited in Bober, "Polykles," 318; I make no mention of those supremely excellent sculptures by the hand of Polyclitus the ancient, which are in the house of Ghiberti, where I saw a large marble vase beautifully carved, which Lorenzo Ghiberti had brought over from Greece, a most beautiful thing). The family connection is with Ghiberti's great grandson, who was a friend of Vasari.

97. *L'Anonimo Magliabecchiano*, ed. A. Ficarra (Florence, 1968), 11.

98. On this question of terminology, see Alberti, *Ten Books on Architecture*, trans. J. Rykwert et al. (Cambridge, Eng., 1989), 420; and S. Lang, "*De lineamenti*: L. B. Alberti's Use of a Technical Term," *Journal of the Warburg and Courtauld Institutes* 28 (1965): 331–35.

99. In his indispensable edition of the *Commentari*, Julius von Schlosser constructs a genealogy of the title term back to Caesar's *Gallic Wars* and Vitruvius, then moving to Ghiberti's own time, the commentaries on Dante, the memoirs of Pius II, the title that Ciriaco d'Ancona gave to his journals and that Leonardo Bruni gave to his reworking of Xenophon (Ghiberti, *Commentari*, ed. Schlosser, 2:10–11; citations to the *Commentari* are drawn from this edition). On the whole issue of Ghiberti's humanism, see the magisterial work of Richard Krautheimer, *Lorenzo Ghiberti* (Princeton, 1982), esp. 277–334.

100. Ghiberti, *Commentari*, ed. Schlosser, 1:31. Cf. his symmetrical account of the collapse of classical art culture at the beginning of the next book (1:35): "tutte le statue et le picture furon disfatte et lacerate di tanta nobiltà et anticha et perfetta dignità et così si consumaron colle statue et picture et uilumi et commentarij et liniamenti et regole dauano amaestramento a tanta et egregia et gentile arte" (all the statues and paintings were destroyed and despoiled of all their nobility and antique and perfect worthiness; similarly dissipated along with the statues and paintings were books and commentaries and principles and rules that offered instruction for such an outstanding and noble art).

101. The best accounts of the multiple provenances are Schlosser, *Leben*, 123–40; Rodolfo Bianchi Bandinelli, "Il Letto di Policleto," *Critica d'arte* 7 (1942): x–xi; and Bober, "Polykles," 317–21.

102. Although there are several valuable studies of individual motifs, some of which will be noted below, the crucial statement on all these issues of artistic influence is Ernst Gombrich, "The Style *all'antica*: Imitation and Assimilation," in *Norm and Form* (London, 1966), 122–28, which uses the *Bed of Polyclitus*, among other works, to establish a graded continuum of Renaissance artistic response to antique motifs. For my own revisiting of these formulations, see below, Chap. 5.

103. The sleeping soldier from the *Resurrection* panel is a precise imitation of the male figure on the *Bed*; it is noteworthy, however, that Krautheimer, though quite interested in classical sources, makes no mention of this connection. Perhaps that is because he relegates the *Resurrection* panel largely to an assistant (*Ghiberti*, 127). The Michelangelo drawing is Windsor cat. 12763, for which see A. E. Popham and J. Wilde, *The Italian Drawings of the XV and XVI Centuries in the Collection of His Majesty the King at Windsor Castle* (London, 1949), cat. 422. The Bandinelli drawing is Louvre 129. On the Dead Christ, see the valuable essay by John Shearman, "The 'Dead Christ' by Rosso Fiorentino," *Bulletin: Museum of Fine Arts, Boston* 64 (1966): 148–72.

104. Two exceptions are a floor mosaic by Niccolò Tribolo at the Laurenziana in Florence, repro-

duced in Bober and Rubinstein, *Renaissance Artists*, fig. 94b, and a drawing, possibly in preparation for the mosaic, possibly by Michelangelo, Casa Buonarotti 53F, reproduced in Bober, "Polykles," fig. 17.4.

105. On a Cupid and Psyche cycle in the Villa Corsini at Mezzomonte near Florence, in which the Bed of Polyclitus composition is for the first time actually used to represent the scene where Psyche uncovers the sleeping Cupid, see Bober and Rubinstein, *Renaissance Artists*, 126–27.

106. Milan, Biblioteca Ambrosiana, F. 214, inf.3. See the valuable discussion of this drawing as well as the whole milieu by Annegrit Schmitt, "Gentile da Fabriano und der Beginn der Antikennachzeichnung," *Münchner Jahrbuch der bildenden Kunst* 11 (1960): 91–151, esp. 91–95. See also Anna Cavallaro's fine work on this same circle in the exhibition catalogue *Da Pisanello alla nascita dei Musei Capitolini* (Rome, 1988), 89–100, 147–60. The drawing discussed here is cat. 23.

107. For such decipherments, see Carl Robert, *Die antiken Sarkophagreliefs* (Berlin, 1904), 3:2., cat. 188.

108. Cat. 106 in Bober and Rubinstein, *Renaissance Artists*; see their voluminous account of its re-use in fifteenth- and sixteenth-century art.

109. See discussion above in Chap. 3.

110. These are cats. 59A and 59B in Bober and Rubinstein, *Renaissance Artists*; see also Haskell and Penny, *Taste*, 195–96. Cf. the interesting discussion of the problem of dancers and muses in relation to Mantegna by Phyllis Williams Lehmann and Karl Lehmann, *Samothracian Reflections: Aspects of the Revival of the Antique* (Princeton, 1973), 98–108.

111. Gombrich, *Norm and Form*, 126.

112. The stucco in the Logge is under arch 2a, according to Dacos's catalogue (*Logge*, pl. 65a). Other examples in the Raphael-Giulio circle, ranging from precise imitations to women in different positions whose bodies nevertheless describe a 180-degree turn, include one of the Three Graces in the Farnesina Loggia di Psiche, as well as the figure of Hebe in the banquet scene atop the room's vault; also in that space are the Venus and an Ariadne; elsewhere in the Palazzo Te is the Deianira from a faux painted relief in the Sala dei Cavalli (our fig. 4.24); on canvas, see Giulio's *Infancy of Jupiter*, National Gallery, London.

113. See Erwin Panofsky's discussion of Federico Zuccari in his *Idea: A Concept in Art Theory*, trans. J. J. S. Peake (New York, 1968), 73–79.

114. Dante, *Inferno*, 20.37–39; trans. Singleton. On the interrelations between Ovidian metamorphosis and Dantean fitting punishment, see Leonard Barkan, *The Gods Made Flesh: Metamorphosis and the Pursuit of Paganism* (New Haven, 1986), 140–49.

115. The Titian repertoire of responses to the *Bed* is almost as varied and interesting as that of Giulio Romano. See Rosand, "Titian and the Bed," n. 74. Otto Brendel ("Borrowings of Ancient Art in Titian," *Art Bulletin* 37 [1955]: 122) omits the *Bed of Polyclitus*—once again, a classicist is less aware of this work than are Renaissance scholars—and ascribes the position of Venus to influences from the Ara Grimani. The drawing is Uffizi 12907Fv. In contrast to Rosand, Harold Wethey (*Titian and His Drawings* [Princeton, 1987], cat. 17) is skeptical about the authorship of the drawing and about its relation to the *Bed*.

116. See Rosand, "Titian and the Bed."

117. The generally available treatment of this project and its subsequent reworkings is Lynne Lawner, *I modi* (Milan, 1984). But see the fine new work by Bette Talvacchia, *Taking Positions: On the Erotic in Renaissance Culture* (Princeton, 1998).

118. "E perchè la Danae, che io mandai già a vostra Maestà, si vedeva tutta dalla parte dinanzi, ho voluto in quest'altra poesia variare, e farle mostrare la contraria parte, acchiocchè riesca il camerino, dove hanno da stare, più grazioso alla vista. Tosto le manderò la Poesia di Perseo e

Andromeda, che avrà un'altra vista diversa da queste; e così Medea e Iasone, e spero con l'aiuto di Dio mandarle, altra queste cose, un'opera devotissima" (Giorgio Bottari and Stefano Ticozzi, *Raccolta di lettere sulla pittura, scultura ed architettura* [Milan, 1822; rpt. 1979], 2:27–28). "And because the *Danaë*, which I have already sent to Your Majesty, could be seen entirely from the front, I decided to do something different in this new *poesia* [i.e., the *Venus and Adonis* now in the Prado] and enable you to see her other side, to make the chamber in which they are placed more agreeable to the eye. I will soon send you the *poesia* of *Perseus and Andromeda* [London, Wallace Collection], which will have yet another vantage point different from these, along with *Medea and Jason* [apparently never painted]; and I hope with God's help to send you, beside these things, a work of the greatest devoutness." For a persuasive discussion of the letter, see David Rosand, "Ut Pictor Poeta: Meaning in Titian's Poesie," *New Literary History* 3 (1971–72): 527–46.

CHAPTER 5: ARTISTS
Epigraph: Galileo Galilei, "Considerazioni al Tasso," in *Scritti letterari*, ed. A. Chiari (Florence, 1943), 96.

1. It may be the clearest indication of the vagaries to which Bandinelli's reputation has been subject that there is to date no major monograph on his work, despite all the discussion he inspired among his contemporaries. Some estimable art historians have considered him in articles or as part of arguments concerning his period. Work of specific relevance will be cited later; here I would signal especially essays by Detlef Heikamp, e.g., "Baccio Bandinelli nel Duomo di Firenze," *Paragone* 175 (1964): 32–42, and "In margine alla *Vita di Baccio Bandinelli del Vasari*," *Paragone* 191 (1966): 51–62; Kathleen Weil-Garris, "Bandinelli and Michelangelo: A Problem of Artistic Identity," in M. Barasch and L. F. Sandler, eds., *Art the Ape of Nature: Studies in Honor of H. W. Janson* (New York, 1981), 223–51, and her *Leonardo and Central Italian Art, 1515–1550* (New York, 1974), 38–41; and John Shearman, "Rosso, Pontormo, Bandinelli and Others at SS. Annunziata," *Burlington Magazine* 102 (1960): 152–56, and *Only Connect* (Princeton, 1992), 44–58. The most succinct overview of his life and career is the fine entry by Michael Hirst in the *Dizionario biografico degli italiani* (Rome, 1963), 5:688–92. The modern scholarly diffidence in regard to the life and work of this artist returns us, as perhaps it should, to Vasari, whose biography of Bandinelli is second only to Michelangelo's in length. For that text, see the valuable annotations by Detlef Heikamp, ed., in *Le vite de' più eccellenti pittori, scultori ed architetti* (Milan, 1964), 6:9–86.

2. See Erwin Panofsky, *Galileo as Critic of the Arts* (The Hague, 1954), 16–20.

3. Galileo's term for matters of dubious value is "cose che abbiano . . . del pellegrino."

4. "Baccio, se questa neve fussi marmo, non se ne caverebbe egli un bel gigante, come Marforio, a giacere? Caverebbesi; rispuose Baccio; ed io voglio che noi facciamo come se fusse marmo; e posata prestamente la cappa, messe nella neve le mani, e da altri fanciulli aiutato, scemando la neve dove era troppa ed altrove aggiungendo, fece una bozza d'un Marforio di braccia otto, a giacere: di che il pittore ed ognuno restorono maravigliati, non tanto di ciò che avesse fatto, quanto dell'animo che egli ebbe di mettersi a sì gran lavoro, così piccolo e fanciullo" (Vasari, *Le vite de' più eccellenti pittori, scultori ed architettori*, ed. G. Milanesi [Florence, 1906], 6:135; trans. G. duC. deVere [New York, 1996], 2:265–66). Subsequent in-text citations to Vasari's *Vite* refer to the Milanesi edition and deVere translation.

5. For the faun and snowman stories, see Ascanio Condivi, *The Life of Michelangelo*, trans. A. S. Wohl, ed. H. Wohl (Baton Rouge, 1976), 12, 15. Vasari's versions are to be found at *Vite*, ed. Milanesi, 7:142–43, 145.

6. On the *Marforio*, see above, Chaps. 3 and 4. The designation gigante goes back to some of the large-scale Donatellian projects for the Florentine Duomo. An Agostino di Duccio terracotta sculpture is called "uno gughante over Erchole"; and by the time of the Michelangelo *David* the expression is almost generic—which is ironic, considering that, narratively speaking, David is the opposite of a giant. Vasari definitively canonizes the term not only by referring to the *David* as a gigante but also by associating it with the *Marforio*, the River Gods, and "i giganti di Montecavallo," i.e., the *Dioscuri* (*Vite*, ed. Milanesi, 7:156).

7. "Sì come era mio padre di vivace ingegnio et attivo, così a pena uscito dalle fasce che mi cominciò ad istruire, e vedendomi con disegni su per fogli e con la neve e con la terra al solito de' fanciulli formare un leone, ora una figura, or un'altra, dalle quali congetturando gli incentivi et inclinazione della natura, che, fomentati, rare volte falliscono, cominciò ad insegniarmi a disegniare" (Since my father was of a lively and active imagination, he began to instruct me when I was barely out of my swaddling clothes. And seeing me go around with drawings on paper and working with snow or dirt, as boys do, carving a lion or some other figure, he was able to perceive the energies and inclinations of nature, which rarely fail one if they are encouraged. So he began to instruct me in drawing). Citations are to *Scritti d'arte del Cinquecento*, ed. P. Barocchi (Milan, 1971), 1369–70.

8. See the subtle iconographic and political analysis of the statue by Karla Langedijk, "Baccio Bandinelli's *Orpheus*: A Political Message," *Mitteilungen des kunsthistorischen Instituts in Florenz* 20 (1976): 32–52; on the limits of Bandinelli's originality, see Hirst, *Dizionario biografico*, 5:691: "per il B. l'antico era solo oggetto d'imitazione e di pura erudizione archeologica senza che egli riuscisse a rielaborarlo in una nuova creazione."

9. "Immitò in questa opera l'Apollo di Belvedere, e fu lodatissima meritamente; perchè, con tutto che l'Orfeo di Baccio non faccia l'attitudine d'Apollo di Belvedere, egli nondimeno immita molto propiamente la maniera del torso e di tutte le membra di quello" (Vasari, *Vite*, ed. Milanesi, 6:143; trans. deVere 2:271).

10. For the comparison with Donatello (unflattering to Bandinelli), see Vasari, *Vite*, ed. Milanesi, 6:144. On the relations of Bandinelli with Donatello, see Langedijk, "Bandinelli's *Orpheus*," 50; and Ulrich Middeldorf, "A Bandinelli Relief," *Burlington Magazine* 57 (1930): 66, 71.

11. See, e.g., in Chap. 1.

12. "Allora il cardinale gli disse: A Sua Maestà si manderà o questo o un simile, che non ci sarà differenza. E risolutosi di farne fare un altro a immitazione di quello, si ricordò di Baccio; e mandato per lui, lo domandò se gli bastava l'anima di fare un Laoconte pari al primo. Baccio rispose che, non che farne un pari, gli bastava l'animo di passare quello di perfezione" (Vasari, *Vite*, ed. Milanesi, 6:145; trans. deVere, 2:272–73). A somewhat different account of the story— one with an even less diplomatic view of Bandinelli's project—is offered by an anonymous Venetian ambassador who has come to Rome during the brief papacy of Adrian VI: "Il re di Francia dimandò in dono quest'opera a papa Leone, essendo a Bologna. Il papa gliela promise; ma per non privare il Belvedere, deliberò di farne fare una copia per dargliela; e già son fatti li putti, che sono lì in una camera; ma il maestro, se anche vivesse cinquecento anni, e ne avesse fatti cento, non potria mai far cosa eguale" (reprinted in Hans Henrik Brummer, *The Statue Court of the Vatican Belvedere* [Stockholm, 1970], 266; The king of France asked for this work as a gift from Pope Leo when he was in Bologna. The pope promised it to him, but, in order not to deprive the Belvedere of it, he decided to have a copy made to give him. The two boys have already been made, and are to be found in a room there. But the artist, even if he lived five hundred years and made a hundred of them, could never equal the original).

13. "Allora io mostrai a Sua Eccellenzia illustrissima con el meglio modo che io seppi, di farlo capace di cotal bellezza e di virtú di intelligenzia, e di rara maniera; sopra le qual cose io aveva discorso assai, e molto piú volentieri lo facevo, conosciuto che Sua Eccellenzia ne pigliava grandissimo piacere"; and "Signore, queste sono di quelle cose che io ho tante volte dette a Vostra Eccellenzia illustrissima. Sappiate che questi antichi non intendevano niente la notomia, e per questo le opere loro sono tutte piene di errori" (Benvenuto Cellini, *La vita*, ed. G. D. Bonino [Turin, 1982], 413–14; translation is cited from *Autobiography of Benvenuto Cellini*, trans. G. Bull [Harmondsworth, 1956], 315).

14. E.g., "In questo mezzo non aveva Baccio atteso mai ad altro, che a mostrare al duca Cosimo, quanto fusse la gloria degli antichi vissuta per le statue e per le fabbriche" (Vasari, *Vite*, ed. Milanesi, 6:170); "During this time Baccio had given his attention to nothing else but demonstrating to Duke Cosimo how much the glory of the ancients had lived through their statues and buildings" (trans. deVere, 2:290).

15. "Così il detto Bandinello cominciò a favellare e disse: —Signore, quando io scopersi il mio Ercole e Cacco, certo che io credo che più di cento sonettacci ei mi fu fatti, i quali dicevano il peggio che immaginar si possa al mondo da questo popolaccio—. Io allora risposi e dissi: —Signore, quando il nostro Michelagnolo Buonaroti scoperse la sua Sacrestia, dove ei si vidde tante belle figure, questa mirabile e virtuosa Scuola, amica della verità e del bene, gli fece più di cento sonetti, a gara l'un l'altro a chi ne poteva dir meglio" (Cellini, *Vita*, 415).

16. "Il quale per le parole anticipate di Baccio s'aspettava che superassi il Davitte del Buonarroto quivi vicino; ma non corrispondendo al dire il fare, nè l'opera al vanto, scemò assai Baccio nel concetto degli artefici e di tutta la città, il quale prima s'aveva di lui."

17. See the illuminating analysis of these relations in Shearman, *Only Connect*, 44–58.

18. The definitive treatment of the subject is Heikamp, "Bandinelli nel Duomo."

19. These verses are cited from Detlef Heikamp, "Poesie in vitupero del Bandinelli," *Paragone* 172 (1964): 64–65. See also the useful note in *Scritti*, ed. Barocchi, 1376.

20. Bernardetto Minerbetti, bishop of Arezzo, writing to Vasari on the occasion of the unveiling of Bandinelli's Christ in August of 1552: "Vi mando uno schizo di queste figure, perché mi diciate, che vi pare di questa postura? Et se quella gamba macha può ragionevolmente star così? Et se quando e' fu crocifisso, voi credete che e' fosse grasso o magro? Perchè ha gran muscoli, grandissime pollice [sic], buon coscioni et insomma è tale, che io non crederò, che e' digiunassi quelli quaranta giorni, ne anche che poi havessi sì gran sete et fame, come ci testifica l'evangelio, se tale era el dì della sua morte" (Karl Frey, *Der literarische Nachlass Giorgio Vasaris* [Munich, 1923], 330; I am sending you a sketch of these figures so that you can tell me what you think of this body position. And whether that leg could reasonably stand up like that? And if when he was crucified you believe he was fat or thin? Why does he have big muscles, huge thumbs, good fat thighs; and in short why is he such that I couldn't believe he had fasted for those forty days, nor that he would have had such great thirst and hunger, as the gospel testifies, if this was the day of his death?). On Adam and Eve being chased out of paradise, see Vasari, *Vite*, ed. Milanesi, 6:180. It should also be noted that there is a plentiful record of positive responses to these works. Francesco Bocchi (cited below, n. 65) places the *Adam and Eve* in the context of Bandinelli's great reputation for disegno, while Raffaello Borghini (*Il Riposo*, written ca. 1584 [Milan, 1807], 1:185–87) includes a dialogue among critics with quite positive reponses to all the Bandinelli Duomo sculpture, though with reservations as well.

21. For the reference to Lutherans, see Heikamp, "Poesie in vitupero," 66; for the anonymous attack

on the *Adam and Eve*, see Giovanni Gaye, *Carteggio inedito d'artisti dei secoli XIV, XV, XVI* (Florence, 1839), 2:500.

22. The letter is to Jacopo Guidi, dated 14 April 1548; it is reprinted in Giorgio Bottari and Stefano Ticozzi, *Raccolta di lettere sulla pittura, scultura ed architettura* (Milan, 1822; rpt. 1979), 1:76.

23. Vasari, *Vite*, ed. Milanesi, 4:10; trans. deVere, 1:619. This passage is discussed in somewhat different terms above in Chap. 2; for the original Italian, see Chap. 2, n. 76.

24. For Armenini, see Giovan Battista Armenini, *De' veri precetti della pittura*, ed. M. Gorreri (Turin, 1988), 253. For Varchi, see *Orazione funerale fatta e recitata nell'essequie di Michelangelo Buonarroti* (Florence, 1564), 39. The expression goes back most particularly to Quintilian, *Institutio oratoria*, trans. H. E. Butler, Loeb Classical Library (Cambridge, Mass., 1989), 10.2.10: "For the man whose aim is to prove himself better than another, even if he does not surpass him, may hope to equal him. But he can never hope to equal him, if he thinks it is his duty merely to tread in his footsteps: for the mere follower must always lag behind." For the whole post-Michelangelo heritage of this topos, see the invaluable Vasari, *La vita di Michelangelo nelle redazioni del 1550 e del 1568*, ed. P. Barocchi (Milan, 1962), 2098–111.

25. For classic treatments of the matter, especially in regard to the imitation of preexisting works, see the third book of Alberti's *On Painting*; Leonardo da Vinci, *Leonardo on Painting*, ed. M. Kemp and M. Walker (New Haven, 1989), 197–98; and Armenini, *De' veri precetti*, 1:8. In connection with Armenini, see the valuable introduction and annotations in *On the True Precepts of the Art of Painting*, trans. E. J. Olszewski (New York, 1977). On the training of artists, see two fine collections of essays: *Children of Mercury: The Education of Artists in the Sixteenth and Seventeenth Centuries* (exh. cat., Providence, 1984); and Andrew Ladis and Carolyn Wood, *The Craft of Art: Originality and Industry in the Italian Renaissance and Baroque Workshop* (Athens, Ga., 1995).

26. On this subject, see Nikolaus Pevsner, *Academies of Art* (Cambridge, Eng., 1940); the Bandinelli section is at 39–42. See also Rudolf Wittkower and Margot Wittkower, *Born under Saturn: The Character and Conduct of Artists* (New York, 1969), 229–34; and Armenini, *True Precepts*, 46–48.

27. For the text, see *Scritti*, ed. Barocchi, 1384–85: Averardo Zati "ritardava le provissioni concesse dal sig(no)re Duca a' giovani che nella mia Accademia particolare del Disegno sotto di me studiavano, come si vede in una carta da me disegnata e fatta stampare in Roma con le parole: *Accademia Baccii ex Senarum comitibus Bandinellis*" (suspended the privileges conceded by His Excellency the Duke to the young men who studied under me in my own personal Academy of Design, as one sees in a drawing I executed and had published in Rome with the caption: *The Academy of Baccio of the family of the Sienese Counts of Bandinelli*).

28. The earlier engraving, by Agostino Veneziano, dated 1531, is explicitly keyed to the Belvedere; the later engraving, undated but probably from the 1550s, was done by Enea Vico. They appear in Adam von Bartsch, *Le peintre graveur* (Würzburg, 1920), 14:167–68 and 15:171.

29. Among the recent contributions to this historiographically complex topic, see Ludovico Borgo and Ann H. Sievers, "The Medici Gardens at San Marco," *Mitteilungen des Kunsthistorischen Instituts in Florenz* 33 (1989): 237–56; and Caroline Elam, "Lorenzo de' Medici's Sculpture Garden," *Mitteilungen des Kunsthistorischen Institutes in Florenz* 36 (1992): 41–84. See also *Il giardino di San Marco: Maestri e compagni del giovane Michelangelo*, ed. P. Barocchi (exh. cat., Florence, 1982).

30. "[Torrigiano] nella sua giovinezza fu da Lorenzo vecchio de'Medici tenuto nel giardino che in sulla piazza di San Marco di Firenze aveva quel magnifico cittadino in guisa d'antiche e buone sculture ripieno, che la loggia, i viali e tutte le stanze erano adorne di buone figure antiche di marmo e di pitture, ed altre così fatte cose, di mano de' migliori maestri che mai fussero stati in

Italia e fuori. Le quali tutte cose, oltre al magnifico ornamento che facevano a quel giardino, erano come una scuola ed accademia ai giovanetti pittori e scultori, ed a tutti gli altri che attendevano al disegno, e particolarmente ai giovani nobili" (Vasari, *Vite*, ed. Milanesi, 4:256; trans. deVere, 1:692–93).

31. The letter to Cosimo dated 7 December 1547 is cited from Bottari and Ticozzi, *Raccolta*, 1:70–71.

32. The undated letter to "Monsignor Maiordomo" is cited from Bottari and Ticozzi, *Raccolta*, 1:104–5. As Krautheimer (*Lorenzo Ghiberti* [Princeton, 1956], 19–20) demonstrates, the decay of Ghiberti's reputation, usually in favor of Donatello or Brunelleschi, had, from the beginning of the sixteenth century, taken the form of reattributing Ghiberti's work—taking away either his personal glory by giving the best work to "better" artists or the glory of his most famous achievement by ascribing it to assistants. See, e.g., *L'Anonimo Magliabecchiano*, ed. A. Ficarra (Florence, 1968), 80.

33. Bottari and Ticozzi, *Raccolta*, 1:71.

34. Though that is Krautheimer's translation (*Ghiberti*, 20).

35. Bottari and Ticozzi, *Raccolta*, 1:74.

36. See my discussion in *Transuming Passion: Ganymede and the Erotics of Humanism* (Stanford, 1991).

37. Anton Francesco Doni, *Disegno* (Venice, 1549), 41.

38. "Ne dì passati m'abbia sollevato il meglio garzone ch'io avessi. . . . Ora pensate che si può fare a aver per emulo questo crudelissimo uomo, che son certo che m'ha sollevato quel garzone, perchè è animosissimo e pronto a fare ogni male" (letter of 7 December 1547 to Jacopo Guidi; Bottari and Ticozzi, *Raccolta*, 1:79; In recent days he filched the best helper that I had. . . . Just imagine what it's like to have as your rival this extremely savage man, since I am sure that he filched that boy because he is utterly determined and ready to do all possible harm).

39. *Il carteggio di Michelangelo*, ed. G. Poggi (Florence, 1973), 3:66.

40. For Michelangelo, see letter of September 1533 to one Niccolò (possibly Tribolo), translated as no. 195 in E. H. Ramsden, *The Letters of Michelangelo* (Stanford, 1963). For Cellini, see, e.g., the episodes in bk. 1, chap. 23, of Cellini's *Vita* concerning the helper Paolino (44–50; *Autobiography*, trans. Bull, 45–49).

41. In fact, Ceccone has been identified with Francesco di Corbignano, about whom there is a considerable paper trail; see next note.

42. In connection with Michelangelo's bevy of assistants, see the fine work of William Wallace, *Michelangelo at San Lorenzo: The Genius as Entrepreneur* (Cambridge, Eng., 1994); for his reconstruction of the career of Ceccone, see 81–82.

43. Bottari and Ticozzi, *Raccolta*, 1:71.

44. For this renunciation, see Ariosto's *Satire 6*, and see the brilliant reading of it by Albert Russell Ascoli, *Ariosto's Bitter Harmony: Crisis and Evasion in the Italian Renaissance* (Princeton, 1987), 107–20.

45. There is a large bibliography devoted to these interactions, which is cited throughout the present volume; among the most important of these studies are Phyllis Lehmann and Karl Lehmann, *Samothracian Reflections* (Princeton, 1973); Roberto Weiss, *The Renaissance Discovery of Antiquity* (Oxford, 1969); and Anna Cavallaro and Enrico Parlato, eds., *Da Pisanello alla nascita dei Musei Capitolini* (Rome, 1988). See also the recent work of Vincenzo Farinella, *Archeologia e pittura a Roma tra Quattrocento e Cinquecento: Il caso di Jacopo Ripanda* (Turin, 1992).

46. On Raphael's projects, see above, Chap. 1.

47. *Carteggio di Michelangelo*, ed. Poggi, 3:216, 233.

48. *Scritti*, ed. Barocchi, 1370–71.

49. For Vasari's discussion of the *Deposition* relief, see *Vite*, ed. Milanesi, 6:153–54; the notes include

a sonnet ridiculing Bandinelli's new title: "Baccio di non so chi scarpellatore, / . . . / Fu facto gentilhuom in due hore"; Baccio from some family of chiselers / . . . / Became a nobleman in two hours. Among the extant versions are a stucco model in the Museo di Stato of San Marino and a bronze casting by Antonio Susini in the Louvre (our fig. 5.14). For a good account of the drawings and their relation to the original(s), see Roger Ward, *Baccio Bandinelli: Drawings from British Collections* (exh. cat., Fitzwilliam Museum, Cambridge, 1988), cat. 27. See also Middeldorf, "A Relief," and the same author's "Allori e Bandinelli," *Rivista d'arte* 9 (1916–18): 483–88; and M. G. Ciardi Duprè, "Il modello originale della *Deposizione* del Bandinelli per Carlo V," in *Festschrift Ulrich Middeldorf* (Berlin, 1968), 1:269–75.

50. On the Andrea Doria commission in this connection, see Heikamp, "In margine alla *Vita*"; see also the same author's long and valuable note in his edition of Vasari, *Vite*, 6:38–40; from the point of view of the drawings, see Ward, *Bandinelli*, cat. 29.

51. Bottari and Ticozzi, *Raccolta*, 1:76.

52. Cited in Heikamp, "In margine alla *Vita*," 58.

53. Doni's text, *Il disegno*, has, so far as I can tell, not been published in its entirety in modern times; a long excerpt—not including most of Bandinelli's speech—appears in *Scritti*, ed. Barocchi, 554–91.

54. *Scritti*, ed. Barocchi, 1374.

55. See, e.g., the letter to Jacopo Guidi dated 6 December 1550 (Bottari and Ticozzi, *Raccolta*, 1:84–85), in which Bandinelli discourses on Roman ruins and on the paving stones that make up the floor of the Pantheon, superior to those of the modern Florentine baptistry.

56. "Restaurò ancora l'antico Laoconte del braccio destro, il quale essendo tronco e non trovandosi, Baccio ne fece uno di cera grande che corrispondeva co' muscoli e con la fierezza e maniera all'antico, e con lui s'univa di sorte, che mostrò quanto Baccio intendeva dell'arte: e questo modello gli servì a fare l'intero braccio al suo" (Vasari, *Vite*, ed. Milanesi, 6:146; trans. deVere, 2:273).

57. For this sequence of events, see Brummer, *Statue Court*, 78–90, and above, Chap. 1.

58. For this episode, see Vasari, *Vite*, ed. Milanesi, 7:151–52; trans. deVere, 2:652. The 1550 edition of the *Vite* offers a somewhat less anecdotal explanation for the signature, relying rather on the artist's unique sense of personal satisfaction with the finished work—perhaps with emphasis on *finished*: "Poté l'amore di Michele Agnolo e la fatica insieme in questa opera tanto, che quivi quello che in altra opera più non fece lasciò il suo nome scritto a traverso una cintola che il petto della Nostra Donna soccigne, come di cosa nella quale e sodisfatto e compiaciuto s'era per se medesimo" (*Le vite de' più eccellenti architetti, pittori, et scultori italiani da Cimabue insino a' tempi nostri*, ed. L. Bellosi and A. Rossi [Turin, 1986], 886; Both Michelangelo's love and his effort were able to accomplish so much in this work that he did there what he never did in any other work, namely, he left his signature written across the strap which supports the breast of Our Lady, as if to indicate a thing in which he was for his own sake satisfied and pleased).

59. It should be noted that in some earlier photographs of the *Adam and Eve* they appear on a pedestal with Bandinelli's name, but none of this installation is original.

60. *Scritti*, ed. Barocchi, 1377. The quotation is from a speech of Virgil to Dante at *Purgatorio* 5.14–15.

61. On the whole complex of portrait representations of Bandinelli, see R. Handley, "A Portrait of Bandinelli," *Fenway Court* 1 (1966): 17–24. As Handley points out, the irony of the Gardner Museum portrait is that it passed during the nineteenth century as a portrait of Michelangelo. On the complexities of these interrelations, see Weil-Garris, "Bandinelli and Michelangelo."

62. On the complex topos of the artist's life, also discussed above in Chap. 2, in addition to Kurz

and Kris, *Legend, Myth, and Magic in the Image of the Artist* (New Haven, 1979), and Wittkower and Wittkower, *Born under Saturn*, see more recent work, including Lawrence Lipking, *The Life of the Poet: Beginning and Ending Poetic Careers* (Chicago, 1981); Patricia Rubin, *Giorgio Vasari: Art and History* (New Haven, 1995); and Catherine Soussloff, *The Absolute Artist: The Historiography of a Concept* (Minneapolis, 1997).

63. Bottari and Ticozzi, *Raccolta*, 1:94–95.

64. *Scritti*, ed. Barocchi, 1395–96.

65. Francesco Bocchi, *Le Bellezze della città di Fiorenza* (Florence, 1591; rpt., ed. J. Shearman, Farmborough, 1971), 24.

66. On the subject of drawing in general, I have benefited from such work as David Rosand, "The Crisis of the Venetian Renaissance Tradition," *L'arte* 3 (1970): 12–40; Francis Ames-Lewis, *Drawing in Early Renaissance Italy* (New Haven, 1981) and *Drawing in the Italian Renaissance Workshop* (London, 1983); Gaspare de Fiore, *I modelli di disegno: Nella bottega del Rinascimento* (Milan, 1984); Alexander Perrig, *Michelangelo's Drawings: The Science of Attribution*, trans. M. Joyce (New Haven, 1991); and E. H. Gombrich, "Leonardo's Method for Working Out Compositions," in his *Norm and Form* (London, 1971), 58–63. As for Bandinelli's drawings in particular, all who study them are much indebted to the research of Roger Ward. In his Ph.D. dissertation, "Baccio Bandinelli as a Draughtsman" (University of London, Courtauld Institute of Art, 1982), in many articles on specific pieces, and in his catalogue, *Baccio Bandinelli*, Ward has done important work in categorizing, dating, and attributing the Bandinelli oeuvre. In the discussion that follows here, I have bracketed the always vexed question of attribution. Most of the drawings that are central to the present arguments have been steadily and convincingly attributed to Bandinelli; when in doubt, I rely on Ward's connoisseurship. On the history of Bandinelli's reputation inside and outside the field of drawing, see the useful survey in Ward, *Bandinelli*, 10–12.

67. The *locus classicus* at the latter end of the Renaissance is Benedetto Varchi's *Due lezzioni*. On the whole philosophical basis for disegno as a mediating term between painting and sculpture, see the subtle analyses in Leatrice Mendelsohn, *Paragoni: Benedetto Varchi's Due Lezzioni and Cinquecento Art Theory* (Ann Arbor, 1982), 79–80, 165–67.

68. For citation and discussion of this letter, see above, Chap. 1.

69. On this form of production, see Arnold Nesselrath, "I libri di disegni di antichità: Tentativo di una tipologia," in Salvatore Settis, ed., *Memoria dell'antico nell'arte italiana* (Turin, 1984), 3:89–147.

70. See Ward, *Bandinelli*, 37.

71. Bandinelli drawings will be cited by their numbers both in Ward's Fitzwilliam catalogue (*Bandinelli*) and in his dissertation ("Draughtsman"), if they appear in both. In this case *Bandinelli*, cat. 8; "Draughtsman," cat. 230.

72. See Roger Ward, "Observations on the Red Chalk Figure Studies of Baccio Bandinelli: Two Examples at Melbourne," *Art Bulletin of Victoria* 23 (1982): 19–37.

73. On the tendency to half-complete the *Torso*, see above, Chap. 3.

74. Ward, *Bandinelli*, cat. 16.

75. See Pliny N.H. 36.20–21.

76. "Fu domandata una gentildonna . . . quello che le paresse di questi corpi ignudi; rispose: Degli uomini non posso dare giudizio. Ed essendo pregata che della donna dicesse il parer suo, rispose: Che le pareva che quella Eva avesse due buone parti da essere commendata assai, perciocchè ella è bianca e soda. Ingegnosamente mostrando di lodare, biasimò copertamente, e morse l'artefice e l'artifizio suo, dando alla statua quelle lode proprie de' corpi femminili, le

quali è necessario intendere della materia del marmo" (Vasari, *Vite*, ed. Milanesi, 6:181). "A lady
. . . , being asked by some gentlemen what she thought of these naked bodies, answered, 'About
the man I can give no judgment'; and, being pressed to give her opinion of the woman, she
replied that in the Eve there were two good points, worthy of considerable praise, in that she
was white and firm; whereby she contrived ingeniously, while seeming to praise, covertly to deal
a shrewd blow to the craftsman and his art, giving to the statue the praise proper to the female
body, which it is also necessary to apply to the marble" (trans. deVere, 2:298).

77. On the drawings connected to the Loreto *Birth of the Virgin*, see Ulrich Middeldorf, "A Group of
Drawings by Baccio Bandinelli," *Print Collector's Quarterly* 24 (1937): 290–304. On the project
itself, see Kathleen Weil-Garris, *The Santa Casa di Loreto* (New York, 1977), 110–56.

78. "Si messe a contraffar di marmo una testa antica d'una femmina, la quale aveva formato in un
modello da una che è in casa Medici" (Vasari, *Vite*, ed. Milanesi, 6:136–37; trans. deVere, 2:266).

79. "Stava tutto il giorno a disegnare nella cappella della Pieve, opera di Fra Filippo Lippi; e non
restò fino a tanto che e' l'ebbe disegnata tutta ne' panni, immitando quel maestro in ciò raro: e
già maneggiava destramente lo stile e la penna e la matita rossa e nera, la quale è una pietra
dolce che viene de'monti di Francia, e segatele le punte, conduce i disegni con molta finezza"
(Vasari, *Vite*, ed. Milanesi, 6:136–37; trans. deVere, 2:266).

80. See, e.g., the work of Kathleen Weil-Garris, *Leonardo*, 21–25; and the same author's "Bandinelli
and Michelangelo," 231–35.

81. On the Michelangelo connection, see Vasari, *Vite*, ed. Milanesi, 6:138. Concerning the whole
episode and its resulting drawings, see Philip Pouncey, "Di alcuni disegni del Bandinelli e di un
suo dipinto smarrito," *Bollettino d'arte* 46 (1961): 323–25. On the connections with Leonardo, see
Ward, *Bandinelli*, 34–35, and Weil-Garris, *Leonardo*, 39.

82. The British Museum drawing is Ward, *Bandinelli*, cat. 13; "Draughtsman," cat. 201. On the
connections to Raphael and the large-scale engravings projects, see M. G. Ciardi Duprè, "Per la
cronologia dei disegni di Baccio Bandinelli fino al 1540," *Commentari* 17 (1966): 146–70.

83. See above, Chap. 4, for discussion of these drawings.

84. Ward, *Bandinelli*, cats. 5, 7; "Draughtsman," cats. 185, 186. On relations between Bandinelli
and Michelangelo as draughtsman, see Ward, *Bandinelli*, 19–20. On the issues of chalk vs. pen
and ink, along with the relations to Michelangelo, see Ward, "Observations."

85. Cellini, *Vita*, 416; *Autobiography*, trans. Bull, 337.

86. The drawing after the *Torso* is Uffizi, 6947F. The Sistine drawings, Louvre, Inv. 118 (pictured),
and Ashmolean. p. II 79, are Ward, "Draughtsman," cats. 275, 342. The images after the
Cascina cartoon, British Museum, pp. 1–60. and Ashmolean, p. II 210, are *Bandinelli*, cats. 5, 33;
"Draughtsman" cats. 185, 283.

87. See Svetlana Alpers, *Rembrandt's Enterprise: The Studio and the Market* (Chicago, 1988), 58–87.

88. The drawing after *Saint Matthew*, Windsor Castle 0454, is *Bandinelli*, cat. 9; "Draughtsman," cat.
422. For the *Moses* drawings, Uffizi, 6916F (pictured) and 6971F, see Roger Ward, "Some Late
Drawings by Baccio Bandinelli," *Master Drawings* 19 (1981): 3–14.

89. The drawing of the boy, Hamburg Kunsthalle 21465, is "Draughtsman," cat. 170, while the
Man Pointing to a Tablet, British Museum 1860-6-16-31, is *Bandinelli*, cat. 22; "Draughtsman,"
cat. 189.

90. For the larger case of the cartoon's influence, see the highly revealing passage (*Vite*, ed. Milanesi,
7:161), in which Vasari describes it as "uno studio d'artefici" and lists the artists, including
Bandinelli, who came under its influence. For the history of repeating this claim as well as an
attempt to authenticate the list of those influenced, see Vasari, *Vita*, ed. Barocchi, 261–69.

91. The pen-and-ink drawing, Louvre 105, is "Draughtsman," cat. 334; it seems to have formed part of Vasari's *Libro dei disegni*, on which see Licia Ragghianti Collobi, *Il libro de' disegni del Vasari* (Florence, 1974), 134. See the discussion of this work as well in Duprè, "Cronologia," 166–67.

92. The classic work on the Cascina project is Johannes Wilde, "The Hall of the Great Council of Florence," *Journal of the Warburg and Courtauld Institutes* 7 (1944): 65–81. Among recent discussions, see *The Genius of the Sculptor in Michelangelo's Work*, ed. P. Théberge (Montreal, 1992), cats. 80–82 (note esp. Antonio Natali's discussion of sketches from life vs. sketches from antiquities in cat. 80); and Michael Hirst, "I disegni di Michelangelo per la Battaglia di Cascina (ca. 1504)," in *Tecnica e stile: Esempi di pittura murale del Rinascimento italiano* (Milan, 1986). On the movements of the cartoon itself, see Charles de Tolnay, *The Youth of Michelangelo* (Princeton, 1957), 105–9, 209–19. Perhaps the most eloquent statement on the Cascina cartoon from the perspective of its loss, contributing possibly more than Vasari to its legendary status, is Cellini's reflection on the disappearance of both the Leonardo and the Michelangelo projects for the Palazzo Vecchio: "Stetteno questi dua cartoni, uno innel palazzo de' Medici, e uno alla sala del Papa. In mentre che gli stetteno in piè, furno la scuola del mondo. Se bene il divino Michelangelo fece la gran cappella di papa Iulio da poi, non arrivò mai a questo segno alla metà; la sua virtú non aggiunse mai da poi alla forza di quei primi studii" (Cellini, *Vita*, 26–27). "One of these cartoons was in the Medici palace, and the other in the Pope's hall: and while they remained intact they served as a school for all the world. Although the divine Michelangelo later on painted the great chapel of Pope Julius he never reached half the same perfection; his genius never again showed the power of those first studies" (*Autobiography*, trans. Bull, 31.)

93. Vasari himself wavers on this last point. The story of Bandinelli destroying the cartoon is told at *Vite*, ed. Milanesi, 6:137–38. At the equivalent moment in the *Life of Michelangelo* (7:161), the prime cause is held to be the illness of Giuliano de' Medici in 1516.

94. "Una storia . . . la quale essendo stata da lui ripiena di molti ignudi di masti e di femmine, di fanciulli vivi e morti, e di diverse attitudini di donne e di soldati, fece conoscere il buon disegno che aveva nelle figure e l'intelligenza de' muscoli e di tutte le membra, e gli recò per tutta Europa gran fama" (Vasari, *Vite*, ed. Milanesi, 6:144; trans. deVere, 2:272).

95. To be fair, it should be pointed out that Vasari's description of the *Saint Lawrence* is sensitive to the picture's emotional content as well as to its forms. See Vasari, *Vite*, ed. Milanesi, 6:147.

96. "Fu mostro al duca questo modello, ed ancora doppi disegni fatti da Baccio; i quali sì per la varietà e quantità, come ancora per la loro bellezza, perciocchè Baccio lavorava di cera fieramente e disegnava bene, piacquero a Sua Eccellenza, ed ordinò che si mettesse subito mano al lavoro di quadro, voltandovi tutte le spese che faceva l'Opera, ed ordinando che gran quantità di marmi si conducessino da Carrara" (Vasari, *Vite*, ed. Milanesi, 6:179; trans. deVere, 2:297).

97. Bottari and Ticozzi, *Raccolta*, 1:63.

98. See *Scritti*, ed. Barocchi, 1393 n.

99. "Per la qual cosa venuto agli orecchi di maestro Andrea tutto quel che detto aveva Baccio di lui, egli come savio lo riprese amorevolmente, dicendo che l'opere si fanno con le mani, non con la lingua; e che 'l buon disegno non sta nelle carte, ma nella perfezione dell'opera finita nel sasso" (Vasari, *Vite*, ed. Milanesi, 6:142–43; trans. deVere, 2:271).

100. On this distinction, see above, Chap. 2.

101. The *Group of Standing Male Nudes*, Christ Church Collection, is *Bandinelli*, cat. 23, recto; "Draughtsman," cat. 284. See also *Drawings and Prints of the First Maniera, 1515–1535* (exh. cat., Rhode Island School of Design, Providence, 1973), cat. 4 (Corcoran Gallery of Art 26.183a), cat. 6 (Woodner Family Collection).

102. See the entry covering this whole series of works in Ward, *Bandinelli*, cat. 39. See also *Bandinelli*, cat. 40. In "Draughtsman," the catalogue nos. are 21 and 195.

103. Bottari and Ticozzi, *Raccolta*, 6:27–28.

104. Ward, *Bandinelli*, cat. 43; and "Draughtsman," cat. 287.

105. For drawings after the *Laocoön*, see Uffizi 14784F and 14785F (pictured); the figure with the exposed musculature is Uffizi 14786F. The drawings after the *Apollo Belvedere* are Hamburg Kunsthalle 21052 and Uffizi 704E; the *Torso* image is *Bandinelli*, cat. 8; "Draughtsman," cat. 230. The double drawing, of *Apollo* and *Torso* (pictured), is Albertina 48.074 Z1 196/65, on which see Ciardi Duprè, "Cronologia," 161–63. Other muscularized figures include Uffizi 526F, 6893F, and 6919F.

106. E.g., Uffizi 6865, Horne Collection 5743v, and British Museum 1946–7-13–268 (pictured) (Ward, *Bandinelli*, cat. 35r; and "Draughtsman," cat. 208).

107. Cf. the famous self-portrait sketch by Michelangelo, Florence, Archivio Buonarroti 13, fol. 111, which accompanies the sonnet "I' ho già fatto un guazzo in questo stento." In this representation, a nude figure in strikingly vertical contrapposto stretches out his brush toward a bit of painting on the ceiling, which looks like a child's rendering of a mutilated individual in recumbent posture. In fact, the "painter" figure in this little sketch is remarkably similar to the "sculptor" figure in Bandinelli's drawing.

108. Vasari has a full, if not entirely accurate, version of the marble's vicissitudes, for which see *Vite*, ed. Milanesi, 7:153 and n. For a more recent version of the documentation, see Charles Seymour, *Michelangelo's David: A Search for Identity* (Pittsburgh, 1967), 21–41.

109. See Vasari, *Vite*, ed. Milanesi, 6:137.

110. "Fece scemare il marmo tanto, secondo che egli aveva disegnato di fare, che lo ridusse molto meschino, e tolse l'occasione a sè ed agli altri, ed il poter farne omai opera molto bella e magnifica" (Vasari, *Vite*, ed. Milanesi, 6:187; trans. deVere, 2:303).

111. On these issues, see, e.g., Lucilla Bardeschi Ciulich, "Michelangelo, Marble and Quarry Expert," in *Genius of the Sculptor*, ed. Théberge, 169–78, and William E. Wallace, "A Week in the Life of Michelangelo," in Sarah Blake McHam, ed., *Looking at Italian Renaissance Sculpture* (Cambridge, Eng., 1998), 203–22.

112. Cellini, *Vita*, 466; *Autobiography*, trans. Bull, 376.

113. "In questo marmo Michelagnolo Buonarroti aveva fatto pensiero di far un gigante in persona d'Ercole che uccidesse Cacco, per metterlo in Piazza a canto al Davitte gigante, fatto già prima da lui, per essere l'uno e l'altro, e Davitte ed Ercole, insegna del palazzo" (Vasari, *Vite*, ed. Milanesi, 6:148; trans. deVere, 2:274–75).

114. "Da questo caso del marmo invitati alcuni, feciono versi toscani e latini ingegnosamente mordendo Baccio . . . , dicendo che 'l marmo, poichè era stato provato dalla virtù di Michelagnolo, conoscendo d'avere a essere storpiato dalle mani di Baccio, disperato per sì cattiva sorte, s'era gittato in fiume" (ibid., 6:150; trans. deVere, 2:276). One poem, by Giorgio Negretti, presented as a dramatic speech by the suicidal marble, has a particularly wide diffusion. It is worth quoting in its entirety: "Ingens marmoreus Lapis, rudisque, / Lune[m] rupibus arduis recisus, / Fato, sideribus, Deis iniquis, / Thusco dum ratibus vehor Liquore, / Qui Florentia labitur per arva, / Bandini fatua manu dolandus, / Memet praecipitem dedi sub undas, / Mersus fluctibus ut semel perirem, / Tortorem fugiens, necesque mille: / Mersum tollere nititur Rosellus, / Funem subjicit, ingemit, laborat, / Contra pondere maximo renitor; / Vincor denique, sublevorque victus / Nil prodest gravitas, onusque, rursus / Imponor ratibus, futurus Orbi / Bandinae feritatis indicator. / Nunc insigne quid imprecar, Roselle, / Dignum pro meritis, tuisque factis? / Fias marmoreus

Lapis, rudisque / Bandini fatua manu dolandus" (from Giorgio Targioni, *Relazione d'alcuni viaggi fatti in diverse parti della Toscana* [Florence, 1768], 1:43; A huge marble stone, and an unhewn one, cut from the sheer Lunean cliffs, by fate, by stars, by the unfavorable gods, while I ride in the ship on the Tuscan stream which glides through Florentine fields, soon to suffer at the foolish hand of Bandinelli, I threw myself headlong under the waters in order that I might perish once and for all, submerged under the waves fleeing the torturer and a thousand deaths. Roselli strives to raise me from my submerged state, he throws a rope under me, he groans, he labors. I strive against it with my very great weight. Finally, I am vanquished and so vanquished I am put on the ship again, a future witness to the world of Bandinelli's savagery. Now, what exceptional curse should I curse, O Roselli, a curse worthy of your deserving and your deeds? May you be turned into a marble stone, and an unhewn one, soon to suffer at the foolish hand of Bandinelli!).

115. "Con intenzione che se il marmo non era scemato troppo, Michelagnolo lo pigliasse, e vi facesse due figure a modo suo. Michelagnolo, considerato il sasso, pensò un'altra invenzione diversa; e lasciato Ercole e Cacco, prese Sansone che tenesse sotto due Filistei."

116. Cellini, *Vita*, 470; *Autobiography*, trans. Bull, 379.

117. Vasari tells this story at *Vite*, ed. Milanesi, 6:186–87. Cellini tells his version at *Vita*, 474–75; *Autobiography*, trans. Bull, 383, suggesting that there is something even worse than Bandinelli: "Oh sventurato marmo! certo che alle mani del Bandinello egli era capitato male, ma alle mani dell'Ammanato gli è capitato cento volte peggio!" ("'Oh, what unfortunate marble!' I replied. 'It would have suffered at the hands of Bandinello, but it's a hundred times worse off with Ammanati!'" [*Autobiography*, trans. Bull, 383]). Cellini also writes poems about the debacle, for which see his *Opere*, ed. G. G. Ferrero (Turin, 1971), poems 59, 60, 63, 64. See the valuable notes on this episode in Vasari, *Vite*, ed. Heikamp, 6:77, as well as Heikamp's "In margine alla Vita."

118. "Perchiocchè aveva inteso che a Roma il Buonarroto ne finiva uno, il quale aveva cominciato in un marmo grande, dove erano cinque figure per metterlo in Santa Maria Maggiore alla sua sepoltura."

119. On this work, see Charles de Tolnay, *Michelangelo* (Princeton, 1960), 5:86–88, 149–52, as well as two essays by Leo Steinberg, "Michelangelo's Florentine 'Pietà': The Missing Leg," *Art Bulletin* 50 (1968): 343–53, and "Animadversions: Michelangelo's Florentine 'Pietà': The Missing Leg Twenty Years After," *Art Bulletin* 71 (1989): 480–505. The issue of Nicodemus has also been at the forefront of discussing the statue. Both Vasari and Condivi use that name for the fourth figure, but, as has often been pointed out, Joseph of Arimathea would make simpler sense. See Wolfgang Stechow, "Joseph of Arimathea or Nicodemus?" in *Studien zur toskanischen Kunst: Festschrift für Ludwig Heinrich Heydenreich*, ed. W. Lotz (Munich, 1963), 289–302; and V. Shrimplin-Evangelidis, "Michelangelo and Nicodemism: The Florentine 'Pietà,'" *Art Bulletin* 71 (1989): 58–66.

120. "Maravigliava che Baccio, sì buono disegnatore, si lasciasse uscir di mano una pittura sì cruda e senza grazia; che aveva veduto ogni cattivo pittore condurre l'opere sue con miglior modo, e che questa non era arte per Baccio" (Vasari, *Vite*, ed. Milanesi, 6:152; trans. deVere, 2:277–78).

121. The present argument is much indebted to the brilliant essay by Irving Lavin, "The Sculptor's Last Will and Testament," *Allen Memorial Art Museum Bulletin* 25 (1977–78): 4–39. On Bandinelli's *Pietà*, see the notes to Vasari, *Vite*, ed. Heikamp, 75; on relations with the Michelangelo *Pietà*, see Weil-Garris, "Bandinelli and Michelangelo," 238–42.

122. Bottari and Ticozzi, *Raccolta*, 3:475. For a fuller discussion, see above, Chaps. 1 and 2.

123. See Vasari, *Vite*, ed. Milanesi, 7:244; trans. deVere, 2:717.

124. Cellini, *Vita*, ed. F. Tassi (Florence, 1829), 3:193. On the Cellini work, see P. Calamandrei,

"Nascita e vicende del 'mio bel Cristo,'" in his *Scritti e inediti celliniani* (Florence, 1971), 55–98.

125. *Carteggio di Michelangelo*, ed. Poggi, 2:216.

126. "Aveva Baccio per costume, nelle statue ch'e' faceva, di mettere de' pezzi piccoli e grandi di marmo, non gli dando noia il fare ciò, e ridendosene: il che egli fece nell'Orfeo a una delle teste di Cerbero, ed a San Piero, che è in Santa Maria del Fiore, rimesse un pezzo di panno; nel gigante di piazza, come si vede, rimesse a Cacco ed appiccò due pezzi, cioè una spalla ed una gamba; ed in molti altri suoi lavori fece il medesimo, tenendo cotali modi, i quali sogliono grandemente dannare gli scultori" (Vasari, *Vite*, ed. Milanesi, 6:174–75; trans. deVere, 2:293).

127. See Lavin, "Sculptor's Last Will," 37.

128. Cellini, *Vita*, 411; *Autobiography*, trans. Bull, 334.

Accademia di Francia, Rome: fig. 3.51

Alinari/Art Resource, N.Y.: title page, figs. 1.6, 1.8, 1.10, 1.14, 1.15, 1.16, 1.20, 2.1, 2.2, 2.5, 2.6, 2.7, 2.8, 3.3b, 3.4, 3.5, 3.7, 3.10, 3.14a, 3.15, 3.21, 3.24, 3.25, 3.26, 3.31, 3.32, 3.33, 3.34, 3.36, 3.38, 3.39, 3.43, 3.44, 3.46, 3.53, 3.57, 3.58, 3.61, 3.63, 3.64, 3.65, 3.66, 3.69, 3.74, 3.86, 3.87, 3.88, 3.90, 3.91, 3.92, 4.1, 4.2, 4.7, 4.9, 4.10, 4.12, 4.21, 4.22, 4.25, 5.1, 5.2, 5.3, 5.5, 5.6, 5.7, 5.8, 5.9, 5.10, 5.11, 5.20, 5.35, 5.41, 5.47, 5.48

Alte Pinakothek, Munich: fig. 3.35

Art Institute of Chicago, Photo ©1998, All Rights Reserved: fig. 1.9

Ashmolean Museum, Oxford: figs. 3.13, 3.30, 3.75, 5.28

Avery Architectural and Fine Arts Library, Columbia University in the City of New York: figs. 1.2, 2.9, 3.73, 4.6, 4.8

Biblioteca Ambrosiana, Milan: fig. 4.19

Biblioteca Estense, Modena, Su Concessione del Ministero per i Beni Culturali ed Ambientali: fig. 1.19

Biblioteca Laurenziana, Florence: fig. 3.11

Biblioteca Reale, Turin: figs. 5.21, 5.22

Bodleian Library, Oxford: fig. 1.21

British Museum, London, Copyright ©The British Museum: figs. 1.11, 3.17, 3.20, 3.45, 3.47, 3.52, 3.56, 3.77, 3.84, 3.89, 5.23, 5.24, 5.25, 5.32, 5.36, 5.39, 5.44

Casa del Vasari, Arezzo: figs. 2.3, 2.4

Courtauld Gallery, London: fig. 5.17

Davison Arts Center, Wesleyan University, Middletown, Connecticut: fig. 5.12

Deutsches Archäologisches Institut, Rome: fig. 4.20

Devonshire Collection, Chatsworth, Reproduced by permission of the Chatsworth Settlement Trustees, Photo: Courtauld Institute of Art: fig. 5.38

Erich Lessing/Art Resource, N.Y.: figs. 1.4, 3.41

Escorial, Madrid, Fotografia cedida y autorizada por el patrimonio nacional ©Patrimonio Nacional: figs. 3.12, 4.11, 5.46

Foto Marburg/Art Resource: fig. 4.16

Frick Art Reference Library; permission to reproduce courtesy of L. Risi, Mantua: fig. 3.70

Galleria degli Uffizi, Florence: figs. 3.9, 4.26, 5.26, 5.30

Giraudon/Art Resource, N.Y.: figs. 1.1, 3.1, 3.37, 5.4

Governing Body, Christ Church, Oxford: figs. 5.37, 5.40

Graphische Sammlung Albertina, Vienna: figs. 3.50, 3.67, 4.27, 5.43

Harvard University Museums, Bequest of Charles A. Loeser, photo: David Mathews: fig. 3.23

Holkham Hall, Norfolk, England, By kind permission of the Earl of Leicester and the Trustees of Holkham Estate: figs. 3.18, 3.28, 5.33

Institute of Fine Arts, New York University: fig. 4.14

Isabella Stuart Gardner Museum, Boston: fig. 5.15

Kunsthalle, Hamburg, ©Elke Walford, Hamburg: fig. 5.31

Kunsthistorisches Museum, Vienna: fig. 1.13

Louvre, Paris, ©Photo RMN: fig. 5.14; Département des arts graphiques: figs. 4.18, 5.27, 5.34

Master and Fellows of Trinity College Library, Cambridge: figs. 3.85, 3.94

Minneapolis Institute of Arts: fig. 4.15

Monumenti Musei e Gallerie Ponteficie, Rome: figs. 1.3, 3.59, 4.23

Musée des Beaux-Arts, Rennes, © Musée des beaux-arts de Rennes: fig. 3.78

Museo Archeologico, Venice, Su Concessione del Ministero per i Beni Culturali ed Ambientali: fig. 3.14b

Museo Capitolino, Rome: figs. 3.3a, 3.8

Museo Civico di Palazzo Te, Mantua: fig. 4.24

Museo Nazionale, Naples: figs. 3.6, 3.42, 3.68

Museum of Fine Arts, Boston, Bequest from the late Washington Irving Jenkins: fig. 5.16

Museum of Fine Arts, Boston, Horatio Greenough Curtis Fund: fig. 5.13

Offentliche Kunstsammlung Basel, photo: Martin Bühler: fig. 3.62

Palazzo dei Conservatori, Rome: fig. 1.18

Scala/Art Resource, N.Y.: figs. 1.5, 1.7, 3.79, 3.83

Schloss Wolfegg, Courtesy of Princely Collection, Wolfegg Castle: figs. 3.49, 3.71, 3.80

Sotheby's: fig. 5.18

Staatliche Antikensammlungen und Glyptothek, Munich: fig. 5.19

Staatliche Museen, Berlin, ©bpk Staatliche Museen, Berlin, photo: Jörg P. Anders: figs. 3.2, 3.22, 3.54, 3.55, 3.60, 3.81, 3.93

Staatliche Museen, Berlin ©bpk Staatliche Museen, Berlin, photo: Ingrid Geske: fig. 3.27

State Hermitage Museum, St. Petersburg: fig. 1.12

Teylers Museum, Haarlem: fig. 3.82

Vanni/Art Resource, N.Y.: fig. 1.17

Welcker Collection, Leiden, Bibliotheck van de Rijksuniversiteit: fig. 3.29

Windsor Castle, The Royal Collection, Courtesy of Her Majesty Queen Elizabeth II: figs. 3.72, 4.17, 5.29

Woburn Abbey, Bedfordshire, England, Photo courtesy of Forschungsarchiv für römische Plastik Köln, reproduced by kind permission of the Marquess of Tavistock and the Trustees of the Bedford Estate: fig. 3.40